STUDIES IN
CONTEMPORARY
JEWRY

The publication of *Studies in Contemporary Jewry* was
made possible through the generous assistance of
the Samuel and Althea Stroum Philanthropic Fund,
Seattle, Washington.

INSTITUTE OF CONTEMPORARY JEWRY
THE HEBREW UNIVERSITY
OF JERUSALEM

STUDIES IN CONTEMPORARY JEWRY

II

1986

Edited by Peter Y. Medding

Published for the Institute by

INDIANA UNIVERSITY PRESS • BLOOMINGTON

To DANIEL G. ROSS
Chairman, International Planning Committee,
Institute of Contemporary Jewry,
on the occasion of his eightieth birthday,
in recognition of his inspiring and valuable service,
and to his wife, GRACE, for her continuing support.

Manufactured in the United States of America

ISBN 0-253-39512-7

ISSN 0740-8625

STUDIES IN CONTEMPORARY JEWRY

Contents

Review Essays

Books in Review/Reviewers

Foreword

The symposium in this volume, "The Challenge of Modernity and Jewish Orthodoxy," covers developments and movements in both the nineteenth and twentieth centuries, in Europe, the new world, Islamic societies, and in Israel, for both Ashkenazic and Sephardic Jewries. If to the external observer Orthodoxy appears to be monolithic and static, the articles in this symposium demonstrate its rich and often deep internal variations, and the dynamic changes which have taken place within it over the last two hundred years. They illustrate differences in religious approach and philosophical interpretation, as well as distinctive patterns of religious behavior based upon fundamentally competing understandings of the inner core of Orthodox values, aspirations, and goals. Thus we are shown how theory and practice are interwoven in different ways, and how particular theories inform varied patterns of behavior.

At the same time, the articles in the symposium serve as a reminder that these variations and differences occur within the framework of a fundamental unity of a common core of beliefs, shared understandings, practices, and rituals which make it meaningful to deal with Orthodoxy as a unitary phenomenon.

More broadly, the symposium raises questions about the relationships between tradition and modernity within Jewry. It suggests that to view these as polar opposites or extremes is mistaken, and that the two have learned to coexist, if somewhat uneasily, within Orthodoxy. What are perhaps most significant are not the many and deep-seated conflicts between them, but the varied ways in which modernity has been harnessed in the pursuit of tradition, and modern methods, skills, and resources have been used in the promotion and furtherance of traditional values and goals. In some cases this constitutes an attempt to hold back, if not eradicate, the impact of modernity for the particular group. Thus the study of Orthodox Jewry provides significant evidence in support of the more general thesis that tradition and modernity are not unitary and discrete categories each consisting of separate variables that cohere together in consistent patterns. The analysis presented here suggests at the very least that allowance must be made for the existence of different forms of tradition and modernity respectively.

Basic questions of the relationship within Jewry between religious authority and political authority are also dealt with extensively in the symposium. Prior to the establishment of Israel these were mainly concerned with three issues: the organization of Jewish communal authority and political organization, and the role of the traditional rabbinical leadership within it in the light of the development of a highly politicized and rival nonobservant leadership; relations with the constituted non-Jewish authority within which Jewry was to be found; and response to the idea of the establishment of a sovereign independent Jewish political entity.

Although the first two questions remained after the state was established, much more emphasis was placed upon the third, and in particular upon the proper relations between religion and politics in the sovereign and independently constituted Jewish political authority. It raised to centrality the role of religion in Jewish nationality, and the role of nationality in the Jewish religion. These were not left to be debated and resolved in the theoretical and intellectual realms, but, as the symposium strikingly illustrates, were given substantive and dramatic social and political expression both in Israel and outside it.

The changes and developments within Orthodox Jewry can also be viewed from the perspective of the contemporary scholarly concern with ethnicity. These constituted Orthodox responses to the new forms of Jewish identity and new patterns of Jewishness and Jewish peoplehood. As such they influenced those forms and patterns in both a direct and a dialectical manner. Insofar as it was widely accepted that the religious, traditional, and cultural component was central to Jewish ethnic definition, the battle was over the view and understanding of religion and tradition to be adopted. Insofar as the religious and traditional component was rejected or deprived of contemporary relevance, the battle was over maintaining their central place in Jewish ethnic definition.

The symposium is also a case study of ethnic revival. Considerable attention is currently focused upon the nonfulfillment of the liberal expectation that ethnicity will pass, and upon the phenomenon of ethnic revival, particularly of the symbolic and external elements. The contribution of our symposium to comparative research in this regard is its analysis and ample documentation of ethnic revival at the core, among those committed to the intrinsic and substantive values and practices of the Jewish religious tradition. In the process of core ethnic revival two aspects are prominent: the capacity of traditional groups within Jewry to maintain and strengthen themselves; and the introduction of a considerable degree of differentiation within Orthodoxy. Ethnic revival, it seems, may consist as much in the elaboration of traditional elements of ethnicity as in the development of new forms.

* * * * *

The first volume of our annual *Studies in Contemporary Jewry* appeared about one year ago, and all those who were associated with its publication were extremely gratified at the warm response which it received. It is therefore with considerable pride and confidence in its future that we present this second volume. This is reinforced by the fact that as I write this foreword, Volume III is in the process of being put together, and Volume IV is already in the advanced planning stages.

The current volume includes contributions from historians, sociologists, anthropologists, demographers, political scientists, philosophers, and scholars of literature, among others. While many and varied disciplines are represented, our primary focus is upon Contemporary Jewry, broadly defined. Like the latter, our effort is also truly international. The annual is prepared and edited in Israel, and published in the United States, while our International Board and our contributors come from many countries around the world.

As in the first two volumes, we intend to continue with the pattern already established of a symposium together with individually contributed articles. Moreover, our practice in the first two volumes has been to publish articles which are generally somewhat longer than journal articles. With this in mind we once again invite scholars to submit manuscripts for publication in future volumes. Similarly, we would welcome suggestions for topics for future symposia. Increasing cooperation in both these regards will greatly assist in consolidating what has already been achieved.

P.Y.M.

STUDIES IN CONTEMPORARY JEWRY

Symposium

The Challenge of Modernity and Jewish Orthodoxy

Orthodoxy in Historical Perspective

Jacob Katz
(HEBREW UNIVERSITY)

Historically, Orthodoxy in Judaism is a product of the late eighteenth century, when Jewish society, on the threshold of modernity, underwent the loosening of the bonds of tradition and the emergence of non-Orthodox tendencies and trends. True, some historians, in dealing with the doctrinal deviations of earlier periods, such as those of the Sabbatean movement, would refer to an "Orthodox" defense of the tenets of Judaism on the part of mainstream representatives of the community. Still, in such contexts "Orthodoxy" means the more or less canonical and at any rate generally accepted teachings current in Jewish society. Applied to later times, however, the term assumes a particular, sociological connotation, referring to a section of Jewish society which deserves this designation because of its specific characteristics. Moreover, these characteristics are not primarily, and certainly not exclusively, of doctrinal relevance. Rather, they relate first and foremost to the measure of observance of traditional ways of life, especially insofar as these are of religious, halakhically grounded significance.

Those who practiced tradition in this way, as opposed to those who to one or another degree relinquished traditional customs (or at least indicated that they did not view them as obligatory), may have remained the majority for quite some time. This was the case in Germany until the mid-nineteenth century, and in Eastern Europe even until the First World War. Nevertheless, it would be incorrect to view the behavior of modern adherents of tradition as simply reproducing what I call tradition-bound society. For the latter, tradition was a self-understood and uncontested guide to both religious observance and religious thought. By comparison, whatever their numerical strength might have been, those who continued to adhere to tradition when its observance ceased to be the universal characteristic of Jewish society were both more self-conscious and less self-confident. Their loyalty to tradition was the result of a conscious decision, or was at the very least a stance assumed in defiance of a possible alternative suggested by the life style of other Jews. In contradistinction to the tradition-bound, therefore, they should be called traditionalists. The awareness of other Jews' rejection of tradition, an option which the traditionalists absolutely denied, was thus an essential and a universal characteristic of all forms and variations of Orthodoxy.

The term "Orthodox," as applied to Jewish traditionalists, was derived from Christian usage, where it referred to those who clung to the official tenets and dogmas of their respective churches. Because in Judaism the correct observance of religious prescriptions, rather than correct belief, was always a surer sign of conformity, "orthoprax" would have been a more accurate designation. The Christian word prevailed, however, though in the Jewish context it acquired a modified connotation. In any event, this was the term which became the accepted label for those who persisted in their traditionalist behavior once a different kind of Jew appeared on the scene—a *maskil* or reformer, who, despite his deviation from the traditional pattern, retained his affiliation to the community.

This analytical distinction aside, the traditionalists themselves, and other contemporaries, did not view Orthodoxy as a new form of Judaism. They appeared simply to adhere to the old ways of thinking and acting, while others turned away from them. This evaluation was prompted, on both sides, by ideological factors. The opponents of the Orthodox accused them of being blind to new realities, and thus incapable of assimilating them into their lives. This very "fault," as it was perceived by the "progressives," was a virtue in Orthodox eyes. Believing Jewish tradition to be a divinely inspired scheme of life, it followed that faithfulness to it superseded the merits of any alternative system.

This consensus on the nature of Orthodoxy was shared even by scholarly observers, including the historians of modern Jewry, who portrayed Orthodoxy merely as a remnant of the premodern period unworthy of attention, or as a convenient foil for dynamic social trends (Haskalah, Reform, Socialism, and Zionism). The exception to this conceptualization was the Neo-Orthodoxy of Samson Raphael Hirsch (1808–1888), which was treated as a novelty on the historical scene because of its modern cultural image.

The equation of tradition-bound and traditionalist Judaism is, however, a form of optical illusion. The claim of the Orthodox to be no more than the guardians of the pure Judaism of old is a fiction. In fact,

Orthodoxy was a method of confronting deviant trends, and of responding to the very same stimuli which produced those trends, albeit with a conscious effort to deny such extrinsic motivations.

The cloak of conservatism certainly did not fit the case of Hirsch's Neo-Orthodoxy, and Hirsch himself regarded his concept of Judaism as different from the merely "traditional" practice of preceding generations. To the outsider, this was obviously from the cultural accommodation made by Neo-Orthodoxy's adherents: their abandonment of special Jewish dress, speech, and mannerisms, changes in taste with regard to decorum during religious worship and the like. The founder of the school explicitly rejected both the mystical and the rational-philosophical vindications of Judaism, as put forth by former generations of rabbis and preachers in what Hirsch viewed as a haphazard homiletical manner. Instead, Hirsch proposed a symbolic interpretation of the minutiae of halakhic injunctions, amounting to a complete and closed system.

Whatever the theological validity of this daring program, it proved its contemporary value in providing inspiration to Hirsch's followers. Convinced of the inner significance of every detail of the Law, they observed it scrupulously while at the same time remaining open to the influence of the non-Jewish environment, to which they belonged, formally at least, by virtue of their civic emancipation. In contrast to the majority of German Jews, who either were becoming de-Judaized or followed the path of Reform or a kind of compromising conservatism, this Orthodox subgroup was characterized mainly by its consistent maintenance of religious observance.

The situation in Russia was entirely different. There, despite a slow but constant growth since the 1830s, the Enlightenment movement remained marginal to Jewish society and fell far short of undermining the traditional attitude of the majority. The trend toward religious reform appeared only in embryonic form. Government support for the Enlightenment was limited to the founding of modern schools and rabbincal seminaries (the latter, in Vilna and Zhitomir in 1847). Although it clearly wished to acculturate the Jews within the Russian majority, it stopped short of adopting the West European pattern of pairing modern education with political emancipation. With few clear social or economic benefits to confer, moreover, education in government schools failed to attract the majority of the Jewish population. Most continued to turn to traditional institutions of learning, the *ḥeder* and the yeshiva, whose students remained for the most part within the fold of traditional Orthodoxy. Wherever Ḥasidism prevailed, the community formed around the *rebbe* also served as a strong if not totally impermeable wall against modernity. Though they deplored the loss of absolute religious unity among Jews, the Orthodox leadership confidently hoped to retain the allegiance of the majority simply by opposing the modernizing efforts of the *maskilim* and the government.

It took the perspicacity of a man like Israel Salanter (Lipkin) (1810–1883), the founder of the Musar movement, to sense that the time of self-understood and unreflecting adherence to the traditional way of life was over, and that only by a conscious act of self-education could the modern Jews internalize traditional values. He prescribed a method of study in which both intellect and spirit were to be cultivated, and rejected the merely mechanical observance of religious precepts. In this he followed in the footsteps of earlier moralists. His innovation in this regard was the proposal that each person set aside a certain hour for secluded and silent meditation, as a means of clarifying what his further self-education required. He even recommended that special quarters be set aside for such contemplation.

The novelty of this idea met, predictably, with the opposition of most traditionalist leaders. The Musar movement remained the preserve of a specific circle of followers and pupils at some of the yeshivot, whose heads recognized the educational potential of Rabbi Salanter's method. These yeshivot then became a stronghold of Orthodoxy, although even here the traditionalists were unable to secure the lasting loyalty of all of the students. Recognition of the possible loss of young people to secular society lay at the basis of Salanter's system, and it is this which ties his approach to that of Hirsch, even if the two stood worlds apart in their respective approaches to non-Jewish culture. Both men sought to bind the Jewish individual to his faith through building up his sense of commitment.

A third set of sociopolitical factors determined the position of Orthodoxy as it emerged in Hungary. There, because of cultural ties to the neighboring German-speaking countries and the political affiliation with Austria, the Jewish population was directly exposed to the influence of the modernizing trends within German Jewry. Founded only recently by emigrants from the countryside or from Bohemia-Moravia, many of the Jewish communities in Hungary were not opposed to the educational reforms which were part of the Enlightenment program since the days of Joseph II (r. 1780–1790). Occasionally, religious reform also made inroads, as in the case of the Arad community under the leadership of Aaron Chorin (1766–1844). Traditionalists, however, were also prominently in evidence. Conspicuous among these was Rabbi Moses Sofer (1762–1839), known as Hatam Sofer, who was a native of Frankfurt but had lived in Moravia since his youth, and served as rabbi in Western Hungarian communities, from 1806 in the country's leading community, Pressburg (Bratislava).

Taking heed of the way traditional Judaism had deteriorated in cities like Frankfurt, and concerned about similar changes in his chosen community, Rabbi Sofer evolved an intellectual and institutional strategy to safeguard tradition. He not only rejected all innovation; he also vested his principled conservatism with religious sanctity, coining the phrase, "Anything new is forbidden according to Biblical Law." Thus, customs such as the exclusive use of the Jewish vernacular in teaching and preaching were elevated, regardless of their inherent religious merit, to the status of dogma. A master of dialectics, the Hatam Sofer persuasively pressed his contention that such interpretations were rooted in halakhic principles. The integrity of the Jewish community, he declared, depended upon the strict adherence of its members to the Orthodox ways of life. Deviators automatically forfeited the right to be called Jews. Although this principle of exclusive Orthodoxy did not reach its full effect for quite some time, Rabbi Sofer was able, in his lifetime, to put it into operation in his own yeshiva, where only those who were prepared to follow the strict rulings of the master were tolerated. Indeed, under his inspiration, the Pressburg Yeshiva became a fountainhead of the militant Orthodox leadership of the next generation in Hungary.

For the clash between traditionalists and innovators gained in intensity during the decades following the death of the Hatam Sofer. In an expanding economy and in the wake of progressive policies which granted the Jews greater liberties (after 1840, for example, Jews were in general free to choose their place of residence), religious practices which seemed obstacles to economic advantage or social ambition were ever more widely discarded. Secular education, mandated by the government, also became generally acceptable in Jewish society. Many communities introduced changes in public worship, thus demonstrating their unwillingness to let tradition be their only guide. Accommodation to current tastes and conformity with non-Jewish practice spurred Reform activity here, as in Germany. From the traditionalists' point of view, all this constituted a deviation from the Law, irrespective of the halakhic standing of the innovations introduced, which therefore were rejected and condemned.

The conflict reached national proportions when the government proposed the establishment of a modern rabbinical seminary, to which the reformers agreed but the Orthodox did not. They wished to maintain the exclusivity of the yeshivas, where talmudic studies were the sole curriculum. The ensuing test of strength culminated in 1868, when, upon granting full emancipation to the Jews, the government called on them to form a national body, along the lines followed by other recognized denominations. At the assembly of representatives convened to form such a body, the traditionalist minority declared that their religious convictions would not permit it to be united with the majority, who, by deviating from the Orthodox norm, had introduced a veritable schism in Judaism. Accordingly, the traditionalists seceded from the assembly.

Although the government as well as liberal public opinion favored progressive tendencies, Hungarian society also contained important conservative elements among the influential aristocracy and the clergy. Relying on these, the Orthodox secured for themselves the right to an independent organization, to be joined by traditional communities or those sections of communities which separated themselves from the reformers. This is the first instance in European Jewish history of an officially recognized Orthodox subgroup. A decade later, Samson Raphael Hirsch secured a similar concession from the Prussian government for his Frankfurt community, and others followed his example.

Organizational affiliation thus became an important basis of modern Orthodoxy, though it was not the only one. Conviction and conduct determined who was Orthodox in such countries as Austria, where separate communities were not permitted. On the other hand, organizational unity did not guarantee uniformity of thought and conduct. In Hungary, for example, the Orthodox differed among themselves, especially with regard to the issue of cultural dissociation from the non-Jewish environment. Even prior to the separation of communities, a group of rabbis from the northeast districts of the country (admittedly, not of the first rank leadership) decided to hold a conference on a number of related matters: All languages but Yiddish were to be forbidden in teaching and preaching; the *ḥeder* was to be preserved as the exclusive educational vehicle for Jewish children—despite government regulations; and of course, no alterations would be permitted in synagogue services.

At the same time, however, Dr. Azriel Hildesheimer (1820–1899), the future founder of the Orthodox rabbinical seminary in Berlin, was running a yeshiva in Eisenstadt on the western border of Hungary, where courses in foreign languages and other secular subjects were taught alongside the Talmud and Codes. Yet, Hildesheimer's enterprise proved to be of short duration, and without lasting effect, in Hungary. Once Orthodox separatism became a fact, the traditionalists developed a *modus vivendi* which entailed sending their children to modern elementary schools, while preserving an exclusively Jewish traditional curriculum on the secondary level, in particular in the old-type yeshivas where future rabbis were trained.

Radical traditionalists rejected even this form of compromise, and some of them took refuge either in Ḥasidic Galicia, or in the as yet unsecularized environment of Palestine. There, the Jewish population, with the aid of world Jewry, maintained a sort of religious reservation, retaining all the characteristics of a premodern community. The Ashkenazic section of the population in Jerusalem contained quite a number of such refugees—not only from Hungary—who sought in the Holy Land a haven from the dissolution they observed in the traditional fabric of Jewish life in their old communities. These elements were naturally predisposed to resist any attempt at innovation, the need for which later began to be felt there, too, and was recommended both by outside observers and by some members of the community.

Though differing from country to country, Jewish Orthodoxy in its various settings retained one common denominator, inherited from premodern, tradition-bound Jewry. This was a far-reaching passivity with respect to long-range planning for the future of the Jewish community.

Ever since its loss of political independence, Jewry had lost faith in its capacity to extricate itself from exile. A basic change could be expected only through an act of miraculous, divine redemption. In the interim, it was taken for granted that the Jews would remain dependent upon the present holders of political power. Action taken to alleviate problems besetting the communities was limited to intervention with these authorities, and were by their very nature of an *ad hoc* character, with but short-range intentions.

The modern era would make it possible to envision more long-range modifications: emancipation, emigration and, later, the establishment of a Jewish commonwealth. But Orthodoxy, apparently unable to shed its premodern mentality, recoiled from taking an active part, much less a leading role, in any of these enterprises. Though they were cognizant of the tangible advantages entailed in free citizenship, or of the compelling reasons for emigration, Orthodox leaders would at best tolerate the steps which others took to achieve these goals. The fear that radical changes in the Jews' external situation might have adverse consequences for their traditional way of life may have reinforced the inbred inclination to passivity.

In the case of the national movement which aimed at the resettlement of Palestine, the Orthodox found theological justification for their opposition. Miraculous messianic expectations, as they were popularly conceived, were so closely associated with the return to Palestine that any human endeavor to achieve this end could easily be presented as premature intervention in the divine scheme of things. One Orthodox interpretation, it is true, argued that, on the contrary, under given circumstances the settlement of Palestine was a necessary first stage in divine redemption. But the majority of Orthodox authorities, and the great bulk of their followers, rejected this point of view. Though this disagreement assumed the form of an ideological controversy, on a deeper level the clash between the two groups reflected basic negative and positive attitudes to modern activism. The activists included Rabbis Zvi Hirsh Kalischer (1795–1874) and Yehuda Alkalay (1798–1878), who later became known as the forerunners of modern Zionism. Although their efforts, in the 1860s and 1870s, had few practical results, their teaching and personal example provided the authority and religious justification for those Orthodox Jews who joined the national movement.

Orthodoxy generally maintained itself, despite the erosive forces of modernity; but until the mid-twentieth century, outsiders as well as its own exponents regarded it as being on the defensive. Orthodox families were everywhere confronted with the likelihood that at least some of their children might leave the fold. This was a common occurrence in Europe, where Jewish life was still comparatively strong. Once mass emigration began, it was almost certain that leaving the home country was tantamount to abandonment of the traditional way of life. Only a small proportion of Jewish immigrants in such major centers as New York or London made the effort to retain their Orthodoxy and to rebuild their institutions accordingly.

Many of the first settlers in Palestine in the late nineteenth century may have intended to maintain traditional practices despite the transition to the unfamiliar life of farmers and laborers. Indeed, Baron Rothschild of Paris, upon whose support the early settlers depended, demanded that certain standards of religious observance be maintained. Yet the more politically motivated among them, beginning with the Biluim of the early eighties and the settlers of the Second Aliyah twenty years later, arrived with the clear idea of founding a new society along secular-national lines, in which religious elements would merely be tolerated. In the long run, the deep cleavage between these almost-revolutionary secularists and the most exclusive wing of Orthodoxy could not be bridged. With the strengthening of the former, in the wake of increased immigration in the decade prior to World War I (from Russia, especially), the conflict broke into the open. Exponents of the so-called Old Yishuv decried the innovators as desecrators who flouted the Law in its most holy abode, the Land of Israel itself. For their part, the radicals among the Zionist pioneers saw themselves as the vanguard of a national renaissance, and dismissed their opponents as vestiges of a waning past.

While rejecting the obligatory character of the Jewish tradition in its Orthodox version, however, the secularists nevertheless were committed to their own vision of the Jewish past, which they identified with the Biblical era, and which embraced ideals of social justice and the value of cultural originality. They were inspired by the conviction that a Jewish society, rebuilt in its ancient land, would somehow reestablish a direct link with its pristine past. This was an obvious and conscious adaptation of a basic feature of Jewish messianism, and was reflected in particular in the symbolic vocabulary employed by the Zionist movement. Paradoxically, it was the Orthodox adherents of Zionism who avoided referring to any messianic meaning inherent in the Zionist enterprise. With an eye toward the arguments of their Orthodox opponents, they resorted to more neutral rationales: the need for a secure place for emigrants and refugees, and the traditional preference for life in the Holy Land for the religious merit attached to its cultivation or for the sake of full halakhic observance.

The one outstanding exception to this reticence was the decidedly messianic view of current events taken by Rabbi Abraham Isaac Kook (1865–1935), later to become the Chief Rabbi of Palestine, who had served the community of Jaffa and the new settlements since 1904. Following in the path of Rabbis Kalischer and Alkalay, Rabbi Kook perceived messianic significance in the work of resettlement. To this he added a mystical-kabbalist element of his own, endowing the Jewish national revival with deep spiritual meaning. He read into the process of Jewish redemption far-reaching implications, not only for the Jews, but for the entire world, which he felt was involved in a basic transmutation. Yet, how could such a view be squared with the fact that the majority of those actually taking part in the work of redemption openly violated the Law? To this difficulty, Kook offered a response which must be seen as the most far-reaching concession made by Orthodoxy to any of the modern, non- or anti-Orthodox trends in Judaism. The resettlement of the ancient home of the Jews and of Judaism, he argued, was a precondition of the ultimate redemption, and would serve the divine purpose even if it were achieved through defiance of the Law. This theory certainly assuaged the consciences of traditionalists who wished to cooperate with the Zionists even though it did not convince the Orthodox anti-Zionists of the Old Yishuv or elsewhere. To them, Kook's daring attempt to harness the messianic idea to what was a license for lawless behavior, if anything, aggravated the situation.

The deep split within Orthodoxy over the issue of cooperation with Zionism was reflected in the organization of Orthodox life, outside Palestine as well. Adherents of cooperation became united in the framework of the Mizrahi party in 1902. Their opponents, led by the successors of Samson Raphael Hirsch, established their own organization, Agudat Israel, in 1912. This group declared its purpose to be the application, to all problems facing the Jews, of the perspective of traditionalism (the "spirit of Torah"). Thus, it emerged as the Orthodox counterweight to the Zionist movement.

In a sense, then, it was Zionism which drew the Orthodox out of their traditional political passivity, while highlighting the latent tension within Orthodoxy. The two extremes were irreducibly divided, as there could be no deeper disagreement than that between the messianic confirmation of Zionism by Rabbi Kook and his followers and its passionate condemnation by his opponents, who went so far as to declare the Zionist enterprise to be Satan's work. The drama of the clash between the two camps was heightened when, in the wake of the Balfour Declaration, the Zionists sought to establish an umbrella organization for all Jews in Palestine. The leaders of the Old Yishuv, with the active assistance of Agudat Israel, fought insistently for its independence, repeating the Hungarian experience. The result, as well, was similar in that, here again, the traditionalist minority seceded from the larger community.

This ultra-Orthodox secession seemed, at the time, of little significance. The Zionist movement had achieved international recognition, and, with the growing support of world Jewry, seemed to be emerging as the exclusive determining factor in the political and cultural life of Palestine. The anti-Zionist Orthodox seemed to have been neutralized, while the Orthodox Zionists had to be content with provisions made for their special needs—in the field of education, for example—and were unable to wield substantial influence in the matter of the public standing of religious law. The dynamic development of the country overwhelmed the Old Yishuv, which, despite some degree of institutional maintenance, was unable to reproduce itself numerically.

This state of affairs was radically altered by the two decisive events of Jewish history in the last generation: the Holocaust and the founding of the State of Israel. At first glance, both of these appeared to augur ill for Orthodoxy—the latter seeming to vindicate the Zionist reading of Jewish history, and the former eliminating Orthodoxy's great demographic reserves. The results, however, ultimately redounded to the renewed vigor of the Orthodox. The remnants of East European Jewry, among them some of its spiritual leaders—rabbis and heads of yeshivot—settled either in Palestine/Israel or abroad. In the course of a generation, new communities were reconstructed along the traditional pattern, complete with institutions of learning which perpetuated and rekindled the Orthodox spirit.

Indeed, the leaders of these communities made it their all-consuming passion and exclusive purpose to rebuild yeshivot and *kollelim,* schools where young men, supported by working wives or by the institution itself, could dedicate themselves to the study of ancient law.

That these efforts succeeded, far more than any previous attempts to transplant East European-type centers of learning to Western cities, is to be attributed to changed conditions: the growing prosperity of the Jewish communities, on the one hand, and the declining attraction of secularist ideologies, on the other.

Nevertheless, while the successes of this effort may be granted, the claim of Orthodox leaders to have rebuilt the destroyed bastions of the Judaism of old requires some correction. While in Europe these institutions may be said to have been an appropriate vehicle of education, existing within a broad social environment, in the new centers of the postwar period they are rather isolated and directed toward a high degree of rejection of the prevailing trends of society. Formerly these institutions catered to the needs of the environment, producing its spiritual leaders and intellectual elite. In their new settings, they are capable of maintaining themselves only by virtue of their cultural dissociation and increasing physical aloofness—a quasi-monastic life. Concrete benefit from their activity accrues only to those in their immediate coterie. If broader circles of Jewish society sometimes support them, it is because of the sentimental appeal they possess as reflections of a tragically lost past.

Not only in their structural and social aspects are these institutions isolationist. This tendency is also marked in their approach to religion. Called upon not only to study the Law but also to interpret it, the students do so only in the narrowest sense of the term. Only the most stringent application of the Law is accepted—a standard to which only the most devoted among the general public are able or willing to adhere. It has often been observed that this generation of Orthodox Jews is more demanding of itself than its predecessors ever were, and at the same time more exclusive and more intransigent toward groups which differ in their interpretation of religious obligations.

"Reconstructionist" Orthodoxy, as it might be called, may appear as a positive phenomenon from the point of view of Jewish group survival in the Diaspora. Its retention of conspicuously Jewish dress, religious posture, and concomitant mental attitudes certainly runs counter to the general pattern of Jewish life in modern European or American society. From the point of view of cultural accommodation in those societies, these may be regarded as disturbing factors. Yet, with the demands of cultural uniformity giving way in so many societies to cultural pluralism, even extreme forms of Jewish particularism may expect to enjoy a measure of tolerance. Moreover, from the study of antisemitism we know that when anti-Jewish reaction sets in, cultural accommodation scarcely makes a difference in any case.

Seen from within Jewish society, the emergence of this new variation of Orthodoxy may be said to enrich the communal scene. Certainly in demographic terms, the high fertility of these groups helps to offset losses in other sectors of the Jewish population. This growth in numbers, apart from directly strengthening Orthodoxy, may come to provide a larger reservoir for the less Orthodox and even the non-Orthodox, as it cannot be certain that Orthodox families will retain the religious fidelity of all their children. At least in the Diaspora, the existence of ultra-Orthodox communities need not interfere with the interests of the broader Jewish public. Ironically, this is not the case in the State of Israel, where Jews themselves constitute the majority culture.

The refugees from Europe who arrived in Palestine in the postwar years included Orthodox elements who reinforced, primarily, the middle of the road Orthodox groups. Yet, it was not they but the heads of reconstructed yeshivot and their students who were to reap the benefits of heightened prestige and religious authority during the first decades of Israeli statehood. At the same time, a related but quite different phenomenon was taking place in Orthodox education in Israel. Rabbi Moshe Zvi Neriah, a former student of Rabbi Kook, earlier found a new type of yeshiva in which Talmud study would be combined with agricultural training. The school catered mainly to members of the religious Zionist youth movement, Bnei Akiva. In time, the Zionist yeshiva idea caught on. Although agricultural training was dropped, the positive—even ardent—commitment to Zionism was maintained.

By the sixties and seventies, the map of Orthodox educational institutions in Israel was completely altered. Whereas in the prewar Yishuv intensive Talmud study had been limited to yeshivot connected with the Yiddish-speaking traditionalist population, now a network of those new institutions existed, which attracted a growing number of pupils from the Orthodox public as a whole. Their success derives partly from conditions affecting postwar Jewry in general, and partly from specific, Israeli factors.

Because Zionism's immediate objective was achieved with the founding of the State of Israel, and it no longer played its previous exclusive role in the public mind, other values and ideas, among them, those of the religious tradition, reasserted themselves.

After the establishment of the state, David Ben-Gurion, as Minister of Defense, exempted yeshiva students—then, a small number of young men—from military service. Non-Zionist yeshivot became attractive to families who viewed military service as a spiritual danger for their sons. At the same time, the Bnei Akiva-connected yeshivot attracted more and more students for whom military service was a supreme national, and hence religious, duty. The success of these yeshivot must be seen in the context of the ideological climate in the country. There were thus two different Orthodox trends which were gaining ground and which could, in the long run, pose a challenge to the secular authority of the state.

The Orthodox of the older variety, though living in the shadow of the Zionist state, could accept its authority only de facto, not de jure, given their ideological reservations. While the small but vociferous group of extremists associated with the Neturei Karta actually refrain from any structural contact with the state's agencies, and indeed refuse to register as citizens, the majority of the separatist Orthodoxy, mostly affiliated with the Agudah, do take advantage of state-provided services. They do not, it is true, "pay" for them in the currency of moral commitment. In their schools, no reference is made to state symbols such as the flag or the national anthem. If Independence Day is observed at all, it is done without any identificational associations. While Orthodox Jewry everywhere in the Diaspora used to go out of its way to demonstrate its loyalty to the powers that be, it is reluctant to do so with regard to the Jewish state. Thus a few years ago, the World Conference of the Agudah in Jerusalem chose not to be greeted by the President of Israel, in order to avoid paying him due deference. In short, these Orthodox groups do not share in the common civic values of the country, which in the last resort guarantee the citizen's loyalty to the state.

The reason most commonly given for this is insufficient submission by the state to the demands of religious law. A deeper reason exists, however. Orthodox Judaism has a fundamental difficulty in coming to terms with a pre-messianic Jewish commonwealth. Jewish tradition did not foresee a middle stage between Exile and Redemption. In this sense, the Jewish state represents an illegitimate offspring of history. This problem, to be sure, did not escape the attention of religious Zionists. Their answer was that a Jewish state, whatever its shortcomings as a religious society, is a first step toward the messianic age. This formula was incorporated in the wording of the prayer for the welfare of the State of Israel, where it is designated as "the beginning of our Redemption." This formula, however, is condemned among the separatist Orthodox. Thus while Orthodox Jews all over the world pray for the welfare of their country, according to the prescribed version of the prayerbook, in Israel of all places the relevant passage is omitted.

Quite a different attitude was taken by some of the Orthodox youth brought up in Zionist frameworks, who were imbued with a belief in the messianic significance of Jewish statehood. Why, they ask, does the road to redemption stop half way, so to speak? Why not take steps to hasten the culmination of the messianic process? Such questions, present ever since the founding of the state, were articulated in their most acute form in the wake of the Six-Day War, when the high-pitched apprehension which preceded the war gave way to an almost supernatural victorious conclusion. Convinced that the messianic era was indeed upon them, some of the Orthodox youth, the founders of Gush Emunim, believed that they knew what steps were necessary in order to consummate the final redemption. In contrast to the leaders of the state, who seemed to be uncertain about what to do with the parts of the historical Land of Israel which had come into Israel's possession, the founders of Gush Emunim, supported by the son and successor of Rabbi Kook at his yeshiva in Jerusalem, had no doubts whatsoever. To them it was evident that full redemption rested on the settling of the whole of Biblical Israel. This irrationally inspired minority outmaneuvered a vacillating government, thus setting into motion those struggles which have dominated public consciousness in Israel ever since.

What we have witnessed is an extraordinary transformation, in which Jewish Orthodoxy, habitually a passive and politically docile element, has, in the context of the Jewish state, displayed an aggressive activism, assailing the state's authority from two flanks. How this came about is clear when one views the present in the light of past developments. Zionism's deep involvement with the messianic expectations of the Jewish people served as its driving force, but this involvement has exacted, and is exacting, its price. It is no light matter for a small and young state to embrace two militant minorities, both avowing the supremacy of divine authority, the one denying the very legitimacy of the state, and the other calling into question the authority of the government, whose policies they feel entitled to defy.

The dangers inherent in such a situation might have been mitigated, at least, had those responsible for state affairs been less prepared to countenance such defiance early on. In this they failed, whether out of lack of foresight, or some latent sympathy on the part of some members of the government for the deviant camps, which prevented them from enforcing the law.

There were those who recognized the overwhelming potential of messianism as a sociopolitical force. Gershom Scholem, for example, demanded an explicit denial of any connection between Zionism and messianism, which was illusory, given the obvious historical link between the two. For without the messianic hopes of restoration to its ancient homeland, why should the Jewish people have chosen this spot of all places on which to reconstruct a national state?

Nevertheless, even with this acknowledged link rooted in the past, there is no compelling reason why the association of Zionism and messianic restorationism could not have been limited to the realistic level. Traditional messianic utopianism, in its different versions, encompassed a variety of elements. Common to all Jewish messianic ideas, however, was the hope for a reestablished Jewish sovereignty in the Jews' own land. Does not the Zionist fulfillment of this hope constitute sufficient realization of the messianic dream? It can only be blindness to the measure of its success—taking into account the obstacles in its path and the sacrifices it took, it was a veritable miracle—that prompts people to make its value dependent on its culmination in some quasi-predetermined political, social, or spiritual perfection. The notion that Jewish political independence would almost automatically lead to the realization of all other ideals, thus saving their exponents the trouble of fighting for them on their own proper grounds, is the great fallacy of contemporary messianism. The commitment to messianic belief may have provided the energy for the establishment of Israel, but the messianic tradition certainly does not contain a blueprint for the conduct of the state. Upon the realization of this fact much in the future of Israel may depend.

Halakhic Responses of Syrian and Egyptian Rabbinical Authorities to Social and Technological Change

Zvi Zohar
(HEBREW UNIVERSITY AND SHALOM HARTMAN INSTITUTE, JERUSALEM)

As intellectuals living and creating within a rich religious-cultural tradition, the Torah scholars of the nineteenth and twentieth centuries did not adopt a revolutionary position in molding their response to the upheavals in Jewish life in their time.[1] However, not all adopted a conservative-reactionary attitude, although a considerable and influential faction of European rabbis did do so, contending that "innovation is prohibited by the Torah."

The image of halakhic scholars in modern times, as a closed and reactionary monolithic school, chiefly serves the current vested interests of groups—whether Orthodox or secular—who find it convenient to treat halakhic society in general, and its leaders in particular, as a single and uniform body, rather than deal with the complex and multifaceted historical reality of this community or culture. In addition, there is a serious lack of basic research in this field. Unfortunately, students of Jewish history who deal with this period as historians or sociologists hardly glance at the abundant halakhic literature. Students of halakhic development, for their part, rarely study modern Halakhah. They also tend to ignore the underlying ideational and value content of rabbinic legal rulings and what these reveal about the attitudes of the rabbis to the statics and dynamics of the societies in which they functioned.

This is true all the more with respect to the study of contemporary Jewish history in Islamic countries. The prevailing image of the Jewish community in the Moslem world is that of a traditional-conservative society, unchanged for hundreds of years, until the sudden shock which it suffered upon being removed from its natural habitat and set down in the modern West during the mid-twentieth century. In point of fact, the Jewish communities in Islamic countries constituted an intricate mosaic of variegated sociocultural situations. While the commonly held image may accurately reflect life in many villages in Yemen, the Atlas Mountains and Kurdistan—it is nevertheless far from accurate with respect to important communities such as those of Algiers, Istanbul, Salonika, Baghdad, Jerusalem, Cairo, and Tunis. The range of halakhic response in these Eastern communities to contemporary problems was, in fact, as broad as was their differing historical experience.

In contrast with Europe, where the modern period split the Jewish people into distinct ideological tendencies and camps, there was almost no fundamental ideological fragmentation of institutional consequence in the Jewish communities in the East. Thus, the rabbis had no need to define themselves as members of one camp or another and, paradoxically, their options in formulating halakhic responses to the new situations evolving in the life of their congregations were therefore more open and diverse.

This study compares modes of response of rabbinical leaders in Egypt and Syria to transformations in their communities, from the last quarter of the nineteenth century to the First World War. The research is based on primary halakhic literature, mainly responsa composed by the rabbis in these countries during the said period.[2] There is an almost complete dearth of secondary monographic research.

One central methodological problem, arising from the use of halakhic literature as historical material, needs to be mentioned at the outset. I do not claim that what comes to light in the responsa represents the practice or even the attitudes of the community; my concern is explicitly with intellectual history, that is: understanding the manner in which the authoritative bearers of Torah culture perceived the changing reality in which they lived and, in particular, analyzing the ways in which they formulated the response of the Jewish symbolic system (the "Torah") to these changes.

I have selected two outstanding rabbinical figures, one in Syria and one in Egypt, who were active during the period in question. One is Rabbi Isaac ben Moses Abulafia, who served as *hakham bashi* of Damascus from 1877 to 1896, and presided over the local rabbinical court both before and after; his *Penei Itzhak* (published between 1870 and 1906) is the most comprehensive collection of responsa published by a Syrian rabbi during this period. The other is Rabbi Elijah Hazzan, who served as *hakham bashi* of Alexandria (1888–1908); his *Taalumot Lev* (published between 1879 and 1907) is the most comprehensive composition of responsa produced by an Egyptian rabbi during the period. These rabbis will be considered to be representative of halakhic approaches typical of the Torah worlds of Syria and Egypt respectively, an assumption borne out by a perusal of the works of other scholars from these countries.[3]

EGYPT AND THE EGYPTIAN JEWISH COMMUNITY

Egypt was brought into close contact with the European world in the wake of Napoleon's campaign, and during the nineteenth century European involvement in the land of the Nile increased steadily. On the one hand, Egyptian rulers sought to adopt Western techniques and science, while on the other, the European powers sought economic and political influence in this pivotal geostrategic area which (from 1869) included the chief route to India and the Far East. Heightened European involvement sparked off Egyptian nationalism which erupted in the 'Arabi Revolt which, in turn, led to a radical intensification of foreign involvement, in the form of a British takeover of the country in 1881–1882.

During the same period, millions of East European Jews emigrated in search of a more comfortable political and social climate. Of these, several thousand reached the shores of Egypt where stable British rule, enlightened and egalitarian with regard to Europeans, combined with economic prosperity to offer an attractive haven from East European persecution and strife.

These two phenomena—British rule and European Jewish immigration—had a synergetic effect on the Jewish community in Egypt. Not only did the community expand at an accelerated pace,[4] but the impact of European influence was all the more forceful. In addition to exposure to European influence from without—via British rule and the encounter with merchants and visitors from across the Mediterranean—the community was exposed to European influence from within: it absorbed into its ranks thousands of European Jews who had internalized the central features of modern Western civilization. Unlike Egypt's Moslem population, the Jews could not defend themselves against these imported influences by fostering a conscious estrangement in the form of "we" and "they."[5] To erect a barrier between themselves and their European brothers would have been to deny the fraternity of the Jewish people, a value which they consistently affirmed.[6] The community leaders, therefore, could not fully or firmly segregate themselves from the influences exerted on the community as a result of European penetration; nor, indeed, were they inclined to do so, for a variety of other reasons.[7] Thus, while researchers may disagree as to the impact of the West on other sectors of the Egyptian population,[8] there can be no question that the Jewish community, in its encounter with the West, was profoundly affected.[9] Significant changes became evident in occupation and education, in the structure and functioning of the community, in marriage and family life, and in the religious sphere.

SYRIA AND THE SYRIAN JEWISH COMMUNITY

The Ottoman Empire, too, underwent significant changes during the nineteenth century. In the first three decades, important foundations were laid for the reform of the army, the bureaucracy and the administration, as well as in education and in the economy. Their effects, however, were felt chiefly in regions close to the capital and less so in the area of Syria.[10] Egypt's conquest of Syria and Ibrahim Pasha's rule (1831–1840) rocked the old order and opened an avenue for far-reaching change. But this golden opportunity was ignored by the Sultan and his government when Ottoman rule resumed, and they reverted to the former status quo. Thus, for the remainder of the nineteenth century, the *Tanzimat* (reforms) which the regime declared and endeavored to realize were to be implemented only partially and in constant struggle against the (generally) latent, though firm and obstinate, opposition of those who had constituted the political and religious power in the old order.[11]

The Empire as a whole was growing increasingly weaker politically, militarily and economically. Against the reformist and centralist initiatives of the government in Constantinople, powerful centrifugal forces were at work, undermining the regime, and leading to the gradual disintegration of the Empire. These opposing tendencies, and the accompanying tension, left their mark on Syria. In the absolute sense, Syria in the nineteenth century undoubtedly developed positively with respect to the safety of persons and property, law and order, the relaxation of despotic rule, greater equality in tax collection, the improved status of minorities and the defense of their rights. However, the greater economic opportunities present elsewhere, both near (as in Egypt) and far off (as in the Americas), led hundreds of thousands to emigrate, including an inordinate proportion of the young, the educated, and the resourceful.[12]

The Jewish community was similarly affected. Although the Jewish population of the urban communities (in Aleppo, Damascus, and Beirut) increased at the end of the nineteenth century,[13] this was due to natural increase and urbanization rather than immigration. In fact, there was a simultaneous wave of emigration to Egypt, Europe, North and South America. As compared with contemporaneous developments in the Egyptian communities, the changes in Syria's Jewish communities, while not insignificant, were nevertheless restricted in depth and scope, due to the relative absence of European influence and the large-scale emigration of the young and educated.[14]

THE RABBINATE AND THE RABBIS

In Egypt as in Syria, the structure of the Jewish communities, as well as the status and function of rabbis, derived from the law of 1865.[15] According to this law, committees were to be established in the major communities to deal with "secular affairs" and "spiritual matters" alongside the rabbis. Nonrabbinical figures comprised the majority in these committees, and therefore the rabbis did not have a free hand in formulating intracommunity policy. In Egypt, the committees clearly took precedence over the rabbis in the administration of community affairs, and cooperation between them was based on mutual recognition of this fact. In Syria, the situation varied. In Aleppo, the rabbis and scholars remained the dominant factor in the community; in Damascus, the forces seemed to be balanced; while only in Beirut (a relatively young community without an established rabbinical base) did the "secular" leadership enjoy the greater power.[16]

The law further stipulated that the rabbinical courts were to be subordinate to the chief rabbis and recognized by the state. Their authority covered only Jews of Ottoman citizenship, and was restricted to matters of "personal status": marriage, divorce, wills, and legacies. Thus the authority of the rabbinical courts over the Jewish population, in matters beyond personal status, depended, as it did in the past, on the voluntary obedience of the members of the community.[17] But now, as distinct from the past, the Jews had recourse to the state courts which handed down rulings according to state law (Ottoman or Egyptian), before which all citizens of the Empire were equal (formally, at least), irrespective of religious affiliation. In Egypt, the Jews became accustomed to submitting all their conflicts and disputes to the jurisdiction of the state courts; in Syria, there was an increasing tendency to do so, although many Jews continued to submit various problems of civil law to the judgment of the rabbis.[18]

State definition of the status of the rabbis and the rabbinical courts, as well as the structure of the communities and the authority of the committees, enhanced the status of the rabbinate and its image in the eyes of the public. A rabbi recognized as the *hakham bashi* of a region and of a regional urban community was therefore generally spared opposition to and questioning of his religious authority and halakhic rulings.

Nevertheless, the complex process of rabbinical appointment, as well as the intricate relationship between the rabbi and the community committees, politicized the rabbinical function, and generated bitter and often protracted contests between various factions over the appointment or dismissal of rabbis.[19]

There were some significant differences between the rabbinical worlds of Egypt and Syria. Egypt, in the eighteenth and nineteenth centuries, was not a focus of significant Torah activity; it did not have Torah centers, and its rabbis did not gather about them yeshivot or large followings of students. In Syria, on the other hand, Torah activity flourished during the eighteenth and the first half of the nineteenth century, particularly in Aleppo, though also in Damascus. Egypt's rabbis during this period had, for the most part, been neither born nor educated locally; whereas most of Syria's rabbis for the same period were natives of that country and products of its *batei midrash.* Thus, Egypt's rabbis in official positions at this time (such as community rabbis, rabbinical judges, or court scribes) had almost total autonomy in their decision-making, and no need to justify themselves before an informal stratum of Torah scholars or to be subject to its criticism. Rabbis in official positions in Syria, on the other hand, had far less autonomy, as their every decision was open to the criticism and potential opposition of a considerable peer group. The absence of local Torah centers, and of local peer control in Egypt, undoubtedly diminished the rabbis' sense of being bound to support local customs and mores, while the opposite can be said of many of Syria's rabbis.

CHANGES IN COMMUNICATION AND TRANSPORTATION

(a) The "Vapors" (Steamships) and Divorce

In the course of the nineteenth century, sea travel in the eastern basin of the Mediterranean was enormously improved as a result of the invention of the steamship and the establishment of permanent sea routes between the major ports in the region. This had a revolutionary impact.[20] Its consequences for Jewish society were equally important, and aroused the attention of halakhic scholars. For example, it contributed directly to increased Jewish migration especially during the latter half of the nineteenth century, one of the side effects of which was the added strain and pressure it put on marriages, leading to an increase in divorce.[21] By Jewish law, a wife is not divorced until the bill of divorce reaches her hands. In the nineteenth century, with the number of cases of divorce involving wide geographical separation rising drastically, it became necessary to provide an overall and efficient solution for the international dispatch of divorce bills (and accompanying documents) between Jewish courts, far removed from each other.[22]

On the face of it, it would seem that the nineteenth century brought not only the affliction but also the remedy, in the form of a modern postal system, which constituted a major turning point in international communication, with respect to reliability, efficiency, speed, and a universal price. Ostensibly, nothing could be simpler than for the rabbinical courts to avail themselves of this innovation and exchange documents, including divorce bills, by means of the mails, and thereby avert the problem of *agunot* (wives deserted without divorce). The difficulty lay in the fact that the modern postal system was run by gentiles; and the early medieval Babylonian Geonim had determined that a bill of divorce was not to be entrusted to a gentile, except ex post facto, in cases of constraint, when there were no Jews who could undertake this sacred task.[23]

What is more, the increase in the number of Jewish travelers along international routes led to a significant decrease in the number of locations which, in principle, could not be reached by a Jewish emissary bearing a bill of divorce. Consequently, there were scholars who argued that there was less justification in the modern period for a bill to be transmitted by gentiles than there had been in former periods. Rabbi Asher Kovo, one of the great scholars of Salonika in the nineteenth century, wrote to the rabbis of Jerusalem who mailed a divorce bill from Jerusalem to Salonika:

> I am astonished by this act of our princely rabbis: whatever induced them to perform the divorce ritual . . . in a manner contrary to the opinion of the Geonim, who forbade sending a bill of divorce by the hand of a Gentile, excepting only cases of great difficulty and constraint. For we see that at present, many travellers and wayfarers come and go from there [Jerusalem] to here [Salonika] by means of the "vapors" [steamships]. Since, then, there is always opportunity for sending the bill of divorce by hand of an Israelite, the route between Jerusalem and Salonika falls nowadays under the category of "a nearby place frequented by caravans" and the situation cannot be considered as "a time of difficulty," according to the majority of authorities, as is well known.[24]

Because of deficient international transportation in the past, it had not been possible to abide by the letter of the ancient norm, requiring a divorce bill to be delivered only by Jews. The onset of modern technology ended this undesirable situation by translating an unachievable ideal into a realistic possibility. Technology is thus seen as a means of enabling the fuller and purer fulfillment of halakhic principles than had been possible in the past.[25]

Most rabbis of the nineteenth century, however, ruled otherwise. Whether consciously or not, they recognized that this issue involved an internal conflict between differing halakhic values, and they preferred resolution of the potentially large-scale problem of *agunot* to the implementation of Gaonic principle.[26] Such a value judgment required halakhic substantiation. A crucial question is, what halakhic-juridical arguments were marshalled to express and establish this position? The nature of these arguments will reflect how the *posek* (rabbinical authority) perceived the possibilities and dynamics inherent in the halakhic system, and indicate how he met contemporary challenges to Halakhah.

Rabbi Isaac Moshe Abulafia, chief rabbi of Damascus, dealt with the issue of the doubtful validity of a divorce bill mailed by a man in Paris to his wife in Damascus, in 1896. Regarding the doubt raised by Rabbi Kovo, which would invalidate the divorce bill, he writes: "I find that all recent rabbinical authorities, blessed be their memory, do not acknowledge—that is, do not analytically accept—this analysis of our great teacher, Rabbi Asher Kovo, blessed be his memory, who had the novel opinion that by means of the 'vapors' all places now stand to each other in the relationship of 'a nearby place frequented by caravans.'. . ."[27] And after referring to several "later" rabbis who adopted such a different attitude, he summarizes: ". . . the reader will see, according to the above [sources quoted] that all recent rabbinic authorities contest the position of the great Rabbi Kovo, blessed be his memory, regarding his novel attitude. . . . Since this is so, we should in this case do nothing but follow the opinion of the majority."[28] In his ruling, Rabbi Abulafia does not present himself as adopting an original or independent stand on the issue, but rather as adjudicating between the diverse positions of past scholars. Furthermore, the position he chooses from among those before him is not based on relevant contextual considerations, but on quantitative formal principles (*Halakhah kerabim*—ruling with the majority).

Yet Rabbi Abulafia did have a stand of his own on the matter, as is disclosed implicitly, in at least two ways. Firstly, his emphasis that Rabbi Kovo's approach is tantamount to a *ḥidush* (innovative breaking of precedent), which he uses, not in the commendable sense, but in the sense of *Bid'aa* (innovation), as it appears in Moslem jurisprudence.[29] Secondly, reference to the sources cited by Rabbi Abulafia to prove that Rabbi Kovo's is the "minority," not the "majority," view, suggests that many—if not all—of these sources fail to demonstrate the desired result, and certainly offer no clear evidence to refute Rabbi Kovo's position.[30]

The comparison between Rabbi Kovo's and Rabbi Abulafia's views yields an interesting contrast: the Salonikan rabbi who (in this instance) upheld the duty of the Halakhah to relate to empirical technological-organizational change by reapplying halakhic principles without formally submitting to precedent, arrived at a halakhic conclusion which resulted in a sharp dissonance between the demands of the Halakhah and the requirements of modern Jewish society. The Damascus rabbi, on the other hand, who sought to have the Halakhah ignore empirical change, and called for a formal-technical verdict, arrived at a conclusion which resolved the potential contradiction between the demands of Halakhah and the needs of the hour.[31] However, his method involves a conscious rejection of any inquiry into the principles guiding the original halakhic formulation, and seems to imply that such rejection is necessary for contemporary functioning of Halakhah.

The approach developed by Rabbi Elijah Hazzan, chief rabbi of Alexandria, resolves the dissonance between the realm of formal halakhic argumentation and the realm of religious-social values. Rabbi Hazzan decided to get to the bottom of the matter and examine a question which had not even been raised by the above-mentioned scholars: what reasoning had originally led the Babylonian Geonim to prohibit a gentile from delivering a divorce bill? The *Rishonim* (medieval rabbinic authorities) had indeed given their attention to this question and, on the whole, had concluded that the approach of the Geonim was not justified. Ashkenazi rabbis had, as a result, openly permitted the conveyance of a divorce bill by means of a gentile. The Radbaz, who lived and wrote in Egypt in the sixteenth century, had supported the European scholars, illustrating his critique of the Geonim with the following example:

> Imagine that the husband were to place the bill of divorce, and the writ of agency, on the back of a donkey, and that the donkey transported them to the home of the agent of transmission [with no human intervention]. Could the agent now not divorce the woman with this bill of divorce, just because it had not come [directly] from the hand of the husband to the hand of the agent?[32]

Thus, the Radbaz argues, the Ashkenazi rabbis were correct in allowing the bill of divorce to be handed to a gentile who, acting solely as instrument, delivers the document to the agent of transmission. Upon further reflection, though, he wondered if there was not perhaps some logic to the decision of the Geonim: "However, it is possible that the Gaon acknowledges this (in the case of a donkey) but decrees against it in the case of a gentile, because of his concern that the husband might rely upon the gentile to act as an agent for him."[33] The Geonim, Radbaz is convinced, could not possibly have dismissed all techniques for conveying a divorce bill by non-Jewish hands. What they demanded was a clear categorical distinction between a purely technical agency, and an agency involving participation and involvement. The latter meant taking part in the process of divorce on the ritual level, a level which was open to Jews only. *In principle,* the Geonim too would have acknowledged that a gentile could serve as a purely technical transmitter. The problem was that *in practice,* the nature of Jewish-gentile interaction could be misconstrued by the Jews, giving rise to a substantive error: treating the gentile as a participant (an agent) would adversely affect the ritual-halakhic validity of the divorce. *For this reason* the Geonim had *decreed* that a bill of divorce was not to be transmitted by a gentile.[34]

On the strength of this explanation for the position of the Geonim, Rabbi Hazzan writes:

> It seems to me, that sending a bill of divorce by mail is less problematic than sending it by the hand of a gentile. For, in the case of a gentile, there is place for concern lest they would come to consider him as acting as an agent, as the Radbaz explained . . . but in the case of the mail, why—it is no gentile who transmits the bill of divorce! But rather, it is deposited in the box of mail and the ship transports the box from city to city, and all the while it is closed and sealed; and when the letter is "registered," the addressee himself must come and get it from the Post Office. So in any case (in this situation) there is no call for a decree against the mail on the grounds of it possibly being considered as an agent. This is quite obvious.[35]

In other words: the postal system is a bureaucracy, and as such is mechanical by nature. Indeed, numerous people work in the system; however, an essential feature of a bureaucracy is the fundamental anonymity of the employees, and the fundamental absence of a personal dimension in the relations between the bureaucracy and its clientele. Therefore, the relations between the user of the postal service and the postal clerks are role relations pure and simple; and there can be no danger that the sender of the letter might come to identify the clerk as an "agent" in the halakhic sense. For an essential condition of legitimizing a person for a halakhic mission is that he have the same basic status as the person charging him with the task, whereas the nature of the defined relationship between the client and the clerks of the postal system prevents the clerks from being perceived as "equals," and regarded (erroneously, if they are gentiles) by the divorcing person as having the same status as himself. Thus, with respect to the mails, the Geonim too would have acknowledged that there was no fear of such a mistake in categories and so their decree did not apply to the modern postal system. The bureaucratization typical of modern organizational systems creates a framework of Jewish-gentile interaction to which halakhic categories, established in the past as regulating relations between Jews and gentiles, do not automatically apply.

(b) The Railway and the Computation of Days of Mourning

The development of modern mechanized transportation in Egypt was remarkable for its high growth rate and geographical span. On the eve of the First World War, Egypt had the highest ratio in the world between inhabited area and overall length of railway line, and occupied a prominent place in records of track length vs. size of population, taking precedence over Japan, Turkey, China, and Greece. She began laying railway tracks in 1853 (before even such developed countries as Sweden and Japan) rapidly altering the popular mode of travel and transportation in the Nile Valley and Delta. Use of the train for interurban travel became so common that in 1900 alone, the state railway authority sold 12.5 million third-class tickets.[36] Little wonder, therefore, that rabbinical scholars were called upon to consider the normative consequences of the train on the halakhic conduct of Egyptian Jewry.

For thousands of years, until the development of mechanized transportation, there had been no significant change in the speed of travel. The ratio between "time" and "distance" had been relatively stable throughout this period, and no special difficulties arose, for instance, when a halakhic verdict in the Shulkhan Aruch was formulated in the following manner:

> If someone's relative died, and he did not find out until he came to the place where he had died, or to the place where he was buried—then: if he had been in a nearby place, that is, one no further than ten parsangs away, so that he could have arrived in one day, then even if he came on the seventh day [of the mourning week] . . . he counts with them . . . but if he had been in a distant place, then even if he came on the second day he must count for himself [the] seven and [the] thirty days [of mourning], starting with the day of his arrival.[37]

The arrival of the train, and its extensive use, altered the time/distance ratio, and confronted the rabbis with the following question: "Now that the railway has been invented, and a person can arrive in one day, even from a distance of more than a hundred parsangs, there arises a question: do we figure the number of parsangs according to the travel speed of railway trains?"[38] Rabbi Elijah Hazzan dealt with the problem in a detailed argument, refuting the position adopted by Rabbi Jospeh Saul Halevi Nathanson (1810–1875), one of Europe's great halakhic scholars of the nineteenth century. The relevant passage in Rabbi Nathanson's verdict is as follows:

> Now: Although today there are railways, and one can travel many parsangs in a day, nevertheless this is not considered "a distance of one day's travel," as I have written in my book Yad Shaul (still in manuscript) [on] section 375. For we reckon only according to natural means, not according to contrivances that have been invented in our times. For, should we do otherwise, the ways of Torah would change, day after day. For continuously do people go by new means: Why, even recently flying balloons were invented, and see (in this connection) B.T. *Makkot* page 5, [where it says] "Should we then take into account a flying camel? We have been taught that the answer is negative." And also according to the statement of the Tosaphot on B.T. *Yevamot* page 116, in the name of R. Menachem—whenever it is not positively otherwise, we reckon "near" and "distant" according to natural means only. . . .[39]

Rabbi Hazzan writes:

> (a) We beg his pardon. Railways are not an "unnatural contrivance," but they are quite natural and comprehensible, and were previously in potentia but have now been brought to realization.
> (b) And regarding his concern, lest the ways of Torah change—(Heaven forbid this!) there is no cause for worry here. For the Rabbis, blessed be their memory, stated a fixed measure: the distance of one day's travel. And this measure is forever constant, like all the rules of our Holy Torah. But, in previous times this measure was specified as ten parsangs—and now, it has grown greater.
> (c) And if it were something rare, not usually present, like a flying camel, we could let the matter rest. But it is well known that wherever the railway is in operation, it does not deviate from its function for any period of time.
> (d) . . . and an incident occurred in this town, involving a man who arrived at the site of his mourning by railway; and automatically the category of "one who arrived from a nearby place" was applied to him without asking a rabbi. And I did not protest against this, for I said: "Let them be, for they are Israelites, the sons of prophets."[40]

Underlying this debate between Rabbi Hazzan and Rabbi Nathanson was a crucial question: What value is to be attributed to the world of culture (and particularly modern and technological culture) as opposed to the world of creation, to "nature"? Rabbi Nathanson's approach implies a negative attitude toward the modern technological world: denying it status as "natural" renders it unworthy of halakhic "recognition." Implicitly, our ancestors, who lived and acted in a manner suited to "nature," and not according to contrivance, lived in a better world than we do; we live in an unnatural world, having exchanged the ways of nature for "novel contrivances." The least we can do is refuse to accord halakhic (normative) status to the degenerate world in which we live.[41]

Unlike Rabbi Nathanson, Rabbi Hazzan feels that "our world" is no less "natural" than that of our ancestors. On the contrary: To the extent that a comparison is valid at all, one might even say that our world is more "natural" than was the case in early generations. Numerous "natural" occurrences which were then only *potentially* possible, are today *actual.* We live in a richer world than our forefathers with respect to the realization of the nature of creation. And there is no reason to withhold halakhic "recognition" from the technological dimensions of the modern world. Our world is no less worthy of halakhic "recognition" than was that of our ancestors.

One of Rabbi Nathanson's basic arguments is that changing halakhic rulings in response to changes in the "external" world contradicts one of the fundamental functions of the Torah, namely: to ensure a stable and permanent normative world. In Rabbi Hazzan's view, the "eternity of the Torah" is not to be identified with "permanence of concrete halakhic statements." The stability of the halakhic world is not measured by the constancy of concrete statements over hundreds and thousands of years, but by the permanence of the principles from, and according to which, the concrete Halakhah is derived.[42] Altering the concrete rulings in response to actual changes in life is thus not a sign of fickleness but rather of profound faithfulness to the principles of Halachah itself.

Rabbi Hazzan's rejection of Rabbi Nathanson's analogy between the railway, the flying balloon, and a "flying camel" reveals the tremendous difficulty in finding Talmudic analogies to the innovations of the modern world.[43] Rabbi Nathanson sought to rest his verdict on Talmudic precedent so as to lend it validity and force. Rabbi Hazzan, however, did not seek any precedent, but analyzed the guiding principles in the *posek*'s original argument, and attempted to show how to remain faithful to the same principles in a different empirical-social context. This may well be illustrative of a deep-set and fundamental controversy over the manner in which the Halakhah of the past is to be projected onto the present. The author of *Shoel Umeshiv* endeavored to base his analysis on the method of analogy, whereby the proposed norm is not "invented" by the *posek* but is found to exist in the ancient writings; that is, the method can subordinate cases, which appear to be far removed from the original incident, to an existing norm. Rabbi Hazzan, on the other hand, attempted to base his argument analytically on the Halakhah itself, in the belief that such an analysis would make it possible to identify the principle or principles which had guided previous scholars in determining a concrete halakhic verdict. Project "classical" Halakhah onto a new empirical situation thus means formulating a *new* concrete Halakhic statement which will ensure the full realization, in the present, of the principles which guided the early composers of Halakhah.

Rabbi Hazzan's concluding reference to an actual incident in which mourners in Alexandria themselves decided the conduct of a family member who arrived from afar by train, without seeking rabbinical advice, expresses a fundamental approach to the nature of the halakhic decision, namely that the Halakhah is not a "closed" rational system of assumptions, claims, arguments, and conclusions.[44] Indeed, it encompasses such a system, but it is not circumscribed by it: Jewry is a living and breathing reality, and the deeds and behavior of the Jewish public have religious value of normative consequence.[45] This, Rabbi Hazzan is persuaded, is true not only of Jewish communities in the past (whose "customs" have been noted in the Codes), but also of Jews in the present: the people of Israel are today, too, the "sons of prophets." Halakhic ruling therefore must be the creative integration of the import of the written halakhic sources for the present, and the "spontaneous" trends of the living Jewish community.

The possible influence of the railway on the connotation of "nearby" for the purposes of mourning, was discussed also by the rabbi of Damascus. However, his motive for dealing with the question was different, because of the vast differences in the development of the infrastructure of transportation in Egypt and in Syria. Until the last decade of the nineteenth century, there was not a single kilometer of railway track in all of Syria; indeed, there were scarcely any roads, and most of the cartage and travel was carried out by means of non-wheeled conveyances. Only in 1895 was a railway line completed between Beirut and Damascus.[46] Rabbi Abulafia's response to the question of the railway's influence on the definition of "nearby" reveals a considerably different approach from that of Rabbi Hazzan.

To begin with, Rabbi Abulafia firmly and unequivocally supports Rabbi Abraham Alkalai of Dubnitsa (Serbia), who had dealt with the question at the end of the eighteenth century.[47]

> For in the sphere of mourning regulations, we do not consider someone as arriving "from a nearby place" unless he arrives from a distance of [not more than] ten parsangs walking by foot, at a moderate pace, not at a run. For thus did our rabbis reckon, that an average person could walk ten parsangs in a day; and these ten parsangs were calculated with regard to a walker, not one who rides by horse or mule. Just as Rabbi Alkalai, in his work "Hessed LeAvraham," has written . . . "We find then, re the case under discussion, that as 'a nearby place' we consider only a place to where an average person could walk by foot, at a moderate pace, in the course of one day, that is, twelve hours . . . thus, if the distance is more than that, it is considered 'a far off place.' . . ."[48]
>
> And according to this—how much more so is it true of one who rides by means of horses of fire and vehicles of fire, that is, by railway, which proceed ten times more rapidly than horses and mules, that such a person certainly cannot be regarded as someone who "arrives from a nearby place" at all.[49]

Rabbi Abulafia's approach is to argue that the problem, in fact, is not new and that, in principle, it had already been decided in early halakhic sources. As Rabbi Alkalai demonstrated, the question of whether "one day's distance" included non-pedestrian forms of travel (such as horses or mules) had already been answered negatively in a Tanaitic Baraita cited in the Babylonian Talmud. That is, the railway was not to be considered a unique innovation, substantially different from forms of transportation familiar since the dawn of history. Although, in practice, his approach is the same as Rabbi Nathanson's (cited earlier), his understanding of the phenomenon of the train is different. The train is not to be disregarded in the calculation of "a day's distance" because of its essential strangeness as an "unnatural contrivance," but because of its essential similarity to horses and mules.

While the two rabbis vary greatly in their assessment of the "naturalness" of the railway, their attitudes to precedents are most similar. As far as Rabbi Abulafia is concerned, it is sufficient that Rabbi Alkalai ruled as he did, basing his analysis on the Talmudic Baraita: he himself is not bound to ponder the inner logic of Rabbi Alkalai's ruling. The decisive fact is the precedent itself, not subject to either the appraisal or analysis of contemporary scholars, but serving as the cornerstone of halakhic projection through analogy onto the present reality.

ROMANTIC VALUES VIS-À-VIS FAMILY DISCIPLINE

Thus far, we have examined two instances in which technological/organizational developments made it necessary to determine how the Halakhah was to respond to these transformations. While it is true that the influences of European civilization left their mark on the Middle East first and foremost in the technical/instrumental sphere, they nevertheless also affected the area of culture, thought, and values, albeit to a lesser degree, and at a later stage.[50] Moreover, these latter influences were more evident among the affluent classes and the intellectual elite, and less so among the general public. Jewish society, however, especially in the large urban centers, seems to have received far greater exposure to Western influence in the field of culture and values for three main reasons. First, many Jews in the East were subjects or protégés of a European power. Second, Eastern Jewish communities maintained political and economic ties with their European counterparts. Finally, there was direct interpersonal contact, whether as a result of European Jewish immigration to the Middle East (chiefly to Palestine and Egypt), and visits there as merchants or tourists, or via the involvement of European Jews in the founding of educational institutions in the Eastern Jewish communities such as those of the Alliance Israélite Universelle. One of the areas affected was that of sexual relations and marriage.[51] Here we will examine the controversy between Rabbi Hazzan and Rabbi Abulafia over one aspect of this sphere: a daughter's refusal to wed the man chosen for her by her family.

In Jewish society of the Middle Ages, marriage was a bond between two families.[52] There were important economic and familial aspects to this bond. The couple, particularly the destined bride, was not a central factor in the detailed and protracted negotiations which preceded marriage. Parental authority was internalized via the socialization process, and it was commonly understood to include the right to choose marriage partners. Nonconformity and noncompliance in regard to the arranged match were clearly the exception rather than the rule and were appropriately treated as deviant by the *poskim*.

One of the features of the modern era in Europe in general, and consequently also among European Jewry, was the growing dominance of the romantic ideal and the heightened consciousness of the individual's importance and opinion. Against this background, we find in European Jewish communities increasing instances of noncompliance on the part of young people with regard to arranged marriages. In the Middle East this phenomenon made its appearance much later, and on a much more limited scale. This, then, is the context of the following dispute between Rabbi Abulafia and Rabbi Hazzan.

Rabbi Abulafia was asked to consider the case below, which occurred in Damascus:

> Reuven became affianced to Leah the granddaughter of Shimon, and the parties signed an engagement agreement, as is customary. Her grandfather Shimon obligated himself to provide a dowry for her, consonant with his status. Also Reuven and Shimon mutually decided upon the sum to be paid by either of them in case of their side causing the annulment of the above-mentioned agreement . . . and explicitly wrote that the payment of this sum would be obligatory without any regard for whom or what caused the annulment. . . .
>
> But now, after several months have passed since the above-mentioned betrothal, during which time the bride was satisfied with her fiance and received him with pleasant countenance—why now, her attitude has changed and she has rejected her fiance and does not want him at all. Her grandfather Shimon took great pains to dissuade her, and to convince her to enter the marriage canopy with the above-mentioned Reuven, that she should not ruin his achievements to his face. Also her mother and uncle and other of her relatives attempted to dissuade her and to convince her, verbally and by monetary inducements; but she was not convinced by them at all. She brazened her face and said: I do not want to take him at all, even if you kill me. Upon seeing this, her grandfather and mother after some time went and affianced her to a different fellow, whom she wanted.
>
> So now Reuven has come and sues Shimon for the sum he obligated himself to pay [in case of annulment]. But Shimon replies thus: "It is indeed true that I obligated myself; but this obligation was only for a case in which I, or another of the bride's relatives, caused the annulment. However, this is not the case now, for we ourselves want him [Reuven] very much, and wish that this could indeed be, for to whom should the treasure of Israel belong [if not to Reuven]? But, what can we do now that the girl has turned a rebellious shoulder and we have exhausted ourselves trying to appease and convince her—to no avail? What now is it within my power to do, that I have not done? Never for a moment did it cross my mind that my own granddaughter would disobey my word and contravene my ruling! I am, therefore, a victim of an unavoidable cause."[53]

In a long and highly detailed response, Rabbi Abulafia justified Shimon and absolved him of paying the sum specified in the betrothal contract. The gist of his argument was as follows: (a) Indeed, according to the contract, the obligation was binding "without any regard for whom or what caused the annulment," (b) However, halakhic literature commonly distinguished between three degrees of "unavoidable causes":

(1) common unavoidable causes; (2) moderately common unavoidable causes; (3) rare unavoidable causes. (c) Furthermore, all the *poskim* are agreed that in the absence of written stipulation as to the special instances included in the obligation, the contract was to be considered binding only with respect to relevant concerns which one might ordinarily imagine could/might happen. (d) The Rashba (Rabbi Abulafia argues), has already determined that a daughter's refusal to comply with an arranged match is a "rare unavoidable cause"; for all daughters accept the marriage arranged for them by their elders.[54] And since this is not a common occurrence which could easily be envisaged, one must interpret the contract to mean that Shimon had not intended in his obligation to be liable for payment in such an instance. A single doubt hovers over this clear-cut decision:

> I noted that the great rabbi Haim Yosef David Azulai, in his aforementioned responsum,[55] related to the issue under discussion in a novel manner: [he suggested that] even if it be conceded that the Rashba considered [the girl's refusal] as "rare" . . . a differentiation should be made between the times of the Early Masters to our time; "For nowadays and in our time, refusal by the girl is not to be considered rare and astonishing; for one's eyes see and one's ears hear, that many maidens refuse, and turn a rebellious shoulder! And if you will, then read of this in the books and the subject matter of the Latter Masters—how many maidens did not follow the words of their father! . . . therefore, this is obviously to be considered "frequent yet infrequent."[56]

Rabbi Haim Yosef David Azulai introduced a new dimension into the argument, an historical dimension: although the Rashba determined that the daughter's refusal to obey was a rare phenomenon, we must not allow his decision to guide us, for social behavior has changed. Rabbi Azulai produced two forms of evidence: one, empirical observation of the conduct of daughters and their disobedience to their parents in arranged matches; and two, the cumulative testimony in the responsa works of the "late" scholars as to the proportions and widespread propagation of this phenomenon.

Rabbi Abulafia finds it difficult to accept this argument and in his analysis he makes two basic criticisms: (a) the *posek* does not have direct access to empirical social reality. One cannot argue that a situation has changed in the course of time when there is no precedent in the halakhic books of such an argument. (b) Rabbi Azulai's "historical" evidence from the books of the "later" scholars, of the increase in the incidence of daughters refusing to comply, is equally unacceptable. The only evidence Rabbi Abulafia is prepared to accept from these books is their halakhic content, and their halakhic content *contradicts*

Rabbi Azulai's innovation; many of the later rabbis did in fact rely on the Rashba's decision, and not one of them suggested that this precedent was invalid because of differences in historical periods![57]

However, later, after a further analysis, Rabbi Abulafia modifies his stand and acknowledges that Rabbi Azulai's assessment of the extent of daughterly recalcitrance might indeed be applicable to European societies, but was irrelevant to the question which had arisen in Damascus.[58] In Europe, he concedes, the local custom based on local etiquette was that the partners of the couple chose one another, independently of the opinion of parents or relatives. Whereas in the countries of Islam—the Middle East and North Africa—the etiquette was and had always been that young people married the mates selected for them by parents or relatives.

The Halakhah, indeed, has always recognized that customs varied according to place (see Mishna, *Pesahim* Chap. 4), and found no difficulty in sustaining a pluralistic Jewish reality, wherein different communities adhered to different customs and even different halakhic rulings, in parallel to one another. Local custom was binding on the local community and their offspring; pluralism in custom was, in principle, synchronic and not diachronic. Rabbi Abulafia could thus clearly accept Rabbi Azulai's explanation of varying customs, but only if these differed from place to place, and not from time to time in *one* and the same location.

Sensitive to these nuances in the analysis of his elder colleague, Rabbi Hazzan adopted and established a very different position regarding the receptiveness of the Halakhah to historical change in the social reality.

> And it would seem to me, that in such a matter, it is not something astonishing or unbelievable. And it is quite possible, that the maiden would refuse. But why then do the Rashba and Rabbi M. MiPano write, that it is an infrequent matter?—because time is a factor. . . . And it would seem that in our time, a maiden's refusal is not to be deemed "infrequent."[59]

He fully identified with Rabbi Azulai: "I find the words of Rabbi Azulai to be full of milk and honey; the words of God are truly in his mouth and my heart rejoices in that I independently reached the same conclusion as did his great mind."[60] And he even argues that accepting the principle of "time is a factor" makes it necessary to recognize, in fact, the continuing dynamism of society during the period which had elapsed between Rabbi Azulai's day and his own: "After we have proved that a differentiation should be made between times and generations, we conclude that in *our* time refusal on the part of a maiden is to be considered '*very* frequent.' "[61]

An approach in which halakhic ruling allows for the historical context demands a corresponding conception of precedents and their significance. Indeed, in his discourse against Rabbi Abulafia's objections to Rabbi Azulai's argument, he directs himself to these two topics: the attitude toward the dimension of time, and the attitude toward precedents. In his view, the principle that it is appropriate to consider time differences in halakhic ruling is not an innovation invented by Rabbi Azulai, but a long-standing and legitimate feature of Halakhah. Furthermore, the use of precedents established by "late" scholars, who lived before Rabbi Azulai, in order to repudiate his position or to present it as a single opinion against many, is an invalid and futile attempt: Rabbi Azulai was specifically concerned with his own period, and evidence from previous generations can prove nothing in a question dependent on time, such as this.[62]

Thus far we have seen Rabbi Abulafia's response and Rabbi Hazzan's criticism. Since the material was published by Rabbi Abulafia, he took the trouble to reply in detail to the criticism directed against him, and made certain that his answer would appear alongside the criticism. A glance at his answer shows on which points, and to what extent, he was willing to credit (if only implicitly) Rabbi Hazzan's approach, and which matters he deemed a question of principle, brooking no compromise.

With respect to the issue of the legitimacy of sociohistorical change as a factor in formulating a halakhic ruling, Rabbi Abulafia writes:

> It is indeed so: in matters where we see that the great masters of the Law differentiated between times, such as in the issue of the depreciation of currencies, and in the issue of impoverishment, as he [R. Hazzan] himself quoted—in such matters do we concede; for they [first] stated [one position] and they themselves [then] stated [a different position].
>
> Not so is the matter under discussion here; for in the words of no authority, even anyone of the Latter Masters who preceded the great R. Azulai by only one generation, do we find such a differentiation. . . . Therefore, in this does R. Azulai cause us great astonishment, in that he makes such a differentiation solely from his own mind and opinion.[63]

Thus, while the principle of sociohistorical change is not foreign to halakhic ruling, it is nonetheless not a general principle. It may be applied only in very specific instances, and these instances are identified by . . . a precedent. It is not the inherent logic of the case under discussion which determines whether its historical context is to be considered, but its formal characteristic as "dependent on time" or "permanent through time." Rabbi Azulai's astounding "innovation" was not that he invented a category of "times have changed," but that he attempted, without precedent, to apply this principle to maidenly refusal of arranged matches; an attempt made "solely from his own mind and opinion,"[64] without any legitimate, formal basis.

Rabbi Hazzan's insistence that "in our time refusal on the part of a maiden is to be considered 'very common'" caused Rabbi Abulafia, reluctantly almost, to directly confront the social reality of his day, and it is plain that he perceives the present through very different eyes than does Rabbi Hazzan:

> And regarding his [R. Hazzan's] statement, that in our time refusal on the part of a maiden is to be considered "very common"—to the contrary! Our own eyes see that all maidens of Israel (excepting only those residing in the Lands of Edom [i.e., Europe] speakers of foreign tongues), why, all the rest—both maidens and youths cover their faces with the veil of shyness at all times. They speak not at all on the subject of the making of their match, and receive in good will whatever is done on their behalf by their father, mother or other relations, without ever turning a rebellious shoulder of refusing. And we have never heard nor seen a maiden or a youth say openly: "We do not want [the match] chosen [for us] by our father and mother" (or other relation). Only, sometimes, in the inner chambers [of the house] they hint to them, in great secrecy, without their voice being heard by others. This fact is so well known as to need no proof. Thus, if sometimes a youth or a maiden do brazen their forehead in public—that surely is a matter "completely infrequent." Such being the case, it is clear now that there is no substance at all to his [R. Hazzan's] words.[65]

In principle, therefore, the rabbis are divided as regards their conception of the historical dimension of Halakhah, and their approach to halakhic precedents. They disagree also in their perception of the reality of the Jewish family in the East of their time.

OVERVIEW

In principle, Rabbi Abulafia feels that Halakhah is, and should be, a closed system of concepts, arguments, and evidence, which operates according to immanent rules and inherent considerations, not dependent or conditional upon any extra-Torah reality.

According to this approach, the *posek* in the present occupies a position of subordination to the conclusions appearing in previous halakhic literature. His procedure should be governed by the axiom that the *posek* does not *create* law, but *decides* law; that is, his function is to determine which of the halakhic conclusions in the literature is applicable to the circumstances about which his judgment is sought. In the best of cases, the *posek* will find that the given problem has already been dealt with in the Torah literature of the past, and that those who dealt with it all agreed as to its solution. A less desirable, though not particularly problematic, possibility is to discover that past scholars dealt with the subject but did not agree on a solution. In this instance, the *posek* must decide which conclusion is valid, and he will do so not on the basis of his personal opinion or understanding, but on the basis of formal principles of ruling.

A more complex halakhic procedure is required when the *posek* finds that the problem has not been dealt with by earlier halakhic scholars. In this case, he must find a similar problem discussed in the literature in order to apply its conclusion to the present problem.

The technique for determining similarity is analogy, which means identifying the same manifest formal characteristics in both instances. (Preferably, these formal elements will be among the essential properties of the incident judged in the past.) When the *posek* finds that an analogy exists, he is entitled to apply the conclusions of the precedent to the case before him.[66]

The common denominator in the foregoing is that the *posek* in the present does not introduce new conclusions (halakhic norms) on the basis of his opinion and understanding, but decides from an existing stock of conclusions which are valid for the situation he faces. Nor is his choice made on the basis of reasonable preference, due to greater substantive, principled or reasoned applicability to the case at hand, but on the basis of formal and technical rules of decision. In the absence of a clear-cut precedent, as well, the precedent is selected by means of a formal-external analogy, without a substantive assessment of the applicability of the first *posek*'s considerations to the present. In short: the substantive-rational-teleological dimension of the halakhic discussions held in the past is, in principle, not open to discussion by the *posek* in the present. Only the conclusions of the past *poskim* are significant and decisive, and these are sifted in a purely formal-legalistic manner.

In the nature of things, this conception of the essence of ruling and the function of the *posek* generates certain tendencies in all aspects of the *posek*'s approach to the social-empirical reality of his Jewish community and the world surrounding it. For the ideal in this method of ruling is the definite and complete similarity between past and present;

and in the absence of total similarity, analogy is purported to bridge the gap between them, and by so doing, render the dissimilarity irrelevant. However, implicit in the very logic of using analogy is the premise that considerable similarity indeed exists between the paradigms of the past and the phenomena of the present. Without this premise, the entire enterprise would become impossible.

This conception of legal judgment channels the *posek*'s thought process toward a minimum recognition of the new or original features of any current phenomenon, and toward a maximum emphasis on old and familiar features. The novel and exceptional properties of a technological, social or cultural phenomenon will be acknowledged only when unavoidable; and then, too, the intrinsic logic of the mode of ruling will make it necessary to stress those elements which are similar to what has occurred in the past, and to determine that it is *these* elements which are significant to the halakhic system.

If we recall the cases analyzed above, we note that the tendency of Rabbi Abulafia is to determine that although steamships have been invented, nevertheless the Mediterranean ports are still "places unfrequented by caravans," so that nothing has changed in principle; that although there is a modern postal system, the non-Jewish postal clerk is still "a gentile," so that nothing has changed in principle; that although trains have been invented, they are analogous to horses, already discussed in the past in the context of defining a "day's distance." Finally, since the Rashba deemed maidenly refusal to wed a groom chosen by her grandfather to be "rare," this decision remains valid even after six hundred years. Rabbi Azulai's attempt to prove otherwise by arguing that times have changed is either incorrect or a dubious innovation, derived from personal opinion. At best, it may be accepted only if strictly circumscribed to particular circumstances (a particular geographic or cultural realm), whereas in the immediate context (all Islamic countries!) the more general rule of the Rashba continues to apply.

Rabbi Hazzan's method is different from the above. In principle, he feels that the Halakhah is, and should be, a system of concepts, arguments and evidence receptive of and reacting to the existing social-empirical reality. The *posek* in the present occupies a position of subordination to the authority of the principles revealed to him in his study of the previous halakhic literature. It is not the conclusions of former *poskim* which obligate him, but the principles underlying their conclusions. The *posek* reaches halakhic rulings by discovering and properly applying the principles embedded in the halakhic works of his predecessors, taking into account the conditions of the concrete reality of his day.

This conception of the essence of ruling and the function of the *posek* generates certain tendencies in its turn. According to this conception, past and present phenomena may differ even when formally similar; in any event, the degree of similarity must be determined in each and every case. Moreover, in principle, the degree of formal-phenomenological similarity, or lack of it, neither enhances nor detracts from the possibility of determining Halakhah. This depends on quite other factors: the *posek*'s ability to understand the underlying considerations and principles which guided *poskim* in the past, and the nature of the society in which he lives. Hence, the *posek* may acknowledge that the train is a novel phenomenon, not analogous to the "flying camel" or any other means of transport discussed in the past; that the stock of past halakhic guidelines for determining the meaning of "nearby" never extended beyond ten parsangs; yet conclude that the specification of "a nearby place" should be extended from ten to one hundred parsangs, or more, since it is the principle ("one day's journey") which binds the *posek,* not the specific precedent.

Similarly, he will admit that steamships have brought about significant change, in that now all places may be said to be "frequented by caravans," yet determine that a divorce bill *may* be sent by the modern mail because its bureaucratic nature renders it different in principle (despite its formal similarity) from reliance on a gentile to act as a husband's agent.

Finally, the *posek* is not obliged to follow the ruling of the Rashba in the matter of a daughter's refusal to accept a chosen match, since the principle behind the contract involves consideration of what is actually common or rare *in the present.* Indeed, it is the *posek*'s agreement with the *principle* behind Rabbi Azulai's analysis that obliges him to disagree with the latter's halakhic conclusion.[67]

It is nonetheless important to avoid schematization. It would not be true, for example, to contend that Rabbi Elijah Hazzan strove to declare every phenomenon that he encountered "novel" and "different" from past halakhic guidelines, requiring the formulation of new ones. For the most part, in fact, he found the historical continuum rather stable. However, in principle, his approach implies a degree of receptivity to prevailing conditions which implies the possibility of specifying the practical-normative consequences of historical change for the corpus of Jewish law.

By the same token, it would be equally incorrect to claim that the mode of ruling adopted by Rabbi Moses Abulafia always left intact the normative guidelines set down in the past. For instance, by ignoring the increase of Jewish passengers on steamships (a function of his tendency to ignore any change in the real world, as far as possible), the rabbi was led to permit the use of the postal system for the transmission of divorce bills, thus providing a more comprehensive and effective solution to the problem of *agunot.*

In sum, formal-legalistic ruling does not *necessarily* lead to de facto conservatism; ruling according to substantive principle does not *necessarily* lead to a radical change in Halakhah. No *intrinsic* monovalent correlation exists between the method of ruling and the halakhic conclusion reached. That such a correlation does, in fact, frequently obtain should then be attributed primarily to other causes, especially those grounded in the historical-cultural context.

UNDERSTANDING THE DIFFERENCES OF APPROACH

There would appear to be several characteristics of the social environment of our two *poskim* which may be singled out as factors reinforcing or encouraging tendencies in favor of a particular method of ruling.

We can point, for example, to the demographic-economic trends in Egypt and Syria, mentioned at the outset, as one such factor. A rabbi in Syria could well have tended to see the reality of the past as normative and desirable to a greater extent than an Egyptian rabbi. The Jewish community in Egypt was undergoing an accelerated process of social-normative change.[68] Technology and modern methods of organization were having a considerable influence on the daily lives of the community's members. It would have been exceedingly difficult for a *posek* in Egypt to take the position that the present was not significantly different from the past. Conversely, the less extensive absorption of modern technology in Syria, combined with the emigration of the potentially more progressive community members (the young and the educated), made it easier, on the whole, for a *posek* to view social reality as essentially unchanging.

In addition to these factors, we must take into account the respective differences in the vectors of development of Jewish intellectual life. During the eighteenth and early nineteenth centuries, Syria had been an important intellectual-Torah center, producing superior rabbis and scholars. Numerous books were written and published. Parallel with signs of decline in the general condition of the community, however, there occurred a waning of its intellectual life. Scholars emigrated (some to Palestine); financial support for them and their students dwindled; many capable young people turned to non-Torah institutions of learning, such as the schools established by the Alliance Israélite.

We can understand the particular significance a Syrian *posek* would attach to the statement "the generations are declining," leading him to ascribe maximum authority to the opinion of past scholars and to establish himself as a purely technical arbitrator of halakhic conclusions.

Although there were still far more scholars in Syria than in Egypt at the beginning of the twentieth century, the situation which obtained in Egypt was not one of deterioration relative to the recent past. In the preceding two centuries, the Egyptian Jewish community had been impoverished, largely illiterate, and had adhered to folk customs which greatly deviated from halakhic norms.[69] There was thus no reason for the rabbis active in Egypt at the end of the nineteenth century and early in the twentieth to feel that, in the Torah world, "the generations are declining," but rather the reverse. Moreover, rabbis in Egypt being relatively few, and for the most part foreign-born, they enjoyed exclusive social-communal authority in the area of Halakhah. Whereas in Syria, as has been noted, a rabbi's function—even in an official position, such as *hakham bashi* or president of the rabbinical court—entailed a degree of dependence on a conservative intellectual class which, despite developmental trends, remained a considerable force. This made it more difficult for a rabbi or *hakham bashi* to show initiative or to set down rulings which were not in complete accord with past precedent.

Looking at factors in the non-Jewish environment, it is hardly likely that the Syrian population, particularly in the towns and villages, would have been impressed by the powerful modernizing forces affecting society in the world at large. The deficiencies and weaknesses of the Ottoman Empire were well evident in Syria.[70] It was an unclear and somewhat contradictory situation, in which a *posek* might understandably persist in operating within a formal-legalistic framework, rather than take a personal stand in assessing how the values of the past were to apply to the present. In this regard, conditions in Egypt were significantly different. The policies of Mehmet Ali and his successors, as well as firm British resolve, left no doubt as to the direction and force of the vectors of change in Egypt during this period.

Another factor of possible relevance was the difference in the attitudes of the Moslem religious leadership *(ulema)* in the two countries. The ten years of Egyptian rule in Syria (1831–41), which entailed the attempt to institute widespread reforms, had left the local *ulema* bitterly opposed to innovation, even after the return of Ottoman rule. In opposing westernization and secularization, they were fairly successful.[71] In Egypt, on the other hand, a modernist school developed, under the influence of Afghani and his students, Muhammad Abduh and

Rashid Rida. This group proclaimed the need to adopt Western science in order to strengthen Islam, and took the position that the principles of true Islam were fundamentally similar (although of course superior) to the concepts of politics and justice in the modern West. To be sure, the modernists were opposed by many in the *ulema*; but they still enjoyed support among a considerable number of Moslems who had been exposed to Western culture and were seeking a platform for an Islam which would not reject European achievements out of hand. Appointed by the British to the Al Azhar administration and, later, to the position of Egyptian Grand Mufti, Abduh wielded great influence over the religious *(shariya)* courts, and published legal opinions, some controversial and innovative, on a wide range of subjects.

That a certain parallel exists between the Jewish and Moslem leadership in the matter of the religious response to modernization may not be coincidental. Without claiming a direct relationship, it is reasonable to argue for the influence of the religious attitudes of the elite of the majority culture on the elites of the religious minorities coexisting in the same area.

Further research may determine that one or both of two final factors may also have been influential in shaping Egyptian and Syrian rabbinical approaches and trends. Firstly, despite my openness to such a possibility, there is not sufficient information to permit me to speak of the adherence of each of our principal rabbis to different traditions or schools in the Sephardi rabbinical world. The second factor is that of biographical differences: their different personal life experiences may well have influenced their attitude as *poskim.* At present, no comprehensive biographical studies exist on either Rabbi Hazzan or Rabbi Abulafia, although each is a worthy subject for such a study.

CONCLUSION

Modern halakhic literature is quite variegated, and reflects differing approaches of modern scholars of the Law in their quest for the way to best mold the specifics of halakhic detail in the rapidly changing modern environment. This characterization of modern Halakhah should be seen as a starting point for detailed research and analysis. It is up to researchers to integrate proficiency in Jewish traditional learning with concepts of modern social studies, to adopt an involved yet critical stance—and so to arrive at a broad and deep understanding of modern halakhic creativity in its cultural and sociohistorical context.

Notes

1. For my description of the rabbis as intellectuals operating within a cultural tradition, I have relied on principles and terms established by Eisenstadt.

2. Thus far, I have located some eighteen volumes of halakhic literature composed by rabbis who were active in Egypt from 1882–1922. For a list of these works, see Zvi Zohar, *Halakhah u-modernizatsiah. Darkei heianut rabbanei mizraim le-etgarei ha-modernizatsiah* (Jerusalem: 1981). Similarly, as part of my research for my dissertation, I have located some twenty volumes of halakhic literature composed by rabbis who operated in Syria during the given period.

3. Rabbi Elijah Hazzan's halakhic approach reflects the approach of other outstanding rabbis who operated in Egypt during this period, primarily Rafael Aharon Ben Shimon, the *hakham bashi* of Cairo; Aharon Mendil Hacohen, Cairo's Ashkenazi rabbi; Rabbi Avraham Avichazir, Rabbi Hazzan's assistant and right-hand man in Alexandria; and Rabbi Masoud Hai Ben Shimon who worked alongside his elder brother, in Cairo. On the approach of Egypt's rabbis to various halakhic problems, and their attitude toward contemporary change, see Zohar, *op. cit.*, and *idem.*, "Mishnatam ha-hilkhatit shel hakhmei yisrael be-miẓraim ha-modernit," *Pe'eamim* XVI (1983), pp. 65–88. My research thus far confirms that Rabbi Abulafia was also a representative and typical figure with respect to the Torah-halakhic activity of Syrian rabbis during the period under discussion. Rabbi Hazzan and Rabbi Abulafia were outstanding scholars. Elijah Hazzan published four volumes of rabbinical responsa under the title *Taalumot Lev* (5639–5667 = 1879–1907), a book of rulings called *Neve Shalom—Minhagei No' Amon* (5654 = 1894), as well as annotations and commentaries to numerous other Torah works. Isaac Moshe Abulafia published six volumes of his *Penei Itzhak* collection of responsa (5630–5666 = 1870–1906), and a book entitled *Lev Nishbar,* in which he replied to rabbis who had raised objections to his first volume of "Penei Itzhak." Both rabbis were important figures in the Sephardic Torah world of their time, and entered into halakhic discussions with the great scholars of Jerusalem and other noted Sephardic rabbis. Elijah Hazzan stemmed from a prestigious family of scholars from Smyrna and was, from an early age, raised in Jerusalem by his grandfather, the Rishon Lezion—a position which he, too, was offered in his later years. Isaac Moshe Abulafia belonged to the illustrious Abulafia family which for generations had produced Torah scholars. One branch of this family settled in Eretz Israel, establishing itself in the holy city of Tiberias (in the district of Damascus). Both scholars were undoubtedly men of strong personality and firm ideas which influenced their rulings and halakhic approach; nevertheless, they were decidedly representative of their time and place: Elijah Hazzan, in his halakhic approach, certainly reflects the typical posture of Egypt's scholars of his day, while Isaac Moshe Abulafia, in his rulings, gives voice to the positions and considerations characteristic of many of Syria's scholars of his generation.

On Rabbi Hazzan, see Zohar, *Halakhah u-modernizatsiah,* pp. 177 ff., and the sources cited there. On Rabbi Abulafia, see Yitzhak Ben-Zvi, in *Oẓar yehudei sfarad* VI (Jerusalem); Weiss, *Hakhmei ha-mizraḥ* (Jerusalem, 1982) pp. 228–237; and with some reservation, M. D. Gaon, *Yehudei ha-mizraḥ be-ereẓ yisrael* vol. II (Jerusalem: 1938).

4. At the time of the British occupation, Egypt had no more than 10–15 thousand Jews. In 1897, over 25,000; in 1907, over 38,500; in 1917, almost

60,000. That is, between 1880–1920, Egypt's Jewish population grew at a relatively stable rate of 50% every ten years. See Landau, J., *Ha-yehudim be mizraim ba-meah ha-XIX* (Jerusalem: 1967) pp. 13 ff; Haim Cohen, *Ha-yehudim be-artzot ha-mizraḥ he-tikhon be-yameinu* (Jerusalem/Tel Aviv: 1972), p. 71; Zohar, *Halakhah u-modernizatsiah,* pp. 7–9.

5. The literature on the modernist movements in Islam in general, and in Egyptian Islam, in particular, is most extensive. What is important for our purposes is that Afghani, Abduh and their students emphasized the essential alienation between the basis of Christian civilization and the basis of Moslem civilization, and when they advocated learning something from Europe, they did so only so as to strengthen Islam in the struggle against European civilization.

6. Typical of the feelings of community leaders in Egypt was the statement made by Senator Joseph de Piccioto Bey, scion of an old distinguished Sephardic family, when asked by the *Today's Post* (1925) for his opinion on the establishment of the "Sephardi Association": "I have always been opposed to separatism, the terms 'Ashkenazi' and 'Sephardi' should be dropped, we are but one people. . . ." This attitude was evident on the community level in the efforts made to absorb the heightened immigration which followed the disturbances in Russia (Taragan, p. 18), and on the religious level, in the close cooperation between the Sephardi and Ashkenazi rabbis (see: Haim Weissblum, "Toldot harav Aharon Mendil Ha-Cohen," in: Aharon Mendil ha-Cohen, *Yad Ra'm* [Tel Aviv: 1960], p. 13; Zohar, *Halakhah u-modernizatsiah,* pp. 197–200).

7. Apart from the principle of "preserving the unity of the Jewish people," there were practical reasons for maintaining positive ties with the Jews of Europe, such as the possibility of their assistance in winning the support and backing of the British government and the European Consuls; the development of trade relations and economic cooperation between Egyptian Jewry and European Jewry, etc. Nor could Egyptian Jews deny that European influence had improved their living conditions, especially their security as a minority group.

8. N. Safran, (*Egypt in Search of Political Community,* Cambridge: 1961, p. 38), contends that "the basic nature of the life of Egyptian society, as well as the form of social organization, underwent a complete transformation." On the other hand, Baer, (G. Baer, "Social Change in Egypt 1800–1914," in P. Holt (ed.), *Political and Social Change in Modern Egypt*; London: 1968, p. 160) feels that the degree of social interaction between Europeans and Egyptians was most limited, even in the urban centers and among the affluent.

9. On the complex of factors which contributed toward the absorption of European influences on the part of Jewish community members in Egypt, see: Zohar, *Halakhah u-modernizatsiah,* pp. 61–66.

10. On the reforms, see S. Shaw and K. Ezel, *History of the Ottoman Empire and Modern Turkey,* vol. II (Cambridge: 1977), pp. 55ff. On their limited influence see M. Maoz, *Ottoman Reform in Syria and Palestine, 1840–1861* (Oxford: 1968), p. 159; S. Shamir, "The Modernization of Syria: Problems and Solutions in the Early Period of Abdulhamid," in Polk (ed.), *Beginnings of Modernization in the Middle East* (Chicago: 1966), p. 351.

11. On the significant influence of the Egyptian regime during this period, and on the restoration of the old order after 1840, see Maoz, *op. cit.* On the partially latent opposition of local power groups to change, see in addition to

Maoz, also R. H. Davison, *Reform in the Ottoman Empire 1856–1876* (Princeton: 1963).

12. On developments within the Empire during this period, see Shaw, *History of the Ottoman Empire and Modern Turkey,* vol. II. On developments in Syria, see Maoz, *Ottoman Reform.* On Syria's relative economic stagnation, and on the emigration from there, see Charles Issawi, *The Economic History of the Middle East 1800–1914* (Chicago: 1968).

13. At the end of the 19th century there were 15–20,000 Jews in Syria. By the eve of the First World War this figure had risen to 30,000.

14. Unfortunately, there is no authoritative scientific study of developments in Syria's Jewish community during this period. My remarks are a summary of what seemed to me reasonable and convincing in the works of J. Sutton, *Magic Carpet in Flatbush* (New York: 1979); W. Zenner, "Hahaim ha-pnimiim shel yehudei suriah be-shalhei ha-tekufah ha- 'otomanit," in: *Pe'amim* vol. III (1980); see also Almaliah, Avraham, *Toldot ha-yehudim be-damesek u-matzavam ha-homri veha-tarbuti* (Jaffa: 1912).

15. On this law, and on the reforms in the structure of the *milets,* and the nature of their status within Ottoman society and vis-à-vis the *Tanzimat* regime, see Shaw, *History* II, pp. 123ff.

16. The powerful role of Syrian rabbis in shaping the political-"secular" life of their congregation, even following the publication of the *Tanzimat* guidelines, corresponds to Maoz's findings in "Ha-ulema ve-tahalikh ha-modernizatsiah be-suriah be-emtsa ha-meah haXIX," in Gavriel Baer (ed.), *Ha-ulema u-veayot dat ba-'olam ha-muslimi* (Jerusalem: 1971) concerning the status of the *Ulema* in Syria. On the rabbis of Aleppo and their status, see Zenner, "Ha-ḥaim ha-pnimiim" and Sutton, *Magic Carpet.* On the development of a new 'secular' leadership in Beirut, see D. Goldman, "Reshit ha-pe'ilut ha-ẓiyonit be-suriah uve-levanon" (forthcoming). The absence of a systematic study of Syrian Jewry is noticeable in this area as well. On the rabbinical leadership in Egypt and its subordination to the "secular" leadership, see Landau, *Ha-yehudim be-miẓraim.*

17. In the premodern era as well, not the authority granted to the Jewish courts by the regime but the voluntary obedience which stemmed from a combination of social and cultural influences constituted the central axis of the independent judicial system of the Jewish communities in Islamic lands. This subject warrants further study and development.

18. On the situation in Egypt, we have the testimony of Rabbi Raphael Aharon ben Shimon: "In our times, the public has no need for a work of practical Halakhah to include civil law. For all such cases are tried in law courts established by the Government, as is well known" (*Tuv Miẓrayim,* 33b). This is also reflected in the small quantity of "Hoshen Mishpat" (civil law) cases discussed in the halakhic compositions of Egyptian rabbis. On the situation in Syria, there is no conclusive study, as mentioned above. However, my findings thus far, from an examination of the responsa of Syrian rabbis, confirm the situation described in the body of the article. But again, there seem to have been differences between the various communities: in Aleppo, few Jews submitted disputes to the state courts, in Beirut there was a tendency to do so, while in Damascus there seems to have been an intermediate situation.

19. On the public image of the *hakham bashi,* and on the discrepancy between this image and the real situation, see Barnai. The most famous conflict surrounding the appointment of a *hakham bashi,* which reflected the degree of

politicization of the function and the complexity of the factors and powers involved in this appointment, took place in Jerusalem following the death of Rabbi Yaacov Shaul Eliashar. This was no more than a familiar and extreme instance of a situation which was by no means unique. Thus, the controversy which arose concerning Rabbi Abulafia's leadership in Damascus (1896) (see Ben-Zvi, *Oẓar yehudei sefarad,* VI.) In Aleppo, too, there was no lack of conflict and power struggles surrounding rabbinical appointments.

20. On the development of sea transport in the area, see Shaw, *History* II, pp. 119–120, and also Issawi, *Economic History.*

21. On the growing divorce rate during the period of large Jewish emigration, see N. Goldberg, in J. Freid, ed., *Jews and Divorce* (1968).

22. On the rabbis' awareness of the issue's urgency, see the remarks made by Rabbi Aharon Mendil Hacohen, Cairo's Ashkenazi rabbi: "Times have changed and generations have changed. And now, in our generation, were it not for the permission to send divorce bills by post—the Jewish people would not be able to endure the daily growing number of abandoned *agunot*" (Aharon Mendil Hacohen, *Yad Rabbi Aharon Mendil,* p. 149a).

23. The earliest source of the Geonim's discussion of the question is to be found in *Halachot Gedolot* (vol. II, p. 165, ed., A. Hildesheimer, Jerusalem: 1978). On the development of their halakhic conclusion, and its subsequent halakhic repercussions, including the rulings by Rabbi M. Isserles (*Shulkhan 'aruch—Even ha-ezer*: #141), see the brief analysis in Zohar, "Psikat halakhah be-'idan shel temurah," in S. Deshen (ed.), *Mizraḥ u-ma'arav be-yisrael,* Jerusalem: 1986.

24. Rabbi Asher Kovo, *Shaar Asher* (Salonika, 5637 = 1877). Even Ha'ezer (folio 113A). Rabbi Kovo was the *hakham bashi* of Salonika; he died in 5636 = 1875. For more information on him see Gaon, *Yehudei ha-mizrah,* p. 617 (note), and the sources listed there.

25. On technology as providing opportunities for the fuller realization of halakhic principles, as it appeared to the Egyptian rabbis, see Zohar, *Halakhah u-modernizatsiah,* pp. 33–34, 55–57.

26. On the manner in which the *poskim* dealt with this question, and the difficulties involved, see the lengthy and detailed analysis by Rabbi Avraham Zvi Hirsch Eisenstadt in *Pithei Tshuva,* Even Ha'ezer section 141, note 35.

27. Rabbi Isaac Moses Abulafia, *Penei Itzhak,* Part V (Smyrna, 5658), p. 116, column c.

28. *Ibid.,* column d.

29. The word is generally translated as "innovation," and refers to invention or fabrication (cf. 1 Kings, 12:33). On *Bid'aa* in Islam, see D. B. MacDonald in *Encyclopedia of Islam,* Vol. I, pp. 712–713 (London, 1913), and compare with J. Robson in *Encyclopedia of Islam,* Vol. I (New Edition), p. 1199 (London and Leiden, 1960).

30. Elsewhere I analyzed his treatment of these sources critically, and at length. My chief finding was that the *poskim* whom he cites did not express any opposition to Rabbi Kovo's opinion, and most of them were even unaware of it; they simply did not discuss the question of the halakhic consequences of modern sea transportation. It would also appear from most of the sources that he cites, that they sincerely demanded that the use of the mails be avoided except in times of difficulty, and they did not spuriously ignore technological developments. One of the *poskim* cited (Rabbi Aharon Azriel [Ozen Aharon] p. 14, col. b) is depicted by Rabbi Abulafia as opposing Rabbi Kovo's position

because he permitted a divorce bill to be sent from Adrianople to Jerusalem, despite the modern means of transportation connecting the two cities, which included on the preliminary section of the route, "a half day's distance of railway track" from Adrianople to Istanbul. However, Rabbi Abulafia, writing in 1896, was insufficiently aware of the diachronic dimension: the divorce bill referred to by Rabbi Azriel, which arrived by post, was sent from Adrianople in 1871—and the railway track between Adrianople and Istanbul was inaugurated only in 1874! (Shaw, *History* II p. 121; C. Morowitz, *Les Finances de la Turquie* [Paris: 1902] pp. 376–377.) In conclusion, the "majority" opinion of which Rabbi Abulafia spoke as opposing Rabbi Kovo's position does not seem to exist when critically examined.

31. This phenomenon should put us on our guard when examining the manner in which the halakhic scholars dealt with change and development. A formal/technical "conservative" approach may yield a solution to a modern problem more effectively than will an essential/substantive approach which demands that the historical-technological circumstances be taken into consideration. Form and content in these matters, do not always correlate.

32. The Radbaz is quoted in: Halevi, *Ginat Veradim* (Istanbul: 5476:1716), p. 84, col. d.

33. *Ibid.*

34. The Radbaz's analysis has interesting halakhic consequences: a glance at Rabbi Hanina's remarks (in *Halachot Gedolot*) shows that he explicitly presented the prohibition for a gentile to participate in the transmission of a divorce bill from husband to wife as a *midrash halakhah* (hermeneutic derivation) from the verse "And he shall give it into her hand": in response to a question posed by the rabbis of the Sura academy, whether it is permissible to transmit a divorce bill by means of a gentile, Rabbi Hanina replied:

> No! For it is written "he shall give it to her hand"—[including also] the hand of her Israelite agent; but not at all to a gentile. It is stipulated that when the bill of divorce leaves the hand of the husband, this can only be (a) to the hand of the wife, or (b) to the hand of an Israelite agent whom the husband has designated as an agent of transmission, and who therefore stands in the husband's stead, or (c) to the hand of an agent of reception who stands in the stead of the wife. But to the hand of a gentile—not at all!

The Radbaz assumes, therefore, that the *literary form (midrash)* does not free the Gaon's remarks from the demand that their *halakhic content* reflect a logical and reasonable stand. The possibility that *midrash halakhah* is not necessarily a purely authoritative source opens up interesting avenues for analysis of midrashic literature, particularly the halakhic midrashim.

35. Elijah Hazzan, *Ta'alumot Lev* II, p. 61, col. a.

36. My description of the development of the railway in Egypt, and its effects, is based in Issawi, *Economic History; idem.,* "Asymmetrical Development and Transport in Egypt, 1800–1914)," in W. Polk (ed.), *Beginnings of Modernization in the Middle East (op. cit.).*

37. *Shulkhan Arukh,* Yoreh Deyah, #375, par. 8.

38. Hazzan, *Neveh Shalom,* p. 48, col. b.

39. Y. Nathanson, *Shoel u-meshiv* (Lemberg, 1869).

40. Hazzan, *op. cit.*

41. Dismissing the deeds of modern man as "unnatural" was fashionable in Europe during the nineteenth century, as was the appreciation of the original

and simple (in any case, happy) world of early man. One should consider possible "romantic" influence on Rabbi Nathanson's attitude.

42. This idea reappears in the writings of Egyptian scholars in various forms and different phrasing. It holds that a distinction should be made between the visible level of concrete halakhic statements, and a deeper level of underlying halakhic principles and values. The *posek*'s function is to remain constant to the deeper level of Halakhah, even if this entails his changing some of the details of the concrete halakhic statments formulated in the past. In certain respects, therefore, the Halakhah is similar to language, with the model of this "religious language" being in many senses analogous to a structural model which distinguishes between superficial configurations and "deep structure," the latter imbuing the former with significance.

43. We will expand on the question of analogy, and its use, below.

44. The view that the Halakhah is a closed system finds its fullest expression in the penetrating essay "Ish ha-halakhah" by Rabbi J. B. Soloveitchik. Rabbi Hazzan, as we saw, does not accept this approach; nor did other composers of responsa works familiar to me accept it, nor does it correspond with what comes to light in an examination of the *halakhah lemaaseh* (case law) determined over generations.

45. On the Halakhah's essential receptiveness to the empirical dimension and natural language see also Zohar, "Al ha-yahas she-bein sefat ha-halakhah le-vein ha-safah ha-tiv'it," *Sefer ha-yovel likhvod ha-Rav J. B. Soloveitchik* (Jerusalem: 1984).

46. On the development of modern overland transportation in Syria, see Hecker's article in Issawi, *Economic History,* and Issawi's introduction.

47. Rabbi Avraham Alkalai was born around 1750, apparently in Salonika where he was raised and educated. He served as a rabbi in Dubnitsa, and at an advanced age settled in Safed where he died in 1811. Apart from his responsa work, *Hessed Avraham,* cited below, he also wrote "Zechor LeAvraham"—in which the laws of the *Shulkhan Arukh* are arranged in alphabetical order.

48. The quotation is from *Hessed Avraham* by Rabbi Avraham Alkalai (Salonika, 5573 = 1813), p. 115, col. b.

49. Abulafia, *Penei Itzhak,* Part V.

50. This opinion is commonly accepted by researchers, and justifiably so; we find a clear statement of it in Issawi, "Asymmetrical Development and Transport," p. 386.

51. Elsewhere I have considered the phenomenon of "private marriage" *(kiddushin pratiyim)* which manifested itself in Egypt, out of the desire of a young couple—when one partner (usually the male) was a European Jewish immigrant—to maintain sexual relations outside the framework of the marriage institution. Zohar, "Mishnatam ha-hilkhatit," *loc. cit.*

52. My remarks on marriage in the Jewish communities of the Middle Ages are based on Jacob Katz, *Masoret u-mashber* (Jerusalem: 1958); *idem,* "Nissuin ve-ḥayei ishah be-motzaei yemei ha-beinayim," *(Zion)* 1950.

53. Abulafia, *Penei Itzhak,* Part I, *Even Ha'ezer* 17, p. 100, cols. c-d.

54. See the Rashba's *Responsa, (She'elot u-teshuvot* Part I (5718 = 1958). The Rashba (Rabbi Shimon Ben Adereth) was one of the great "early" scholars; he lived in Spain in the thirteenth century.

55. Haim Joseph David Azulai, one of the great Sephardi scholars of the eighteenth century, and perhaps the greatest. The passages quoted here are from his book *Haim Sheal* (Livorno, 5552), 11.

56. Abulafia, *op. cit.,* p. 102, col. d.
57. *Ibid.*
58. *Ibid.,* p. 106, col. a.
59. *Ibid.,* p. 113, col. d.–p. 114, col. a.
60. *Ibid.,* p. 115, col. b.
61. *Ibid.,* p. 116, col. b.
62. *Ibid.,* p. 115, cols. b–g.
63. *Ibid.,* p. 115, col. c.
64. Cf. above, note 29, regarding Bid'aa.
65. Abulafia, *op. cit.,* p. 115, col. d.–p. 116, col. a.
66. The term "analogy" has different senses. I refer to an analogy between terms and not an analogy between proportions. In the past, situation 'a' necessitated halakhic action 'x'. Today, we have before us not situation 'a' but situation 'b', which apparently is not dealt with in the sources. But there is a significant similarity between 'b' and 'a'. On the basis of this similarity (analogy), we will determine now, that just as situation 'a' in the past called for action 'x', so in the present situation 'b' (which is similar to 'a', as stated) also calls for action 'x'.
67. This attitude toward the present is reflected also in the attitude toward community custom in the present: Rabbi Elijah Hazzan tended to ascribe normative significance to public behavior in the present, while those who adopted the formal approach took the patterns determined in the past as decisive, and viewed the present public as either behaving as did their forefathers or as straying and deviant. See above.
68. In taking the *rate* of change as an important factor, I refer to A. Toffler, *Future Shock* (New York: 1971).
69. See Zohar, *Halakhah u-modernizatsiah,* pp. 63–63, 94–97.
70. Apart from Shaw, see also Maoz, *Ottoman Reform*; R. Davison, *Reform in the Ottoman Empire.*
71. Maoz, "Ha-ulema ve-tahalikh ha-modernizatsiah be-suriah," *loc. cit.*

Responses to Modernity in Orthodox Jewish Thought

Eliezer Goldman
(BAR-ILAN UNIVERSITY)

As construed in this paper, "Orthodox Jewish Thought" will refer to the thought of Orthodox Jews. We will consider as an Orthodox Jew one who is personally committed to Halakhah as traditionally interpreted and applied and is not associated with a non-Orthodox establishment. To many, inclusions and exclusions so determined may appear arbitrary. Since, in any event, selection is unavoidable, such arbitrariness seems preferable to adoption of a controversial criterion of Orthodox thought. The selection has not been limited to contemporaries, although all those whose ideas are here described did their mature work in the present century.

Modernity is many-faceted and poses a variety of questions for the Orthodox. Specifically, I have chosen to deal with a variety of responses to questions raised by secularization of the life-world and by secularization of Jewish peoplehood. I am not unaware of the controversies of historians and sociologists as to whether the social and cultural processes which go by the name of "secularization" ought properly so to be understood. But in this study we are concerned with a specific religious tradition. By "secularization" we shall mean abandonment of norms, criteria of legitimacy, forms of life, and perceptions of reality which have characterized that tradition.

THE SECULARIZED LIFE-WORLD*

In the confrontation of modernity by Orthodox Jewish thought, a critical problem is posed by the secularization of the life-world, the

*I am employing the term "life-world" somewhat freely, without binding myself to the implications of its Husserlian usage.

world we take for granted in everyday life, the kinds of entity assumed to exist, the factors believed to direct the course of events and which are taken into account when projecting courses of action, the institutional structure of human activity, the normative order accepted as binding.

The life-world of the premodern cultures of Jews, and of the societies in which they lived, was permeated with elements derived from the dominant religious traditions. In a world which was not generally perceived as possessing causal structure, much that transpired was, as a matter of course, imputed to divine providence. Disease and misfortune could be considered acts of divine retribution in a literal sense. The social and political order were divinely ordained. One's work, whether exalted or menial, was a vocation, one's wealth a trust. In the medieval ages, conceptions of a natural world order, albeit in an Aristotelian rather than in a modern sense, were entertained by a small intellectual élite who adjusted their religious world view and their interpretations of Scripture accordingly. Hence, medieval religious philosophy was an esoteric discipline. Maimonides found it necessary to warn his disciple that even natural philosophy must be withheld from the public. Both intellectually and morally, the readjustment of religious conceptions to the "true" philosophy of nature was too sophisticated an undertaking for all but the chosen few.

Modern man conceives events in his natural and social environment as causally connected. When something goes wrong, his unmediated reaction is to seek out the natural causes. He regards the social and political order either as artifacts to be manipulated or as outgrowths of a sociocultural tradition. Neither one's social position nor his occupation are foreordained. Like Laplace, in his cosmology, he does not tend to invoke divine action as an explanatory hypothesis. The normative order is considered to be open to criticism and historically variable. The upshot is a secularized life-world. Religion, in the proper sense, is either a matter for sectarians who repudiate the modern outlook, or for the sophisticated, whose perception extends beyond the life-world. The common man rarely construes his everyday experience in religious terms. If religious elements enter at all into his life, it is more by way of attachment to a social tradition than in an authentically religious manner. Only in extremity does he sense insufficiencies in his basically secular outlook.

How do the Orthodox react to this situation?

They have, of course, the option of rejecting modernity. At the purely intellectual level this is possible by preventing direct contact with the literature, art, and thought of the secular environment. This was the policy of the Orthodox leadership in Eastern Europe during the struggle against the Haskalah. They built upon the relative segregation of the Jewish masses and the intellectual stimulation offered scholars by traditional Jewish learning. In due time this came to be supplemented with the intensive indoctrination of the Musarists. Their outstanding success was in fostering an intellectual élite steeped in traditional learning and relatively impervious to outside intellectual influence. It is from such élites that the rabbinic leadership continues to be recruited in Israel, and to a growing extent in the United States.

Such insulation could never be complete, especially in Israel and in the West. Even among the leaders of the Musar movement we find men who were to some extent conversant with contemporary thinking. They appreciated that one could not simply ignore the ambient culture, and in their own way attempted to come to grips with it. This is not always apparent at first glance. The relevant discussions are usually conducted in terms applicable to premodern conditions as well. Yet careful reading reveals their relevance to the confrontation with modernity.

Common to most Orthodox thinkers is the opinion that there is something wrongheaded about the secular outlook. Their thinking in this matter is largely shaped by traditional theological arguments from design. Denial of their force is imputed to a distorting effect of inclination. Even so philosophically sophisticated a thinker as Rabbi J. B. Soloveitchik, who is well aware of the inadequacies of the classical arguments of rational theology, believes that is true only insofar as we are concerned with the quantitative physical world of the scientist, but that the everyday world perceived in its qualitative splendor requires "explanation" in theological terms.[1] The secular outlook on the natural world is in reality an aberration. How are we to account for it? Rabbi Soloveitchik regards this as a consequence of sin.[2] In like manner, Rabbi Eliyahu Dessler, a leading Musarist in recent times, attributed unbelief to a cognitive distortion. The naturalistic heretic is suppressing what in the secrecy of his heart he knows to be the truth.[3]

Rabbi A. I. Kook, who devoted much thought to the subject of contemporary disbelief, went so far as to interpret it as a reaction to the shortcomings of the prevalent Orthodox religiosity, and even assigned it a historic role in the religious education of Israel. Yet he failed to perceive the significance of the fact that, as directly apprehended by modern man, the world in which he leads his daily life is devoid of sacral elements, that the religious is not part of what he takes for granted. There is good reason to believe that Rabbi Kook himself was simply unable to imagine how the world could be observed in such a light. Interestingly enough, the therapy which Rabbi Kook prescribed for the then current irreligiosity goes to the heart of the matter. The Torah and the religion of Israel must be presented in the light of the most profound religious thought. Talmudic scholarship must be supplemented by careful study of the great Jewish thinkers, whether of the philosophical, ethical, or mystical traditions. Only thus could a point of departure be attained for a needed rejuvenation of religious Jewish thinking. Even the more recondite aspects of religious thought must be popularized, since naive theological conceptions are unacceptable even to the uneducated. In terms of the problem being discussed here, Rabbi Kook maintained that, in our time, any tenable religiosity must go beyond the life-world. Religion without sophistication is no longer viable.

THE OPTION OF TOTAL REJECTION

A strategy employed by some Musarists is to deny the reality of the natural order. There is no governing principle except divine providence. We have here what is tantamount to a revival of the *Weltanschauung* of the Kalâm in medieval Islam. Once the Musar movement retreated from the community at large to the yeshivot, the Musarists concentrated upon building up motivation for Torah study. In this, they had to contend with the normal ambition to set up a secure basis for one's livelihood as well as with political and other civilizatory interests, which of necessity divert time and interest from Torah. To this end they fostered an ideology of complete trust in Providence, a readiness to live from hand to mouth, and an ethic of irresponsibility for future welfare. It is said of the Hafetz Hayim that he dissuaded donors from setting up endowments, future proceeds from which would go to supporting the yeshivot. The arguments are set forth in terms applicable to men in any time or place, and the paradigms appealed to are Biblical and Talmudic. In the case of some of these Musarists, however, it is quite clear that we have a frontal attack upon the modern ethos with its emphasis upon foresight, calculation, planning, and domination of nature through knowledge of its workings. But to undermine the practical normative aspects of the modern life-world, one must also negate its cognitive premises. An exceptionally clear and unambiguous attempt at this may be found in the published discourses of Rabbi Eliyahu Dessler.

Rabbi Dessler opens his discussion of nature and miracle with a Humean gambit. Causality is a matter of habit. We conceive as causally related those kinds of events which we are accustomed to observe concomitantly. We tend to regard as miraculous only that which occurs in unaccustomed ways. From these premises he continues in a vein reminiscent of the Kalâm. In reality there is no causation save that of direct providential action. Nature, as an immanently ordered system, is an illusion, the purpose of which is to test our faith. "The being of each new moment is due to an originative action of His will, intended by Him, blessed be He, for some specific purpose, and, with respect to its material aspects, completely independent of the preceding moments." The physical world, which appears to us in the guise of a temporal continuum, has, in reality, a discrete structure which, like the pictures of a strip of movie film, produces only the illusion of connected motion and change. The only true cause is the divine will, which, from one discrete moment to the next, renews the creation. In a sense, human achievement is also illusory. "The general did not vanquish his enemy because he was heroic, but because his victory was foreordained. To this end he was granted valor. And when it is ordained that he shall no longer be successful and victorious, he will no longer succeed and no longer overcome his enemies. Where then are his craft and prowess?"[4] In Rabbi Dessler's view, it is not sufficient to deny the autonomy of the natural order. One must recognize that there is no necessity for it even as an agency of the divine action.

The practical upshot is a radically deontological view of the religious life. One's sole responsibility is for the performance of his religious duties in the present. Central to these is the study of the Torah. Some effort and time is required to provide the necessities of life. This, however, is also an exercise in faith. Is a person able to recognize, even while exerting himself to provide his basic needs, that it is not his effort but the divine ordinance which makes this possible?

None of these ideas are novel. They can all be traced to Rabbi Dessler's teachers and predecessors in the Musar movement, and even further back. But they are formulated clearly and systematically in a way which makes them relevant not only to the perennial struggle against too great a preoccupation with material needs and interests, but as an expression of the resistance to the world picture and activist ethos of modern man. This counter-ethos has deeply influenced the community of yeshiva scholars. Understanding it takes one a long way toward comprehending the position of this community vis-à-vis the events of recent Jewish history and its attitudes toward current movements in Jewish life.

In the classical literature of Jewish thought there is a vigorous critique of just such a theology and its associated ethic in Maimonides' polemic with the Kalâm.[5] For him, the natural order constituted the preeminent expression of the divine governance of the world. Aside from the order of nature all providential guidance is mediated by Intellect, the most perfect exemplification of which, in the sub-lunar world, is the prophetic instruction. The ordinary course of events, except insofar as it is determined by the free choice of men, is governed by natural law, and, in its details, subject to chance. On any plausible interpretation, Maimonides denied the familiar conception of Providence as direct intervention at specific moments of time. That Maimonides could consider his own conception to be an authentic interpretation of the idea of Providence is due to his cosmology. In his world picture, any event occurring in accordance with natural laws and any intellectually guided action could be regarded as resulting from the divine influence mediated by the heavens (the spheres and intelligences), and in the absence of which the world could not subsist for even a moment. On the modern cosmic model, the world, even when considered to be created, is construed as self-subsistent. The human intellect is unique in the sense that there are no intellects on the cosmic level to mediate between God and the human mind. If man is at all able to confront God, it must be in the immediacy of His presence. We have men and the natural world on the one hand, the Creator in His transcendence on the other. There is nothing in the cosmic order capable of mediation. It follows that, granted the modern world picture, the philosophically concerned religious person confronts a problem of the relation of the wholly transcendent to the created world.

MAN'S RELATION TO THE TRANSCENDENT

Possible religious constructions of this relation are taken up in Rabbi Joseph B. Soloveitchik's essay, "Halakhic Man,"[6] in which the religiosity of *Homo halakhicus,* taken as an ideal type, is contrasted with that of the mystic type. For both, establishment of a relationship with the transcendent is a central religious task. The latter attempts to do so by attaining freedom from the fetters of this world and ascending inwardly to the Beyond. The former would have the this-worldly permeated by the transcendent. Ultimately this is possible only through an act of God whereby the divine presence is concentrated in this world. Rabbi Soloveitchik analyzes the disparity between the original Midrashic use of the idea of *Tsimtsum* and the concept as employed in Lurianic Kabbalah. On the Kabbalistic account, which, for the purpose of his essay, Rabbi Soloveitchik interprets in accordance with Habad doctrine, *Tsimtsum* is a withdrawal of the divine, without which the mundane and finite could not have attained its relative being, for in its infinitude the divine negates all finite being. Hence, this-worldliness is alienation from the divine. It can be overcome only by the inward action through which finite being can be transcended and man reinstated with the divine source of his being. In the original midrashic concept, the reality of the this-worldly as God's creature is taken for granted. The theological problem concerns the possibility that the transcendent be localized and the divine presence be concentrated at specific places as on Sinai or in the Sanctuary or Temple or even wherever Torah is being studied. The truly paradigmatic instance is that of the Sinaitic revelation which brought with it the Halakhah and effects the permanent permeation of this world by the transcendent through the *outward* action of man.

For halakhic man, the world perceived in everyday life is a datum, but not one to be taken for granted in every respect. Even as the scientist, in order to understand how events in the world are related, must reorganize the initial data within the framework of his own specially designed concepts, so does the halakhist, in order to operate halakhically within the world, conceive it within a special halakhic framework. Natural events acquire meaning as signals for halakhic action. At the same time, natural objects are cognitively restructured in terms of halakhic categories. The manner in which halakhic thought and, consequently, halakhic practice operate with the categories of space and time, for example, differs from that employed in everyday life and that of the physicist. Halakhic norms are heteronomously given but their conceptual organization and systematization has remained over the ages a matter for the creative intellectual activity of the halakhic virtuosi. Halakhic man, by his very subjection to the halakhic norm, rejects the pretension of modern man to absolute spiritual and moral sovereignty. Yet in application of the Halakhah, and especially in its intellectual elaboration, he manifests the creativity and autonomy so highly prized in modernity. The ethos of halakhic theory and practice is not one of passive obedience, but of actively shaping a sacral life. Its deontic structure subserves an end which dominates it, sanctification of the life of man in this world. This is the halakhic response to the basic religious question: How is the this-worldly related to the transcendent? Halakhah is concerned primarily with the mundane activity of man. Although theory is distinguishable from practice, and halakhic theorizing is in itself regarded as a central form of religious practice, halakhic theory is intended for application in the natural life of man. In his orientation to transcendence and his concern with the sanctification of life halakhic man is at odds with the trend of modernity. His commitment to this-worldly action, his transformative ethos and the creative drive in the field of halakhic theory are quite consonant with the modern stance.

In "The Lonely Man of Faith," Rabbi Soloveitchik delineates another typological contrast, that of majestic man as against the man of faith. Majestic man seems to be deliberately intended to represent modern man's urge to dominate nature and, thereby, his own fate. His antithetical figure, the lonely man of faith, is not evoked as a contrasted traditional figure. He represents a specific dilemma of contemporary man, who after all his achievements in domination finds himself bereft of genuine communion with his fellow men. As Rabbi Soloveitchik sees it, the natural community of active men is instrumental and external. In the depth of their being, the members of this community are isolated. They become aware of their loneliness when they seek redemption, a condition described as one in which "the individual intuits his existence as worthwhile, legitimate, and adequate, anchored in something stable and unchangeable."[7]

Two aspects of this presentation are noteworthy. In the first place, man is ordained by his Creator to be both majestic man and man of faith. Typologically, the two seem opposed. In fact, man was intended to be both. It is his vocation to dominate nature and, within the bounds of his condition, master his fate. But dissatisfaction with the superficial community of which alone majestic man is capable, is built into his nature. Without in-depth communion man is lonely, and this loneliness can be relieved only in response to God's revelation. This response is described as one of humility and defeat, as opposed to domination. Yet it neither cancels nor delegitimates his urge to creativity and the masterly attitude toward his *natural* condition. If man is but an *image* of God, he is nonetheless an image of *God.*

Secondly, the man of faith, as described by Rabbi Soloveitchik, is not a regression to premodernity. His stance seems to be a reaction to postmodernity. Rabbi Soloveitchik is attempting to disclose what he regards as the in-depth sources of the anxieties of contemporary man. These he considers universal to humanity and only highlighted in the contemporary situation.

Students of his writings have sometimes been puzzled by the question, how Rabbi Soloveitchik understands the relation between halakhic man and the two types described in "The Lonely Man of Faith." Between halakhic man and majestic man there are obvious resemblances. But, in his subordination to the divine will, halakhic man deviates greatly from the majestic pattern. This question is never explicitly answered. From Rabbi Soloveitchik's latest writing, one senses that he is attempting to trace the basic religious dilemmas from the surface to ever-deeper strata. The affinity of halakhic man to majestic man is striking only so long as we refrain from examining what is taken for granted by the former, namely the normative authority of the Halakhah. The autonomy of halakhic man vis-à-vis his sources is strikingly brought out by many Aggadic passages, some of which are cited in this connection by Rabbi Soloveitchik. But it is a heteronomously based autonomy, one deriving ultimately from revelation. For a full understanding of halakhic man it is insufficient to delineate his characteristic manner of proceeding within the frame of reference which is taken for granted. Surely, in the modern context one must uncover the grounds for accepting such a framework. In this respect, it would seem that the essay on "The Lonely Man of Faith" contributes to an understanding of halakhic man. To attain this specific form of majesty, one must possess the humility of the man of faith.

Rabbi Soloveitchik's discussions are, of course, more generalized and the typological dichotomies such as that of majestic man and the man of faith are meant to represent possibilities inherent in the human situation as such. There can be no doubt, however, as to their special relevance to the contemporary human situation.

A DOUBLY RADICAL ORTHODOXY

Yeshayahu Leibowitz would probably challenge the contention that he has any interest in the confrontation between the Orthodox Jew and modernity. Nevertheless, his writings are important for any examination of what Orthodox Jewish thinkers have contributed to this subject.[8] In Leibowitz's thought we have both the most radical acceptance and the most radical rejection of the modern stance. This is a consequence of the extreme consistency with which he pushes the fact-value dichotomy. At the cognitive level, our world is more or less that reported to us by scientific workers. Leibowitz's conception of science is thoroughly empirical. However much of our knowledge may be imported into it by our intellectual schemes, the final arbiter in all questions of fact is our experience, and this is forced upon us. In the popular sense of the word, the world picture we all really accept when we do not delude ourselves is "secular." For example, there is no room in it for acts of Providence. This applies not only to nature, but to human history in its factuality. In truth, however, the world of given facts may be called secular only in the sense of religion being indifferent to it and its being indifferent to religion. Pragmatically, facts are of the utmost importance for action. Given our purposes, these can only be achieved by due attention to the means-consequence relations which are, of course, factual. But nothing concerning the desirability of ultimate purposes, the identity of intrinsic values, or the validity of categorical norms can be inferred from the factually existent. Since it is precisely with these that religion is concerned, questions concerning the facticities of the world are religiously irrelevant. Hence, in its cognitive aspects, the contemporary life-world has no bearing whatsoever upon religion.

It is otherwise with the normative aspect of the "modern" outlook. Its general tenor has been dubbed "humanistic," thereby implying that the source of values and norms is to be located in individual men or in human communities. But the terms "humanist" and "humanism" have been employed in at least two other senses: (a) as referring to the normative position that only the humanly significant ought to be our concern; (b) as signifying the moral demand that in all our decisions and actions due attention be paid to considerations of human welfare, dignity and freedom. This ambiguity of "humanism" has confused readers and critics of Leibowitz, who declares that Jewish religiosity is the negation of humanism. Obviously, what he has in mind are the first two senses of "humanism." There is no contradiction between his rejection of humanism and his deep concern for the rights and the dignity of subjected populations.

Yet another thesis which is fundamental in Leibowitz's thought on Jewish matters has failed to attract the attention it deserves, probably because it is explicitly stated only once or twice in his writings: the claim that the purely inward experience is incommunicable. This assumption is made to account for what Leibowitz regards as an empirically verified fact, that Jewish religion as a collective and historic phenomenon is constituted by the Halakhah. This has generally, but unjustifiably, been construed as a denial of the inward dimension of Jewish religiosity. What Leibowitz has argued is that, no matter how great the importance it may have for the individual, the personal living experience cannot constitute the basis for a publicly instituted religion. Halakhah has been the common form of religious life for Jews. The inner experience has differed from individual to individual, the theology from one philosophic culture to another. Coming to terms with Jewish religiosity as such means embracing the life of the Halakhah.

What is usually called "faith" cannot be a concern with the factual, but arises only in the domain of the normative. The datum of Jewish religion is the Halakhah. Whatever beliefs and dogmas are associated with it are essentially attempts to place this datum within a context, attempts which will vary from one cultural milieu to another. The inner religious experience in Judaism is an epiphenomenon of halakhic practice and varies from person to person. Only the institutional framework of the Halakhah is common, permanent, and definitive.

The radical heteronomy of Halakhah is subject to several qualifications. The first derives from the fact that interpretation, analysis and application of the Halakhah are human activities, and were intended so to be. As Leibowitz puts it, the divinely ordained Torah has been given over to human manipulation. The second qualification goes even deeper. If norms cannot be derived from facts, they can be adopted only by what is tantamount to a decision; not necessarily by an arbitrary decision, but, nevertheless, by an act of free choice. Even if we ignore the problems associated with revelation, obedience to the revealed will of God is not forced upon us by revelation unless we have accepted obedience to the will of God as a principle or as an end.

Such a conception is not entirely foreign to traditional rabbinic thought. If the concept of acceptance of the Torah as a convenantal act be taken seriously, it would appear to be an act of free choice. There is indeed an Amoraic opinion that only to the extent that the Torah was freely accepted could it be truly binding. But Leibowitz's notion of faith and commitment to the Torah as decisions goes much farther. He is fully cognizant of the obvious secular alternatives. We seem to have the following situation: From the "internal" point of view of one who has already accepted the Halakhah, he must be regarded as subject to heteronomous regulation. From an "external" point of view, acceptance of the Halakhah is an autonomous act. True enough, as a matter of biography, most Torah-observant Jews are never faced by an *actual* choice. They are born into Torah-observance. Yet even for them there is an ever-present *virtual* choice which experience or reflection may impel one to actualize.

In spite of the great difference between the kind of conceptual schemes with which Rabbi Soloveitchik and Professor Leibowitz work and the Kabbalistic frame of reference of Rabbi Hayim of Volozhin, there is a sense in which the two, within a modern context, are presenting their respective versions of Rabbi Hayim's thesis that the Deity in His full transcendence enters into the human world only through the Torah and its commandments. If the presentation in "Halakhic Man" were to be taken as Rabbi Soloveitchik's definitive view, the difference between the two versions would not be too great. But when "The Lonely Man of Faith" and subsequent writings are taken into account, the two versions indeed diverge. The difference becomes most evident in the respective treatment of prayer. According to Leibowitz, man is not really able to address God. His doing so is a purely halakhic act. Aside from the halakhic demand it has no justification and makes no sense. To stand before God in prayer means to accept a stance imposed by the Halakhah. This is exhaustive of the intention of prayer. There is no overcoming the ontological gap between God and man. Prayer cannot be considered a form of communication, let alone of communion with God. In Rabbi Soloveitchik's account, man truly addresses God, even as, in prophecy, God addresses man.

DIVINE IMMANENCE AS THE DRIVE TO PERFECTION

We have thus far considered theological positions which emphasize the transcendence of God, a life-world dominated by technological interest, and a corresponding model of the physical world. On the theological side we still have to consider the rival viewpoint which focuses upon the immanent aspects of the divine, a viewpoint which may be traced back to the Kabbalah and its ḥasidic offshoots. The divine transcendence, though all-encompassing, is totally beyond our ken. Whatever relation we have with God is through the mediation of the Sefirot, or divine emanations, which, though uncreated, represent the attributes of God as creator. From here it is only a step to a theology which attributes immanence in this created world to the divine action. We have seen that such a view, though quite appropriate within the frame of medieval cosmology does not quite jibe with the model of the physical world as perceived by the modern layman.

It is quite otherwise with a strand of thought which dominated the European mind in the nineteenth century and the early years of the twentieth century, an outlook which infiltrated the life-world from the philosophy of culture and history in which it originated: the idea of human society and culture as progressing according to an immanent principle from "lower" to "higher" planes. No matter how many the *caveats* of the theorists, at the commonsense level this was construed teleologically. Human history was perceived as progressing inevitably towards a goal inherent in it. Was it farfetched to offer a religious interpretation of this drive towards perfection as the innerworldly divine action?

In the very first years of this century, Rabbi A. I. Kook was strongly influenced by Moses Hess's *Rome and Jerusalem,* which contributed to the shaping of his own views on Jewish nationalism.[9] Hess's "Zionism" was embedded in a teleological conception of evolution through which, by the direction of what he conceived as divine providence, the organic evolved from the cosmic, and the social (spiritual) from the organic. Humanity itself evolves towards an ideal community of nations, a brotherhood of man. This drive of the world toward an ideal unity was identified by Hess with God, thus suppressing any idea of divine transcendence. Rabbi Kook adopted this evolutionary model, but adapted it to a theological scheme which recognized a transcendent Deity, God-in-Himself, and His immanence in the created world, manifested in its drive towards perfection, and in the propensities implanted in individual and collective souls. This teleological trend of the world was toward ever-greater unity, in which respect it was attempting to emulate the absolute unity of the Creator.

The religious life of man is properly oriented to the immanent aspect of Deity, to what Rabbi Kook calls "the Divine Ideals." Originally, this was argued on epistemological grounds.[10] All human knowledge is knowledge of the object as related to the knower, and the known object reflects the knowing subject. Only for this reason is knowledge possible. The known object is not completely alien to the subject. This is as true of conceptual knowledge as it is of sense perception. Even on the level of ordinary knowledge, the thing-in-itself is unknowable. It is no mere theological peculiarity that God-in-Himself is inscrutable. When man encounters the divine through the medium of His cognizable attributes, he realizes that they correspond to what is exalted and lofty in his own soul, but infinitely more sublime. By its very presence in the mind, the divine enlivens whatever is worthy in man's soul and raises it to ever higher levels.

Any attempt to know God as substance must lead to a religious collapse. In itself, the divine, which is totally other than the knowing subject and ever beyond him, threatens his very being. The desire to confront God in His transcendence leads to an experience of nothingness and to feelings of despair. The result is either a melancholy religion reflecting the experience of alienation, or else a retreat from God in defense of one's own threatened being. Man comes to terms with God only through the medium of the divine ideals and worships Him truly by doing his share in furthering their realization. Israel's vocation is to exemplify such a realization, which is possible only in the totality of a national life. The Torah and its commandments constitute a program of education which fosters the dispositions required in those who would realize the ideals.

In Rabbi Kook's later writings these ideas are overlayed with a symbolism and terminology taken from Kabbalistic sources. Nevertheless they remained the live kernel of his thought—an interpretation of the life of Judaism in terms of the evolutionary concepts of the nineteenth century. Intellectual and moral progress, and hence the increasing adequacy of religious conceptions, occurred by way of dialectically transcending ostensible oppositions. Within the divine plan for history, even the secular heresy has its uses as an incentive to go beyond primitive theological concepts and promote a more profound religiosity. The contemporary (early twentieth century) preoccupation of secular movements with moral and social ideals was a one-sided participation in the moral growth of humanity. Its ultimate religious meaning was only temporarily obscured.

Rabbi Kook, a prevalent misconception notwithstanding, never wearied of warning against blurring the boundary separating the sacred from the profane. However, the stereotyped criteria for classifying the religiously significant and the secular were considered by him to be inadequate. He could thus write: "How wretched are men who are unaware that their concern with a higher morality and search for the good is, in reality, the quest for God."[11] This consists in promotion of the divine ideals implanted in the creature and in the souls of men.

THE SECULARIZATION OF JEWISH PEOPLEHOOD

Intellectual redefinitions or reorientations are required not only because of a secularized life-world. The modern situation has given rise to a new Jewish self-perception which runs counter to that of Orthodoxy. The emergence of secular Jewish nationalism and the foundation of the state of Israel have raised issues far deeper than those which have been the subject of current controversy. The basic question concerns the very nature of Jewish peoplehood.

Traditionally, there was never a question as to the unique national identity of the Jewish people. Jews regarded themselves and non-Jews looked upon them as a people apart. Their unity and distinctiveness were constituted by devotion to Torah as a way of life for the individual and as the basis for the communal and legal organization. By dint of this they were distinguished from the communities within which they resided and, at the same time, were able to maintain communication and solidarity over the diaspora. The gist of the matter was put by Saadia Gaon in the tenth century when he stated that "our Umma, Bnei Israel, is an Umma only in its Laws." I have deliberately left the word "Umma" in its Arabic form to indicate that the context of Jewish peoplehood, as conceived by Saadia, included the communities of Islam and Christianity. Nations in the modern sense were nonexistent at the time.

Zionism arose within the context of modern European nationalism. Those who sought to develop a concept of Jewish peoplehood on the model of the European nationality of the time appealed to a paradigm which was foreign to traditional conceptions. Many, of course, consciously attempted to introduce a new basis for Jewish national life. While Orthodox opposition to Zionism was part of a broader struggle against change in the forms and observances of Jewish life, the particularly stubborn resistance of the Orthodox leadership suggests an awareness that the very concept of Jewish peoplehood was at stake. Thus certain rabbinic figures declared Zionism a greater danger than the Enlightenment. The latter only led individual Jews astray, but the former undermined the very foundations of Jewish life.

COMMUNITY OF LAW OR STATE SOVEREIGNTY?

The anti-Zionist Orthodox leadership in Eastern Europe was too detached from the currents of contemporary life and culture to articulate its opposition in a manner relevant to the issues of the time. They were certainly not equipped to formulate their position in terms of a political philosophy or a philosophy of history. This was done by Isaac Breuer in a series of essays and books, culminating in his work, *Weltwende,* written in 1938 but first published in 1979.[12] His statement is all the more impressive in view of the fact that, after the promulgation of the Palestine Mandate by the League of Nations he had urged Agudat Israel to participate in the upbuilding of the National Home, albeit outside the frame of the Zionist Organization.

Breuer distinguished phenomenal history from history-in-itself, which he also termed metahistory. Phenomenal history is the actual course of history with its wars, catastrophes, class struggles, cruelties; one might almost add—holocausts. There have been impressive advances in culture and in the level of personal morality. The ugly nature of the history of nations reflects the domination of politics by power and violence. This will always be the case so long as nations are regarded as the source of law. Worship of the sovereign national state is the idolatry of modern times. Within the state, the will of the powerful is imposed upon the weak; without, war constantly recurs. One might almost say that the sovereign national state has realized the evils of the Hobbesian state of nature in a maximal degree. So long as national states do not recognize that they are subject to a law independent of their authority no amelioration of this condition may be expected.

Phenomenal history is godless. Within it religion can have its place only in the lives of individuals. God can be recognized as Father but not as King. Kingdom of God implies recognition of His sovereignty over nations, and this is incompatible with the sovereignty of the national state. The Kingdom of God cannot obtain in phenomenal history but only in history-in-itself. This is not an eschatological vision. It is realizable in the history of nations and has in fact been realized in the history of Israel and brought about by Israel's acceptance of the Torah at Sinai. By thus accepting the Law of God, Israel was constituted a nation. It thereby responded to the vocation of realizing the Torah in the world. The Jewish religion is not a national religion in the sense that it is expressive of the national spirit. Such religion is a form of heathenism. It is a national religion in the sense that the religion is constitutive of the nation. Such a religion cannot be a "faith," since a nation is not a community of faith but a community of will. Between a nation and God no other relation is possible other than that of law. The community of law is primary for Israel as a nation. It precedes the state, which, like the territory, is only an instrument of the national life; a function of the law-community. Drawing on Biblical paradigms, Breuer declared:

> *The community of law remains in existence also within the state,* at all times prepared to oppose it, and, indeed, to fight the state, should it abuse the power entrusted to it; at all times prepared, too, to resume its desert existence, should the state succumb to abuse of its function and draw the national territory to its ruin.[13]

Subjection to the law of God of his own free will is the vocation of man as such. But, among nations, only Israel has accepted this destiny. For two thousand years it has maintained itself as a national community of law without state and without territory. Its pariah position was a consequence of refusing to give up its vocation as a nation constituted by acceptance of the law revealed by God, by virtue of which God, not the state, was sovereign. Only through Israel is God the God of history, and history a realization of the human vocation. One may perhaps actualize Breuer's point by indicating that, contrary to a common Zionist position that Israel was now called upon to reenter history, it was the nations of the world who must liberate themselves from the bonds of phenomenal history and its reign of violence to enter history-in-itself where God was the God of history by virtue of His sovereignty over the nations. The attempt to adapt Jewish peoplehood to the pattern of European nationalism was a betrayal of Israel's vocation. This, of course, is not to delegitimate Jewish statehood as such, but to deny the legitimacy of the claim to sovereignty of any state, including the Jewish state.

RABBI KOOK'S CONCEPTION OF JEWISH NATIONALISM

Between the ideas just outlined and the views of Rabbi A. I. Kook on Jewish nationalism there are interesting contrasts and surprising similarities.

In a series of essays written in the early years of the present century, in which he first developed his conception of the vocation of Israel, Rabbi Kook also delivered a scathing critique of secular Zionism. Its basic weakness was its irrationality. If we forego the religious vocation of Israel, what plausible motive remains for the struggle to ensure Jewish survival? The disappearance of nations which were assimilated by others possessing greater vitality is a familiar occurrence in world history. No one regards it as tragic. The incentives which bind individuals to nations and their states are largely of a utilitarian nature, namely the benefits which accrue from membership. Participation in Jewish peoplehood affords no benefits. There are only disadvantages. The severe persecution to which individual Jews are subjected can readily be avoided by renouncing their Jewishness. On purely secular grounds, what justifies the heavy emotional involvement in the issue of Jewish national survival?

This is not to deny historic significance to the revival of Jewish nationalism in secular form. Like many religious Zionists of the time, Rabbi Kook considered secular Zionism a first step in a process of repentance. He goes so far as to attribute a definite function to secular Zionism. Every spiritual movement must have a natural basis. The source, in human nature, of the aspiration to the divine ideals[14] is located in familial love, which has its natural extension in feelings of national solidarity. Rabbi Kook concurred in the judgment of secular nationalists such as Ahad Ha'am that contemporary Jewry was woefully lacking in a sense of mutual responsibility and national solidarity, that Jews tended to be egoistically individualistic. The natural feelings of Jewish solidarity must be awakened before one could expect a spiritual revival. Love for members of one's national community and a sense of solidarity with them was the natural spring of morality. Hence it was also the natural origin for love of "the God of Israel," the name he employs in the wake of Kabbalistic usage to designate the immanent aspect of Deity as manifest in the divine ideals. In this respect, the ultimate vocation of Israel is not particularistic. It envisions a further generalization of the love of kind to a love of humanity. Rabbi Kook fears that without the spirit of the Torah we are likely to be trapped into

> the imbecility which may be engendered by the excitement of a nationalism which has become morally disoriented. A nationalism which has no more exalted feeling than itself from which to derive vitality and illumination, can easily be degraded to a brutish and ugly self-love.[15]

The upsurge of Jewish nationalism, even in its secular form, could thus be regarded as a first stage in a renascence of Israel. At times Rabbi Kook even spoke of a division of labor between those laying the material foundations for a revival of the national life and those concerned with a spiritual awakening. Even in matters spiritual and moral the "younger generation," its "secularism" notwithstanding, displayed qualities which were lacking in its elders, especially in its dedication to ideal causes, both national and universal. Rabbi Kook distinguished two levels of morality. In the first place, there was practical morality, that which was binding given the prevailing intellectual conceptions and institutional structures. These, however, were not static. Hence the need for an "ideal morality" concerned with the moral progress of institutional arrangements and, in part, promoted by intellectual advance.[16] In its ideal yearnings the younger generation could claim superiority over its elders. Their deviation from the path of Torah is attributed by him to dissatisfaction with the gap between their ideal morality and the pedestrian nature of current religiosity, especially the Halakhah as presently understood. This is their strength, but also their basic weakness; the reason they have so little to offer by way of achievement in realizing their ideals. Aspiration to the ideal cannot proceed by way of abandoning the practically oriented norms, but only by their enhancement, universalization, and search for their deeper significance.

In a most interesting essay, Rabbi Kook describes the history of Israel subsequent to the age of Solomon as a fall from an ideal state characterized by the unity of what he calls "the divine idea" and "the national idea."[17] The latter is embodied in the social organization of the community, the former in its spiritual culture. Israel, from its very inception, aspired to an all-encompassing community which in all ramifications of its activity would be inspired by the divine idea. Such a community required a political structure, a socioeconomic organization, and a developed culture. Its fundamental conception was that the divine idea was to be the guiding light of the national community, not of individuals alone. The divine idea and the national idea were, in reality one, the former representing its spiritual aspect, the latter its civilizatory orientation. Political exigencies eventually brought about the severance of the spiritual from the civilizatory, by dint of which the latter acquired a life of its own and was alienated from the spiritual. In consequence, the divine idea degenerated into what Rabbi Kook called "the religious idea" which is constricted to the domain of individual religiosity. Concurrently, the national ideal was corrupted and assumed the form of the political idea, which is devoid of ideal aspirations and governed by purely utilitarian considerations. Different periods in the history of Israel were characterized by the ascendency of one or the other of these degraded ideas. In exile, the religious idea alone dominated. The conception of a polity informed by the divine ideals fell into oblivion. The redemption of Israel will consist in the reunification of the two ideas and recovery of their original forms.

The aspiration to unite the divine and the national ideas is the unique attribute of Israel. One finds *individuals* with lofty moral ideals and even saintly lives among all people. Among the nations, only Israel has set before itself the goal of a national life which, in all its aspects, is guided by the divine ideals. This is its national idea which is at one with the divine idea. But one might object that Israel, as we know it, hardly displays such characteristics. Thus, Rabbi Kook's own criticisms of the Jewry of his time, the egoistic individualism which he bemoans, appear to contradict his views about the unique qualities of Israel. Similarly, during the two thousand years of exile, the Jews, according to Rabbi Kook, seem to have been content with a religious life addressed primarily to the individual. He counters such objections by the introduction of the concept of "the communal Israelitic soul." Though aspiration toward the divine ideals has been dormant for centuries, it continues to animate the communal soul and by virtue of this is potentially present in the souls of Jewish individuals. Any Jew need only plumb the depths of his own soul to discover therein the workings of the communal soul. The negative verdict of experience is thus circumvented by myth.

On the surface, Rabbi Kook and Isaac Breuer present contrasting temperaments and divergent views. One has a positive overall evaluation of the Zionist endeavor, the other is anti-Zionist. The idiom of one tends to the mystic, the other's thought is formulated in Kantian terms. Yet there are some highly significant similarities. Both believe that the religious uniqueness of Israel as well as its national singularity consist in the fact that its religion is that of a nation and is effectuated in the life of the national community. Its most complete expression is obtained in the condition of statehood when the entire institutional structure is geared to Israel's religious vocation. Both regard this vocation as universalistic rather than particularistic in orientation, and attribute the evil in history to the autonomy of the political order.

They differ profoundly with respect to the identity of Israel's vocation and the nature of ideal religiosity. Rabbi Kook conceives the vocation as teleologically informed. The Law possesses an instrumental function. Breuer, on the other hand, regards the Law as the only relation which a nation, as distinct from the individual, may have with God. The divergence in their assessment of Israel's condition in Exile is a consequence of this. Rabbi Kook perceives the exile as a fallen state in which the life of Israel is inspired by its religious and national ideas only in their degenerate form. Breuer would admit that, ideally, the Law's domain of application would include state and territory. However, even in exile, by retaining its character as a community of Law, Israel lived up to its vocation.

There remains yet another point of disagreement which is no less profound. Breuer considers the election of Israel to be a function of its voluntary acceptance of the Torah—an act of free will which, in principle is repeated by everyone who commits himself to observance of the Torah. The significance of the sovereignty of the divine law consists in its transcendent origin. Any conception of the Torah as embodying the national spirit would render it incapable of its function of negating the sovereignty of the nation. Rabbi Kook, on the other hand, imputes the aspiration toward the divine ideals to the very nature of the Israelitic soul in which it is implanted. Israel discovers its vocation as an *idea innata.* In this sense, at least, it is an outgrowth of the national spirit.

In either view, the religious status of a Jewish nationality with a secular self-perception becomes problematic. The emergence of the State of Israel only intensifies such problems. How, in such views, does one construe a Jewish state in which Jews differ over the very conception of Jewish peoplehood; in which divergent answers are given to the question: What does it mean to be a member of the Jewish people? All this, when only a minority would agree explicitly that the Torah is constitutive of Jewish nationality. The moral aspirations which may have been characteristic of Rabbi Kook's time are hardly felt today. In that case, much of what he had to say by way of religious legitimation of Zionism, even in its secular version, would seem to have lost its validity. Can religious significance be attached to a nation whose self-perception is secular and to a state in which the criteria of legitimate authority and domain of jurisdiction are secular?

THE AUTONOMOUS STATUS OF JEWISH NATIONALITY

An interesting attempt to come to grips, from a religious point of view, with the real situation of Jewry today was made by Rabbi Hayim Hirschensohn, who, admittedly, was regarded as an eccentric by his rabbinic colleagues as well as by his fellow members in the Mizrahi movement.[18] Rabbi Hirschensohn questions the assumption made by almost all religious Zionists that the Jewish religion was constitutive of Jewish nationhood. True, the Jewish religion is a national religion in the sense that it is addressed to a nation rather than to a set of individuals, and requires implementation in the national life. Moreover, a Jewish nation bereft of its religion is spiritually impoverished and has lost much of its significance. Nonetheless, it has not lost its identity as the Jewish nation. He contends that those who maintain, as he himself once did, that Jewish nationality is constituted by its religion were misled by the model of Jewish life in Palestine, Russia, and Poland into regarding the "sinners" as marginal to the Jewish community. Only upon arrival in the United States did he appreciate the possibility that a major portion of that community might be alienated from the Torah and, nevertheless, remain attached to the Jewish people.

Rabbi Hirschensohn goes on to argue that, even on a basis of halakhic analysis, Jewish nationality, as such, has an autonomous status. The Jewish nation is a covenanted community. By the covenant it is bound to observe the Torah which was accepted freely. By the same covenant it was also constituted as a nation. As such it has a corporate unity extending into the future and a power of enactment binding upon future generations. The national unity established at Sinai is independent of the actual observance of the commandments. Their violation is punishable, but does not disrupt the corporate unity of Israel. Thus, two aspects of the Sinaitic covenant may be distinguished, the commitment to observance of the Torah and the founding of the nation of Israel. Historically, the two coincided. In principle, the latter is presupposed by the former since the Torah is addressed, in the first place, to the corporate body of Israel. The bond of Jewish nationality, though derived from the Sinaitic covenant, is not abrogated by secularization of large portions of the Jewish community. The mutual responsibility of individual Jews and the warranty of the community for its individual members remain in force.

The basic implications of such a position may perhaps be formulated independently of the specific conception of the covenant as developed by Rabbi Hirschensohn. The Jewish people in its collectivity is the addressee and bearer of the Torah, which can be adequately realized only in the life of the national community. Hence, there is a *religious* interest in the welfare of the Jewish people, in their national survival and their organization as an independent political entity. Though the Orthodox must persist in their aim of realizing the Torah within the national life and its state, non-realization of that aim need not impair the solidarity of Jews in the corporate sphere.

National solidarity is one thing, tensionless accord quite another. On any of the three views here outlined, the Orthodox conception will conflict with the idea that religion is an individual concern. Even Rabbi Hirschensohn envisages an ongoing struggle over the character of the Jewish state. However, of the three responses here outlined, his alone offers the Orthodox Jew a perspective in which the secular attitude can be taken at face value and, yet, as one with which one may contend within the framework of a common political life.

Notes

1. See J. B. Soloveitchik, "The Lonely Man of Faith," in *Tradition* (Summer 1965), p. 17, and especially "U-vikashtem mi-sham," in *Ish ha-halakhah—galui ve-nistar* (Jerusalem: 1968), pp. 125ff., p. 132 n. 7. For Rabbi

Soloveitchik, this is not a matter of logical inference. It is part of one's immediate living experience upon contemplation of nature.

2. "U-vikashtem mi-sham," pp. 140–41.

3. Rav Eliahu Eliezer Dessler, *Mikhtav me-eliahu* (Jerusalem: 1958), vol. I, pp. 171–76.

4. *Ibid.*, p. 163.

5. *Guide of the Perplexed,* Part 1, chap. 73; Part 3, chap. 17.

6. Originally published in *Talpioth* (1944), this essay has since been published in several collections of essays by Rabbi Soloveitchik, most recently in *Ish ha-halakhah.*

7. "The Lonely Man of Faith," p. 24.

8. Leibowitz's writings on Jewish issues have been collected in *Yahadut, 'am yehudi, u-medinat yisrael* (Jerusalem/Tel-Aviv: 1975) and *Emunah, historiah ve-'arakhim* (Jerusalem: 1982).

9. Concerning Hess's influence on Rabbi Kook, see: Eliezer Goldman, "Ziyonut hilonit, te'udat yisrael ve-takhlit ha-torah: maamarei ha-rav Kook be-*Peles* 5661–5664 (1901–1904)," *Da'at* (Summer 1983).

10. See the article "Da'at elokim" in *Ikvei ha-tzon,* first published in 1906, subsequently in the volume *Eder ha-hayakar ve-ikvei ha-tzon* (Jerusalem: 1967) pp. 130–31.

11. In a set of aphorisms published under a pseudonym, Rabai, "Peirurim mi-shulkhan gavoha," *Yizreel* 5673 (1913).

12. Breuer's major work is *Der Neue Kusari; ein Weg zum Judentum* (Frankfurt a/M: 1934). A collection of writings, including a section of *Der Neue Kusari,* has been published in English translation: *Concepts of Judaism,* edited by Jacob S. Levinger (Jerusalem: 1974).

13. "Judaism and the National Home," (presented to the Anglo-American Committee of Inquiry, 1946), *Concepts of Judaism,* pp. 90–91.

14. See above.

15. "Te'udat yisrael u-le'umiyuto," *Peles* 5661 (1901) p. 227.

16. See: "Da'at elokim," p. 135.

17. "Le-mahalakh ha-ideiot be-yisrael," *Orot* (Jerusalem: 5723 = 1963) pp. 102–111. The article was originally published in *Ha-ivri*, 5672 (1912).

18. For a rounded description of Rabbi Hirschensohn's ideas on Jewish nationalism and questions concerning a Jewish state in the contemporary world, see Prof. Eliezer Schweid's monograph, *Demokratiah ve-halakhah* (Jerusalem: 1978). The most important sources are Rabbi Hirschensohn's four volumes of responsa, *Malki ba-kodesh* and the three-volume book, *Eileh divrei ha-brit* (Jerusalem: 5686/5688 = 1926–28).

Ḥaredim Confront the Modern City

Menachem Friedman
(BAR-ILAN UNIVERSITY AND HEBREW UNIVERSITY)

> "Many have dwelt on the problem of our age—that the sons do not carry on the tradition of the fathers." *Ha-Homah* (The Rampart)[1] 20 Ellul 5707 (5 September 1947)

> "It is an undeniable fact that not only has the strength of faithful Judaism not dwindled in our holy land . . . [but] a youth has risen up here, great in numbers and high in quality, with an unprecedented erect spiritual bearing and an extremely firm self-awareness." *Ha-Edah* (The Community)[2] 20 Sivan 5742 (11 June 1982)

The contrast between these two quotations clearly indicates the change that has taken place in the ability of what is known as ḥaredi Jewry to maintain continuity over generations, despite the erosive factors which have threatened its continued existence since the end of the eighteenth century. In its confrontation with the process of the "tide of erosion" against religion in the past, traditional Orthodoxy did not have a great deal of success, to put it mildly.

The "erosion" that broke down the hegemony of religion and tradition had a traumatic significance which in large measure shaped the main conceptions of ḥaredi religiosity and set its attitude to the "hostile" environment.[3] The second quotation points to the change which has occurred, as expressed not only in the fact that the "erosion" has been arrested, but also in the creation of an ambience of stricter piety —what is called "religious extremism" by some, but "erect spiritual bearing and firm self-awareness" in the words of the quotation.

Part of a book-length study on traditional-orthodox Judaism: continuity and change, which will be published shortly under the auspices of the Jerusalem Institute for Israel Studies.

Ḥaredi (pl., Ḥaredim) is a collective, generic term for a specific grouping of ultra-Orthodox Jews. The Hebrew word connotes "the Godfearing."

In ḥaredi circles, the concept of "erosion" connotes not simply leaving the traditional-religious way of life, but also its occurrence as a broad and rapid social process, which brings with it a clear feeling of disintegration among those who seek to remain faithful to the religion and tradition, and apprehension about the survival of Judaism as they understand it.

The sense of a "current" sweeping things away percolated into the Jewish communities of Eastern Europe toward the end of the nineteenth century, and as a result of World War I, it was heightened in the 1920s and '30s. An analysis of the content of the writings of the spokesmen ("heroes") of religious Jewry in the period between the wars reveals the extent to which they had absorbed the notion that religious Jewry had lost its supremacy in the Jewish world in the sociopolitical and economic spheres to the radical movements in East European Jewish society.

This is most clearly conveyed in Nathan Birnbaum's Yiddish pamphlet of 1920 entitled *In goles bay yidn* (In Exile among Jews). The title itself is strong evidence of the loss of primacy and the taking over of the leadership by the bearers of change and modernity: whether those who, in their sociopolitical movements sought an overall and unequivocal solution to the existential problems of Jewish society, or those who, as individuals, stood for the adoption of modern European values and norms through the abandonment of basic elements of traditional Jewish identity.

This, I believe, is where we must locate the genesis of ḥaredi religiosity as a social phenomenon—based, it is true, on a traditional way of life which it seeks to preserve, but tinged by a form of revolt against the pattern of life of traditional-religious society. It is a revolt directed toward "liberation" from the "mass" *(hamoyn)* and from established members of the community, and dedicated to the creation of the voluntary ḥaredi community as an elite religious society.[4] Ḥaredi religiosity can thus be defined as the religiosity of an elite. This definition signifies that norms of religious conduct are set more according to individual ability—"completeness" *(shleymus)* and "ascending levels" *(madreygeh)*—and less on the basis of "traditions of the forefathers." Ḥaredi religion sees the norms of religious conduct (Halakhah) as a dynamic category, and religious change thus becomes an essential part of ḥaredi self-perception.[5]

In the historical context of the erosion of traditionalism and traditional structures in the early part of the twentieth century, Ḥaredism represents a distinct socioreligious phenomenon. It is the product of the increasing tension between two legitimate sources of religious conduct[6]: the quotidian norms of traditional life, and the literary tradition of Halakah (the latter frequently presenting maximal alternatives). The growing influence of ḥaredi religiosity, i.e., the trend toward the maximalist position derived from halakhic literature, is reflected in the appearance of the commentary "Mishna Brura" on the *Shulkhan arukh—oraḥ ḥaim,* by Rabbi Israel Meir Hacohen (Kagan),[7] which so quickly became authoritative for all of traditional-Orthodox society.

Ḥaredism arose in a dialectical relationship with the simultaneous processes of modernization and secularization in Jewish society that accompanied the uprooting and migration of Jews from small towns to big cities, and from East to West (Western Europe and America). These processes inevitably undermined the hold of local traditions, as Jews increasingly encountered different traditions of life in new and often alien geographical and social contexts. Among those who wished to remain loyal to tradition, the sole agreed basis common to them all was a commitment to uphold the written codes of religious behavior: that is, the literature of halakhic rulings. The Holocaust which wiped out that Jewry within which traditions of religious life were preserved was the background against which ḥaredi religiosity became the dominant expression of traditional Orthodoxy among the surviving elements of East European Jewry.

This analysis is intended to convey a sense of the dialectical and, at first sight, paradoxical character of the development of ḥaredi Jewry. This community could only have developed against the background of the "erosion" of the strength of religion and tradition among East European Jews. On the other hand, it was able to entrench itself and develop mechanisms to block further erosion and to establish a new ḥaredi society specifically because of the context and framework of the post–World War II modern city. In short, while the westward migration and urbanization that preceded the Second World War were manifestations of the eroding current working against traditionalism, they also served as important factors in producing the phenomenon of Ḥaredism.

When East European Jewry was annihilated, practically all the surviving members of the traditional-religious sector went either to Israel or to the big cities of the West, and it was precisely then that the process of reconstruction occurred the success of which is alluded to in the second citation above.

THE VOLUNTARY COMMUNITY

Ḥaredi society is organized in a network of "voluntary communities," which in ḥaredi terminology are called "publics," "circles," and the like. The idea of the voluntary community represents an innovation in the historical context of the traditional Ashkenazi community. The latter is defined geographically, in the sense that everyone residing within the boundaries of the community is considered to be a member of it. As a community, it is fairly homogeneous in the practice of customs and traditions.

The voluntary community, on the other hand, introduces a form of belonging that is in principle not imposed but chosen. It shapes and fixes the religious norms of those who wish to belong, and is thus selective. It was precisely the trend away from religion and tradition in the wider Jewish society that enabled traditional-religious groups to "free" themselves from religious responsibility to a larger community. Where the territorial community placed a premium on homogeneity of practice, the voluntary community is free to develop an elite religiosity. Moreover, the multiplicity of voluntary, selective communities living by self-imposed norms allows for the coexistence in one territory of different expressions and nuances of religious practice—as long as the differences are perceived as legitimate in the ḥaredi framework. Thus, different ḥaredi congregations can maintain their own specific customs and traditions or relative levels of piety. Such an accommodation is an advantage in a social context in which the processes of uprooting and migration have created tensions by bringing together Ḥaredim of different backgrounds.

In addition, Ḥaredism, as the piety of an elite practiced within voluntary sub-communities, can exist only against the background of other, more or less legitimate, Jewish frameworks which serve the non-ḥaredi community or those who have dropped out of ḥaredi circles. Thus, the voluntary ḥaredi community finds its fullest expression in a big city with a considerable and varied ḥaredi and non-ḥaredi population.[8]

THE CLOISTERED COMMUNITY

Along with the voluntary community, there developed in Poland and Lithuania what we shall call the "cloistered community." This framework, more than any other, created the basis for the reconstruction of ḥaredi society and for ending the drift away from traditionalism. This is the term we apply here to the larger yeshiva of the Volozhin type as it took shape in the latter part of the nineteenth century, under the growing influence of the *Musar* movement.[9] This type of yeshiva is distinguished from past models in the Ashkenazi cultural orbit in two important ways: (1) It is a supra-congregational institution, drawing most of its students from outside its immediate vicinity, and supported financially by private benefactors from many communities. (2) The head of the yeshiva and the other leading teachers are independent from other, local rabbis. The post of head of the yeshiva is distinct from that of Rabbi in the community in which the yeshiva is located. In actual fact there are instances of congruence between the two roles, in which case the yeshiva headship is perceived both by the holder of the post and the pupils, as by the learned public at large, as primary, while the function of the rabbi is attached to it as a secondary role.

The Volozhin-type yeshiva became an independent community by bringing together in one place a group of young men, unmarried for the most part and cut off from their families, in an all-encompassing setting where they live all day, every day, for nearly the whole year. This community is specifically established as a framework for the fulfillment of the ideal of learning *(talmud torah),* and this sets it apart from its surroundings. The yeshiva's purpose is seen not only to educate the students in depth, but to form them intellectually and spiritually. Almost by definition, this situation—all-day study in a collective life cut off from the everyday secular world—is marked by a special strictness, a search for "completeness" *(shleymus),* or, in other words, a degree of religious tension characteristic of the monastery.

The Volozhin-type yeshiva was also a focus of social and religious ferment, and one might say that it was here that many students from the smaller and more isolated townlets of the "Pale of Settlement" brought into contact with young men from the larger cities, first discovered the culture of the Haskalah movement and the social and spiritual problems that were being discussed at the time. This, of course, was an unintended effect of the system. In terms of the yeshiva's inherent characteristics, the stronger the anti-religious current in the general society became, the more the yeshiva departed from the older community-rooted pattern, becoming more and more estranged from its social environment. It became the standardbearer of traditional religiosity and a bulwark against the countercurrent. The more the traditional community crumbled, the more the Volozhin-type yeshiva became the expression of traditionalism.

Finally, the Volozhin-type yeshiva, too, is forced by the opposing current to change and adapt itself. One result of this is a reorientation of purpose, so that the yeshiva exists not only for educating its students in Talmud and the Commentaries, but also, and perhaps more so, for nurturing their spirit in the ḥaredi mold. In this connection, we must take note of the Musar movement's penetration into the yeshivot at the end of the nineteenth century. In the final analysis, the followers of Musar sought to turn life in the yeshivot into a primarily religious experience of unremitting striving for spiritual perfection. In this scheme, studying Torah was but a means to that end, rather than a process of acquiring knowledge. Thus, the large Volozhin-type yeshiva as it was shaped by the Musar movement constitutes the clearest and most complete expression of ḥaredi religiosity, as we have defined it.

Just as this yeshiva turned into the standard bearer of traditional piety, it provided a solid base for the "revolt" of the religious elite against the traditional life of the Orthodox community at large. The cloistered community of learned youth was in fact built on the ruins of the traditional Ashkenazi community, which was no longer able to ensure its own continuity. Removing the young men from the authority of their parents, from contact with everyday secular life, from involvement in the life of a larger community with its compromises with reality, the yeshiva of the sort we are describing brings together students of the same generation and places them under the tutelage of leaders who, often endowed with personal magnetism and radiating authority, serve as role models of the complete religious life. This setting fosters an ambiance of piety in which the quest for religious wholeness must inevitably lead, consciously or unconsciously, to an elitist sense of superiority over the ordinary "mass" of traditional Jews. Revolt against the lower standards found outside—even in their family and in the community of origin—is not only tolerated but encouraged, as long as it is governed by the striving for "completeness" in the religious sense. Thus is formed the ideal ḥaredi community, one which sees itself always as striving for an ever-greater achievement and ever-higher level in the expression of the Jew's duty to God.

In the seclusion that it cultivates, the yeshiva is not, in principle, part of a supportive environment, but perceives itself as an island in a hostile sea, as if the "whole world" (the "street," the "mass") were on one side and the yeshiva on the other. This self-image is reflected in the attitude of the yeshiva to economic and other mundane matters. The idea of attaching value to "the practical" *(takhlis)*, in the sense of acquiring skills and training in order to fit oneself into the modern economy, is seen as the main manifestation of contrast between the yeshiva and the "street"; so much so that the yeshiva consciously denied that it existed at all as an institution for the training of rabbis.[10] The yeshiva took a stand, essentially, in opposition to the principle of productivity. This added yet another layer in crystallizing the "heroic" religiosity, the readiness for sacrifice for the sake of realizing spiritual ideals, which ḥaredi society sees as its vocation.

The extreme and stubborn opposition to "things practical"[11] in the prewar Volozhin-type yeshiva was a principal cause of its failure. Until the 1950s, it was unable to prevent even those who entered its doors from later giving up the religious way of life. The students' stay in the cloistered community was but a moratorium of limited duration, during which the tension grew between the yeshiva's ordering of priorities and the economic concerns looming outside. No mechanisms were developed to ease the students' unavoidable encounter with "the practical." Yet, after the 1950s, in a clear example of dialectical social development, foundations which were laid earlier in the century enabled a reconstruction of the yeshiva, and with it, ḥaredi society, which halted the defection from within.

1. The Heroic Elite

Against the background of the anti-religious current on the one hand and the opposition to mundane affairs on the other, the yeshivot produced a tempered elite which saw its aim and purpose in absolute—"heroic"—dedication to the ideal of Torah study as expressing Judaism in its fullness, and to the yeshiva as the core from which Jewish existence would draw sustenance. This elite continued to make repeated attempts in every place it reached, at times under intolerable conditions, to set up yeshivot that would serve as nuclei of a ḥaredi community.[12]

2. Center of Torah

The Volozhin-type yeshivot, with their total dedication to Torah study, helped to bring about a burgeoning of intellectual creation in this sphere which could not fail to impress the whole Jewish world. The relative isolation of the yeshivot made it possible to elaborate new structures of theoretical, halakhic-juridical thinking, without having to concern themselves with the practical consequences of these innovations on practical rulings. These conditions of almost absolute intellectual freedom attracted brilliant intellects fascinated by the intellectual adventure that the yeshiva setting offered. In the history of Torah study, the big Volozhin-type yeshivot marked a breakthrough in Talmudic-halakhic thought, and became world Torah centers.[13] These yeshivot, and their heads, in particular, were placed in a position of "pan-Jewish" religious leadership. This, combined with the collapse of traditional religious life around them, generated a partial or even full delegitimization of other rabbis and Torah study institutions, perceived in the yeshivot as representing relative weakness, inconsistency, and readiness for compromise.

3. An Alternative to Modernism

The Volozhin-type yeshivot, under the influence of Musar movement ideas, stressed the dissonance between the religious-intellectual values in whose name they educated students, and the practical, material, anti-spiritual values of modern society. The duality of the two realms (modernity = material shallowness; the yeshiva = spirituality, holiness) was fostered in the yeshiva.

In the wake of World War I, the positions taken on these issues played a part in the renewed encounter between German and East European Jewry. For the first time since the mid-eighteenth century, young German Jews (albeit few in number), from families that accepted the way of life of modern society even as they accepted the authority of halakhah, found their way to large Volozhin-type yeshivot (Mir, for example).[14] In these young men's eyes, the yeshiva represented the antithesis of their parents' modernity (i.e., worldliness), their willingness to compromise—and in their stead offered a spiritual wholeness that was unique in its unequivocal demand for total dedication. It is true, however, that in this case there was no categorical rejection of modern culture and education, or the trend of self-isolation, which is so widespread in ḥaredi circles today.

As the traditional life came more and more to be perceived through a cloud of romanticism, and as modern society sank deeper into materialist preoccupations, the anti-materialism of the yeshiva emerged as the expression of a new existential philosophy (to be discussed below).

In the spring of 1954, Moshe Scheinfeld, one of the ideologues of the postwar Ḥaredism that was developing in Israel and the West, published an article in the Agudat Israel youth journal, *Digleinu* (Nisan 5714), entitled, "And He Shall Turn the Hearts of the Fathers unto the Children," in which he stated:

> Anyone with clear perception will see an extraordinary phenomenon—*the children are more complete than their fathers*. . . . The young man founds a new world among the ruins, leaping, as it were, over his bewildered father and returning to his grandfather, who was whole and sure of himself. . . . The young man of faith seeks completeness . . .; he finds it within the walls of the (holy) yeshivas. . . . In his parents' home, as against this, he very often comes up against contradictions . . . There is punctilious observance of what is subsidiary and neglect of the essentials . . . observance by rote, and the entertainment of views that are tainted with apostasy and atheism. . . . [This] is the source of the "tragedies" that take place in many homes when the parents feel that their sons learning in yeshivas and daughters finishing their studies in

> Beit Yaakov seminaries are in their hearts rebelling against them and openly or tacitly demanding *more completeness, more sacrifice and more consistency in deed and thought.* . . . The young man with faith today is entirely free of the spell of the false solutions that previously held him in thrall. He believes that the crown of Torah is above all else. . . . There once again, like a hundred years ago, there are girls who set their hearts on marrying a scholar and joyfully undertake the burden of providing for their families. This fact is no less than miraculous in today's crassly materialistic reality. . . . "He shall turn the hearts of the fathers unto the children"—[i.e.] the hearts of the fathers shall turn unto the Lord because of the children. . . . [emphasis added]

An atmosphere of youthful rebellion pervades this description of the renewal of ḥaredi religiosity in the mid-1950s. The setting for this renewal were the yeshivot reestablished after the Holocaust in Israel (Ponivezh, Mir), England (Gateshead), and the United States (Telz and Lakewood) by yeshiva heads who succeeded in escaping from the vale of slaughter. This new trend, which had had no success in earlier years, was spoken of by Scheinfeld and others in terms of miracles wrought by Divine Providence. "It is impossible to explain this by any natural explanation. In this phenomenon we see the hand of the Lord," writes Rabbi Shmuel Barazovsky, head (Admor) of the Slonimer Ḥasidim (*Digleinu,* Nisan 5743/1983).

RENEWED EQUILIBRIUM BETWEEN THE YESHIVA AND THE ECONOMY

The Volozhin-type yeshiva that was implanted afresh in the West and in Israel did not actually change the structure of Torah study. The principle of opposition to "the practical" remains valid in all the yeshivas calling themselves ḥaredi.[16] Any yeshiva in which the student receives secular training of any kind is not a "holy" yeshiva and is disqualified in the eyes of ḥaredi authorities.[17] All the same, this opposition is not quite what it was in Eastern Europe. The structure of modern society has made possible the development of a "bridge" between the yeshiva and the surrounding material world.

1. Beit Yaakov: The First Step

The development of an educational network for girls (Beit Yaakov) was perhaps the most revolutionary change in the framework of traditional-religious Jewry. On the strength of the fact that the Halakhah and tradition did not lay down limitations in principle to the content of girls' education—except for the study of Talmud—the Beit Yaakov school made it possible to transmit the content of relatively modern studies. The schools of the Beit Yaakov network, which are influenced somewhat by the Neo-Orthodox movement in Germany, were unique in the East European traditional setting. The need to provide teachers for this school system led to the establishment of teachers' seminaries even before the Second World War (Cracow, 1927).[18] Such schools were established in Palestine in the 1930s, and teacher training seminaries followed here, too.[19]

Although there were only a few such schools in pre-state Palestine, with the establishment of the state of Israel this situation altered dramatically. Like other institutions under the auspices of Agudat Israel, Beit Yaakov soon became part of the Israeli educational system, enjoying supplementary budgets which made possible a wide expansion. In turn, the increased number of schools necessitated a greater number of teachers' institutes, which in fact absorbed a decisive majority of female Ashkenazi school graduates. In 1950 a new teachers' seminary was established in Bene Berak, which three years later came under the direction of Avraham Yosef Wolf. His influence on the seminary came to be felt throughout ḥaredi society. As was later noted, "It is no secret that the Beit Yaakov seminary in Bene-Berak has a very special reputation in comparison with all the other seminaries in the country as regards 'extremism' " (*Beit Yaakov,* Ellul 5719 = 1959). One of the principal manifestations of this changed atmosphere was the fostering of the kind of aspirations mentioned by Scheinfeld: to marry Torah scholars and to undertake the burden of maintaining the family. Norms set in Bene-Berak were subsequently adopted at other Beit Yaakov seminaries in Israel and abroad.

That women should take the breadwinner's role in the family, so as to enable their husbands to study Torah, is certainly not a new concept, and I have discussed the metamorphosis of this issue elsewhere. In the present context, the idea was promoted first of all by Rabbi Avraham Karlitz ("Ḥazon Ish"), but his influence alone is not a sufficient explanation for its wide acceptance in the ḥaredi community. Instead, the phenomenon has its roots in a conjuncture of several forces: an outstanding charismatic personality (the Hazon Ish), the trauma of the Holocaust, and special socioeconomic conditions. We turn our attention now to this last factor in particular.

The teaching profession is one in which working conditions are almost ideal for the married women of the ḥaredi community. The school, as an institution which imparts values, is also one that calls for control of personal conduct. It is entirely under the supervision of ḥaredi institutions—a fact that obviates many questions which arise when married women are employed outside the home.[20] Hours are suited to the demands of household work and can be reduced or increased in accordance with varying conditions at home.

The increasing demand for teachers ensures employment for almost all the graduates of the seminaries. Outside employment, bringing a reasonable salary, can thus be combined with responsibility for the household for a large segment of the community's women. In contrast, the husband's yeshiva training does not prepare him at all to assume an economic role in the family—a point to which we will revert later. He has, in fact, three options. (1) He can go into his father's business, or that of his father-in-law (which, for obvious reasons, is not possible in all cases). (2) He can begin to train for some occupation. This, too, is problematic: work that demands a relatively simple level of skill has low status, while work that demands a higher level of skill presupposes a higher level of general education than that attained by most graduates of ḥaredi yeshivas. (3) His most realistic choice is to continue his Torah studies and train for a position in the religious sphere.*

The wife's work outside the home is generally seen as temporary, to last until the husband completes his training and finds a suitable position. Thus, while the wife's work outside the home is perceived as a realization of a religious ideal, it is also based on the fact that suitable and relatively convenient sources of employment existed, and on rational calculations regarding the future prospects of the family.

The fact that a woman whose status as a match is relatively high will show a willingness to work so that her husband can go on studying Torah has had an inestimable moral influence on yeshiva students. Indeed, one can say that by this means, Torah studies became "practical." Outside employment for women has come to be viewed as a necessity,[21] and this has had a dramatic effect on the structure of ḥaredi society that goes beyond the confines of the present article.

2. *Background Conditions: The Modern Welfare State*

The transition to modern Western society after World War II brought traditional-religious Jewry into the era of the welfare state. The concept of the welfare state entails a rising standard of living and health services, underwritten by health insurance, national insurance (social security), free education, and the like. These benefits are complemented by insurance programs provided in the private sphere, which are adaptable to family income levels. This situation makes it possible for a middle class family to do without the employment of

*Military service is, of course, not considered to be an option.

their children, and ensures the family's economic stability in times of crisis (illness or death of the father).

In these conditions, the years of schooling can be extended to the completion of secondary education and beyond. While modern society utilizes this period of time for training as broad strata as possible for functions in the economy calling for a high degree of proficiency, ḥaredi society utilizes it for Torah study in the yeshiva setting. This is consistent with the rejection of productivity-oriented "practical" values built into the ḥaredi system of socialization.

In the newer conditions of modern Western society, however, this state of affairs has even greater significance and impact. First, yeshiva study now embraces all of the younger members of ḥaredi society (apart from those who lack even a minimal capability), who remain at their studies until marriage and beyond. Second, owing to technological advance, the gap in education between ḥaredi and non-ḥaredi youth is steadily widening. As more types of work become the exclusive preserve of low-level social strata, and a growing proportion of the population enters the various educational networks, the effect of seclusion, of being cut off from "the practical," becomes greater than in the past.

This is not the entire picture, however, and while the conclusion is correct as far as it goes, this state of affairs is more likely to keep the younger ḥaredi generation within the cloistered setting of the yeshiva than to propel them outwards, as was the case in the past. It is precisely because education and technology have combined to restrict the range of callings which demand only low-level skills and make them the preserve of lower, failed strata that the modern welfare state has helped to put these jobs outside the bounds of what is considered acceptable for students of the yeshivas. Thus it is in the context of modern Western society that the yeshivas have been able to mobilize the decisive majority of ḥaredi youth, for whom the possibility of leaving their studies before marriage—i.e., revolting against the ḥaredi concept of the world and against parental authority—has become more unrealistic than ever.

To leave the "holy" yeshiva is necessarily to cut one's social ties, usually one's family ties as well. Such a step has immediate economic consequences, but above and beyond this, for one who leaves the yeshiva, the prospects of finding an alternative social setting that fits his expectations and his self-image in relation to the world around him are extremely slim. In the past, such alternative social settings existed, making it possible for young people from the traditional-religious community to transfer to a different one. One can point here to secular, political movements that pursued an aggressive policy of recruitment among young people from traditional-religious circles and that then resocialized and absorbed those who wished to free themselves of the "yoke of Torah." Such groups, pioneer youth groups in particular, which may be referred to as "moratorium" groups, acted as surrogate families and provided the setting for adjustment to the norms and values of the surrounding society. Underground political movements, as well as the kibbutz, also provided such a moratorium in the past. These settings now either no longer exist or else no longer function in the same manner. The dropout from the yeshiva world must now face the outside world on his own, without an economic base and without a general education.

3. The Practical Alternative: The "World of Torah"

Since the 1950s, the sole pattern of socialization in ḥaredi society has been, as we have stated, the rejection of the "practical" in favor of a viable alternative. Yeshiva students today, unlike in the past, have confidence that their economic future is assured in one way or another. Rabbi Eliezer Shach, for example, writes: "And the truth [is], with God's help the sons of the Torah [i.e., students of the yeshivas] set themselves up well afterwards."[22] This remark reflects not just a personal opinion, but a state of affairs about which we hear repeatedly from other Ḥaredim and their leaders. Anyone who has read memoirs and letters from the nineteenth and early twentieth century, in which the problem of "the practical" figures so importantly for fathers and sons who wished to remain true to tradition, cannot but recognize the dramatic change that has taken place in the last generation in this regard. This, despite the fact that Torah study remains the exclusive content of the yeshiva curriculum, and despite the extension of yeshiva education over almost the entire ḥaredi society and over a longer period of time for both single and married students.

Rabbi Shach's remark is a good illustration of the prevailing attitude in ḥaredi circles to the economic question: "setting themselves up" implies that the problem of material welfare is irrelevant as long as the young man is studying, and moreover, that he need not feel troubled on that account. "Setting themselves up" does not signify, however, that tension no longer exists between the yeshiva as a cloistered community and the economic world outside; on the contrary, this tension is perceived as functional in achieving the aim of Torah study—attainments in Talmudic erudition ("greatness in Torah").

Finally, this general attitude may be said to embrace an element of the irrational—a lack of planning—which has a very important function. The rational approach, that is, general education, is not highly rated, given the fact that many who pursued the "practical" have not succeeded, while those who pursue Torah study have done well. It follows, according to this argument, that material success is not necessarily linked to rational planning, but rather to the providence of the Creator. The duty of the yeshiva student, therefore, is to trust in God, who will provide the economic support that he deserves.[23]

This brings us back to the question of just how ḥaredi society found a way to ensure the material welfare of its sons, precisely in the context of modern, urban society.

1. Ḥaredim in International Trade

The large Western city is a meeting place of international business, where social connections can provide the basis of commercial connections. When the Ḥaredim settled in the metropolitan centers after World War II, the entrepreneurs among them found conditions in which they could put their connections to best advantage. Not only did they all share a distinctive lifestyle, but most often they also belonged to one or another religious subcommunity (e.g., a ḥasidic group with its own leader). This made it easier for them to find a niche in certain branches of international trade (diamonds and the like).*

The success of certain individuals had a broader impact on the ḥaredi social system. First, it undermined the conventional notion that the ḥaredi way of life and traditional dress make participation in modern international trade almost impossible.[24] Second, the fact that the majority of the successful ones began with "nothing" reinforced the argument relating to the unreliability of modern education. Third, those who succeeded in the business realm helped others to enter. Finally, the emergence of a stratum of wealthy Ḥaredim had an immediate effect on the economic standing of the religious leaders in the community and on ḥaredi institutions—yeshivas in particular.

2. The Monopoly of Religious Services

The combined impact of past anti-religious trends and the Holocaust of European Jewry reduced the traditional-religious communities to a minority of the Jewish population. This, of course, has not meant that all the links binding the rest of the Jews to their religious

Incidentally, the perception of the leader as one with the power to "act" (i.e., to influence superior forces to bring their power to bear in the material realm—children, health, material needs), may be part of what makes difficult decisions in business activity psychologically easier.

traditions have been severed. The link with tradition is seen, among other things, in the continuing demand for a variety of religious services: *kashrut* supervision, ritual accessories (phylacteries, *mezuzot,* Torah scrolls, wine goblets, etc.), and religious functionaries. After World War II, the supply of these services and accessories became more and more the monopoly of Ḥaredim. Potential competition was reduced by the processes of widening education and the acceptance of aspects of modern life in the larger, non-ḥaredi circles where the need to fit into a technological economy is not considered to be in opposition to a religious lifestyle.

In Israel, the economic implications of this monopoly has yet another dimension. Here, religious services (rabbis, judges in the religious courts, kashrut services, army chaplains, teachers in ḥaredi schools, etc.) are part of the state budget. This has opened secure career paths for those whose exclusive preoccupation with Torah study over a long period of years has made them the most likely candidates for these posts. From this point of view, it is particularly important to make mention of the post of *dayan* (judge) in the state rabbinical courts, which parallels that of the civil court's district judge in salary and status. The institutionalization of this office, which is open, in practice, to the better yeshiva students, has made a direct contribution toward reinforcing the idea that Torah study in ḥaredi yeshivot is eminently practical, in the long run.

Thus, ironically, it is their very minority status that functions for the Ḥaredim as an advantage in securing their economic basis.

3. The "Kollel": The Extended Moratorium

The *kollel* is an institution on a small scale (usually embracing thirty to fifty students), intended for yeshiva graduates after marriage. The length of study in the *kollel* is not fixed, and depends in large measure on the inclinations of the student himself.

A separate setting for young married men *(avrekhim)* for extended study, as a continuation of the Volozhin-type yeshiva, first appeared in Poland and Lithuania. In 1877, funds provided by Ovadia (Emil) Lahmann of Germany, at the urging of Rabbi Israel Salanter (founder of the Musar movement), helped to establish the "Kibutz avrekhim—kollel prushim" (society of scholars in ascetic seclusion) in Kovno.[25] From the beginning, this institution and those which were modelled upon it were intended for the few, for men of sublime spirituality. When Rabbi Avraham Karlitz founded the "Torah students' group" in Bene Berak (better known as the "*kollel* of the Ḥazon Ish") in 1942, he also intended it for the "spiritually sublime few . . . those who cast aside all the vain delights of this world and choose the path of Torah, obeying the injunction: 'Tarry in the house [of the Lord] all your days.' "[26]

However, after the 1950s the *kollel* became a place where almost anyone who had studied in a ḥaredi yeshiva could stay on after his marriage.[27] Furthermore, the *kollel* is a temporary setting (five to ten years) for the decisive majority of the students, after which they leave in order to go into business or to become a religious functionary.

The development of these institutions was only possible against the background of the rise in the standard of living of the Jewish population in the Western world in general, and of the ḥaredi population in particular; as well as against the background of the change that took place in women's education and in their ability to earn the family's keep at least for the initial period after marriage.

There is no doubt that the introduction of the *kollel* as a teaching institution intended for all ḥaredi yeshiva students has had a wide socioreligious significance, which cannot be discussed here. Apart from this, however, the institution is of decisive importance in prolonging the "moratorium" period, during which entry into the economy is postponed. As was noted above, the moratorium period is liable to increase the tension between the yeshiva and the "economic life." And yet, extending the period of study after marriage paradoxically lowers this tension and facilitates the process of transition. This is so because the explicit function of the *kollel* is to create a setting for study that will enable the young man to deepen his learning until he becomes "great in Torah." Since it is clear that at least some of the students will not reach this stage, and that some will eventually start preparing to enter the economy, the *kollel* enables them to plan this gradually. The young man can leave the *kollel* at a time convenient to him and under conditions which he deems suitable.

Indeed, once ḥaredi society succeeded in putting all its sons into the "cloistered community" of the yeshiva, where Torah is the sole legitimate subject of study, it was forced to institute the *kollel* in order to provide a moratorium for the ill-prepared *avrekh* before his assumption of material responsibilities. It is impossible to evaluate the proportion of students like this, for whom the *kollel* functions as a shelter from confrontation with "the practical."

4. Resources for the "Holy Yeshiva" and the Kollel: Mobilizing the Jewish World

The maintenance of these institutions demands considerable resources. We have already noted the fact that the success in business of part of the younger ḥaredi generation enables them to increase their share in the maintenance budget of yeshivot and *kollelim.* In view of the fact that, after the Holocaust, ḥaredi Jewry represents for many Jews the culture that was wiped out, ḥaredi communities have also been able to mobilize resources from the whole Jewish world. All of traditionalist Jewry is thus perceived as a kind of living museum of the past, in whose continued existence the nation has an interest. Many also see a contribution to a yeshiva as an appropriate gesture in memory of traditional-religious members of their families killed in the Holocaust.

Israeli government assistance must also be taken into account. It is impossible to know the precise amount of financial support that flows into the yeshivot and other ḥaredi institutions, but the fact that additional students are accepted every year and that the standard of living in the yeshivot rises steadily while new institutions are constantly being established is testimony to the fact that the scale of funds coming from various sources is not small, but quite the opposite.

THE METROPOLITAN CITY: HEDONISM, ALIENATION, CRIME

As we have said, living in the modern metropolitan city enables Ḥaredim to enjoy the benefits of the welfare state, while also providing the opportunity for some of them to fit into the business world. The large city, however, also represents the secular spirit and is the place where the ills of modern society are more in evidence than anywhere else. From this point of view, the modern city, more so than in the past, constitutes a serious threat to the traditional-religious way of life.[28] For the purpose of this discussion, we shall define "the secular" as accepted norms of daily behavior running counter to traditional-religious conceptions. The best example is the permissiveness manifested in women's dress. Secular society and mores are not only evident in public places; they reach into the private home by way of the media (television, etc.). The more permissive modern society becomes, the more the feeling of being "threatened" by the modern city becomes characteristic for the Ḥaredim.

1. Toleration and Alienation

Perhaps the most characteristic feature of the big modern city is the variegated composition of its population. The different groups live and function side by side on the basis of a relative tolerance—which is at least partly the result of the constantly deepening alienation affecting urban social relations. This state of affairs allows population groups like the Ḥaredim which stand out as "strangers" in and alienated from the dominant way of life, to fit into certain sectors of economic life on the one hand and on the other to separate themselves in their residential quarters and their social life.

2. The Ghetto—A Territorial Base

The primary condition for ḥaredi existence in the big city is the creation and demarcation of a territorial base—a ghetto. This not only facilitates effective social control within the community, but also lowers the tension stemming from the fundamental and highly visible opposition between the ḥaredi Jew and the dominant surrounding culture. The ghetto takes the edge off the sense of being strange, and at the same time makes it possible to create a complex system of parallel and complementary social compensations (social status, leisure pastimes, and entertainment) that enable the ḥaredi Jew to live simultaneously in two opposing worlds.

The development of the urban ḥaredi ghetto owes much to postwar affluent conditions which facilitate large-scale residential mobility. Those who move from one neighborhood to another in search of a more homogeneous environment create space in turn for others whose lifestyle fits more closely with those around them.

As the standard of living rises in modern society in general and in ḥaredi groups in particular, new residential quarters (ghettos) for Ḥaredim are built, combining togetherness and isolation: ideal conditions for ḥaredi life in the modern city.

3. Varieties of Ḥaredism in the Modern City

The varied and variegated character of ḥaredi Judaism stems both from the nature of ḥaredi religiosity and from the fact that Ḥaredism is based on an East European tradition which incorporated a wide diversity of custom and local practice. These origins may be seen in the subcommunities which exist today, each with its own practices, leadership, dress, and even, in part, religious perceptions.

Certainly potential and actual tensions exist between the various groups, but the modern city's constantly expanding living space makes it possible to limit these tensions. The territorial base maintained by each group makes for a maximum of internal homogeneity while allowing for internal "nomadism." Moreover, the existence of large Jewish populations in the same city makes for an easier "division of labor," whereby the Ḥaredim provide religious services and accessories, leaving to the others all the activities calling for a greater involvement in modern secular culture.

4. *Ḥaredi Religiosity as an Antidote to the City's Maladies*

In the past, against the background of the poverty and the existential crisis of East European Jewry, the "modern" was perceived as the alternative to the "decaying" old world, which would bring a better future and a solution to pressing human problems. Traditional religion was identified with the "old world" which was falling to pieces, and so was delegitimized.

Today, against the background of a hedonistic culture of entertainment and consumption, which has elevated permissiveness to a principle and led to increased crime and a plague of drugs, modern culture as expressed in big city life finds itself in crisis. This necessarily generates feelings of apprehension, alienation, and insecurity among wide strata of the urban population. In this situation, ḥaredi Judaism can present itself as an alternative that has succeeded in maintaining social institutions which preserve values and norms of modesty, spiritual riches, social togetherness, and an attitude of respect for tradition and the older generation, in the absence of crime and drugs. The "success" of ḥaredi society is compared to the "failure" of modern culture, and this tends to reinforce the sense of superiority of ḥaredi Judaism in the eyes of those faithful to its ways.

CONCLUSION

The existential crisis of traditional-religious Jewish society in Eastern Europe grew more and more acute from the mid-nineteenth century on. The flight from religion and tradition was accelerated by the processes of uprooting and migration from small town to big town, and from Eastern Europe to the West. Here, the encounter with modern Western society swelled the anti-religious current still more. Ḥaredi religiosity developed against this background and as a reaction against it. It found its expression mainly in the large yeshivas of the Volozhin type, which were under the influence of the Musar movement. These have been described here as "cloistered communities," inasmuch as they have been based on a life of study, separate from family and community, meant to imbue students with a sense of being a religious elite, and championing a "heroic" piety of absolute dedication to the study of Torah through the denigration of material concerns.

The Holocaust of European Jewry, which dealt its heaviest blow to the traditional-religious community of Eastern Europe, turned this way of life into the preserve of a small minority in the Jewish world. This minority then moved to metropolitan centers in the countries of the West and Israel. It was precisely here, strangely enough, that ḥaredi society, based on groups of surviving remnants from Eastern Europe, succeeded in developing social mechanisms which enabled it to block the hitherto chronic outflow of members and to build up a new ḥaredi culture. This dialectical development was linked to a rise in the standard of living in Western countries after World War II and the development of the modern welfare state, which allowed students to prolong their stay in educational institutions. Thus, it became possible to adopt the "cloistered community" as the sole educational model in ḥaredi society.

While the city provided easy opportunities for Ḥaredim in certain spheres of business, at the same time the Ḥaredim became the almost exclusive suppliers of services and accessories connected with religious practice. These factors made it possible to decrease the tension between the anti-economism of the yeshiva and the pragmatic values of the economy, thus facilitating the move from one to the other. The *kollel* also made such a transition easier by preventing a sharp crisis for those not yet capable of making it.

The revolution in women's education and vocational training meant that they could find suitable employment as teachers, which was consonant with ḥaredi social values and also contributed decisively to making yeshiva—and *kollel*—study "practical."

In the setting of the big city, the ḥaredi ghetto provides a solid territorial base for the various subgroups in the community. It enables the Ḥaredim to maintain an independent culture which can borrow selectively elements from the surrounding culture, and to maintain a large measure of internal social control. The modern city thus affords the chance to sustain the ḥaredi voluntary community in a dialectical balance of isolation from, and mingling with, the rest of the population.

What is more, given the crisis of modern urban culture, as expressed in alienation, crime, and drugs, ḥaredi Jewry can present itself as a viable alternative, while at the same time it derives much benefit from the fruits of "the modern"—in terms of living standard, modern technology, and the relative tolerance among urban groups.

It should be remembered that the continuation of this lifestyle is contingent upon an ongoing division of labor between the Ḥaredim and the modern culture around them, and between the Ḥaredim and other Jews.

The main condition for Ḥaredism's continuity is the maintenance of the "cloistered community" as the exclusive educational institution, where the younger generation is not given access to training for most of the tasks of modern society. The life of such institutions depends on the capacity of the ḥaredi society to ensure an alternative system of material support for the younger generation. This, in turn, depends on providing teaching posts or equivalent employment for the women of the community, on the availability of posts in the rabbinate and in teaching institutions for the men, and on a continuing market for religious services and accessories which the community can dominate.[29] There are already signs that not all of these conditions may last over the long term.

Ḥaredi society's very success in ensuring the entry of all of its younger generation into the "cloistered community," its large natural increase and the "mobilization" of "newly Orthodox" Jews from outside the community *(ḥozrim bi-tshuvah),* together may create preconditions for a future crisis.

Notes

1. The organ of "Neturei Karta." See *Encyclopedia Judaica* vol. XII, col. 1002, and my book, *Hevrah va-dat* (Jerusalem: 1978), p. 366.

2. The organ of the anti-Zionist ḥaredi community in Jerusalem, with a relatively broad readership in the ḥaredi community at large. See *Encyclopedia Judaica* vol. IX, col. 892, and *Hevrah va-dat,* chaps. 1, 2, 4.

3. On this, see also M. Friedman, "The Changing Role of the Community Rabbinate," *The Jerusalem Quarterly* 25 (1982), pp. 79–99; M. Freidman, "The National Religious Party in Crisis," in D. Caspi *et al.* (eds.), *The Roots of Begin's Success: The 1981 Israeli Elections* (London and New York, 1984), pp. 141–168.

4. The conscious opposition of the ḥaredi elite to what is called "the mass," the "bourgeois community" *(baalei-batim)* and so on, finds expression in almost all the writings (including halakhic studies) produced by the spokesmen of ḥaredi religiosity, both in Eastern Europe, prior to the Holocaust, and afterwards as well. In a forthcoming article, I intend to deal with this matter at length.

5. This definition is somewhat different from that of M. Samet, who views ḥaredi Judaism as one expression of the Jewish Orthodoxy that arose upon the demise of traditional Jewry, and thus places Ḥaredism in the same historical context as German neo-Orthodoxy and Hungarian Orthodoxy on the Hatam Sofer model. See Samet, "Ha-yahadut ba-zeman he-hadash," *Mahalakhim* I (1969), pp. 29–40, and III (1970), pp. 15–27; and *ibid.*, "Ha-konflikt odot misud erkei ha-yahadut bimedinat yisrael," *Mehkarim be-soziologiah* (Hebrew University, 1979), pp. 42–49.

6. See note 4.

7. Better known by the name Hafetz Haim, the title of his book (Vilna, 1873).

8. On this, see below, and my article cited in note 3.

9. On the *yeshivah gedolah* see S. Stampfer, *Shalosh yeshivot litaiyot ba meah ha-19* (Ph.D. dissertation, The Hebrew University of Jerusalem, 1981). On the Musar movement, see esp. E. Etkes, *Rabbi Yisrael Salanter ve-reshitah shel tnu'at ha-musar* (Jerusalem: 1982).

10. The schools for rabbinical ordination in the West (seminaries)—those which adhered to halakhah—were contemptuously dubbed "rabbi-factories." See the letter of Rabbi Haim Oyzer Grodzensky to Rabbi Meir Hildesheimer, head of the rabbinical seminary in Berlin, dated 27 Kislev 5694 (= 15 December 1934). The letter dealt with Hildesheimer's proposal to transfer the seminary to Tel-Aviv.

11. Opposition to the introduction of any secular learning within the yeshiva framework became an article of faith in the ḥaredi community: "It is absolutely clear in the teachings of our greatest rabbis that foreign learning [i.e., secular knowledge] not be taught to yeshiva students. . . . They saw this as a certain loss . . . and determined to wage a holy war against this . . ." (Rabbi Yeshaya Karlitz, "Hazon Ish," *Kovez̧ igrot* vol. 2: Bene-Berak, 1956, pp. 50, 56). In this connection, the story of the closure of the Volozhin yeshiva (in 1892), when the Russian authorities tried to introduce secular studies, was turned into a myth of sacrifice in defense of principle. See Rabbi M. M. Yashar, *Ḥafetz Ḥaim* vol. I: Tel-Aviv, 1958, pp. 223–25.

12. A good example of this activity is given by the case of Rabbi Haim Moshe Yehudah Schneider. Although he is not an especially well-known figure even in ḥaredi circles, he can serve as an archetype of this "heroic" elite. Schneider, deeply influenced by the Hafetz Haim, fled to Germany in 1905 to avoid conscription into the Russian army. He dedicated his life to establishing yeshivas in Germany on the Volozhin model. In the end, he succeeded in establishing one in England, the first of its kind there (the Torath-Emet Schneider Yeshiva). See G. Schneider, *Sefer zikaron:* Bene-Berak: 5725 (= 1965), pp. 9–24.

13. See S. Y. Zevin, *Ishim ve-shitot* (2nd ed., Tel-Aviv: 1967), esp. the introduction (unpaginated): "It was as if the yeshivas of Lithuania had created a 'revolution' in the study of halacha, and from Lithuania, this spread to other countries. . . ."

14. Approximately twenty students from Germany were enrolled in the Mir Yeshiva in 1929. See Mark Wischnitzer, "Ḥomer le-toldot ha-yeshivot be-eiropah ha-mizraḥit," *Talpiot* VI, nos. 1–2 (1953), p. 362. Cf. M. Zinovich, "le-toldot yeshivat Mir," in *Sefer Mir* (Jerusalem: 1962), p. 110.

15. The Ponivezh Yeshiva was reestablshed in Bene-Berak by Rabbi Joseph Cahanman in 1943. The Mir Yeshiva was similarly reestablished, at about the same time, by Rabbi Eliezer Yehudah Finkel in Jerusalem. The Gateshead Yeshiva in England was formally opened in 1927, but only became a center of Torah study after the Second World War. The Lakewood Yeshiva in New Jersey was founded by Rabbi Aaron Kotler in 1941. The Telz Yeshiva was founded in Cleveland in 1942.

16. When Rabbi Kotler founded the yeshiva in Lakewood he strenuously opposed secular studies. On the dramatic scene when the issue was decided, see Z. Sorotzkin, *Ha-deah ve-ha-dibur* vol. 3 (Jerusalem: 1965), p. 201; A. Sorsky, *Toldot ha-ḥinukh ha-torati* (Bnei Brak: 1967), p. 286.

17. See, for example, the comments of Rabbi Yehezkel Sarna, head of the Hebron Yeshiva, on the high school yeshivas, in *Digleinu* (Iyar-Sivan 5721 = 1961): "The name of a yeshiva is holy. . . ."

18. See: L. Deutschlander (ed.), *History of the Beth Jacob Girls' Schools* (Vienna: 1933); D. R. Weissman, "Bais Yaakov, A Women's Educational Movement in the Polish Jewish Community: A Case Study in Tradition and Modernity," (M.A. thesis, New York University, 1979).

19. See *Ḥevrah va-dat* p. 362; Sorsky, *Toldot ha-ḥinukh,* pp. 455–56.

20. See Sarah Koplowitz, "Kavanatam reẓuyah aval ha-maasim einam reẓuyim," *Ha-Modi'a* (21 Shvat 5743 = 4.2.1983); I. Beharav, "Va-taas be-ḥefeẓ kfiah," *Tmurah* (11 Nisan 5743 = 25.3.1983).

21. "We must bear in mind that today it is necessary that women work, in order to maintain Torah study" (I. Beharav, see note 20).

22. In a letter dated 15 Heshvan 5738 (= 27.10.1977), and published in *Ḥeshek patenu* 2, p. 106.

23. See, e.g., Rabbi Moshe Feinstein's remarks in a letter to "heads of *metivtot*" (undated), private archive, and cf. Rabbi Jacob Kneivsky ("Stapler"), *Sefer ḥayei olam* (Bene-Berak: 5717 = 1957), pp. 7–8.

24. The case of Yisrael Zupnik, one of the important wealthy members of the Satmar ḥasidic community in New York, is an excellent example. He began with trade in sacred books, a strictly Jewish business. During the war he began to go into the food industry, which included dealings with non-Jews. His success aroused a good deal of interest and seemed to prove to others that it was indeed possible even in America to appear as a traditional Jew and to conduct business in a modern city. See M. M. Gerlitz, *Yisrael oseh ḥayil* (Jerusalem: 5735 = 1975), pp. 8–9.

25. See J. Lifshitz, *Zikhron yaakov,* part 3 (Kovno: 1930), pp. 222–226; S. S. Bialoblotsky, *Merkazei ha-torah be-lita. Eim lamasoret* (Ramat-Gan: 1971), p. 232.

26. *Koveẓ igrot* vol. 1 (Jerusalem: 5715 = 1955), pp. 96–97.

27. I.e., *avrekhim.*

28. See M. Friedman, "The National Religious Party in Crisis," p. 2.

29. The reference here is to the growing number of religious functionaries from the *"hesder"* yeshivas, where once the members of the ḥaredi community dominated.

The Religious Kibbutz Movement: The Pursuit of a Complete Life within an Orthodox Framework

Aryei Fishman
(BAR-ILAN UNIVERSITY)

The Religious Kibbutz Movement (HaKibbutz HaDati, hereafter the RKM), consisting of sixteen settlements and a population of about 7,500 in 1984, was founded in Palestine in the early 1930s by graduates of the religious pioneering movements in Germany and Eastern Europe.[1] They, too, were motivated by those national and socialist values which had led the secular Zionist pioneering movement to found and evolve the kibbutz pattern of life.[2] Underlying this ideological rationale, however, lay another value: to reestablish, within the parameters of a modern self-contained social framework, the religious community that had been disrupted by nineteenth-century emancipation.[3]

The RKM's pursuit of this goal must be set against the background of the major modernizing movements within Orthodox Judaism which preceded it: nineteenth century Torah-im-Derekh Eretz,[4] which was created in post-emancipation Germany and propelled the breakthrough of Orthodox Judaism into the modern world; and Religious Zionism,[5] which was formally founded at the turn of the century in the pre-emancipation setting of Eastern Europe, in the very midst of the collapse of the Jewish traditional order. As part of their aim of integrating the Orthodox Jew into universal society, both movements sought to reestablish the religious unity that had prevailed within the circumscribed traditional society, by expanding that unity to encompass a comprehensive framework that constituted a "full and complete life."[6] This article seeks to present the modern religious community created by the RKM as a distinct and advanced stage in the realization of that goal.

The key to the innovative thrust of Torah-im-Derekh Eretz and Religious Zionism—and of the RKM after them—was Torah as an innovative power.[7] In both movements we find the notion that Torah is inherently related to a "complete and full life" and, in order to be observed properly, must be realized in such a life.[8] The traditional religious order was incomplete to the extent that it was not receptive to general culture and its structure lacked some of the key spheres with which to lead a complete life,[9] such as primary occupations and sovereign political institutions. On the other hand, emancipation for Torah-im-Derekh Eretz and Religious Zionism, and modern nationalism in particular for Religious Zionism, implied the "return" of the Jewish people to a complete life characteristic of humanity at large, and its participation in a society possessing all the institutions necessary for the maintenance of a fully self-contained life.[10] This return to a universal life would influence Torah to activate its creative power in order to relate organically to it.

Torah-im-Derekh Eretz sought to attain this integration between Torah and universal life by identifying with the general German society and participating in its institutions. Religious Zionism sought to achieve it within the framework of a national Jewish society. Each one influenced the formation and development of the RKM in its own particular fashion.

II

Samson Raphael Hirsch (1808–1888), the father of Torah-im-Derekh Eretz and of modern Orthodoxy in general, responded to the challenge of the values of emancipation and universal culture which had led to mass abandonment of traditional religion by seeking to incorporate them within Judaism. Two slogans epitomized the endeavor of Torah-im-Derekh Eretz to achieve religious unity within a universal framework. The first, "Mensch-Jissroél"[11] (man-Israel) implied that a Jew could realize himself religiously as "Israel" only through the universal dimension of "man."[12] In order for the religious Jew to realize his universal component, he must integrate himself within the general society, and work for its improvement. The second slogan, "Torah-im-Derekh Eretz" (Torah and civic life), implied that the participation in the civic life of the society was a necessary condition for the realization of Torah.[13] Civic life was regarded as a raw substance to be molded by Torah; Torah, by leaving its imprint upon this substance, transmuted it into a religious reality. Thus, Rabbi Yehiel Weinberg commented on Hirsch's perception of Torah: "It is within the power of Torah not only to accommodate all cultural contents, but also to constitute the force that molds them . . . and even to transform them in Torah [as a cultural system]."[14]

Through Toram-im-Derekh Eretz, Orthodox German Jews developed a new self-awareness as religious Jews and as human beings. They absorbed the general culture and participated actively in the economic and political institutions of the general society about them.[15] The religious ideology of Torah-im-Derekh Eretz successfully effected the transition of the Orthodox Jew from a tradition-bound to a modern, open world. The feeling that Torah is inherently related to a complete life and could sustain such a life within its purview was so deep among the ideologues of Torah-im-Derekh Eretz that they even spoke of realizing "the dominion of Torah" in the general life of their society.[16]

German Orthodoxy made a seminal contribution to the modernizing thrust of the RKM through the pioneering youth who were brought up in its culture and constituted the dominant element of the RKM.[17] But the very familiarity of Orthodox German Jewish youth with the modern world, through their secular education and participation in the institutions of a general society, sharpened their sensitivity to the limitations of modern Orthodoxy's attempt to integrate the universal and the particular cultures.[18] Already at the turn of the century the seemingly unified religious pattern of German Jewish religious life had come under question.[19] Orthodox youth become aware of the prevailing structural dualism of Jewish and general life. In the 1920s the recognition of this dualism constituted a subject of growing concern in the emerging religious pioneering movement that was to organize formally in 1928 as "Bachad" (Brith Chalutzim Datiim).

The structural dualism prevailed at two levels. (a) The integrated relationship that Torah-im-Derekh Eretz had worked out between traditional and universal values was chiefly in an ideational context; in practice this integration did not and could not exist. While the Orthodox Jewish population shared universal values with the general German public, which helped cultivate a sense of social solidarity, this sharing could not be realized at the more meaningful religious level. (b) It was on the normative social level in particular that the Orthodox Jew could not integrate his two meaningful worlds. Most of the institutions in which the Orthodox Jew participated, particularly in the economic and political spheres, were subject to non-Jewish authority and molded by the values of the non-Jewish population. Hence, the Orthodox Jew had no control over the regulation of these institutions through his Torah values. Furthermore, at the occupational level the Orthodox Jew could assume only those roles that did not clash with halakhah, i.e., that did not involve working on the Sabbath and Jewish holidays. On the other hand, the institutions over which the Orthodox Jew could exert control, in the halakhically ordered Kehillah, affected only limited aspects of his life. Whereas in traditional society, the Kehillah had encompassed almost all of Jewish life, in the wake of emancipation it was restricted by the German state chiefly to the ritual sphere.[20] Yet, this halakhically ordered community was more deeply meaningful for the Orthodox Jew because it constituted the religious social framework of Jewish public life. In effect, the modern Orthodox Jew found himself a member of two diverse and unbridgeable social orders; that of the all-embracing general society and that of the contracted halakhically ordered community.

The structural dualism and tension within Orthodox youth is poignantly expressed, as is the direction of its resolution, in 1932, in the bulletin of Bachad:

> Judaism is becoming more and more a matter of cognition, observed artificially alongside real life. . . . Orthodoxy ignores the fact that proclaiming "the dominion of the Torah" is condemned to remain merely a slogan if not accompanied by the obligation to struggle for a national, social and cultural *Gemeinschaft* in a closed system. Only such a community can constitute a base for enabling Torah to be an all-embracing value influencing (general) culture and Jewish learning, and a factor that molds the whole person.[21]

III

Gemeinschaft was the key concept among German Jewish youth for the realization of a "complete life" in a religious framework.[22] This concept, adopted from the German youth culture,[23] was cultivated within Bachad, many of whose members were graduates of Jewish youth movements. Influenced by German idealistic philosophy, *Gemeinschaft,* among other things, represented a closed social system that encompassed the total life of the individual in a unified meaningful framework. It conveyed the notion that a person can fully realize himself as a "whole person" only if he is "organically" integrated within a community whose members share a common value system that guides them in fulfilling all the social roles necessary for the independent existence of the community. The community was conceived as expressing the ideals of its members through the symbolic world and institutions that it forms and sustains.

Applying the concept of *Gemeinschaft* to the modern Jewish Orthodox reality, the pioneering youth reached the conclusion that observant Jews who identified with modern life were not in a position to realize the unity between the particular Jewish and universal components of their identity, unless they participated in a social order that was both complete in the institutional sense, and ordered by their religious values.

Hence, the specific value of Zionism for enabling the Orthodox Jew to lead a completely integrated life. As stated in 1934 by Ernst Simon: "The heart of Zionism is the restoration of a complete life to Judaism."[24] Zionism's goal of creating a national Jewish society that would also be modern provided a potential framework for an Orthodox Jew to fulfill himself as a whole person without impairing the observance of his religious culture. Religious Zionism outlined the path toward the realization of that potential. Its ideology rested on the beliefs that religion and nationalism are interwoven in Jewish life, and that traditional Jewish culture could be transformed sufficiently to enable it to sustain a modern self-contained national life.

IV

Established formally in 1902, with the founding of Mizrahi in Vilna, Religious Zionism legitimated universal values at two levels. The nineteenth century progenitors of the movement had implied that Jewish nationalism suggested the return of the Jewish people to the family of nations; the creation of a modern Jewish national community was regarded as complementing West European emancipation by providing a particularistic mold for organizing participation in a general life.[25] At the turn of the century, the leaders of Mizrahi conceived the modern national Jewish society as a vehicle for the preservation of the Jewish people and of Torah, in the face of the mass abandonment of traditional culture and spreading assimilation. In the words of the founding proclamation of Mizrahi: "For the return to Zion will provide a sure base . . . for our people . . . and security for our Torah."[26]

Mizrahi, however, did not attempt to come to grips with the basic economic and colonizing needs of the emerging national society in Palestine and was not motivated to sustain those needs in basic religious terms. Middle class in membership orientation, Mizrahi did not advocate the transformation of the occupational structure of Jewish life in order to develop a complete life in a national framework.[27] For that matter, Mizrahi did not develop an articulate and coherent ideology for defining the relationship between religious and universal values in the framework of Torah[28]—as did Torah-im-Derekh Eretz. But its approach to establish meaningful unity between the two spheres was explicitly articulated in its ideology. Thus, Zeev Yaavetz in 1904 perceived the

Jewish national community as a framework conducive for encouraging Torah to relate to all aspects of life and to sustain them within its system:

> The sense of unity that dominates the spirit of our religion . . . embraces life in its entirety and renders it an essential part [of this unity]. . . . Only in the land of our fathers can Torah branch out in its own way, without hindrance. For there it will be the matron. . . . Only there will the Torah be able to revive itself and restore its people to a real life, a life of complete unity.[29]

Such sentiments, however, remained little more than a theoretical formulation in the life of Mizrahi.

It was left to HaPoel HaMizrahi, the labor offshoot of Mizrahi founded in Palestine in 1922, to make an innovative practical attempt to integrate universal and traditional religious values in a self-contained society. Conceiving Torah as "the national spirit of the Jewish people, the source of its culture"[30] and inspired by the ideology of "Torah vaAvodah" (Torah and Labor), HaPoel HaMizrahi legitimated the pioneering values of secular Zionism, such as self-labor in primary occupations—especially in farming—and cooperative settlement, and transmuted them into religious values.[31] Through the new religious norms, roles and institutions which it created, HaPoel HaMizrahi sought to build "a complete and authentic Jewish life . . . an all-encompassing life"[32] in the framework of the emerging Jewish national society in Palestine. In the 1920s, HaPoel HaMizrahi regarded the moshav, the small-holder cooperative settlement, as the preeminent social-economic pattern by which to realize its values.

The goal of the Torah vaAvodah ideology to create new religious norms and roles so as to contain a national society within the framework of Torah fitted in neatly with the Bachad ideal of creating a complete life ordered by religious values. As stated in 1932:

> Our slogan, "Torah vaAvodah" does not imply Torah plus a certain attitude towards labor and social problems. We perceive Torah as an [operative] method, a legal structure and a form of life that is intended to encompass and define the occupational sphere, a life of labor and all the problems that a social structure encounters.[33]

V

By and large, however, Religious Zionism was not capable of ordering the Jewish national society according to religious values, for the majority of this society was secular in outlook, and opposed religious patterns of organization. Hence, while the national society provided a particular Jewish framework for realizing universal values, the religious dimension of this particularity was tenuous. A further and more significant challenge to the complete integration of universal and traditional values, however, derived from the gap that existed between the normative demands of the emerging Jewish national institutions and the norms of Halakhah.

Halakhic dynamics had been greatly restrained since the end of the eighteenth century,[34] and the Rabbinate, the institutionalized authority for the interpretation of Halakhah, was generally unresponsive to the national values and did not try to come to grips with the conflicts between halakhic and national norms. Not only did the social reality of the twentieth century differ immensely from that of the eighteenth century, but the functional needs of a self-sustaining national society were far more complicated than those of the pre-emancipation Kehillah. In effect, the gap between established Halakhah and the needs of the modern national society implied that observant Jews could not fulfill all the roles necessary for the autonomous functioning of that society. In 1942, a leading HaPoel HaMizrahi figure was to express the corollary of this situation: "[This means] forfeiting [a complete] life, leaving the building of the land to secular Jews, confirming thereby that there is a contradiction between Torah and life."[35]

For the members of Bachad in Germany, the very notion of a contradiction between Torah and a complete life was unacceptable. Their point of departure was that a complete life is a hallmark of the true religious life, in which all aspects of this life are meaningfully and functionally consistent. Torah was conceived of as inherently related to such a life, "For without a complete life there cannot be a complete [realization of] Torah."[36] Indeed, if Halakhah proved incapable of sustaining the roles and institutions necessary for the complete functioning of a national society, then the flaw was not in the structure of that society. The burden of proof lay with Halakhah, which was challenged to activate its ability to sustain a self-contained modern Jewish society.

Hence, the significance of the closed social system that the *Gemeinschaft* represented. In Jewish religious terms, such a system constituted a self-contained society which created conditions for the reinvigoration of Torah in general, and of Halakhah in particular, by grappling with the basic functions of that society.

> The absence of a self-contained Jewish national and cultural Gemeinschaft prevents a Jewish perception of life based on the Torah. . . . We should not seek the blame for this situation in the Torah, but

> in our historical situation, which does not enable us to activate the tremendous forces hidden in the Torah. In this situation we must redeem the Torah by our own efforts. . . .[37]

This approach suggested that the dynamics of Halakhah could be served by the praxis stemming from the functional needs of the self-contained society. The closed all-encompassing social system would promote a direct confrontation between Torah and a complete life, thus inducing Torah, by means of the Oral Law, to respond to the needs of the national community.

> The dynamics of Oral Law cannot be restored by the personal efforts of many individuals, nor by the resolution of any conference of a hundred and twenty rabbis. Only a free independent Jewish society that creates its life within itself offers the opportunity to revive Oral Law.[38]

The socialist values of the Jewish youth movements in Germany in the 1920s and early 1930s reinforced the national values that Bachad espoused in its quest for a universal frame of living. Socialism implied direct identification with all of mankind and cooperating in building a better world. Paul Tillich's philosophy of a meaningful religious socialism, expounded at that time in Germany, encouraged Orthodox youth to seek a Jewish religious underpinning for socialist values.[39] Bachad found it in the social doctrine of Torah vaAvodah, which held the social precepts of the Pentateuch and prophets to represent the true intention of the Torah with regard to the ordering of human society. Religious pioneering youth, accordingly, interpreted socialist values as Torah values which called for their realization in social institutions. The educational program of Brith HaNoar HaDati, the religious pioneering youth movement affiliated with Bachad, gave clear expression to this in 1933:

> The awareness that the realization of Torah is a collective task should be included in an early stage of our educational work. This awareness should be deepened by the explanation that the Torah cannot be fully realized in every Jewish collective, but only in a Gemeinschaft of free workers in which there is no exploitation. The universal goal of education for socialism complements the specific [national-religious] Jewish goal.[40]

VI

These seminal ideas which developed within Bachad during its formative period in the late 1920s and early 1930s had not yet crystalized into a coherent ideology when the first graduates of the movement immigrated to Palestine at the end of 1929 with the intention of establishing a kibbutz. But the general idea of utilizing this social pattern to attain the life of religious unity that they sought had already begun to take shape. If it was beyond their control to achieve this unity on a macronational scale, the collective structure of the kibbutz was vaguely conceived of as an instrument for achieving that unity on a micronational scale. The thoughts of a member expressed in a letter written immediately after the group's arrival in Palestine convey that feeling:

> Ever since we established [our training farms] we have been working for the creation of a communal group of Orthodox workers. We believe that it is the only way to live a productive and independent life according to the spirit of the Torah. Today [Jewish] Orthodoxy is content if it can maintain its positions against other streams; if it can save the . . . Sabbath from the complexities of the economy. We cannot rest content with that. We aspire to a Jewish atmosphere that is central to our future—one that encompasses the whole man in his economic and cultural life. We believe that this constitutes the only direction that the Orthodox offensive must take.[41]

The first group of Bachad graduates established itself in a work camp immediately after its arrival in Palestine and called itself "Rodges," after one of their training farms in Germany.[42] In the course of the 1930s and 1940s, other religious pioneering groups were formed, of German and East European immigrants, and of native Palestinians. In 1937 Tirat Tzvi, the first religious kibbutz settlement was created. When the State of Israel was established in 1948, the RKM numbered ten settlements, concentrated for the most part in three separate blocs on the frontiers of the Jewish national community.[43]

VII

The settlement conditions which confronted the RKM—acute security problems and unfamiliar agricultural territory—severely tested their idea of achieving a viable integration between universal and particular values in a self-contained system. We have noted earlier that the gap which existed between the norms of Halakhah and the needs of a self-contained national macrocommunity limited the capacity of Religious Zionism to establish a unified religious life in a national setting. The RKM experienced that same gap on a microcommunity scale when its groups set about developing their farm economies. Thus the creation of a complete and unified religious life was contingent upon on bridging that rift. However, inspired by "faith in the Torah and its omnipotence,"[44] and conceiving of the kibbutz as the preeminent social vehicle for that purpose, the members of the RKM believed, nevertheless, that they could achieve the desired unity within the parameters of a pioneering life.

The outstanding halakhic problem facing the religious kibbutzim concerned the functioning of community life on the Sabbath. According to the established Halakhah, the milking of cows, the activation of security arrangements, and repairs to disrupted water or electricity systems were forbidden on the Sabbath. The Orthodox pioneers rejected the use of the "Shabbes goy" (the gentile who is called upon to perform activities on the Sabbath that were forbidden to Jews) because it contradicted the concepts of self-labor and of a self-contained community. Other halakhic problems involved the observance of the agricultural precepts which apply to the Land of Israel, such as the suspension of agricultural work on the sabbatical year. The centrality of these problems in the life of the young religious kibbutzim is reflected in a statement written in 1938:

> The national renaissance . . . has opened to the religious pioneer, spheres of life that were hitherto unfamiliar . . . self-labor, . . . the development of a farm-economy, and the problem of guard duty, are among the outstanding characteristics of this revolution . . . in Jewish life. . . . Today these matters constitute the significant background of our life and being . . . and of the realization of our goal: to create a full religious life that is based on the thrust to regenerate Torah, our people and the land.[45]

VIII

It is beyond the scope of this article to demonstrate how the RKM went about solving each of the halakhic problems that it encountered. Suffice it to say that most of these problems were eventually solved in a fashion that was consistent with the ideal of a self-contained micronational community, yet within the framework of Halakhah. Through these solutions the RKM achieved a religious breakthrough, extending Torah legitimation to sectors and roles of life from which Orthodox Jews had hitherto been exluded by Halakhah. Nor is it within the scope of this article to analyze the structure of religious authority within Orthodox Judaism. Basically, however, as we indicated above, the ultimate solution to halakhic problems depended on the rabbinate, whose authority the RKM accepted in principle. In order to achieve the religious breakthrough, however, there were times when the RKM temporarily blurred the line of allegiance to rabbinic authority, without overstepping it in the long run. Many of the solutions which the RKM was instrumental in achieving contained several stages, each of which was legitimated by a different mode of authorization.

To demonstrate one specific multistage solution to a halakhic problem, we shall describe in some detail the evolution of the answer to the question of milking cows on the Sabbath and utilizing their milk.[46]

When dairy farming was introduced into the Jewish agricultural sector of Palestine in the 1920s, cows were milked by hand. Established Halakhah, however, forbade milking by Jews on the Sabbath, as well as the use of the milk that was produced. Before the establishment of the religious kibbutzim, Orthodox farmers who kept milch cows solved the problem by employing Arab laborers to do the milking on the Sabbath. Such a solution, however, created security problems and also endangered the herds, because the laborers could transmit diseases which were then prevalent among Arab cattle. The rabbis to whom this problem was first addressed gave due consideration to the difficulties, and proposed milking onto the ground in order to prevent suffering to the animals and, at the same time, to prevent the use of the milk. This solution, however, meant wasting one-seventh of the milk produced and threatened the viability of the dairy economy of the Orthodox farmers. The RKM, in accordance with their belief in "a Torah of life which encompasses every facet of life and makes life possible,"[47] sought an economically rational solution that would be compatible with Halakhah.

The first stage of the solution (1933–42) involved milking on the Sabbath into a vessel containing a cereal. This solution was based on a dispensation that a member of a Frankfurt rabbinical court had given the Rodges commune in 1933 when it established its first dairy shed. This dispensation, however, was conditional upon its endorsement by a local Palestinian rabbi. Indeed, the then Ashkenazi Chief Rabbi of Tel-Aviv, Rabbi Shlomo Aronson, gave his verbal approval to that dispensation several months later, and on the Sabbath the dairymen in Rodges would milk the kibbutz's small milch herd into a pail containing oats, rice, or some other cereal. The members of the kibbutz would themselves consume the entire product.

However, when word of this dispensation spread in 1934, it was impugned by Rabbi Avraham H. Kook, the Ashkenazi Chief Rabbi of Palestine, as well as by other leading figures in the rabbinical world.[48] As a result, the Tel-Aviv Chief Rabbi withdrew his endorsement, and no other local rabbi was willing to support it. Nonetheless, the Rodges dairymen continued to milk on the Sabbath into a pail containing food, and other religious kibbutzim that were forming and establishing dairy sheds during this period followed the same pattern. This Sabbath milking practice *was* approved in 1937 by Rabbi Eliezer S. Rosenthal, whom Rodges had then appointed to serve as its religious leader, but the general rabbinical consensus continued to oppose it.

At the same time, the young RKM was aware that such a solution was only temporary, from both the halakhic and economic standpoints. Not only did the rabbinical consensus reject it, but it would not be practical once the dairy herds expanded.

The growth of the dairy sheds in the religious kibbutzim led to a second stage in the search for a solution to the question of Sabbath milking (1942–50). Based on ḥalakhic research conducted by Torah scholars within the RKM, the Chief Rabbi of Jerusalem, Rabbi Tzvi Pessah Frank, in 1942 gave a dispensation to milk on the Sabbath into a pail containing chlorophyll.[49] This material prevented its consumption as milk, but not its use in the manufacture of dairy products such as butter and yellow cheese. Indeed, Tnuva, the national marketing agency of the collective settlements, purchased the milk for these purposes. However, although this dispensation was issued by a highly esteemed rabbinical figure, other important rabbis opposed it.

The introduction of the automatic milking machine into the dairy sheds of the RKM around 1950 constituted the third and final stage. The machine was introduced because economically it was more rational; however, it was also endorsed by a general rabbinical consensus. The introduction of the milking machine was the culmination of a sixteen-year search for a solution to the problem of Sabbath milking that would be both economically sound and completely legitimated by the rabbinate.

We have noted, however, that in its attempt to achieve a breakthrough in solving the problem, the RKM did not always accept the weight of rabbinic authority. It did so in the self-awareness that it constituted a community empowered to act as a non-formal religious authority.[50] A RKM member commented retrospectively in 1951 upon this type of religious authority.

> We assumed the authority to determine . . . practices even though they were not always in accord with what is written in the *Shulhan Arukh*. . . . We did this . . . because of our religious feeling . . . that a community is able to withstand the violation of an accepted religious practice. If an individual trangresses that which is written in the *Shulhan Arukh*, his religious outlook may be utterly destroyed. However, a religious community that lives a communal life with collective responsibility could assume responsibility in this sphere too. Only thus can we

> explain to ourselves how we dared to touch areas which, from the formal point of view, we were unqualified to touch.[51]

Basically, the community acted on its own by invoking Torah as charisma. Torah in this sense invested the community with a sense of religious authority,[52] enabling it to suspend the established religious norm and to replace it with a new norm that was conceived of as expressing the true intention of Torah in the particular situation.[53] This sense of authority was inspired by the spirit of "the preeminent principle, 'It is time to act for the Lord, for they have violated His Law'; [i.e.,] there are times that the transgression of Torah is the very observance of Torah."[54] The exercise of charismatic communal authority temporarily bridges the gap between halakhic and pioneering norms; the religious community was enabled to establish a foothold in a new reality from which it was possible to work out a more rational solution to the problem of milking on the Sabbath by technological means, and eventually to obtain the approval of the institutionalized religious authority.

Charismatic communal authority also provided the initial legitimation for the maintenance of security on the Sabbath. A member of Tirat Tzvi, writing in 1958, described the process involved in working out that solution:

> [Just as a rabbi to whom we referred the problem of milking on the Sabbath answered]: "Do you really have to maintian a dairy shed? Why don't you occupy yourselves with other matters, without becoming involved in matters of Halakhah?" . . . we probably would have received an answer in the same vein had we asked rabbis whether we were permitted to settle in the Beit Shean Valley and [thereby] place ourselves in situations which would compel us to violate the Sabbath for reasons of security. But we did not ask the rabbinate whether we were permitted to settle there. And when we created facts—the rabbinate proceeded to confirm them and even permitted the violation of the Sabbath [for security reasons] by the rationale of saving endangered life. Many other problems of this sort were not solved *a priori,* but only after we created facts.[55]

Charismatic religious authority was temporarily exercised in situations involving the ideological principle of self-labor until the rabbis closed the gap between halakhic and pioneering norms at the religious institutional level. It seems that this type of authority was not invoked for other situations, which did not involve the immediate utilization of non-Jewish labor. In some such situations, halakhic solutions congruent with pioneering values were found by the utilization of technological means, such as avoiding the sowing of "diverse seeds" *(kilayim)*.[56] In others, however, satisfactory solutions have yet to be found. A notable example in the latter category is the sabbatical year, when the settlements of the RKM continue to work the land according to a dispensation whereby the land is sold fictitiously to a gentile.[57] While such a solution enables orderly economic functioning, it also mars the ideal of a self-contained community.

IX

It was only by directly confronting Halakhah with the practical realities of a micronational community that the RKM could realize its basic goal of creating a unified religious life in a general social framework by means of a self-contained community. In this process it went beyond the accepted parameters of Orthodox Judaism. Indeed, at first the RKM was generally looked upon askance by Orthodox Jewry: eventually, however, it was accepted, and Religious Zionist circles even acclaimed it. As one RKM member stated in 1939, when reviewing the religious pioneering policy of the RKM:

> Our group enterprise would not have come into being had we not acted upon our will to create by boldly taking matters into our own hands, and had we waited for a formal solution. . . . When we first began our enterprise we were taken to task, regarded as transgressors in the accepted traditional sphere. Then [traditional Jewry] became reconciled to us, and finally [today], many religious circles look upon us as the creators of a new religious reality.[58]

Indeed, in the process of working out the operative integration between traditional and universal cultures, the Orthodox kibbutzim formed a social base—what Berger and Luckmann call a "plausibility structure"[59]—for the creation of a new religious reality expressing this integration. Nurtured by the symbols and social practices of both general and religious cultures, this reality was crystalized by the very experience of building and defending a religious pioneering community. In creating this new reality, the RKM outstripped the earlier modernizing movements which sought to create a unified religious life in the modern era. The self-contained microcommunity enabled the individual kibbutz member to participate with others who shared his basic religious and universal values in the interactive processes sustaining community life, and thus realize existentially the unity that he sought.

Historically, the significance of the new religious reality that the

RKM created transcended the confines of the kibbutz community in that it seems to have had a far-reaching effect upon the national religious identity of Orthodox youth. The majority of Orthodox Jewry in pre-state Palestine came from traditional East European communities, and it was chiefly through involvement in the life of the national community in Palestine that it became conversant with a modern social order. During the 1920s and 1930s, however, Orthodox youth felt itself marginal in relation to national society, because its ideological sector lagged behind the secular Zionist group with regard to participation in the cardinal activities of national society, such as settlement and defense. Indeed, from the founding of HaPoel HaMizrahi in 1922 until the establishment of Tirat Tzvi in 1937, the theme of "casting off the shame from religious Jewry" recurs again and again in Religious Zionist literature,[60] in the context of its meager practical contribution to the building of the national society, particularly in pioneering settlement. As a result, it was difficult for national religious youth to synthesize the two components of its identity.

Although a systematic study has yet to be made, there is strong evidence to suggest that the new social reality created by the RKM exerted a crucial influence on the positive self-image of Orthodox youth. The outstanding defense record of the religious kibbutzim,[61] the high level of their economic performance,[62] and—perhaps what is most important—their integration of universal and traditional elements within the social reality, established a positive reference group with which national religious youth could strongly identify in the process of its adaptation to and integration within Jewish national society.

On the face of it, the post-emancipation cultural background of the German Orthodox pioneers might appear to explain the secret of the success of the RKM in serving as a pacesetter for other Orthodox youth in pre-State Palestine. But this factor in itself does not seem to be sufficient; to it must be added the resolution to directly come to grips with the problems of a self-contained pioneering life. As an RKM leader maintained as early as 1934:

> It is not ideologies or theories, schools of thought or lectures, that are decisive in creating the [national religious] reality in Palestine. It is the life that one lives, that calls for a practical solution to all its problems and activities—only such a life can determine the form of the synthesis between Torah and labor.[63]

Notes

I am grateful to Priscilla B. Fishman for her editorial advice.

1. This article deals with the development of the RKM in a broad context. For a more specific analysis and evaluation, see the following publications of the author: (a) (ed.), *The Religious Kibbutz Movement* (Jerusalem, 1957); (b) "HaKibbutz HaDati," *Encyclopedia of Zionism,* Vol. I (New York, 1971), pp. 452–453; (c) "Al Hithavuta shel HaTnuah HaKibbutzit HaDatit," *HaKibbutz* 6–7 (1978/79), pp. 69–87; (d) "'Torah and Labor': the Radicalization of Religion in a National Framework," *Studies in Zionism* 6 (Autumn, 1982), pp. 255–271; (e) "The Religious Kibbutz: Religion, Nationalism and Socialism in a Communal Framework," in E. Krausz (ed.), *The Sociology of the Kibbutz* (New Brunswick, 1983), pp. 115–123; (f) "Judaism and Modernization: The Case of the Religious Kibbutzim," *Social Forces* 62 (1983), pp. 9–31.

2. For these values in the kibbutz context see, for example, H. Darin-Drapkin, *The Other Society* (New York, 1963).

3. For the centrality of the religious community in the ideology of the RKM, see Fishman (e).

4. See M. Breuer, *The "Torah-im-Derekh Eretz" of Samson Raphael Hirsch* (New York, 1970); I. Grunfeld, "Samson Raphael Hirsch—the Man and his Mission," in S. R. Hirsch, *Judaism Eternal,* vol. I (London, 1956), pp. xiii–xlvii.

5. For perceptions of Religious Zionism in the historic context of European emancipation, see M. Waxman, *The Mizrachi, Its Aims and Purposes* (New York, 1918); I. Wolfsberg, *HaMizrachi-HaPoel* HaMizrachi (Jerusalem, 1946), pp. 20ff. (Hebrew).

6. We shall adduce below references to this phrase. For the general Jewish post-emancipation yearning for "a full and complete life," see Yehezkel Kaufman, *Golah veNeikhar,* vol. II (Tel-Aviv, 1930), p. 42.

7. Torah as an innovative power constitutes a component of Torah as charisma. In the latter sense, Torah constitutes a creative ordering power emanating from the sacred and investing its possessors with the sense of authority to revoke the legitimacy of established religious cultural elements and social roles and institutions and legitimate new ones. This conception of Torah has been developed in A. Fishman, "The Religious Kibbutz: a Study in Interrelationship of Religion and Ideology in the Context of Modernization" (Ph.D. dissertation, Hebrew University, Jerusalem, 1975) (Hebrew).

On charisma in the sense of creative ordering power, see E. Shils, "Charisma, Order and Status," *American Sociological Review* 30 (1965), pp. 199–213, and S. N. Eisenstadt (ed.), "Introduction," *Max Weber on Charisma and Institution Building* (Chicago, 1968). For charisma in the double-edged sense of a power capable of revoking the validity of the established sacred and investing new elements with sacredness, see Eisenstadt, p. xix. For a detailed analysis of the role of Torah as charisma in the formation of HaPoel HaMizrahi, the labor wing of Religious Zionism, see Fishman (d). For the exercise of Torah in the charismatic sense of a double edged power in the RKM, see below, section VIII.

8. In Torah-im-Derekh Eretz see *The Psalms,* S. R. Hirsch edition, English translation by G. Hirschler (New York, 1966), Psalm 119:99; in the thought of Religious Zionism, see B. Berahyahu, "Mahu HaPoel HaMizrachi?" in N. Avinoah and Y. Bernstein, *Yalkut* (Jerusalem, 1931), p. 56.

9. S. R. Hirsch, *The Nineteen Letters of Ben Uziel,* translated by B. Drachman, (New York, 1899), Letters 10 and 18; S. H. Landau, *Ketavim* (Warsaw, 1935), p. 29.

10. See, for example, S. R. Hirsch, *Judaism Eternal,* translated by I. Grunfeld, vol. II (London, 1956), p. 39; Landau, pp. 42–43.

11. *Nineteen Letters,* p. 16.

12. See Breuer (note 4), pp. 24–25; N. Rosenblum, *Jewish Social Studies* 24 (1962), pp. 226–228.

13. *The Pentateuch,* S. R. Hirsch edition, English translation by I. Levy (New York, 1971), vol. I, 3:24.

14. Yaakov Yehiel Weinberg, "A Torah of Life," in Y. Emmanuel (ed.), *HaRav Shimshon Raphael Hirsch, Mishnato veShitato* (Jerusalem, 1962), p. 192.

15. See I. Grunfeld, *Three Generations: The Influence of S. R. Hirsch on Jewish Life and Thought* (London, 1958).

16. I. Breuer, "Rabbiner Hirsch als Wegweiser in die Judische Geshichtes" *Nachlath Z'wi* V (1935), p. 77. The English translation of this essay appears in L. Jung (ed.), *Jewish Leaders 1750–1940* (Jerusalem, 1964), pp. 163–177.

17. In 1941 the German element constituted 55 percent of the members and candidates for membership in HaKibbutz HaDati. See *Likrat HaMoetza HaShelishit* (Tel-Aviv, 1945), p. 58.

18. The sensitivity of *East European* Orthodox youth that was emerging from traditional Jewish society to the gap between their Jewish religious and human identities is concisely expressed in the following statement of a graduate of the Bnei Akiva youth movement in Eastern Galicia: "The creation of a type of whole person is the task of kibbutz life. If this is difficult for others, for us it is far more difficult. For despite our heavy emphasis on 'man,' the task of creating a religious person in whom humanity and religion go hand in hand and blend into one, will always confront us." B. Imber, "Our Kibbutz Education," *Tikwa* (Lwow, 1935 [?], stencil).

19. See Breuer, pp. 41–44.

20. See K. Wilhelm, "The Jewish Community in the Post-Emancipation Period," *Leo Baeck Institute Yearbook* II (1957), pp. 47–75.

21. J. Leibowitz, "Zur Tarbuth-Frage," *Choser Bachad* 2 (Neue Folge), (Gerhingshof, Av, 5692 [1932], stencil). Yeshayahu Leibowitz and Ernst Simon (see the referent of note 24 below) had a considerable influence over the development of the Bachad ideology.

22. On the centrality of the concept of *Gemeinschaft* in the life of the Zionist youth movement in Germany, see Y. Shimoni (Simon), "Al HaNoar HaYehudi BeGermania," in G. Hanokh (ed.), *Darkhei HaNoar* (Jerusalem, 1937), pp. 150–151.

23. See H. Becker, *German Youth, Bond or Free* (London, 1946). For the influence of nineteenth century German Volk ideology on the German youth movement culture, see G. L. Mosse, *The Crisis of German Ideology* (New York, 1964), pp. 272–273.

24. E. Simon, *Zion* (Berlin) VI (1934), p. 46.

25. See J. Katz, "The Jewish National Movement: A Sociological Analysis," *Journal of World History* XI (1968), pp. 267–283, passim.

26. "The First Proclamation of Mizrachi," in P. Churgin and L. Gellman (eds.), *Jubilee Publication of the Mizrachi Organization of America* (New York, 1936), p. 33 (Hebrew).

27. For an analysis of the structural difficulties of Mizrachi in establishing a

national religious subculture within Orthodox Judaism, see Fishman (d), pp. 257–258.

28. See, for example, Rabbi M. A. Amiel, *HaYesodot HaIdyologiim shel HaMizrachi* (Warsaw, 1934), pp. 3–4.

29. Z. Yaavetz, "HaAhdut," in *HaMizrah* (Cracow, 1903), pp. 16–17.

30. S. H. Landau, p. 38. This quotation is taken from an English translation of the article in A. Hertzberg, ed., *The Zionist Idea* (New York, 1966), pp. 434–439.

31. See Fishman (d).

32. Landau, p. 39.

33. Leibowitz.

34. M. Elon, *The Principles of Jewish Law* (Jerusalem, 1973), p. 35.

35. Reprinted in S. Z. Shragai, *Hazon VeHagshama* (Jerusalem, 1956), p. 109.

36. J. Leibowitz, "Thoratreuer Zionismus," *Zion* II (1930), p. 64.

37. J. Leibowitz, "Zur Tarbuth Frage," *Choser Bachad* 1–2 (Adar II and Av, 5692 [1932]).

38. J. Leibowitz, "Ein Versuch zur Klaerung," *Zion* II (1930), p. 143.

39. See, for example, H. Abt, "Juedische Jugenbewegung," *Nachlat Z'wi* III (1933), pp. 375–376.

40. *Grundriss eines Erziehungsprogramms* (Hamburg, 1933; stencil), p. 12.

41. Sch. B., *Rundschreiben* 5 (December, 1929; stencil).

42. This group formally adopted the kibbutz pattern of living at the beginning of 1931. In 1941 it settled on its permanent site as Kvutzat Yavne.

43. For a history of HaKibbutz HaDati until 1966, see Fishman (b).

44. E. S. Rosenthal, *Alonim,* Sivan, 5703 [1943].

45. "Din veHeshbon miYeshivat HaVaadah leVeirur Sheelot Datiyot," *HaHed,* Tamuz, 5698 [1938], p. 11.

46. The following discussion is treated more extensively in Fishman, note 7, pp. 205–207. For a historical overview of the Sabbath milking problem and its solution in the Orthodox settlements in general, see Haim Y. Peles, "Baayot HaHalivah BeShabbat BaHityashvut HaDatit BeEretz Yisrael," *Barkai* 2 (Fall, 5745–1984), pp. 108–131.

47. T. Admanit, "On the Religious Significance of the Community," in Fishman (a), p. 31.

48. See Zvi Yehuda Kook, *HaHed,* Tammuz, 5696 (July, 1936), p. 16; A. Sursky, *Or Elhanan* (Wasserman), Los Angeles, 1970), p. 75 (Hebrew); Rabbi Haim Ozer Grodzensky, *Kovetz iggrot* (Bene-Berak, 1970), pp. 457–461.

49. See S. Friedman, "The Extension of the Scope of Halakha," in Fishman (a), pp. 48–49.

50. On the authority of a community to depart from an established Halakhah when the needs of the hour dictate such a practice, see M. Elon (note 34), pp. 658ff.

51. M. Or, "Protocol of the Fifth Council of HaKibbutz HaDati," 1951 (unpublished). See also T. Admanit in Fishman (a), p. 31.

52. For the concept of a charismatic community see Max Weber, *Economy and Society,* edited by G. Roth and C. Wittich (New York, 1968), pp. 243, 1119.

53. See note 7.

54. M. Or, *Netivah,* Shvat, 5711 (1951), p. 7. Cf. M. Elon, *HaMishpat HaIvri,* vol. II (Jerusalem, 1973), p. 412.

55. M. Or, *Amudim* 152 (Sivan, 5718 = 1958), p. 19.

56. See T. Admanit, "The Observance of the Agricultural Mitzvot Today," in Fishman (a), p. 123.

57. See Y. Heinemann, "Contemporary Observance of the Sabbatical Year," in Fishman (a), pp. 130–136.

58. Reuven, V., *BaTirah* (Tirat Tzvi), 5 Av, 5699 (1939, stencil).

59. P. L. Berger and T. Luckmann, *The Social Construction of Reality* (New York, 1967), pp. 154ff.

60. See Fishman (c), p. 82, note 4.

61. See Fishman (b).

62. For a recent account and analysis of the economic success of the RKM settlements, see Fishman (f).

63. R. Herz, *Zion* VI (1934), p. 54.

From Religious Zionism to Zionist Religion: The Roots of Gush Emunim

Gideon Aran
(HEBREW UNIVERSITY)

In the early 1950s, in a secluded spot among the citrus groves of the Israeli coastal plain, a dozen or so teenagers held regular meetings in the conspiratorial manner of a secret sect. There, in a fervent state of heightened emotional consciousness, they would reveal to each other their deepest, heretical thoughts and together weave plans for a glorious future. Youthful dreams soon became the basis for a tight-knit social core, built around a daring and ambitious set of ideas. The group called itself "the Embers" (in Hebrew, *Gahelet*). It appears that even then they sensed the symbolic significance of their activities. They soon left off merely talking about their shared spiritual *Angst* and sought ways to root their mission in practical contexts, and to set about the systematic fulfillment of their dreams. Eventually, from these beginnings, they wrought a revolution in religious Zionism. Their path led them first to a transformation of the "Merkaz Harav" yeshiva in Jerusalem, and to a more general transformation of religious Zionist youth as a whole. The result, ultimately, was the creation of a unique nationalist-religious culture that crystallized in an active political and institutional framework. Thirty years later, almost all the members of *Gahelet* are to be found among the top leaders of Gush Emunim. A direct line led from naive youthful adventure to decisive influence over the entire national-religious sector; indeed, over the very identity of Israeli society and its governing institutions.[1]

Gahelet was the forerunner of Gush Emunim, and therefore it will serve as the axis of our discussion. The story of Gush Emunim begins with *Gahelet* not only because of the personal and historical continuity between the two, but also because we find revealed in *Gahelet,* for the first time, some of the typical patterns and unique features that later would come to characterize the Gush. Thus, *Gahelet* is the precursor of Gush Emunim in the symbolic sense as well as in the institutional one: here one finds both the structural and the ideological foundations of Gush Emunim as a politico-religious phenomenon. The underlying problem of both *Gahelet* and Gush Emunim in historical terms is the tension between traditional religion and modern, secular society, in general, and between Jewish Orthodoxy and nationally sovereign Judaism (i.e., Zionism) in particular.

Thus, for example, one finds expressed in *Gahelet* the same mystification of the Israeli experience of exalted statehood and, flowing directly from that, the same tension between faithfulness to Halakhah and *mizvot* on the one hand and faith in the reality of redemption, on the other, as one finds later in Gush Emunim. Similarly, one can point to the tension between the entrenchment of an institution of Torah learning, on the one hand, and the explosive momentum of a public movement, on the other, which characterized both the early and later incarnations of *Gahelet.* Many other points of contact and indeed identity between the two phenomena also exist: more specifically, e.g., the nature of the relationship between Rabbi Zvi Yehuda Hacohen Kook and his students in which the line between leader and the led is very difficult to trace; or, again, a similar recourse to a kabbalistic dialectic system permitting the simultaneous acceptance and rejection of the Zionist political enterprise.

In *Gahelet* we find that first encounter between the thought of Rav Abraham Isaac Kook and the personality of his son R. Zvi Yehuda, on the one hand, as they came to be personified in the Merkaz Harav yeshiva, and that small, unique group of young people, on the other; unique in the quality of their religious and national sensitivity, struggling with the tension between the two, against the background of a profound crisis in religious Zionism.

Gahelet represents the beginning of the trend toward radicalization among national-religious youth in Israel, a process which heightened both their religiosity and their nationalism, and thus the tension inherent in their identity containing both dissonant elements. This heightened consciousness became the basis of their strength and pride, and in due course, of their demands for leadership in the national-religious sector and beyond it, in Israeli society in general. In this paper we will be concerned chiefly with the role of *Gahelet* in the rejuvenation of Merkaz Harav and in the creation of the Kookist school of thought, more than with its role in the transformation of the national-religious sector of Israeli society. In any event, the two processes are closely linked. They are both the cause and the result of the growing internal tensions rooted in two parallel trends: the "Orthodoxization" of Zionism, and the "zionization" of Orthodoxy.

Gahelet had its beginnings in the first four years of Israeli statehood, and it ended roughly two to three years after the 1956 Sinai Campaign. Thus, it overlaps to a great extent with the early years of the new state. Most observers of Gush Emunim place its origins in the aftermath of the 1967 war or of the Yom Kippur War of 1973.[2] In my view, the roots of Gush Emunim lie buried further back in the past, in the decade after 1948. *Gahelet* and Gush Emunim have their origins in the establishment of the state.[3] Thus while the events of 1967 and 1973 are necessary for any explanation of the rise of Gush Emunim, they are not sufficient.

Gahelet and Gush Emunim were not created by one climactic event, as fateful as it may have been. Rather, their emergence was conditioned by a given long-term reality. The link between Gush Emunim and the wars of 1948, 1967, and 1973 is analogous to the relationship between the Sabbatean movement and the events of 1648–49.[4] In addition, of course, such climactic events are themselves the products or focused, sharpened expressions of broader historical developments. Where Sabbateanism was born within a Jewish religious context, conditioned by the experience of Exile,[5] "Emunism" can be viewed as a religious response to the experience of Redemption. The political fulfillment of Zionism was the underlying cause of a great crisis in Jewish Orthodoxy, caught between tradition and modernity, religion and nationhood.

The Six-Day War reinforced the development of national-religious trends and channelled it in a certain direction. The Yom Kippur War lent added stature and recognition to an already existing mood and a previously articulated set of ideas. But fundamentally these factors were superimposed upon a bedrock of preexisting concepts and tendencies. In 1967, the important new factors were the resurgence of the "whole Land of Israel" concept, and a heightened conviction of the imminence of messianic redemption. In the wake of 1973, political activism became more central, expressing with growing force the desire to lead the nation as a whole, secularists included.

Beyond these elements, however, the one dominant focal point of this complex of ideas was the fact of Jewish sovereignty itself: the reality of the national experience—modern and, essentially, secular. The establishment of the state was itself a symbol for a broader phenomenon. Political sovereignty, concretized in a network of governing institutions resting on a modern, secular basis, spelled the end of any illusion that Jewish secularism could be dismissed as a passing phenomenon. *Gahelet* was not a product of a historic event, but rather a function of a historic era, one which seemed to herald the triumph of the secular spirit.

Thus, it is possible to view *Gahelet* as a reaction to political secularism born within a defeated and bewildered Orthodoxy. Withdrawing somewhat from their previous interest in their social and cultural surroundings, those who reacted in this way also tended toward self-segregation and, naturally enough, to an extremism of their own distinctive kind. That is, one can point to a congruence between the dynamics at work in the birth of Gush Emunim and the real or perceived inferiority of religion and marginality of the religious sector in Israel.

While the achievement of statehood took place under the banner of secular Zionism, it was also the case, however, that the advent of national independence could be understood as a fact of supreme religious significance. Religious Zionists saw the establishment of the State of Israel as an unmistakable sign of the beginnings of a messianic fulfillment, a necessary first step toward complete redemption. The ingathering of the exiles, the return of the people to its land and the setting up of a sovereign government were all, traditionally, indicators of the approach of the messianic era.[6] A certain amount of religious excitement accompanied these events. It was indeed a time of exaltation, even intoxication, during which the more Orthodox sector went out of its way to cooperate with the secular public in Israel, and was welcomed in a spirit of acceptance and good will. Politically, this was expressed in the presence of Agudat Israel in the first cabinet.

Thus, the national state was accorded a certain sanctified status. It was precisely this point which became the stumbling block for religious nationalists. The new situation posed a direct challenge to Orthodoxy, demanding that it realize to the full the opportunity presented. The spiritual exaltation of 1948, if anything, made the religious dilemma more severe than would have been the case had no religious significance been assigned to Jewish statehood. *Gahelet,* then, must be seen not only as a reaction to antagonistic forces from without, but also—perhaps primarily—as a response to internal tensions within Orthodoxy, which had to be addressed on its own terms. This aspect did nothing to mitigate the problem: if anything, it made it all the more difficult. Ultimately, and paradoxically, the understanding of Israeli independence as a religious fact would help to reinforce the tendency to withdraw from direct involvement with the state as such into a mode of life increasingly segregated and alienated from its environment.

In our discussion of "religion" and Judaism in confrontation with modern nationalism, we refer specifically to traditional religion, more or less identified here with the terms "Orthodoxy" or "neo-Orthodoxy." It is the gap or opposition between traditional Judaism and Zionism that is the starting point for our examination of *Gahelet* and, ultimately, Gush Emunim as well.

As both the proponents and detractors of Zionism among the Jews will at least implicitly attest, Zionism is the great challenge facing Judaism. What is at stake is not only one or another abstract philosophical position, but an actual (and often bitter) encounter between two camps. To a great extent, for many, Zionism is the "positive expression" of the decline of Judaism.[7] This is the root of the troubled relationship between the two, and this is the problem for which Gush Emunim purports to provide a radical solution. Thus, although Gush Emunim hoists aloft the slogan, "There is no Zionism without Judaism, and no Judaism without Zionism," there is no doubt that they are fully aware of the divisions and antagonisms between the two. They do not deny, for example, that for the most part traditional Orthodoxy remained outside the Zionist camp in its early years, both in the Diaspora and in the *yishuv*. Despite the fact that they sometimes engage in a celebration of the religious "forerunners of Zionism," blowing up their historical role out of all proportion, their awareness of the general traditionalist attitude toward early Zionism is implicit in their championing of the Kookist position as a unique expression of national-religious thought.

Moreover, the Kookists cannot escape the other side of the coin: namely, that the Zionist enterprise and its prime motive forces were essentially secular, and that it self-consciously proclaimed its rebellion against traditional Judaism. On the contrary, they assign to this rebellion a paramount spiritual value.[8] The lesson they derive from the emergence of Zionism, accordingly, is that the bond between the Jew, his people, and his land does not rest on the piety that finds expression only in the routine of religious observance and study; but that this bond comes from a deeper, hidden source of religiosity. The Zionists possess a hidden spiritual "spark," and Zionism is itself an unconditionally religious quality of spirit, regardless of subjective intent.[9] It is no accident that the spokesmen for Gush Emunim explicitly celebrate the secularism of Zionism: the Kookist outlook is expressly built upon this paradox, and seeks to provide the explanation for it. In the process of giving Zionism religious sanction, it sanctifies it.

In highlighting the frictions between Judaism and Zionism, it is certainly not my intention to argue that there is no underlying affinity between the two, or that Judaism and Zionism are polar opposites. The contrary is the case. The link between Judaism and Zionism is built on strong, positive elements, so that ambivalence better describes their mutual relationship than does conflict. Zionism, for all that it constitutes a revolution in Judaism, also derives its strength from it. Zionism aspires to a revitalization of Jewish life. Nothing illustrates better Zionism's dependence on religion-laden values than the most basic of all Zionist concepts: the yearning of the Jews for Zion. Zionism celebrates, and is nourished by, symbols that are prominently situated in the matrix of tradition.

But here precisely is the point at which Zionism constitutes a threat to traditional religion. Orthodoxy in fact recognizes that Zionism encompasses an element of "return" to Judaism. This element is at once positive and encouraging, and negative and threatening, from the traditionalist point of view. The Orthodox response to Zionism is therefore fractured, at times pointing with pride to Zionism's need to identify with traditional values, which may be taken as an indication of the primacy of religion; while at other times, in pursuit of the same argument, Orthodoxy denies any substantive link with Zionism.

In fact, however, Zionism's reliance on traditional Judaism is very selective. In searching for a usable past, it has gone very far back—to symbols of Jewish life prior to the destruction of the Second Temple—skipping over the heritage of almost two thousand years of Diaspora existence, as expressed in the Orthodox Judaism of our day. Thus, beneath the tension between Zionism and Orthodox Judaism *per se,* one can discern a much older fissure in Judaism: that line dividing rabbinic, halakhic Judaism on the one hand from the Biblical, politically sovereign Judaism of ancient Israel on the other.

Only in a later stage in the realization of the Zionist idea, when some of its initial self-assurance was lost, did there emerge a tendency to reorient Zionism toward some Jewish Diaspora values. This, however, intensified rather than dispelled the tension with Orthodoxy. Zionism still poses a problem for Judaism, in that while it borrows traditional symbols, Zionism turns them "on their head." Orthodoxy understands this very well. Take, as a prime example, the transvaluation of messianism—a central feature of Zionism as it took shape historically. The reestablishment of the Jewish nation was predicated on removing supernatural elements from the national consciousness. Nationalism was inspired by traditional messianism, from which it derived both ideological force and emotional momentum. But first, a critical transformation had to take place, from a "miraculous" to a "realistic" messianic idea. This is what Zionism accomplished, and in fact one may say that this was its essential role in Jewish history.[10] The heritage of traditional Judaism had to undergo a process of secularization and modernization before it could be turned into a unifying and driving force for modern Jewish nationalism. The revolution this involved is summed up in the phrase, "modern, secular messianism." Thus, Zionism does indeed hark back to the traditional foundations of Judaism, but it removes them from their original context and formerly accepted understandings.

Secularization has at least two important connotations, which are not mutually exclusive.[11] The term refers, first of all, to the emancipation of the social-cultural sphere from the religious sphere. Society as such is vested with an autonomous existence, and, indeed, claims priority over the religious sphere. Religion remains but one among many sectors of society, within strictly defined boundaries. Secularization in this sense takes place both on the structural and the ideational level: the state, for example, separates itself from the religious establishment, while philosophy, ethical thought, art, and science similarly no longer are founded on a belief in God. This separation usually (though not necessarily) is bound up with a decline of the authority of religion, in its now-restricted purview. At the height of this process, religion appears in a pluralistic social context and becomes a purely "private" matter for each individual or sub-group choosing to define itself religiously in a "free market" situation.[12]

The other sense in which secularization may be understood refers to the transfer of religious values—symbols, especially—from their "natural" original context, where they fit into a belief in the supernatural, to a new social sphere where they serve other purposes entirely. The new content of such symbols is foreign to their traditional forms, altering their essential character and orienting them in this-worldly directions. The best illustration here is the transformation of the Judeo-Christian messianic theology into socialist, liberal, or nationalist ideologies. Once the religious symbolism is harnessed to a secular framework, the attendant emotional baggage and overall mentality are similarly removed and enlisted in causes whose aims directly or indirectly subvert those originally associated with these symbols.

Secularization in the first sense would seem to be a necessary precondition for secularization of the second kind, although it is the second which carries the graver implications for religion. This is particularly the case when a modern, secular society takes as its primary object the preservation and faithful realization of those traditional values which it has taken over and claimed for itself. This is what Zionism has done to traditional Judaism. But Zionism was only the second stage of a secularization process that began in the context of European Jewish emancipation and the Enlightenment.

What emerges from our discussion is that the tension between Judaism and Zionism encompasses several layers of conflict: the one between religion and society and that between tradition and modernity, in addition to the old-new ones, i.e., that between religion and nationality and that between religion and the state. We are dealing with two phenomena which are, after all, close to one another and yet the distinction between them is crucial.

From the traditional religious point of view, Zionism is secular in that its basic drive is toward this-worldly sovereignty. Zionism wants the Jew to be the master of his fate—where traditional Judaism saw only God as the ultimate Master, necessarily imposing limitations on both the individual and society. The Zionist state makes its own laws, which Orthodoxy must to some extent view as competition with or rejection of divine law (i.e., Torah law). Zionism is based upon the *a priori* definition of man and the national collective as autonomous entities. The principles and causations of man's behavior are immanent rather than transcendent. This is the procrustean secular understanding that enabled Zionism to lead Judaism back into history and to bring the Jews to political independence.

But Orthodoxy is aware of the dualism inherent in Zionism: not only continuity for the sake of revolution, but a revolution for the sake of continuity, as it were. Zionism is, certainly, a reassertion of Jewishness. This good intention, however, is the source of the problem insofar as it sets up nationalism as a substitute Judaism. In this sense, in comparison with Reform Judaism, Zionism is judged to be the greater threat, because Reform resulted (so the traditionalist argument goes) in the alienation of individual Jews from the proper paths of Torah; while Zionism leads astray the national collective as such—a form of mass assimilation.[13]

This critical evaluation of Zionism stems from the kind of analytical virtuosity so characteristic of traditional Judaism. The Orthodox are sensitive to the nature of the threat to tradition constituted by the transplantation of religious elements to the secular realm:

> Our opposition to Zionism and to the state is not based on any objection to Jewish settlement in the Land of Israel, which is a *mizva,* and is certainly not founded on enmity towards the Jewish people, God forbid. Quite the contrary. It comes out of a desire to purify and sanctify these values which Zionism reduces and empties of significance, giving them meanings which are foreign (i.e., not Jewish).[14]

Here is a perceptive understanding of the nature of the secularization process that is inseparable from Zionism precisely where it champions the assertion of Jewish identity. Rather than offering a set of alternative, secular values, Zionism effects a transposition and hence a transformation of significant meanings derived from religious tradition.

The result is a blurring of the distinction between traditional religion and secular nationalism—a dangerous development from the Orthodox point of view. Gush Emunim, on the other hand, has been able to put this blurring of the lines to good effect. Nevertheless, ironically, any future success on its part will contribute to the sharpening of the lines of division.

At this point it should be noted that tradition itself was altered in the course of its confrontation with modernization and secularization. At about the end of the eighteenth century, the encounter gave birth to a new social phenomenon: Orthodoxy.[15] While Orthodoxy represents itself as the sole legitimate heir of traditional Judaism, it is in fact only one stream among others—although it is arguably the closest to the original medieval rabbinic mold. Orthodoxy, in practice, is a defensive reaction against the other modern trends in Judaism which it views as contrary to tradition.

We have thus far referred to Orthodoxy in its broadest sense in speaking of traditionalist Jewry as a whole. In fact, however, it will be necessary to refine the concept and narrow it for the purposes of this discussion.

Beginning in the second half of the nineteenth century, one can discern two distinct trends emerging within Orthodoxy. Each of these two Orthodoxies subdivided still further along a range of positions, but the significant differences between the two major camps were the overriding ones, and indeed, the gap between the two continued to widen. Ultimately, each came to reject the other's position as unacceptable. On the one side, we find the neo-Orthodox, whose origins go back to the school of thought enunciated by Samson Raphael Hirsch ("Torah and worldliness") and among whose products we can point to the Zionists of Mizrahi and HaPoel Hamizrahi ("Torah and labor"). On the other side, we find the ultra-Orthodox, represented by a variety of subgroups (generically known in Hebrew as Ḥaredim), both in Israel and in the Diaspora. These groups oppose any significant innovation in religious life or indeed in any sphere of their social activity. While the first camp attempts to come to grips with modernity and its secularity, internalizing some of its aspects to some degree, the second seeks to avoid this encounter as far as possible. Among the modern or neo-Orthodox are the religious Zionists; religious anti-Zionists are typically located in the ultra-Orthodox wing.

In theory there is little difference between the "neo" and the "ultra": both are firm in their commitment to the Orthodox tenet of *torah min hashamayim* (the Torah as divine law) and a complete acceptance of the binding nature of the *mizvot*. In practice, however, they differ considerably in terms of life style.

Gush Emunim occupies a position somewhere between these two extremes. Its direct lineage, of course, lies within neo-Orthodoxy; however, the Gush understands itself as an opposition to the mainstream of modern Orthodoxy and in some ways takes up positions that are close to those of the ultra-Orthodox camp.

It is noteworthy that those Orthodox elements who identified with Zionism in its early years favored an alignment with the Central and West European sections of the Zionist movement—which by and large were not actively involved in matters of religion and many of whose members might be called assimilated to a considerable degree—rather than with the East European Zionists, with whom they found it difficult to achieve a modicum of dialogue and cooperation. The tension between the religious Zionists and the (other) East Europeans in the movement stemmed from the fact that many of the latter were consciously and outspokenly antireligious, having themselves rebelled against the traditional life.

In addition to this, however, one must consider that the East European secularists presented greater problems for the Orthodox, because of the secularists' attitude to the question of the content of Zionism. Their predilection to think about the Zionist reassertion of Jewish nationhood as a matter of cultural consciousness implied a search for something that might replace religion. This sort of Zionism was aimed at providing a solution not only for the "Jewish Question," but also to the "question of Judaism." Those who saw Zionism's goal as the creation of a "new Jew" could hardly serve as proper partners for the Orthodox, who, rather, were more readily able to find a common language with those who attached little importance to the matter of *kultur.*[16] This paradoxical alliance reached its most ironic point when the Orthodox Zionists supported the Herzlian faction in the debate over Uganda (1903). Here were Orthodox Jews willing to relinquish, if only temporarily, the Holy Land.

One way or another, Orthodox Jews have had difficulties in coming to terms with Zionism. True, the regnant tendency among religious Zionists has been to deny that an inherent paradox exists in their position. Nevertheless, a number of leading figures among them, while fully committed to both their Orthodoxy and their Zionism, have acknowledged that some such tension exists.[17]

It should come as no surprise that the confrontation between Zionism and Judaism has been particularly acute in Israel itself. Here the basic problem has been complicated and exacerbated by the variety of points at which the two cultural visions meet and collide on a concrete level: in social relations, economics, and politics. We have only to look at the vexed relations that developed in pre-state days between the so-called old *yishuv* and the new *yishuv*.[18] On the one side, the Ḥaredim of the older settlement had come to live in the Holy Land out of motivations which surely included the desire to escape from the challenge of the non-Jewish European environment (and the radically changing Jewish environment, at that), to seek a refuge of traditionalism and fortify themselves there against the tide of modernity. On the other side stood the pioneering settlers of the new *yishuv* who were fulfilling their vision of Zionism by building a country and a nation.

The land of Israel was not just the scene of contention between the two factions: it was, in itself, the bone of contention. It was the real and symbolic focus of the conflict, serving both the Zionists and the traditionalists as the linchpin of their ideology. Orthodox opposition to Zionism derived from Orthodox attachment to the land—and this, of course, predated the rise of Zionism and the reaction against it.

The developing relationship between Zionism and Orthodoxy was put to its definitive test when the State of Israel was established. The dilemma was institutionalized, and theoretical issues became practical questions. At stake was the matter of what constituted law for the people of Israel: would a sovereign Jewry be ruled by Torah law, as religious tradition demanded, or not?

Israel is, after all, a *Jewish* state. That is its official self-definition, that is the substance and essence of its public identity, and that is how the overwhelming majority of its citizens perceive it. Hence, Orthodoxy cannot treat it as if it were simply another state. Moreover, statehood restored to Judaism a public dimension, gave it properties of civil society, that had been all but lost under the blows of secularization, modernization, and emancipation.[19] The new state filled the vacuum that was created by the crumbling of the traditional religious structure in the Diaspora.

Yet it was in Israel that—after a somewhat euphoric but brief respite around the time of the War of Independence—the tensions that existed before Israeli statehood were intensified. This may be attributed to a variety of causes, from the sociodemographic to the symbolic. For one thing, only with statehood were conditions created that mandated the taking of binding decisions for the entire population of the country. Previously, there had not been—nor could there have been—binding obligations, as there had not existed any political sovereign entity encompassing the various subcommunities of the *yishuv*. Rather, these voluntary communities had pursued parallel but essentially autonomous paths, while cooperating to a greater or lesser degree out of practical necessity. Statehood, by its nature, limited the self-determination of each subgroup.

A second factor was mass immigration. This not only altered the scale on which the society operated, but also increased the heterogeneity of culture and social mentality in the population, necessarily arousing issues of national identity. For example, broad new sectors of the population now existed whose stance vis-à-vis religious tradition was basically positive.

Finally, with a new generation born into the reality of Israeli statehood, it was only natural that the previous, paramount goal of establishing a state would now be replaced by a questioning and rethinking of concepts and positions taken for granted in the past.

The duality of nation and religion has existed within Judaism from its very beginnings, and has accompanied it through history as a distinguishing feature. The tension between religion and the state is also one of its classic leitmotifs. Hence the fundamental opposition between the priest or prophet and the Israelite king. Exilic existence in many ways freed Judaism of these internal conflicts. The restoration of Jewish independence, naturally enough, has brought them once more to the fore. But this time, the problem is different, quite unprecedented in Jewish history, and therefore all the more difficult. The State of Israel confronts Orthodox Jewry with a reality never before encountered by Judaism—nor even imagined: the existence of a *Jewish secular* state. Traditional sources offer no guidance in the case of a sovereign Jewish polity that is also secular.

In theory, Orthodox Judaism has two archetypal options in responding to this situation. The one alternative is that usually associated with the ultra-Orthodox. The extreme Ḥaredim reject the Zionist state out of hand and refuse to cooperate with it on any level. This is a well-defined religious position, with its own internal logic. The other available position, generally speaking that of religious Zionism, borders on the sanctification of the state. Israel, despite its secular character, is the bearer of such religious significance that any faithful Jew becomes obligated to take an active role in its life and share in the responsibilities of citizenship, almost on a par with the obligations imposed by the Torah.

Of course, in practice the majority of Orthodox Israelis refrain from taking either position to its logical conclusion, adopting mutually incompatible elements from both archetypal options, and this compounds the tensions within Orthodoxy. In the process. Israeli Orthodoxy has fallen in the esteem of the broader public, in its own esteem, and particularly in that of its younger generation.

Nonetheless, it must be emphasized that the two extreme positions are not abstract "ideal types," but really exist in the form of known groups in the Israeli population. They serve as points of orientation for the rest of the religious sector, who place themselves along a spectrum stretching between the two. One widespread "compromise" position is the one that affirms Jewish statehood as a positive development, not because the state is viewed as a religious end in itself, but because it is seen as a means to an end. The state, despite its secular character, creates the preconditions that allow for the observance of the *mizvot* that are obligatory only in Israel, helps in fostering a fully Jewish life style, and assures the safety, well-being, and pride of the Jews.

Some members of the religious Zionist camp recognize, however, that such compromises were bought at the price of a certain amount of self-deception. Moreover, the delicate balance thus achieved was not destined to last very long. Orthodox nationalists could only be satisfied on a very superficial level by promises and guarantees of narrow party interests which avoided making religious demands upon the general public. Critics charged that religious Zionism had made its peace with the secularity of the Jewish state—had indeed placed on it its stamp of approval—all for the sake of its own social and political welfare: in a word, it had "sold out." Such charges became characteristic of the Kookist camp, first in *Gahelet* and later in Gush Emunim, to which we now turn our direct attention.

As noted at the outset, *Gahelet* was the creation of a group of youngsters who were students at religious Zionist schools in Israel in the 1950s. The group, associated with the Orthodox Bnei Akiva youth movement, displayed an unusual degree of social and religious commitment and activism, and was deeply troubled by the predicament of religious Zionism. *Gahelet* was at once an expression of the Orthodox Zionist dilemma and an attempt to offer a solution to it. *Gahelet* emerged from the ranks of Orthodox Zionism and in opposition to it. Aside from anything else, it was an authentic religious response to the challenge of Zionism.

Gahelet began at Kfar Haroeh, a well-established agricultural settlement affiliated with Hapoel Hamizrachi that maintained an Orthodox boarding school. It was the only such school in the country at the time, headed and founded by Rabbi Moshe Zvi Neria, and destined to become the model for the network of Bnei Akiva-linked yeshiva high schools. Rabbi Neria was a chief spokesman and an outstanding personality of the religious Zionist movement. In 1951–52, the school was involved in the campaign to counter what the Orthodox camp saw as an "anti-religious war." Those years were characterized by a depressed spirit that followed hard upon the ecstatic first year of Israeli independence.

The entering class of 1951 included members of the "Eitanim" branch of Bnei Akiva, from the Tel Aviv area, who arrived at the school as an established social unit. Among them, however, were a number of exceptional individuals who, from the very first, kept their distance from the rest and formed a school "aristocracy." Their group consciousness and ideological development took on a distinct form, based on purist aspirations. Their meetings were marked by intense and intimate outpourings of thought and feeling, and were generally conducted at night in secluded spots. There was much frank soul-searching and heated argument, informed by what they felt was the fatefulness—even holiness—of the hour at hand. They quickly became a closed, selective community with a highly developed sense of mutual responsibility.

These were youngsters aged thirteen to fifteen, and their youth certainly played a crucial role. *Gahelet* was, among other things, an adolescent rebellion against parents whose moderation and compromises were viewed with disdain. (Indeed, the sons, by and large, were to become more strictly Orthodox than their parents.) Their rebellion was also expressed in the challenge they threw down to their youth movement's leadership—both the group leaders with whom they had direct contact and the national leadership; a rebellion that began modestly from minor infractions but which ended in an open conflict over principles, that created a revolution in the movement. And one can also say that they rebelled against the authority of their teacher, Rabbi Neria, whom they held in the highest regard, but whom they quite consciously coopted and led in their own direction more than they allowed themselves to be guided by him. This blurring of the distinction between rabbi and followers was to be repeated later in the early growth of Gush Emunim.

Their age manifested itself in a number of other group traits, among which one can point to a naive romanticism. Thus, for example, there were group "confessions," often revolving around a newly discovered attraction for the opposite sex, something which resulted in their partnership with a girls' group called *Nogah.*[20] Their romanticism found expression also in their preference for picturesque settings full of magic and drama. Important in this regard, as well, was the conspiratorial air that they fostered, from the very beginning, which often had no instrumental purpose.

To all this we must add the exaggerated seriousness with which they viewed their every word and deed, which was a factor in the frequent internal quarrels and threatened splits. They were plagued by typical adolescent identity crises, but they also (again, typically for their age) displayed very little patience or tolerance for middle-of-the-road positions, moderation, or compromise. They demanded clear-cut definitions, total consistency. Their radicalism was inspired by a world-embracing idealism, breadth of vision, spontaneity and originality, exuberance and chutzpah—as well as ambition and self-confidence. There was undoubtedly an element of delicious excitement too, with all their youthful innocence. Hence their exclusivity and elitism, with regard to those outside the group, and their far from modest self-image among themselves, which was reinforced by the admiration of outsiders. They were treated as something special, regarded as somehow older than the others, and given greater latitude.

Gahelet's romanticism, rebelliousness, and radicalism are well-known qualities of youth culture and typify the classical youth movement. Thus, the group "confessions" of adolescent boys in a male-only educational setting; the long nights around the campfire; the compulsive searchings for a higher sense and order in the world and for the meaning of God—all of this also took place in the early days of the socialist Zionist youth movements, perhaps no less so among the more right-wing nationalists, in the style of "Young Germany" of the 20s.[21]

About a half-year after the inception of *Gahelet,* the group published its first newsletter, a primitive attempt in mimeograph. In it, they declared their intention to "kindle the flame of future generations, to look forward to the day on which every man in Israel will sit under his vine and fig tree in full observance of the Torah of Israel."[22] Among the other guiding principles mentioned in this first issue of *Gahelet,* one finds "love of all the Jewish people and mutual responsibility for all Jews"; "nationalism and patriotism"; "dedication to the nation and loyalty to the state"; "readiness to sacrifice for the sake of the nation." One also finds a strong sense of their confidence in being able to reach out and affect the general public and to lead it in the prescribed direction.

These very closely linked ideas may, in the Israeli context, be subsumed under the word *halutziut* (inadequately rendered in English as "pioneering spirit"), and it is this highly untypical juxtaposition of Torah and *halutziut* that *Gahelet* placed on its banner. In addition to its classical symbolic connotation, the name *Gahelet* was an acronym for "Nucleus of Torah-Learning Pioneers." Later on, they formulated very specific goals, among which was the founding of a new religious kibbutz in which to put their ideals into practice. The center of their kibbutz was to be the yeshiva, where the male members of the collective would spend the bulk of their time in study while the community's economy was looked after by the women.

The original group grew from a founding trio who gathered around them a dozen students, selected from the cream of their seventy classmates, and an additional five from the school at Pardes Hannah. At the end of the first year, the group numbered twenty members; by the end of the second year, it had doubled in size. When the class graduated after four years, *Gahelet* claimed a membership of close to one hundred.

Qualifications for membership were strict. The two main criteria were the social compatibility of the candidate with the group and his standards of religious observance. In the group's publications of the time it was argued that the two criteria were in fact integrally linked, as the distinction between the social and religious elements was difficult to establish. A candidate was accepted only by a two-thirds majority vote, and he then could take four days to reconsider his fateful step. No one remembers a single instance, however, in which an accepted candidate changed his mind.

In the first years, only graduates of yeshiva schools were accepted. Afterwards, when the group came to value quantity as well as quality, in line with the drive for wider influence (in the Bnei Akiva movement, first of all), it opened its ranks to the "better" members of the local youth groups.[23]

Heavier demands were made of members than of potential candidates. Peer pressure was exerted to maintain the most stringent standards, particularly in the realm of religious behavior. Laxity or infringements carried a heavy social cost, which could include warnings, public reprimand, even "excommunication." All this, of course, merely heightened the prestige and group consciousness of the members, and the lines drawn around the insiders became ever sharper. This accounts for the superiority and even the snobbery with which outsiders were treated. The cultivation of secrecy also helped tie the group together. Indeed, it was quite some time before wider youth movement circles became aware of what was happening.

Another method of social control and indoctrination was the introduction, unusual in the Israeli context, of regular exhortatory sermons. Such *musar* talks, to be sure, had a long tradition in the yeshiva framework, going back to Rabbi Israel Salanter in the late nineteenth century, and are still a part of ultra-Orthodox yeshiva life today. The use of this specific method for rekindling the commitment of the faithful points up the somewhat dissonant combination of a spontaneous, open-ended spiritual experience and a drive toward a strict, conformist regimen. The history of religions provides several examples of initial charismatic outbursts and mystical yearnings which are gradually harnessed into Orthodox patterns, reinforcing and sanctioning old norms and ritual obligations.

This "Orthodoxization" was expressed, as well, in the adoption of a style of speaking, writing, even dressing, that emphasized the didactic, the spiritual, the pious. "Modest dress," speech studded with expressions from the yeshiva world and scriptural allusions—all were characteristic of this behavior and were elevated in importance almost to the level of ritual observance itself. The calculated spirituality came across in the sermons, too, which were almost entirely devoted to "religion and ideology." This atmosphere was clearly felt by members and outsiders to be the special quality of the group, and had a most profound impact on the girls who became associated with it. As they themselves claim, they transformed their life style radically to conform to the standards set by the boys.

Aside from such psychosocial factors, it is worth noting that the setting at Kfar Haroeh lent itself particularly well to a process of separation from the outside world. The yeshiva was a "total" educational environment, socially and institutionally, which made for a heightened separation from parental homes and a concomitantly enhanced influence exercised by teachers and mentors. Even its ecological situation fostered separateness: the yeshiva was located relatively far from the community of Kfar Haroeh itself. It was, in effect, a "hothouse" that allowed the students in some sense to avoid confronting the Israeli reality of the time, and permitted them to construct a religious ideology that had no need to face "historical" tests. In later years, this sort of "monastic" setting would be recreated in the Gush Emunim West Bank settlements, where the purist standards of a sacred code could be maintained.

With the yeshiva boys as the dominant and guiding element, the emphasis of the group's ideas shifted from "Torah and labor" to "Torah," exclusively, with Torah-study as the ideal. Scrutiny of the day-to-day life of the religious kibbutzim revealed the disappointing fact that study was not as central a concern as *Gahelet* members believed it ought to be. Nor, as they found to their chagrin, was religious behavior strictly monitored—particularly in the area of socializing with women.

Returning during vacation periods to the mainly urban, local branches of the youth movement, *Gahelet* members took on roles of group leadership, acting as guides to those their own age. In this way, their experience began to communicate itself to a wider periphery. The impact of *Gahelet* on Bnei Akiva is reflected in the youth movement's bulletin, *Zeraim,* of those years.[24] *Gahelet* members were also sent as representatives to national conferences. Their crowning achievement was the decision taken by the movement, in conjunction with the army, to permit the graduating members to study at a yeshiva for a year before doing their military service.

This was a radical departure from previous Bnei Akiva policy, and in retrospect marked the beginning of a new radicalism. From here on, the emphasis shifts away from the values of kibbutz settlement and focuses on Torah education.[25] High school yeshivas of Bnei Akiva were now established, followed by the *"hesder"* yeshivas which attracted the best of religious high school graduates. The direction that many students took was toward becoming teachers, raising the status of the yeshiva faculty that previously had kept itself outside the more influential and authoritative circles of the rabbinate. In the process of "Orthodoxization," the movement developed a more positive self-image, a greater confidence in confronting the broader public, and what may be called "religious pride."

The success of *Gahelet* in transforming the values of the religious-Zionist youth movement can also be read in the fate of the "losing side": the religious kibbutz. Originally intended to expand and continue its development, *Gahelet* and the youth movement as a whole reached a point of downgrading the kibbutz as an ideal, if not actually rejecting it. Bnei Akiva, educating youngsters toward "Torah and labor," had been intended as the main reservoir of future religious kibbutz members. The new spirit in the movement, although not yet completely dominant, had already alienated many members from the original message.

The advances made by the *Gahelet* group and its sympathizers aroused a good deal of opposition at the time: local branches of the youth movement were divided ideologically and socially by the competing camps. There was palpable tension between the smaller group and the general membership. A more serious problem developed, however, between the radicals and the national leadership and its institutions. *Gahelet* had in fact anticipated opposition, and had therefore initially kept its activities in recruiting adherents secret. Its fears were well-justified: when the existence of the group became known, it was charged with creating a private organization, inimical to the unity and aims of the movement. Differences also arose over the character of the group's intentions for its post-graduation goals, as well as their timing. The conflict came to a head when the national leadership demanded the immediate dismantling of *Gahelet.*

In the end, the group was in fact split up, but by that time the influence of its ideas within the movement was an accomplished fact—

felt even in the top echelons. The very man sent to oversee the dismantling of *Gahelet* was won over to its point of view and in fact joined it—or at least the faction that broke its ties with Bnei Akiva. That man was Haim Druckman, who later became one of the most influential educators of religious Zionist youth and a leader of Gush Emunim.

In their eleventh-grade year, the *Gahelet* group helped to initiate a twelfth-year study program at Kfar Haroeh, in the framework of a *beit midrash* (study center) established there. The following year they helped to found a new yeshiva at Kerem Beyavneh. The latter's importance as an innovation—one which grew directly out of the *Gahelet* experience—was that the aim was not merely to add another year of study prior to military service, but to establish an independent yeshiva to serve as the center of the new ideology.

Most of the group's members, however, including the original founders, chose to study at already established yeshivas, where they hoped to mold the character of the schools to their own way of thinking. In the main there were three yeshivas that attracted the *Gahelet* alumni: "Netiv Meir" and "Merkaz Harav" in Jerusalem, and "Hadarom" in Rehovot.[26] Kerem Beyavneh was the creation of those who remained, and was the first yeshiva founded by young Israelis.

At Kerem Beyavneh the *Gahelet* group continued to stick together, maintaining a distinct identity. It was during this period that a chain of events—perhaps coincidental, perhaps inevitable—led the Kerem Beyavneh group to meet with their former classmates in Jerusalem, and through them, to a personal encounter with R. Zvi Yehuda Hacohen Kook of Merkaz Harav. Long discussions took place about the relationship between the Jewish people, its land and the Torah. R. Zvi Yehuda's character and ideas left a profound impression on the group, and when (in the early spring of that year) the yeshiva at Kerem Beyavneh was left without a head, it was only natural that the students should gravitate toward Merkaz Harav.

A second meeting with R. Zvi Yehuda was arranged at Passover, during which the group asked him to provide instruction in the thought of his father, the late R. Abraham Isaac Hacohen Kook. This was the decisive juncture at which the link with "Merkaz Harav" took shape, and with it came the feeling among members of the group that they had finally found themselves an appropriate mentor.

Even the proudest "Kookist" will admit that, until the coming of the *Gahelet* group, the Merkaz Harav yeshiva was not widely regarded as an important center of Torah study. Even in religious Zionist circles it tended to be ignored or actually forgotten. R. Zvi Yehuda's own status, both inside and outside the yeshiva, was not particularly high. The truth of the matter is that even during the lifetime of Rav Kook himself, whose personality was certainly outstanding, both in the yeshiva and in society in general, the yeshiva itself did not achieve the kind of central importance which its founders had hoped for. It certainly did not achieve its original intention of serving as a bridge between the traditionalist "old *yishuv*" and the "new," Zionist settlers.

In the twenty years after Rav Kook's time, the yeshiva had lost track of the distinctive role it had intended to play in Zionism and in the secular world in general, and lapsed into the routine of a typical yeshiva. Its financial and its physical condition deteriorated, and it lacked connections with any public body or faction that might have supported it. It had very few students, of rather poor quality, and a staff of mediocre teachers.[27]

The *Gahelet* alumni generally maintain that they came "not to the yeshiva, but to the rabbi." This implies, of course, a negative judgment of the spirit which existed at "Merkaz" before their coming; but it equally reveals the personal and intimate quality of their encounter with its principal. Indeed, almost from the very first, the group took to spending long hours in study and discussion with R. Zvi Yehuda, developing warm and especially close ties with him. His preference for these students over the others was marked, and it soon became apparent that an "in" group existed. To borrow a ḥasidic term, they made R. Zvi Yehuda their "rebbe." He became their discovery: a hidden genius, previously unappreciated, now revealed in all his glory as an exceptional personality. They surrounded him with a myth of their own creation: he became a towering figure of irresistable magnetism. His was a charisma that owed more to the veneration of his followers than to his own qualities.

The "love at first sight" between *Gahelet* and R. Zvi Yehuda proved to be of lasting duration—not least because each side of the partnership had found in the other exactly what it had been looking for. They fulfilled each other's needs almost perfectly, and the relationship enjoyed a singular mutuality, even a completeness. To the young men, R. Zvi Yehuda was their teacher, their leader, their father; to him, they were disciples, sons, a public.

With their attachment to "Merkaz" and to R. Zvi Yehuda, the group had seemingly given up its original ideal, that of combining *halutziut* and Torah—although in time they would develop the argument that the path they had chosen indeed represented this combination, in its highest expression. However, for the moment, the group excused itself from the religious-Zionist challenge. This withdrawal from activity in the public arena to the sphere of traditional learning, nonetheless, did not solve for them the basic tension between Zionism and Orthodoxy.

Instead, they brought that tension with them as they penetrated further into the world of Torah. The contradictions were expressed not only on an ideological level, but on the social-institutional level as well.

Although there is something to be said for a number of interesting similarities between the yeshiva world and a youth movement—the common elements of youth culture, elitism, strict devotion to the cause, etc.—the entry of *Gahelet* into a traditional yeshiva structure was fraught with incongruities and tensions.

The first effect on the group was the abandonment of those qualities which were specific to the youth movement: the social-political activism, the focus on the surrounding society. They entered the yeshiva environment wholeheartedly, concentrating solely on the study of Torah. They justified this, at the time, by arguing that the building of the yeshiva "from within" had to precede any attempt to affect the society outside the yeshiva. They were indeed aware of the nature of the turnabout they had made, if only from the attitude of the religious kibbutz movement, Bnei Akiva, and the religious Zionist party circles towards them. The youth movement and the kibbutzim were not quite sure what to do with *Gahelet* any more, while the party assumed that, as yeshiva boys, they no longer had a voice in political matters. Only they themselves still considered themselves to be "political." It was in this unique position, straddling the two worlds, that the group set out to develop its distinctive philosophy, based on the paradoxical belief that it was here, enclosed within the four walls of the house of study, that they would reach the full meaning of the political.

Not quite ten years after the start of their yeshiva career, some *Gahelet* members emerged from their study hall to organize a faction within the National Religious Party. Criticizing the party's policies in general, and the role played by its "Young Guard" in particular, they pulled together a number of young yeshiva men interested in a revival of the spirit of "Torah and labor." Their actual power was minimal, but they were convinced that "quality"—i.e., the fact that they were scholars—would weigh heavily in their favor. The faction was recruited from Merkaz Harav and elements drawn from Bnei Akiva and the religious kibbutz movement, and their first challenge were the party elections in the N.R.P. in 1963–64. They called the faction *Hug Emunim* ("circle" or faction of the faithful).

Their effort was stillborn, and this fact was no less significant than that of their embarking on the project in the first place. R. Zvi Yehuda forbade the leaders of the faction—R. Zephaniah Drori and R. Haim Druckman, in particular—to continue their political activities. "Either politics or Torah," he told them, stating what was the traditionalist view, though he thus negated some basic mystic-messianic principles of his father's philosophy. He did, in fact, soften his ultimatum, arguing that it was important to strive to influence the state and Israeli society, but that this did not include the formation of anything as formal as a party faction. The fledgling politicians heeded his instruction, and returned to their studies.

The forerunners of Gush Emunim, thwarted and disillusioned in their confrontation with their society and with Zionism in its secular, political terms, sought refuge in the religious tradition. Seeking a basis for the Zionist component of their identity, they turned to the religious component which their parents had to some extent compromised in creating the religious Zionist option. In identifying more with Zionism, they had distanced themselves somewhat from traditionalist values and style. Gush Emunim, on the other hand, having gone the route of distancing itself from practical Zionism as a way of rediscovering the world of tradition, would later find it necessary to "rediscover" Zionism. The path of *Gahelet* led—not inevitably, nor did members at the time foresee what lay ahead—to a heightened political consciousness.

With *Gahelet,* we have a small, even marginal, group withdrawing from the fray, paradoxically because of its zealous devotion to state and nation. It did not abandon its attachment to them, but the ambivalent nature of its attitude to them became more extreme. From within the Orthodox yeshiva world, they were both increasingly attracted and repelled by the political world outside. It took twenty-five years, but the alumni of *Gahelet* finally did break into the political arena, eager to capture it for religious Judaism via the fulfillment of Zionism. One may say that if *Gahelet* represented "Orthodoxization" for the sake of Zionism, Gush Emunim was "Zionization" for the sake of Orthodoxy.

Gahelet is a historic turning point for religious Zionism. A group that is zealously devoted to a set of traditional values, even if marginal or small, can have a disproportionate influence on the general public. This is particularly true with regard to the influence of such a group upon those sectors of society which themselves owe allegiance to those same values. The compromisers are in effect "held captive" by those on the extreme who demand consistency between theory and practice.

Against the background of the challenge of a secular modernity (in the guise of Zionism) poised to conquer Judaism, and of the seeming inability of the "national religious" option to meet it, *Gahelet* offered a new solution to the problem. It approached Judaism and Zionism as a unity, and embarked on a course of dual radicalization: a more extreme Orthodoxy together with a more extreme nationalism. Though involved in the state and its society, the members of *Gahelet* came to view them from an external vantage point. *Gahelet* admired the ultra-Orthodox, just as they admired the secularists, for what they saw as their self-sufficiency and the faithfulness to principles which endowed them with authority and legitimacy.

The solution offered by *Gahelet* embraced a nationalist-political experience clothed in mystical-messianic terms; it was a deep and authentic religious revival that used Zionism as its medium. In *Gahelet* we see the beginnings of the change from "religious Zionism" to "Zionist religion." This reversal is the essence of what I have called "Kookism." Kookism is a value and idea complex—an ideology, mentality, and life style—that originated in *Gahelet* and became in the course of time the characteristic feature of the radical activist sector of religious, land-settling Zionism. The roots of the phenomenon lie in the encounter between Rav Kook's theological system, mediated through the personality and educational endeavors of his son, and the individuals of a small "sect."

Gahelet, however, was not the inevitable product of any earlier developments, but rather an independent, original phenomenon. It may be surprising to learn that until they came to the old house on Rav Kook Street in Jerusalem, the youths of *Gahelet* were not familiar with the thought of Rav Kook. With R. Zvi Yehuda as their guide, this now became an overriding preoccupation. Today, the graduates of the group cite Rav Kook's thought as the source of their emergence—even if only through indirect and hidden influences of which, at the time, they were not aware. But in precise historical terms, it is clear that they were believers in search of a dogma. The matching of the spiritual doctrine and its cult was a case of "elective affinity."[28] Kookism led them to the mystical-messianic solution of the Zionism-Judaism dilemma, and at the same time brought them further into the traditionalist world. This, of course, heightened the tension which they experienced as nationalists and as Orthodox Jews in the State of Israel.

The meeting of the group's search for a solution and the thought of Rav Kook transformed the latter from a theology to an ideology. *Gahelet* benefitted from the added depth—both spiritual and ideological—as well as the added strength afforded by the weight of tradition, when they attached themselves to Kook's ideas. Those ideas, on the other hand, benefited from the place of honor they received in an actual social-political framework, when in their original context they had exerted little real influence. At last translated into a platform for action, the mystical-messianic complex faced the challenge of historical reality. At first, Kookism was a rationalization for the group's set of ideas, an external or instrumental tool for the articulation of an independently developed consciousness. In due course, however, the ideology took on an independent existence, with a considerable potential of its own. It took the Zionism-Judaism dilemma out of its this-worldly context and placed it in the transcendental realm of Torah, kabbalistically interpreted.

Until the advent of *Gahelet,* in its Kookist phase, the mystical messianism of Rav Kook was understood as an individualistic and esoteric doctrine.[29] To the extent that it had achieved prior recognition, it was generally an object of bitter criticism, from the "right" (i.e., the ultra-Orthodox camp), or exploited and patronized by the "left" (secular Zionists) which romanticized it without understanding it.[30]

Rav Kook's great stature as a thinker notwithstanding, in his ambition to apply his conception to all sectors in the *yishuv,* to unite them finally under an all-embracing "sacred canopy"—containing the profane as well—his enterprise was a dismal failure. His messianic mysticism, appropriating Zionism within its folds, was never accepted by the secular camp. It was, at the same time, repulsed by large and important parts of the Orthodox community. Consequently, it was only natural that Rav Kook's most important public project—the establishment of the chief rabbinate, which meant the institutionalization of his theology—turned out to be, at the very least, less than successful. To this day, its authority is not quite accepted by the secular public while the Orthodox right wing (from Agudat Israel rightwards) totally denies it. Instead of serving to bridge the gap between the Orthodox and the non-Orthodox, it actually emphasizes the differences dividing them.[31]

Such was the fate of Rav Kook's tragic attempt to break through toward the Zionist pole of his ingenious synthesis. His more modest enterprise, the yeshiva which he founded, not only did not live up to the classical standards of an institution of halakhic learning, but also failed to play any role in the general social and political system. It took nearly thirty years before *Gahelet* discovered Rav Kook's legacy and revealed its enormous potential—even while altering it in the process.

Once the encounter occurred between *Gahelet* and the teachings of Rav Kook—between social experience and civil consciousness on the one hand and the religious idea and emotion on the other—each became linked to the other in a relationship which revealed new dimensions on both sides. Rav Kook's thought took on the aspect of a platform for political involvement and was harnessed to the aspirations of an active social force. In a parallel development, those aspirations took on spiritual depth and enjoyed a new legitimation for what had until then been merely dreams and feelings. In the process, both assumed an essentially new and different significance, which could not then have been appreciated, and cannot now be exaggerated. Its distinctive and lasting expression is Gush Emunim.

Notes

This paper is a condensed and translated version of a chapter in a Ph.D. dissertation to be submitted to the Department of Sociology and Social Anthropology of the Hebrew University (1984). The broader study consists of description and analysis of Gush Emunim, its social dimensions and cultural significance. It is based primarily on three years of field research which included intensive participant observation, open in-depth interviews, and documentary analysis. Although Gush Emunim, as a social movement, is usually analyzed in terms of political sociology, extensive use is made here of the analytical perspective of the sociology of religion.

It is my contention that the activist public face of Gush Emunim, salient and important as it is, is basically a function of the religious nature of the group. Elucidation of this less obvious and more complex aspect is essential for an understanding of the way in which the movement presents itself in public life. The analysis of Gush Emunim as a religious movement sheds light on some basic features of Israeli society, in its relationship with the traditional Jewish heritage in particular, and on the problematics of the relationship between society and religion in general. The chapter from which excerpts are presented here is followed by a chapter analyzing the teachings and activity of Rabbi Abraham I. Kook (Rav Kook), and another devoted to his son and his Merkaz Harav yeshiva. Together, these three chapters form the framework in which we deal with the origins of Gush Emunim. This is followed by a study of the culture, values, and characteristic ideas of Gush Emunim, and finally by chapters dealing with its structure, dynamics, organizational, and political patterns.

The term "Zionist religion" has been used previously, though in a different sense, by Y. Eilam, "Mashber ha-ziyonut—mashber ha-yahadut," *Bitfutsot hagolah* (1975).

My thanks are due to the editors of *Studies in Contemporary Jewry* for their initiative and counsel, and particularly to Eli Lederhendler for his help in translation and editing.

1. *Gahelet* is practically unknown outside a very limited circle of those who were directly involved in it. It has been ignored in the literature, with the one exception of the forthcoming book (1985) by M. Bar-Lev, which deals with *Gahelet* in the context of the development of the Bnei Akiva movement.

2. See, e.g., J. Odea, "Gush Emunim: shorashim ve-du-mashma'uyot," *Bitfutsot hagolah* 1979/80, and A. Rubinstein, *Mi-Herzl ad gush emunim u-behazarah* (Tel-Aviv: 1980).

3. E. Goldman used a similar chronology, with reasons closely approximating my own. Though he did not pursue the subject historically or sociologically, as an educator and thinker with a close familiarity with the subject he raises very interesting points, from the perspective of religious Zionism and of the religious kibbutz movement in particular. See his "Meshihiyut pashtanit," *bit-*

futsot hagolah 1979/80. Without citing it by name, Goldman alludes to the *Gahelet* phenomenon as an early manifestation of what later developed into Gush Emunim. His perceptive comments were necessarily brief, coming as a reaction to the first piece of research on Gush Emunim (Odea, see note 2 above). He did not go into details, nor did those who adopted his analysis in subsequent discussions. See e.g., E. Sprinzak, "Gush Emunim: model ha-karhon shel ha-kizoniyut ha-politit," *Medinah, mimshal, ve-yahasim bein le'umiim* 17 (1981).

4. See Gershom Scholem, *Shabbetai Zvi ve-hatnu'ah ha-shabtait biyemei hayav* (Tel-Aviv: 1974), esp. chapter 1.

5. *Ibid.*

6. Gershom Scholem, "Le-havanat ha-ra'ayon ha-meshihi be-yisrael," in *Dvarim bago* (Tel-Aviv: 1975).

7. Such a view is expressed, for example, by B. Kurzweil, "Mahutah u-mekoroteha shel tnu'at ha-kna'anim," *Luah ha-aretz* (Tel-Aviv: 1953).

8. See, e.g., Hanan Porat, " 'Ayin be-'ayin yir'u be-shuv ha-shem ziyon," *Petahim* 1975.

9. *Ibid.*

10. See J. Katz, *Le'umiyut yehudit* (Jerusalem: 1979), esp. pp. 15–36.

11. For the distinction between the two senses of secularization and their application in Jewish history, see *ibid.*, pp. 72–85, 132–154.

12. For the definitive expression of this idea, see P. Berger, *The Sacred Canopy* (New York: 1969 [1967]); T. Parsons, *Social Structure and Personality* (New York: 1970).

13. The Lubavicher Rebbe, as quoted by Y. Eilam. "Mashber ha-ziyonut—mashber ha-yahadut," *Bitfutsot hagolah* 1975.

14. *Ibid.*, p. 46. Cf. I. Gitlin (of the extreme right-wing ultra-Orthodox camp) in his critical essay, *Yahadut ha-torah ve-ha-medinah* (Jerusalem: 1959), p. 26.

15. My brief and general discussion of Orthodoxy is based on the historical-typological description by M. Samet (mimeo., no date), "Ortodoksiah—tipologiah ve-historiah," and particularly on Eliezer Schweid's analysis in *Ortodoksiah ve-humanizm dati* (Jerusalem: 1977).

16. This motif is repeated to a certain degree in the Gush Emunim experience: the Gush also tends to prefer the non-ideologically secular over those non-Orthodox Israelis who have their own articulated approach to Jewish culture and identity.

17. Aside from the controversial views of Leibovitz (e.g., as presented in *Yahadut, am yehudi u-medinat yisrael* [Tel-Aviv: 1976]), for whom the tensions between religion and secular nationalism are central, we can cite a number of figures who have enjoyed a much greater acceptance, despite their unusual candor: Baruch Kurzweil (e.g., in his already-cited essay on the Canaanites—see above, note 7); Rabbi Adin Steinsaltz, who stated that Zionism is "the negation not only of the Diaspora but of Jewish tradition itself" (in *Petahim* 23 [1972]).

18. On the Orthodox community's attitude toward Zionism in the pre-state *yishuv,* see M. Friedman, *Hevrah va-dat* (Jerusalem: 1978) and "Yahasei datiim—hiloniim likrat hakamat ha-medinah," in A. Shapira (ed.), *Sugiyot be-toldot ha-ziyonut ve-ha-yishuv* (Tel-Aviv: 1982/83).

19. The terms are used by S. Avineri: *Ha-ra'ayon ha-ziyoni ligvanav* (Tel-Aviv: 1980), see esp. his "Epilogue."

20. Among the more first-hand accounts which I was able to gather (from

interviews and the writings of the *Gahelet* members from those years), I found the testimony of a young woman who was close to one of the founding members of *Gahelet,* and who afterward joined the group with the rest of her group of girls, to be of particular importance. In the course of her own subsequent career, as a student of social psychology at the Hebrew University, she wrote a term paper on *Gahelet* as a case study of a "small group." A copy of the paper, written twenty years ago (and thus still close in time to the actual events) is in my possession.

21. See, e.g., W. Laqueur, *Young Germany* (London: 1962).

22. The wrinkled and yellowed pages of *Gahelet*'s bulletins of thirty years ago were of particular use to me in my research.

23. Among the first members of *Gahelet* who later played an influential role in Bnei Akiva, in the Merkaz Harav yeshiva, and finally in Gush Emunim (or the "Kookist" camp out of which it grew), all of them well-known rabbis today, we can cite the following: Zephaniah Drori, Yaakov Filber, Zalman Melamed, Ariel Fuchs, Shabbetai Zelikovich. All of them began their political careers at age fourteen. Other prominent personalities who associated themselves early on with the group are: Haim Druckman, the Bnei Akiva group leader who became a "follower" of the boys he ostensibly led; and Moshe Levinger, then affiliated with the "Ezra" group in Jerusalem. After his military service, he turned to Torah studies and fell under the spell of the group at Kfar Haroeh, still in its formative stage. Later, at the Merkaz Harav, he formally joined the group. One might also mention Rabbi Waldman, who arrived from the United States at about that time and encountered the group during the founding of the yeshiva at Kerem Beyavneh.

24. See, e.g., *Zeraim* of 1954/55.

25. *Zeraim* no. 1,1954/55. The Bnei Akiva bulletin at the time published a revealing cartoon, depicting a boxing arena: the defeated fighter, lying on the floor, bears the caption, "kibbutz"; his elated victor stands above him, arms aloft, bearing the label, "yeshiva." *Zeraim* no. 2, 1954/55.

26. Their choice was limited, as most of the yeshivas belonged to the ultra-Orthodox camp (the so-called black yeshivas), and were not quite what they had in mind in terms of developing the *Gahelet* point of view. It should be noted that in the early stages of choosing a school for the group as a whole, Merkaz Harav was considered but rejected. They felt that it was loosely organized and "not serious," giving the impression of being on the level of a European "ḥeder"—and not for Israelis like themselves. Rav Zvi Yehuda sent two representatives to Tel-Aviv to speak with the group and attempt to convince them to study at his yeshiva, but they sent the two men back without as much as granting them an interview. Within a generation, these very youths became central figures at Merkaz Harav and took part in founding a "ḥeder" for their own children, attached to the yeshiva.

27. At the time that *Gahelet* became part of Markaz Harav, there were some twenty other students there, who conducted their studies in a very traditional fashion. See M. Z. Nahorai, "Lihyot yehudi," *Amudim* (May 1976).

28. On the role of "elective affinity" in social processes, see Max Weber, in H. Gerth and C. Mills (eds.), *From Max Weber* (London: 1948), pp. 284–85. Cf. E. Fischoff, "The Protestant Ethic—History of a Controversy," in S. N. Eisenstadt (ed.), *The Protestant Ethic and Modernization* (New York: 1948); and P. Berger, "Charisma and Religious Innovation," *American Sociological Review* no. 28 (1963).

29. For a description in similar terms, see G. Scholem, *Major Trends in Jewish Mysticism* (New York: 1971 [1941]).

30. See M. Friedman, *Hevrah va-dat;* Rivka Shatz, "Reshit ha-masa neged ha-rav Kook," *Molad* 1973/74; David Kna'ani, *Ha-aliyah ha-shniyah ve-yahasah la-dat ve-lamasoret* (Tel-Aviv: 1976); Muki Tzur, *Le-lo kutonet pasim* (Tel-Aviv: 1976).

31. See Friedman, *Hevrah va-dat.*

The Politics of Tradition: Agudat Israel in Polish Politics, 1916–1939

Gershon C. Bacon
(BAR-ILAN UNIVERSITY)

In interwar Poland, Jewish political activity reached a highly developed state. Political parties arose representing practically every point on the political spectrum. For the most part, these parties set up a full range of auxiliary services, such as youth movements, a periodical press, and the like. In the period in question they carried on an intense political struggle among themselves for hegemony within the Jewish community and the chance to chart the future of Polish Jewry through the setting of ideological, educational, and economic priorities.

In the sphere of general Polish politics, despite great ideological and tactical differences, there was agreement among the main Jewish parties on basic goals. These were the implementation of the political and cultural rights guaranteed to the Jews by the Minority Treaties and the relevant clauses of the Polish constitution, elimination of legal and bureaucratic discrimination, and ensuring the full participation of Jews in the life of the newly independent Polish state.

Of the major political parties active within Polish Jewry, the Orthodox Agudat Israel has merited little serious scholarly attention. Instead, it has usually served as the target of the polemical ire of historians and publicists identified with Agudah's opponents or as the subject of apologetic presentations by Agudah's partisans.[1] As the second largest vote-getter after the Zionists and the party in control of the two major communities of Warsaw and Lodz for considerable periods

This article is part of a larger, comprehensive survey of the history of the Agudat Israel movement in interwar Poland. Research for this project was aided at various stages by grants from the National Foundation for Jewish Culture, the Memorial Foundation for Jewish Culture, and the International Research and Exchanges Board (IREX), to whom I express my thanks.

of time, Agudat Israel was a major factor on the Polish Jewish scene, and as such deserves a more balanced assessment of its leadership, goals, tactics, and achievements.

ORIGINS

In the highly politicized atmosphere of Polish Jewry, the Orthodox were late, reluctant entrants into party politics. Internal Jewish developments, rather than the general political situation, proved to be the decisive factor in spurring some elements in the Orthodox community to organize politically.

Despite concern over the growing strength of secularist parties which threatened to take over the Jewish community, important elements of the Orthodox community continued to oppose politicizing Orthodoxy, for they viewed the politicization as a betrayal of the religious tradition that Orthodox politicians would be defending. Politics by its very nature would lead to bargaining and compromise, and to the penetration of new and unwanted modern ideas into the traditional community. On the other hand, lay and rabbinic supporters of political activity argued that the interests and feelings of the vast majority of traditional Jews should not go unrepresented.

It is not surprising, then, that the political organization of Polish Orthodoxy proceeded at a slow pace. The initial decision came after much hesitation and with ambivalent feelings. Once the decision was made, the mechanics of electioneering, fundraising, and canvassing for membership had to be learned. The cautious, moderate political stance that Agudah would exhibit stemmed in part from the feelings of ambivalence regarding politics in general. If circumstances forced the Orthodox into politics, they tried their utmost to transfer age-old modes of Jewish political behavior into the realm of modern parliamentary politics.

The official history of the Agudat Israel movement begins with the May 1912 Katowice Conference. At that conference, Orthodox Jews from Eastern and Western Europe decided to form an organization for the promotion and defense of Orthodox Judaism. For all practical purposes, however, Agudat Israel in Poland began its organizational efforts only in 1916, during the German occupation.

In the relatively free political atmosphere which then prevailed, Jewish and Polish political parties commenced open political work that had generally been impossible under the Tsarist Russian regime. Two Orthodox rabbis from Germany, Kohn and Carlebach, came to Warsaw in 1916 as advisors to the occupation authorities.[2] They met with ḥasidic leaders, promoting the idea of Orthodox organization.[3] Among the followers of the Gerer Rebbe[4] in particular they found a receptive audience. That ḥasidic group had a long history of struggle against modernist tendencies in Judaism and viewed with concern the rise of Zionist and Jewish socialist parties. In Lithuania, as well, major rabbinic figures had made several abortive attempts at founding an Orthodox political movement. Thus the founding of Agudat Israel in Poland (called at first Agudat Ha-Ortodoksim) was not a totally imported foreign concept,[5] but was a combination of local needs and the organizational talents and political connections of the German rabbis.

Though the German rabbis may have had their own agenda, deriving from German interests in the area[6] as well as the internal Jewish issues relevant to both Germany and Poland, the Polish Agudah fairly quickly developed an independent stance that had as much in common with its Zionist and Bundist opponents as it did with Frankfurt Orthodoxy. It wanted no part of the distinctive approach of Frankfurt Orthodoxy, namely the formation of a separatist Orthodox community. Polish Orthodoxy turned to politics not in order to preserve a dwindling minority group, but to provide a spokesman for a hitherto silent majority. Nor did the Polish Agudah condone a separation of religion and nation. Religion served as the basis of Jewish nationality, but it was a nationality all the same, even if the Agudah rarely used the term "national minority rights" so resented by the Poles.

The basic components of the Orthodox political posture are evident in the very first contacts between Agudah and the emerging Polish state apparatus in the immediate pre-independence years, 1916–18. Thus, for example, Agudat Israel (under its earlier name) sent a greeting and declaration of loyalty to the newly named Provisional State Council. In his response, Marshal Niemojowski expressed satisfaction with the Orthodox declaration of loyalty, and promised that the new Polish state would adhere to ancient traditions of tolerance, allowing the Jews to serve their ancestral faith as equal citizens.[7] But from the beginning, the Polish authorities refused to acknowledge any national element in Jewish existence in Poland, and even the moderately worded declarations of Agudat Israel, laced with patriotic proclamations, were unacceptable.

In this transitional period, while downplaying any Jewish national claims, the Agudah, on several occasions, stated its demands for legal equality and an end to religious discrimination, as, for example, in a July 1917 memorandum to the Warsaw municipality.[8] Similarly, an Agudah representative in the State Council declared that Orthodox Jews would walk hand in hand with the Polish public as useful and worthy citizens. He laid down no conditions, since he did not wish to burden the new government, and because he knew that only through mutual compromise would Jews and Poles have normal relations. He noted that his restrained declaration did not mean that Orthodox Jews had no demands. Instead, it demonstrated a realistic view of the situation and a desire to reach agreement based on trust. He believed that "without a doubt the Polish state will treat all parts of the population equally, including Jews, following the exalted traditions of old Poland which promised Jews equality and religious toleration."[9]

These basic themes characterize the political stance of Agudat Israel throughout the period under consideration. While affirming its loyalty to the state and its confidence in the good intentions of the Polish people, Agudah also espoused a moderate, religion-centered Jewish nationalism and quietly enunciated political demands. Such a stance had a superficial resemblance to the position of the Jewish assimilationists, and on occasion served as ammunition for Polish spokesmen at Versailles in their campaign against national minority rights for Polish Jewry. Polish politicians claimed that the majority of Polish Jews regarded the Jewish question as a strictly religious one, and only a small minority of "separatists" wished to create a nation within a nation and to perpetuate differences between Jewish and non-Jewish Poles.[10] Thus, in the context of this polemic the traditionally garbed, Yiddish-speaking Orthodox Jews emerged as less "separatist" than secularist Zionists or Bundists, a somewhat strange turn of events.

For its part, Agudah made no effort to eschew its super-patriotic outlook, but consistently denied that it compromised the struggle for Jewish rights. In part, the whole controversy was semantic. Both sides in this intra-Jewish polemic accepted some notion of Jewish nationality, but Agudah based its concept of Jewish nationhood on religious criteria. For Zionists, Folkists, or Bundists, this religious definition was either outmoded or too restricted and could too easily be misinterpreted by Polish authorities.

LEADERSHIP

In 1919, as Jews prepared to go to the polls for the first time in an independent Polish state, the various Jewish parties presented their programs to the electorate. In this and subsequent campaigns, the Agudah party program—centered on the primacy of religious interests and religious leadership and a quiet, dignified struggle for Jewish rights—remained remarkably consistent. Its electoral strategy favored Jewish political unity as the best tactic to gain the maximum number of Jewish deputies. Yet Agudah made its entry into any wider coalition conditional upon being granted freedom of action on crucial religious and political matters.

Agudah was far from unique in this respect. The fractious nature of Jewish politics in Poland, characterized as it was by strong personal and ideological antagonisms, precluded any lasting united Jewish political front. Prior to the 1919 Sejm elections, discussions took place among the middle-class parties over a united election list. These negotiations ultimately faltered on two basic issues. Agudah refused to make its religious demands a matter of lower priority, and refused to come either directly or indirectly under the aegis of the Zionist-dominated Temporary Jewish National Council.[11]

A proclamation of leading ḥasidic rebbes in support of Agudah demonstrated this stance. Agudah had wanted a united Jewish front, but circumstances prevented this; so now Orthodox Jews must back Agudah in this first test of strength:

> give your votes only to the election lists of your pious brethren wherever there are such lists of these pious ones. Let the various parties see that you do not wish to surrender even the slightest bit in matters of religion. By your deeds you will give strength to your brothers to defend all the interests of Judaism in material and spiritual affairs. . . .[12]

Even in national elections, the major Jewish parties devoted much of their propaganda effort to the internal Jewish debate. Each party tried to carve out some constituency in the Jewish community and use that political base to promote its philosophy of Jewishness. Agudah claimed the Orthodox masses as its fiefdom, although both religious Zionists and nonpartisan Orthodox groups challenged this claim.[13] Nevertheless, Agudah went to the voters claiming to be the voice of traditional Judaism. It promised to defend Jewish interests and rights with dignity and to protect Jewish tradition against onslaughts from within or without.

All of the Jewish parties, Agudah included, chose their candidates with an eye toward presenting a distinct party image to the Jewish voting public. In the case of Agudah, those men chosen as candidates for the Sejm, Senate, or local offices represented the special political approach of Agudat Israel. This included combining the aura of religious tradition with a rabbinic stamp of approval and the age-old image of the Jewish intercessor *(shtadlan)*—a proud, dignified figure who went to the corridors of power to plead the case of the Jews. To fulfill these ends and others to be noted below, Agudah ran three major types of candidate.

Prominent among them were, first of all, rabbis, particularly in the first election campaigns in 1919 and 1922, but continuing throughout the period. Besides making the obvious point about the religious character of the party, rabbinical political candidates symbolized other ideas as well. Traditionally garbed, long-bearded rabbis sounding patriotic declarations in eloquent Polish harked back to the idyll of Jewish-Polish cooperation during the Polish revolts against Russian rule—a not unimportant symbol in the period of independent Poland's rebirth, when Jewish demands for minority rights were denounced as unpatriotic by Polish spokesmen. Indeed, Agudah played upon this association by sending to the Constituent Sejm Rabbi Abraham Perlmutter,[14] a student and colleague of the legendary patriotic figure Rabbi Dov Berish Meisels of Warsaw. The Agudah leaders considered selecting rabbinical candidates not just a vote-winning tactic but an educational tool as well. Such Jewish representatives in the Sejm showed Orthodox Jewish youth that they could continue in the old ways yet still be part of a modern state.[15] In some cases (e.g., the noted Rabbi Meir Shapira who ran and was elected in 1922) the rabbinic candidates did not even speak Polish. Finally, Agudah maintained that rabbinic figures made the best *shtadlanim* in times of crisis, since their dignified demeanor and bearing best expressed Jewish anguish.

The second type of Agudah candidate and representative, the mainstay of the party leadership, was the wealthy Orthodox businessman and communal leader. These men, who combined traditional education with some (usually informal) secular knowledge, had the wherewithal to devote most of their time to communal work. In the nineteenth century they had often been in the shadow of the even wealthier assimilationists who dominated the Jewish Kehillah boards. In the newer democratic conditions which prevailed after independence, the Orthodox plutocracy came into its own. The feeling of an obligation to serve the public was a strong one, and we can find the same man serving simultaneously in the Sejm, the city council and on his local Kehillah board.[16] Both the rabbi and businessman type representatives were cautious, conservative figures who wished to continue the "old politics" of *shtadlanut* in the newer forums of a democratically elected Kehillah and the Polish parliament.

Upon the formation of Agudat Israel, there emerged a third type of leader in the Orthodox community. This was the party functionary, the young Orthodox Jew recruited by the German rabbis during World War I or who grew up in the Agudah youth movement.[17] These young men, who sometimes even possessed university degrees, took to partisan politics in a much more natural manner than their elders, and functioned in editorial, secretarial, educational, and other staff capacities. Though leaders of this new type did not enter parliament, by the 1930s they made their political debut on the local level—in the Kehillahs and city councils.

Table 1. Votes for Jewish Parties, 26 January 1919

	Jewish National Council	Ortho-dox	Folk-ists	Bund	Poale Zion	Others	Total
Former Russian Poland	180,234	97,293	59,229	16,366	27,063	16,622	396,807
Former Austrian Poland	52,661	—	—	—	951	4,422	58,034
Totals:	232,895	97,293	59,229	16,366	28,014	21,044	454,841

ELECTORATE

It is difficult to identify with any degree of precision the exact social and religious strata of the Polish Jewish community which supported Agudah. Researchers have done district-by-district analyses of voting patterns in several elections,[18] but neither these nor analyses of the Polish censuses of 1921 and 1931 provide data about the voting patterns or demographic makeup of the various ḥasidic groups. A peculiar kind of "ticket splitting" by Polish Jews complicates the picture still further. The same individual who supported the Zionists in the Sejm elections might support Agudah in the Kehillah elections and the Bund in municipal or union elections.[19]

With all this, the general pattern that emerged in the 1919 elections remained more or less stable throughout the interwar period. Votes for the Jewish parties in the election of 26 January 1919 are shown in Table 1.[20]

Eleven Jewish deputies were returned in this first Polish parliamentary election: 6 National Council (Zionists); 2 Orthodox (Agudah); 2 Folkists; and 1 Poale Zion. Deputies elected to the former Austrian parliament represented the still-disputed Eastern Galicia region, and they included two Jewish assimilationists.[21]

Agudah's electoral strength lay mostly in the area of former Congress Poland. In this area lived the Gerer Ḥasidim and some other smaller ḥasidic groups which, according to contemporary and retrospective accounts, formed the backbone of Agudah support. In later elections, when voting took place in all of the Polish territory, the general picture changed little, though the Agudah did develop some pockets of support in Eastern Galicia and Polish Lithuania. With some local variations (e.g., the strong popularity of the Folkists and their leader Prylucki in Warsaw), Agudah established itself in a solid if distant second place to the Zionists in Congress Poland.[22] In 1919 it returned deputies from the Lodz and Lublin districts (Rabbis Halpern and Perlmutter). Lack of a vote-sharing agreement with the Zionists prevented the election of a third Orthodox deputy (from the capital).

In Congress Poland, the most developed area of the country, the struggle between traditional and modernist ideologies was most intense, and lines were clearly drawn. Religious Jews found a more congenial atmosphere in the Zionist movement in Galicia and Polish Lithuania than in Congress Poland.[23] In addition, significant segments of Orthodox Jewry in Galicia maintained an anti-political or apolitical stance, preferring to leave politics to non-Jews or to secularist Jews. Personal factors may also account for Agudah's weakness outside Congress Poland. The Rebbe of Belz, leader of Galician Ḥasidism, did not wish to yield to the leadership of the Gerer Rebbe. Non-ḥasidic Lithuanian Orthodox Jews may have avoided associating with a party so clearly under ḥasidic domination, even if the heads of the major Lithuanian yeshivas also appeared in Agudah rabbinical councils.

In the elections of 1919, the political lineup of Polish Jewry had drastically changed. Jewish nationalists of various types swept the field and, with the exception of the holdovers from the Austrian parliament, assimilationism practically disappeared as a political force within Polish Jewry. If Agudah's claim to speak for the majority of Polish Jewry did not reflect political realities,[24] it had established itself as a major factor on the Polish Jewish political scene.

POLITICAL ORIENTATION AND STRATEGY

Jewish political strategy in independent Poland took two major directions: cooperation and confrontation. With some exceptions, the Galician Zionists, merchant groups, and Agudah tried to protect Jewish interests through cooperation with the government, while the Congress Poland Zionists, Bundists, and Folkists demonstratively opposed government policies.[25] Whichever strategy the parties adopted, they aimed at similar goals: protection of Jewish political rights, social-cultural autonomy, and national identity.

Within this general framework, Agudat Israel took its stand as a proud representative of the "old" Jewish politics and the political wisdom of past centuries. This stemmed both from the generally conservative tendencies of Agudah's leadership and its assessment of Jewish political clout as severely limited. Thus Agudah, with one major exception, pursued a minimalist political strategy based on the recognition that Jews still lived in a hostile environment. Legal emancipation and democratic elections did not alter the fact that the Jews were a people in Exile, the tent-dwelling Jacob dependent on the good graces of his wild brother Esau for survival. On numerous occasions, Agudah spokesmen enunciated this principle as the most realistic stance for Polish Jews:

> Orthodoxy sent its representatives to the Sejm and Senate to improve the Jewish situation in Poland. . . . But we must conduct our fight in a way which will enable us to come to an understanding. Our fight for our rights must be *tactical, honorable,* as befitting a people such as we are. *We* must be the ones to be sure to shape a better atmosphere for us in the Sejm. . . .[26]

Opposition for the sake of opposition was useless. Nor did intervention on behalf of individuals deserve the contempt heaped upon it. In an undated memorandum to the American Jewish Joint Distribution Committee (which appears to be from the early period of Polish independence), Agudah in Poland made the same points in a slightly different manner: Agudah represented Jews who wished to regulate all aspects of life according to tradition. Part of that tradition was for Jews to maintain a loyal attitude of peace and goodwill to the state. Jewish nationalist parties aimed at stimulating a secular national consciousness and weakening the hold of religion. Their struggle for national minority rights cast them into conflict with the policies of the state. This involved grave risks, particularly in a newly created state like Poland.[27]

Opponents of Agudah scoffed at its position as a shameful relic of a bygone era. For Zionist leader Yitzhak Gruenbaum, quiet diplomacy and personal intervention constituted craven submission by men who lacked the strength to speak in a loud voice about their suffering and could "only look with begging eyes at the Polish lord."[28]

For its part, Agudah regarded the activity of intercession *(shtadlanut)* as a necessary and honorable part of the work of any dedicated Jewish representative, and more effective than the "empty demonstrations" of its Zionist adversaries. It set as its goal the defense of Jewish rights in every way possible, to prevent injustice or harm to individual Jews or entire communities. If the circumstances demanded, personal intercession was a proper activity for a Jewish politician who daily heard the pleas and cries of the wronged.[29] This may partly explain why Agudah had some parliamentary representatives not fluent in Polish, since an important part of their job was providing a sympathetic ear for Jews' suffering, and the rabbis were admirably suited for this task.

The emphasis on behind-the-scenes intercession also makes it difficult to evaluate Agudah's successes and failures in this period. As the one-time secretary to the Agudah Sejm faction put it: Agudah claimed that its major successes lay in *preventing* worse things from happening, a difficult claim to disprove or substantiate.[30]

Acutely aware of both their vulnerability and their visibility as minority representatives, the small group of Jewish deputies prepared themselves for the opening of the Constituent Sejm. Symbolic of their uncomfortable position was their concern that Rabbi Perlmutter, as the oldest deputy present, would have to chair the Sejm until election of the marshal (speaker). The prospect of an elderly rabbi presiding over the first freely elected Polish parliament did not appeal to the sense of discretion of the Jewish deputies. Luckily the arrival of old Prince Radziwill in Warsaw ended the problem, as he preempted the position by seniority. Press reports noted, however, that Polish deputies were aware of the discomfiture of their Jewish colleagues.[31]

From the outset, Agudat Israel maintained a general policy of cooperation with other Jewish parties, while reserving for itself freedom of action and making no programmatic commitments. Thus, Agudah joined the Zionists and Folkists in the so-called Free Union of Deputies of Jewish Nationality, but would not accede to Zionist requests for an agreed-upon political program. Finally, all the factions agreed on urgent goals to be pursued in the immediate future. These included placement of Jewish representatives on key Sejm committees. The deputies decided to work to place Zionist deputy Yitzhak Gruenbaum on the constitution committee where he could safeguard Jewish interests during formulation of the new constitution. Rabbi Halpern of Agudah sought a seat on the military affairs committee where he believed he could best serve his Orthodox constituents by ensuring that Orthodox recruits could continue their religious observances whenever possible.[32]

Since the operating rules of the Sejm limited membership in the house committee (the so-called Konwent Seniorow) to clubs with twelve or more members, the Jewish deputies appeared to be shut out of important decisions, including committee assignments. A deadlock between the major Polish parties over the election of the marshal, however, enabled them to use their eleven votes to decide the issue, and thus gain some concessions. In this case, the candidate of the Polish Right promised the Jews the committee assignments they desired while the Center-Left candidate would not, so the Jewish club supported the right-wing candidate.[33] At least on this occasion, the limited prospects for achieving their major political demands forced all the Jewish parties into the position of bargaining for some concessions from the Polish majority.

Though they often decried the minimalist and moderate stance of Agudat Israel, the Zionists and Folkists also indulged in the same kind of intercessionary politics on an almost daily basis. Jewish politics in interwar Poland was conducted on two different planes: the "exalted" plane which related to minority rights, government subsidies, and equal participation in all aspects of Polish life; and the everyday plane which dealt with bureaucratic discrimination and softening the impact on individual Jews and Jewish institutions of burdensome legislation. The difference between Agudah and its adversaries lay in the fact that Agudah treated the everyday plane as an almost sacred calling while the Zionists regarded the "exalted" plane as their essential task and work on the more prosaic level as an unavoidable necessity.

The incident of the election of the Sejm marshal also brings out another point of the dispute between Agudah and its rivals. From the outset, Agudah questioned one of the axioms of the new Jewish parties, namely that the progressive forces on the Polish Left were natural allies of the Jews and would support their demands, and that the Jews should support the Left on general political and social questions.[34] The Sejm marshal incident proved that even the antisemitic Right could make concessions to the Jews, but it was generally regarded as a one-time exception. Agudah considered the identification with the Left as against Jewish interests, as *a priori* Jewish identification with one Polish political camp weakened their leverage. In addition, Agudah leaders wondered whether Jews necessarily had common interests with the Left. After all, the Jews were mostly small businessmen and artisans and their interests could conceivably clash with those of the workers and peasants.[35]

Agudah differed with other Jewish parties and the Left on the issue of a bicameral legislature, and supported proposals for an upper house. A Senate of more educated people could be expected to look beyond partisan concerns and realize the injurious effects on Poland of anti-Jewish regulations, as opposed to the "mass of half-illiterate peasants from Witos' party, who are always ready to vote for all decrees against Jews."[36]

Association with the Left was also opposed on the grounds that on crucial social issues, nether the Left nor the Right would support the Jews. The socialists might sign a few appeals or parliamentary questions to ministers, but for their own ideological reasons they, too, opposed Jewish national aspirations.[37] Moreover, implementation of the socialist program would lead to economic ruination of the Jewish community.[38] Agudah therefore followed an independent strategy, voting sometimes with the Left, sometimes with the Right, but in accordance with the Jewish interest in each case.[39]

In speeches from the Sejm rostrum, Agudah representatives tried to exemplify the ideal of *shtadlanut*: the general expression of confidence in the goodwill of the Polish majority, the statement of Jewish demands in non-provocative language, and vigorous responses to attacks on Judaism and Jewry.[40] Often Agudah deputy Rabbi Halpern responded with demonstrative applause or catcalls, neither of which found their way into the protocols, but which were noted by journalists.[41]

In general, though, Agudah's intercessionary tactics dictated that Orthodox representatives not make a determined public stand on most issues. Though they supported their Jewish colleagues in almost every case, Agudah deputies themselves took a public stand only when they believed a fundamental matter of Jewish dignity was at stake. Otherwise, they tried to win concessions either at the committee level or through intervention with public officials. Thus, Rabbi Perlmutter took the rostrum to denounce the not uncommon suggestion that Jews to "go to Palestine," and to assert that Jews might hope for the messianic call to return to Palestine but that in the present "it is our duty to live in this land, with the same rights and obligations as all others, in agreement and harmony with society as a whole."[42]

On another notable occasion, Rabbi Halpern took the floor to respond to a speech by Father Lutoslawski of the National Democrats, who had accused Judaism of teaching hatred for non-Jews.[43] Agudah could not let such charges go unanswered, despite a great reluctance to dignify them by making a formal reply. Rabbi Halpern delivered a fairly standard defense of supposedly anti-gentile passages in the Talmud, noting that since the Sejm was not a proper forum for theological dispute, these would be his only remarks on the subject.[44]

While working in their own way to promote general Jewish political goals, Agudah representatives made special efforts to defend the specific interests of the Orthodox community against perceived threats. For example, they denounced Yitzhak Gruenbaum's proposal to exclude clerics from the Sejm as an insult to Orthodoxy.[45] They also opposed the motion by socialists and some Jewish deputies that public schools be secular.[46] In interventions with government ministers, Agudah spokesman asked for protection of synagogues requisitioned by the army during the Polish-Soviet war,[47] and complained that, contrary to orders, Jewish soldiers did not receive leave for the holidays while in one camp Jewish soldiers were forced to sing Christian hymns.[48]

Their major effort in the religious field centered around achieivng official recognition of the ḥeder as fulfilling the requirements of the compulsory education law, an effort eventually crowned with success.[49]

The one major deviation from Agudah's established political approach took place in 1922. Lack of government action on even the most minimal Jewish demands plus an election law clearly designed to limit minority representation led a reluctant Agudat Israel to join, along with the Zionists, a larger National Minorities Bloc. On many occasions, Agudah spokesmen noted that joining the Bloc was a last resort, and that they preferred a united Jewish list, even if that meant reduced representation, rather than an association with other minority groups that openly expressed their hostility to the Polish state. Finally convinced that in the prevailing circumstances a separate Jewish list would lead to electoral disaster, Agudah assented to a purely technical bloc without programmatic elements.[50]

Even within the proposed Jewish club in the Sejm, Agudah demanded the right to follow its own views on matters of principle. In its election propaganda Agudat Israel tried to minimize the break from its earlier political line. Despite its entry into the coalition of minorities, Agudah claimed it had no further obligations to the other Jewish parties or national minorities: "Our policy in the Sejm remains the same—understanding with the Polish government and Polish society. We want to build our lives on the basis of friendly coexistence with our Polish fellow citizens for which we will spare no sacrifice."[51]

Because the Jewish parties took part in the Minorities Bloc, it is impossible to gauge the actual electoral strength of each party in the Bloc, but the positioning of Agudah candidates on election lists and the number of mandates Aguda received does give a general idea of its relative strength. On the basis of party affiliation, the thirty-five Jewish Sejm deputies divided up as follows:[52]

General Zionists	
a. E. Galicia	9
b. Minorities Bloc	6
Agudah	6
Mizrachi	6
Hitachdut Poale Zion	4
Nonpartisan	2
Merchants Union	1
Folkists	1

The strong Jewish showing was due in part to an election boycott by Ukrainians in East Galicia, which left the field open for the Jewish parties. Agudah was in a tie for second place ranking with the religious Zionist Mizrachi party. In December 1922, Agudah's representatives joined all other Jewish deputies (with the exception of Folkist deputy Prylucki) in the so-called *Kolo Zydowskie* (Jewish Circle) of the Sejm and Senate.

Both in the Sejm and within the *Kolo,* Agudah usually preferred to do its work quietly. In the period until the 1926 Pilsudski coup d'état, Agudah deputies spoke infrequently from the Sejm rostrum and generally did not embark on policy initiatives. They occasionally did dissent vociferously if policies under consideration directly threatened Orthodox interests. On such matters they continued to lobby government officials and to propose amendments in Sejm committees or in the Sejm chamber.[53] Their concerns included national standards for minimum salaries for rabbis,[54] noncombatant service for clergymen and theological students,[55] and provision of kosher food for Jewish prisoners.[56] An area of particular concern was that of Orthodox education, which, like other Jewish school systems, suffered from bureaucratic obstructionism and Polish noncompliance with commitments to provide proportional allocations of funds. Another part of Agudah parliamentary work involved representing the Jewish club on those committees assigned to Agudah by the *Kolo.*[57]

Despite a general commitment to Jewish political solidarity, Agudah could and did vote differently from its colleagues in the *Kolo.* On one notable occasion, both Agudah and some Mizrachi deputies split with the Kolo over a religious issue, and their votes determined the fate of the legislation in question. This occurred in 1924, when these religious deputies voted in favor of an amendment which struck from the law a paragraph allowing a religionless oath of allegiance for nonreligious recruits. The other Jewish deputies opposed the amendment.[58]

Agudah's one major political initiative in the interwar period was its alliance with the Pilsudski camp in the wake of the 1926 coup. Although the new regime did not carry out any quick solution of Jewish grievances, the changed atmosphere led Agudah to seek an alliance with the regime as an alternative to its reluctant membership in the Minorities Bloc. This did not mean that Agudah abandoned independent politics altogether. In the elections of 1928 and 1930, Agudah candidates ran on the list of the Non-Party Bloc in Cooperation with the Government (BBWR) as well as on an independent Jewish national list. This mixed strategy fitted in with Agudah's general aim of seeking an accommodation with the Polish majority while standing up for Jewish interests. From its pragmatic view of politics, Agudah saw little future for Minorities Bloc politics. Despite the impressive electoral achievements of 1922, the Bloc had gained little on the legislative front, while deputies working on a private level had done much to better the situation of Jews. Jewish deputies elected on a list the government regarded as hostile could not expect much success in intercessionary activity.[59]

The alliance between Aguda and the Pilsudski camp was based on common values and ideologies, optimism and wishful thinking. As a fairly conservative, business-backed, "nonpartisan" Jewish political movement, Agudah did not find it hard to identify in principle with a regime that preached nonpartisan, competent government for the whole country and made imprecise but frequent proclamations about a just Polish society.[60] For its part, the BBWR wished to line up sympathetic representatives of the national minorities behind its call for national solidarity.

Though still pessimistic about the possibilities of immediate major changes in the Jewish situation in Poland, Agudah regarded the invitation to join the BBWR list as an unprecedented action by a major Polish group, a move toward ending chauvinistic politics and towards carrying out the provisions of the Polish constitution.[61]

The moderate, loyalist stance of Agudah may have misled the Pilsudski camp into thinking that Agudah had no significant political demands of its own. Government reports and publications on Jewish political groups stressed that Agudah regarded loyalty to the government as a religious duty and that its ideology was dominated by the religious factor to the virtual exclusion of social and political matters.[62] In the long run, neither side got what it expected from this pact. Agudah could not "deliver" the Jewish vote for the Sanacja, while it continued to voice frequent criticism of government policies. The Pilsudski camp, though it was far preferable to the National Democrats, still did little to deal with longstanding Jewish political grievances. In 1928 and in 1930, however, Agudah saw an alliance with the Sanacja as the best possible option.

In the elections of 1928 and 1930, all the Jewish parties suffered major setbacks, but Agudah suffered more than most. In 1928 its list received a respectable 184,000 votes (in alliance with the Folkists and Merchants Union), but returned no deputies. One Agudah deputy was returned on the BBWR list.[63] Total Jewish Sejm representation fell from thirty-five to fifteen. The elections of 1930 witnessed a further diminution of Jewish representation (seven elected on independent lists, three on the BBWR list). Agudah returned two deputies (one independent, one BBWR).[64]

In this period, Agudah activity in the Sejm followed the tactics introduced by its deputy Eliahu Kirshbraun, one of the major architects of the pact with the Sanacja: careful cataloging of Jewish needs and grievances accompanied by expressions of trust in the goodwill of the Pilsudski camp. From the Sejm rostrum its deputies complained of anti-Jewish discrimination in government service,[65] in the universities, and in taxation policies.[66] They noted the laughable sums allocated by the Religions Ministry for Jewish religious needs.[67] They tempered these laments with expressions of confidence in the regime.

The Agudah press blamed the failure of the government to act on Jewish demands on such factors as the heritage of the pre-Pilsudski coup era,[68] interference by lower-echelon bureaucrats,[69] or preoccupation with the economic crisis.[70] In the end, Agudah deputies could only express hopes for fulfillment of the ideal of Polish-Jewish cooperation.[71] and redouble their efforts at intercession to aid individuals in distress.

Throughout the entire interwar period, Agudat Israel was also active in the sphere of municipal government.[72] The scattered and partial sources available demonstrate that the nature of municipal politics differed in several important respects from national parliamentary politics, and this had a direct effect on Agudah's activities in this sphere. Jewish population concentrations in Polish cities[73] meant potentially fairer Jewish representation in the municipalities than in the national elections where minority group strength was diluted. On the other hand, municipal elections strongly reflected local concerns, which meant that in addition to the usual political parties a host of neighborhood or local professional and splinter religious groups participated.[74] Furthermore, in the major cities, the Jewish Left (Bund and Poale Zion) consistently showed greater strength in municipal elections than in Sejm elections.

Agudah policies on the municipal level were in part a reaction to these different conditions. First of all, there was a constantly shifting array of alliances between the various Jewish parties, which had no relation to the situation in Sejm, and at times even ran counter to the coalition in the Sejm.[75] The strong presence of the Jewish Left gave Agudah an additional serious rival which, what is more, made no effort to conceal its hostility to Orthodoxy. The Left made anti-Orthodox proposals in the city councils and did its best to prevent the granting of allocations to Orthodox institutions.[76]

As in the parliament, Jewish municipal representatives had to carry on a continuous struggle to get even a semblance of equal treatment for the Jewish areas. The rough-and-tumble politics of the Polish Right was even less restrained in the city councils than in the Sejm; hence, in the mid-twenties we find attempts to outlaw Jewish ritual slaughter on the local level, a decade before attempts to do so on the national level.[77] The more openly antisemitic tenor of some of the debates generated a slightly more militant stance on the part of Agudah.[78] On the other hand, the fact that the city council dealt with bread-and-butter issues of streets, lighting, hospital care, etc., meant that the Jewish councilmen could achieve a modicum of success in getting their requests accepted. Agudah councilmen such as Eliahu Kirshbraun excelled in presenting

Jewish needs in a manner which showed not just what Jews demanded from the city, but the economic advantages to the city administration brought by the Jewish institutions whose support was sought.[79] At least until official antisemitism began to prevail in the mid-thirties, such pragmatic arguments could on occasion bring results.

In the last four years of the interwar period the Jewish position in Poland deteriorated greatly. Anti-Jewish agitation increased, and calls for boycotting Jews and for Jewish emigration came from the government camp as well as from the right-wing opposition. The influence of parliament in general and of the reduced Jewish delegation in particular declined still further.[80] In the case of Agudah, after the death of Pilsudski in 1935, the alliance with the Sanacja lost most of its luster, and finally broke down when its successor movement—the Camp of National Unity (OZON)—became openly anti-Jewish.

Agudah continued its policies of speaking out on matters of Jewish honor and pursuing personal intervention on all manner of grievances, but with little success. The final blow to the policy of trust was the 1936 campaign waged against *shehita* which culminated in restrictive legislation.[81] Agudah suffered a great defeat in this affair, and it suffered some reversals in the Kehillah elections of 1936, as did all the other Jewish parties which had representatives in the Sejm. The Bund, on the other hand, greatly increased its electoral strength on the basis of protest votes. Until the outbreak of the war, the few remaining Agudah deputies continued their activities of intercession, although with greatly lowered expectations. Both in the Sejm and the city councils, they sounded the Jewish cry of distress.

Agudat Israel, the party of tradition, followed the political tactics used throughout the centuries of Diaspora Jewish history. The policy of *shtadlanut* was designed for protecting Jewish interests in a hostile political atmosphere. By patiently, proudly but tactfully presenting Jewish needs, Agudah hoped to meet some of those needs—or, failing that, to protect Orthodox institutions and prevent any further erosion of the Jewish position. Seen in this light, Agudah's historic alliance with the Pilsudski camp was the one potentially attractive alternative among the limited political options open to Orthodox Jewry.

Agudah hoped for much, but expected little. Agudah's failure was part of a more general failure of all the Jewish parties, right and left, Zionist and non-Zionist, socialist and non-socialist, and reflects the failure of the Second Polish Republic to reach a modus vivendi with the numerous minorities within its borders. In such an atmosphere, neither militance nor moderation had any chance of success. Even in failure, though, Agudah leaders felt that they had performed their religious mission as faithful emissaries of the community and, as such, served as an "address" and rallying point for traditional Jews trying to cope with political, economic and ideological upheaval.

Notes

1. See the contemporary accounts by A. Hafftka in I. Schiper *et al.* (eds.), *Zydzi w Polsce Odrodzonej* (Warsaw, 1933), vol. 2, pp. 249–311; Leopold Halpern, *Polityka Zydowska w Sejmie i Senacie Rzeczypospolitej 1919–1933;* Simon Segal, *The New Poland and the Jews* (New York, 1938), pp. 181–85. Most later accounts draw heavily on these surveys. A series of partisan essays on Jewish political ideologies can be found in Basil Vlavianos and Feliks Gross (eds.), *Struggle for Tomorrow* (New York, 1954). The pioneering work on Agudat Israel was done by Ezra Mendelsohn in his article, "The Politics of Agudas Yisroel in Inter-War Poland," *Soviet Jewish Affairs* vol. II, no. 2 (1972) pp. 47–60.

2. Alexander Carlebach, "A German Rabbi Goes East," *Leo Baeck Institute Year Book* VI (1961), p. 62.

3. David Flinker, *Varsha* (Jerusalem, 1947/48), pp. 134–35.

4. Ḥasidic leader Abraham Mordecai Alter (1866–1948) whose headquarters was in the Polish city Gora Kalwaria (Hebrew, Gur; Yiddish, Ger).

5. Cf. Salo W. Baron, *A Social and Religious History of the Jews* (first edition: New York, 1937), vol. II, p. 393.

6. See *Morgen-Zhurnal* (New York), 10 August 1941, p. 5.

7. Letter of Crown Marshal W. Niemojowski of 20 February 1917, reproduced in Hillel Seidman, *Zydowskie Szkolnictwo Religijne* (Warsaw, 1937), pp. 9–10.

8. N. Zohar, "Agudat Yisrael be-Varsha," in Y. Grunbaum (ed.), *Entsiklopedia shel galuyot: Varsha,* vol. VI, part 2 (Jerusalem, 1959), col. 242.

9. Letter by Polish observer dated 28 June 1918, appendix to Moshe Landau, *Ha-yehudim kemi'ut le'umi be-folin* (Ph.D. diss., Hebrew University, Jerusalem, 1972), p. 271.

10. *Jewish Chronicle* (London) 21 March 1919, p. 8.

11. *Der Moment,* 9 January 1919, p. 3.

12. *Ibid.,* 23 January 1919, p. 2.

13. See, e.g., *Haynt* (afternoon edition), 26 January 1919, p. 1.

14. *Der Moment,* 9 February 1919, pp. 3–4.

15. Interview with Dr. Hillel Seidman (one-time secretary to the Agudah Sejm delegation) 29 January 1976.

16. For personal data on Agudah deputies, see Tadeusz Rzepecki, *Sejm i Senat 1922–27,* pp. 186, 297, 305, 334, 375–76. See also Hillel Seidman, *Ishim she-hikarti* (Jerusalem, 1970), pp. 271–75; personal archive of Lejzor Sirkis, Central Archives for the History of the Jewish People (Jerusalem), microfilm HM 9976.

17. See, e.g., *Eleh ezkera* (New York, 1956), vol. I, p. 110.

18. See Ludwik Hass, *Wybory Warszawskie 1918–1926* (Warsaw, 1972).

19. Ezra Mendelsohn, "Polin," in Jacob Tsur (ed.), *Hatefutsah: mizrah eiropah* (Jerusalem, 1976), p. 207.

20. A. Hafftka, "Zycie Parlamentarne Zydow," in I. Schiper (ed.), *Zydzi w Polsce Odrodzonej,* vol. II, p. 289. At the time of the elections for the Constituent Sejm in 1919, the borders of the newly independent Polish republic were far from fixed, with large territories under dispute with several neighboring countries. The areas of signficant Jewish population where the 1919 elections did take place were former Congress Poland and part of former Austrian Poland (Western Galicia). Congress Poland signifies the area of central Poland which, after the Congress of Vienna, was reconstituted as a kingdom under the tsar of Russia, but with certain limited autonomy (until 1863). Its territory includes the major centers Warsaw and Lodz. The province of Galicia constitutes former Austrian Poland. At the time of the 1919 elections, only the western part of the province was under Polish control, while in the eastern half of the province Poles and Ukrainians struggled for hegemony. Since no vote took place in Eastern Galicia, members of the Austrian Reichsrat from that region were coopted into the Constituent Sejm.

21. L. Halpern, *Polityka Zydowska,* pp. 7–8.

22. L. Hass, *Wybory Warszawskie,* Table 17 (between pp. 68–69).

23. Ezra Mendelsohn, *Zionism in Poland—The Formative Years, 1915–1926* (New Haven, 1981), pp. 177–78.

24. *Haynt,* 31 January 1919, p. 3.

25. See Ezra Mendelsohn, "The Dilemma of Jewish Politics in Poland: Four Responses," in B. Vago and G. Mosse (eds.), *Jews and Non-Jews in Eastern Europe 1918–1945* (New York, 1974), pp. 203–19.

26. *Der Yid,* 30 March 1923 (yr. 5, # 76 [956]).

27. Archives of the American Jewish Joint Distribution Committee (New York), File 346, "Poland—Culture and Religion."

28. Y. Grunbaum, *Milhamot yehudei polania* (Jerusalem, 1941), p. 289.

29. *Der Moment,* 14 February 1922, p. 3.

30. Interview with Dr. Hillel Seidman, 29 January 1976.

31. *Haynt,* 13 February 1919, p. 3.

32. Jacob Shatzky, "Yidishe politik in Poilen," in *Algemeyne entsiklopedie* (New York, 1950), vol. IX, col. 219; *Haynt,* 10 February 1919, p. 2; 19 February 1919, p. 3.

33. A. Hartglass, "Milhamot yehudei polen," in I. Halpern (ed.), *Beit yisrael be-folin* (Jerusalem, 1948), vol. I, p. 136.

34. Y. Grunbaum, "Yidishe politik," in *Haynt yubiley-bukh* (Warsaw, 1928), pp. 64–65; L. Halpern, *Polityka Zydowska,* p. 15.

35. *Der Yid,* 2 November 1920, pp. 3–4.

36. *Ibid.,* 21 October 1920, p. 2.

37. *Ibid.,* 17 November 1920, p. 3.

38. *Ibid.,* 24 November 1920, p. 2.

39. *Ibid.,* 12 November 1920, p. 4.

40. See the speech by Rabbi Perlmutter, *Sprawozdanie Stenograficzne Sejmu Ustawodawczego* [SSSU], 24 February 1919; see also Isaac Lewin, *Tsu der geshikhte fun Agudas Yisroel* (New York, 1963/64), pp. 24–25.

41. *Haynt,* 24 February 1919, p. 3.

42. SSSU, 27 May 1919, cols. 4–6.

43. *Der Yid,* 29 October 1920, p. 4.

44. SSSU, 2 December 1920, col. 41.

45. *Der Yid,* 29 October 1920, p. 4.

46. *Ibid.,* 17 March 1921, p. 3.

47. *Ibid.,* 10 October 1920, p. 4.
48. *Ibid.,* 11 October 1920, p. 4.
49. *Ibid.,* 6 July 1921, p. 3.
50. *Ibid.,* 13 October 1922, p. 6.
51. *Ibid.,* 20 October 1922, p. 5.
52. A. Hafftka, "Zycie Parlamentarne Zydow," pp. 293–95.
53. For committee assignments, see *Haynt,* 15 December 1922, p. 2.
54. *Der Yid,* 19 March 1923, p. 3.
55. SSSU, okres I, session 97; 8 February 1924, cols. 8–9, 23.
56. *Haynt,* 7 February 1924, p. 3.
57. *Ibid.,* 10 February 1924, p. 4.
58. SSSU, okres I, session 123, 3 June 1924, col. 23 and appendix; *Haynt,* 4 June 1924, p. 3.
59. *Der Yid,* 16 December 1927.
60. Joseph Rothschild, *East Central Europe Between the Two World Wars* (Seattle, 1974), pp. 57–59. See *Der Yid,* 26 September 1927, p. 6.
61. L. Halpern, *Polityka Zydowska,* pp. 32–33; *Der Yid,* 29 January 1928, p. 6; 27 March 1928.
62. See report on Jewish political parties, "Archiwum Akt Nowych" (Warsaw)—Interior Ministry, Organizational Department, Nationalities Division, file 1062. See also S. J. Paprocki (ed.), *Minority Affairs and Poland* (Warsaw, 1935), pp. 148–49.
63. A. Hafftka, "Zycie Parlamentarne Zydow," pp. 299–300.
64. L. Halpern, *Polityka Zydowska,* pp. 41–42.
65. *Dos Yidishe Togblat,* 16 December 1933, p. 1.
66. *Ibid.,* 7 November 1932, p. 4; 8 November 1932, p. 4; 6 November 1933, p. 3.
67. SSSU, session 3, 16 December 1930, col. 102.
68. *Dos Yidishe Togblat,* 12 February 1932, p. 2.
69. *Ibid.,* 8 November 1934, p. 4.
70. *Ibid.,* 4 March 1932, p. 4.
71. *Ibid.,* 6 November 1933, p. 3; 8 November 1934, p. 4; 8 February 1935, p. 10.
72. See, e.g., Joseph Kermisz, "Di yidishe reprezentants in varshever shtotrat," in A. Tartakower (ed.), *Sefer ha-shanah/Yorbukh* III (1970), pp. 279–93.
73. See Jacob Lestchinsky, "The Jews in the Cities of the Republic," *YIVO Annual of Jewish Social Science* I (1946), pp. 156–77.
74. L. Hass, *Wybory Warszawskie,* p. 87.
75. See, e.g., *Haynt,* 13 May 1923, p. 4.
76. See, e.g., *Haynt,* 1 December 1922, p. 9; *Moment,* 6 December 1921, p. 5.
77. *Moment,* 5 March 1926, p. 2; *Der Yid,* 29 January 1928, p. 4.
78. See, e.g., *Der Yid,* 21 January 1921, p. 3.
79. *Der Yid,* 15 May 1921, p. 3; *Dos Yidishe Togblat,* 21 February 1932, p. 8; 7 March 1933, p. 5.
80. J. Shatzky, "Yidishe politik," col. 237; Antony Polonsky, *Politics in Independent Poland* (Oxford, 1972), p. 397.
81. *Dos Yidishe Togblat,* 27 February 1936, p. 2; 6 March 1936, pp. 1–2, 10, 12; 19 March 1936, p. 6.

Ritual Variation among Modern Orthodox Jews in the United States

Samuel C. Heilman and Steven M. Cohen
(QUEENS COLLEGE, CUNY)

While many outsiders view Orthodox Jewry as a monolith, the Orthodox, like Jewry in general, are characterized by distinctions and divisions. Many of the important differences among them can be arrayed on a continuum. On one end are those who wish to be *of* as well as *in* the larger society; at the other end are those who seek *segregation.* "In order to protect their souls [they have] attempted to fence in their members and fence out the secular."[1] And in the center are those who dualistically and with ambivalence try to be both cosmopolitan and parochial, modern and Orthodox.

For contemporary Orthodox Jews, many of whom see themselves as living a life guided by Halakhah (Jewish law, literally, the way) and shaped by its observances—a life which many of them call "Torah-true"—the great challenge has been to come to terms with the situation of modernity in which all of them find themselves. Some, the "modern Orthodox," have tried to find a middle course, a way to remain true to what they see as the demands of sacred tradition while avoiding social insularity. They seek to be both cosmopolitan and parochial, an approach once enunciated by Moses Mendelsohn: "Comply with the customs and civil constitutions of the countries in which you are transplanted, but at the same time, be constant to the faith of your forefathers."[2] Many would agree with Ephraim Sturm, executive director of the Young Israel movement, that "the Torah as a divine document must perforce be livable and applicable in all societies. The trick of course is to separate the eternal concepts of Torah from those things which were products of Europe and its self-contained Jewish community."[3] And many would undoubtedly also concur with Rabbi Dr. Norman Lamm, president of Yeshiva University, a major modern

Orthodox institution, who wrote that they "must be receptive to new ideas, honest questions, and novel situations."[4]

Others, the "traditionalist Orthodox," emphatically reject in their rhetoric an obligation to be a part of secular culture. For them, the modern world and host society are at best a "background setting for Torah" but by no means something of which they wish to be actively a part.[5] These are Jews who see "the worlds of Halakhah and American life as mutually exclusive paths incapable of integration within the lifestyle of the individual."[6] "The 'traditionalists' are characterized by an attitude of disdain toward any attempt at compromising ritual with the demands of the contemporary outside world. Unlike the 'modern Orthodox' they feel perfectly at home with the most rigid of halakhic prescriptions."[7]

Yet while there may be differences between the modernist and traditionalist trends in Orthodoxy, "they agree in making the symbol of the Torah, representing the element of continuity, primary to Judaism and central to the definition of a Jew."[8] "When confronted with a contradiction between a halakhic statement and a sociological trend or scientific 'truth', Torah, as it has always been understood, must prevail."[9] That is, the official rhetoric of Orthodoxy, traditionalist and modern, articulates an ideological commitment to the way of tradition, ritual, and Halakhah.

Heretofore, a considerable literature has explored traditionalist Orthodox Jews (particularly the Ḥasidim), those who seek to remain culturally and socially (although not economically) apart from the contemporary world. However, only recently have some social scientists turned their attention to those whom we have called the modern Orthodox Jews, those who fashion an accommodation between the perceived ideal of Judaism as an all-encompassing life-form and the contemporary world.

On some matters modern Orthodox Jews conform to the beliefs and practices of their traditionalist counterparts. In others, the two groups diverge. Insofar as they do, we might surmise that some modern Orthodox Jews experience a sense of "falling short" or "not living up to" their self-imposed obligation to follow traditional Jewish laws and practices to the letter. On the other hand, many of them resemble, in several ways, those who may be called nominally Orthodox or even non-Orthodox. In each instance, modern Orthodox Jews distinguish themselves from what they perceive to be the extremes of the modernist "left" and the traditionalist "right." Precisely how they relate their accommodation to the extremes, the nature of their compromises, and the limits of flexibility are analyzed below.

One area crucial to the lives of modern Orthodox Jews and to distinctions among them is, of course, that of ritual practice. In this paper, we try to accomplish two related research aims in this area. First, we attempt to simply demonstrate the existence of a perceivable and structured gradient of ritual observance among the modern Orthodox. For those (primarily outsiders) who are unclear as to how highly ordered distinctions among modern Orthodox Jews manifest themselves in ritual practice (or who may be unclear about whether significant distinctions in religious practice even characterize the modern Orthodox), our documentation and description of ritual distinctions among those we shall term "nominal," "mainstream," and "traditionalist" Orthodox should prove instructive.

Second, we also demonstrate how social factors other than the symbolic or religious significance of certain ritual practices operate to influence the frequency with which they are performed by various subgroups within the modern Orthodox. Thus, many (including, perhaps, most insiders) might think that modern Orthodox Jews, whose rhetoric speaks of devoted adherence to ancient Jewish religious law and whose practice sets them apart not only from the larger society but from other American Jews as well, are primarily influenced in their choice of which religious norms to follow primarily by symbolic considerations. We demonstrate that other factors—such as the ability of the Orthodox community to punish transgression or award compliance with religious law or the social costs entailed in performing certain practices—have powerful influences upon the frequency with which many rituals are undertaken.

This paper, then, focuses on important differences in ritual practice among varieties of modern Orthodox Jews.[10] We will attempt to derive from the analysis of our data a sense of how people come to grips with tradition in the contemporary context, of how those we term "cosmopolitan parochials" cope with and commonly resolve the tensions of simultaneously living in different worlds.

THE DATA

In 1979 and 1980 we conducted surveys of several samples of American Jews, most of whom were Orthodox. We began by administering mail-back questionnaires to mailing lists supplied by an association of Orthodox professionals, an Orthodox periodical, a Young Israel synagogue in the Boston area, and a modern Orthodox synagogue in northern New Jersey. We also administered the questionnaire to students in a Queens College class in the sociology of American Jewry and we surveyed the membership (again through the mails) of a "right-wing" Conservative synagogue in Queens, New York.

From these samples we collected approximately 570 interviews in roughly equal number from all sources, with the exception of the college class, which supplied only 18 completed questionnaires. We then initiated a preliminary analysis of the data, modifying our conceptualization of the study. As a result, we made some minor changes in the questionnaire, dropping a few items and adding some others.[11]

We then mailed the revised questionnaire to approximately 1,000 members of Lincoln Square Synagogue on Manhattan's fashionable Upper West Side. The synagogue is a vital congregation with large numbers of young couples and singles, many of whom, it is thought, derive from non-Orthodox backgrounds and prior affiliations. After mailing two waves of questionnaires, we obtained completed interviews from approximately 490 respondents. These comprise the largest single source of the 1,023 usable interviews.[12]

Very traditional Orthodox Jews are almost totally unrepresented in our study. We have few, if any, ḥasidic Jews or those affiliated with the traditionalist Agudat Israel movement. Thus, most of our sample is from the more modern wing of Orthodoxy in the northeastern United States. Our best educated guess is that the type of Orthodox Jews we are examining represents not more than 5% of American Jewry (about 8%–10% of American Jewry is Orthodox and we have largely excluded the 5% or so who are highly traditional and insulated).

We make no claim to accurately represent this universe, vague as its definition might be. Modern Orthodox Jews in the New York and Boston areas may well be more or less observant, insular, or politically conservative (or liberal). We simply do not know either how to define precisely the boundaries of American modern Orthodoxy or, as a result, whether our sample accurately represents that community. We therefore make only very modest demands of our data, demands which we believe are commensurate with the very modest quality of our sampling. That is, as we discuss below, we have defined within our sample a non-Orthodox control group, one which neither regards itself as Orthodox nor meets our criteria for Orthodox observance. We have divided the remaining 665 Orthodox respondents into three subgroups (nominals, centrists, and traditionalists) on the basis of their ritual observance. Our analysis focuses upon differences between these four groups. We readily admit that the distribution of these groups in the American Orthodox community may well differ from that found in our sample (we have placed about 60% of our Orthodox respondents in the middle group of "centrists" with roughly equal proportions of about 20% in the two wings of "nominals" and "traditionalists"). However, we do contend that the patterns of variation and the broad conclusions we draw are generally applicable to the larger world of contemporary modern Orthodoxy in the United States.

THE CENTRALITY OF RITUAL PRACTICES: COUNTING MITZVAS

Our decision to contrast centrist or mainstream modern Orthodox with traditionalists and the nominally Orthodox immediately raised the question of how to find boundaries (somewhat real, somewhat imputed) among these groups. There are various ways of going about this task. We could define the groups for research purposes solely in terms of their theological beliefs, that is, the extent of commitment to particular fundamental tenets of faith (such as belief in God, confidence in revelation at Mount Sinai, or conviction about the coming of the Messiah). Alternatively, we could have measured social involvement in a segregated Orthodox community consisting of family, friends, neighbors, coworkers, and communal institutions.

We chose instead to define the three Orthodox groups—the "traditionalists," "centrists," and "nominals"—in terms of ritual practice, what insiders call "the observance of mitzvas." We felt that we had good substantive reasons for preferring ritual practice—mitzvas—over beliefs and social ties as a starting point. Most critically, Orthodox norms strongly emphasize practice, and the ethos of praxis has become an integral part of the taken-for-granted reality of Orthodox Jewish life.

The centrality of ritual practice is also apparent in the extraordinary attention Orthodox Jews pay not only to their own ritual practice, but also to that of their neighbors, friends, and kin.[13] Insiders easily locate themselves and others on the traditionalist-modern continuum by noting performance of key indicator rituals in conjunction with an implicit standard of ritual observance. Particular observances may not be the most important in the doctrinal sphere, but they do indicate to the insider a pattern of ritual behavior which is usually consistent with a particular religious profile.

We demonstrate that between the ritually very active traditionalists and the relatively less observant nominals lies a complex middle ground occupied by the mainstream of the modern Orthodox. Although they vary considerably among themselves in several aspects of Jewish identity and commitment, they also differ considerably in several crucial ways from their Orthodox counterparts to the modernist "left" or traditionalist "right."

THE CENTER AND THE EXTREMES: BOUNDARY-SETTING RITUALS

Our questionnaire asks respondents about a wide range of Jewish ritual practices. Some of these are in fact observed by many, if not most, American Jews; others are practiced by very few, primarily the traditionalist Orthodox. We could have chosen to classify our respondents in terms of all the available ritual practices. However, such a procedure would have precluded further examining variation in ritual practice among Orthodox Jews. One of our key research questions—the one we address in this paper—is to discover which rituals in fact typify each of the three Orthodox groups. By using only a few indicator rituals to define all three groups, we can still examine how the observance of other rituals—the ones we left out of our index—varies across Orthodoxy.

With this strategy in mind, we first separated the Orthodox (N = 665) from the non-Orthodox (N = 358). Respondents were asked whether they saw themselves as "Orthodox," "Conservative," "Reform," or something else. Only those who answered "Orthodox" qualified for inclusion in one of the three Orthodox groups.

Among the self-defined Orthodox, we constructed our index by counting the practice of seven indicative observances. We make no claims for the theological centrality of these observances; we simply find them to be useful and statistically reliable sociological indicators of Orthodoxy. As such, they must be viewed not as ends in and of themselves but rather as research tools. Two of them (1 and 2 below) deal with fasting on commemorative holidays, three (3, 4, and 5) pertain to dietary laws, and the last two (6 and 7) concern observance of the Sabbath.

(1) *Fasting on the Tenth of Tevet:* This is a minor fast day commemorating the first siege of Jerusalem by the Babylonian king Nebuchadnezzar. Consistent with sex-linked patterns in our data as well as cultural norms of Orthodoxy, we awarded one point in our index to men who fasted a whole day on this holiday and one point to women who fasted at least part of the day.

(2) *Fasting on Tisha B'av:* This a major fast day which commemorates the destruction of the two Holy Temples in 586 B.C.E. and 70 C.E. respectively. Men who fasted the entire fast and women who fasted at least part of the day received one point on our index of Orthodoxy.

(3) *Refraining from eating cold salads at the home of a friend where kashrut is not observed:* Distinctions between "recipe knowledge" and formal religious laws of behavior abound in connection with

Jewish dietary laws and customs. In practice, some Orthodox Jews make use of a degree of latitude provided in the formal legal system in connection with cold foods such as salads which are not rendered unkosher by contact with non-kosher utensils. Those who refrained from utilizing this latitude received a point on our index.

(4) *Refraining from eating warm "kosher" food cooked at the home of a friend where kashrut is not observed:* Eating food which is kosher prior to cooking but which has been cooked in a non-kosher kitchen entails for most Orthodox a breach of traditional religious law and contemporary custom. Those who refrained from doing so received a point on our index.

(5) *Maintaining two sets of dishes for meat and dairy:* Those who observed this prescription have what most Orthodox regard as the minimal requisites of a kosher home, and received a point on our index.

(6) *Refraining from turning lights on during the Sabbath:* Commensurate with prevailing Orthodox interpretation of Biblical and rabbinic prohibitions against using fire on the Sabbath, those who practiced this observance received one point on our index.

(7) *Refraining from "going to work on your job" on the Sabbath:* This observance, based on the premise that the Sabbath is a holy day of rest, also earned the respondent one point on the index of Orthodoxy.

Both empirical and substantive reasons led us to choose these particular indicators of Orthodoxy. Empirically, we found wide variations in the frequencies of performance. Two of the practices—fasting on the Tenth of Tevet and refraining from eating even a cold salad in a non-kosher home—were observed infrequently in our sample. (The proportions are only 43% and 35% among all our Orthodox respondents.) The Tisha B'Av fast, refraining from turning lights on and off on the Sabbath, and refraining from eating warm foods in a non-kosher home were observed with about the same high level of frequency among the Orthodox (85%, 82%, and 74% respectively). Virtually all those who called themselves "Orthodox" kept the last two practices (not going to work on the Sabbath = 93%, and two sets of dishes = 96%). Thus we can speak of "hard" and "easy" criteria of Orthodoxy. To qualify as "traditionalist Orthodox" on our scale, respondents had to pass hard as well as easy tests; they had to observe all seven rituals. Those we called "centrist Orthodox" performed most (four) of the rituals; that is, they passed moderate to easy tests. Finally, those whom we defined as "nominally Orthodox" performed a minority (three or fewer) of these rituals, clustered around the "easy" set of observances, but nevertheless identified themselves denominationally as "Orthodox."

Our substantive reasons for choosing these particular rituals derive

Table 1. Seven Ritual Practices Used to Construct the Orthodoxy Index

	Degree of Orthodoxy			
	% Non-Orth.	% Nominal	% Centrist	% Traditional
Fasting on the 10th of Tevet				
Men (whole day/part day)	0/2	3/18	53/26	100/0
Women (whole day/part day)	0/1	0/0	15/27	66/34
Fasting on Tisha B'Av				
Men (whole day/part day)	7/19	31/34	95/3	100/0
Women (whole day/part day)	8/17	29/34	78/18	100/0
No cold salads at non-kosher friends' homes	6	5	20	100
No warm "kosher" foods at non-kosher friends' homes	8	16	79	100
Two sets of dishes	54	80	99	100
Never goes to work on Sabbath	47	70	97	100
Never turns on lights on the Sabbath	2	18	92	100
Approx. N =	358	110	410	145

in part from our understanding of community norms and practices—recipe knowledge. According to it, Orthodox Jews see keeping kosher and Sabbath observance as cornerstones of religious commitment. Their transgression virtually guarantees exclusion from Orthodoxy. Insiders also recognize different degrees of keeping kosher and Sabbath observances; gradations which they use, at least tacitly, to label and identify themselves and one another.

The other components in the scale revolve around two fast days—Tisha B'Av and the Tenth of Tevet. "The general effect of fasting, apart from its obvious physiological consequences, is to produce a kind of corporate solidarity among those who manage to hold out."[14] Thus, fasting serves as a kind of boundary mechanism, a means by which those who fast separate themselves from others.

Table 1 permits a clearer understanding of how we defined the three groups of Orthodox Jews, and by implication, how we constructed the ritual observance boundaries separating them.

As noted above, traditionalist Orthodox Jews, by definition and in line with the strict demands of Jewish tradition, performed all rituals. The centrist modern Orthodox differed from them primarily in their failure to perform the two most stringent, least popular practices (the Tevet fast and eating no cold salads in non-kosher homes). Only about half the centrist modern Orthodox met the sex-specific criteria for fasting on the minor fast day, and as few as 20% claimed that they do not eat cold salads in non-kosher homes. (Clearly, they must fail to meet at least one of these "hard" tests, otherwise they would probably qualify as traditionalist Orthodox.) These practices, then, are the two rituals in our index which served most frequently to separate traditionalists from the centrists.

While divided on the two "hard" rituals, nearly all the centrists qualified on all the other rituals. Thus, almost every one (95%) of the centrist men reported fasting the entire day of Tisha B'Av and a similar number (96%) of the centrist women fasted at least a part of the day. Almost all (92%) of the centrists "never" turned lights on and off on the Sabbath. Similarly nearly all (97%) never went to their job on that day and 99% kept two sets of dishes. A substantial majority (79%) did not eat warm kosher foods in non-kosher homes. (Apparently, more centrists maintain ties with the non-kosher world than do traditionalists.)

The two most widely observed practices in the table—not going to work on the Sabbath and keeping two sets of dishes—distinguished the nominally Orthodox from both the non-Orthodox and from the rest of the Orthodox. These two practices were almost universally observed among the traditionalists and centrists, but among the nominals—those who at the very least call themselves Orthodox—a noticeable minority worked on the Sabbath or had no separate dishes. Nevertheless, more of them observed these practices (70% and 80%) than the non-Orthodox (47% and 54%).

In short, typical centrist Orthodox respondents never worked on the Sabbath, had two sets of dishes (for meat and dairy), fasted on Tisha B'Av (and possibly although not necessarily on the Tenth of Tevet), did not turn lights on and off on the Sabbath, and were unlikely to eat warm foods in non-kosher homes, but would eat cold salads there. Hardly any nominally Orthodox Jews fasted on the Tenth of Tevet, or refrained from either eating in non-kosher places or from turning lights on and off on the Sabbath. Most nominals fasted at least part of Tisha B'Av, while large majorities did not work on their jobs on Sabbath and had two sets of dishes.

Lastly, we may discover how the non-Orthodox differed from the Orthodox in terms of the rituals reported in Table 1. Few non-Orthodox observed fast days other than Yom Kippur; most ate in non-kosher homes; and most turned lights on and off on the Sabbath. However, roughly half of these (most of whom in our sample belong to an Orthodox or Conservative synagogue) observed the more popular practices of refraining from Sabbath work on the job and maintaining meat and dairy dishes.

We make no claim for the inviolability of these distinctions. In fact, we suggest quite the opposite by drawing upon sociologist Paul Lazarsfeld's concept of "the interchangeability of indices." Our selection of questions may strike some persons as arbitrary—another group of tests could do as well. Moreover, the location of our intergroup boundaries is also arbitrary. One may certainly raise or lower the criteria of observance which demarcate the traditionalists from the centrist modern Orthodox, or the centrists from the nominals. That judgment largely depends upon the size of the sample and the distribution of respondents over the traditionalist-nominal Orthodox continuum. Moreover, those who may be relatively traditionalist in one community or sample may be fairly centrist in another context and vice-versa.

We fully appreciate the element of arbitrariness, therefore, in distinguishing among Orthodox subgroups. However, we still contend that studying differences among these groups is both possible and fruitful. Even though our ritual-based distinctions may seem arbitrary to some, we shall show that they are nevertheless associated with all sorts of patterned variations and therefore are useful indices. In fact, if we do admit to a degree of arbitrariness in our definitions of these various Orthodox types, whatever differences we do find among them are that much more impressive in light of the crude techniques available for distinguishing varying levels of religious Orthodoxy.

VALIDATION BY THE RESPONDENTS

One immediate way of confirming that we have adequately distinguished groups with differing levels of Orthodoxy is to turn to the respondents themselves and see whether they agree with our evaluations. Accordingly, we asked them to reckon their own degree of Orthodoxy with the question: "Would you characterize yourself as 'Strictly Orthodox,' 'Fairly Orthodox,' 'Slightly Orthodox,' or 'Not Orthodox'?" As Table 2 demonstrates, the respondents' evaluations did indeed accord with our own.

Nearly all (90%) of those we called "traditionalist Orthodox" deemed themselves "Strictly Orthodox." At the other end of the spectrum, hardly any (10%) of the nominally Orthodox referred to themselves as "Strictly Orthodox." Most (64%) called themselves "Fairly Orthodox." Interestingly, those we defined as centrist divided in the way they viewed themselves, a hint of the ambivalent character of the group in the middle which is *both* modern *and* Orthodox; half characterized themselves as "Strictly Orthodox" (50%) a proportion halfway between that of the other two Orthodox groups.

The close correspondence between the respondents' own evalua-

Table 2. "Strictness" of Orthodoxy (Self-Evaluated): "Would you characterize yourself as . . . Orthodox?"

	Degree of Orthodoxy			
	% Non-Orth.	% Nominal	% Centrist	% Traditional
Strictly	2	10	50	90
Fairly	5	64	46	10
Slightly	20	23	4	0
Not	73	3	0	0
	100	100	100	100
N =	176	107	404	142

tions and our ritual-based classification suggests something about the respondents and about our classification. About the respondents, it indicates that members of the Orthodox community know that certain ritual practices are expected of the Orthodox Jew. To be sure, the reference points for determining whether one is "Strictly," "Fairly," "Slightly," or "Not Orthodox" varies from one person or community to another; but within the boundaries of their community, individuals know more or less where they belong.

With regard to our classification, the correspondence with self-evaluations shows that we have captured in our index a reasonable representation of social reality. In other words, the respondents agree not only that there are varying degrees of Orthodoxy; they also concur in general terms with the ways—faulty as they may be—in which we have divided them.

THE HIERARCHICAL STRUCTURE OF RITUAL PRACTICE

Previous studies of American Jewish religious behavior have documented what cultural natives and insiders well understand: there is a hierarchical structure to ritual observance. Very simply, not every ritual commandment is practiced with equal attention and regularity.[15] Not only does the frequency of observance of certain rituals vary considerably, but particular observances are commonly linked to one another in predictable ways. Jews who observe the "hard" rituals (for example, refusing to ride, spend money, or use electricity on the Sabbath) will almost certainly perform the "easy" and most popular ones (for example, fasting on Yom Kippur or lighting Ḥanukkah candles). Conversely, Jews who fail to perform the "easy" practices are highly unlikely to carry out the "hard" ones. These linkages constitute a hierarchy of ritual practice among American Jews.

Traditionalist Orthodox Jews

Accordingly, we would expect to find a similar structuring of ritual practices among Orthodox Jews. In the hierarchy of practice we would expect that almost all traditionalists would observe all the ritual items found in our survey. Sometimes the logic is quite direct and obvious. Since traditionalists by our definition fast on one of the minor fast days, they should also fast on all the others; since they refrain from eating even a cold salad in a non-kosher home, there is no reason to believe that they would do so at a restaurant. But, we would also expect the traditionalists' observance to extend beyond the domain of just those rituals which are conceptually proximate to those embodied in our operational definition of a traditional Orthodox Jew. We would expect their observance to extend to areas further afield such as dress, ritualized text study, synagogue attendance, Sabbath observance, and the laws of "family purity" which among other things require monthly immersion in a *mikveh* (ritual bath) by married women, following the menstrual period. In fact, Table 3 demonstrates nearly universal compliance by traditionalists with all these areas of observance.

Among traditionalists, 95% or more of the men fasted not only on the Tenth of Tevet (the observance contained in our definition of a traditionalist) but also on the three other minor fast days. Similarly among the women, nearly all observed the fasts at least part of the day.

The traditionalists' compliance with the strictest interpretation of the dietary regulations was almost universal as was their observance of the Sabbath. In fact, almost all the men (95%) reported usual attendance at all three Sabbath services (Friday evening, Saturday morning, and Saturday afternoon).

Significantly, as we suggested and as any insider would anticipate, the punctilious observance by traditionalists extends to areas far removed from those explicitly contained in our operational definition of Orthodox traditionalism. Virtually all (99%) of the traditionalists reported that the women of the house used the *mikveh* (ritual bath); almost all of the men (94%) studied sacred texts weekly, usually on the Sabbath (90%)—in line with their respective halakhic obligations.

Perhaps the most telling pieces of evidence of the traditionalists' commitment to Orthodoxy came from those practices which visibly distinguish the Orthodox Jews from their contemporaries. All (100%) of the traditionalist respondents reported that the man of the house kept his head covered (with a hat or yarmulke) "on the street" and that he wore *tzitzit,* fringes mandated in the Bible (Num. 15). (Only among the traditionalists did we find a sizeable proportion—15%—who wore their *tzitzit* outside their shirt where it is easily visible.) Traditionalist

Table 3. Ritual Practices

	Degree of Orthodoxy			
	% Non-Orth.	% Nominal	% Centrist	% Traditional
Fasting (% whole/% part day)				
17th of Tammuz				
Men	0/4	5/18	60/26	99/1
Women	0/2	3/13	21/31	80/20
Tzom Gedalia				
Men	0/3	5/15	53/21	95/3
Women	1/1	0/0	15/27	66/27
Fast of Esther				
Men	2/5	8/22	63/21	97/3
Women	2/6	5/17	31/33	77/23
Yom Kippur (% whole day only)				
Men	78	97	100	100
Women	84	91	98	100
Kashrut				
Buy only from kosher butchers	56	81	100	100
No warm foods in non-kosher restaurants	13	24	81	99
No salads in non-kosher restaurants	6	8	23	91
Sabbath				
Never do housework	30	70	93	96
Never watch television	8	34	92	99
Attend Sabbath morning services (% usually/% sometimes)				
Men	25/47	59/38	93/5	100/0
Women	18/53	51/37	70/24	75/23
Attend all 3 Sabbath services (% usually/% sometimes)				
Men	4/20	23/43	61/32	95/4
Women	4/7	18/25	10/34	9/37
Other practices				
Woman regularly goes to mikveh	3	26	79	99
Studies texts weekly (% usually/% sometimes)				
Men	14/34	30/35	62/33	90/10
Women	6/32	23/49	35/45	30/68
Usually studies texts on Sabbath				
Men	28	56	81	94
Women	17	60	56	67
Man keeps his head covered "on the street"	3	22	71	100
Man wears tzitzit (% inside/% outside shirt)	2/0	19/0	73/2	85/15
Married woman covers head in public	0	5	34	91
Synagogue Attendance				
Men (daily)	1	9	26	66
(more than once a week)	6	21	39	28
(once a week)	15	28	26	4
Women (once a week or more)	15	28	57	48

married women also were distinguished in their practice of the religious custom of covering their hair in public (either with a kerchief [*tikhl*], wig [*shaytl*], or hat).

In short, there are no rituals in our survey where the traditionalist Orthodox departed from traditional norms.

The Centrist Modern Orthodox

The centrist modern Orthodox, on the other hand, while substantially complying with many if not most ritual norms, nevertheless displayed markedly lower rates of observance in certain areas. One difference for example between the centrists and traditionalists concerns the observance of the minor fast days. The centrists fasted about 30 to 40 percentage points less often than the traditionalists.

Similarly, the centrists deviated from the traditionalists in their pattern of compliance with the dietary laws. Only about 4 in 5 (81%) would not eat warm nominally kosher foods in non-kosher restaurants. The discrepancy with respect to cold salads was even greater. Less than a quarter of this group refrained from eating cold salads in non-kosher places of dining, compared with 100% of the traditionalists. We may assume the centrists were aware of the nuances of religious law and the legalistic distinctions drawn between hot and cold foods. Although they were more compromising in both regards than were the traditionalists, they were significantly more accommodating to modern norms of eating anywhere and with anyone when they believe the law provides some latitude, some discretion for individual decision-making.

A similar case can be discerned in the case of Sabbath prayer service attendance. The centrist men attended the synagogue on Sabbath mornings almost as often as the traditionalists (93% versus 100%). However, fewer attended all three services (61% versus 95%). Here, as with fasting and observance of the restrictive dietary laws, the more demanding the practice, the greater the discrepancy between the traditionalists and centrists. Moreover, they treated Sabbath morning as a holy day—therefore going to prayers—and the afternoon as a holiday—therefore staying at home, reading the paper, visiting friends, etc.

Interestingly, centrist women attended Sabbath services at least as often as their traditionalist counterparts. Apparently the mutually offsetting effects of two factors combined to maintain a relatively high rate of attendance among the former. On the one hand, these women exhibited lower rates of ritual observance than the traditionalist women. They were, for example, much less likely to fast a whole day on the Seventeenth of Tammuz (21% versus 80%) and fewer used the *mikveh* (79% versus 99%). We might therefore expect lower service attendance rates among centrist women. However, not only were they less ritually oriented than the traditionalists, they were also more distant from the traditionalist cultural heritage which regards communal religious practice such as synagogue attendance as a predominantly male preserve. Thus, the centrists' greater laxity in overall ritual observance (which would diminish attendance rates) was counterbalanced by modernity's relatively greater sexual egalitarianism which promotes female participation in such aspects of public Jewish life as synagogue attendance.

The centrists differed from the traditionalists in numerous other ways. Significantly fewer men (by 25 to 30 percentage points) studied sacred texts on the Sabbath, kept their heads covered on the street, and wore *tzitzit* (fringes). As noted, fewer centrist women used the *mikveh.* Consistent with earlier findings in connection with "harder" observances, only about a third of the centrist wives kept their hair covered in public as compared with 91% of their traditionalist counterparts.

Just as centrists were substantially less observant than the traditionalists, so nominally Orthodox Jews were less ritually active than the centrists. Looking to the left, then, centrists see themselves as stricter in their Orthodoxy. Looking to the right, they assume, in the words of one: "We probably don't come up to specs."[16]

The Nominally Orthodox

Aside from fasting on Yom Kippur, the rates of ritual observance among the nominally Orthodox in no case approach those among the centrists. For example, about 50 percentage points separated the two groups' rates of fasting on minor fast days; hardly any nominally Orthodox fasted a whole day on those occasions. Men among these two types of Orthodox differed greatly with regard to keeping their heads covered in public or wearing *tzitzit.* Only about a fifth of the nominals observed these practices, whereas two-thirds to three-fourths of the centrists did. Hardly any nominally Orthodox refrained from eating cold salads in non-kosher restaurants and only a quarter (24%) refrained from eating warm kosher foods in such places. Although a large majority (70%) of the nominally Orthodox did not do housework on the Sabbath and most of the men and women (59% and 51%) usually attended Sabbath morning services, these figures are still substantially lower than those found among the centrists.

Even greater variations between the two groups can be found with regard to Sabbath observances. Whereas almost all the centrists (92%)

reported never watching television on the Sabbath, only a third (34%) of the nominals made such a claim. Apparently, those who identify with Orthodoxy but reside on its marginal left wing keep the Sabbath as a special day, but not entirely in traditional terms. While they faithfully attend synagogue services on Sabbath morning, they do not refrain from watching television. That is, the Sabbath for these Jews has become largely a family day set aside for rest, relaxation, synagogue attendance, and leisure, as expressed, in addition to other forms of activity, by television viewing.

While the nominally Orthodox performed ritual practices less often than other Orthodox groups, the religious behavior of the women in this group is especially noteworthy. Among the centrists and traditionalists, women fasted, studied texts, and attended synagogue services much less often than did men, keeping with sex-linked differences in the traditional normative expectations. As noted earlier, the discrepancy between the sexes was smaller among the centrists than among the traditionalists; but among the nominals, these sex-linked differences in ritual practice disappeared almost entirely. Nominally Orthodox women fasted on minor fast days, studied sacred texts, and attended Sabbath services at about the same levels as their male counterparts. Nominally Orthodox women were much less likely to use the *mikveh* (26%) than the centrists (79%) or traditionalists (99%). Thus, relative to their more observant peers, the nominally Orthodox women have substantially departed from traditional norms regarding the use of the *mikveh,* where there are special obligations for the Jewish woman, but have maintained a similar level of observance in areas which among the traditionals produces higher male observance (i.e., fasting, studying, and synagogue prayer). Clearly, while the nominals were less observant, so too were they here also more sexually egalitarian (a reflection of their attachment to liberal American [rather than Jewish] values) as evidenced in the similar levels of Jewish practice among nominally Orthodox men and women.

The Non-Orthodox

The non-Orthodox in our sample, although more observant than most American Jews, had a substantially lower rate of ritual performance than Orthodox Jews. Hardly any of the non-Orthodox fasted on the minor fast days. None of the married women covered their hair in public and almost none of the men kept their head covered on the street or wore *tzitzit.* Nearly all ate salads or heated kosher foods in non-kosher restaurants. In fact, they were probably as likely to eat *non-*kosher foods there as well. Few regularly studied sacred texts and few refrained from watching television on the Sabbath. Indeed, on that day, only 30% refrained from housework. Relatively few attended Sabbath morning services with regularity—25% for the men and 18% for the women.

Substantial compliance with traditional law and custom among these non-Orthodox was evident only with regard to those practices kept by a large proportion of American Jews in general: Yom Kippur fasting and the purchase of kosher meat. This finding highlights the existence of a distinctive set of ritual practices which sets apart all varieties of Orthodox from the remainder of American Jews.

SOCIOLOGY VERSUS HALAKHAH: EXPLAINING VARIATION IN RITUAL OBSERVANCE

While the foregoing discussion has focused on different patterns of practice among Orthodox Jews of varying degrees of ritual observance, we have yet to concentrate on the rituals themselves and why some are more readily observed than others. The centrist modern Orthodox offers an ideal locus in which to study this question. They seemingly exercise some discretion in choosing which ritual commandments to follow and which to ignore, trying to find a middle course.

Most centrists are thoroughly socialized into Orthodox society and tradition and thus know what is expected of them. Many, in fact, have friends or family from the more traditionalist wing to their ideological right, and on occasion conform in their behavior to their most stringent demands. Why, then, do many—if not most—centrist modern Orthodox Jews choose to keep some religious prescriptions and violate others, of whose significance they must be aware?

The obverse of this question is of equal interest. Many centrists are also intimately connected through ties of family and friendship with the more marginal, nominally Orthodox Jews who hold out a much laxer model of religious observance. Why then do the centrists shun that model, and instead remain more punctilious in their observances of certain rituals? In short, we ask, why and how does the center exist?

A similar concern has been raised by sociologists and historians in examining the experience of post-emancipation Jews. Many such Jews sought to balance the demands of citizenship in the host culture with commitments toward the parochial obligations of Judaism. Many modern Jews sought to overcome their historically stigmatized pariah status and to enter civil society with their Jewish identities intact; nonetheless they often modified their religious behavior with an eye to social acceptance. Practices which severely inhibited integration—or at least appeared to do so—were among those which modernizing Jews most readily abandoned. The dietary restrictions, for example, created a barrier to socializing between Jews and other citizens; the prohibitions of work on the Sabbath had direct economic consequences for Jewish workers and Jewish employers. On the other hand, many Jews maintained practices which they believed could be reinterpreted to comport with, or which could be understood and accepted by, the host culture. Those they felt they could not reinterpret or explain, they sometimes changed or at the very least kept from public view.

In some ways, the centrist modern Orthodox have adopted a similar approach. Their ritual practices are influenced somewhat by social acceptance criteria similar to those once used by the emancipated Jews. Not wishing to be too remote from the host American culture, they—more than non-Orthodox Jews who also try to be both traditionally Jewish and modern American—reinterpret, compartmentalize, and sometimes modify their Jewish existence in the light of contemporary patterns of culture, even as they place great emphasis on their ties to Orthodox beliefs and practices.

We believe three sorts of influences explain variation in ritual observance among the Orthodox in general and among the centrists in particular: (1) religious meaning, that is, the import of the rituals within the traditional culture and heritage; (2) concern with a sense of belonging to the Orthodox community; and (3) concern about a sense of belonging to the larger non-Jewish society. In short, modern centrist Orthodox Jews (like non-Orthodox Jews) observe specific practices more or less frequently because of variations in the practices' religious, communal, and social implications. To them the public institutions of the Orthodox remain anchored to tradition while the private and individual domain is attached to American modern social norms.

As noted earlier, relative to the traditionalists, centrists were lax with certain ritual norms, especially practices that tend to symbolize and induce social segregation, and that are invested with what may be perceived as a discretionary element in terms of religious law and custom. Some interpretations of the law, for example, do not specifically forbid eating cold salads in non-kosher restaurants. Nevertheless, traditionalists find eating even technically kosher foods in a non-kosher milieu troubling. Their very presence in such a place might erroneously convey Orthodox approval of eating any foods in such places, or to sanction being in a non-Orthodox setting. Thus, while eating cold salads in a non-kosher restaurant may not technically transgress the letter of the law, for the traditionalist it transgresses its spirit. But for centrists—whose spirit is a mix of modern America and the parochial traditions of Orthodoxy—the solution of eating kosher food without making halakhic contact with the non-kosher but making spiritual contact with it is ideal.

Similar considerations apply to the wearing of head coverings by married women. The centrists interpret the religiously based requirements for this practice as being ambiguous at best and more likely discretionary. The wearing of such coverings is seen as serving to sharply differentiate and ultimately segregate the Orthodox Jews from all others. (Interestingly, those centrist women who do wear headcovers—34%—often wear wigs with stylish coiffures which are unrecognizable as wigs to the untrained eye. This is a far cry from the obvious *peruke* worn by many Orthodox women with more insular proclivities.)

The data on synagogue attendance and on observing minor fast days reflect the limitations which centrists place on their embrace of parochial Jewish life. For example, many resort to fallback options rather than totally abandon certain practices. Many more centrists than traditionalists "usually" attended all three Sabbath services, but more still did so "sometimes." None said they "never" go, as did some nominals and non-Orthodox. A similar pattern appears with regard to behavior on minor fast days. While almost all traditionalist men fasted a whole day on the minor fast days, only a majority of centrists did so, and about a quarter fasted part days.

Communal controls are at work here. The norms of Orthodox culture as interpreted by the centrists demand male attendance at the main Sabbath service on Saturday morning; but they are effectively relaxed with respect to Friday evening or Saturday afternoon attendance. The presence of a significant quorum seems to satisfy the centrist community.[17] This is perfect ambivalence; the community wants a quorum so all services will take place; the individuals however, are less willing to commit themselves to coming to each of the services.

Similarly, fasting on minor fast days is often a non-public act. Those who do not fast or fast only part days are not publicly challenging the tenets of Orthodox Jewish practice as they would by undertaking other religious transgressions. This too reflects the ambivalence of the centrist. The fast remains legitimate in line with Orthodox norm; the individuals themselves do not always fast on them.

In fact, of all the minor fasts, the Fast of Esther is most closely tied to public performance, in that it is followed by the popular and well-attended synagogue celebration of Purim and the reading of the Scroll of Esther. At this gathering, those who have fasted a full day either can be distinguished or testify to their having fasted. Thus, of all the minor fasts, the Fast of Esther is, not surprisingly, the one centrist men observed most often for the public place remains framed and determined by institutional and traditional Orthodoxy.

The interplay of concern with traditional religion and acceptance by the Orthodox community and concern with acceptance by the larger society is well illustrated in a group of observances where the centrists' behavior differed less substantially from that of the traditionalists. Roughly three-quarters of the centrist men kept their heads covered in public; the same proportion wore the *tzitzit* (albeit under their shirts and out of public view); and about the same percentage of centrist wives followed religious law with regard to the *mikveh*. Practice of these activities among the traditionalists was nearly universal—99% to 100%.[18] What is significant about these patterns of centrist observance is that they exceed those of the other ritual practices discussed, and yet they are still less than those of the traditionalists. In each case, we must ask why the level of practice of this ritual is as high as it is, but still lower than the traditionalist rate.

Consider the covering of the head first. In principle, hats can be worn without especially distinguishing the wearer, but in practice they do set off the Orthodox Jew from the vast majority of men who do not wear them.[19] Yarmulkes on the other hand unmistakably distinguish the Orthodox male from the non-Orthodox.[20] As such, they are a recognized demarcating symbol. Since wearing a yarmulke is akin to making a public statement about one's attachment to the Orthodox community, failing to wear one may be symbolically understood as making an opposite assertion. The principal inhibition against publicly wearing a yarmulke, then, is that it creates an overt barrier between Orthodox and others, both non-Orthodox and gentile. The male who wears one thus expresses solidarity with his fellow Orthodox, while setting himself apart as something of an outsider. Hence there is both a high social cost and a high communal reward in wearing a yarmulke.

Unpredictably, the modernists among the Orthodox increasingly prefer the yarmulke to the hat. The former—particularly the small knitted type which modernists prefer to the larger, old-fashioned black velvet or cotton yarmulke—is seemingly not as stigmatizing as a hat in hatless America. As Jews have come to feel more at ease in expressing their distinctiveness in a contemporary America which exhibits a growing tolerance for symbolic expressions of ethnicity, they have increasingly begun to wear yarmulkes in public. That is, social cost has decreased, and consequently the rate of yarmulke wearing has increased. As we show elsewhere in our larger study, more younger centrist Orthodox kept their heads covered in public than their older counterparts. But the meaning attached to wearing that headcover may alter over the generations. In fact, the older man who does not cover his head in public may be, in many ways, more traditionalist in outlook and behavior than the son who wears a small knitted yarmulke. Today, however, that little headcover has become the cultural *sine qua non* among younger Orthodox Jews, for all but the nominals. Yet its smallness and near-invisibility is again the reflection of centrist ambivalence.

The wearing of *tzitzit* and attendance at the *mikveh* are both essentially non-public, and as a result have few consequences for social integration. At the same time, they are invested with high religious significance deriving from the role ascribed to them by the Scriptures.[21] Wearing *tzitzit* is a symbolic medallion of Jewish Orthodoxy entailing minimal social cost. Going to the *mikveh* also has high religious and symbolic significance for Orthodox Jews with few adverse consequences for acceptance by the larger society. The Talmud and Halakhah have a great deal to say about the sexual conduct of married couples. According to Jewish law, the woman goes to the *mikveh* at night, unobtrusively. No one but she and her husband need know that she observes this ritual, and commonly they do not. To be sure, the user of the *mikveh* may interpret the meaning of her practice in any way she chooses; in traditional religious terms as a divine commandment, in symbolic terms as a dramatic enactment of her own bodily rebirth, in psychological terms as a way of renewing her husband's and her own sexual appetites, and so on. But the act itself is viewed as religiously essential while entailing little social cost. It is therefore performed by most centrists.

We have also seen that majorities of all three types of Orthodox men study religious texts, at least on the Sabbath (the rates were 94%, 81%, and 56% for the three groups of men). At the same time, however, such involvement clearly drops as one moves from the traditionalists to the nominals. Religious text study among Orthodox men is a highly social act, reflective of and generative of social ties to other Orthodox men. Increasing marginality from traditional Jewish social involvement or, put differently, social involvement with the larger or less traditionally Jewish world apparently diminishes involvement in ritual study. Among the traditionalists, as we show elsewhere in the larger study, communal ties to other Orthodox Jews abound and hence the vast majority of them engage in regular study.

In short, committed to a life somewhat apart, the centrists—like other modernists—seek whenever possible to mitigate their segregation. Where discretion seems possible, where the Jewish law appears to allow for latitude in the direction of participation in the host culture and contemporary life patterns, or where the Orthodox community can exercise few social sanctions for noncompliance with traditionalist norms, the centrist Orthodox sometimes adjust their behavior to that of the less observant world outside the strictly Orthodox one.

Table 4. Childbearing Variables

	Degree of Orthodoxy			
	Non-Orth.	Nominal	Centrist	Traditional
Number of children				
Married, 35+ years old	2.0	2.1	2.9	4.2
Married, 18–35 years old	1.1	0.7	1.5	2.1
Wrong to limit number of children (%)	9	14	27	60

CHILDBEARING VARIATIONS AMONG THE ORTHODOX

The biblical injunction to "be fruitful and multiply" is a norm taken to be of central significance in the Orthodox community. Not only is there a distinctive religious/symbolic significance attached to bearing and rearing children, there are other aspects of cultural significance as well. Jews have had a past of high fertility. Their adaptation to the modern world meant diminished birthrates and the adoption of lower fertility ideals of middle-class society. However, for Jews—as for some other religious groups—involvement in the contemporary traditionalist religious community has meant an affirmation of the pro-natalist, high fertility heritage.[22]

Accordingly, we would expect Orthodox traditionalism to be associated with higher than average childbearing rates. Table 4 presents data relating to number of children born (separating those over and those under 35 years old). Within age categories, the traditionalists had more children than the centrists, who in turn exceeded the nominally Orthodox.

Among those 35 or over (i.e., those with completed families), reading from right (traditionalists) to left (non-Orthodox), we find the mean number of children declining as follows: 4.2, 2.9, 2.1, 2.0. The younger adults (under 35) exhibit a similar pattern: 2.1, 1.5, 0.7, 1.1. Evidently the traditionalists not only have more children throughout their lives, but they have them earlier. Since we know that Jews are highly efficient at avoiding unwanted pregnancies (they are adept at contraception), we can infer that the different Orthodox groups are having different numbers of children precisely because they so choose.

More evidence to this effect can be gleaned from the results pertaining to the question of the advisability of voluntarily limiting the number of one's children. There are small increases in the proportions opposing this view (i.e., the use of contraception) as we move from non-Orthodox (9%) to the nominal Orthodox (14%), and to the centrists (27%). When we reach the traditionalists, the figure jumps dramatically upward to 60% who believed that limiting childbirths is wrong. Clearly, traditionalists had the most pro-natalist attitudes among the Orthodox.

However, the traditionalists' actual birthrate, although the highest of all our groups, suggests that they do practice some form of birth control. Even those traditionalists over 35 with pro-natalist views had "only" a mean of 4.5 children (data not shown in the table). Obviously even Orthodox traditionalists have adapted to contemporary fertility norms by practicing some form of contraception, despite their stated support of high fertility ideals. They too share in the ambivalences that emerge in the contact between Orthodoxy and the modern world.

A general conclusion we can draw from these results is that even the traditionalists have adjusted their behavior—at least in the case of childbearing—to the modern world more readily than they have changed their attitudes—at least toward contraception. Lip service to ideals seems, at the very least in this case, to outlive their practice.

CONCLUSION

The essential lesson to be derived from this discussion of ritual variation within modern Orthodoxy is that religious/symbolic issues, communal ties, and social factors all play important roles in determining ritual performance. Thus modern centrist Orthodox Jews are not, as some have claimed, a world apart, but are rather similar to other American Jews in their desire to be both Jewish and American, both parochial and cosmopolitan, particular and universal. Ritual practices which inhibit integration and are perceived to be of low religious/symbolic importance are less likely to be undertaken and even the observance of important *mitzvas* shows some effects of cultural dualism.

Notes

This is a collaborative work and the order of the authors' names is not intended to indicate seniority.

We thank Professors Calvin Goldscheider and Charles Liebman for their critical comments.

1. Milton Himmelfarb, "Secular Society? A Jewish Perspective," *Daedalus* no. 12 (1968), p. 283; Leo Jung, "What Is Orthodox Judaism?" *The Jewish Library* second series, Leo Jung (ed.), (New York: 1930), pp. 113–132; Alan

Fisher, "The Outsider and Orthodox Judaism," *Tradition* vol. XIII, no. 3, Winter 1973, pp. 66–98; cf. Charles Liebman, "A Sociological Analysis of Contemporary Orthodoxy," *Judaism* (Summer 1964), pp. 285–304.

2. J. L. Blau, *Modern Varieties of Judaism* (New York: 1966), p. 27.

3. Ephraim Sturm, "Social and Religious Philosophies of the Early 1900s Which Influenced the Formation of the Young Israel Movement" (no date) unpublished, p. 9.

4. Norman Lamm, "The Voice of Torah in the Battle of Ideas," *Jewish Life* (March–April 1967), p. 30.

5. David Singer, "Voices of Orthodoxy," *Commentary* (July 1974), p. 58.

6. Saul J. Berman, "The Jewish Day School: A Symposium," *Tradition* vol. XIII, no. 1 (Summer 1972), p. 97.

7. Liebman, "A Sociological Analysis," p. 295.

8. Blau, *Modern Varieties,* p. 308.

9. Rabbi Nisson Wolpin, "Letters," *Commentary* (November 1974), p. 24.

10. As an aside, it is drawn from a larger study, now under way, which also delineates variations in religious beliefs, community involvement, and social attitudes.

11. Most of the additions concerned social and political items, areas we cover elsewhere in the larger study from which this paper is drawn.

12. We discarded from the published analyses an additional group of forty ritually observant respondents who called themselves non-Orthodox—generally Conservative—Jews. Though substantively intriguing, their small number precluded our obtaining stable statistics.

13. Samuel C. Heilman, *Synagogue Life: A Study in Symbolic Interaction* (Chicago: 1976).

14. Brian M. Bullivant, *Competing Values Traditions in an Orthodox Jewish Day School: A Study of Enculturation Dissonance* (Ph.D. dissertation, Monash University, 1975), p. 338.

15. Although regularity and attention are not identical—one may be "regular" in performance of a ritual but not give it much "attention," carrying it out mechanically and without devotion *(kavvanah)*—among Orthodox Jews there is a tacit understanding that while regularity is not sufficient for guaranteeing attention to ritual behavior, it is nevertheless necessary. Out of regularity, attention and intention may come. We could not survey pure attention and so we settled for regularity.

16. Heilman, *Synagogue Life,* p. 19.

17. Ibid., pp. 95–103.

18. The missing 1% could easily have resulted from errors by respondents, coders, or keypunchers.

19. Among Orthodox Jews even styles of hats and the way they are worn may serve as signals of one's affiliation. Thus, for example, black stetsons worn in a skewed fashion are headgear often associated with yeshiva students.

20. Cf. Heilman, *Synagogue Life,* pp. 53–56.

21. Numbers 15:37–39.

22. S. M. Cohen and P. Ritterband, in Paul Ritterband (ed.), *Modern Jewish Fertility* (Leiden: 1981), "Why Contemporary American Jews Want Small Families: An Interreligious Comparison of College Graduates."

Essays

Self-Employment and Jewish Continuity

Calvin Goldscheider
(HEBREW UNIVERSITY AND BROWN UNIVERSITY)

Imprinted on American popular culture is the image of the immigrant Jews striving to "make it" in America. Part of the imagery relates to the desire to be independent—from family and country of origin as well as from the control of non-Jews, though it is doubtful whether in reality Jews fully disassociated themselves from kinship ties or their communities of origin. Here we shall focus on a small corner of that reality—occupational independence. Specifically, we shall analyze some evidence on patterns of Jewish self-employment. The data reported in this article were derived from a 1975 Boston metropolitan area study. They allow for the systematic analysis of the self-employment patterns of Jews and other ethnics (see Fowler, 1977; Cohen, 1983; Goldscheider, 1985).

In our context, self-employment implies two interrelated facets of Jewish cohesion. First, self-employment means direct control over one's own job. Indirectly, it implies greater reliance on family for resources and connections as well as power over resources to be distributed to others, and, where appropriate, to coethnics. Moreover, to the extent that Jews are more likely to be working for themselves, they may be more likely to form networks and contacts with other Jews in similar positions. The basic issue focuses on the identification of social and economic structures in which Jews interact in large part with other Jews.

Economic networks are one basis of ethnic cohesion when they

The data reported in this article were analyzed as part of a larger project on the demography of American Jews supported by the Center for Modern Jewish Studies, Brandeis University. In somewhat different form, this paper will appear in a forthcoming volume, *Social Change and Jewish Continuity*, 1985. Frances E. Kobrin, Steven M. Cohen, and Peter Y. Medding made valuable comments on an earlier version.

involve greater interaction among Jews than between Jews and non-Jews. The greater the in-group interaction, the greater the group cohesion. The changing extent of self-employment over time is an indicator of the changing cohesiveness of the Jewish community.

This perspective moves us beyond oversimplified explanations of Jewish self-employment patterns. It has been argued, for example, that the Jewish propensity for self-employment derives from fear of non-Jewish control over the jobs Jews have. This concern relates to potential antisemitism and ostensibly explains the consequent desire to be independent. Over time, so the argument goes, there developed a Jewish cultural preference for autonomous or independent occupations. This tendency stems from, and is continuous with, the pattern of occupational concentration and segregation characteristic of their East European origins (see Goldscheider and Zuckerman, 1984). However, the transformation of Jewish socioeconomic conditions over the last century, the radical differences between the status of Jews in America and in nineteenth-century Europe, and the general economic and social differences between European and American societies make such interpretations of direct continuity superficial.

We assume, therefore, that the sources of self-employment primarily reflect the economic and social contexts Jews confront in America and only secondarily the socioeconomic (educational and occupational) backgrounds their grandfathers and fathers brought with them to America. Our question is not on the past but on the present: what are the current patterns and recent changes in self-employment and what significance do they have for Jewish continuity?

Previous studies of ethnic variation in self-employment have been based on limited data. While inconsistent self-employment differences between Protestants and Catholics have been reported in the literature (cf. Lenski, 1961; Goldstein, 1969; Goldscheider and Kobrin, 1980), for Jews, the evidence has been consistent, although never analyzed in detail. Lenski notes in his combined sample of Detroit in the 1950s that Jews had significantly higher rates of self-employment than non-Jews. He concludes: "In short, it appears that even in the bureaucratized modern metropolis there are real and significant differences among the major socioreligious groups in the degree to which they value occupational independence and autonomy, with the Jews ranking first, White Protestants second, and Catholics third" (p. 104). While the findings of higher self-employment levels among Jews are clear, Lenski's conclusions about the value Jews placed on occupational independence are inferential.

National data based on the Current Population Survey of 1957 confirm the findings for Jews. For example, 37 percent of Jewish professionals were self-employed compared to about 15 percent of Roman

Catholics and White Protestants. Self-employment was even higher for managers but the same patterns emerge: 69 percent of Jewish managers were self-employed compared to about 50 percent of the non-Jews. These differences remain when years of schooling and urban residence are controlled (Goldstein, 1969, Tables 6 and 7). Hence, differences between Jews and non-Jews in the level of self-employment do not appear to be limited to a particular community, nor can they simply be attributed to the different levels of education and urban concentration characteristic of Jews, Protestants, and Catholics.

More recently, a detailed analysis of self-employment for religious and ethnic groups focused on Rhode Island data collected in the late 1960s (Goldscheider and Kobrin, 1980; cf. Kobrin and Goldscheider, 1978). There were only 65 Jews in the Rhode Island survey and detailed analysis was limited. Nevertheless, some insights into variations in self-employment across communities may be gained by comparing the Boston and Rhode Island data. Since the question asked was identical, the timing of the studies was close, and the ethnic compositions of Rhode Island and the Boston metropolitan area are similar, these comparisons are analytically valuable.

The Boston data allow us to examine several key issues associated with self-employment patterns. First, differences in self-employment between Jews and non-Jews can be explored and patterns of convergence among religious groups can be examined. In particular, we shall focus on the direction and intensity of change in self-employment for Jews and other ethnic/religious groups. In addition, we shall examine what changes in self-employment occur for contemporary Jews as occupational and educational levels change. Once these relationships are analyzed, we then can clarify to what extent self-employment patterns are solely a reflection of educational, occupational, and other differences in the personal backgrounds of Jews and non-Jews.

All male respondents (and husbands of female respondents) were asked whether they worked for themselves or someone else. A question on whether the father of the respondent worked for himself when the respondent was growing up was also included. This, however, was asked only of those below age forty. Data on the self-employment patterns of Jewish women were also collected. No previous research on ethnic differences in self-employment patterns of women has been carried out.

JEWISH AND NON-JEWISH SELF-EMPLOYMENT

The basic pattern of higher levels of self-employment among Jews may be observed in Table 1. Over one-third of the Jewish males who

Table 1. Proportion Self-Employed by Age, Religion, and Ethnicity: Males

	Total	18–29	30–39	40–49	50–59	60+
Jews	36.6	16.3	43.2	32.9	54.7	46.3
Non-Jews	11.2	6.2	10.1	18.5	12.3	11.9
Blacks	6.4	4.5	8.3	*	*	*
White Protestants	14.5	5.9	17.6	8.3	25.0	18.5
Irish Catholics	7.0	16.7	7.7	*	*	*
Italian Catholics	14.5	0.0	14.3	38.5	21.4	7.1
Other Catholics	11.7	6.7	16.7	17.6	5.3	18.8
Protestants	13.2	6.7	23.5	5.6	18.2	18.5
Catholics	11.1	6.2	10.9	20.5	11.6	10.0

*Insufficient data for presentation

are working are self-employed, three times the level among non-Jews. This pattern characterizes all the detailed racial, religious, and ethnic groups.

The absolute level of Jewish self-employment is lower in Boston than in Rhode Island, where over half the Jews were self-employed. In part, this difference reflects the age-generational differences in the composition of the Jewish communities of Boston and Rhode Island—the latter are significantly older, with a higher percentage of the foreign-born. However, the particular demographic differences between these Jewish communities are not the entire explanation. A detailed examination of self-employment among non-Jews shows that self-employment among Protestants and Catholics (Irish and Italians) in Rhode Island is also higher than in Boston. This forces us to search for explanations of self-employment differences beyond the specific features of the Jewish communities. These include the different occupational markets and economies of the two areas, their opportunity structures, and, in turn, the nature of in- and out-migration patterns and their socioeconomic selectivity.

The Boston data further indicate, as did the Rhode Island study, that the most conspicuous ethnic, racial, and religious differences in self-employment are between Jews and non-Jews. The lower rates of Irish Catholic self-employment and the higher rates among Italian Catholics are consistent in both studies.

Patterns of in- and out-migration are of critical importance in understanding differences between Boston and Rhode Island. Many of the Jews in Rhode Island are selective stayers, who may be more likely to enter into family businesses. Fully 70 percent of the children of Rhode Island Jews move out of the state (Kobrin and Goldscheider, 1978, pp. 220–24). This is clearly not the pattern of Jews in Boston, where there are high rates of in-migration (Goldscheider, 1985, chapter 4).

These patterns also characterize the non-Jews of these areas, although not to the same extent. In Rhode Island, the Italians remain in much larger numbers than the Irish and a much larger proportion of Italians are involved in ethnic community networks, including those formed among the self-employed. These migration patterns have direct implications for self-employment in the community. The generational networks of Jewish self-employment are weaker in Boston than in Rhode Island, although stronger than among non-Jews. Jews who remain in Rhode Island are more likely to connect up with family and kin networks which involve working for oneself.

These comparisons between communities and between Jews and non-Jews clearly point to the importance of the broader demographic and economic structure of communities as key determinants of self-employment. Neither universal values of occupational independence nor uniform patterns across communities characterize American Jews. At the same time, we should not lose sight of the similarities. Despite demographic and economic differences between Boston and Rhode Island, self-employment patterns are remarkably similar.

Changes in self-employment may be inferred from age variation. These data show that, without exception, Jews of all age cohorts have significantly higher self-employment levels than non-Jews. This characterizes, with but one minor exception, every comparison between Jews and other racial, ethnic, and religious subgroups. However, the age data do not provide a clear indication of the direction of change in self-employment. Over 40 percent of Jews age 30–39 are self-employed, a higher proportion than among those age 40–49 but lower than among those age 50–59. Similar fluctuations characterize non-Jews. Among those 18–29 years of age, there is a sharp drop of self-employment levels. This appears to reflect a life cycle factor, careers at this age only beginning, and the fact that many of the males age 18–29 remain in school and have not yet permanently entered the labor force.

Among those age 30–39, there appears to be no convergence in self-employment levels between Jews and non-Jews relative to previous age cohorts. Ethnic-religious differences in self-employment in Boston remain strong. A similar conclusion emerged from the Rhode Island data. Clearly there is no basis in these two sets of data for concluding that ethnic differences are converging toward some uniform, undifferentiated level. This holds true despite changes over time and variations in levels between communities.

While the age data suggest that Jewish–non-Jewish differences in self-employment have not disappeared, the issue of generational change may be addressed more directly. The Boston data collected information on the self-employment of fathers. Aggregate and indi-

Table 2. Generational Self-Employment by Age and Religion: Males

	Son's Age			
	Jews			Non-Jews
	18–29	30–39	18–39	18–39
Father Self-Employed	69.6	49.4	62.8	32.2
Son Self-Employed	15.6	42.6	22.8	5.1
Son Not Self-Employed	84.4	57.4	77.2	94.9
Father Not Self-Employed	30.4	50.6	37.2	67.8
Son Self-Employed	19.1	44.4	30.6	11.0
Son Not Self-Employed	80.9	55.6	69.4	89.0
Son Self-Employed	16.7	43.5	25.7	9.1
Father Self-Employed	65.2	48.4	55.6	18.2
Father Not Self-Employed	34.8	51.6	44.4	81.8
Son Not Self-Employed	83.3	56.5	74.3	90.9
Father Self-Employed	70.5	50.2	65.2	33.6
Father Not Self-Employed	29.5	49.8	34.8	66.4

vidual level change can be identified by comparing the self-employment distributions of fathers and sons. It should be clear that we do not have an unbiased sample of fathers' self-employment. Differential migration, mortality, and fertility of fathers and differential survivorship and migration of sons, affect the representativeness of data on fathers derived from the sample (cf. Blau and Duncan, 1967; Matras, 1975; Kobrin and Goldscheider, 1978). However, given the powerful effects of selective in-migration, age comparisons may not reveal changes in self-employment. Hence, the direct generational patterns take on particular significance.

These comparisons show that 63 percent of the Jewish fathers, but only 26 percent of the sons, were self-employed, a relative decline of 59 percent (Table 2). For non-Jews, the decline is from 32 percent to 9 percent, a relative decrease of 72 percent. Thus, despite the lower starting level of self-employment among non-Jews, the rate of generational decline is sharper. Since the decline in self-employment by generation is greater for non-Jews, differences in self-employment between Jews and non-Jews have widened. The differences are not small, as Jewish sons have levels of self-employment almost three times as high as non-Jewish sons. Neither age cohort variations nor generational changes in self-employment indicate convergence of Jewish–non-Jewish differences, despite a common trend toward declining levels of self-employment.

A summary of these generational flows in self-employment at the individual level focuses on the proportion of fathers and sons who were both self-employed, both working for others, or had changed generationally (Table 3). These data show that 14 percent of Jewish fathers and sons were both self-employed compared to less than 2 percent of non-Jews. This level is significantly lower in Boston than in Rhode Island where the level of self-employment over two generations of Jews is very high (43%). However, the percent for non-Jews is also higher. The ratio of Jews and non-Jews who are self-employed in two generations is exactly the same in both studies (7 to 1). Again, while the pattern is identical, the level varies.

At the other end of the continuum, the proportion of two generations working for others is twice as common for non-Jews as for Jews. The flow from self-employment to working for others characterizes 46 percent of the Jews and the ratio of that pattern to the flow from employed fathers to self-employed sons is about the same for Jews and non-Jews.

The low proportion of two-generational Jewish self-employment reflects, in part, the small percentage of the self-employed among Jews age 18–29. The proportion of two-generational self-employment is much higher for those age 30–39, where the proportion of those enrolled in school is reduced. Life cycle factors distort and accentuate the downward generational decline in Jewish self-employment.

The shift toward an individual rather than an aggregate level of analysis allows us to examine the dynamics associated with the attainment and maintenance of self-employment (Table 2). The self-employment of Jewish sons does not follow directly from the self-employment of their fathers. While 23 percent of fathers who were self-employed had sons who were self-employed, 31 percent of fathers who were not self-employed had sons who were self-employed. The same pattern characterizes non-Jews. There is, therefore, no greater probability of being self-employed if the father was self-employed than if the father worked for others. In this sense, self-employment is not inherited generationally. This further suggests that contemporary pat-

Table 3. Self-Employment of Fathers and Sons by Age and Religion

		Jews			Non-Jews
Father	Son	18–29	30–39	Total*	Total
Self-Employed	Self-Employed	10.9	21.0	13.9	1.7
Self-Employed	Not Self-Employed	58.8	28.3	46.1	30.6
Not Self-Employed	Self-Employed	5.8	22.5	11.9	7.4
Not Self-Employed	Not Self-Employed	24.6	28.2	28.2	60.3

*Includes a small number of cases 40–49.

Table 4. Proportion Self-Employed by Age, Religion, and Father's Education: Males

	Son's Age					
	Jews			Non-Jews		
Father's Education	18–39	18–29	30–39	18–39	18–29	30–39
<High School	27.9	31.5	*	9.3	5.7	15.8
High School	25.1	11.3	42.0	14.0	10.0	23.1
Some College	50.7	34.8	67.8	22.2	23.1	*
College Grad	16.1	10.3	31.6	3.8	4.8	*
Post-Grad	16.2	11.5	28.0	*	*	*

*Insufficient data for presentation

terns of Jewish self-employment involve new jobs in a transformed economy.

The lack of direct effects of family employment history on current self-employment in Boston differs significantly from the Rhode Island data, where direct generational continuity in self-employment might be called a characteristic of the Jewish community. A major factor in this difference is the pattern of high out-migration from Rhode Island, resulting in a greater continuity in self-employment among those who remain. The higher in-migration rates of Jews to Boston (and their lower rates of two-generational self-employment) contribute to the different findings in the two communities. Since it is a community characteristic (rather than a specific ethnic or religious trait), the pattern characterizes non-Jews as well. Nevertheless, the major finding is that Jewish sons are more likely to be self-employed than non-Jewish ones, irrespective of the employment patterns of their fathers.

These conclusions are reinforced when we examine these data from a somewhat different angle. We ask, what are the self-employment origins of sons who are self-employed? The bottom half of Table 2 shows these recruitment patterns. Over 55 percent of all Jewish sons who are currently self-employed had fathers who were self-employed when they were growing up. However, an even higher proportion of those currently working for others had fathers who were self-employed. The lack of direct self-employment recruitment characterizes non-Jews as well, and is not restricted to a particular life cycle segment.

Given the relative unimportance of fathers' self-employment for the self-employment of sons, we can explore whether the self-employment of sons derives from the educational attainment of fathers. The data to answer this question are presented in Table 4. Among Jews, the lowest levels of self-employment characterize those whose fathers graduated from college and did post-graduate work. It is these fathers who have the lowest probability of transferring directly to their sons their specific occupational self-employment. The highest level of sons' self-employment is among those whose fathers had some college education. Fully half of Jewish sons whose fathers had some college education were self-employed, about twice as high as sons whose fathers had higher or lower educational levels. This characterizes both age groups and is particularly pronounced among those age 30–39, where 68 percent are self-employed. The sons of fathers with lower educational levels are less likely to be self-employed than those whose fathers had some college education.

The influence of educational attainment of fathers on sons' self-employment is similar for Jews and non-Jews. The highest self-employment among non-Jewish sons occurs among those whose fathers had some college education, and the lowest, among those whose fathers were college graduates. However, the effects of fathers' education on the self-employment of sons are less pronounced among non-Jews than among Jews.

While current self-employment patterns of Jews and non-Jews are related to the educational attainment of fathers in similar ways, self-employment differences between Jews and non-Jews cannot be accounted for by educational differences in their family backgrounds. The higher self-employment level among Jews is not primarily a reflection of the particular educational levels of Jewish fathers. For example, comparing the self-employment levels of those whose fathers were college graduates shows that the level is four times higher for Jews than non-Jews. Similarly, over 90 percent of the non-Jews whose fathers had fewer years of education worked for others, compared to about 70 percent of the Jews.

EXPLAINING SELF-EMPLOYMENT

The explanation of self-employment differences between Jews and non-Jews does not reside in the educational or self-employment patterns of their fathers. How, then, can we account for the exceptional Jewish concentration in self-employment? There are few theoretical guidelines for formulating specific explanations. From the more general sociological literature we can deduce two alternative arguments (cf. Goldscheider and Kobrin, 1980). One theme suggests that ethnic differences generally are transitional and spurious. To the extent that self-employment patterns differ for Jews and non-Jews, the source of variation should be explored in these groups' patterns of social class concentration. Since Jews have very different socioeconomic characteristics than those of non-Jews, it seems reasonable to hypothesize that such variation may account for self-employment differences. This argument parallels the "characteristics" hypothesis which has been postulated for the explanation of the unique patterns of Jewish fertility. This hypothesis argues that the particular fertility behavior of Jews is the result of their unique combination of urban and socioeconomic characteristics (see Goldscheider, 1971; Goldscheider, 1985, chapter 6).

Alternatively, it can be argued that ethnicity is an independent and continuing feature of American life which cannot be reduced solely to socioeconomic characteristics. Specifically, self-employment differences between Jews and non-Jews are not the result of the particular educational and occupational concentration of Jews. Rather, other factors may be operating: Jewish community ties and networks reinforce the particular concentration of Jews in self-employed categories. This structural argument will be referred to as the "ethnicity" hypothesis.

There is yet a third possibility, which posits a specific value which Jews place on occupational independence. This value is continuous with the historical European experience of Jewish vulnerability and the particular status of Jews in the European stratification system. The continuity of this value in America reflects continuing concern about antisemitism and Jewish dependence on non-Jews. This "self-protection" cultural hypothesis cannot be tested directly from the available data. But it seems likely that variations in self-employment over time and among communities as well as within the Jewish population could not be attributed solely to variations in the intensity of adherence to such culturally transmitted values.

The characteristics and ethnicity hypotheses may be partially evaluated by examining Jewish–non-Jewish differences in self-employment, controlling for education, occupation, and related factors. If the socioeconomic characteristics hypothesis is correct, then we would expect no differences in self-employment to remain when the effects of socioeconomic status are controlled. If, on the other hand, differences in self-employment remain within socioeconomic categories, then the argument that specific ethnic factors are operating is strengthened. We cannot test whether the remaining differences are structural or cultural. That would require a different research design with specific questions addressed directly to this issue.

Here we examine variation in self-employment levels among Jews by educational level, not of fathers, but of sons (Table 5). In this generation college graduates have the highest levels of self-employment (45%) and post-graduates (mainly professionals) the lowest (31%). While there is no clear pattern relating education to self-employment among Protestants and Catholics, it is plainly different from the Jewish

Table 5. Proportion Self-Employed by Education, Religion, and Ethnicity: Males

	Less than High School	High School	Some College	College Grad	Post Grad
Jews	39.2	37.0	32.7	45.2	31.1
Blacks	7.1	6.7	10.0	*	*
White Protestants	6.3	17.2	14.3	16.7	20.0
Irish Catholics	5.6	14.3	*	*	*
Italian Catholics	14.3	4.2	33.3	*	*
Other Catholics	16.1	15.2	0.0	*	*
Protestant	8.0	11.4	18.2	15.2	20.0
Catholic	12.2	11.3	13.2	8.3	5.3

*Insufficient data for presentation

pattern. Nor do differences in self-employment levels between Jews and non-Jews reflect their differential educational levels. Self-employment differences are most clear, and the gap is greatest, among the less educated. Among those with less than a high school education, self-employment is three to four times higher for Jews than for non-Jews.

To examine whether these educational differences are related to life cycle factors, we compared Jews and non-Jews within educational levels by age. In no case are self-employment levels similar for any educational level-age group (Table 6).

The same conclusion emerges when self-employment is related to occupation, although the differences are often reduced (Table 7). Half the Jewish managers are self-employed compared to about 30 percent of the non-Jewish managers; 35 percent of the Jewish professionals are self-employed compared to about 20 percent of the non-Jewish professionals. Even more striking patterns appear for those in clerical-sales occupations: 36 percent of the Jews are self-employed compared to less than five percent of the non-Jews. The proportion of Jewish workers who are self-employed is over two and a half times that of non-Jews. These patterns hold within age groups as well.

Since the occupational concentration of Jews is so skewed, particularly by age, more detailed comparisons for specific occupations are difficult. Two interesting findings are revealing. First, fully 30 percent of the Jewish physicians are self-employed, almost twice as high as among non-Jewish physicians. Second, the general category of clerical-sales can be subdivided to locate the specific occupational sources of Jewish self-employment. The high rate relative to non-Jews reflects the very heavy concentration of Jewish men in outside saleswork (largely real estate and insurance) and the direct link between that and self-employment. Fully half of the Jewish men in outside saleswork

Table 6. Proportion Self-Employed by Education, Age, and Religion: Males

Jews	High School	Some College	College Grad	Post-Grad
18–29	*	22.2	33.0	1.9
30–39	*	57.3	44.2	44.6
40–49	27.8	62.5	31.8	29.3
50–59	46.8	34.9	81.7	51.5
60+	42.8	30.7	52.5	70.2
Non-Jews				
18–29	9.3	3.8	4.2	5.9
30–39	15.9	*	11.1	*
40–49	13.5	*	18.2	*
50–59	7.0	30.8	*	*
60+	10.9	*	*	*

*Insufficient data for presentation

work for themselves. Nevertheless, examining other clerical-sales jobs, about 15 percent of the Jews are self-employed, which is still three times the non-Jewish rate.

In sum, there is no evidence to support the socioeconomic characteristics explanation of Jewish self-employment. It remains unclear what specific structural and cultural factors are operating. Multivariate analysis examining several religious and ethnic variables shows no relationship to Jewish self-employment when education, occupation, and age factors are controlled. A regression analysis combining the socioeconomic origin variables (fathers' education, occupation, and self-employment) and current education, occupation, and demographic characteristics shows few effects on current self-employment. By inference, therefore, other factors associated with ethnic networks, economic ties and perhaps some cultural features of the Jewish community are operating to influence self-employment patterns (cf. the conclusions in Goldscheider and Kobrin, 1980).

THE SELF-EMPLOYMENT OF JEWISH WOMEN

Until now, no research has examined the particular features of self-employment among Jewish women. Yet the extent to which women work for themselves has two important implications. First, the disruption to traditional family roles may be less among self-employed women than among women working for others. Self-employed women may have much more flexible work schedules and may be better able to regulate their participation in the labor force over the life cycle. Second, self-employment may link women to family, friends, and coethnics much as it does for men.

We address several elementary questions to the Boston data. First, we ask whether self-employment patterns of Jewish women are exceptional relative to non-Jewish women. We find that, as with men, Jewish women have higher rates of self-employment than their non-Jewish counterparts of each age cohort (Table 8). Of all Jewish women who ever worked, 9.3 percent were self-employed; almost 15 percent of the Jewish women currently working are self-employed. The respective proportions for non-Jewish women were 4.1 percent and 6.8 percent. The differences between the levels of self-employment for women currently working and those who have ever worked imply that more sporadic workers are less likely to be self-employed. To the extent that a higher proportion of Jewish women are self-employed than non-Jewish women, their work patterns may be less sporadic. Those not currently working are much less likely to have ever been self-employed. The largest difference between Jewish and non-Jewish women is among the 40–49 age cohort, where the proportion of the self-employed among Jewish women is 28 percent compared to less than 9 percent for non-Jewish women. It is this age cohort which is characterized by the highest level of labor force participation.

A second question relates to the impact of education and occupation on these patterns. The data show a higher concentration in self-employment among those Jewish women who completed high school compared to those with more (or less) education. For each educational level, Jewish women have higher levels of self-employment than non-Jewish women. The largest self-employment difference between Jews and non-Jews is for women who graduated from high school. Self-employment variation by education is much greater among Jewish than

Table 7. Proportion Self-Employed by Occupation, Religion, and Ethnicity: Males

	Professionals		Managers	Clerical-Sales	Workers
Jews	34.5		48.8	36.0	19.0
White Protestant	25.8		26.1	0.0	9.4
Irish Catholic		16.7		0.0	4.5
Italian Catholic		42.1		5.0	6.3
Other Catholic	21.4		28.6	10.0	4.9
Protestant	26.5		20.8	3.4	7.5
Catholic	14.3		36.8	5.3	4.9

Table 8. Proportion Self-Employed of Those Who Ever Worked, by Age, Education, and Occupation: Females

	Jews	Non-Jews
All Ages	9.3	4.1
18–29	2.9	0.5
30–39	4.8	3.9
40–49	27.9	8.7
50–59	15.5	8.5
60+	6.2	2.8
Education		
<High School	2.9	2.1
High School Grad	14.3	5.1
Some College	5.2	3.9
College Grad	8.8	5.3
Post-Grad	9.6	5.1
Occupation		
Professional	6.3	1.9
Managers	41.7	38.6
Clerical-Sales	2.2	1.3
Workers	11.8	3.1

among non-Jewish women. In large measure, differences between the self-employment levels of Jewish and non-Jewish women are independent of life cycle effects and dependent on educational level.

An analysis of the impact of occupation on the self-employment of women shows higher levels of self-employment among Jewish women within broad occupational catagories. There is clearly an enormous range: from 42 percent of the managers to 2 percent of the clerical-sales workers. The same characterizes non-Jews. Only small differences in the level of self-employment separate Jewish and non-Jewish managers (42%–32%) and Jewish and non-Jewish women in clerical-sales (2.2%–1.3%). Hence, the pattern of Jewish exceptionalism in self-employment is bimodal—among both professionals and workers.

We can extend the analysis in two directions. First we can examine occupation in greater detail. These show very high levels of variability, as might be expected. Teachers and social workers—Jews and non-Jews—have very low proportions of self-employed; medical and medical-related professionals have higher levels (about 12%). The key, therefore, to understanding the self-employment patterns of Jewish women is to focus on their occupational concentration. Unlike the consistently high levels of self-employment among men over a detailed range of occupational categories, the variance is much greater among women.

Another extension of our analysis focuses on the relationship between education and female self-employment within age cohorts (Table 8). The general higher level of self-employment of Jewish women holds for 12 out of the 16 age-educational comparisons. Adding in occupational controls, however, again reduces the self-employed differences between Jewish and non-Jewish women. The high level of self-employment among high school graduates age 40–49 (47%) is concentrated in managerial positions. Jewish women are much more likely to have access to those positions—through families and kin networks—than are non-Jews. Similarly, 36 percent of the Jewish women age 50–59 with high levels of education are self-employed. This is twice the level that obtains among non-Jews and is heavily concentrated in the professions.

Hence, unlike in the case of Jewish men, the unique patterns of self-employment of Jewish women reflect occupation-education-cohort factors. Nevertheless, an examination of the most educated professional women and the managers of family businesses suggests continuing differences for the employment pattern of Jewish women compared to non-Jewish women. To the extent that self-employment is less disruptive to childbearing, child rearing and family life, there would be less conflict between working and family roles among Jewish women. Clearly, there is no reason to argue that the self-employment patterns of Jewish women result in a particular disadvantage for Jewish continuity. On the contrary: the self-employment of women, in conjunction with the patterns noted for males, reinforces kin and community networks.

SELF-EMPLOYMENT, SOCIAL CLASS, AND ETHNICITY

One concomitant of the development of modern industrial society is the reduced level of self-employment. In the United States, the level of self-employment among men has fallen by over 55 percent in the period from 1940 to 1970, from over one-fourth to one-ninth of the labor force (Goldscheider and Kobrin, 1980). Working for oneself has become a marginal phenomenon. The scale of enterprise has increased, large chains have replaced small businesses, and other transformations in the occupational economic structure no longer favor working for oneself. Yet, there is some evidence that self-employment patterns remain an important dimension of the stratification system (Robinson and Kelley, 1979; Wright and Perrone, 1977; Kluegel, 1978). Control over resources may increase for managers and employers as the economy changes. Access to jobs, the segmentation of labor markets, occupational concentration, and differential opportunity structure are connected with self-employment and with ethnic stratification. Neither job authority nor class position can be predicted using measures of socioeconomic status (cf. Robinson and Kelley, 1979; Goldscheider and Kobrin, 1980). Previous research has concluded that, on both theoretical and empirical grounds, there is a need to separate status (the occupational achievement model) from class factors (authority and control over the means of production). If we conceptualize self-employment as one aspect of the class rather than the status system, we expect variables affecting self-employment to be different from those associated with occupation. Our argument is that ethnic groups provide differential access to self-employment opportunities and are, therefore, a key to understanding the class system.

We cannot test directly whether self-employment is primarily a dimension of class or status, or what the particular links are between self-employment and ethnicity. A detailed multivariate model reveals that the factors affecting the stratification system associated with occupational, educational, and income levels are not predictors of self-employment. By inference we suggest that ethnic networks are important considerations both in determining self-employment and in understanding its consequences.

While ethnic groups vary in occupational, educational, and demographic characteristics, self-employment variation is not accounted for by these differences. The cohort and generational data suggest that levels of Jewish self-employment are not static but vary with broader social and economic opportunities. Community variations reflect demographic compositional issues, migratory selectivity, and economic structural factors. It is not likely that community variation and changes over time in self-employment reflect variation and change in norms and values about self-employment.

The ethnic factor in self-employment involves specific networks maintained by ethnic subcommunities. These networks facilitate the process of ethnic variation and change in self-employment. They are also reinforced by self-employment patterns. The higher levels of self-employment characteristic of Jews may represent one mechanism by which contacts and interactions within the Jewish community are maintained and reinforced. Whether self-employment differences between Jews and others primarily reflect basic structural or cultural differences cannot be determined with the evidence available. The choice to work in a particular job, for oneself or for others, is complex, and constrained by the structure of opportunity, career goals, and values of autonomy and independence. Whatever the specific mix of determinants of self-employment, these patterns have wider repercussions and implications. For many Jews, self-employment reinforces ties and bonds that are powerful forces for ethnic continuity. As with occupational and educational concentration, high levels of self-employment have characterized Jewish men and women for at least two generations. These patterns are part of existing networks across generations and establish continuing bonds within the Jewish community.

References

Blau, Peter and O. D. Duncan. 1967. *The American Occupational Structure.* New York: Wiley.

Cohen, Steven M. 1983. *American Modernity and Jewish Identity.* New York: Tavistock Publications.

Fowler, F. J. 1977. *1975 Community Survey: A Study of the Jewish Population of Greater Boston.* Combined Jewish Philanthropies of Greater Boston.

Goldscheider, Calvin. 1971. *Population, Modernization and Social Structure.* Boston: Little, Brown.

Goldscheider, Calvin. 1985. *Social Change and Jewish Continuity.* Bloomington: Indiana University Press.

Goldscheider, C. and F. Kobrin. 1980. "Ethnic Continuity and the Process of Self-Employment." *Ethnicity* 7:256–78.

Goldscheider, C. and Alan S. Zuckerman. 1984. *The Transformation of the Jews.* Chicago: University of Chicago Press.

Goldstein, Sidney. 1969. "Socioeconomic Differentials among Religious Groups in the United States." *American Journal of Sociology,* May, pp. 612–31.

Kluegel, J. R. 1978. Causes and Cost of Racial Exclusion from Job Authority. *American Sociologial Review* 43:285–301.

Kobrin, Frances and Calvin Goldscheider. 1978. *The Ethnic Factor in Family Structure and Mobility.* Cambridge, Mass.: Ballinger Press.

Lenski, Gerhard. 1963. *The Religious Factor.* Garden City, N.Y.: Doubleday.

Matras, Judah. 1975. *Social Inequality, Stratification and Mobility.* Englewood Cliffs, N.J.: Prentice-Hall.

Robinson, R. and J. Kelley. 1979. "Class as Conceived by Marx and Dahrendorf." *American Sociological Review* 44 (February), pp. 38–58.

Wright, E. and L. Perrone. 1977. "Marxist Class Categories and Income Inequality." *American Sociological Review* 42:32–55.

Herzl and the Russian Zionists: The Unavoidable Crisis?

Yossi Goldstein
(HEBREW UNIVERSITY)

The generally accepted view in Zionist historiography has been that relations between the Russian Zionists and the founder of the Zionist Organization, Theodor Herzl, were cordial until the dramatic turn of events surrounding the "Uganda" controversy.[1] Strains in the relationship between the two main centers of Zionist activity—Vienna and Russia—have been depicted as mere growing pains accompanied by a degree, perhaps, of a more basic ambivalence. This essay will attempt to demonstrate that, in fact, the relationship between Herzl and the Russian Zionists was flawed almost from the first, apart from a very brief initial period. This state of affairs continued to worsen as time went on, reaching a climax in the summer of 1903. "Uganda," therefore, was not a conflict due to unique and peculiar circumstances, but rather the inevitable result of underlying processes.

Rumors of Herzl's political activities began to reach Russia during the fall and winter of 1895.[2] The nationalists of Hibbat Zion, who had declared as their goal the Jewish settlement of Palestine, were then marking their fourteenth year. The "Odessa Committee," which had developed out of Hibbat Zion, was then in its sixth year of activity. Their thinking and activities coincided somewhat with those of Herzl. Thus, consideration had been given to the idea of calling a Zionist congress, and there are clear similarities between Pinsker's "political" ideology and Herzl's basic ideas.[3]

Not surprisingly, Herzl's ideas and activities aroused a great deal of interest among those in Russia with Zionist inclinations, and he quickly became the focus of attention in the Jewish national movement in Eastern Europe.[4] His journeys to Constantinople, London, and Paris in search of support for the Zionist idea captured the imagination of many even when details were scanty, and they created the impression of someone whose words had a sound basis in deeds.[5] The prevailing image of Herzl was that of seriousness and reliability.[6] The mounting interest in his affairs was well reflected in the Jewish press, beginning in the winter of 1896. *Der Judenstaat* was translated into Russian and rapidly distributed. The activists of Hibbat Zion who met with Herzl reported back very favorably. Initial negative responses to some of Herzl's ideas—among the Russian Jewish intelligentsia[7] and the veteran leadership of Hibbat Zion—did little to dampen the enthusiasm for Herzl among the rank and file and most of the leaders of Hibbat Zion. Indeed, interest in and attention to Herzl increased during the first half of 1896.[8]

In July of that year the "Odessa Committee," reflecting the general mood, made Herzl's advent the main topic of its discussion.[9] That meeting called for support for Herzl's projects and the establishment of regular contact with him. Lawyer Z. Belkowsky, a member of the "Odessa Committee" and considered to be "Herzl's man," reported that "the Committee is behind him."[10]

Herzl was probably aware of his popularity in Eastern Europe, but apparently did not attach any real importance to it. He did not, at this stage, view his Eastern supporters as a force potentially capable of aiding in the carrying out of his grand plans. In the first half of 1896 he still believed that he could win over the Western Jewish aristocracy. The product of a Western education, who shared the social views of the Central European Jews around him, Herzl viewed the Jews of Eastern Europe with a degree of disdain.[11] Even at a later stage when, having despaired of recruiting the wealth of the Jewish financial elite for the task of winning over the Turks, he turned to the masses of his East European Jewish admirers for support, he was not particularly warmly disposed toward the *Ostjuden.* He undertook his *"Ostpolitik"* without real enthusiasm. It was his close advisors, themselves from Eastern Europe—Z. Belkowsky, M. Berkovitz, Z. Zaidner—who pointed out to him the vast potential of the massive Jewish population in the East, which alone could ensure the success of the Congress.[12]

The first hints of opposition to Herzl within the "Odessa Committee" were discernible in the fall of 1896. This early friction stemmed from several factors: the growing feeling on the part of the older leadership of Hibbat Zion that Herzl was slighting them; discontent in Hibbat Zion circles outside of Russia (in Germany, Britain, and France);[13] and Herzl's failure to win over Rothschild.[14] For his part, Herzl conveyed the (accurate) impression that he had little regard for Hibbat Zion's activities.[15] He aroused the ire of Hibbat Zion circles even more when he publicly criticized the Jewish settlement projects in Palestine, then supported by Rothschild. While the leaders of the "Odessa Committee" were sharply critical of Herzl at this point,[16] they nevertheles continued to cooperate fully with Herzl, until April–May 1897, but with growing misgivings and ambivalence. Although they agreed with and supported Herzl's pursuit of political contacts, they found fault with his tactics, and were skeptical of his chances of success.[17]

The opposition to Herzl was led by the head of the "Odessa Committee," the banker A. Greenberg, and by the "Committee's" Warsaw representative, Shmuel Pinchas Rabinovich ("Shefer"). They argued that Herzl's activity would lead to the eclipse of Hibbat Zion and its projects:[18] "Vienna is not Odessa, and when it comes to the Congress, we will have to take a back seat."[19] The Jews of the West—and Herzl was regarded as an authentic representative of the *Westjuden*—would undoubtedly wield the greater influence in any joint venture of East and West European Jews. The "superiority" of the latter was assumed by Westerners and Easterners alike[20]:

> Russian speech, which has served us so well, will not be heard at the Congress, nor will we readily be able to find among us many who can measure up to the fine manners of Europe. In the midst of all the excitement of the Congress, we will be forced to play the passive role of onlookers.[21]

As the Congress approached, ambivalence turned into antagonism which reached a high pitch among "Committee" members and was openly expressed in the Russian-Jewish press.

However, none of the "Odessa Committee" was willing to be accused of thwarting Zionist activity, or of preventing a Zionist Congress. Moreover they did not wish to put a brake on the positive impact of Herzl's charismatic ideas and personality upon many who had not previously been drawn to Hibbat Zion. They thus decided neither to block Herzl nor to support his plans.

The deterioration in relations between them stemmed from a number of factors. Without doubt Herzl disagreed with the path chosen by Hibbat Zion fifteen years earlier, and he rejected the view that Jewish colonies in Palestine represented the solution to the problems that he had outlined: "Our efforts must be concentrated on gaining our acknowledgement as a State. . . . We do not need a colony, nor a series of colonies. . . ."[22]

But, beyond these ideological considerations, Herzl had no confidence in the ability of the Ḥovevei Zion to achieve their declared aims. His letters and his diary suggest that he was abysmally ignorant about the extent of Hibbat Zion's activities in Palestine. Moreover, just as he knew little if anything of the Jewish situation in Russia, and just as he had previously been unaware of Pinsker's *Autoemancipation,* so too did he fail to grasp the nature of the Hibbat Zion leadership. Zvi Belkowsky had to explain to him the importance of Rabbi Shmuel Mohilever's role as one of the guiding spirits of Hibbat Zion and as chief spokesman for the Orthodox camp in the nationalist movement.[23] His contacts with the Russian Zionist leadership were restricted, in the main, to those individuals who met his western standards of culture and civility. Belkowsky, a professor of law; Zaidman, the engineer from the Ukraine; and the successful lumber merchant David Wolffsohn, were the sole Eastern "types" with whom he could comfortably associate. These men, of course, were hardly representative of the majority of Herzl's East European admirers.

Although in retrospect it might seem that Herzl's "Eastern maneuver" might have been a deliberate attempt to replace the old Hibbat Zion leadership with new men, closer to him in ideas and tactics, a careful examination of the facts reveals that such was not the case. The fact is that Herzl did not know even one of the Russian Zionists who formed the new leadership group in the wake of the first Zionist Congress: men like I. Bernstein-Cohen, M. Ussishkin, V. Jakobson, J. Tschlenow, and M. Mandelstamm. Herzl, and his close advisors as well, were simply unacquainted with these future leaders of the movement.

There was some doubt, even a short time prior to the convening of the first Congress, whether the Russian Hovevei Zion would participate.[24] A significant group within the "Odessa Committee" did not trust the Viennese journalist. There was also some apprehension about how the Russian government might regard the participation of Russian Zionists in such a gathering. It was also feared that the Congress might injure Turkish sensibilities, with possibly adverse consequences for the Jewish colonies in Palestine.[25] Some were opposed to participation on the grounds of distance and expense[26]—and, indeed, many of those invited failed to attend the Congress.

Many leading activists, on the other hand, stressed the necessity of attending the proposed Congress. They believed that the "only hope" for the Congress and its leader lay in the kind of influence which only the vast majority of the movement was capable of exerting.[27]

Herzl, aware of these cross-currents, made every effort to allay the suspicions of the Zionist leadership in Russia and, in a flurry of letters and articles, tried to convince them of the importance of the Congress. Despite his good intentions, however, Herzl proved once again to be insensitive and ill-informed on Russian Zionist matters. His letters and invitations were too often addressed to the wrong people, and he showed poor judgment in his choice of emissaries to Russia. At first, of all the members of the "Odessa Committee," he intended to invite only Lilienblum to the Congress. One of his biggest mistakes was, of course, the site selected for the Congress.[28]

The leaders of Hibbat Zion viewed Herzl's choice of Basle as further indication of his lack of regard for the East Europeans. Prior to the selection of Basle, in fact, Herzl considered several other Swiss cities: Zurich and Geneva. The Russian leaders protested sharply, believing that the proximity of anti-Tsarist revolutionary groups in the Swiss university towns would lead the Russian government to suspect the Zionists of subversive conspiracy. In consideration of the importance of the Russian Zionists to the success of the Congress, Herzl agreed to move it to Munich, but the strenuous opposition of the Munich Jewish community led him to revert to Switzerland.

The leadership of the "Odessa Committee" finally decided, as noted above, not to oppose the Congress but to lend only tacit support. Very few actually traveled to Basle, among them Lilienblum, Shefer, and Ahad Ha-Am.[29] Many others, including the leading Orthodox supporters of Hibbat Zion, decided to remain at home and await its results. Even the group of delegates who came to the Congress were still somewhat angry and discontented with their own decision prior to the opening, and waited with apprehension for events to take their course. As it happened, their negative mood was changed by the end of the Congress into one of "exaltation," as one participant put it, brought about by Herzl's dramatic performance as orchestrator and star attraction.

In his dealings with the Russian Zionists at the Congress, Herzl made every effort to appear flexible and to accept their demands. Thus, he was not publicly critical of the Rothschild colonies, and was able to ensure the absence of any anti-Russian speeches or declarations. He appeased the Orthodox elements, who had been concerned over the secular character of Herzl's ideas, by declaring that "Zionism does not intend to do anything that might injure the religious sensibilities of any Jewish group." At the same time, the faction of *"maskilim,"* under the tutelage of Ahad Ha-Am, could derive satisfaction from Herzl's statement that "Zionism is the return to Jewishness even before the return to the Jewish land." The Ḥovevei Zion saw the inclusion of the first paragraph of the Basle Program as a victory for their point of view ("the settlement of Palestine by [Jewish] farmers, craftsmen and workers in industry, to the extent that this furthers the general aim"). Those, finally, who wished to see the Zionist movement as a party dedicated to the struggle for political rights for Jews in the Diaspora could point to the third paragraph of the Program, which included the phrase: "Zionism will do the utmost possible to enhance Jewish self-esteem."

Further examples of Herzl's conciliatory tactics abound, but their sum effect was to satisfy Herzl's overriding desire to forge a stable and broad coalition for an effective Zionist organization. He was willing to pay almost any price in order to produce a platform that would win the loyalty of any Jew who might sympathize with the Zionist program, regardless of his particular commitments or point of view. At the Congress, it seems, Herzl reached the conclusion that, in order to achieve the goals he had outlined, he would need the support of a significant portion of the Jewish population. In expressing the view that at the Congress, he "discovered" the Jews of Russia, he accepted them as a necessary element in his plans for the future. But this did not dispel the latent and basic ambivalence of the Russian delegates.

The Zionist Organization, unlike Hibbat Zion before it, began to spread to ever-widening circles in Russian Jewry. Even the Russian secret police, the *Okhrana,* termed the phenomenon "astonishingly powerful." The vociferous opposition of the anti-Zionist Orthodox traditionalists was unable, despite its best efforts, to block the progress Zionism made following the Congress.

Aside from Herzl's own image, a variety of factors attracted Jews to the movement and fuelled its growth. The primary factor was the need for radical changes if a solution to the Jews' difficult socioeconomic situation was to be found. Zionism offered one such solution: the establishment of a Jewish society freed from the pressures imposed by the hostile environment. There were elements in the Zionist ideology which clearly drew on the traditional faith in a return to Zion. These served to augment the legitimacy of Zionism in the eyes of many Jews, even if Herzl had stressed the fundamentally materialistic—as opposed to spiritual—character of his answer to the Jews' problems.

During this early phase of expansion, the leadership and organization of the movement passed into the hands of several local representatives of the Zionist executive committee who headed liaison offices. The primacy of the "postal bureau" in Kishinev, run by Bernstein-Cohen, was very quickly established. This was the office that served as the nerve center of the organization in Russia, as well as the direct link with the central office in Vienna. As time went on, it arrogated to itself more and more administrative functions, formerly in the purview of other offices and local representatives.[30]

The delegates who had returned from the three dramatic days in Basle continued to convey their excitement to audiences at home for about two years, during which they described the leader from Vienna in superlative terms. Internal criticism of Herzl's "political" strategy and his paternalism, however, did not abate. But the dominant tone remained one of full cooperation, in the interests of unity and the successful building of a strong organization.

Despite the respect that he commanded in Jewish intellectual circles—especially in southern Russia—Ahad Ha-Am's critique of Herzl's position was not at this time (1897–99) politically significant. Herzl was riding the crest of a wave of popularity, and there were those among the rank and file and the leadership, as well, who saw him in the role of a modern seer who could bring the redemption. Against such emotional considerations, the rational arguments of the critic from Odessa made but a limited impression. There were also rumblings against Herzl within the Zionist leadership, but they can be ascribed to factional rivalry. These grievances were not taken, at the time, as signs of a fundamental divergence of views or escalating crisis.

The Zionist representatives in Russia decided, for example, to withhold half of the membership dues *(shekalim)* collected in order to finance the movement in Russia[31]—a decision which met with the stiff opposition of Herzl and his colleagues in Vienna, who counted heavily on the aggregate financial strength represented by the Russian Jews' *shekalim.* The executive in Vienna quickly issued a directive which demanded that membership dues be sent to the central office *in toto,* to be used at Vienna's discretion.[32] But when the Russians insisted on the use of locally raised funds, the central office had little choice but to accede to their demands[33] even though Herzl personally intervened in the affair.

Herzl and the Russian Zionists also clashed in this initial period over the frequency of future Congresses,[34] the weight to be given to the Russian movement in the councils of the organization,[35] the importance of engaging in "cultural work" and of devoting serious discussion to "practical work" in Palestine—a discussion which Herzl viewed as premature.[36] To the Russian Zionists, settlement activity in Palestine was the essence of Zionism, and cultural activity its soul. Herzl's refusal to treat these subjects seriously almost produced a crisis at the second Zionist Congress.[37]

A review of the initial period of Zionist organizational activity (1897–99) shows that in these years Herzl sought to avoid confrontation with the Russian leaders, and met their demands in at least some cases. While he insisted on such matters as the need for reconvening the Congress annually, he demonstrated flexibility in the question of financing the Russian organization, in bridging the gap that existed on the question of "culture," and on raising the Russian representation on the Zionist executive committee from four to ten, and later to twelve.[38] These actions undoubtedly stemmed from the increased dependence of the Zionist endeavor on support by large numbers of East European Jews, following Herzl's shift in strategy away from the unsuccessful wooing of the Jewish aristocracy of Western and Central Europe, to the organizing of congresses and the establishment of a Zionist bank.

Herzl began to speak of the Russian Jews as a qualitative, as well as quantitative, potential reservoir of Zionist strength. He wrote, for example, that he "discovered" in the Russian Jews "a great cultural force, the likes of which we had not expected."[39] Such expressions aside, however, which were largely a matter of lip service, Herzl did not succeed in getting along with *Ostjuden* on a personal level. He understood the necessity of winning their support, but remained ever convinced of their inferiority.

The third Zionist Congress (15–18 August 1899) proved to be a crucial indicator of the coming trend in Herzl's relations with the Russian Zionists. It is from this time that one perceives a growing lack of confidence on their part in Herzl's diplomatic activity. This gradual disillusionment contrasted sharply with the enthusiasm with which they had greeted his speech at the mass meeting held in London on 3 October 1898 and his audience with the German Kaiser (2 November of the same year).[40]

The delegates from Russia came back from the third Congress with mixed reactions. The disappointment and dissatisfaction which some of them expressed[41] were tempered by a sense of encouragement derived from the new energy displayed at the Congress and the enhanced status of the Russian representation.[42] But this soon gave way to alarm. They developed serious doubts about Herzl's ability to win Turkish approval for the Zionist project, and became increasingly distressed at his absolute denigration of a strategy of gradual settlement.

It was this issue, above all others, which radically divided Herzl and the Russian Zionists. They firmly believed that Jewish settlement in Palestine (termed "practical work" in the language of the day) was "beneficial to the Zionist cause." It followed that the subject of Palestine had to be brought to the center of Jewish consciousness, through the dissemination of pamphlets and through "constant efforts to create a fund for redeeming the land, until such time as we receive the hoped-for charter."[43] Moreover, the Russian Zionists tended to view the new "engine" created by Herzl (the Zionist Organization) as a splendid means to further the colonization activity begun by Hibbat Zion. Indeed, there were some—Ussishkin, for example—who argued that only settlement activity, undertaken in broader and broader scope even prior to receiving a charter, would capture the hearts and minds of the Jewish people.[44]

Herzl was convinced that such ad hoc colonization could not lead to the realization of Zionist aims. Without securing a legal foundation for the endeavor, the point would inevitably come when the government would cut off Jewish immigration, in response to demands by the local population, which might view the influx of Jews as a threat. Immigration made sense to Herzl only under conditions of "our assured sovereignty."[45]

In contrast, the Russian Zionists, viewing immediate settlement as the *sine qua non* of Zionism, passed resolutions to this effect regularly from 1897 onwards. For example, at their meeting in Bialystok, held three months after the first Zionist Congress, they declared that: "Work to promote the colonies in the Holy Land falls within the terms of the Basle Program, and it is the responsibility of the Zionists to ensure the success of this work."[46]

Symptomatic of this growing conflict were the differences between the two sides over the running of the Zionist bank. Herzl's view of the proper function of the bank was naturally determined by his overriding dedication to the charter idea. Thus, the bank was to serve as the chief fiscal tool in negotiating an agreement with the Turks. In the event that the Turks proved obdurate, the bank could provide the means for securing some other parcel of land for Jewish settlement. Hence, Herzl did not oppose investing bank funds outside Palestine. The Russian Zionists, who viewed the bank primarily as a tool to aid the development of the Jewish settlement in Palestine, objected in principle to any bank involvement outside Palestine (or Syria).[47] This prolonged dispute (lasting until the fifth Congress—1901) was finally resolved when Herzl conceded most of the Russian Zionists' arguments. Despite his unequivocal resistance to "old Ḥovevim-style" settlement activity, he was unwilling to continue this confrontation with the Russians.[48]

Despite such fundamental differences in outlook on ideological and practical questions, Herzl demonstrated an ability to find a way around these difficulties and to win allies in the leading circles of Russian Zionism: men like I. Jasinowsky, S. I. Rabinovich, and M. Mandelstamm. Moreover, he was able to placate those among them who were often critical of him: J. Tschlenow, Z. Belkowsky, and even M. Ussishkin.[49] To this end, Herzl had recourse to personal conversations and frank written exchanges. But it would seem that, over and above his undisputed talents in persuasion, his charm and his celebrated "charisma," all of which had a good deal of influence among the East European Zionists, another decisive factor in Herzl's favor was the fact that he simply was irreplaceable. While a number of alternatives could be envisaged in the area of program and ideology, any alternative to Herzl as leader of the Zionist Organization seemed to offer nothing but a return to the days of Hibbat Zion, in terms of the level of activity. This was a prospect which the Russians were eager to avoid.

An example of Herzl's ability to maneuver politically among the leaders of the movement in Russia was the episode in which Bernstein-Cohen was deposed as leader of the Russian Zionist organization. Though they had initially viewed Bernstein-Cohen's rising influence with equanimity, Herzl and his advisors in Vienna were disturbed at the Russian representative's growing penchant for public criticism of Herzl's policy.[50] Particularly following the fourth Zionist Congress (1900), they began to feel that Bernstein-Cohen, based in his postal bureau in Kishinev, constituted a real threat to the hegemony of the central office in Vienna.

Bernstein-Cohen had aroused the antagonism of some of his Russian colleagues as well, such as Jasinowsky, Mandelstamm, and Rabinovich. Herzl was able to capitalize on this discontent, and thus secured Bernstein-Cohen's removal from office (December 1901).[51]

The entire episode gives an indication of Herzl's political perspicacity in his dealings with the Russians. He decided to act only when it became clear that Bernstein-Cohen, had he remained in office, would have endangered the delicate network of relations between Russia and Vienna. At the same time, he was well aware of the considerable support Bernstein-Cohen enjoyed at home, and was careful to avoid any public attack against the Kishinev leader. Such attacks in the press or in internal circulars to the membership could well have proven counterproductive.[52]

Another example of Herzl's ability to cope with challenges from the Russian camp was his handling of the group of young intellectuals, led by Weizmann and Motzkin, who formed a fighting opposition dedicated to the ideas of Ahad Ha-Am.

At first, following a consistent policy, Herzl sharply opposed the formation of an identifiable opposition group within the Zionist organization. Thus, he was absolutely against the meeting of the "youth conference" held by Weizmann and his friends in April 1901. When, despite Herzl's efforts to block it, the group decided to establish the "democratic faction," Herzl switched tactics. He avoided a head-on clash, preferring instead to minimize the group's influence as far as possible. He rejected a suggestion that he take steps against the young "rebels." He maintained contact with their leaders, opposing them when his interests were directly at stake, and gave in to some of their demands.[53]

For their part, the Russian Zionists continued at this stage to display toward Herzl the same ambivalence, based on the perceived necessity of keeping the Viennese writer at the helm of the organization, as they had in the past. Thus, although Ahad Ha-Am's incisive critique of Herzl's *Altneuland* (July 1902) found a ready ear among many of the Russians, they stopped short of an all-out attack. They, along with the ideologue from Odessa, viewed *Altneuland* as an unmistakably Western vision of the Zionist future, one quite different from their own view. If they were unwilling to come to Herzl's defense, however (as did some Western intellectual figures such as Max Nordau), they were nonetheless unprepared to mount the barricades against him.[54]

In August 1903, Herzl met with leading figures in the Russian government (notably, Plehve and Witte). The reaction among the Zionist activists in Russia to these discussions provides one final and instructive example of the manner in which relations between Herzl and the Russian Zionists developed.

Herzl had sought a meeting with leaders of the Russian regime for some time, and the Zionist representatives in Russia had made a considerable effort to achieve such an encounter.[55] When word was received that a visit by Herzl would be welcomed, they tried to ensure that it would indeed be a success. This, despite the fact that such a visit might be taken as a Jewish rehabilitation of Plehve, coming as it did only five months after the Kishinev pogrom (19–21 April 1903), for which the Minister of the Interior was being blamed in Jewish circles.

Upon his arrival in Russia, and everywhere he stopped along his route, Herzl was received by the Zionists with due honor and, indeed, warm enthusiasm. Many among them even helped him spread the idea that the visit was part and parcel of the diplomacy aimed at securing a charter from the Turks. As an added advantage, they argued, the visit would improve the regime's view of Zionist activity in Russia. It was hoped that the Minister of the Interior would cancel the order of 7 July 1903 in which he had prohibited such activity throughout the Pale. No opposition to the visit was evident, for example, at the meeting of the Russian Zionist leadership held one month before Herzl's arrival.[56] This situation contrasted sharply with the anger expressed among many movement activists *after* the visit, when they criticized Herzl for meeting with Plehve. *Ex post facto,* they saw the meeting as a lapse in judgment and tact; decried the supposed rehabilitation of Plehve as "a stab in the back"; and mocked Herzl's much-vaunted successes with the ministers.[57]

In sum, it may be said that, from the third Congress on, Herzl and the Russian representatives of the movement failed to resolve the inherent dualism that plagued their relationship. The executive committee in Vienna was accused of "using us only when it needs money," and of "making light of our proposals."[58] Vienna (read Herzl) was charged with "neglecting crucial needs" and with "failing to involve the Russian Zionists even in decisions directly affecting them."[59] Yet, paradoxically, the lack of a viable alternative to Herzl's leadership led the Russian Zionists to feel an ever greater dependence on him.

On Herzl's part, it rankled that the Russians gave him no peace. Given their role as an opposition, it seemed to him that none of what he was trying to do was able to escape criticism. He complained (in his diary and to personal friends) of the continuing obsession of men like Ussishkin and Bernstein-Cohen with "practical" details, in the old spirit of Hibbat Zion which "always led to defeats."[60] Yet he was aware that the Russian Zionists were the soul of the movement. The Russian Pale was the only potential source of mass support and funds.

This mutual dependence which continued to grow did nothing to halt the escalation of tensions between the two sides. The Uganda affair brought the process to its climax.

From the ideological standpoint, the Russian Zionists rejected Herzl's territorialist-political emphasis. This was clear already at the conference in Bialystok, mentioned above, which took place shortly after the first Zionist Congress, and continued to find expression in successive resolutions adopted by the Russians. As time went on and Herzl's main effort continued to be focused on Constantinople and Palestine, it seemed evident that the dual option for the solution of the "Jewish problem" mentioned in one passage of *Der Judenstaat*—that of Argentina alongside that of Palestine—was no longer under consideration. Beginning with the third Congress, however, Herzl seemed to be trying to turn back the clock. It was in this period that Herzl lent practical support to three "territorialist" plans for Jewish settlement outside Palestine: first in Cyprus, then in El Arish, and the third in East Africa.

The rumors about such plans that circulated in Russian Zionist circles, even before the Uganda controversy, reawakened the conviction that Herzl had after all remained true to his "territorialist" notions. His declarations to the effect that "the principal and ultimate goal is Palestine" no longer elicited much confidence. On the contrary, Herzl's statements in the wake of the Uganda affair, that present political conditions dictated the settlement of the Jewish people on any territory at all, served as "proof" that many of the initial suspicions which he had aroused had been justified. His renewed contacts with the Turkish government were widely received apathetically—even coldly—except among such loyal supporters as Mandelstamm.[61] Indeed, those of his strongest critics, such as Bernstein-Cohen and Shimshon Rosenbaum, voiced the opinion that a charter, even were Herzl to succeed in obtaining one, would be useless because the Jewish people was not yet in a position to take advantage of such a document. They argued that activities oriented toward such a goal were premature, and possibly damaging at that stage.[62] Until the Uganda affair, this view did not win majority support among the Russians. Afterwards, many were convinced of the truth of this contention, agreeing with Ussishkin's attack against "those who have been carried away by over-inflated diplomacy."[63]

The crisis over Uganda was symptomatic of a fundamentally weak relationship between Herzl and the Russian Zionists, one in which the fissures had been widening over the course of several years at least. But it is important to add to this an additional factor: the weakness and inner division of the Russian Zionist movement itself, increasingly evident for two years before the outbreak of the controversy over Uganda.

The removal of Bernstein-Cohen from his leading position in the organization had resulted in a change in the movement's activities in Russia. Decentralization led to a lack of coordination and cooperation among the various leaders. This factionalism came sharply into focus in the Uganda affair.[64] Indeed, were it not for the fact that the conflict was exploited for internal political purposes, the entire affair might have vanished "like a soap bubble" (in the words of Yehiel Tschlenow, one of the central characters in the drama).[65] In ideological terms, Uganda differed very little from the previous conflicts over Cyprus and El Arish.

It ought to be noted, at the same time, that in this case Herzl failed to display his former political sensitivity and deft handling of the Russian leadership. Where previously (as in the case of Bernstein-Cohen) he had shown remarkable astuteness and an instinctive sense of timing, he now committed every possible error. His rather brutal attack against Ussishkin, spokesman for the "nay-sayers," was one of the more egregious of these.[66] Things might well have turned out differently had Herzl employed some of his characteristic diplomatic talents. He erred in failing to win the favor of Ussishkin's camp even before things came to a head. He stubbornly closed ranks with his Russian supporters, led by Jasinowsky, when he might have built a few bridges to those in the opposing group, such as Tschlenow, who would have welcomed such a move. Through four months of polemics (August–November 1903), Herzl failed to discern the nuances separating the extremists from the moderates among his Russian opponents.

By mid-December, when he began to change his tactics,[67] it was too late. By then the lines were too firmly drawn; the opposing camp had had its conference in Kharkov (11–14 November 1903) and had made its demands public. Jasinowsky convened the "pro-Organization" faction, announced its formal establishment, and declared his nonrecognition of the Russian Zionist executive committee led by Ussishkin.[68] Too many opposing interests were involved for Herzl to have been able at this point to appease both sides, and in fact, his attempt to do so at the expanded executive meeting in Vienna (11–15 April 1904) failed.

The Uganda crisis was also an indicator of Herzl's basic attitude to the Jews of Eastern Europe. Six years before, he had publicly "discovered" their "cultural-spiritual strength." Now, as the crisis reached its dramatic climax, Herzl's fundamentally negative attitude to East European Jewry reasserted itself. His conduct during the entire affair reveals an underlying—perhaps even subconscious—lack of confidence in the abilities of the Russian representatives. This, indeed, may have been the root cause of his many errors. His former ability to maneuver with judgment and tact failed him completely this time. Instead, he made ill-considered decisions based largely on emotional and irrational reactions, if not on prejudices that were as deeply rooted in his own mind as they were among broad segments of educated Central European Jews.

CONCLUSION

The relations between Herzl and the Russian Zionists during the early years of the Zionist movement were based on two primary factors. One was the practical failure of Hibbat Zion as a mass movement, and the consequent desire of the Russian Zionists to find a totally new organizational framework for their program. The second was the nature of the link between Herzl, the crucial motive force in the Zionist Organization, and the Russian Zionists, representing the potential of mass support for the movement.

Herzl's success in establishing the World Zionist Organization, the flocking of Jews to join the movement, and the creation of an effective administrative apparatus served only to highlight the previous failure of Hibbat Zion in these areas. At the same time, most of the Russian Zionists believed that, despite Herzl's grand political vision and his determination to adhere to the course of diplomacy, the primary significance of the Zionist Organization was precisely its effectiveness as a vehicle for the realization of the old ideology of the Ḥovevei

Zion.[69] They regarded the essential difference between Hibbat Zion and the Zionist Organization as a matter of form rather than content, and attributed this salutary change to Herzl's influence.

The Russian Zionists' fear of yet another failure was the key to their approach to Herzl. Without him, they felt, the Zionist movement would return to the days of the "Odessa Committee." They hoped to alter the dominant "political" trend in the Zionist Organization, and to make "practical" settlement activity and cultural work in the Diaspora the focus of the movement's program. But they were unwilling to attempt to dislodge Herzl himself from his leading position, even when they found themselves at loggerheads with him.

Herzl, for his part, could not do without the Russians, in spite of what he may have felt about *Ostjuden.* These, after all, were the very Jews whom he planned to save through the establishment of a Jewish state. By any standard of measurement, the East Europeans constituted the most significant part of the Zionist Organization: they accounted for the lion's share of dues-paying members, shareholders in the Colonial Bank, delegates to the Congresses, and members of the executive committee. Herzl appreciated his dependence on the Russian Zionists and acted accordingly—even after the Uganda crisis. If anything, the crisis demonstrated all the more the indispensability of the Russians to the maintenance of a unified world movement. Moreover, Herzl had proven unsuccessful in replacing the militant Russian leadership, a fact that only reinforced their position and underscored their influence.

In effect, they had left behind the situation that had prevailed during the period of the first two Zionist Congresses, when the Westerners provided the natural leaders and the Easterners provided the members, delegates, and funds. From now on, even if the Westerners based in Vienna continued to hold sway officially, the Russian leadership with its own ideological orientations was firmly established as an alternative leading force: a force working for change in the Zionist Organization, and one with realistic expectations in that regard.

Notes

1. Cf. A. Böhm, *Die Zionistische Bewegung,* Band 1 (Tel-Aviv, 1935), pp. 185–98; M. Heymann, *The Uganda Controversy,* 2 vols. (Jerusalem: 1973, 1977); D. Vital, *Zionism, The Formative Years* (Oxford, 1982) pp. 267–367; M. Heymann, "Herzl veẓiyonei rusiah: maḥloket vehaskamah," *Ha-ẓiyonut* III (Tel-Aviv, 1973) pp. 56–96.

2. Herzl's first published expression of his views appeared in *Ha-tsefirah* issues 11, 14, 15 (January 1896).

3. Herzl wrote in his diary, after reading *Autoemancipation,* that he found "a remarkable similarity in terms of the critique, and much that is similar in the constructive program . . . a pity that I did not read this before sending my pamphlet to press. On the other hand, it is just as well that I did not—perhaps I might not have written my own work." *The Complete Diaries of Theodor Herzl* ed. R. Palai (New York and London: 1960), vol. 1, p. 222.

4. Cf. *Voskhod,* no. 8, 1896; *Ha-melits* no. 49 (27 February = 12 March 1896); *Ha-tsefirah* no. 11 (12 = 25 January 1896; A. Lopukhin, *Sionism: Vozniknovenie sionistkogo dvizhenie i ego pervonachal'nyi kharakter* (1903), pp. 4–8.

5. Cf. Lopukhin, pp. 8–9; *Ha-tsefirah* no. 62 (13 = 25 March 1896); *Ha-melits* no. 34 (10 = 22 March 1896), no. 49 (27 February = 12 March 1896).

6. Cf. D. Shimshi, *Zikhronot* (Jerusalem: 1938), pp. 82–83; S. Saltzman, *Zikhronot ve-rishumim* (Tel-Aviv: 1943), p. 138.

7. *Voskhod* no. 8, 14, 32 (1896).

8. *Ha-tsefirah* no. 62, 228 (1896); Shimshi, p. 83.

9. The "Odessa Committee" convened its regular meeting in July 1896. No public discussion of Herzl took place, for fear of government displeasure, but Zvi Belkowsky reported on Herzl's ideas at an unofficial session, and urged his colleagues to support Herzl. After an exhaustive discussion, during which (even at this stage) some criticism was raised, it was decided to encourage Herzl in his proposals. Compare the minutes of the meeting, 27 Tamuz–3 Av, 5656 (1896), Central Zionist Archives (CZA) A-9/18; *Ha-tsefirah* no. 152 (9 = 21 July 1896); *Ha-melits* nos. 147–169 (2 = 14 July—28 July = 9 August 1896); Z. Belkowsky to T. Herzl, 20 Sept. 1896 (German) CZA A-171/20.

10. G. Belkowsky to T. Herzl, 20 Sept. 1896 (Ger.), CZA A-171/20.

11. *Die Welt* (18 October 1897).

12. Belkowsky to Herzl, 17 April 1897, 23 May 1897 (Ger.), CZA A-171/20.

13. Cf. Ludvipol to Ussishkin, July 1896 (Heb.), CZA A-24/4-55.

14. Sh. P. Rabinovich to Y. Goldberg, *Sefer ha-kongres* (Jerusalem, 1940) pp. 485–87.

15. Lopukhin, p. 11.

16. *Ha-tsefirah* no. 228 (1896); *Luaḥ aḥiasaf* 1897, p. 254; *Ha-shiloaḥ* I, pp. 177–82.

17. Cf. *Ha-tsefirah* no. 263 (1896).

18. M. Ben-Hillel Hakohen, *Olami* (Jerusalem: 1927), vol. III, p. 51.

19. *Sefer ha-kongres,* p. 102.

20. Cf. *Zionisten-kongress in Basel (29–31 August 1897). Offizialles Protokoll* (Wien: 1898) [=Protokoll I], pp. 82–84.

21. *Sefer ha-kongres,* p. 107.

22. *Jewish Chronicle* (17 July 1896).

23. Belkowsky to Herzl, 23 May 1897 (Ger.), CZA A-171/20.

24. Cf. *Ha-tsefirah* nos. 105–107, 124, 137, 139, 153–154, 162, 172–177 (1897); Belkowsky to Herzl, 29 April 1897 (Ger.), CZA A-171/20; Nissenbaum to Epel, February 1897, CZA A-19/62–63; *Ha-melits* nos. 124, 130, 137–146, 169 (1897).

25. Belkowsky to Herzl, 10 April 1897 (Ger.), CZA A-171/20; Ussishkin to Kaminka, 13 = 25 April 1897 (Heb.), CZA A-147/32–3.

26. Y. Nissenbaum, *Ali' Haldi* (Heb.) (Jerusalem: 1969), p. 115.

27. *Sefer ha-kongres,* 417–18.

28. Cf. Herzl to Shtand, 18 February 1897 in Herzl, p. 330; *Ha-tsefirah* no. 92 (1897); Y. Nissenbaum, pp. 112–13; Belkowsky to Herzl, 9 May 1897 (Ger.), CZA A-171/20.

Ahad Ha-Am to Aarenpries, 8 July 1897, Iggerot *Ahad Ha-Am* (Tel-Aviv: 1960), vol. I, p. 235; on Bukhmil and his visit to Russia on Herzl's behalf, see *Sefer ha-kongres,* pp. 93–96, 132–33; Sefer *Bernstein-Cohen* (Tel-Aviv: 1946), p. 119; *Ha-aretz* (24 September 1938); M. Ben-Hillel Hakohen, *Olami,* vol. III, p. 55.

29. Cf. *Die Welt* no. 14 (1897).

30. Cf. Y. Goldstein, "The Zionist Movement in Russia (1897–1904)," Ph.D. dissertation, Hebrew University (Jerusalem) 1982, pp. 1–97. Bernstein-Cohen to Herzl, 19 = 31 December 1899, CZA Z_1-233.

31. Circular letter no. 7 from "Postal Bureau" (March 1898, 2) (Rus.), CZA A-24/5-347.

32. *Ibid.*

33. Bernstein-Cohen to M. Mandelstamm, 30 November (=12 December) 1897 (Rus.), CZA A-3/6; Bernstein-Cohen to A.C. (= Actions Comité), Vienna 18 (=30) March 1898 (Rus.), CZA Z_1-260.

34. Bernstein-Cohen to Motzkin, 18 (=30) June 1898 (Rus.), CZA A-126/31–30; Mandelstamm to Herzl, 1 (=13) July 1898; *Ha-olam* no. 40 (1938). Cf. Mandelstamm to A.C., 29 January (=10 February) 1898, CZA Z_1-260; Bernstein-Cohen to A.C., 6 (=18) April 1898 (Ger.), CZA A-126/31–33.

35. Mandelstamm to A.C., 6 (=18) October 1898 (Ger.), CZA Z_1-260; *Stenographisches Protokoll der Verhandlungen des II. Zionisten-Congresses gehalten zu Basel vom 28. bis 31. August 1898* (Protokoll II) (Vienna: 1898), p. 64.

36. Herzl to V. Jacobson, 4 July 1903 (Ger.), CZA H-VIII/41.

37. Cf. Y. Goldstein, pp. 65–81.

38. Cf. *Ha-meliẓ* no. 196 (1897); Y. Chlenov, *Pirkei ḥayyav ufeulato: ketavim, neumim, mikhtavim* (ed.) S. Eisenstadt (Tel-Aviv: 1937), p. 129; Bernstein-Cohen to A.C., 6 (=18) April 1898 (Ger.), CZA A-126/31–33.

39. *Die Welt* no. 19 (1897).

40. Tschlenow to A.C., 7 (=19) December 1898 (Ger.), CZA Z_1-276; Ussishkin to A.C., 8 (=20) December 1898 (Ger.), CZA Z_1-276; *Ha-tsefirah,* nos. 243–45 (1898). Cf. Circular Letter from Postal Bureau, May 1900 (?) (Heb.), CZA A-24/15-807; no. 9 (28 December (=10 January) 1900 (1901) (Rus.), CZA Z_1-378; Y. Rabinovich to A.C., February 1900 (Heb.), CZA Z_1-266.

41. *Stenographisches Protokoll der Verhandlungen des III. Zionisten-Kongresses Basel, 15 bis. 18 August 1899* (Protokoll III) (Vienna: 1899), p. 69.

42. Cf. Circular Letter from Postal Bureau, No. 4 (September 1899) (Heb.), CZA A-24/9-4/309; from Ekaterinoslav, No. 1 (September 1899) CZA A-24/8-292.

43. Y. Tschlenow in *Ha-melits,* no. 229 (1903); *Protokoll* III, p. 229.

44. Ussishkin to A.C., 3(=16) March 1900 (Heb.), CZA Z_1-276.

45. T. Herzl, *The Jewish State: An Attempt at a Modern Solution of the Jewish Question* (trans.) Sylvie Avigdor, 6th edition (London: 1972), pp. 65–67; A. Bein, *Theodor Herzl: biografiah* (Tel-Aviv: 1961), p. 129.

46. *The Bialystok Decision,* CZA A-24/51 and Z_1-383.

47. Cf. Tschlenow to A.C., 7(=19) December 1899 (Ger.), CZA Z_1-275.

48. *Ha-melits,* nos. 24–26, 28, 34 (1890).

49. Cf. Ussishkin to A.C., 13(=26) July 1903 (Heb.), CZA Z_1-276; Tschlenow to Herzl, 4(=16) January 1900, CZA Z_1-275.

50. Cf. Y. Goldstein, pp. 32–42. On Bernstein-Cohen's criticism of Herzl, see, for example, his letter to the A.C. in Vienna (June 1899), CZA A/26/3; Circular Letter No. 4 of the Postal Bureau (October 1899), CZA A-24/9/4-309; Circular Letter No. 8 (January 1900), CZA printed material 2/7/32; Circular Letter (May 1900), CZA A-24/5–8/807. His criticism of Herzl, the Zionist leadership in Vienna and the management of the Bank reached its peak in a circular he sent in August 1901: ". . . Many local [Zionist] groups have inquired at this office as to the veracity of reports in the press concerning the successes of Herzl, the Bank, etc. To my regret, it must be stated that the Bank does not see the Postal Bureau as the central institution of Russian Zionism. . . . In this instance, the Bank takes its cue from the Actions Comité in Vienna, which also turns to us and takes us into account only when it is in need of funds . . ." Circular Letter No. 18 (1901), CZA HV/A3. It was after the circulation of this letter that a fiery exchange of letters took place between Herzl and Bernstein-Cohen. Herzl also wrote an exceptionally sharp letter to the A.C. (23 August 1901), CZA Z_1-210 (Ger.). Cf. letters from Bernstein-Cohen to Herzl, 5(=18) July 1901 and 19 July (=1 August) 1901, CZA Z_1-233; and from Herzl to Bernstein-Cohen, 6 August 1901, CZA A^1-180. The battle between the two continued at the expanded session of the A.C. held 9–10 November 1901, at which a great deal of rancor was expressed. See the minutes, CZA Z_1-191.

51. *Ha-tsefirah,* no. 284 (1901); *Der Jude,* no. 2 (1901). Bernstein-Cohen was removed from office at the pre-Congress meeting of the Russian Zionist organization that took place 25 December 1901, prior to the fifth Zionist Congress.

52. Cf. Mandelstamm to Herzl, 14(=20) August 1901; *Ha-olam,* no. 47 (1901); Minutes of the A.C.'s meeting of 1 January 1901 in CZA Z_1-174; and the Grosses Actions Comité (GAC) meeting of 9–10 October 1901, CZA Z_1-191.

53. Bernstein-Cohen to Herzl, 19 July (=1 August) 1901, CZA Z_1-233; Herzl to Bernstein-Cohen, CZA Z_1-180.

54. *Die Welt* (13 August 1903). Cf. Tschlenow to O. Kokesch, 17(=30) April 1903, CZA Z_1-276.

55. Cf. M. Heymann, *The Uganda Controversy* II, pp. 25–39; T. Herzl, *Diaries,* III, pp. 293–305.

56. M. Heymann, *ibid.*

57. Cf. *Sefer Bernstein-Cohen,* p. 136 and minutes of the GAC meeting of 21–22 August 1903 in CZA Z_1-193.

58. Circular Letter No. 9 from Postal Bureau, 28 December 1900 (=11 January 1901), CZA Z_1-379; Circular Letter No. 11 from Postal Bureau, 28 January (=10 February) 1900, CZA Z_1-379.

59. Circular Letter No. 9 from Postal Bureau; Lopukhin, p. 98; Circular Letter No. 26 from Postal Bureau, CZA Z_1-378; cf. Circular Letter No. 7 from the Information Bureau, 5(=18) April 1902, CZA Z_1-380.

60. T. Herzl, *Diaries* II, p. 280.

61. Herzl to Mandelstamm, 28 May 1901; *Ha-olam* no 53 (1938); Circular Letter No. 3 from St. Petersburg (Russ.), 20 February (=6 March) 1902, CZA A-171/20; cf. Circular Letter from Simferopol (Russ.), 2(=15) February 1902, CZA Z_1-386; *Ha-tsefirah,* no. 31 (1902).

62. M. Heymann, "Herzl ve-ẓiyonei rusiah," *loc. cit.,* p. 58.

63. *Ha-tsofeh,* no. 228 (1903); *Die Welt* (3 October 1903).

64. Cf. Y. Goldstein, pp. 24–32, 107–31.

65. Tschlenow to Gaster, 6(=19) November 1903, in Heymann, *The Uganda Controversy,* II, p. 162.

66. Cf. *Die Welt* (30 October 1903).

67. Cf. Herzl to Y. Reines, 5 December 1903, in *Ha-tsofeh* no. 296 (1903).

68. I. Jasinowsky to Herzl, 12(=25) December 1903, CZA H VIII/397.

69. Cf. Ussishkin to A.C., 9(=21) September 1897, CZA Z_1-276 and *Ha-meliz,* no. 28 (1898), no. 34 (1899).

Poale Zion: A Zionist Transplant in Britain (1905–1945)

Gideon Shimoni
(HEBREW UNIVERSITY)

Not long after taking up residence in London, where he was to stay for some fourteen years, Ahad Ha'am conveyed to his friend, the historian Simon Dubnow, his impressions of Jewish life and Zionist activity in England:

> What shall I write to you about Jewish life here? . . . Judaism, in our sense of the word, is in *Galut* here much more than in Russia. There are Zionist "meetings." . . . But in all these things there is no breath of life and you feel at once that the whole thing is only an exotic plant which has been brought from abroad and artificially stuck in the ground, without any deep roots.[1]

Poale Zion was just such a transplant of early Socialist Zionist manifestations in Tsarist Russia. Notwithstanding Ahad Ha'am's skeptical observations, the present study seeks to trace the development of this transplant in Anglo-Jewry, and to inquire into its significance, if any, in the composite history of Zionism. Although attitudes and policies toward Zionism on the part of the British labor movement will, of necessity, be touched upon, this inquiry focuses upon Poale Zion, its ideological content and its political activities, as an aspect of the history of Zionism in Britain.[2]

ORIGINS OF POALE ZION IN ENGLAND

A dearth of sources makes it difficult to document precisely the origins of Poale Zion as an organized group in England.[3] However, it is evident that among the Jewish immigrants from Eastern Europe who found their way to Manchester, Leeds, and London there emerged sporadically, between 1900 and 1905, a number of small groups animated by a synthesis of socialist and Zionist ideas. From the earliest extant publication, *Di Yudishe Frayhayt,* only three issues of which appeared, all during 1905, it is possible to cull something of the ideological tenor which informed those early groups. Its editor, Kalman Marmor, was an East European emigré. He expounded a socialism which was essentially idealistic and did not shrink from drawing heavily upon the Jewish heritage, particularly from "the great teachers of truth, the fighters for freedom and justice, the Prophets." Rejecting extreme Marxist materialism, he argued that the history of mankind was "not only the history of 'class struggle' as Karl Marx held":

> The soul of human development is the unceasing striving for the "end of days," for a world of happiness and freedom, truth and justice! Man is better than we think. Man is created in "the image of God" and if he will eat of the "tree of life" (as the Torah itself says) he can uplift himself, to Godliness itself.[4]

Whilst recognizing universal workers' solidarity, Marmor's socialism refused to abnegate particularist Jewish national needs. It neither acquiesced in the patriotic Zionist demand "that every Zionist should suppress his personal opinions and class interests and be a purely nationalist Jew," nor accepted the insistence of the cosmopolitan socialist "that every socialist should suppress his national sentiments and the overall interests of all Jews."

Immigrant Jews who, in the fashion of Kalman Marmor, sought to synthesize Zionism with socialism did not enjoy a congenial relationship with the leadership of the English Zionist Federation which had been founded in 1899. Marmor complains that on the one hand, the Socialist Zionists had difficulty gaining entrée into the general socialist movement, while on the other hand they "don't fare much better in the Zionist camp—the clericals and the insincere honour-seekers incite the Zionist mass against them with the charge that 'since the socialists and anarchists have failed to break the Zionist movement from the outside, they have penetrated to disturb it from within.' "

As reflected in the columns of *Di Yudishe Frayhayt,* in the years 1902 and 1903 considerable tensions marred the relationship between the Yiddish-speaking Zionists of the East End who included socialist-minded working class immigrants, and the acculturated, philanthropically oriented West End Jews who constituted the executive of the English Zionist Federation. Part of the East End opposition coalesced in mid-1902 to form a new Zionist society under the name *Ma'aravi* [Western].[5]

The *Ma'aravi* society appears to have been composed mainly of socialist Zionists, one of whom was the ubiquitous Kalman Marmor. It charged the executive of the Zionist Federation with promulgating what it bitterly termed an internal Zionist "aliens bill" which disqualified persons not permanently domiciled in England from being delegates to the World Zionist Congress. This, it claimed, was aimed at preventing supporters of the Democratic Faction (an incipient party in opposition to aspects of Herzl's policies) from being chosen by the immigrant Zionist societies in England. Itself identifying with the ideas of the Democratic Faction, the *Ma'aravi* society upheld the conception of Zionism as a national cultural revival. It opposed any territorialist alternatives to Eretz Israel and stressed practical colonization there and Hebrew cultural work in the Diaspora: "We must know that it is an impossibility to revive a people without reviving its national language and without Hebrew there can be no united spiritually free Jewish nation." Moreover, it emphasized the rejection of the *Galut* arguing somewhat sharply that "one who feels at home in *Galut,* loves his masters and says 'I do not wish to go free,' yet wishes to assist us 'out of pity' is not welcome in our organization. . . . We feel ourselves to be strangers everywhere, even where we are given full rights of citizenship."[6]

The *Ma'aravi* society appears to have faded away after the Fifth World Zionist Congress in August 1903. At the same time, Kalman Marmor and other socialist-inclined immigrant Jews in the East End of London and in Leeds formed the first clearly defined Socialist Zionist groups in England going under the name Poale Zion. By 1905 there were such groups in London, Leeds, Liverpool, and Manchester. The platform of the Leeds group provides an indication of their ideological orientation. It upheld "the standpoint of the general proletariat which strives to replace the individualist capitalist order with a socialist order." Hence, it undertook the task of "struggling against the present economic order together with other proletarian organizations." At the same time, it recognized "the right of every nation to self-determination" and therefore the "necessity to create a national political center in Eretz Israel" for the Jews. It also sought to participate in the "struggle for civil and national rights in *Galut* lands."[7]

The great controversy over Uganda and Territorialism which dominated the World Zionist Organization's affairs between 1903 and 1906 also divided Poale Zion in Britain. One London group, designating itself "Poale Zion No. 1" took a firm stand against all territorialist notions outside of Eretz Israel.[8] It also favored close cooperation with the Zionist Federation at whose conference in June 1905 Kalman Marmor called for an unequivocal resolution assuring that "there be no repetition of the Uganda turmoil."[9]

However, another section of Poale Zion in London turned fully territorialist and published in 1906 one issue of an organ called *Dos Naye Leben.* This organ was intensely ideological but oriented exclusively to the East European scene. Thus it carried an unsigned thirty-three-page exposition of the socialist-territorialist *Weltanschauung,* but no information relating specifically to activities in London. It found the notion of historical rights to the land quite unacceptable. "From a socialist standpoint," argued these territorialists, "all means of production belong to the class which works them. The earth, from this standpoint, belongs to those who now work it; not to those whose forefathers at one time worked it." Only in a place "where there was no native, hungering population; where large stretches of land have not yet been worked by anyone," was it feasible and legitimate, from a socialist standpoint, to develop a Jewish territorial home.[10]

Another divisive ideological question was whether Poale Zion ought to adhere purely to British trade unionism or adopt a vigorous socialist program. This issue was aired at a conference in Manchester on April 14, 1906. No agreement was reached but the socialist group was granted freedom of propaganda.[11]

For the period from 1906 to 1912 very few sources are available. It appears to have been one of "decline and dejection,"[12] and it was only toward the end of that period that the diminutive Poale Zion societies in England were somewhat invigorated by the lecture visits of leading Socialist Zionist personages, notably Dr. Chaim Zhitlowsky, who drew large crowds to a series of public meetings in 1912. A conference held at the end of December 1912 set up a more stable party apparatus and Jacob Zerubavel was invited to conduct a lecture tour in 1913. Ber Borochov, the brilliant Poale Zion theorist, also visited London in the spring of 1914, attracting large audiences of radically minded Jews. At the St. George's town hall Borochov participated in a public debate with Rudolf Rocker, the egregious Gentile leader of Jewish anarchism in London, and Morris Myer, editor of *Di Tsayt.*[13]

After the outbreak of the First World War, Poale Zion played a prominent role in the creation of a common front of all Jewish labor bodies dedicated to the struggle for Jewish equality in all countries. Established in April 1915 as the *Arbeter Farband far Idishe Rechten* [Labor Organization for Jewish Rights], the main plank in its platform was the demand for equal rights in Russia and Romania, but at its conference held in Leeds in late 1915, the Poale Zion delegates, with

Morris Myer as spokesman, managed to include in their platform a demand for "free immigration and colonization in Palestine and in other lands."[14] That this moderate gesture toward Zionism could be hailed as an achievement by Poale Zion is indicative of its difficult upstream struggle within the Jewish labor camp in Britain.

At about this time, Leon Chazanovitch, of the central office of the World Confederation of Poale Zion in The Hague, visited England and stimulated the first concerted efforts to put the Zionist-Socialist case to British trade union and labor leaders.[15] Indeed, in late 1915, Poale Zion applied for affiliation to the Independent Labour Party. However, this application was turned down owing to the influence of the Bund in Russia, which had informed the Independent Labour Party's leaders that the Russian Social Democratic Party had repudiated Poale Zion.[16]

The picture which can be composed from existing sources reveals in 1915 a congeries of Poale Zion groups with a fragile central committee shifting from London to Edinburgh and then to Leeds. The London and Leeds branches had only some forty members each, attending meetings twice a week. They were active in the *Arbeter Farband far Idishe Rechten,* in the sale of the *shekel* (membership certificate entitling its purchaser to voting rights to the World Zionist Congress), and in raising funds for the local Workers Fund and for the Palestine Workers Fund. Other branches existed in Manchester, Edinburgh, and Glasgow, but they numbered no more than ten to fifteen members each.[17]

In sum, all of this amounted to a little over a hundred members—a rather diminutive presence of Socialist Zionism. Yet it was not devoid of some significance considering the modest scale of Poale Zion membership in other lands. Thus contemporary Poale Zion in *Eretz Israel* had only some 200 members, while there were only some 600 in Russia, 1,000 in Austria and 1,200 in the United States. Moreover, in 1915 the Zionist organization as a whole commanded no more than some 5,000 members in Britain, while the *Arbeter Ring* [the Workers' Circle] had no more than 831 members in 1914.[18] The Workers' Circle had been in existence since 1909 and was a secular mutual aid society with strong socialist affinities. Its branches were free to choose their own cultural program and forms of political alignment, but these were in the main not in sympathy with Zionism.

Prior to 1915, support for Poale Zion in the East End was certainly overshadowed by that enjoyed both by the socialist but anti-Zionist General Jewish Workers Bund, and by Jewish anarchists, led by Rudolf Rocker (not himself a Jew), which reached their pinnacle during the Jewish garment trades strike of June 1914. Yet the anarchists disintegrated precipitously within a year of that peak.[19] So much so that by August 1915 Poale Zion could credibly report to its World Confederation that "Here we now have great opportunities. Anarchism is as good as dead. . . ." Furthermore, they could take pride in the fact that the Bundists—although still a force—had been outmaneuvered by Poale Zion in the formation of the *Arbeter Farband far Idishe Rechten.*[20]

THE BRITISH LABOUR PARTY'S WAR AIMS MEMORANDUM

The turning point in the history of Poale Zion in Britain came in the wake of the British Labour Party's War Aims Memorandum, a first draft of which was publicized in August 1917, preceding by three months the Balfour Declaration. Labour's memorandum, as finally formulated in December 1917, contained a clause which stated:

> The British Labour movement demands for the Jews in all countries the same elementary rights of tolerance, freedom of residence and trade and equal citizenship that ought to be extended to all the inhabitants of every nation.
>
> It furthermore expresses the opinion that Palestine should be set free from the harsh and oppressive government of the Turk, in order that this country may form a Free State, under international guarantee to which such of the Jewish people as desire to do so may return, and may work out their salvation free from interference by those of alien race or religion.[21]

To be sure, this statement fell far short of Zionist aspirations, since it did not include support of the right to Jewish national autonomy over and above civil equality. Moreover, it was vague and ambiguous over the right of the Jews to "return" and the nature of the "Free State" to be formed; it could be interpreted merely as a sanctuary offering civil rights for persecuted Jews, and not necessarily as a state fulfilling Jewish national aspirations. Its ambiguity thus exceeded even that of the Balfour Declaration which was issued a little later. Nevertheless, the Labour statement was essentially favorable to Zionism and constituted the first official expression of sympathy for the Zionist case given by a political party in Britain.

The authors of the labor statement were Sidney Webb and Arthur Henderson, especially the former,[22] but the precise motives behind the clause concerning the Jews are difficult to ascertain owing to the absence of relevant references in the available Labour Party sources. One can no more than surmise that a contributing factor was the efforts of Poale Zion to influence trade union and labor leaders, issuing from the initiative of Leon Chazanovitch to which we have referred. Through the efforts of its *Arbeter Farband* which, as a united front of Jewish workers groups, carried more weight than Poale Zion alone, English trade union congresses had already considered the Jewish Question in 1915 and passed resolutions calling for the "civil and political equality of the Jews in all lands." Also the success of the World Confederation of Poale Zion in presenting its case within the international socialist forum may have influenced the British labor leaders.[23] Quite independently of these possible factors, Harry Sacher claimed the credit on behalf of the "Manchester Group" of Weizmann's associates (of which he was one in the company of Israel Sieff and Simon Marks) who had lobbied labor leaders.[24]

Whatever may have been the genesis of the Labour Declaration's Jewish clause, Poale Zion certainly regarded it as a signal attainment. In December 1917 it distributed to the Yiddish-speaking public a "Declaration to all Jewish Workers" in which it stressed that

> even before the government, the executive committee of the English Labour Party incorporated in its peace demands, a demand for full equality for Jews generally and concerning the formation of Palestine as a Free State in which the Jews would be able to undisturbedly develop their own national life.[25]

In this declaration, Poale Zion appealed with much pathos to the Jewish workers to join its ranks as the truest representative of the Jewish working class. It declared that a new era had dawned—"the great hour of the national awakening of our people"—and that "a yet greater hour of the reconstruction of our national home in Palestine" was imminent. Arguing that whereas opposition to Zionism was not unexpected from the Jewish bourgeoisie, it wondered how any Jewish worker could find it in him to oppose the freeing of the Jews from "national enslavement." Moreover, the Jewish worker had a special role to play in the task of national reconstruction, just as did the workers in all nations. For Palestine was to be reconstructed, "not according to the principles and standpoints of the middle classes, which seek only profit out of private interests, but . . . on socialist foundations, in tune with the strivings and ideals of the proletariat in general."

Extant records of Poale Zion indicate a significant spurt of activity in the wake of the Labour Party Memorandum and the Balfour Declaration, and the momentum was sustained throughout 1918 and 1919. New groups were formed in North London, Liverpool, Birmingham, and Swansea; Jewish labor conferences were held in a number of cities and passed resolutions acclaiming the Labour Party's statement; and for the first time Poale Zion mobilized its supporters to campaign intensely for labor candidates in the elections of 1918. Also evident for the first time were efforts to create a register of Hechalutz candidates in England aimed at joining pioneer settlements in Palestine (although nothing much seems to have issued from this). Moreover, for the first time, efforts were initiated to form English-speaking branches. A printed leaflet in English was issued by Poale Zion's information bureau, which had been entrusted to the Edinburgh branch, appealing dramatically for English speakers to join the party:

> The momentous hour has struck. . . . Apathy and indifference at this momentous period is a sin against our national dignity, against our great and glorious heritage, against the blood of our fathers who suffered the anguish of martyrdom in order to preserve their integrity. . . . We want a Palestine that will reflect all the principles of freedom and social justice; not a Palestine that will be an exploiting ground for the capitalist.[26]

At the Poale Zion conference in Manchester at the end of April 1918, the gathering reconfirmed its independence of the Zionist Federation and rejected the idea of Palestine becoming a British crown land as this would be "annexationist in the full meaning of the word." Rather, echoing labor's War Aims Memorandum, it preferred "the creation of a Free State for the Jewish people in Palestine and the immediate removal of obstacles to Jewish colonization."[27]

In October 1918 Poale Zion announced a major reorganization to gear the party to cope with what it described as the "extremely important historical moment" in which it found itself, situated as it was in Britain at the center of those events which would determine the fate of the Jewish people. The central committee handed over authority to a special work committee headed by Morris Myer which was entrusted with the task of planning and implementing certain key objectives. These included closer cooperation with what Poale Zion described as middle class Zionist elements headed by Chaim Weizmann, while at the same time endeavoring to make Zionism "more democratic and representative of the Jewish masses."[28]

At a Poale Zion conference in Leeds during April 1919 the considerable expansion of the party was evident. The Leeds branch, regarded as Poale Zion's "mother" branch in England, had all but collapsed during the war years owing both to mobilization and to the return of many of its members to Russia (in many cases leaving wives and families behind for whom Poale Zion found it necessary to create a special fund). Having virtually started anew after the war, it reached a membership of about one hundred by May 1919. New branches had been established in Woolwich (with some sixty members) and in Cardiff, while the veteran Manchester branch had reached a membership of two hundred. At this point the total active membership may be estimated to have been at least seven hundred. The conference of April 1919 was attended by forty-two delegates from nine branches (East London, North London, Manchester, Leeds, Glasgow, Edinburgh, Birmingham, Liverpool, Swansea). It took a stand in defense of the use of Yiddish in Palestine; called for the attraction to its ranks of the English-speaking generation in Britain, and reaffirmed the intention to seek affiliation with the Labour Party in Britain.[29]

Most significant of all was the initiative Poale Zion took in assembling a broad common front of all Jewish workers' organizations in Britain. Its purposes included not only the demand, held in common by almost all segments of Jewish labor, for "national autonomy for the Jews in those countries where they are concentrated in large masses" and "political rights for Jews in all countries," but also for the specifically Zionist purpose of "fostering national ideas amongst the Jewish workers," and demanding "a national home for the Jewish people in Palestine." The program it recommended for local matters included support and further fostering of Jewish trade unions, improving the material and cultural status of Jewish workers, and formation of a Jewish national workers' committee which "shall establish intimate relations with the British Labour Party . . . and when necessary and possible, attach ourselves as a Jewish section to the British Labour Party."[30] Out of this conference there emerged the Jewish National Labour Council which became a significant force in the Jewish labor camp of Britain. Its moving spirits were Poale Zion leaders, above all Morris Myer who acted as honorary secretary. By the time it held its second conference in June 1919 it could boast of delegates from twenty-eight workers' organizations throughout Britain—trade unions, Workers' Circle branches, Poale Zion branches and the Socialist Territorialists. It could with credibility claim to incorporate "the largest number of Jewish Labour organisations and trade unions in this country."[31]

It was in the form of the "Jewish Social Democratic Organisation" that Poale Zion confronted its most zealous ideological opponent in the Jewish workers' camp. Like Poale Zion, it had small branches in the major concentrations of immigrant Jewish workers—London, Manchester, Liverpool, Glasgow, and Leeds. Moreover, it preceded Poale Zion in attaining official status of some sort within the English labor movement when it was accepted in December 1916 as an affiliate of the British Socialist Party. The latter was the most left wing of the groups incorporated in the Labour Party and subsequently, in 1920, was to participate in the formation of the Communist Party.[32]

The Jewish Social Democratic Organisation lost no opportunity to disparage Poale Zion and influenced the British Socialist Party's Conference held in April 1918 to pass a resolution censuring Zionism. It asserted that Poale Zion was "a body as small in number as they are in influence on the Jewish labouring population," and had "no right to speak on behalf of organised Jewish labour either in this country or in any other . . . they have never been authorised by the Jewish Trade Unions to speak on their behalf, and if anything, these Unions are indifferent or even hostile to Zionism." To this challenge Poale Zion responded in a public statement impressively listing all the Jewish trade unions which had lent their support to a program for a national home in Palestine.[33] It was able to prove that, with the formation of the Jewish National Labour Council, in all of London only four Jewish trade unions "did not openly express themselves in favour of a National Home for Jews in Palestine, neither did they declare against it; a great number of members even of these Unions sympathise with our National Ideal." Poale Zion also refuted as "a mean calumny" the Jewish Social Democratic Organisation's assertion that "when Jewish workers become Zionist they neglect their economic and political struggles." "We can give at least the names of ten chairmen of Jewish Trade Unions who are members of our Party," claimed Poale Zion.

At least one important personality of Jewish extraction in the leadership of the British Socialist Party evinced sympathy with the cause of Poale Zion. He was Henry Alexander, a man who had undergone a rediscovery of his Jewish identity which was to eventuate in his joining Poale Zion. Advised by him, on 6 July 1918 Morris Myer led a deputation of the Jewish National Labour Council to the British Socialist Party's organizing committee.[34] This deputation argued that only two minor groups of Jews opposed the ideal of a Jewish national home in Palestine—"the extreme Jewish reactionaries and great magnates, who are represented in this country by such men as Major Lionel Rothschild, Lord Swaythling and others, on the one side, and on the other side by Jewish Socialists who have strong inclinations to assimilation."[35] Although there is no indication that the British Socialist Party revised its negative view of Zionism, events soon eclipsed the influence of the Jewish Social Democratic Organisation. In October 1918 two of its leaders were arrested and subsequently deported, while some other prominent members returned to Russia of their own accord.[36]

In the British labor movement, as also internationally, a period of ideological polarization ensued, culminating in the founding of the British Communist Party in 1920, in which the British Socialist Party participated. Thenceforward it was from the ranks of the Communist Party that the main working class opposition to Zionism issued rather than from any purely Jewish anti-Zionist body in the labor camp.

It appears that by dint of the same process of polarization, the

Independent Labour Party became somewhat better disposed to Poale Zion. As we have already noted, in the past it had rejected Poale Zion's application for affiliation. It had also evinced reservations about the Palestine clause of the Labour Party's 1917 War Aims Memorandum on the grounds that it implied dismemberment of the Turkish realm and would inflict injustice on the Arabs in Palestine.[37] Now, after mid-1918, Poale Zion information circulars began to report on a more sympathetic attitude by the Independent Labour Party.[38] Moreover, Poale Zion's aspiration to be officially accepted as an affiliate of the British labor movement was finally capped with success when the Labour Party acceded to the request in February 1920.[39]

It was in the category of "Socialist Societies" that Poale Zion now became a part of the Labour Party in the company of the Independent Labour Party itself, of the Fabian Society and also of less significant societies such as the Herald League and the Teachers Labour League. Owing to a dearth of references to the event in the available sources, it is not possible to document the exact circumstances in which this affiliation was effected. One may no more than infer that recent contacts between Labour Party leaders and representatives of the World Confederation of Poale Zion facilitated a favorable predisposition on the part of the Labour Party's executive. In late 1919 a number of leaders of the World Confederation visited London en route to and from their conference in Stockholm. On 25 October two of these leaders, Nahman Syrkin (at the time representing American Poale Zion) and Efraim Blumenfeld from Palestine, were very sympathetically received by the secretary of the British Labour Party, Arthur Henderson. Two days later, Syrkin and another Palestinian Poale Zion leader, Israel Shochat, were invited to a sitting of the party's Advisory Committee on International Affairs chaired by Norman Angell.[40]

At about the same time the desirability of gaining affiliation to the Labour Party was being earnestly discussed in the executive committee of the local Poale Zion. Henry Alexander, the prominent Anglo-Jewish socialist who had by now joined Poale Zion, appears to have played some role in advising the Poale Zion executive or perhaps even negotiating on its behalf in the matter of its affiliation.[41]

Be that as it may, Poale Zion's affiliation to the British Labour Party was hailed by the World Confederation of Poale Zion as a very important development—an evaluation well justified by later events: "This direct organic connection with the Labour Party will be," it announced, "in view of the growing political importance of that party, of considerable weight especially for the Jewish proletariat's efforts concerning Palestine."[42]

The ideological dissonance throughout the socialist world surrounding the formation of the Third International (the Comintern) did not leave English Poale Zion unaffected. During 1919 a rift began to develop between some members of the branch in the East End of London who advocated alignment with the Comintern's revolutionary socialism and the executive committee of Poale Zion which was loyal to Shlomo Kaplansky's search for alignment with the less revolutionary forces which eventually reformed the Second International. In late 1919 tensions led to insults, and even an exchange of blows, at a meeting of the executive committee. This occurred in the wake of the East London branch's submission of a resolution condemning Morris Myer and A. Z. Romanovsky (respectively editor and correspondent of *Di Tsayt* and both members of the executive committee) for publishing what was described as anti-Socialist articles.[43] Not long after, "an organized left faction of the Jewish Socialist Party Poale Zion" announced its formation in a printed brochure entitled *Vos Villen Mir* [What Do We Want]. Declaring itself for "revolutionary Poale Zionism," the class struggle and recognition of the necessity for a dictatorship of the proletariat, it arraigned the World Confederation's Bureau with a series of accusations: binding up the cause of Jewish freedom with the imperialist, capitalist powers; cooperating too closely with bourgeois Zionism; accepting the Ahdut Haavoda of Palestine as a sister party despite the fact that it contained non-socialist elements; concurring in the suppression of Yiddish in Palestine and in the exclusion of Arab laborers from its ranks.[44]

However, the Left Poale Zion was to remain but a tiny splinter group in England. In 1933 it went on to form its own branch of the Workers' Circle in whose general development the Left Poale Zion leaders Itzhak Nathani and Noah Barou played important roles. Barou was also prominent in the founding of the World Jewish Congress in 1936. After 1935 the minuscule Left Poale Zion presence in Britain was to perform something of a mediating role for contacts between its counterpart in Palestine, known as "Poale Zion-Marxist Circles," and the Independent Labour Party in Britain, particularly with Fenner Brockway and James Maxton.[45] In concert with the Palestinian Left Poale Zion leaders Zeev Abramovitch and Itzhak Itzhaki (who spent some time in Britain on the eve of the Second World War), the participation of various extreme left-wing labor leaders in Britain was won over for a "Committee for Socialist Jewish-Arab Solidarity and Workers' Unity in Palestine."

POALE ZION INSIDE THE LABOUR PARTY

Mindful of the centrality of London as the capital of the mandatory power in whose hands rested the fate of Palestine, in 1920 the World

Confederation of Poale Zion opened a Political Bureau in London out of which the important Poale Zion leader, Shlomo Kaplansky, began to operate together with David Ben-Gurion (who was there from spring 1920 until summer 1921). Quite naturally, the local Poale Zion leadership now deferred to Kaplansky and Ben-Gurion in the conduct of political affairs. Indeed, at the Labour Party's conference in June 1921 Kaplansky was able to address the plenum as a Poale Zion delegate.[46] At this time Moshe Shertok who had come from Palestine to study at the London School of Economics also took part in Poale Zion activities and was instrumental in the formation during 1923 of the first consequential English-speaking branch in London with some forty members.[47]

Its freshly gained status within the Labour Party henceforth enabled Poale Zion to plead its case for socialist Zionism in a spirit of intimate comradeship. Thus, in the wake of the Arab riots against Jews in 1921 one finds Poale Zion appealing in this passionate vein to its Labour Party comrades:

> In all the world, we have only organised Labour to whom we can tell our grievances and before whom we can enter our protest against the cruel injustices to which we have been subject. We hereby ask you to listen to our pleas and demands so that these may be sounded through you from the tribunes of English public opinion before the whole world.[48]

For their part, Poale Zion's branches energetically threw themselves into electoral canvassing for labor candidates in the elections of late 1922. Poale Zion's printed organ *Unzer Veg* (which appeared, with long interruptions, between 1919 and 1923) described its election campaign, organized by the new party secretary Chasin-Arnoni, as "the first time that our party has taken part in a political action of this country . . . mobilizing all its forces to support, to the best of its ability, the brother party in its difficult struggle."[49] To the Jewish electorate Poale Zion appealed in the following vein: "Tories and Liberals come to you without a program, without a liberating thought, only with the old empty promises. They wish to continue along the old paths, they wish to leave the rich rich and the poor poor; they were capable of disturbing the world, they are incapable of rebuilding it." Poale Zion argued that the Labour Party was "the only party which actively supported the struggle of the Jewish masses against civil and national suppression in Eastern Europe and for our right to national existence and development in Eretz Israel . . . only the Labour Party takes seriously its duties and promises to the Jewish people."[50] The members of Poale Zion were also intensely mobilized in early 1923 to canvass in the Whitechapel by-election for labor's candidate, Harry Gosling, who was successful, and again in the 1924 elections which issued in the first Labour government.[51]

Throughout the 1920s relations between the British Labour Party and the Zionist labor movement in Palestine were greatly facilitated by visits of British labor leaders to Palestine. One such visitor was Josiah Wedgewood, the Liberal turned Labour, and a devoted supporter of Zionism. Another was Ramsay MacDonald, soon to become Britain's first Labour prime minister, whose enthusiastic account of his visit was republished by Poale Zion as a pamphlet entitled "A Socialist in Palestine."[52]

The local Poale Zion itself, however, appears to have declined in activities between 1923 and 1928. After J. Pomerantz's period as secretary ended in 1921, the party suffered from frequent changes of secretaries and it declined in membership. Whereas the Labour Party's annual conference report of 1924 accredited Poale Zion with 1,500 members, that of 1928 gave only 600.[53] Between 1924 and 1928 the World Confederation's direct political endeavors in London also waned in the absence of Kaplansky who was deputed for work elsewhere. It was not until 1928 that efforts were resumed with the assignment of Dov Hos, a dynamic Palestinian-educated personality, to the task of fostering relations with the British Labour Party. Hos had guided Ramsay MacDonald on his tour of Palestine and established very friendly relations with Herbert Morrison and a number of other British labor leaders.

Yet the advantages of Poale Zion's affiliation to the Labour Party, and of the direct contact with the Zionist labor movement through visits to Palestine more than made up for the decline in local activities. These advantages were reflected in a series of Labour Party pronouncements and conference resolutions expressing support for the Zionist case. One such pronouncement was made in unison by major constituent organizations of the British labor movement who urged upon the British government's representative at the San Remo Conference in 1921 "the necessity of redeeming" Balfour's pledge "by the acceptance of a Mandate under the League of Nations for the administration of Palestine with a view of its being reconstituted the National Home of the Jewish People."[54] The Labour Party's 1920 conference in Scarborough passed a resolution moved by the Poale Zion's representative J. Pomerantz urging the government, in view of the San Remo decision to give Great Britain the Mandate over Palestine, "to remove the restrictions placed upon the immigration of Jews."

At the 1921 conference in Brighton, a resolution moved by Poale Zion's S. Kaplansky was unanimously carried. It urged, in conformity with current Poale Zion ideology, that the upbuilding of Palestine "be effected, not upon the foundation of capitalist exploitation, but in the interests of Labour"; called for the unification under British mandate of all of Palestine, including the Upper Galilee and Trans-Jordan, and for the furtherance of parallel, autonomous institutions for Jews and Arabs. Finally, in 1930, the Labour conference held in Llandudno carried a resolution moved by Poale Zion's Maurice Rosette, which reaffirmed all past pronouncements and added "that the time has come for the Government (at the time a Labour-led government) to apply all the resources at their command in order to promote the policy of the Mandate by the development of the economic possibilities of the whole of the Mandated Territory and thus to encourage Jewish immigration and the close settlement on the land to its utmost capacity."

THE WHITECHAPEL BY-ELECTION OF 1930

After its rather uneventful passage through the 1920s, Poale Zion in Britain suddenly was exposed to great turbulence in late 1930. The occasion was a by-election in the constituency of Whitechapel and St. George which had a large Jewish electorate estimated by contemporaries at nearly 40 percent of the total.[55] The by-election resulted from the untimely death of Harry Gosling, who had gained an overwhelming victory for labor in the recent general election of May 1929. It so happened that the somewhat fragile position of MacDonald's labor government invested this by-election with more than usual significance at this point in time. For its electoral campaign in Whitechapel and St. George, the Labour Party relied heavily upon the influence of the Transport and General Workers' Union, whose general secretary was the formidable Ernest Bevin. Harry Gosling had himself been president of that union, and had largely owed his electoral success to its support.

Under normal circumstances the Labour candidate could confidently have relied on wholehearted election support from Poale Zion. But only a month earlier, in October 1930, the Labour government had issued the Passfield White Paper which augured new restrictions of Jewish immigration and of land purchase and commented upon Zionist endeavors in Palestine in critical terms. In Zionist eyes this was perceived as a betrayal of Britain's mandatory responsibility for the development of the Jewish national home. Consequently, some leading Zionists seized the opportunity to express their indignation by rallying an anti-government Jewish vote in Whitechapel. Concurrently, the Liberal Party pointedly chose as its contestant for the Whitechapel seat Barnett Janner, a Jew and prominent leader of the English Zionist

Federation. The Conservative Party's candidate was Noel Guiness, while Harry Pollitt stood for the Communist Party.

Under the auspices of the East London Zionist League, a "Palestine Protest Committee" was formed. One of the protest leaders, Rabbi Louis Rabinowitz, declared explicitly that "they were using the present by-election in Whitechapel as a legitimate means of registering a protest against the Government."[56]

In common with all Zionists, Poale Zion had left no doubt as to its grave disappointment with the Passfield White Paper. Communicating its objections to Arthur Henderson, secretary of the Labour Party, it pointed out that the White Paper was in direct contradiction to the party's conference resolution passed as recently as a few weeks earlier at Llandudno. Arguing further that in the past "the sympathy of British Labour with the national aspirations of the Jewish people . . . was a powerful argument in our hands which we used to win over the Jewish masses to the cause of Labour," Poale Zion averred that the White Paper had now shaken confidence in the sincerity of the British labor movement and "done incalculable harm to the Poale Zion as advocates of Labour policy." Hence it had decided to call upon the executive of the British Labour Party "to use its influence for securing the withdrawal of the White Paper even if this involves the resignation of the Minister responsible." Finally, Poale Zion linked the matter quite blatantly to the forthcoming by-election "in an area which has a substantial Jewish vote." "We feel bound to add," it stated, "that your reply will largely influence the Jewish vote in that constituency."[57]

Furthermore, when Poale Zion's central committee got wind of the Labour Party's intention to nominate the candidacy of Stafford Cripps (at the time Solicitor-General) for the by-election, it decided unanimously that it could not support a candidate who was actually a member of the government responsible for the White Paper. This decision having been communicated to Ernest Bevin, he duly saw to the replacement of Stafford Cripps's contemplated candidacy by that of James Hall, himself an executive member of the Transport Workers' Union.[58]

It is evident that the executive committee of the Labour Party took Zionist protestations seriously, for it appointed a deputation "to consult with various interests concerned with the Palestinian policy, and to seek an interview with the Prime Minister." This deputation duly consulted with Shlomo Kaplansky and Dov Hos who were in London at the time.[59] The matter was also extensively aired with Lord Passfield himself, who tried somewhat disingenuously to assure them "that the Government statement of policy has been subjected to considerable misunderstanding and misinterpretation, and not a little misrepresentation, in certain quarters."[60] Although Passfield offered to publicize "some sort of reassuring statement," the Party's executive committee felt that this was inadequate and therefore directly urged Prime Minister Ramsay MacDonald to remedy the situation immediately, lest the delay "render a position already peculiarly awkward almost beyond recovery."[61]

Meanwhile, a spate of letters to the editor of the *Jewish Chronicle* urged the Jews of Whitechapel to express their protest at the Labour government's White Paper on Palestine by voting for non-Labour candidates. "The small but vigorous voice of Jewry in Whitechapel must now give its emphatic No!" wrote one indignant correspondent, "when it will shortly be asked to give its support to the Government that has violated and abrogated every principle of good faith to the Jewish people."[62]

Poale Zion now informed the Labour Party of its decision that "before any steps be taken by the Party [Poale Zion] in the matter of the Whitechapel by-election, a clear and unequivocal statement be sought from the Labour Party executive regarding its attitude to the White Paper."[63] Meanwhile James Hall prudently rose to the occasion by announcing that there indeed were certain inferences in the White Paper which he could not reconcile with the Labour Party's past declarations. Moreover, he gave an undertaking:

> If any attempt is made either by this Government or by any other Government to depart from the spirit of the resolution of the Llandudno Conference which so clearly expressed the policy of our party, I will regard it as my duty to my Jewish constituents to vote against any such action.[64]

In the light of Hall's statement, a special joint meeting of Poale Zion's central committee and the committees of all London branches now decided to actively campaign on behalf of the Labour Party's candidate. It explained its decision in these terms:

> The policy best calculated to safeguard the interests of the Jewish masses and the rights of the Jewish people in Palestine is to return Mr. James Hall to Parliament, thus adding to the group of devoted labour friends in Parliament one more supporter who will, like his predecessor in the Whitechapel division, represent in the House of Commons in the best possible way the interests and aspirations of the Jewish people.[65]

This decision exposed Poale Zion to a barrage of reproachful criticism from other Zionists. The *Jewish Chronicle* reported caustically on Poale Zion's decision under the heading " 'Ratting' from Zionism." Its columnist called Poale Zion's policy a "traitorous course." They had "decided to oppose Jewish interests and vote for the Labour candidate," he commented, "doubtless because they are far more concerned with the interests of Labour, as they see them, than with the interests of Judaism as every Jew knows them to be at this crisis in Jewish affairs."[66]

Editorially, the *Jewish Chronicle* appealed to Jewish electors not to give their votes to the Labour candidate, "for his success, should the votes he obtains be as great as or greater than those given to the late member for the Division, will mean the triumph of the Government who will draw from it an approval by a largely Jewish constituency, of their Palestine policy, and will in consequence pursue it." In contradiction to Poale Zion's reasoning it insisted that only Jewish refusal to give support to the Labour candidate would "inflict such a moral defeat on the Government as will induce them seriously to reconsider, and maybe withdraw altogether, the White Paper."[67]

In response to these abusive criticisms, J. L. Cohen of Poale Zion argued that "Poale Zion, more than any other section of Zionists, have felt the recent blow," but they were convinced that only by continuing their work within the Labour Party, would they be enabled "to fight for the carrying through by the Government of the official policy of that Party, and to insist on the proper application of their avowed principles of internationalism and democracy in their treatment of Jews and Palestine."[68]

As the election date drew near, Poale Zion called a public meeting in Whitechapel for 28 November, with the dual object of protesting against the Palestine White Paper and clarifying its attitude in the Whitechapel by-election. The speakers invited to address the meeting included Ernest Bevin and James Hall. Feelings in the East End were by now highly inflamed and a group of rowdy hecklers attempted to disrupt the meeting and convert it into a demonstration of support for the Liberal candidate, Barnett Janner. The first speaker, Harry Snell, was prevented from being heard, as was Michael Marcus. At that point Ernest Bevin took over the chair and made himself heard by dint of his indomitable presence. Declaring that the Transport Workers' Union alone had twenty-six members in the House of Commons, he pledged that "if the White Paper came up before the House they would all vote against it, as would also Mr. Hall when he got there." "The Jewish workers," he urged, "could not afford to be separated from the rest of the working class and from the Labour Party, and should stand by the Labour candidates and the solidarity of the workers."[69]

When the by-election finally took place on 3 December 1930 the result was a victory for Labour's James Hall. However, the Labour majority was drastically reduced to a margin of 1,099 over the Liberals' Barnett Janner.[70] In the inclement circumstances which the White Paper had precipitated, Bevin could justifiably be highly satisfied with the result. As for Poale Zion, its newsletter claimed that "the firm stand of the Poale Zion was largely responsible for the defeat of the enemies of socialism in Whitechapel."[71] To be sure, Palestine policy was certainly not the only important issue at play in this by-election; the constituency also included a significant Irish vote concerned with the question of support for Roman Catholic schools. The problem of unemployment in the East End was also at issue.[72] However, the fact that Barnett Janner, who as a political novice but a Jew and known Zionist drew his support mainly from the Jews, was able to increase the Liberal poll from 4,521 in May 1929 to 7,445 (whereas the Conservative poll rose only by 318 votes), suggests a real swing of the Jewish vote away from Labour. Such a swing, rightly feared by the Labour Party, might well have lost it the election.

In these circumstances, therefore, it is reasonable to infer that even a limited success of Poale Zion in dissuading a few hundred members and sympathizers from deserting Labour might well have sufficed to save the Labour candidate from defeat. As for the Passfield White Paper, it was to all intents and purposes rendered nugatory through a Zionist diplomatic triumph conducted by Weizmann and his colleagues of the World Zionist Organization—a development beyond the scope of the present study, and in which the Whitechapel by-election affair played only an ancillary role.[73]

FROM THE WHITE PAPER OF 1930 TO THE WHITE PAPER OF 1939

If it is credible that in the 1930 Whitechapel by-election Poale Zion played a crucial role in tipping the electoral scales in Labour's favor, it is equally credible that its role was no longer significant in the two election contests which followed in that constituency. For in 1931, notwithstanding Poale Zion's sustained support for Labour's James Hall, he was defeated by the Liberal candidate Barnett Janner, who again explicitly appealed to the Jewish electorate. As for the next general election, in 1935, although Hall gained election to his seat in a straight contest with Janner—gaining 13,374 votes to Janner's 11,093—it is by no means evident that Poale Zion activity, or any Zionist influence for that matter, was crucial for this Labour victory.[74]

During 1931 both Dov Hos and Shlomo Kaplansky returned to Palestine to undertake other tasks and for a few years the conduct of political and ideological work was left almost entirely to the local Poale Zion, the main role being played by Joseph L. Cohen. To be sure, Dov Hos persevered from afar in the cultivation of friendly relations with James S. Middleton and William Gillies, respectively secretary and international secretary of the Labour Party, not least of all by sending from time to time gift cases of Jaffa oranges.[75] In contrast to the difficult period the British Labour Party was experiencing, having suffered severe losses in the 1931 election only partially recouped in 1935, the Zionist labor movement was fast rising to its zenith as the dominant force in Zionism. Relationships beween the two movements were much enhanced by the continuation of visits to Palestine on the part of leading British trade unionists and Labour Party personalities, arranged through the efforts of J. L. Cohen. The visitors to the Zionist labor movement in Palestine included, in 1933, the trade unionist Creech-Jones, later to be Colonial Secretary in Attlee's labor government; Frederick Pethick Lawrence in 1934; and Herbert Morrison and Susan Lawrence in 1935.[76] The cumulative influence of internal Poale Zion lobbying and external relationships with the Zionist labor movement in Palestine sustained the essentially pro-Zionist policies of the British Labour Party throughout the period from 1931 to 1935.

One major success related to the proposal revived after 1934 by High Commissioner for Palestine Sir Arthur Wauchope that a Legislative Council be convened reflecting the ratio of Jews to Arabs in the population of Palestine. Both in the World Zionist Organization's leadership and in the Palestine Labor Party (Mapai) opinion was overwhelmingly opposed to the precipitate creation of such a body. It was deemed potentially disastrous since the Arab majority in such a council would inevitably thwart Jewish immigration and the Zionist aspiration eventually to become a majority in Palestine. Ideologically, however, it was no simple task to oppose a proposal which was bound to commend itself to socialists as democratic and progressive.

In its lobbying for Labour opposition to the proposal, Poale Zion adopted the somewhat disingenuous line of argument that "by no stretch of the imagination, would it be possible to consider the proposed Legislative Council as a democratic institution," since it would represent only the vested interests of the big Arab landlords rather than the Arab masses who in "their present primitive state would have no effective voice in the elections to that council." It averred that "the attempt to inaugurate a legislative council in a country whose population has as yet not enlisted even the meagre opportunities afforded it for municipal government, is at the least premature . . . it would merely provide a tribune for Arab agitation against the work of upbuilding and create a grave source for friction between the two peoples." Moreover, argued Poale Zion:

> As a preliminary condition to any attempt to establish a legislative council, all parties concerned must accept the Mandate and the obligations imposed thereby. The present Arab leadership, however, openly and categorically repudiates the Mandate. It is inconsistent with the obligations imposed by the Mandate to entrust the legislation of the country to a majority which is opposed to the very foundation upon which the whole legislative structure of Palestine rests.[77]

The controversial proposal for a Legislative Council coincided with the first attempt of the Labour Party to go beyond the various pronouncements and resolutions on record and systematically to formulate a long term policy on Palestine. The task of drafting such a policy fell to the party's Advisory Committee on Imperial Questions. Its recommendations, formulated in February 1936, were far from committing Labour to carte blanche support for Zionists aspirations. However, to the credit of Poale Zion's propaganda and protestations against the proposed legislative council, the recommendations did at least reject the proposal as inopportune on the grounds that it "would probably promote irresponsibility and discord, without satisfying Jews or Arabs or facilitating good government."[78]

The concerted efforts of Poale Zion in Britain and labor leaders from the *Yishuv* also met with success in the propaganda clash over the significance of the Arab strikes and violence which broke out in 1936. These events marked the beginning of a protracted Arab rebellion. Among other things, this fresh Arab onslaught found expression for the first time in something of an ideological offensive against Zionism on the labor front in Britain. Certainly the records of the Labour Party reveal an increase of incoming correspondence from Palestinian Arab sources purporting to represent a socialist workers' case. The major emanation of this genre issued from George Mansour of the Arab Center in London, who identified himself in letters to the Labour Party as "former secretary" of the Arab Labour Federation in Palestine, and claimed to represent "the Arab case from the point of view of Arab labour and the Arab masses." Mansour complained that the British Labour Party had failed to understand the Arab case. However, the arguments marshalled by him bore very little ideological imprint of a socialist character. They appealed primarily to the conventional principle of national self-determination—insisting that the Arab population had the exclusive right to such self-determination in Palestine—and to the democratic principle that a majority not be subjected to the will of a minority.

While on the one hand charging the British government with selfish imperialist motives "for occupying a country of strategic importance" on behalf of the Jews, Mansour did not refrain from invoking the British imperial power's pledges to the Arabs in return for their assistance in the World War. Challenging the Labour Party's sympathy for the Zionist cause, Mansour asked: "Why, then, should it not be considered possible for the Jews to live amongst the Arabs as a minority?" He averred that "there is every possibility of Jews and Arabs living together in harmony, provided only that the Jews look upon themselves as ordinary citizens among their Arab neighbours, like all other minorities. But there is no chance for Jewish nationalism to live side by side with Arab nationalism. And Arab nationalism means the Arab lands for the Arab people." Mansour's arguments were not untainted by an antisemitic motif, for he charged that "the promise to make Palestine a Jewish National Home was made to international Jewry—in other words, to Jewish international capitalists—in return for favours received."[79]

Poale Zion's propaganda line on the Arab unrest and rebellion was articulated in socialist ideological terms. It argued that the so-called General Strike in Palestine was no more than a reactionary manifestation of "organised murder, pillage and incendiarism," more akin to fascist tactics in Italy and Germany than to true working class action. "Instigated by the Arab capitalists, the landlords and notables, who exploit the Arab workers the more brazenly as these workers are backward and unorganised," claimed Poale Zion, "it is a nationalist adventure by Arab exploiters of labour on approved Fascist lines, which, posing as a popular movement, has obtained the support of Tories and Communists alike." Poale Zion contended that it was not the Jews whom the Arab workers had to fear, but "the Arab employers, seeing the danger to their class, realising that the influence of organised Jewish labour on the exploited Arab masses and the advance of the Arab Jewish Working Class Movement must culminate in the overthrow of their feudal domination, fight it with every weapon they can lay hands on, as reaction invariably fights the advance of new ideas and modes of life."[80]

Notwithstanding the growth of the pro-Arab elements within the Labour Party[81] there can be no doubt that the Zionist case, at least in essentials, commanded far more support. The 1936 Labour Party conference already saw the passing of a pro-Zionist resolution, proposed by Susan Lawrence and seconded by Maurice Rosette of the local

Poale Zion. A pro-Arab counterresolution was rejected. Recalling "the continuance of support given by the British Labour Movement to the establishment of a National Home for the Jewish People in Palestine," the resolution as passed deplored what it described as "the outbreak of racial and religious strife which threatens to destroy this great humanitarian project and to deprive the Jewish people of the opportunity of developing their own political, social and cultural institutions."[82] When Parliament debated the situation in Palestine in June 1936, all three of the Labour members who participated in the debate, Tom Williams, Arthur Creech-Jones and Herbert Morrison, had been fully briefed by David Ben-Gurion who was in London at the time. Each thoroughly endorsed the Zionist case against the Arab strike.[83]

On the whole, the records of the Labour Party's International Department in the late 1930s show that Arab representations were thoroughly outflanked and outclassed by the compound Zionist lobbying of the local Poale Zion and the emissaries from the Zionist labor movement in Palestine. Indeed, the Arab case barely got a hearing and was, besides, very poorly presented. The contents of a tedious letter to the chairman of the Labour Party, claiming to represent over seven hundred workers from the Palestine Workers' Society in Haifa, and the treatment it received from William Gillies, secretary of the International Department, typified the situation. In poor English, the letter protested against what it described as "the unlimited and unreserved support of your Party to the Zionist cause which is but a capitalist and imperialist movement . . . against the Arab masses of workmen and peasants." It charged the Zionists with forbidding Jews of all classes "to have any dealings with Arabs at all." By its attitude toward the Arabs, the letter stated, the Labour Party was "undoubtedly endeavouring to exterminate [sic] a historically and politically established nation, namely the Arabs, in favour of a race alien to the Arabs and to their mother country."

Revealing its true colors, the letter went on to warn that if their disillusionment with British labor were not allayed, Arab workers might

> throw away this Socialism of which we have been apparently deceived and embrace National Socialism . . . We have already the conviction in any case that every International movement of any sort is submind [sic—subverted or undermined?] by Jews. As a minority every where [sic] Jews, since they have become race minded and religiously political conscious, they are trying to over rule [sic] the world by undermining every international movement in which they make it their duty to indulge.[84]

Far from being impressed by this memorandum, William Gillies referred it to the Zionist labor movement's spokesman in London, Berl Locker, for comment. Little effort was required to discredit the letter's claims to represent an Arab worker's movement of any significance. Identifying the so-called Palestine Arab Workers' Society as "one of the numerous groups established by the Mufti party with the object of hitching the Arab workers to its wagon and of spoiling any attempts at co-operation between Jewish and Arab workers," Locker pointed to the obvious Nazi influences evident in the memorandum.[85]

In marked contrast to the International Department's scant attention to Arab representations, those of the Zionists received a sympathetic hearing throughout this period, personalities such as Dov Hos and Ben-Gurion being invited on occasion to address the meetings of its International Subcommittee.[86] After protracted consideration of various proposals, in 1937 the special subcommittee on Palestine which had been set up to formulate a long-term policy, produced recommendations favorable to the Zionist case although not devoid of reservations. They stated: "The Arabs desire a stoppage of Jewish immigration but the mandatory power cannot agree to this. The pledge of the National Home must be honoured." They opposed both division of Palestine into Jewish and Arab cantons and formation of a legislative council, at least until "there is evidence that Jews and Arabs will work together in amity." They supported continued Jewish immigration to Palestine, while adhering to the principle that it should be limited by the country's absorptive capacity. However, in Zionist eyes, these essentially positive formulations were somewhat vitiated by the fact that, in the course of the committee's deliberations a majority had favored a proviso, aimed at allaying Arab fears, that for a period of ten years immigration should not be permitted to upset the relative proportion of Jews to Arabs.[87]

THE INVIGORATION OF POALE ZION AND ITS PLACE IN ANGLO-JEWISH ZIONISM

In the course of the 1930s Poale Zion in Britain increasingly gained the adherence of a new generation of locally born personalities. Like Maurice Rosette, who in the 1920s had been the forerunner of this phenomenon, they were mostly the first-generation offspring of immigrants from Eastern Europe who had been attracted to the British labor movement but sought to synthesize that affinity with their strong Jewish identification. These included Nathan Jackson, Maurice Pearlman, Max Easterman and Sydney Silverman. Another invigorating factor was the accession of expatriates from Europe who had been associated with labor Zionism there. Foremost amongst them was Schneier Levenberg, who arrived from Eastern Europe in 1936 and soon became a key figure in the ideological and practical work of Poale Zion. Finally, in 1938, there was the arrival in London of Berl Locker as head of the Political Bureau of the Jewish Agency in London. For many years a major organizer of the World Confederation of Poale Zion, Locker was now assigned the task of acting as representative of the labor leadership in Palestine, a function akin to that fulfilled by Dov Hoz and Shlomo Kaplansky prior to 1932. Not long before Locker's arrival, Berl Katznelson, whilst in England in 1937, had initiated the idea of establishing a "Palestine Labour Studies Group," with the aim of publishing propaganda literature in English. This issued in a series of twelve booklets on various aspects of labor Zionism, climaxed by the publication in 1938 of a collection of documents, speeches and articles which highlighted the positive attitude towards Zionism of the British labor movement from 1917 until 1938. J. S. Middleton, secretary of the Labour Party, provided an enthusiastic introduction to this booklet.[88]

At about the same time, in 1938, a body called the "Palestine Labour Political Committee" was established with Berl Locker as chairman, and the participation of S. Levenberg, J. L. Cohen, M. Rosette, M. Pearlman, and N. Jackson as professional secretary. The committee undertook intensive lobbying and liaison activities with all segments of British labor, trade unions, and cooperative movements, and sought the cooperation of other Jewish labor organizations. In addition, Poale Zion launched, in late 1938, a major propaganda venture in the form of a "Petition for Jewish Immigration into Palestine," in cooperation with a number of Workers' Circle branches and Jewish trade unions. It collected about a quarter of a million signatures for presentation to the British government.[89]

By the late 1930s Poale Zion was conducting its activities mostly in English and its membership was mainly lower middle class. An examination of the occupations of the leading personalities in Poale Zion in the 1930s and 1940s reveals among the foreign-born no working class persons, but rather a prominence of persons with business and manufacturing occupations and of Yiddish journalists. The locally born generation of leading personalities included a number of lawyers (some of whom entered labor politics), a few university teachers, and rather more business occupations.[90]

The ideological clash with communism for the allegiance of the leftist element in the English-speaking generation presented Poale Zion with its greatest challenge in the 1930s. In a series of English articles written in 1935 Joseph L. Cohen gave an exposition illustrative of the main lines of Poale Zion's answer to communist arguments. Cohen argued that communism offered no real alternative to Zionism: "Communism is not interested in the Jewish position as such. The Jews are not an end in themselves, but the means to an end." All that the communists offered was that the Jews "be the first to be sacrified on the altar of international socialism." Moreover, he contended, whereas in Russia itself Soviet practice had gone back to "a nationalist Russian policy," only the Jewish communists maintained an out of date cosmopolitan Orthodoxy. "While the Bolsheviks of Russia have changed their minds, or at least, their tactics, the suggestion to apply this change to the Jewish question would be regarded by the Jewish communists as in the nature of a religious heresy." Hence the Jewish communists in England adhered to the outdated cosmopolitan ideal but only with reference to the Jews. They were wilfully blind to the experiments in socialism being made in Palestine, to the benefits brought in the labor emancipation of the Arabs there and to the fact that it was labor Zionism, not the bourgeoisie, which was leading the Zionist endeavor in Palestine towards a socialist society which would ultimately take its place alongside of all other socialist societies. Cohen averred that Zionist socialists too "believe in the dominating future of internationalism, but regional consciousness in all degrees is an attribute of mankind, and internationalism, in so far as it attempts to stifle regional expression, is a fallacy. . . . Internationalism is therefore interpreted by Zionists to mean not the destruction of nations but closer co-operation between them for the good of all."[91]

Poale Zion's calculated attempts to penetrate the Workers' Circle dated back to a party leadership consultation held on 22 October 1922 with the participation of Shlomo Kaplansky and Berl Katznelson.[92] By 1937 there were four Workers' Circle branches which were aligned with Poale Zion. They were branches 15 and 19 in London, branch 12 in Leeds, and branch 18 in Glasgow. However, the communist presence was strongly felt in the Workers' Circle and the dominant tone was one of indifference if not opposition to Zionism.

To be sure, Poale Zion made repeated attempts to gain a larger following in the East End. A particularly concerted effort was made after the formation of the Palestine Labour Political Committee in 1938 when a consultation was held there with secretaries of several Jewish trade unions and the chairmen of a number of branches of the Workers' Circle. Schneier Levenberg presided and the gathering was addressed by Berl Locker and Dov Hos. The *Zionist Review* reported that

> in the course of the discussion it was made clear that much opposition was to be expected from the strong Communist element in East London;

> nevertheless a general consensus of opinion seemed to be that the average Jewish worker was not in sympathy with that party's attitude to Zionism and that an individual approach to Jewish Trade Unionists on the basis of the right of free immigration was certain of success.[93]

As in the past, it was only through the creation of front organizations on the basis of a lower ideological common denominator that Poale Zion was in fact able to promote its influence. In the 1940s it was able to mobilize sympathetic elements in the Workers' Circle branches and the trade unions within the loose framework of "Friends of Jewish Labour in Palestine." This was served by the publication of *Jewish Labour News,* a weekly information sheet sent to over two hundred British trade union and cooperative journals. Likewise, the formation of a "United Jewish Labour Committee" facilitated fund-raising for efforts to rescue Jews from Nazi Europe operated by the Histadrut (the General Federation of Jewish Labor in Palestine). However, by the Poale Zion leadership's own admission, these initiatives fell far short of making a major impact upon the working class Jewish population. As late as 1946, its secretary Nathan Jackson had to report to a Poale Zion conference: "Much is still to be done to bring over to our side the Jewish workers' organisations, particularly the Workers' Circle."[94]

Throughout the entire period of Poale Zion's existence, it had functioned as an independent group outside of the mainstream Zionist Federation which identified itself politically with General Zionism. In the atmosphere of crisis precipitated by the 1939 White Paper and the tragedy of world war, negotiations were at last entered into with a view to Poale Zion's affiliation to the Zionist Federation. In January 1942 an agreement was announced. Its terms included the statement that "Poale Zion will retain their present character and relations with the World Poale Zion movement and the British Labour Party. They will work in complete co-operation with all other forces in the Zionist Federation for the furthering and strengthening of the Zionist cause."[95]

Poale Zion's affiliation had an immediately beneficial impact upon the Zionist Federation. Indeed, so energetic were Poale Zion's representatives in the Federation's councils that by late 1945 a group of General Zionists, whose main spokesman was Phineas Horowitz, launched a bitter protest at what they described as Poale Zion's "stranglehold over the offices, machinery and instruments of propaganda of the wider Organisation." Whereas General Zionist societies constituted over eighty percent and other parties something less than twenty percent, argued Horowitz, the General Zionists had in fact become a minority on the Federation's Council and "a good many of the key positions, and particularly those in relation to political propaganda, have passed out of General Zionist hands."[96]

Although these charges were exaggerated, and were in fact repudiated by General Zionism's most prominent leaders Selig Brodetsky and Lavy Bakstansky, certainly one key position, that of editor of the Federation's organ, the *Zionist Review,* was occupied by Poale Zion's Shneier Levenberg. In that capacity he served as the leading ideological exponent of the controversial campaign for what came to be known as the "capture" of the Jewish Board of Deputies by means of a "caucus" created by the Zionist Federation. Engineered mainly by the Federation's secretary, Lavy Bakstansky, but with the energetic cooperation of Poale Zion, this campaign resulted not only in the election of Selig Brodetsky as president of the Board—the first avowedly Zionist leader to hold that position—but also in the election in July 1943 of an overwhelming majority of Zionist members in all of the Board's committees. Moreover, it also abolished the Board's fifty-year-old partnership with the non-Zionist Anglo-Jewish Association in the body known as the Joint Foreign Committee which customarily represented Anglo-Jewry on matters within the purview of the British Foreign Office.[97]

In quantitative terms, Poale Zion remained only a small component of the Zionist Federation whose nominal membership reached 31,000 by 1946. Nevertheless, Poale Zion increased the number of its affiliated branches from 16 in 1943 to 27 in 1946. Its membership in this period rose from 1,300 to 2,000.[98] In addition, since 1938 Poale Zion had been fostering a Young Poale Zion movement whose members ranged from 18 years of age into their 20s. It began with five societies in the provinces and one in London, but its growth was disturbed during the Second World War and it was only after 1945 that it developed further.[99]

To be sure, since the mid 1930s, labor Zionism in forms ideologically aligned with Poale Zion, although not affiliated with it, became the predominant influence amongst the organized Jewish youth in Britain. This was especially manifest in the senior ranks of the Habonim youth movement, in the more left-wing Hashomer Hatzair movement formed in 1939, and in the attendant surge of *chalutz* groups preparing for settlement in *kibbutzim* in Palestine. These were greatly augmented and stimulated by the influx from the continent of aspiring *chalutzim* who found temporary asylum in Britain. By 1944 the amalgamated strength of the English and continental sections of Hechalutz reached 850, with eight *kibbutz* training centers [*hachsharot*], seven engaged in agriculture and one in mining occupations. In addition, there were in London four *chalutz* houses, which were communes of prospective *chalutzim* seconded for youth work in the city. In the same year, the unification of Habonim with Mishmar Habonim (the framework encompassing *chalutzim* from the continent) recorded a membership of 3,000 youth.[100] The heightened significance of Poale Zion within Anglo-Jewish Zionism in the 1940s cannot be adequately appreciated in isolation from the broader context of these allied labor Zionist manifestations in Britain.

LABOUR'S "INTERNATIONAL POST-WAR SETTLEMENT" CLAUSE ON PALESTINE

Poale Zion in Britain was not significantly involved in local lobbying over the partition proposals emanating from the Peel Commission of Inquiry, which dominated Zionist concerns in 1937. Since Dov Hoz, Berl Katznelson, and Ben-Gurion himself, now chairman of the Jewish Agency Executive, came to London to engage in intensive political activity, the local Poale Zion was relegated to a back seat. The not entirely intended outcome of Ben-Gurion's tactical maneuverings was the Labour Party's tendency "to adopt a non-committal attitude as regards the principle of partition."[101] As it happened, however, in the wake of the Woodhead Commission's Report in November 1938, the British government in fact shelved the partition idea and moved toward the distinctly pro-Arab policy finally adumbrated in the White Paper of May 1939. It was then that the reinvigorated Poale Zion organization in Britain began to make itself felt and the Labour Party's receptivity to Poale Zion's solicitations reached its apex.

Throughout the war years Poale Zion relentlessly lobbied within the Labour Party against the White Paper; it presented a memorandum to the executive of the party, its representatives met with the party's international subcommittee, it published information pamphlets, and it proposed resolutions at the party's successive annual conferences.[102] In 1939, at the conference held at Southport, a resolution formulated by Poale Zion but moved by Barbara Ayrton Gould (a member of the Labour Party's national executive) and seconded by Maurice Rosette, was carried by a show of hands, only two hands being raised against it. It endorsed the stand taken by the Parliamentary Labour Party against the government's White Paper policy, and declared in unequivocal terms that

> the White Paper by imposing minority status on the Jews; by departing from the principles of economic absorptive capacity governing Jewish immigration; by making Jewish entry dependent upon Arab consent, and by restricting Jewish land settlement, violates the solemn pledges contained in the Balfour Declaration and in the Mandate.[103]

In 1940, at Bournemouth, Nathan Jackson of Poale Zion successfully moved a similar resolution and called for "the continued growth of the Jewish National Home in Palestine by immigration and settlement." At the 1943 conference held in London, Maurice Rosette even successfully moved a resolution whose wording went beyond the conventional formulation—it stated that the conference "reaffirms the traditional policy of the Labour Party in favour of building Palestine as the Jewish National Home" (rather than the usual "a Jewish National Home *in* Palestine").

Finally, the Labour Party's 1944 conference passed a plan for a new international postwar order containing a clause on Palestine which reached the apex of support for the Zionist case: "There is surely neither hope nor meaning in a 'Jewish National Home,'" it stated, "unless we are prepared to let Jews, if they wish, enter this tiny land in such numbers as to become a majority." Furthermore, the clause went on to make what was for the Labour Party an unprecedented proposal: "In Palestine surely is a case on human grounds," it stated, "to promote a stable settlement for transfer of populations."

> Let the Arabs be encouraged to move out as the Jews move in. Let them be compensated handsomely for their land and let their settlement elsewhere be carefully organised and generously financed. The Arabs have many wide territories of their own; they must not claim to exclude the Jews from this small area of Palestine, less than the size of Wales. Indeed, we should re-examine also the possibility of extending the present Palestinian boundaries by agreement with Egypt, Syria or Transjordan.[104]

The genesis of this remarkable clause may be traced in the papers and diaries left by its author, Hugh Dalton, the Labour Party leader who was later to become Chancellor of the Exchequer in Attlee's postwar labor government. They make it evident that the formulation was very much his own and not the direct result of Zionist lobbying, whether by the Jewish Agency leadership or by Poale Zion.[105] Its far-reaching pro-Zionist stance took all of the Zionists, from Weizmann through to Berl Locker, by surprise. Indeed, its advocacy of "transfer" of Arab population was a source of considerable embarrassment since it gratuitously went beyond the consensus of Zionist policy. Owing to war conditions in London, the Labour Party conference at which the statement was to be approved had been postponed from May to December 1944. When the Zionist leadership got wind of the proposed text in May, their delight with the general tenor of the proposed clause was much dampened by concern lest the stress placed on transfer might create the impression that without so radical a measure, Palestine could not possibly accommodate all the Jews who wished to settle there.

Weizmann afterwards wrote in his memoirs: "I remember that my Labour Zionist friends were, like myself, greatly concerned about this proposal. We had never contemplated the removal of the Arabs, and the British Labourites, in their pro-Zionist enthusiasm, went far beyond our intentions."[106] Hence Locker was at pains to tell W. Gillies, secretary of the Labour Party's international department, that transfer was "not a prerequisite condition for a large-scale Jewish settlement, and it is necessary and wise that we should make all our future plans for the rebuilding of Palestine on the assumption that we have to reckon with the presence of something like a million Arabs, their rights and needs." Locker would have preferred the notion to have been omitted. However, "now that it has appeared," he wrote to Gillies, it would be a mistake to leave out the transfer clause, because "its removal might be interpreted as admission that the Labour Party's proposal involves an injustice to the Arabs." In extenuation, Locker suggested that the operative words were "should be encouraged," which every unbiased reader would interpret as the suggestion of a voluntary transfer by agreement, not compulsion. The clause thus remained unchanged when the Post-War Settlement statement was passed at the party's conference in December 1944. Indeed, as if to emphasize that no change had taken place, at its pre-election conference of May 1945, Hugh Dalton declared on behalf of the national executive council, labor's support for a "free and prosperous Jewish State in Palestine."[107]

CONCLUSION

By 1945 Poale Zion in Britain had thus reached the pinnacle of its development both within the Zionist movement in Britain and in relation to the British Labour Party. Ironically, all the promise which this fact held out for the future rapidly evaporated after the Labour Party came to power in the elections of July 1945. The irony was all the more bitter in that this election also swept an unprecedently large number of Jewish MPs, almost all Labour, into Parliament: twenty-six, of which no less than five were themselves members of Poale Zion, namely S. Silverman, I. Mikardo, M. Orbach, H. Lever and J. Mack.[108] Furthermore, in the same year Harold Laski became chairman of the Labour Party's national executive. Laski was a Jew whose brilliant intellectual odyssey had only recently brought him, as he himself phrased it, "like a prodigal son returning home," utterly to the Zionist conviction "of the need for the rebirth of the Jewish nation in Palestine."[109]

The frustrating struggle of Poale Zion from 1945 to 1949 against the new Labour government's reversals of the spirit if not the letter of all previous Labour Party resolutions and pronouncements on Palestine falls outside the purview of the present article. Suffice it to note that, in the final analysis, neither the internal presence of a Poale Zion entity in the Labour Party nor the long record of sympathetic relationships with the Zionist labor movement in Palestine were able to stand the test of adverse political realities at the level of high policy after 1945. It transpired that the successful lobbying of labor Zionism in the Labour Party was one thing and the policies followed by the Labour government were quite another. As Joseph Gorny's *The British Labour Movement and Zionism* has shown, an undercurrent of ambiguity is in fact traceable throughout the Labour Party's relationship with the labor Zionist movement. It was the negative strain in that ambiguity which came to the fore under the constraints of Labour's governmental responsibility.

In retrospect, it is evident that the significance of Labour Party conference resolutions in particular could easily be overrated. In later years Arthur Creech-Jones, at pains to plead extenuating circumstances for Labour's apparent volte-face, explained that the conference forum was never "constituted for careful study, deliberation and consideration." He noted that delegates too often cast their votes in ignorance of many of the facets concerning the matter on which they were making policy. "In the case of Palestine," he observed, "Zionist activity among constituency parties, affiliated organisations and delegates did not contribute to calm reflection. The Arab case was never understood or discussed or publicised."[110] Reflecting on the process by which resolutions on Palestine were passed at the many conferences he attended, Maurice Rosette has provided much the same evaluation.[111]

In quantitative terms Poale Zion was never more than a small component of the Zionist movement. Originating among Yiddish-speaking immigrants in the early years of this century, its membership reached only a few hundreds in all of Britain before 1917. Even in peak years of activity such as Poale Zion attained between 1917 and 1923, in 1930, and after 1938 (by which time it conducted its affairs primarily in English) its membership never exceeded some two thousand. These numbers must be considered in the context of total nominal membership of the Zionist organization in Britain which rose from about 4,000 in 1899, to some 7,000 in 1902, then declined again to about 4,000 in 1917. In the wake of the Balfour Declaration it rose rather dramatically to some

25,000 by 1920. Judging by sales of shekels—a gauge which, however, provides an overly generous estimate—19,353 Jews associated themselves with Zionism in 1939 and 31,000 by the end of 1945.[112]

Although ideologically socialist and devoted to working class interests, Poale Zion's social composition was not substantially working class. If its early membership included a fair number of employees in workers' occupations, mainly in the needle industry, they tended to upward mobility. Certainly by the 1930s almost all the leading figures in Poale Zion were lower middle class, and often enough themselves employers of labor in various manufacturing and business occupations. In addition, the British-born generation of Poale Zion members included many who had acquired a university education and professional occupations. Despite repeated efforts to expand its working class membership, especially in the East End of London, Poale Zion gained a commanding position only in a few branches of the Jewish Workers' Circle, which was itself no more than a workers' friendly society possessed of a broad sense of identification with socialism and working class interests. However, a considerable reservoir of sympathy for the achievements of Jewish labor in Palestine was to be found in some of the Jewish trade unions, and among the Jewish working class population in general. By the strategy of creating a series of loose common-front organizations, Poale Zion was able to tap this reservoir repeatedly throughout the period we have surveyed. Initially, in 1915, the common denominator was provided by the struggle for equality in Eastern Europe, to which Poale Zion appended a plea for "free immigration and colonization in Palestine and in other lands." In the next stage, commencing in 1918, the common platform broadened to include local Jewish trade union interests, the demand for national autonomy in Eastern Europe and an explicit plea for "a national home for the Jewish people in Palestine." This found expression in the Jewish National Labour Council. By the late 1930s, Poale Zion could draw more directly upon a great fund of goodwill and admiration for the Zionist labor movement in Palestine prevalent among Gentiles and Jews within the British labor camp. To this end, Poale Zion bent its efforts through the medium of its Palestine Labour Political Committee and the creation of bodies such as the Friends of Jewish Labour in Palestine.

The emancipated status of Jews in Britain and the non–working class social composition of Poale Zion endowed it with a doubly vicarious character. It was vicarious, first, in its passionate espousal of immigration to Palestine and the creation there of a national Jewish homeland, without perceiving this as a personal imperative or applying it programmatically to the Jews situated in Britain. Second, it was vicarious in its advocacy of a working class ideology without real applicability to its own social composition or to the actual Jewish situation in Britain. Reflecting on the peculiarities of Poale Zion in England in an article written in 1944, Schneier Levenberg (who only eight years earlier had left the East European ambience of Zionist Socialism) commented perceptively:

> Labour-Zionist practice was greatly modified, but its theory remained almost unaltered. As far as I know, no serious effort had even been made to adapt Zionist-Socialist ideology to the circumstances under which Jews are living in Anglo-Saxon countries. . . . Where Labour Zionism has been introduced to the Jewish masses in England, it was explained to them mainly in its bearings upon Palestine or as an old theory which Borochov and Syrkin had successfully applied to Jewish life in Eastern Europe. Seldom has it been used as the best possible means for the understanding of Jewish problems in this country.[113]

Levenberg was reluctantly obliged to observe that Poale Zion activity in England amounted to not much more than "General Zionism somewhat influenced by Labour ideas, an ideological bond with the Histadrut and political contacts with British Labour."

Yet whatever its inadequacies as an expression of Socialist Zionism in theory and practice, and notwithstanding its diminutive size, Poale Zion in Britain fulfilled a very distinctive role in the history of Zionism. This was fortuitously facilitated by its being situated in the country which held the mandate over Palestine, and in which a broadly based, democratic labor movement was on the ascendent. Poale Zion in Britain was enabled to promote the Zionist case to a degree quite disproportionate to its size and in a manner ideologically palatable to the British labor movement. Moreover, it was well placed to mediate an ongoing relationship between the leadership of that labor movement and of its small but dynamic counterpart in Jewish Palestine.

This distinctive role of Poale Zion was well recognized by the broader Zionist movement. To be sure, there were occasions when the Zionist Executive in London asserted its primacy in representing Zionist policy not only to the British government in power, but also to the Labour Party.[114] However, as early as the period of the Balfour Declaration, Weizmann was cognizant of Poale Zion's lobbying endeavors with the Labour Party[115] and *a fortiori* after Poale Zion's official affiliation to the Labour Party in 1920 was its special role acknowledged. Participating in November 1921 in the deliberations of a "Zionist Committee for Relations with the Labour Movement," Joseph L. Cohen of Poale Zion was able to credibly put the proposition that

> as the Labour Party wished to deal with the Poale Zion and not with the Zionist Organisation, the work of interesting the Party in Zionism would

> have to be done either through the existing or an improved Poale Zion. Any statement put forward by the Zionist Organisation might be challenged by the Labour Party in a way which would be impossible in the case of an affiliated body like the Poale Zion.[116]

The historical record leaves no doubt that labor Zionism's lobbying and ideological expositions completely outstripped that of the Arabs throughout the period we have surveyed. In determining the credit for this it is artificial to separate the labor movement in Palestine from Poale Zion in Britain. While the large fund of sympathy for the Zionist case evinced by the Labour Party must be attributed directly to the impressive achievements of the Zionist labor movement in Palestine, Poale Zion was of considerable significance in exposing British labor to those achievements and in facilitating the relationship between the two labor movements. Indeed, the historical record makes it clear that the activities of local Poale Zion leaders such as Pomerantz, Joseph L. Cohen, Maurice Rosette, and Schneier Levenberg cannot correctly be perceived separately from that of the World Confederation's leaders or of the emissaries from Palestine who periodically spent some time in London. To all intents and purposes, Shlomo Kaplansky, Dov Hos, and later Berl Locker functioned while in Britain as integral members of the local Poale Zion. Also short-term visitors from Palestine like Moshe Shertok, Berl Katznelson, and David Ben-Gurion relied on the local Poale Zion to facilitate their activities in relation to the Labour Party.

If in the final analysis, events after 1945 rendered futile Poale Zion's lobbying throughout the years, this is an observation which can be applied no less to the lobbying activities of the Zionist organization as a whole. It should not blind our historical inquiry to the perception that what had begun at the beginning of the century as a fragile transplant of socialist Zionism by a handful of Jewish immigrants from Eastern Europe developed qualitatively into a major manifestation of Zionist activities in Britain.

Notes

Abbreviations:

CZ Central Zionist Archives, Jerusalem
LM Archives of the Labor Movement, Tel Aviv
LP Archives of the British Labour Party, London
  JSM James S. Middleton Papers
  WG William Gillies Papers
  IMPAC Advisory Committee on Imperial Questions
JC The Jewish Chronicle
ZR The Zionist Review
JL Jewish Labour

English transliteration of Yiddish periodicals follows Leonard Prager, "A Bibliography of Yiddish Periodicals in Great Britain (1867–1967)," *Studies in Bibliography and Booklore.* IX, no. 1, 1969, pp. 3–33.

1. Ahad Ha'am to S. Dubnow, 18 December 1907, Aryeh Simon (ed.), *Letters of Ahad Ha'am* [Hebrew], IV, (Tel Aviv 1958) 99.

2. The policies of the British Labour Party in relation to Zionism have been admirably traced and analyzed in two recent works: Joseph Gorny, *The British Labour Movement and Zionism 1917–1948* (London, 1983) and Andrew Sargent, "The British Labour Party and Palestine 1917–1949," Ph.D. Dissertation, University of Nottingham, 1980. I wish particularly to thank Dr. Sargent for his permission to consult this work and to acknowledge its valuable contribution to the subject. I wish also to thank Dr. S. Levenberg for his insightful comments on the MS of this article and for correcting some factual errors.

3. It is generally acknowledged that the first Jewish Socialist society in the world was that formed in 1876 by Aaron Lieberman in London's East End. However, our reference is to *Zionist* Socialism as manifest in Poale Zion.

4. Kalman Marmor, "Zionist Socialists," in *Di Yudishe Frayhayt,* no. 2/3, May/June 1905. The quotations which follow are from the same source. Particularly instructive is an article entitled "The Aliens Bill of the English Zionist Federation," which provides many footnoted quotations from earlier Yiddish journalistic sources, notably *Der Koysel Maarovi* which appeared in 1902 (also edited by Marmor) and *Der Idisher Ekspres* of which issues dated in 1902 and 1903 are cited. Kalman Marmor was born near Vilna in 1879, studied at universities in Switzerland and was one of the founders of the World Union of Poale Zion in 1907. In 1906 he came to the USA where he was active in Poale Zion. However, in 1922 he joined the New York Yiddish Communist daily, the *Morning Frayhayt,* to which he remained a contributor until his death in 1956.

5. The publicist Dr. Ezekiel Wortsmann and Kalman Marmor were the leading lights of the *Ma'aravi* society. It produced the above mentioned short-lived organ called *Der Koysel Maarovi* (Western Wall). A similar development in Leeds led to the formation of a society called *Ḥalutzei Zion* (Pioneers of Zion).

This article forms part of a broader research project on Zionism in Anglo-Jewry which has been made possible by research grants from the Israel Academy of Science and Humanities and the Hebrew University's Rachel Kelly, Ben-Eli (Honig), and Sheinborn, and Berl Locker funds.

6. *Der Koysel Maarovi,* no. 2, Dec. 1902, cited in *Di Yudishe Frayhayt, ibid.,* p. 17. On the Democratic Faction's relationship to the *Ma'aravi* society, see Israel Klausner, *The Opposition to Herzl* [Hebrew] (Jerusalem, 1951) p. 225, and M. Zinger, *The Origins of Zionist Socialism* [Hebrew] (Haifa, 1957), p. 384.

7. *Di Yudishe Frayhayt, ibid.,* p. 38.

8. See the section "Yiddish Chronik" in *Di Yudishe Tsukunft,* no. 2, 1904, p. 118.

9. *Di Yudishe Frayhayt,* no. 2/3, May/June 1905, p. 39.

10. *Dos Naye Leben,* no. 1, March 1906, pp. 30–31.

11. See S. Levenberg, *The Jews and Palestine: A Study in Labour Zionism* (London, 1945), p. 127.

12. According to J. Pomerantz, who became active in 1912. See J. Pomerantz, "Fifty Years Poale Zionism in England," *Jewish Vanguard,* 24 Nov. 1950, p. 3. (This article formed part of a series which appeared in successive issues of this paper.) However, in a communication to the present writer in June 1984, Dr. S. Levenburg has pointed to evidence that even in this period Poale Zion was active.

13. J. Pomerantz, *Jewish Vanguard,* 5 Jan. 1951, p. 3. *Ha'achdut* [organ of Poale Zion in Eretz Israel], V, 1913/14, no. 26, pp. 29, 30, and no. 32/33, p. 54, report briefly on Borochov's visit and tell that it attracted new members to Poale Zion and that "of late many locally-born workers have joined our party."

14. Circular Report of the Committee of the Jewish Socialist Labour Party Poale Zion [Yiddish, handwritten], Leeds, 28 Sept. 1915, LM (42) 12 III/1; *Yedios* [mimeographed bulletin of World Confederation of Poale Zion in Yiddish], no. 1, Aug. 1915, in CZ; *Di Tsayt,* Supplement on the Workers' World, 3 Oct. 1915.

15. As recollected by J. Pomerantz (who was at the time secretary of Poale Zion). Leon Chazanovitch was the first to make real progress in this task. See J. Pomerantz in *Jewish Vanguard,* 18 Jan. 1951, p. 3.

16. See A. Sargent, p. 26, citing Independent Labour Party, National Administrative Council Minutes, 22 Oct. 1915, 6 June 1916.

17. Circular Report of the Committee of the Jewish Socialist Labour Party Poale Zion, *ibid.*

18. The figures for Poale Zion are given in I. Kolatt's entry on "Poale Zion" in *The Encyclopaedia Judaica,* XIII, 662. On the strength of the Zionist Organization see Stuart Cohen, *English Zionists and British Jews* (Princeton, 1983), pp. 56–57, 282. The Workers' Circle figures are given in its brochure: *The Workers' Circle, Diamond Jubilee 1909–1969.*

19. See William J. Fishman, *East End Jewish Radicals 1875–1914* (London, 1975).

20. *Yedios, ibid.,* p. 6: "We have great influence in the *Farband.* The Bundists find themselves in the opposition in it—quite the opposite of their position in America. . . ."

21. S. Levenberg, pp. 204–205.

22. See A. Sargent, p. 14. Henderson was a member of Lloyd George's war cabinet from late 1916 until July 1917, hence he must have been aware of the deliberations which culminated in the Balfour Declaration. His role in formulating the memorandum's clause on the Jews accords well with his later record of consistent moderate sympathy for Zionism. Although Webb's later record, including his 1930 White Paper, was far less sympathetic to Zionism it

too was hardly incompatible with the rather ambiguous form of the Labour Memorandum's clause.

23. The world confederation of Poale Zion reported in 1915 upon some successes in bringing the Jewish question before the British trade unions. See *Jüdaische Arbeiterkorrespondenz* [mimeographed bulletin in German] Den Haag, no. 2, 1915, pp. 11, 12, in CZ. See also the memorandum prepared by S. Kaplansky and presented to the International Socialist Bureau: *The Jews and the War, Memorandum of the Jewish Socialist Labour Confederation-Poale Zion,* The Hague, 1916. This English translation from the original German was distributed by Poale Zion in Britain.

24. See I. Friedman, *The Question of Palestine 1914–1918* (London, 1973), p. 254.

25. *A Declaration Concerning a National Home for the Jewish People in Palestine in Accordance with Our Own Proletarian Outlook* [Yiddish], Central Committee of the Jewish Socialist Workers Party Poale Zion, England, London, Dec. 1917, pp. 2–3.

26. *Jewish Socialist Labour Party Poale Zion, Appeal no. 1,* Information Bureau, Edinburgh [n.d.], in LM (42) 12 III/4.

27. These events are reported in mimeographed circulars [handwritten in Yiddish by J. Pomerantz] issued by Poale Zion. Central Committee Circulars of 20 June 1918, 1 Nov. 1919, in LM (42) 12 III/3.

28. *Work-Committee Announcement,* Central Committee of the Jewish Socialist Workers Party Poale Zion in England [Yiddish], Oct. 1918, LM (42) 12 III/4.

29. *Unzer Veg,* I, no. 1, 1 May 1919; no. 2, 16 May 1919; no. 8, 24 Sept. 1919.

30. It called a conference in May 1918, to which it invited "two delegates from every Jewish trade union, Jewish political labour organisation and every other Jewish workers association." *Memorandum and Invitation Issued to all the Jewish Trade Unions, Jewish Political Labour Organisations and Other Jewish Workers' Societies, Workers Ring Branches* [*et al.*], Central Committee of the Jewish Socialist Labour Party Poale Zion of Great Britain and the Jewish National Trade Union Committee [n.d.], in LM (42) 12 III.

31. The Council made efforts to counteract anti-aliens agitation. It helped to found or revive two trade unions, the Leather Workers and Stick Makers, and it energetically supported a general strike of the London Mantle Makers. The resolutions of its conference of 8th and 9th June 1919 included the continuation of the fight against anti-aliens agitation; a decision to seek representation in the Jewish Board of Deputies, the demand that the Board pay more attention to internal questions in the country and fight antisemitism and a protest against "those Jews [the Jewish plutocracy] who were hostile to the interests of the Jewish masses in Britain." See printed *Invitation to all Jewish Workers' Organisations to the Annual Conference of the Jewish National Labour Council of Great Britain,* May 1919, in CZ Z4/119; also *Unzer Veg,* no. 4, 16 June 1919, pp. 12, 13.

32. A. Sargent, p. 23, citing *The Call,* 7 Dec. 1916 and *British Socialist Party, Annual Conference Report* (London 1917).

33. *A Calumny Repudiated* [mimeographed], Statement by the Jewish Socialist Labour Party, Poale Zion, Central Committee [n.d.] in LM (42) 12 III/4. The Unions mentioned included the Jewish Bakers Union, the National Boot and Shoe Union (Branch No. 2), the Diamond Workers 'Bond,' the United

Garment Workers Trade Union (Jewish Branch), the National Amalgamated Furnishing Trade Union (Branch 61), the Cigarette Makers Union, the Hat and Cap Makers Trade Union.

34. Poale Zion Circular [Yiddish, handwritten], 20 June 1918 in LM (42) 12 III/4. According to this source another extreme left-wing figure who actively lent his support to Poale Zion was the Gentile Tom Mann.

35. *The Jewish Working Class and the Demand for a Jewish National Home: Report of a Deputation of the Jewish National Labour Council of Great Britain to the Organising Committee of the British Socialist Party* [printed brochure], [n.d.] LM (42) 12 III/3.

36. A. Sargent, p. 32.

37. *Ibid.,* p. 26.

38. See handwritten circular, 20 June 1918 in LM (42) 12 III/4.

39. A. Sargent, p. 42 citing Executive Council Minutes of the Labour Party, 9 Feb. 1920. Strangely, the event does not appear to have made any impression on the contemporary Jewish press. Neither the *Zionist Review,* nor the *Jewish Chronicle,* nor even *Di Tsayt* (whose editor Morris Myer was on the executive of Poale Zion) mention it.

40. *Jewish Labour Correspondence* [Bulletin issued by the Bureau of Jewish Socialist Labor Confederation Poale Zion] Stockholm, II, no. 1, Jan. 1920. Also *Unzer Veg,* I, no. 11/12, Dec. 1919, pp. 19, 20. The questions discussed in these contacts concerned the organization of an international commission for investigating the pogroms in Eastern Europe and the difficulties being placed in the way of Jewish immigration into Palestine. However, they may well have raised the Labour Party's regard for Poale Zion in England.

41. J. Pomerantz to S. Kaplansky [handwritten letter in Yiddish], 5 Jan. 1920, LM (104) IV 28. The letter mentions that Henry Alexander was present at the meeting in order to participate in the discussion on affiliation to the Labour Party. Alexander had by then fallen out with the executive of the British Socialist Party on account of disagreement with the dominant tendency to follow East European models rather than seek an independent British course in building socialism. See L. J. Macfarlane, *The British Communist Party: Its Origins and Development until 1929* (London, 1966), p. 22.

42. *Jewish Labour Correspondence,* II, no. 2/3, June 1920.

43. The incident is vividly described in J. Pomerantz to S. Kaplansky, 5 Jan. 1920, *ibid.*

44. *Vos Villen Mir,* Committee of the Left Faction in the Jewish Socialist Party Poale Zion in England [n.d.], [printed booklet] in LM.

45. See James Maxton's sympathetic but noncommital introduction to Left Poale Zion's booklet: Z. Abramovitch, *Whither Palestine* (London, 1936), and on its relationship with the Independent Labour Party, see Elkana Margalit, *The Anatomy of the Left: The Left Poale Zion in Eretz-Israel* [Hebrew] (Tel Aviv, 1976), pp. 196–202; also J. Gorny, pp. 154–160.

46. See S. Levenberg, p. 216.

47. *Unzer Veg,* no. 1, 1 Feb. 1923, and no. 3, April 1923.

48. Statement submitted by the Jewish Socialist Labour Party Poale Zion of England to the Executive Committee of the British Labour Party, 20 April 1920 [mimeographed typescript], in LM (42) 12 III/4.

49. *Unzer Veg,* no. 1, 1 Feb. 1923.

50. *Towards the General Elections 15 Nov. 1922,* Jewish Socialist Workers Party Poale Zion, England [Yiddish], printed leaflet in LM (42) 12 III/3.

51. *Unzer Veg,* no. 2, March 1923, and election pamphlets issued by Poale Zion for the 1924 election in LM, *ibid.*

52. *A Socialist in Palestine,* Jewish Socialist Labour Party Poale Zion, London 1922. On these various visits see J. Gorny, pp. 29ff.

53. See *Labour Party Report of the 24th Annual Conference,* 1924, p. 258; *28th Annual Conference,* 1928, p. 111.

54. For a summary of this and the following pronouncements and resolutions, see S. Levenberg, pp. 206–219.

55. See *Di Tsayt,* 16 Nov. 1930, which reports on an estimated 37,012 eligible voters in Whitechapel, of which 12,000 were Jews.

56. *JC,* 28 Nov. 1930, reporting on the public meeting of the Palestine Protest Committee.

57. Jewish Socialist Labour Party Poale Zion to Arthur Henderson, 28 Oct. 1930, LP JSM/210/41.

58. These events are chronicled in a Poale Zion Newsletter, Jan. 1931, a copy of which is in LP JSM/210/79. Also in *Jewish Socialist Labour Party Poale Zion, Report of the National Executive Submitted to the Annual Conference,* Manchester, 4–6 April 1931, in LM. See also *Di Tsayt,* 27 Oct. 1930, 4 Nov. 1930.

59. Assistant Secretary of Labour Party to Rossette (Hon. Sec. of Poale Zion), 29 Oct. 1930, LP JSM/210/42.

60. Assistant Secretary to Kaplansky, 31 Oct. 1930, LP JSM/210/46.

61. Exec. Committee to the Prime Minister, 30 Oct. 1930, LP JSM/210/45.

62. *JC,* 31 Oct. 1930, pp. 27, 28.

63. Rosette (Hon. Sec. of Poale Zion), to Middleton (Sec. Labour Party), 7 Nov. 1930, LP JSM/210/47. In a similar vein, the National Labour Council urged the Labour Party secretary "to send a message to the Jewish electorate of Whitechapel, clarifying the position and assuring them of the sympathy of the Party on this specifically Jewish question." L. Liff (Hon. Sec. Jewish Labour Council), to Middleton, 10 Nov. 1930, LP JSM/210/48.

64. Poale Zion Newsletter, Jan. 1931, in LP JSM/210/79.

65. *Ibid.,* and also Poale Zion Statement reported in *JC,* 28 Nov. 1930. See also *Di Tsayt,* 17 Nov. 1930, which reported on a public meeting convened by Poale Zion at which James Hall went so far as to hint that Lord Passfield would probably have to resign on account of his misguided White Paper.

66. *JC,* 21 Nov. 1930.

67. One particularly acerbic letter-to-the-editor writer in the aforementioned issue, protesting at the "traitorous decision of Poale Zion to support the Government in the Whitechapel election," pointed out that the budget of Poale Zion as a *Sonderverband* was covered by the Zionist Organization. "It thus follows," he argued, "that Jewish money given to *Keren Hayesod* for the express purpose of upbuilding the Land of Israel, will be used by the Poale Zion for the patriotic purpose of supporting a Government which, by word and deed, is doing everything in its power to render that purpose futile."

68. *JC, ibid.*

69. Poale Zion Newsletter, *ibid.*

70. Whereas the 1924 election results were H. Gosling (Labour) 13,701; F. H. Sedgewick (Liberal) 4,521, and L. Guiness (Conservative) 3,417; the 1930 results were James Hall (Labour) 8,544; B. Janner (Liberal) 7,445; L. Guiness (Conservative) 3,735, and H. Pollitt (Communist) 2,106.

71. Poale Zion Newsletter, *ibid.*

72. See Morris Myer's analyses of the electoral situation in *Di Tsayt,* 28 Nov. 1930, 5 Dec. 1930.

73. See N. A. Rose, *The Gentile Zionists* (London, 1973), pp. 1–29.

74. See Geoffrey Alderman, *The Jewish Community in British Politics* (Oxford, 1983), p. 114. In 1931 the Conservatives did not contest the seat, but the Communist Harry Pollitt did, gaining 2,658 votes largely at Hall's expense. Hence the Liberal's Janner was able to win with 11,013 votes. In 1935, with no Communist candidate, Janner gained little more than in 1931, whereas Hall was able to win with a comfortable majority of over 2,000. This is not to say that Poale Zion was tardy in supporting Labour in the elections. Indicative of its energetic campaign are the election broadsheets it distributed in 1935. See LP JSM/210/124 & 123.

75. LP JSM/210/100. Middleton to Hos, 14 March 1933; also WG/PAL/19–21.

76. See J. Gorny, pp. 124–125.

77. *Memorandum to British Labour Party on Proposed Legislative Council for Palestine,* Jewish Socialist Labour Party *Poale Zion* of Gt. Britain, January 1936 [mimeographed typescript]. The international subcommittee circulated copies of this memorandum to the Parliamentary Labour Party. See A. Sargent, p. 138.

78. International Department (Private and Confidential), Advisory Committee on Imperial Questions No. 160 A, Amended Version, Feb. 1936, in LP IMPAC/3/32 (Palestine Sub-Committee Minutes and Memos 1935–1937). See also J. Gorny, citing Labour Party/National Exec. Council/Advisory Committee on Imperial Questions—Palestine No. 160 A, Feb. 1936. Also Labour spokesmen in the House of Commons Debate, 24 March 1936, cited in S. Levenberg and J. Podro (eds.), *British Labour Policy on Palestine* (London, 1938), pp. 167–83.

79. "Statement of the Arab Case," attached to letter, Mansour to Exec. Committee of the Labour Party, 31 May 1939. LP WG/PAL/182.

80. *Palestine Jewish Labour and the Arab "Strike,"* The Jewish Socialist Labour Party Poale Zion of Great Britain, Central Committee [n.d.], copy in LP WG/91.

81. See J. Gorny, pp. 132–134. Gorny relates that when Berl Katznelson came to attend the Labour Party conference of October 1936 in Edinburgh, he was told by Susan Lawrence that some members of the national executive were "influenced by Arab propaganda and have doubts on Zionism."

82. Cited in S. Levenberg, p. 224.

83. See J. Gorny, p. 130, and Sargent, p. 145, citing Parliamentary Debates, House of Commons, vol. 313, no. 106, 19 June 1936, and Ben-Gurion, *Diary,* note 18, June 1936.

84. Palestine Arab Workers' Society to Chairman, British Labour Party, 27 June 1939, LP WG/PAL/192.

85. B. Locker to W. Gillies, 31 July 1939, LP WG/PAL/195. Similarly, Locker was able to discredit George Mansour of the Arab Centre in London by pointing to his appearance under the auspices of the antisemitic "The Patriot." *Ibid.*

86. See Sargent, pp. 179, 180, who amply shows the "commanding position of the Zionists in their dealings with the Labour Party," in contrast to the fragmented Arab groups who "were generally ignored or dismissed as creatures of the Mufti."

87. LP/International Department/Advisory Committee on Imperial Questions/Palestine Subcommittee with covering letter by Middleton, 12 April 1937, in JSM 210/134. Also see J. Gorny, pp. 135–136. In the Palestine Subcommittee Susan Lawrence was the main initiator of proposals essentially pro-Zionist in character. In T. Reid the Arab case had an advocate but he was in the minority.

88. See S. Levenberg and J. Podro (eds.), *British Labour Policy on Palestine* (London, 1938). Among the members of the "Palestine Labour Studies Group" were Abba Eban and Abe Harman.

89. See S. Levenberg, *The Jews and Palestine* (London, 1945), pp. 130, 131. (Hereafter citations from S. Levenberg refer to this work.)

90. I am indebted to Maurice Rosette for aiding me in identifying the occupations of some forty of the leading personalities in Poale Zion as reflected in the sources for the 1930s and 1940s. Examples of the Yiddish journalists are Morris Myer, Y. Kapitanchik, and A. Z. Ruminovsky. The business and manufacturing occupations included L. Gildesgame (who owned a hosiery factory), A. Richtiger who had an interest in the same, I. Jesiersky who represented a trading company, A. Perlmutt who owned a dress factory, and Ben Shaw who was a businessman. Even Sam Dreen who had a working class background and had once been very active in the legendary Rudolf Rocker's circle of East End anarchists, came to own a tailoring workshop. The university teachers included J. L. Cohen, who lectured in economics at Cambridge and later worked for Marks and Spencer, and J. Rumyanek (later Romney) who lectured at L.S.E. The professionals who entered labor politics included Ian Mikardo and Sidney Silverman.

91. J. L. Cohen, "The Communist Challenge and a Zionist Reply," *ZR*, Aug/Sept. 1935, Oct. 1935, Nov. 1935. These were also reissued by the Federation of Zionist Youth as a booklet, *The Communist Challenge and a Zionist Reply* (London, 1936).

92. *Unzer Veg*, no. 1, 1 Feb. 1923, p. 15.

93. *ZR*, 21 Oct. 1938, p. 17.

94. *Poale Zion Information*, Dec. 1946, pp. 5, 6.

95. S. Levenberg, p. 132; also *ZR*, 9 Jan. 1942.

96. See P. Horowitz, "General Zionist Actions Group," *ZR*, 11 Jan. 1946 and "Letters to the Editor," 18 Jan. 1946.

97. On these important developments see G. Shimoni, "Selig Brodetsky and the Ascendancy of Zionism in Anglo-Jewry 1939–1945," in *The Jewish Journal of Sociology*, XII, 2 Dec. 1980, pp. 125–161. For examples of S. Levenberg's ideological contribution to the "capture" see his articles in *ZR*, 16 April, 4 June, 18 June 1943.

98. *Zionist Federation of Great Britain and Ireland Annual Reports*, 42nd (1942) to 46th (1946) and *Labour Party Annual Conference Report*, 1946, p. 67.

99. *ZR*, 30 Sept. 1938 and *Poale Zion Information*, Dec. 1946.

100. *Zionist Federation of Great Britain and Ireland Annual Reports*, 44th (1944), p. 38ff.

101. On these political activities in London, see J. Gorny, pp. 142–143.

102. See especially Jewish Socialists Party (Poale Zion) of Great Britain, "The Jewish People and Palestine," Memorandum submitted to the Executive of the Labour Party, 10 July 1941, in LP/Int. Dept. Papers Correspondence 1932–1946/Box 5P. See also Poale Zion's pamphlet, *Under Sentence of Death*, London, 1942, which told of Nazi crimes against the Jews and called for the rescue of Jewish refugees and their entry into Palestine and other countries.

103. This and the following quotations are taken from the survey of all the relevant resolutions and comments at the Labour Party's annual conferences in S. Levenberg, pp. 229–251.

104. S. Levenberg, *ibid.,* citing from the Report "International Post-War Settlement" submitted by the Labour Party Executive to the 43rd Annual Conference, London, 1944.

105. H. Dalton Papers, London School of Economics, 7/10, pp. 42 ff., and Diaries, 16th November 1943. For an extensive discussion of Dalton's role see A. Sargent, pp. 258ff.

106. C. Weizmann, Trial and Error (New York, 1966), p. 436.

107. LP/Int. Dept. Papers Correspondence 1932–1946/Box 5P, Locker to Gillies, 15 May 1944. Copy also in H. Dalton Papers, 7/10. Emphasis on the essentially voluntary nature of the contemplated "transfer" of population was the line also adopted by the *Zionist Review,* whose editor at this time was Poale Zion's Shneier Levenberg. See *ZR,* 28 April 1944, 5 May 1944. For Dalton's May 1945 statement see *Labour Party Annual Conference Reports,* 1945, p. 104.

108. See G. Alderman, p. 126. In addition, another two Jews were elected, Phil Piratin of the Communist Party and Daniel Lipson as an Independent. In the previous general election, held in 1935, only five Jews were elected to parliament.

109. *ZR,* 11 May 1945; also J. Gorny, "The Jewishness and Zionism of Harold Laski," *Midstream,* Nov. 1977, pp. 72–78. Gorny explains the essence of Laski's ideological conversion to Zionism thus: "Since he saw assimilation not as a negation of the existence of the Jewish people, but as an abolition of its separatism, he was to find a common language with Zionism."

110. Cited by A. Sargent, p. 271, from a draft of a book on Palestine by A. Creech-Jones, left incomplete at his death and to be found in Creech-Jones' papers, St. Anthony's College, Oxford 32/2/50.

111. See interview with Maurice Rosette, Feb. 1981 in Oral Records Centre of the Institute of Contemporary Jewry, Hebrew University.

112. These figures, if not cited earlier in this article, are derived from *English Zionist Federation, Annual Reports,* for 1919–1920; 1939; 1945.

113. S. Levenberg, "Poale Zionism in England: Some Reflections on the Past and the Future," *JL,* June 1944, pp. 6, 7.

114. E.g., in 1920 when the Executive of the Zionist Organization objected to Poale Zion's independent representations to the British Labour Party on the subject of Arab riots against Jews in Palestine. Secretary of Zionist Organization to Secretary of Poale Zion, 24 March 1920, CZ Z4/584.

115. See J. Gorny, p. 8.

116. Minutes of Meeting, Zionist Committee for Relations with the Labour Movement, 29 Nov. 1921 in S. Kaplansky Papers, CZ A137/75.

Review Essays

French Antisemitism and French Jewish Identity

André Harris and Alain de Sédouy, *Juifs et français.* Paris: Bernard Grasset, 1979. 345 pp.
Jean Laloum, *La France antisémite de Darquier de Pellepoix.* Paris: Syros, 1979. vii + 214 pp.
Lazare Landau, *De l'aversion à l'estime: juifs et catholiques en France de 1919 à 1939.* Paris: Le Centurion, 1980. 352 pp.
Shmuel Trigano, *La République et les juifs: après Copernic.* Paris: Les Presses d'Aujourd'hui, 1982. 274 pp.
Stephen Wilson, *Ideology and Experience: Antisemitism in France at the Time of the Dreyfus Affair.* East Brunswick: Fairleigh Dickinson University Press, 1982. xviii + 812 pp.
Michel Winock, *Edouard Drumont et cie: antisémitisme et fascisme en France.* Paris: Editions du Seuil, 1982. 221 pp.

In the nearly two hundred years since their emancipation, French Jews have continued to debate the success of the 1791 legal act granting them citizenship. Disagreement in attitude, action, and organization has characterized their reactions to the major historical tests of their collective experience: becoming the first Jewish citizens of a modern European republic, dealing with the contradictions of the Napoleonic regime, modernizing their institutions, dealing with the persistence of hostility whose depth they continually tried to gauge during such traumatic episodes as the Dreyfus Affair and the years of the Vichy regime. Legal and social obstacles to their full integration have not been lacking, and yet their experience has included sufficient positive elements to nourish the optimistic side of the debate.

In the face of this ambiguous history, French Jews today remain divided on all the relevant major questions: the significance of antisemitism, the tactics to follow in responding to hostility, and the relationship between Jewish identity and such hostility. The last problem has given rise to an important discussion about the nature of Jewish identity at both an individual and communal level, and the manner in which Jewish particularism can be reconciled with French identity.

The questions that repeatedly arise include: is there a French antisemitism of significantly dangerous proportions? What share, not of the French population alone, but of French political groups and institutions, is involved? Is the real France the France of the Revolution, the Dreyfusards, and the Resistance, or is it the France of Napoleon's "Infamous Decrees," the anti-Dreyfusards, and Vichy? Is *Minute,* which currently sells well in the French kiosks, as dangerously antisemitic as was *Je suis partout?* Are the security precautions now taken at all Jewish institutions and synagogues a sign that Jewish vulnerability to physical danger has not abated?

This debate continues to animate much of the writing about and by French Jews, and the six books under consideration here are a sample of this flourishing literature. They do not deal exclusively with antisemitism, but all derive more or less from this central concern. The books reviewed here are mainly historical and sociological in nature, although the volume by Trigano is also largely polemical. They all shed light on aspects of Jewish existence, identity, relationships with non-Jews, and responses to the hostility and misunderstandings which Jews have experienced in the course of their relations with the French people since the Dreyfus Affair. These studies are themselves based on an already extensive literature, and find their natural context in current intellectual debates. The works of Robert Byrnes, Arthur Hertzberg, and Edmond Silberner laid the groundwork for all recent studies of anti-Jewish sentiment emanating from the French political Left.[1] Pierre Pierrard's *Juifs et catholiques français* described Catholic antisemitism from Dreyfus to 1945. The book is rich in detail and documentation, and includes a critical bibliography. It is a virtual *mea culpa* for his Catholic coreligionists, while offering hope for future progress toward a more enlightened attitude.[2] Philippe Ganier-Raymond's 1975 publication detailed numerous aspects of antisemitism during the Vichy period. Motivated to publish largely by a fear that the situation had not sufficiently changed, he concluded that nowhere else in Europe did local antisemitic measures exceed the demands of Berlin and assist the Nazis so efficiently.[3] A more detailed study of Vichy anti-Jewish policies, by Michael Marrus and Robert Paxton, followed a few years later, and reached the same conclusion. It fuelled the debate over the nature of French antisemitism, suggesting that a major factor in its longevity has been the apathy of the masses.[4] Jean Laloum's book, considered below, deals with the same period, and although it is written from a different perspective, confirms these findings.

For more than two decades, French Jews have been examining the nature of their identity in works that display the intellectual diversity of this community. We should cite especially Pierre Aubery's *Milieux juifs de la France contemporaine à travers leurs écrivains* (1957), which presented the first systematic postwar discussions of Jewish "difference," of antisemitism, and of Jews and politics;[5] Rabi's *Anatomie du judaïsme français* (1962), which analyzed institutions and ideologies within the community;[6] and Albert Memmi's *Portrait d'un juif* (1962), in which the term *judéité* (Jewishness)—recently accepted by the Académie Française—was first introduced.[7] In 1968, Roger Ikor described the "end of marranism" in his *Peut-on être juif aujourd'hui?*, which described the evolution of "new Jews," Jews without complexes.[8] In 1971, Alain Guichard, a non-Jewish reporter for *Le Monde,* called for an end to the spurious problem of Jewish dual loyalty, and endorsed the Jews' right to be different, and to live in a France conceived along culturally pluralistic lines.[9] Through this volume, the general public became aware of questions of Jewish identity, the dilemma of assimilation, the tensions in Israel-Diaspora relations, the relationship between Sephardim and Ashkenazim in France, their respective self-perceptions and ideologies.

Even greater growth in the literature on these topics took place over the past ten years. There has been a veritable deluge of novels, memoirs, books of philosophy, programs, and ideological statements.[10] Basic research on the social aspects of the community has been provided by sociologists Freddy Raphael, Dominique Schnapper, and Doris Bensimon-Donath.[11] Perhaps the most popular young Jewish writer today is Alain Finkielkraut, following the publication of his *Le Juif imaginaire.*[12] Although critics viewed his Jewish identity as essentially negative, an argument made by Shmuel Trigano in the book discussed below, Finkielkraut actually wrote that he was moving from what had been an essentially negative conception of Jewishness to a position of positive understanding and involvement. His book seems to have struck a chord among many Jews in France born after the Second World War.

The systematic study of French Jewish history since the Enlightenment, on the other hand, has been the province of North Americans, beginning with Arthur Hertzberg, and including Michael Marrus, Paula Hyman, David Weinberg, and myself.[13]

It is in the context of this growing literature on French antisemitism and the development of French Jewish ideas that the present six books ought to be considered.

Stephen Wilson's very large, very dense, and enormously rich volume, *Ideology and Experience: Antisemitism in France at the Time of the Dreyfus Affair,* is extensively documented with excellent notes and bibliography. In keeping with the trend to find the antecedents of modern political antisemitism in left-wing as well as right-wing traditions, Wilson develops and substantiates this thesis through a detailed study of literature, ideology, public activity, and institutions. He separates and examines individually various forms of antisemitism: economic, social, national, racial, religious and "sexual." His wide-ranging yet in-depth study provides ample documentation for the theory that antisemitic ideology was a "negative reaction to modern secular and 'capitalistic' society and to social change" (p. 739).

As suggested by his title, it is the development of ideological antisemitism that interests him, rather than the traditional anti-Jewish religious sentiment of the Church. He discusses the social function of antisemitism and insists on a sociohistorical explanation for its emergence as an ideology in the last decade of the nineteenth century. He shows that, as a long-term phenomenon, it is not related to the density of Jewish population nor to its social-professional structure.

He offers a judgment on the Jewish response to antisemitism that is more moderate than that made by Michael Marrus in his volume on the same topic. Marrus, in stressing the existence of a "politics of assimilation," had given support to charges of Jewish passivity and political blindness. Wilson responds that in many cases, as he demonstrates, it made sense for French Jews to seek support in existing political and social structures rather than strike out on their own. Because the government frequently took a stand against antisemitism, because the Jews often won legal suits against printed antisemitic calumnies, because the police (according to archives examined by Wilson) did not show any antisemitism, this Jewish political judgment was not irrational. Moreover, Jews found support in many sectors of French society, and could reasonably consider antisemitism a minority phenomenon.

This exemplary case study of antisemitism will disappoint only those seeking ultimate explanations for a persistent phenomenon, for Wilson disavows any such aim, arguing that tendencies to seek general theories based on psychology or sociology fail in the required task of placing the emphasis on the specific sociohistorical context.

Lazare Landau's *De l'aversion à l'estime: juifs et catholiques en France de 1919 à 1939* could almost be read as a continuation of the broader Pierrard volume, cited above, which treated this period only briefly. Landau argues that despite their socioeconomic mobility, Jews were hampered in their integration into French society. Only intermarriage, in which the children were brought up as nominal Christians, allowed Jews to enter French society. Made up essentially of non-practicing Catholics, French society could absorb only Jews who adopted an analogous position.

It is in the context of these assumptions about the requirements for integration that Landau develops his historical analysis of the relationship between Catholics and Jews during the two decades preceding World War II. He shows that Jews and the issue of Jewish identity were kept constantly before the public by a large segment of the press. It was in this period, in fact, that the crucial debate was begun over Jewish "dual loyalty," which of course took on even greater significance after the establishment of the State of Israel. In response to this challenge, Jews in pre–World War II France argued that no more conflict exists between loyalty to two communities than between loyalty to two parents.

A large part of Landau's study is dedicated to examining the Jewish stereotypes which appear in French literature. The Jew invariably emerges as the quintessential foreigner, revolutionary, subverter of French traditional culture, and manipulator of wealth in the service of his political designs.

Landau emphasizes, however, that during this very period there was also a growth of Catholic empathy for Jews and of ecumenical contact. Intellectual collaboration in scientific religious studies, especially in the critical study of the Bible and the life of Jesus, fostered improved mutual understanding. Landau focuses on three important Catholic figures, Jacques Maritain, Georges Bernanos, and Emmanuel Mounier, who, through very different political paths, assisted in the development of a more positive Catholic attitude toward Jews. For Maritain, a mysterious link existed between Jews and Christians, and therefore antisemitism could not avoid hurting the core of the Church itself. Bernanos, while never renouncing Drumont, was explicit in his rejection of contemporary antisemitism. Mounier, alone of the three, acted in the tradition of left-wing Catholicism, and called for resistance to antisemitism as part of the general fight against fascism.

Landau believes, as does Wilson, that the explanation of antisemitism cannot be found outside the sociohistorical context. He argues that the political instability of the period turned people against the parliamentary regime, and assisted in the development of antisemitism, because the Jews were inseparably bound to the republic.

This useful volume is unfortunately flawed in a number of respects. Inexcusably, it lacks both an index and a bibliography. It also perpetuates certain distortions about French Jewish history, which are partly based on an insufficient appreciation of the role of immigrant Jews. Landau endorses, for example, the discredited theory propagated by the Jewish consistorial leadership of the time that antisemitism was exacerbated by the immigrants' foreignness and failure to assimilate. He underestimates the contribution of the immigrant Jews in combatting antisemitism, and echoes the tendency to exaggerate French Jewish assimilationism, when he claims that only a small minority wanted to fight antisemitism. He seems unaware of the work of Paula Hyman and David Weinberg, who showed that if the native Jewish "establishment" was reluctant to see French antisemitism as anything but a transient aberration imported from Germany, the larger immigrant population, for all its internal divisiveness, was united in the desire to fight antisemitism overtly and politically.

The next volume under consideration advances our study of antisemitism into the period of World War II. In his *La France antisémite de Darquier de Pellepoix,* Jean Laloum establishes the personal responsibility of Darquier, the commissioner for Jewish questions, in the persecution of the Jews. This well-researched and thoroughly documented case study, which predates the more ambitious and better-known Marrus and Paxton book on the same period, reaches a similar conclusion about the responsibility of Vichy France in the deportations of Jews from France.

Laloum's work focuses on the antisemitic propaganda of the period, and he argues convincingly that the diffusion of this propaganda was an essential step in the preparation of the French public for the implementation of Vichy programs. Laloum supplies much detail about the institutions charged with this task, the *Office Français d'Information,* and the *Agence Française de Presse.* He describes the activites of other central figures in this endeavor, such as Joseph Antignac.

Darquier de Pellepoix died quietly in Spain in 1981, a fact which came to public attention two years later. Yet he had stirred a great public controversy only a few years earlier when an interview with him was published in *L'Express* (October, 1978). Darquier gave the French reporter a clear picture of an unrepentant antisemite, and asserted that only vermin had been gassed during the war. Laloum fills us in on Darquier's antisemitic ideology and early extremist activities, from 1934. He supplies numerous quotations from the press with which Darquier was directly or indirectly associated, photographs of some of the literature, posters, and antisemitic demonstrations. Curiously, we learn that Darquier may have been the first to accuse the Jews of being "the most racist people in the world" (p. 15). Laloum's research suggests that public opinion was sufficiently ambivalent that had it not been so successfully manipulated by Darquier's propaganda, it might have produced a popular outcry in favor of the Jews.

Somewhat less satisfying than these three monographs is Michel

Winock's collection of previously published articles grouped under the rather misleading title *Edouard Drumont et cie: antisémitisme et fascisme en France.* In fact, the volume offers little that is new on Drumont himself, although the title might lead one to expect an extended study on Drumont's relationship to French fascism—an area that remains to be thoroughly examined. Aside from the article on the catastrophic fire at the Paris Charity Bazaar in 1897, which seems to have wandered into the book by accident, most of the articles do contribute, although not in any unified fashion, to elucidating aspects of the history of French antisemitism and fascism. The volume offers no synthesis, nor any new approach to the history of either antisemitism or fascism. The addition of a brief introduction and conclusion to the articles does not go far toward knitting the pieces together. Yet many of the essays are of undeniable value, and the contribution of this publication is to have made them considerably more accessible.

The article on Drumont studies the man whose slogan, "France for the French," still intrudes its way onto many a French wall. Drumont's long-term influence is undeniable, and the essay discusses the varied and contradictory sources of Drumont's antisemitism, including the right-wing, Catholic tradition, the anticapitalism of the populist Left, and "scientific" racism.

Far more interesting are his case studies on Georges Bernanos, on the Joan of Arc cult, and on the novel *Gilles* by Drieu la Rochelle. The Bernanos article is included in order to rule Bernanos out of the fascist company of Drumont. Winock explains what Lazare asserts, that Bernanos, an avowed follower of Drumont, nevertheles rejected contemporary antisemitism. Bernanos, Winock shows, read Drumont selectively, refusing to see the fanaticism or racism in his mentor, and concentrating on Drumont's anticapitalism and opposition to the negative social effects of capitalism. Winock argues that although Bernanos never became a philosemite, his opposition to the Nazis and to Vichy was far stronger than his antisemitism, and he opposed the murder of Jews. Winock invites us to reread carefully *La Grande peur* and to conclude that Bernanos was not at all the precursor of fascism he is often assumed to be, but a serious opponent of modern totalitarianism.

The fascinating, detailed analysis of the political philosophy that permeates the novel *Gilles* makes it evident that Pierre Drieu La Rochelle wrote a thoroughly fascist autobiographical novel. Winock shows the book to be a mine of information on fascist and antisemitic theory, myth and values, "a rich catalogue of fascist ideas." Although the article is convincing in its interpretation of the text, we are left with a fascinating case somewhat out of context. If some of the obvious sources of ideas are briefly alluded to, no suggestion is made about the influence this work may have had on the course of political and literary events.

Perhaps the most original and most satisfying article of the volume, "Jeanne d'Arc et les Juifs," makes a very strong, clear case for the "essential antagonism between Joan of Arc and the Jews." In his excellent delineation of the elements in the myth of Joan of Arc and those in the countermyth of the Jews, Joan is described as an "anti-Jew." Winock might instead have called the Jew an "anti-Joan," as symbolic of his being an anti-Frenchman (and, of course, an anti-Christ). Joan represents rootedness, hard work, health, nature, peoplehood, national unity, spirituality, piety, virginity, and racial superiority. The Jew represented the opposite of all these, nomadism, capitalism and speculation, illness, subversion of the nation, materialism, deicide, utilitarianism, prostitution, and the inferior race. The contrast between Joan and the Jew is not theoretical; Winock shows that the annual May celebration of Joan of Arc has been a frequent occasion for antisemitic events, and he traces some of the relevant history from 1871 to the inclusion of the rites of this cult in the Pétainist regime.

The investigative report by André Harris and Alain de Sédouy, *Juifs et français,* is composed of lively and revealing interviews with close to fifty representatives from various sectors of the Jewish community. The authors present much of the material in the words of those they interviewed, but the quotations are interspersed with their own perceptive observations and comments, and occasionally even with summaries of relevant published research.

As the title indicates, the unifying theme of the volume is Jewish existence and identity in the context of French society. What emerges from these interviews is a ubiquitous sense of insecurity. This feeling is manifested equally by those who recall that neighbors took their furniture when they themselves sought refuge during the war; by others who conduct sociological studies of contemporary attitudes toward Jews; by the doctor's wife who reveals that her husband believes his career is blocked because he has heard colleagues say that there are too many Jews in high positions at his hospital; by the description of an antisemitic bias in a history course at a *lycée.*

Even people whom the authors had assumed would represent the stereotypical assimilated French Jew revealed a keen sense of alienation from mainstream French society. Thus, Pierre Dreyfus, former director of Renault, who subsequent to the interview even became Mitterrand's Minister of Industry, and who evoked for the interviewers the long history of secularism and republicanism in several generations of his family, recounted that despite his having felt "not 99% French, but 100%, . . . life and events showed me that even if you forget you are a Jew, others do not forget it . . . we Jews experienced the events of 1940–44 differently from the non-Jews . . ." (pp. 40–41).

The rest of the volume is a valuable mine of further detail in this vein, of fascinating material on prominent Jewish individuals and archetypical experiences, of insight into Jewish institutions and political attitudes of Jews since the 1930s. The interview with Jacob Kaplan, for example, provides the former Chief Rabbi of France with an opportunity to defend his participation at meetings of the fascist Croix de Feu, and to explain the political analyses and positions of French Jewish leaders in the 1930s. The authors also correctly point out that the increase in overt Jewish activity and concern with matters of Jewish identity and antisemitism are not restricted to the young. In fact, a discovery of one's Jewishness and of the relevant existential problems has frequently been a phenomenon of the middle-aged population.

Once again we must deplore the fact that French books frequently omit an index. Because of the way this volume is organized, an index of the people interviewed would have been a most useful tool, greatly increasing the facility with which the book is consulted.

The final volume under consideration is a sociopolitical polemic, based on a religious perspective, which presents a specific historical interpretation of the French Revolution and the legal emancipation of the Jews in republican France. Shmuel Trigano's book, *La République et les juifs: après Copernic,* written in the aftermath of the bombing of the rue Copernic synagogue, is an indictment of republican France for having failed to keep its side of the bargain with the Jews. Trigano argues that France's Jews, in agreeing to relinquish their specificity, were entitled to expect full equality and protection. Instead, they have been repeatedly frustrated by a continuing pattern of antisemitism.

The contemporary popular fear of French antisemitism is widespread; it is not to be dismissed as the perspective of a single author. Yet we are obliged to note that there is a certain lack of rigor in the logic of the argument as presented here. Is it really true, as Trigano would have us believe, that the Republic has abandoned its Jews? Is it true that in the Dreyfus Affair, Vichy, and Copernic the Republic was at fault? Is it not, rather, the case in each of these events that the responsibility for antisemitism lay elsewhere? In the Dreyfus Affair, as historians since Hannah Arendt have argued, the antisemitic forces were those that were hostile to democratic values and were attempting to replace the Republic with a reactionary regime. In the case of Vichy France there was no Republic at all.

Another problem with Trigano's assault on the republican tradition in France is that he has a perspective in which the Jews' centrality figures constantly. He assumes that the Jews were uppermost in the minds of Frenchmen, and gives insufficient respect to accident, blunder, and indirect consequence. For example, he writes, "It is as if the French felt the need to maintain the Jews as a fixed point, an immovable reference point, in order to continue to believe in France and live there" (p. 89). He even argues that without the Jews there would be no Republic at all, because they are the last Frenchmen who still believe in the Republic. To prove this point, he quotes several prominent French Jews, including Jacques Attali, Roger Gérard Schwartzenberg, and Michel Debré ("d'origine juive") on the French national idea.

The Jew's role, Trigano complains, is to be "hostage for the Republic." He is asked to refrain from defending himself when attacked, and thereby to uphold at his own expense the myth of the liberal republican idea. Trigano pushes this even further. The only reason the French turned out in large numbers to demonstrate solidarity with the Jews after Copernic, he says, was to maintain the Jews' illusions and prevent them from abandoning their essential role of hostage of the Republic.

As distressed as he is by culturally monolithic Jacobinism, Shmuel Trigano is equally frightened by the tendency of contemporary socialist France to lend support to minority cultural groups. Although he rejects the Emancipation, he deplores the danger of a possible return to the *ancien régime,* in which the Jews had no place. Cultural minorities in France, he warns, mean regional, territorial groups. As a nonterritorial group the Jews will be disfavored. Since the publication of the book, Trigano has continued to argue in this vein, claiming that the government's advisory report on cultural minorities lumped Jews together with Gypsies and foreign laborers, denying them the same sympathy accorded to territorial minorities.

The clue to understanding Trigano, I think, is to realize that the real tragedy for him was the destruction of the Jew *qua* Jew. The Republic is blamed precisely because the Republic, through its gift of emancipation, eliminated the traditional Jewish community. This meant the end of the authentic evolution of Jewish life and culture relatively sheltered from outside frames of reference.

Trigano argues that what is now necessary is a renunciation of the broken revolutionary contract and the creation of a new status for the Jews. He calls for the establishment of an authentic Jewish existence in which Jewish history is allowed to evolve from its own tradition rather than that of its host country. The return to Jewish sources is his recommendation for a new direction for Jews. In this book, as throughout all his writings, he calls for a re-examination of Jewish identity and urges Jews to seek an understanding of what constitutes their cultural heritage and how it may be propagated in the future.

Trigano writes in a prophetic vein. In a previous work he recognized this explicitly, calling Jews to move "toward a prophetic life," which he defined as "seeing and saying."[14] His is a frankly religious perspective, and the cultural renaissance he seeks is religious. The bearers of the religious tradition in France today, he argues, are the Sephardim. He specifically rejects the Ashkenazic orientation of certain prominent thinkers, such as Bernard-Henri Lévy, Blandine Barret-Kriegel, André Glucksmann, Richard Marienstras, and Alain Finkielkraut, for whom, he says, Judaism is defined by the Christian world. They are Jews because they are running from antisemitism. Their Judaism has little or no content, being reduced at best to the Bible. He contrasts the "Sephardic" view of Judaism, which includes philosophy, spiritualism, and mysticism, with the "Ashkenazic" tradition of Haskalah, politics, and Zionism. The Sephardim are seen as the real link between French Jews and their authentic past.

In what should probably be read symbolically, French Jews are invited to call a new Sanhedrin to undo the work of the Napoleonic Sanhedrin, and to find a new political path which will reestablish the tradition of Jewish self-government. This volume and the small corpus of work already produced by this young philosopher offer a fully developed, however controversial, program for Jewish communal existence.[15]

The point of departure of all six volumes reviewed here is French antisemitism. We have seen a variety of appreciations of the threat Jews have faced in France at varying times since the Dreyfus Affair. A large proportion of the people interviewed by Harris and de Sedouy exhibited both fear and alienation, even those who might have been expected to be the stereotype of the "assimilated" Jew.

When we turn to the religiously based political philosophy of Shmuel Trigano, we find confirmation of the ubiquitous influence of antisemitism on Jewish identity. Trigano himself criticizes empty Jewish identities which consist solely of opposition to antisemitism, and yet his own seeking for a meaningful spiritual and cultural continuity of Jewish existence also derives from a sense that France has betrayed the Jews. Until we solve a number of methodological problems, conclusions regarding levels of antisemitism will remain to a certain degree speculative. What is certain, however, is that the perceived threat of antisemitism underlies many ideologies.

PHYLLIS COHEN ALBERT
Harvard University

Notes

1. Robert F. Byrnes, *Antisemitism in Modern France: The Prologue to the Dreyfus Affair,* New Brunswick, New Jersey, Rutgers University Press, 1950. Arthur Hertzberg, *The French Enlightenment and the Jews,* New York, London, Columbia University Press; Philadelphia, Jewish Publication Society of America, 1968. Edmond Silberner, *Sozialisten zur Judenfrage, ein Beitrag zur Geschichte des Sozialismus vom Anfang des 19 Jahrhunderts bis 1914,* Berlin, Colloquium Verlag, 1962.

2. Pierre Pierrard, *Juifs et Catholiques Français: De Drumont à Jules Isaac (1886–1945),* Paris, Fayard, 1970.

3. Philippe Ganier-Raymond, *Une Certaine France: L'Anti-sémitisme, 40–44,* Paris, Ballard, 1975.

4. Michael Marrus and Robert Paxton, *Vichy France and the Jews,* New York, Basic Books, 1981.

5. Pierre Aubery, *Milieux Juifs de la France Contemporain à Travers Leurs Ecrivains,* Paris, Plon, 1957.

6. Rabi, *Anatomie du Judaisme Français,* Paris, Les Editions de Minuit, 1962.

7. Albert Memmi, *Portrait d'un Juif,* Paris, Gallimard, 1962 (the last chapters) and *La Libération du Juif,* Paris Gallimard, 1966. Cf. his article, "Negritude and Judeity," *European Judaism,* vol. 3, No. 2, winter 1968–1969.

8. Roger Ikor, *Peut-on être juif aujourd'hui?,* Paris, Grasset, 1968.

9. Alain Guichard, *Les Juifs,* Paris, Grasset, 1971.

10. Among the ideological works, mention must be made of Richard Marienstras's seminal essay on Jews as a minority. Even many of the French Jews who continue to reject the term "minority," are moving closer to this concept of cultural pluralism. (Richard Marienstras, "Les Juifs ou la vocation minoritaire," in *Les Temps Modernes,* number 324-325-326, August–September 1973; reprinted in his *Etre un peuple en diaspora,* Paris, Maspéro, 1975).

11. Freddy Raphael has written, among many articles and books, *Juifs en Alsace,* Toulouse, Privat, 1978; and *Nouveaux Régards sur les Juifs d'Alsace,* Strasbourg, Istra, 1980; Dominique Schnapper, *Juifs et Israelites,* Paris, Gallimard, 1980; Doris Bensimon-Donath has written, among others, *L'Intégration des Juifs Nord-Africains en France,* Paris, La Haye, Mouton, 1971.

12. Alain Finkielkraut, *Le Juif Imaginaire,* Paris, Seuil, 1980.

13. Michael Marrus, *The Politics of Assimilation,* New York, Oxford University Press, 1971; Phyllis Cohen Albert, *The Modernization of French Jewry: Consistory and Community in the Nineteenth Century,* Hanover, New Hampshire, Brandeis University Press, 1977; Paula Hyman, *From Dreyfus to Vichy: The Remaking of French Jewry, 1906–1939,* New York, Columbia University Press, 1979; David Weinberg, *A Community on Trial: The Jews of Paris in the 1930's,* Chicago and London, The University of Chicago Press, 1977.

14. Shmuel Trigano, *La Nouvelle Question Juive, L'Avenir d'un Espoir,* Paris, Gallimard, 1979, pp. 284–286.

15. Before *La Nouvelle Question Juive,* cited above, Trigano published *Le Récit de la Disparue: Essai sur l'Identité Juive,* Paris, Gallimard, 1977. His thesis, on the national idea in Judaism, is being readied for publication.

North American Books on Latin American Jewry

Judith Laikin Elkin, *Jews of the Latin American Republics.* Chapel Hill: University of North Carolina Press, 1980.
Eugene Sofer, *From Pale to Pampa: A Social History of the Jews of Buenos Aires.* New York: Holmes & Meier, 1982.
Robert Weisbrot, *The Jews in Argentina from the Inquisition to Perón.* Philadelphia: Jewish Publication Society, 1979.

During the last five years, three major volumes on Latin American Jewry have been published in English in the United States. The three authors all emphasized the dearth of previously published works in this field—a claim which might be more accurate if the reference is to books in English only, as has been demonstrated by Martin Sabel's *Latin American Jewry: A Research Guide* (Cincinnati: 1978). For this reason their publication is particularly welcome.

Judith Laikin Elkin's *Jews of the Latin American Republics* is the most comprehensive of the three, attempting to cover the entire geographical area from the southern border of the United States to Tierra del Fuego, and the whole historical period from pre-Columbian times to the present.

The wide range and scope of her study create diffficult problems for the author. Thus, in a single chapter ("Community Life on the Jewish Street"), Elkin describes such diverse phenomena as burial societies, credit organizations, publishing enterprises, religious practices, and education (her sequence). This solution to the problem of thematic organization seems less than adequate. Similarly, on the geographic plane, Elkin is compelled to offer us a cumbersome mosaic of data compiled from various countries. The resulting collage of places and issues is sometimes coherent and sound—in particular, the section on peddling in the chapter on economic pursuits. In many other instances, however, the approach raises serious methodological and conceptual questions.

First and foremost, this book raises the question whether the Jewish experience in Latin America is essentially one phenomenon, emanating from a basic common reality, or is a multiple experience reflecting a variety of separate histories. Until reinforced by evidence and sound argument, the case for the generalization of the Latin American Jewish experience cannot be accepted. Unfortunately, Elkin does not address this crucial issue. Thus, the non-specialist reader may overlook the profound gap separating Argentina, a primarily European society which almost from its inception provided a benevolent reception for European immigrants, on the one hand, and Guatemala, Peru, and Mexico on the other—societies of predominantly native and Indian character which barely encouraged immigration.

Second, this book fails to take note of two major themes in Latin American Jewish life. One is the existence of strong, nationwide representative umbrella organizations which make the organizational patterns of most Jewish communities in Latin America diametrically different from that in the United States. In Argentina, apart from the Communists, who were affiliated for only a short time, the whole community participated in the Delegación de Asociaciones Israelitas Argentinas—DAIA—almost from that body's establishment in 1935. The same is true of the Federación Sionista and the Comité Representativo (founded in 1919 and 1940, respectively) in Chile, for the Comité Central in Mexico and Uruguay (founded in 1938 and 1939), and for many other communities as well. The other theme missing here is the centrality of Zionism and the State of Israel for these communities' institutional structures. To overlook them, as does the author, is to miss issues which dominate much of the internal life of these Jewish communities as well as their relationships with the host societies.

Overall, the author provides the reader with much enlightening information and many valuable insights, mostly based on secondary and printed materials. In several instances, conclusions based on such sources ought to have been more tentative; or, indeed, presented not as conclusions at all, but rather as hypotheses, open questions calling for further study.

The narrative reads easily and avoids the pitfalls of a catalogue style. The book's final chapter offers an interesting analytical comparison of Jews "North and South"—referring to U.S. Jewry and the Latin American communities. The bibliographical appendix is a welcome update to older guides to the literature. As a well-written summary, however flawed, and as a ground-breaking book as far as the English reader is concerned, this book is an important contribution to the field.

Robert Weisbrot's study of Argentinian Jewry, which is an expanded version of an M.A. thesis, did not face the geographical problem with which Elkin had to wrestle, but his time span (from the Inquisition to Perón) presented similar thematic-structural difficulties. The author opted for a subdivision into three "parts," entitled "The Settlers," "The Culture," and "The Country," comprising ten chapters.

Very early on, Weisbrot abandons chronological-historical description in favor of a rather anecdotal account of events, personalities, and problems. The choice of material lacks balance, however, and is weighted toward the more "colorful," regardless of historical significance or reliability of documentation.

Thus, the white slave trade among Jews in Buenos Aires takes up a disproportionate amount of space in the section entitled "Political Evolution." True, white slavery was a very real problem in the Jewish community until it was successfully overcome in 1930, as Weisbrot correctly indicates. However, this hardly justifies devoting two-thirds of the entire section to this one issue, at the expense of other significant factors in Jewish political development.

Similarly, when discussing the impact of Zionism on the Argentinian community, he included a detailed description of Julio Popper, a young Jewish adventurer from Romania who, in the 1880s, tried to make his fortune in the antarctic region of Tierra del Fuego. His importance to Zionism, however, remains unexplained.

Another individual figure whom Weisbrot treats at length is Rabbi Amram Blum. A Hungarian Orthodox rabbi who was invited to serve the ultra-Orthodox Arabic-speaking community of immigrants from Aleppo, he was later nominated, through the direct influence of President Perón, as chief of the Ashkenazi Rabbinical Tribunal. The close relationship between the populist and authoritarian Argentinian leader and the foreign Orthodox rabbi has as yet not been adequately dealt with. It is noteworthy that when Perón was ousted, Rabbi Blum had very few friends and had to leave Argentina without delay. Weisbrot's account, which fills almost all the pages dedicated to "The Rabbinate," does not go beyond a one-sided summary of the events. This story is allowed to overshadow other issues of religious leadership, no less important.

The problem of thematic organization is particularly apparent in the author's treatment of antisemitism. Chapter Eight, "The Roots of Antisemitism," deals mainly with events in the 1960s (and is based on data from a number of field studies published in 1971 by a then-pro-Perónist writer, Juan José Sebreli). The real origins of antisemitism in Argentina—the anti-Jewish outbreaks of 1910 and the "pogrom" of January 1919—are dealt with in a previous chapter, "Acculturation," under the subheading of "Politics." The thread is picked up again in various other contexts in a way that suggests that the theme is an ever-present concern.

Elsewhere in this book, the author presents outdated information, even where more recent and thorough research is available. Thus, he might have drawn upon the present reviewer's history of the Baron de Hirsch–sponsored agricultural colonies (Haim Avni, *Argentina, ha-aretz ha-yeudah* [Argentina, the Promised Land]: Jerusalem, 1973), and on U. O. Schmelz and S. DellaPergola's study of Jewish demography in Argentina and other Latin American countries (*Ha-demografiah shel ha-yehudim be-argentina uve-aratzot aherot shel amerikah ha-latinit:* Jerusalem and Tel-Aviv, 1974). The latter study, in particular, has dramatically altered our perceptions of the demographic features of Argentinian Jewry.

These shortcomings are only partly compensated for by the author's colorful and fluent prose and the excellent illustrations. The field of Latin American Jewish studies would have been better served had the author produced a more balanced and better documented work, or one which was the product of advanced and sustained research.

Eugene Sofer's social history of the Jews of Buenos Aires, on the other hand, is based on an extensively rewritten Ph.D. dissertation, of which only a part has been incorporated in the present volume. The author deals with the East European background of the Jewish immigrants (the "Pale" mentioned in the title is, of course, the Russian Pale of Settlement); the development of both Argentinian Jewry and the host society until 1945; and the changes in the urban-geographic residence patterns and socioeconomic mobility of the Jews in that period. The concluding chapter deals briefly with the period between the first election of Juan Perón (1946) and the end of the 1970s.

The author's most innovative work is to be found in the sections dealing with spatial and socioeconomic mobility. These chapters are largely based on archival and primary sources, whereas the historical material on "Pale" and "Pampa" is based almost exclusively on secondary and published material.

In order to study the social history of the Buenos Aires community, Sofer constructed a large sample of its members from the membership lists, questionnaires and files of the largest and most comprehensive central Askhenazi organization, the Asociación Mutual Israelita

Argentina (AMIA, also known as the Ashkenazi Kehillah of Buenos Aires, founded in 1895 as the Ashkenazi Burial Society). Sofer's contribution lies especially in his empirical approach to the subject of Jewish mobility, and in his endeavor to collect field data.

Along with the Jewish sources, the author collected and made skilful use of relevant demographic and economic data from Argentinian official censuses and from American and English official reports. On this basis he endeavored to present an integrated description of the development of the Jewish and the host society in Argentina. This approach he shares with Elkin, but he has taken it significantly further, especially in Chapters Four and Five, where he has applied it to a defined range of themes and phenomena.

Nevertheless, some aspects of the study are open to question. For one thing, there are some doubts about whether the author's sample from which he deduced much of his data is representative of the Ashkenazi population of Buenos Aires between 1895 to 1947. As there is no methodological appendix, one does not know whether he utilized membership lists other than those of the AMIA. To use only the latter is to make the questionable assumption that this body occupied as central a position in its early years as it did more recently.

Similar inadequacies affect Sofer's description of Jewish economic pursuits. Relying on a limited number of Jewish sources, his list falls short of a comprehensive treatment of Jewish activity in this realm during the long period under review. This might have been remedied by reference to the Schmelz-DellaPergola study of Jewish demography and socioecomic status, which would also have saved much of the data of the final chapter from obsolescence.

Finally, the main chapters of the book would have gained in depth had the author utilized the Yiddish and Spanish Argentinian Jewish press in order to corroborate the findings based on his sample.

Nevertheless, Eugene Sofer's book is an important contribution to the field of Latin American Jewish studies, so long as his conclusions, like the one regarding Jewish socioeconomic mobility ("over the first half century of Jewish life in Buenos Aires, most workers experienced mobility only fleetingly if at all . . . I have called this phenomenon 'inconsistent mobility,' " p. 96) are regarded as well-based hypotheses, laying the groundwork for further and more comprehensive studies in this field.

The volumes by Elkin and Sofer are worthwhile contributions, while Weisbrot's could hardly satisfy the nonacademically inclined readers. All three rely heavily on secondary sources, which means that the English-reading public still does not have access to primary and basic research in this field. Such studies already exist as doctoral dissertations, and together with research written in Hebrew and Spanish, they await adaptation for wider readerships. This specialized research, based on primary sources, reveals that the Latin American Jewish experience has striking relevance for the understanding of other Jewish communities and cultural minorities. It is to be hoped that English-language publishers will soon make these works available to the public.

Haim Avni
Hebrew University

The "Führer State": Myth and Reality

Gerhard Hirschfeld and Lothar Kettenacker (eds.), *Der "Führerstaat": Mythos und Realität. Studien zur Struktur und Politik des Dritten Reiches/The "Führer State": Myth and Reality.* Veröffentlichungen des Deutschen Historischen Instituts London, Vol. 8. Introduction by Wolfgang J. Mommsen. Stuttgart: Klett-Cotta Verlag, 1981. 465 pp.

This volume is the product of a conference convened in May 1979 by the German Historical Institute in London. Although none of the contributions deals specifically with the subject, several participants devote a considerable part of their exposition to the persecution and genocide of the Jews in the Third Reich. Consequently, the book presents a good outline of the current controversy among German historians about what they describe as "the genesis of the Final Solution."

Tim Mason introduces the series of articles with an overview of the debate which has split German historians of National Socialism for almost a decade. Mason's categorization of the different positions into two separate camps of "functionalists" and "intentionalists" has meanwhile been so widely disseminated and schematically overstated as to have become almost meaningless. Mason designates as "functionalists" those historians who try to explain the evolution of the Nazi regime by referring to the accruing momentum of uncoordinated decisions: "The cumulative radicalization of Nazi policies which ended in total war and genocide" appear as arbitrary, as it were "self developing" mechanisms, without a causal connection to ideological factors (p. 24). The "intentionalists," on the other hand, are those historians who ascribe the decisive role (hence, also the responsibility) to the Führer-dictatorship and its ideology.

Mason criticizes this latter approach for ignoring significant questions of political development, administrative structure, and the dynamics of interorganizational rivalry. Hitler's world view—in which living-space imperialism and hatred of Jews were preeminent—is the explanation of all political decisions. This is in his opinion a moralist analysis, in which the historians "meditate on the enormity of the regime's crimes . . . [and] invite the readers to hate and abhor, too" (p. 29). Mason sees this as a relapse into the "methodological individualism" which neglects the "dynamics of organizational rivalries" characteristic of the administrative and political structure of the Third Reich. He sees Hitler's actual role in his "function as Führer," i.e., as an integrating factor among multilayered political and economic interests.

His critique of the "functionalists" is a great deal milder. He takes them somewhat to task for their insufficient attention to economic relationships. Recommending Marxist interpretations, he vaguely attributes the confused strategy and tactics of the war of expansion to the "politico-economic need for plunder. . . . Genocide was the most distinctively Nazi, the most terrible part of an over-arching politics of struggle. And these were the politics of a whole capitalist epoch" (pp. 39–40).

These are familiar tunes, in unfavorable contrast even to Mason's own earlier and more subtle Marxist approach. In a series of articles in the Berlin *Das Argument* in the 1960s Mason refuted the Orthodox "Agent-Theory" prevailing then and even now in Soviet and East German historiography. In comparison, his later utterances, as in this article, appear as a retreat to earlier positions more secure against attacks from the "old" or "new" Left.

How the National Socialist regime actually functioned is not resolved by Mason's "Literaturbericht," or by the contributions by Hans Mommsen and Klaus Hildebrand which follow, representing respectively the "functionalist" and "intentionalist" interpretations. Which was the decisive factor? The abundance of competing authorities in an intended or merely tolerated confusion of jurisdictions, or the finally decisive "Führer"-dictatorship? After all that has been said, it is still not clear why both elements, side by side and complementing each other, could not have contributed to the process of political decisions.

To its credit, modern scholarship has revised earlier theories of a monolithic, tightly-organized-down-to-the-last-detail central system of power. This has led to the realization that in the National Socialist state, too, social and political interest conflicts existed and were fought out by the means available within the given framework of dictatorship. Nevertheless, the resultant confusion over lines of responsibility and bureaucratic intrigues can by no means be considered as *the* characteristic feature par excellence of the Nazi system of government. Similar traits were no less common in Western democracies, even in wartime.

To the contrary, the Nazi regime is, in my opinion, characterized by the combined effect of tactically pragmatic improvization and ideologically determined objectives—with regard to which Hitler played a decisive, but not the only decisive, part. Under these conditions, this system functioned with amazing efficiency, so that the ideologically postulated objectives were in fact attained—sometimes with the help, other times in spite of the "administrative chaos." Hans Mommsen's contention that the system was condemned to be "self-destructive" is by no means substantiated (pp. 68ff.). Klaus Hildebrand and Lothar Kettenacker argue rather convincingly that the Nazi regime collapsed only after military defeat.

A historical discussion can advance our understanding only if it confronts empirically researched aspects of the Nazi regime, which some of the contributors to this volume actually tried to do. In this context the war and the murder of Jews by the millions—or the "Final Solution," as the Nazis euphemistically called it and as it was subsequently taken over by historians—refuse to be neglected, although here and there one finds attempts to do so, even in this volume.

Hans Mommsen refers to Martin Broszat's statement of 1970 that no formal order of genocide by the Führer was found anywhere. However, Mommsen stresses the "cumulative process of radicalization . . . the gradual getting used to the systematically practiced abrogation of law and to acts of violence, which produced passive resignation and irresponsible indifference, long before the regime conducted its policy of extermination . . . with cynical perfection" (p. 59). According to Mommsen, this was the result of

> numerous intermediate stages . . . which, only in retrospect, appear as the consistent realization of a fixed intention, and though individually they had resulted from widely differing initiatives. . . . [T]he 'idea', that is to say, Hitler's fanatical expressions of racial antisemitism alone, did not suffice to set the methodical extermination of Jews into motion. It required the escalating acts of violence by which to accustom the henchmen to become professional murderers and to blunt [the sensibilities of] witnesses, for systematic murder to become concrete reality. (p. 63)

Mommsen's propensity for overstated formulations, in my view, frequently leads to a misunderstanding of his thesis, as for example, at the March 1983 Yad Vashem conference in Jerusalem. In all of the discussions of the "pre-planning" of Hitler's direct and verifiable order in the mass murder committed in the occupied eastern territories, and of the precise process of decision-making, the far more essential matter of identifying the groups of people who participated and who shared responsibility is often lost sight of. Mommsen's analysis of the momentum that carried executive bodies, once set in motion, toward the implementation of Hitler's ideologically dictated decisions is open to debate. His thesis cannot, however, be interpreted as a revisionist rehabilitation of the German people or of individual groups and functionaries. The "dynamics of radicalization" of which he speaks in fact widen the circle of responsibility rather than the opposite.

> It cannot be argued that Hitler did not wholly approve of the policy of extermination in the east, [or] that he did not directly or indirectly urge [it] upon his subordinates. [But by the same token] no less bitter is the realization that without the bustling competition of dignitaries currying the dictator's favor, along with the secondary bureaucracies working with automaton-like objectless perfection, Hitler's fanatic racial objectives could hardly have been translated into the horrifying truth of the extermination of more than five-and-a-half million Jews and several million Slavs and other victims of the regime. (p. 62)

On the "Way to Auschwitz" and its "Intermediate Stations," as described by Mommsen, there were tens and hundreds of thousands of accomplices or at least silent onlookers. "A large group of military men, officials and technocrats as well as representatives of the major industries willingly placed themselves at the service of inhumanity and the barbaric use of violence . . ." (p. 64). Accordingly, Mommsen draws the circle of cooperation and responsibility rather wide. On the other hand, his emphasized separation between technocratic obedience and over-servility and any ideological motivation must induce an almost instinctive rejection, especially in Jewish audiences. It is indeed hard to escape the impression that by his interpretation the perfectionist implementation of mass murder may be conceivable even in the absence of any antisemitic ideology and tradition. (Actually this has been implied more than once in the heat of argument by extreme "functionalists.")

Mommsen is, however, more cautious: "The concrete implementation of the regime's criminal intentions was . . . left to men of eager and servile underling mentality. . . . Some were blindly racist anti-Semites and anti-Communists, but these were outweighed by mere assiduous executors and power-technicians" (p. 65). Mommsen does mention the ideological dimensions of the genocide, but he obviously tends to underestimate their importance. In a later article he is indeed more explicit: "The influence of antisemitic propaganda or the authoritarian inclination of the German political culture can explain only inadequately why the Holocaust could become reality" (*Geschichte und*

Gesellschaft, vol. 9 [1983], p. 420). Even if this is true, the decisive point remains, in my opinion, that without those elements the Holocaust cannot be explained at all! And this is exactly what Mommsen tries to do—at least implicitly—with the help of his concept of "self-propagating mechanisms."

The question of how German public opinion might have altered Hitler's course in this matter, despite his ideological fixation on the Jews, will probably never be answered unambiguously. It is doubtful (although not impossible) that "massive protests by the Christian churches . . . and by the officer corps would have contained the policy of the 'Final Solution' . . . within strictly circumscribed limits" (p. 66). The fact is that Hitler did not have to come to grips with any such thing. In any event, the responsibility of the wider circles mentioned above, as argued by Mommsen, is not reduced by the possibility that protests which were not voiced would in any case have proved ineffectual.

It is probably this one aspect of—if one insists—the "functionalist" explanatory model which elicits the most vociferous opposition on the part of other German historians. Klaus Hildebrand opposes the "revisionist view of the National Socialist state," which overrates the "polycratic chaos in the internal and external political sphere," and which seeks to depict Hitler as the mere "representative" of fascism in Germany rather than as an autonomous actor. Citing Karl Dietrich Bracher, Hildebrand castigates "New Left and Marxist dogmatism" for its sweeping generalizations and lashes out at

> revisionist interpretations opposed to the 'old-liberal' research of totalitarianism . . . which would like to heave behind . . . the questions of guilt and responsibility but thereby risk an underestimation and trivialization of National Socialism. . . . The revisionists . . . unintentionally run the risk of minimizing the ideological and totalitarian dimension of National Socialism . . . while unduly incriminating the liberal western constitutional and social order. (p. 77)

While Hildebrand's argument against wholesale theoretical generalization seems convincing, it remains questionable why his own no less sweeping concept of "totalitarianism" should be more acceptable. Not unlike Marxist—and other—concepts of "fascism," this model, born and raised in the wake of the Cold War, obscures the singularity of Nazism and its racist dogma and is too all-inclusive. Hildebrand rightly points out that the "destruction of European Jews derived from Hitler's programmatic deliberations . . . and the existence of racism in the National Socialist 'Weltanschauung'" (pp. 86ff.). Unfortunately, he remains vague in regard to the mass appeal of this ideology for the German population, leaving us with the uneasy impression of Hitler-centric evasion. Neither Hitler's "ideas of the destruction of the Jews and of racist supremacy . . ." nor his "specific pathological anti-Semitism" can solely be blamed for all that happened. The persecution and mass murder of the Jews were simply unthinkable without the wide consensus, or at least the tacit toleration, not only of his "ideas" but also of their gruesome realization.

In this regard Lothar Kettenacker's contribution is definitely a step in the right direction, stating as it does that "Research has disregarded the connection between Hitler's prejudice [against Jews] and the ideological dispositions among the masses . . ." (p. 102). Whether Nazism can really be defined as a "revolution," or more specifically, a "petty bourgeois revolution," as Kettenacker attempts to do (building on earlier work by Ralf Dahrendorf and David Schoenbaum), is rather more of a semantic problem. On the other hand, his analysis of the "National Socialist seizure of power within and the extension of power without"—that is to say, the entire twelve-year period of Nazi rule—as "a single *levée en masse* [such] as German history had not known before or since" (p. 107) is of fundamental significance.

Kettenacker argues that the appeal of the ideology of *Volksgemeinschaft* had a historic effectiveness which must not be underestimated. Manipulatory techniques practiced by the regime to great effect had the impact they did because they appealed to this mentality (p. 113). The susceptibility to such appeals on the part of a broad stratum of the population, increasingly distancing itself from the Prussian-German traditional elite, made it possible for Hitler, soon after 1933, to induce the majority of the upper stratum to "curry favor, to disband voluntarily and toe the line, and, if need be, to resign and emigrate." This was a decisive factor in the Nazi seizure of power (p. 107). The priority which Kettenacker allots to sociopsychological motives, especially ideological ones, forms an interesting basis for discussion.

His treatment of the extermination of the Jews deserves a more critical examination. It is hardly accidental that he mentions it only very briefly, almost incidentally—perhaps aware of its collision with his own thesis. After introducing, on the basis of "popular sentiment" *(Volksempfinden),* the concept of the "*Volksmoral* . . . corrupting the individual's sense of justice," he immediately adds that here "one needs to guard against establishing a direct causal connection with the enormous crimes of the regime, the extermination of the Jews, and the *Lebensraum* imperialism which also bears a genocidal quality" (p. 116). Here Kettenacker obviously shrinks back from the conclusions of his own argument: one simply cannot plead, for pages on end, the case of the broadest agreement of the *Volksgemeinschaft* with the Führer, right to the bitter end, and then in two short, unsubstantiated sentences, exclude antisemitism, *Lebensraum* imperialism, and genocide from this consensus. If the *Volksgemeinschaft,* grouping itself around its Führer, is declared to be the central integrating factor of Nazi rule, then the exclusion from it of German Jewry was as integrally basic to this ideology as was the "enemy" concept which declared "international Jewry" to be its principal political opponent. These were fundamental and constant elements in Hitler's world view—and, according to Eberhard Jäckel, whom Kettenacker often cites, the most and, actually, the only constant ones.

These concepts formed the leitmotif of Nazi propaganda from the founding of the NSDAP until the end of the Third Reich, and were definitely "popular." With them the seeds of the later crimes were already sown in the *Volksempfinden.* Without this, the obedient and perfectionist execution of crimes, which clearly contradicted all traditional human norms of behavior, by tens of thousands of people who were directly involved, and the tacit connivance of the majority of the population, is simply inexplicable. According to Adalbert Rückerl, since the end of the war more than fifty thousand Germans have been sentenced by foreign courts for war crimes and for their participation in crimes against humanity. In the Federal Republic, close to 88,000 preliminary proceedings were instituted for suspicion of responsibility for or participation in Nazi crimes (Cf. *Aus Politik und Zeitgeschichte* B 43/82). In comparison, microscopic investigation of the "genesis" or the successive stages in the decision-making process relating to the "Final Solution," though not superfluous, seems almost trivial. For this reason, and in spite of the criticism stated here, Kettenacker's approach opens new vistas and deserves profound and further study.

It is, certainly, far more convincing than Ian Kershaw's attempt (in this volume) to ascribe Hitler's popularity to nothing more than his conservative-nationalist successes, in contrast to the alleged lack of general acceptance of his ideology of conquest and his racial policies. It is not merely that Kershaw's evidence is of questionable value—police reports may deal with exceptions, and court records hardly reflect attitudes among the general population—it is also open to doubt because of the fact that Hitler's appeal continued long after there could be any further talk of "successes."

Other contributions to the volume present the results of specialized research and are well worth reading. Special mention should be made of the expert study by Horst Gies on the *Reichsnährstand* (farmers), as well as the papers by Horst Matzerath and Jeremy Noakes on the relationship between the Party and the bureaucracy on the local level. The third part of the book is largely taken up by a discussion on the National Socialist "expansionist economy," between Alan S. Milward and Bernd-Jürgen Wendt. This is a subject which deserves separate and more detailed treatment.

AVRAHAM BARKAI
Lehavot Habashan

Book Reviews

Steven E. Aschheim, *Brothers and Strangers: The Eastern European Jew in German and German Jewish Consciousness, 1800–1923.* Madison: University of Wisconsin Press, 1982. xiv + 331 pp.

Steven Aschheim has written an enormously rich and stimulating study of the attitudes of Germans, and specifically German Jews, toward the *Ostjuden,* the Jews of Eastern Europe. But this is no circumscribed monograph. Instead, Aschheim has succeeded in turning his subject into a prism through which to view the tortuous identity of the German Jews themselves as they confronted the problem of integration into German society. For the way the Jews of Central Europe saw their brothers in the East became a mirror for their own ambivalent relationship to Judaism. As Aschheim writes in the concluding lines of his book:

> most of post-Enlightenment Jewish history was conditioned by the dialectics of the rift between [emancipated and unemancipated Jewry]. The existence of the ghetto, as myth and reality, colored profoundly the fate and disposition of emancipated Western Jewry. The "Ostjude" and "German Jew" were archetypal representations of the dichotomy. . . . Mirror opposites, they remained bound to each other. Whether negatively or positively conceived, idealized or despised, the Ostjude was regarded as the 'real' Jew and the living model of *Ur* Jewishness lost to German Jewry. . . . Their power as cultural symbols made them essential ingredients of German Jewish self-definition. Their changing image reflected the complex and contradictory face of German Jewry itself.

Cast in this light, Aschheim's book becomes nothing less than a history of German Jewish culture in the nineteenth and early twentieth centuries. Using a wide variety of literature, newspapers, journals, and, to a lesser extent, examining German Jewish organizations and institutions, he has reconstructed the mentality of the German Jews from the Enlightenment to Weimar. Despite the plethora of other studies of the Jews of this period, there is no one work that has succeeded to such a great measure in capturing both the richness and ambiguities of this subject. This book therefore stands as perhaps the most definitive current work on German Jewish culture since the Enlightenment.

It is, to be sure, problematic to define a whole culture on the basis of intellectual expressions (a criticism made already of Aschheim's book by Ismar Schorsch). Yet Aschheim has examined not only the products of "high culture" but also those of popular culture such as pulp novels (more work might be done on the popular German Jewish press). In addition, he has devoted attention to the actions and attitudes of a host of Jewish organizations such as the *Centralverein,* the *Deutsches Komitee zur Befreiung der russischen Juden,* and the attempted umbrella organization, the *Vereinigung jüdischer Organisationen Deutschlands.* This is intellectual history at its best, demonstrating the continuum between "high" culture, "low" culture, and institutional history.

Aschheim starts his work with the German Jewish Enlightenment and argues that the adoption of the idea of *Bildung* from the German *Aufklärung* served to give German Jewry its unique ethos and to cause it to distinguish itself from the Jews of the East (the use of *Bildung* by the German Jews is the subject of a separate study by David Sorkin). The period up to 1880 was one of relatively little contact between the Ostjuden and their German brothers. The stereotype of the Ostjuden was developed in particular by the writers of the *Ghettogeschichten,* the romantic tales of the Ghetto which often served as a thinly veiled cloak for Enlightenment preaching. Once the immigration of Eastern Jews into and through Germany began, the Ostjuden came to be seen as a threat to German Jewish integration.

The encounter with the Ostjuden coincided with the rise of the new antisemitism of the late nineteenth century. Aschheim shows how the antisemites exploited the negative image of the Ostjude, which had been in part created by the German Jews themselves, in their polemics and caricatures. Yet, in a very subtle argument, he points out that although the antisemites attacked equally (if not more) the assimilated Jew, their hostility to these opposite types of Jews was really part of a continuum: the Ostjude serves as a symbol for the "true" identity of the assimilated Jew, hidden under the surface.

The Zionist movement ostensibly changed the image of the Ostjuden by treating them as part of the unified Jewish nation. Yet, the Central European Jews who led the early Zionist movement, such as Herzl and Nordau, adopted many of the negative sterotypes of those Jews who constituted the main following of the movement. They patronizingly saw the Ostjuden as pathetic and backward people who could only be saved and modernized by being transported to Palestine. In the years directly preceding and, even more, following World War I, the more radical young Zionists in Germany went much farther in changing the image of the Ostjuden. They created what Aschheim felicitously calls a "counter-myth," turning disdain into idealization.

The Ostjuden became the source of true Jewish culture against the vapid and vacuous bourgeois culture of German Jewry. Martin Buber's version of Ḥasidism played a particularly important role in this counter-myth by presenting an "authentic" nonrational religion as opposed to the liberal rationalism of the Judaism regnant in Germany. Yet, even here, the Jews most admired by these young Zionists were modern intellectuals such as Ahad Ha-Am and Bialik.

Aschheim devotes a long chapter to discussing the impact of World War I on the image of the Ostjuden. Germans and German Jews came face to face with the Jews of the East. This encounter promoted certain antisemitic images but also sparked tremendous sympathy and identification in many Jewish soldiers. One result of the encounter was the "cult of the Ostjuden" which captured the imaginations of many in the Jewish renaissance that followed the War.

Finally, Aschheim shows how the antisemites of the early Weimar Republic focused much of their hostility on the Ostjuden in Germany and how this hostility manifested itself in several pogroms. The question of the Ostjuden in Weimar thus became the focus for the Jewish question in Germany and foreshadowed the fate of all the German Jews in the next decade, for the very qualities in the Eastern Jew which excited the enmity of the antisemites were presumed to inhabit all Jews, no matter how assimilated. The question of the Ostjuden became a dress rehearsal for the Holocaust. The argument of Aschheim's book thus sweeps relentlessly from the rosy hopes of the Enlightenment period to the dark days of the early 1920s. And even though it ends in Weimar, the issues which the question of the Ostjuden raised for both Germans and German Jews make the Holocaust its true coda.

I would only offer one note of criticism of this otherwise superb achievement. Aschheim assumes, along with many other Jewish historians, that the Ashkenazic Jewish world before the Enlightenment was unified. In fact, the sense of division between East and West preceded the *Haskalah* by at least a century, if not more. Many Eastern European Jewish customs, such as the early age of marriage, were less common among German Jews. The decline of German Jewish *yeshivot* and consequent travel of students to the East or importation of teachers from the East can be documented in the sixteenth and seventeenth centuries. While the disdain Aschheim finds in the late eighteenth and nineteenth centuries is most probably new, the sense of foreignness begins earlier and serves as a necessary background to understanding the emergence of the image of the Ostjuden. Yet, Aschheim is surely correct that the Enlightenment and emancipation created "national" Jewish communities (French Jews, German Jews, etc.) and that it was precisely the ambiguities of these new entities that symbolize the quintessential problem of the modern Jew.

David Biale
State University of New York
at Binghamton

David Berger (ed.), *The Legacy of Jewish Migration: 1881 and its Impact.* Introduction by Irving Howe. New York: Brooklyn College/Columbia University Press, 1983. 187 pp.

Proceedings of the Eighth World Congress of Jewish Studies. Panel Sessions: Jewish History (Hebrew and English). Jerusalem: World Union of Jewish Studies/Magnes Press, 1984. 104 pp.

East European Jewry in the nineteenth century was a vast reservoir of Jewish cultural and demographic strength. Even while two and a half million emigrants from this community made their way westward, the Jewish population in Eastern Europe remained the single most important center of Jewish life. It took the combined might of the most awesome totalitarian powers in human history—Soviet Russia and Nazi Germany—to bring East European Jewry to the threshold of complete extinction in the twentieth century.

An awareness of these basic facts, attesting to a large measure of inner vitality and stability, is necessary in order to retain a sense of perspective when one considers the social, economic, and political changes that made the nineteenth century what can easily be viewed as an era of rampant turmoil and dislocation for East European Jews. Urbanization, the impoverishment and proletarization of growing sectors in the Jewish population, the cultural modernization conventionally tagged with the label *haskalah,* political radicalization and, of course, the mass emigration itself all deeply affected Jewish society on all levels. This must be viewed as a process of change—sometimes dramatic—but not one of inner collapse.

The two volumes reviewed here consist of twenty papers read in 1981 at two conferences—one in New York, the other in Jerusalem—in which these changes are examined one by one. About half of the papers deal with the East European immigrant experience in America; two papers, both in *Legacy of Jewish Migration,* deal with developments in other immigrant centers (London and Palestine); and the remaining ones concern various facets of social, political, and intellectual modernization in nineteenth-century Russia. All of the papers, therefore, are integrally linked to a common set of themes, so that reading the volumes cover to cover does not become a hapless exercise in trying to follow unrelated arguments. Moreover, since almost all of the contributors are historians, the papers maintain a similarity of discourse which makes for smoother reading. This much said, it should not be imagined that either book completely escapes from the unevenness inherent in published collections of conference papers.

A good conference should represent the state of the art; and, indeed, most of the papers presented offer new insights, ask new questions, or analyze new data. Deborah Dash Moore and Paula Hyman, for example, cover new ground: Jewish urban ecology, and the nexus between immigrant ethnicity and women's social history, respectively (Moore, *Proceedings;* Hyman, *Legacy*). Jonathan Frankel and Israel Bartal (both in *Proceedings*) reexamine old assumptions about Jewish radical ideologies as they developed from the 1860s through the 1880s, noting that in this formative stage different strands of nationalist, populist, and socialist thought cross-fertilized each other and drew on a little-studied inner tradition of ideas cultivated by the "radical *haskalah*." In another paper that takes a revisionist tack, Arthur Goren *(Proceedings)* argues that Orthodox immigrants in New York practiced a politics derived from the traditions of Eastern Europe which was more "American" than the ideological politics waged by other, more frequently studied, sectors of the immigrant community. Naomi Cohen also challenges regnant Orthodoxies in her paper on the effect of the immigration on the German-Jewish establishment in America *(Legacy)*.

In contrast, Yitzhak Maor's paper on the attitude of Russian Jewish liberals toward Russia prior to the crisis of 1881–82 (in *Proceedings*) is rather old-fashioned in its approach. Jonathan Frankel's analysis of the way the crisis propelled a new cadre of leaders to the forefront of Jewish political activity offers richer insight here *(Legacy)*.

The fruits of recent research are offered by Michael Stanislawski *(Legacy)* and by Thomas Kessner *(Legacy* and *Proceedings)*. Stanislawski elaborates on the crisis of traditional authority in Russian Jewry, a theme now familiar to readers of his *Tsar Nicholas I and the Jews* (Philadelphia, 1983). Kessner's paper updates to 1925 his findings on immigrant economic mobility (see his *The Golden Door: Italian and Jewish Immigrant Mobility in New York City, 1880–1915*: New York, 1977).

Others give us a hint, and more, of work in progress: Moses Rischin's paper on Abe Cahan *(Legacy)* is, one hopes, a foretaste of his promised book-length biography, and Steve Zipperstein's thoughtful consideration of the dynamics of the *maskilic* attitude toward the modern city *(Legacy)* will figure in his new book on nineteenth century Odessa Jewry (forthcoming: Stanford, 1985).

Although each of the twenty papers cannot be considered here, one final word ought to be said about the interesting contrast between the conclusions reached by two of the intellectual historians represented in these volumes: Arthur Hertzberg *(Proceedings)* and Robert Seltzer *(Legacy)*. Hertzberg finds that American Jewry was largely bereft of local rabbinic or intellectual leaders of European caliber and education during the formative era of immigration. "The history of American Jewry . . . is largely that of one East European class, the next to the poorest element with little Jewish and secular education . . . whose labor prepared the way for their immediate descendants both to rise in America and to create a different kind of Jewish community than had ever existed before." The unstated implication is that if American Jewry seems to lack direction and purpose today, its past as a community of *baalei melakhah*-turned-*baalei batim,* with scholars (traditionalists and rebels) relegated to its margins, may be a partial explanation.

On the other hand, Robert Seltzer's stimulating essay on Simon Dubnow offers, as a parting shot, the idea that although Dubnow himself did not immigrate to America, American Jewry nonetheless partakes of his guiding spirit in its own "implicit ideology": "Affirmation of *this galut* (together, to be sure, with support of the State of Israel), veneration of the Jewish ethnic heritage (together with acculturation to the American language, manners, and political culture, and with the cultivation of a Jewish literature in the English vernacular), advocacy of intellectual freedom and political liberalism, . . . the primacy of *klal yisrael* and toleration of a wide range of Jewish ideologies. . . ."

One may detect here the traces of older, East European, battle lines. In this, at least, continuity has been preserved in spite of all that has changed.

ELI LEDERHENDLER
Jewish Theological Seminary of America
Hebrew University

Gary Dean Best, *To Free a People. American Jewish Leaders and the Jewish Problem in Eastern Europe, 1890–1914*. Westport, Conn./ London: Greenwood Press, 1982. 240 pp.

"Almost every study of the American Jewish immigration," wrote Zosa Szajkowski in 1973,* "criticizes the attitude of the American Jews of German origin toward the East European immigrants. The wealthy "Uptown Jews," the *Yahudim* as they were called derogatorily, are blamed . . . for their paternalistic attitude toward philanthropy, for their use of *shtadlones* . . . instead of open protests." And he, of course, was right. Nationalist, populist, folkist, socialist, or simply democratic sentiments, singly or in combination, had long come to dominate modern Jewish historiography. The masses and their leaders or would-be leaders attracted the limelight as the oligarchs were bundled off into the wings. This was true not only of Dubnow, Dinur, Mahler, and Tcherikower but also, to a large extent, even of Rischin. However, as Szajkowski himself then pointed out in his classic study of New York Jewry, a revisionist trend could already be detected.

Naomi Cohen's article "The Abrogation of the Russo-American Treaty of 1832" as well as her book on the American Jewish Committee; Lloyd Gartner's study "Roumania, America and World Jewry: Consul Peixotto in Bucharest 1870–1876"; and Arthur Goren's work on Magnes and the New York Kehillah had all been recently published. Since then, just to note one of the most important studies, we have seen the appearance of Yehuda Bauer's two volumes on the Joint Distribution Committee. (Of related interest is Fritz Stern's fascinating study of Bleichröder in his *Gold and Iron.*)

Gary Dean Best's *To Free a People* belongs firmly within this ongoing enterprise which, after a lapse of two generations, has again taken up themes which had so engaged Lucien Wolf and Cyrus Adler. In the preface, he explains that although his book goes up to 1914 (actually, even further) he is primarily concerned with the decade and a half before the establishment of the American Jewish Committee in 1906, a period which, as he rightly says, has hitherto been relatively neglected.

What Best sets out to study is the patrician as political lobbyist. He concentrates primarily on three men who, by 1890, had already achieved great public prominence—Simon Wolf, Oscar Straus, Jacob

*Z. Szajkowski, "The *Yahudi* and the Immigrant: A Reappraisal," *The American Jewish Historical Quarterly* LXIII (1973–74), p. 13.

Schiff—and on their efforts to cajole the United States government into helping the Jewish people in Russia and Romania. They acted sometimes, but not always, in concert, as individuals and in their own name (with the partial exception of Wolf who, in theory at least, represented the Union of American Hebrew Congregations and B'nai B'rith). But their ready access to a succession of Presidents and Secretaries of State made it possible for them to be seen widely as they saw themselves—the spokesmen of American Jewry on all that concerned the plight of Jewish communities overseas.

The great advantage of the approach adopted by Best is that it brings out how little their interventions at the White House and the Department of State were really sporadic gestures of good will, but rather constituted part of a self-conscious political tradition. Every act of governmental intervention on behalf of Jews in one foreign country or another was well recorded, remembered, and trundled forth as a precedent to justify renewed diplomatic action in a new crisis. To work from an ever broader basis of case lore was regarded as a major key to success. The fact that both Wolf and Straus were lawyers by training no doubt encouraged this *modus operandi.*

A central problem with which they always had to grapple was the fact that in accord with diplomatic usage, at least as understood prior to World War I, the United States government had no standing when it came to the "internal" affairs of Russia and Romania. The natural response of every administration when faced by some new anti-Jewish outrage in those two countries was therefore, however regretfully, to do nothing. And it fell to the lobbyists to demonstrate that, nonetheless, where there was a will there was a way.

Thus, in the case of the anti-Jewish measures taken by the Tsarist regime in 1891–1892 (above all, the expulsion of Jews from Moscow), President Harrison and Secretary of State James Blaine were induced to despatch a protest to St. Petersburg on the grounds that the mass of hapless refugees from Russia was bound to end up on American shores. When it came to a renewed crisis in Romania in 1900, Straus could recall the fact that as early as 1872, a United States President (Ulysses S. Grant) had protested against the treatment of the Jews in that country. In the final analysis, Roosevelt and Hay decided, however hesitantly, to do likewise, basing their intervention on the relevant clauses of the Berlin Treaty of 1878. At the time of the Kishinev pogrom, the United States government again took up the Jewish cause, seeking to forward a petition of protest from American Jewry to the Russian regime. The culminating act in this series was, of course, the abrogation of the Russo-American Commercial Treaty in 1912, a move forced on President Taft by Congress.

Similarly, there was development, as well as continuity, in the means employed by Schiff and the others to bring their influence to bear. Their preference was clearly for private and discreet channels of communication. But they proved ready to call public protest meetings (at the time of Kishinev, for example); to work openly to punish enemies and reward friends on the international financial markets (Schiff's part in raising massive loans for Japan while denying them to Russia during their war of 1904–1905); and to institutionalize their lobby, opening it up to a broader membership (the American Jewish Committee).

By choosing a narrow focus, Gary Best has succeeded admirably in showing how his chosen trio conducted their relations with the Presidents and their men. There is a wealth of documentation, from both private and government archives, used here systematically for the first time.

But the reader will find very little about anything which falls beyond the line illuminated by this single beam. He will hope in vain to learn anything significant about the relationship of the three to the American Jewish community at large or to their counterparts in Western Europe (the Rothschilds, Paul Nathan, Samuel Montagu). Even the personalities of these unusual individuals remain shadowy and one-dimensional, revealed primarily through their letters, which were usually drawn up in the language of a legal brief. Only Schiff, with his quick temper, passionately held feelings, his pride, his occasional impulsiveness and occasional arrogance sometimes breaks through the screen of diplomatic discretion. (In a letter of December 1905 to Theodore Roosevelt, he virtually proposed that the United States threaten Russia with war unless an end be put to the anti-Jewish massacres.)

Best, understandably enough, makes no systematic attempt to ascertain what effect all the diplomatic notes and financial pressures actually had on the Russian and Romanian governments. This, after all, would require extensive research in the archives of those countries. However, he seems disinclined to repeat the judgment pronounced by Fritz Stern on similar activity during the 1870s—that it was in the nature of a cruel caricature permitting statesmen to pay mere lip service to Jewish interests while actually betraying them, and thus to create the impression of Jewish power where there was only Jewish impotence.

If anything, Best probably tends to exaggerate somewhat the actual influence which the patrician Jews enjoyed, just as Stern probably underestimated it. The truth seems to be that they were more than a *quantité négligeable* and could make quite a nuisance of themselves. But at bottom, their power was extremely limited. Schiff and the

Rothschilds acting together in 1906, as Best describes, could not prevent the regime of Nicholas II from raising a huge loan in Europe. All they could do was to make this undertaking much more difficult. And the same pattern repeated itself during World War I. Nor, of course, could the American Jewish leadership prevent or even modify the anti-immigration laws passed by the United States Congress in the 1920s.

If the question of their effectiveness must thus remain open, this book certainly reconfirms what Szajkowski argued. The German Jews, at least as represented by Schiff, Straus, and Wolf, were profoundly engaged by the plight of the Jews in Eastern Europe. The *yidn* had no cause to complain about these particular *yahudim*.

JONATHAN FRANKEL
Hebrew University

Edward J. Bristow, *Prostitution and Prejudice: The Jewish Fight against White Slavery, 1870–1939*. London: Oxford University Press, 1982. £15.00.

Starting in the 1870s, Jews played an increasingly conspicuous role in commercial prostitution. By the twentieth century, Yiddish-speaking Jews dominated the international white slavery traffic, especially in Jewish women, out of Eastern Europe, and Jews maintained an important position as brothelkeepers and procurers in parts of Eastern Europe, Argentina, New York, Constantinople, and elsewhere. These traffickers, their women, and their opponents form the subject of this book.

Nineteenth-century Jewish prostitution stemmed from the same factors which led to prostitution in the general community, namely disorientation and rootlessness following migration from country to city, rapid urbanization, the disruption of family life, working-class poverty and low wages, and the breakdown of traditional faith. Antisemitism played a role to the extent that it distorted the Jewish economy, impoverished the people, and led young women into taking risks with suitors from abroad who turned out to be procurers.

These social conditions provided opportunities for street-wise young Jews and members of the Jewish underworld to prey on their own people for gain. Just as the American gangster Lepke Buchalter found it convenient to extort Jewish businesses in New York, so did

Jewish procurers in Minsk, Lodz, Warsaw, Odessa, Cracow, Vienna, and Lemberg turn inward to their community for recruits.

While most of the Jewish women in the brothels of Asia, Africa, and Latin America were recruited in Eastern Europe, their North American sisters, although foreign born, were recruited locally. Popular wisdom depicted the prostitutes as having been seduced, tricked, or forced into the profession, but this was not always so. Bristow shows that many of the women knew exactly what they were getting into, preferring the higher material rewards of a life of vice to the drudgery and low wages of the sweatshop or factory. As an American recruiter in Lincoln Steffen's story "Schloma, Daughter of Schmul" put it, prostitution "ist besser wie packin pants."

The Jewish communities' and leaders' response to the "unclean ones," as they were called, was motivated by their desire to rescue and help the victims, convict the pimps, and confront the antisemites head on. This was based on the faulty assumption that visible Jewish efforts against white slavery would deny the use of the "Jewish trafficker" stereotype to the racist. At the formal and institutional level, philanthropists like the Rothschilds, social workers such as David Blaustein, feminists like Bertha Pappenheim, rabbis like Henry Berkowitz, and journalists like Abraham Cahan debated the problem in the press and at international conferences and formed the anti–white slavery committees around the world. At the same time, Jews participated actively in the interdenominational anti–white slavery crusade. On the local level, where the Jewish population was small, such as in Buenos Aires, Rio de Janeiro, and Constantinople, the respectable Jews did not allow the pimps and prostitutes to participate in the religious life of the community. Exclusion and ostracism in these places led the outcasts to establish their own institutions, synagogues, and cemeteries. In larger Jewish centers, where total segregation proved impossible, communal action ranged from physical assault on the brothels, as in Warsaw, to political pressure on city governments to investigate and deal with the problem, as in Chicago and New York.

The decline in Jewish commercial vice in places like the United States, Great Britain, and South Africa after World War I resulted from upward Jewish social and economic mobility. In other more closed societies, Jewish white slavery persisted until 1939, to be halted by the war and the destruction of European Jewry.

In compiling his study, Bristow drew upon archives and collections located in eight countries and utilized an impressive array of primary and secondary sources: government reports and surveys, judicial proceedings, police files, newspapers and journals, organizational reports, correspondence, memoirs, and popular literature in English, German,

French, Polish, Spanish, Yiddish and Hebrew. The book is exhaustive, covering North and South America, Europe, Asia, and Africa; readable, with the narrative enlivened by vivid portrayals of the procurers and their victims; and convincing, with Bristow making effective use of statistical data (the 1889 Russian census of prostitution in the Empire, municipal surveys of licensed brothels, and police lists of convicted traffickers) to buttress his contention about the extent and scope of Jewish involvement in white slavery.

Although the volume contains a number of stylistic errors—titles printed one way in the text and another in the footnote (p. 27); the tea magnate Kalonymus Wissotzky's name is spelled Wissovsky (p. 227)—they do not detract from the work's importance. Bristow's book contributes a good deal to our knowledge of the nature and extent of the Jewish underworld, and helps us gain a more realistic picture of Diaspora Jewry in the late nineteenth and early twentieth century.

ROBERT ROCKAWAY
Tel-Aviv University

Joseph Buckman, *Immigrants and the Class Struggle: The Jewish Immigrant in Leeds, 1880–1914*. Manchester University Press, 1983. £17.50

In his pioneering work, *Di geshichte fun der yidishe arbayter bavegung,* Hertz Burgin emphasized the weakness of Jewish labor organizations in England, comparing them unfavorably with their counterparts in Russia and the United States. Subsequent historians have not contested this judgment except to note that Jewish trade unionism was stronger in the provinces, and particularly in Leeds, than in London. Most notably, Lloyd Gartner argued that the existence of large clothing factories distinguished the tailoring industry in Leeds from that in the capital. These factories, he suggested, produced a steady flow of orders for Jewish workshops, enabling them to attain a size and stability not possible in London. These industrial conditions are seen as having favored the growth of a stable trade unionism.

In *Immigrants and the Class Struggle* the Jewish labor movement in Leeds and the economic conditions which produced it are the subject of close historical scrutiny. Buckman demonstrates that far from creating conditions of stability, the Leeds clothing factories had the reverse effect upon Jewish labor. He shows that workshops were always ancillary to, and dependent upon, factory production and so were always the first to suffer whenever trade was disturbed. Furthermore, the pattern of industrial development led to a progressive concentration of the industry in highly mechanized factories. As this occurred, the dependent Jewish workshops became increasingly marginal and thus less stable. Having thus disposed of the economic determinist explanation of Jewish trade unionism in Leeds, Buckman goes on to describe the thirty-five years of arduous struggle via which the Leeds Jewish Tailors, Pressers and Machinists Trade Union finally achieved a mass membership and won a significant victory over the masters in the years just before the First World War (p. 116).

Buckman's account splendidly fulfills his goal of recovering a too long ignored portion of Anglo-Jewish history. This restoration has an additional strategic role, to overthrow what he terms the "unitary" interpretation of East European Jewish settlement in Britain. In other words, the ties of religion and ethnicity emphasized by Gartner and others are here seen to have been "incidental" (p. 86), and are replaced by the class struggle as the dynamic organizing principle of immigrant life in the Leeds ghetto. Certainly, Buckman's acerbic historiographical survey amply demonstrates that the existence of profound social and political divisions within Anglo-Jewry, and their frequent location in economic struggles, have too often been understated or not explored. Typically, the bitter struggles of immigrant workers in Leeds to establish a trade union in the tailoring industry have been ignored and the union itself has been reduced to the happy outcome of a benign industrial structure. Buckman's revisionism is even more wide-ranging. For example, he uses his story of tenacious and ultimately successful trade unionism to challenge images of the essential "individualism" of Jewish immigrants.

Nevertheless, *Immigrants and the Class Struggle* leaves some questions ill-resolved and others unposed. The most important historical omission is of the role of Jewish women. Here, both conventional and radical histories of Anglo-Jewry are united in silence. Buckman also argues persuasively that Jewish trade unions played an important role in gaining acceptance for immigrants in Leeds by allaying fears that they would undercut wages. But in *Immigrants and the Class Struggle* there is a general reluctance to recognize the particularity of the situation and politics of the Jewish working classes. As a result, important aspects of Jewish working class culture and politics—such as religious Orthodoxy—which fall outside preconceived ideas of the parameters of trade unionism and revolutionary politics are barely considered.

These caveats notwithstanding, Buckman has produced an important and closely argued book which should act as a stimulus and a challenge to other historians. By demonstrating that Jewish tailoring trade unionism in Leeds developed in workplace conditions not fundamentally different from those in London, Buckman has rendered problematic the accepted accounts of the Jewish labor movement in the capital.

David Feldman
Cambridge University

Michael Checinski, *Poland: Communism—Nationalism—Anti-Semitism*. New York: Karz-Cohl, 1982. viii + 289 pp. $22.95.

According to its title, this is supposed to be a book about Communism, nationalism and antisemitism in Poland. In the words of the author, his study analyzes "three intertwining strands in postwar Polish history: the Communist Party, the security forces, and the Jews." According to the book's flyleaf, Mr. Checinski, having reconstructed the rise of the security service in postwar Poland, "provides a rare inside look into the mechanics of political power in a Communist country. . . ." Thus it can be seen that the book offers a rather rich menu and indeed, it does touch upon most of the topics listed above.

Having said this, the question still remains as to what the book is really all about. Disregarding the different claims, it is clear that the main focus of the book is an analysis of Polish-Jewish relations in post–World War II Poland. Anyone attempting even to touch upon this highly controversial and emotion-laden topic must be commended for undertaking what may be called a "mission impossible." The history of Polish-Jewish relations prior to World War II is difficult enough and still awaits an objective and scholarly treatment. However, in comparison with what has been written about the relations between the Poles and the Jews since 1939, the former task seems easy. The progressive deterioration in that relationship, culminating in the antisemitic paroxysm of March 1968, has most likely discouraged many scholars from attempting to deal with this topic for fear of being accused of prejudice and lack of objectivity, if not worse.

It may be assumed that Mr. Checinski was very much aware of the hazardous nature of his enterprise and it is much to his credit that he decided to undertake it despite the risk. I wish I could report that his effort proved successful: I am afraid that it has not and that Polish-Jewish relations in the postwar period still await their historian. In fact, I found the book rather disappointing, considering the background and credentials of the author who, in addition, claims to have interviewed eighty high-ranking Communist Party officials, secret police and military officers, and leaders of Jewish cultural and economic institutions in Poland.

Mr. Checinski apparently hoped to throw new light on such key stages and events in Communist Poland as the Stalinist period, the so-called Polish October of 1956, the factional conflicts in the 1960s, including the outburst of antisemitism in the spring of 1968, and finally, "what was behind the crackdown on Solidarity in December 1981." The last desire turned out to be wishful thinking since the author ends his narrative in the late 1970s and mentions "Solidarity" only in passing. His discussion of the other events is essentially based on secondary sources and to this reviewer, at least, the references to personal interviews mentioned earlier do not substantially affect the gist of the argument. To put it differently, with some minor exceptions, unfortunately the author did not, despite his specialized experience, succeed in providing us with a "deeper understanding" of various events. Altogether a unique opportunity was missed to contribute to a better understanding of the highly complex question of Polish-Jewish relations in a historical perspective.

ANDRZEJ KORBONSKI
University of California at
Los Angeles

Michael J. Cohen, *Palestine and the Great Powers, 1945–1948*. Princeton: Princeton University Press, 1982. 417 pp.

Eleven minutes after the State of Israel was proclaimed on May 15, 1948, President Truman announced American recognition of the new-born state. This dramatic step stunned the diplomatic community. Even the American Ambassador to the United Nations, Philip Jessup, was caught by surprise. Jessup was at the rostrum of the General Assembly in the midst of proposing an American-sponsored trusteeship scheme for Palestine when someone brought him news of the act of recognition. He dismissed the report as a poor joke, only to be corrected by his assistant who had, in the meantime, retrieved a crumpled wire-service ticker tape from the wastepaper basket confirming the report. Near-pandemonium broke out on the floor of the General Assembly. In Jerusalem, Walter Eytan, the director of the newly formed Israeli Foreign Ministry, also reacted with complete disbelief to the report of U.S. recognition conveyed to him by a BBC reporter. But, as Cohen relates, Truman had earlier informed Chaim Weizmann that upon the establishment of the Jewish state he would accord it recognition.

In effect, the present study represents an attempt to portray the background to the President's dramatic pronouncement and to place it in historical perspective. This book is a successor volume to the author's earlier study, *Palestine: Retreat from the Mandate,* which left off the story in 1945. Cohen, in the present volume, traces the American role in the Palestine issue from the end of World War II in 1945, when Truman assumed the presidency upon the death of Roosevelt, through the various vicissitudes which marked American policy up to the act of recognition. He illustrates the manner in which Washington ultimately assumed the primary role at the United Nations in seeking an international solution to the Palestine problem.

Historians have long been divided over President Truman's motives in promoting partition and according diplomatic recognition to the fledgling Jewish state in 1948. One school argues that it was all politics—that in succeeding to the presidency in 1945 Truman immediately set his sights on election to the presidency in his own right. Cultivation of the Jewish vote was crucial, and from the very beginning Truman acted in a manner designed to endear himself to the Jewish electorate. A second school maintains that, while not unaware of the political implications of his pro-Jewish actions, Truman was deeply stirred by the horrors of the Holocaust and was sincerely dedicated to alleviating the plight of the thousands of DPs incarcerated in the refugee camps in Europe. This compassionate concern for the fate of the Holocaust victims was subsequently linked to implementation of the partition plan for Palestine adopted by the General Assembly of the United Nations. The world organization, according to Truman, was created precisely to resolve such issues as the Palestine problem, and there was a moral, if not a legal, obligation to see the plan through if the United Nations was to succeed in its primary task of preserving international peace and security. Thus, humanitarianism combined with a dedication to international organization dictated the need to promote the U.N. partition plan for Palestine.

Cohen, it would appear, had some difficulty in deciding between these two schools of thought. Thus, in the matter of recognition, Cohen writes (p. 389): "Truman's decision on May 14 [1948] to recognize the State of Israel derived from a rare mixture of common sense and political opportunism." And yet on p. 395 we read: "Truman's precipitate recognition of Israel, masterminded by Clifford, seems to have been motivated primarily by the . . . desire to forestall the Soviets."

However, Cohen's overall assessment is decidedly negative. He attributes Truman's Palestine policy more to politics than to goodwill. Thus, on p. 389 we read:

> Truman is generally recognized to have been one of the great presidents of the United States. But his reputation must stand on spheres other than Palestine. . . . "Despite his great attachment to the Bible, Truman lacked the vision, the perception and the historical outlook to grasp fully the significance of his act" [of recognition].

In reaching this conclusion, however, Cohen seems to have relied on some evidence which must be regarded, at best, as dubious. At the same time, he has surprisingly neglected to examine the one aspect of Truman's policy which, more than anything else, raises serious questions regarding the measure of the President's commitment to the cause of Jewish statehood, namely, the American arms embargo imposed on Palestine and the Middle East on December 5, 1947. This matter and its critical bearing on the fate of the Yishuv are barely mentioned by Cohen (there is no reference to the embargo in the index) and yet it is no exaggeration to say that if arms had not been forthcoming from other (mainly eastern) sources, the Jewish state might never have survived. The embargo, it might be noted, was retained even after diplomatic recognition was granted the Jewish state. Any assessment of the Truman Administration's Palestine policy requires a careful review of the embargo episode; a perfunctory reference hardly suffices.

On the other hand, Cohen's analysis of the May 12, 1948, meeting at the White House on the issue of recognition suffers from reliance on a totally unsubstantiated source. This meeting was summoned by the President to decide whether to announce *in advance* an American intention to recognize the Jewish state upon its proclamation. Present at the meeting were leading State Department officials—Secretary of State Marshall, Under Secretary of State Lovett, Robert McClintock of the U.N. desk—and key assistants to the President Clark Clifford and David Niles. According to Cohen [p. 383], "the main thrust of Clifford's argument, in addition to stressing the wisdom of recognizing reality, was that a prompt American recognition of the new Jewish state would restore the president's standing with the Jews to where it had been prior to the State Department's trusteeship initiative on March 19." As authority for this assertion Cohen cites John Snetsinger's *Truman, the Jewish Vote, and the State of Israel,* in which it is claimed that Clifford argued that "with a national election less than six months away [the President] should move towards redeeming himself with Jewish voters by immediately recognizing the existence of the Jewish state." But the Snetsinger work was published *before* the secret State Department documents of this period were opened, and unless corroborated from other sources, cannot be depended upon. The Snetsinger book is essentially based on interviews with participants years after the events took place and is therefore quite unreliable. As an illustration, one should note the following: In footnote 42 on p. 183 Snetsinger, on the basis of an interview with Robert McClintock, states that "during the conference on May 12, 1948 . . . [the] desire to beat the Soviet Union before she could recognize the Jewish state, was never even brought up as a reason for immediate recognition." The files of the State Department, as recorded in at least three places in *FRUS 1948* (pp. 906, 974–75, and 976), demonstrate that the Russian argument was central to Clifford's presentation to the conference. (Interestingly enough, McClintock himself drafted the State Department minutes.) These same State Department minutes confirm quite clearly that Clifford did *not* highlight any domestic political consideration for recognition. This emerges from the charge by Lovett and Marshall that Clifford's counsel represented "a very transparent attempt to win the Jewish vote." If Clifford had said what Snetsinger attributed to him, there would have been no sense in referring to his suggestion as "a transparent attempt." Clifford's reference to recognition having "distinct value in restoring the President's position for support of the partition of Palestine" related to the utter confusion which marked America's Palestine policy at that point as a result of the State Department's introduction of the trusteeship scheme. Recognition, Clifford argued, would reconfirm basic support for partition. The statement had no bearing on domestic political considerations.

Similarly, Cohen's treatment of the March 19, 1948, debacle on trusteeship regrettably fails to take into account significant evidence relevant to the issue. On that date, it will be recalled, Warren Austin, U.S. Ambassador to the United Nations, had informed the Security Council of American abandonment of the partition scheme in favor of a temporary trusteeship for Palestine. Just a day earlier, on March 18, Truman had met with Chaim Weizmann and had pledged continued U.S. support for partition. Upon learning of the Austin pronouncement, Truman was furious and charged the State Department officials (the lower echelons) with wilful insubordination out of a desire "to cut his throat." But the President had authorized the text of the Austin speech on a contingency basis (if the Security Council failed to adopt the partition scheme) and since the contingency was fulfilled, how account for the presidential consternation? Cohen documents the episode but omits to take into account clear evidence of State Department stratagems to ensure Security Council refusal to accept the partition plan. This evidence serves to place the whole episode in a new light and to confirm Truman's charge of State Department duplicity. It lends support to the view that State Department officials (even senior ones) were unabashedly working to undermine the President's pro-Jewish state policy.

This is an informative and interesting book, written with style and verve. Cohen's analysis is invariably challenging and thought-provoking. For instance, he makes out an excellent case for the impact of Irgun and Lehi activities, culminating in the hanging of the two British sergeants, on Britain's resolve to abandon Palestine. He also notes how utterly indifferent British and American officials were to the Holocaust as a factor underlying the drive to establish a Jewish state. Although one can on occasion take issue with the author's interpretations of the intentions of some of the leading actors—especially Truman—this work represents a notable contribution to the field and will assuredly command the attention of all those who study this period.

Shlomo Slonim
Hebrew University

Percy S. Cohen, *Jewish Radicals and Radical Jews.* London and New York: Academic Press, 1981. 224 pp. $26.00.

Percy S. Cohen sets as his purpose in *Jewish Radicals and Radical Jews* to explore the relationship between being Jewish and being radical. He focuses on two questions: "whether or not Jewishness and radicalism coexist" and "whether there is a causal connection between Jewishness and radicalism and why, if there is, this should be the case." These questions are explored largely in relation to the radical student movements between 1962 to 1972. The data utilized consists of secondary sources and interviews. The latter were collected between 1971 and 1973 from 52 young radicals of Jewish origin located in the

United States (18), Britain (6), France (11), Germany (4), Italy (5), and Argentina (8).

Jewish Radicals and Radical Jews suffers from numerous methodological, substantive, and theoretical problems. On the level of methodology, the weakness is most glaring with respect to the interviews. Cohen wants to investigate Jews who are radicals. Yet he never defines what he means by radical other than the cryptic statement: "The term radical . . . means 'left-wing radical.' " As used throughout the book, radical comes to mean anything, typically perjorative, Cohen wishes it to mean. Then, there is the issue of the interview data and its analysis. No information is provided as to how the radical Jewish interviewees were selected. No interview schedule is presented and thus we are ignorant as to the wording of the questions. Cohen intimates that the interview data are primarily qualitative in nature but then proceeds to analyze them as if he were dealing with data from a large survey. Generally, the most simple of tabular analysis is used to confirm ad hoc and post hoc hypotheses but seldom does the author convert raw numbers into percentages and never are the data treated to any basic statistical analysis. This does not, however, inhibit Cohen from making sweeping generalizations and "important" points on the basis of numerical differences on the order of 3.

Most of the time Cohen divides his respondents into two categories—Jewish Radical (JR) and Radical Jew (RJ). The difference between these radicals is that JRs (28) did not belong to a Jewish organization and that RJs (24) did. This one indicator is supposed to differentiate between radicals with a weak and a strong Jewish identity. Cohen generates a variety of hypotheses to account for or to explain differences between these two categories. Again, he deals primarily with raw figures, typically very small numbers.

Another glaring weakness is Cohen's historical explication. The author fails to develop a historical context within which to root his data or observations. Never does Cohen adequately deal with the social, economic, and political forces that influenced young Jews' political choices. Instead, he provides the reader with abbreviated, abstract, and shallow historical synopses. It is also evident from his footnotes that he has not bothered to thoroughly inform himself on the development of the many radical groups that appear in his book. This leads him in the American case to confuse the Trotskyite Young Socialist Alliance with the Socialist Young People's Socialist League.

Cohen essentially tries to make a psychological argument to explain why a disproportionate number of Jews supported leftist radicalism: Jews as a vulnerable minority developed a compensatory sense of superiority. An integral element of this superiority has been the emphasis on literacy and ideas. This, in turn, has "produced an exaggerated belief in the role of ideas . . . in the moral transformation of the world." This fantasy has taken a "moral-justificatory" form involving the destruction of a hated authoritarian body politic and the creation of a new egalitarian order. In sum, Cohen contends that Jews were propelled toward radicalism as a result of being a minority group that engaged in compensatory utopian fantasizing.

Cohen's thesis is flawed on several grounds. It cannot explain why utopian compensatory fantasizing found a political, much less a radical political focus. If Jews did engage in such fantasizing, they could just as likely find a religious and/or nationalist outlet. Cohen's thesis, which applies to Jews as a collectivity, cannot account for the fact that only a minority of Jews in any country in the post-emancipation period devoted themselves to radical causes. It also does not assist us in ascertaining which Jews would be most likely to choose to make a leftist commitment. Furthermore, the thesis has nothing to say about the variations over time and place in the number and relative proportion of Jewish radicals. An ahistorical and static thesis such as Cohen's is fundamentally incapable of dealing with these important issues.

Incredibly, Cohen has very little to say about the role of exploitation, oppression, class, and particularly politics in the generation of Jewish radicals. There is scarcely any mention of the activist role of a Jewish working class in Europe and America in the late nineteenth and twentieth centuries that did so much to bring Jews to the left. Only a brief mention is made of the fact that the radical movements often fought against antisemitism and opened their ranks to Jews and on these legitimate grounds attracted Jews.

A partial explanation for Cohen's theoretical shortcomings may be his anti-radical bias. After stripping away his numerous modifiers and qualifications, it is clear that the author regards radicalism as a dangerous phenomenon, particularly for Jews. Cohen views the left as a threat to Israel and to Judaism. Jews who are attracted to and remain within radical movements are defined as having a flaw, like self-hatred. (He levies the charge of self-hatred as a factor in the radicalizing process and insinuates "that some, most, or even all Jews who join radical movements . . . tend to be self-hating" without providing one shred of evidence.) The positive contributions that Jewish and non-Jewish radicals made to Jews and non-Jews alike in raising living standards through union and political struggles, improving intergroup relations and economic opportunities for minorities, and in the building of democratic and socialist institutions in Israel receive short shrift from Cohen.

Flawed by inadequate methodology, insensitivity to local facts, and inadmissible blanket psychologizing, Cohen's book is less an academic treatise than an anti-radical tract.

ARTHUR LIEBMAN*
State University of New York
at Binghamton

Arnold M. Eisen, *The Chosen People in America: A Study in Jewish Religious Ideology.* Bloomington: Indiana University Press, 1983. x + 237 pp.

It was Spinoza who first uncoupled the religious from the political, and it is significant that his *Tractatus* on the subject opens with an assault on the notion of the chosenness of Israel. Ever since then, both his conscious and his inadvertent heirs have wrestled with the civil status of a people believing itself to have been divinely elected. Biblical in origin, this belief has somehow resisted the corrosive effects of secular scepticism, democratic impulses, and universalist aspirations. Jewish religious thought has continued to acknowledge, however ruefully, the pertinence of *am segulah* because, as Arnold Eisen points out, it accentuates the three points strategic to the meaning of Judaism. The idea of chosenness defines the covenant that God transacted with the Jewish people itself; it shapes how Jews are bound to one another; and it has profoundly affected the relations of Jews with the peoples among whom they have dwelled.

So pivotal an idea has been especially vulnerable in the atmosphere of an America which advanced a competing claim to election and mission, which sponsored a nationalism also based upon particularity if not historical exceptionalism, and which exhibited so much freedom and hospitality that it called into question the Jews' own sense of separatism and uniqueness. A feeling of peoplehood nevertheless endured, and therefore chosenness was reinterpreted so as to reinforce some sense of distinctive Jewish identity. Eisen's book is an account of how such revisions were formulated, how a decisive element of the Jewish faith was preserved without disturbing the place of its adherents in the United States. This was the special function of theology, although the author prefers the term "ideology," so that the transformation of a Judaic belief can be understood as a consequence of the

*Arthur Liebman died in February 1985 while this volume was in press.

circumstances of Diaspora life. Primarily a treatment of the doctrinal enigmas and logical tensions with which Jewish thinkers have struggled, Eisen's book renders the changed meaning of election intelligible in the light of the actualities of American Jewish experience.

He has made a valuable—and valiant—effort to categorize the history of this idea according to three generations of rabbis and other religious spokesmen, from 1920 to the present, and according to the denominations that emerged in the United States, including Reconstructionism. Reform rabbis in particular underscored the parallel between the Judaic sense of mission and the American trust in a unique historical destiny. Among their congregants such a harmonization provided the reassurance that they were no longer in exile. Reconstructionism went even further, at least initially, and explicitly repudiated the collective self-portrait of *am segulah.* Since supernaturalism could not be reconciled with the scientific spirit, and since a particularism defined in terms of divine election conflicted with the modern proclamation of the spiritual worthiness of all human souls, Mordecai Kaplan and his followers excised chosenness from their conception of Jewish civilization.

Orthodoxy joined this debate rather late; and even then, Eisen writes, a rabbi like Joseph Soloveitchik "does not argue for chosenness, because he does not need to" (page 104). Largely an immigrant community, at least until fairly recently, Orthodoxy steadfastly affirmed election rather than defended it. Sandwiched between such dogmatic persistence and Reform redefinition of election as commitment to social justice, the Conservative enterprise appeared equivocal—and indeed was so variegated that its views on the subject defy easy summarization. But perhaps Robert Gordis's voice was representative. The depth and force of the Hebraic religious insight, he asserted, licensed Israel to reveal God's message to humanity. Chosenness therefore could not be taken for the sort of divine favoritism which in others produced chauvinism or even racism. In a pluralistic society the credentials of the Jews received further recognition: religious genius could be invoked as the Jewish contribution to civilization.

The third generation (1945–1980) provided perhaps the most arresting reformulations of election. By then Jewish minority life had become so comfortable and so complacent that its intellectuals and theologians felt obliged to make alienation the main entry in their lexicon. Eisen suggests that chosenness became one formula for sustaining a connection with the Jewish past, and for responding to the existentialist tenet that the fate of man is fragility and estrangement. For in the aftermath of the Holocaust, Jewish thinkers could present the experience of their people's unredeemed exile and unfathomable suffering as the human condition pushed to its extreme limits. Chosenness could be invested with new meaning, as special sensitivity to the ferocity of history. The revelation enunciated at Mount Sinai posed an alternative to the terrors of the age and to the emptiness of suburbia, thus raising the stakes of the "half-way covenant" that the Jews had negotiated with America.

Eisen may well have exaggerated the relevance of chosenness to the third generation, and indeed may overestimate the importance of his topic. For in the calendar of American Jewry, Shavuot is the least resonant of the major festivals; and its reminders of revelation, covenant, and mission might have been even more neglected had confirmation ceremonies not pumped life into holiday observance. So long as the God of Sinai is considered the deity of personal encounter, cognate ideas like election can be only as strong as the immediacy of such experiences, which most congregants seem too modest to proclaim. So long as God remains for most moderns that obscure object of desire, chosenness and mission are less likely to be felt than to be defended, however acrobatically. And there, ambiguously and problematically, an ancient idea seems to rest.

It was nevertheless an inspired scholarly project to make chosenness a measure of the vicissitudes of American Jewish life over the past half century, even though the religious thought of that community is not its most impressive feature. That is why the execution of the project is rather unsatisfactory, because the evidence upon which Eisen relies is simply neither rich nor subtle enough to sustain elaborate historical criticism. Some thinkers who might have re-charged the debate, like Milton Steinberg and Abraham Joshua Heschel, abstained. And by tracing the revisions of belief to the social world of American Jewry, Eisen traps himself into raising issues that neither his training nor his methods—he teaches religion at Columbia—are likely to freshen. Phrases are plucked from modern masters from Durkheim to Wittgenstein; but there is no mention of Tocqueville, for whom egalitarianism as the axial principle of American democracy made the pressure upon the belief in chosenness ineluctable. The national suspicion of whatever smacked of a unique ethnic relationship to God threatened to exclude Sinai from a usable past and made the mission that originated there seem so intellectually inconvenient.

Stephen J. Whitfield
Brandeis University

Emil L. Fackenheim, *To Mend the World.* New York: Schocken, 1982.

"There is a moment of truth," Nadezhda Mandelstam realized in 1934, "when you are overcome by sheer astonishment. 'So that's where I'm living, and the sort of people I'm living with! So that is what they're capable of! So this is the world I live in!' We are so stupefied that we even lose the power to scream." In the wake of the Holocaust kingdom, Emil Fackenheim adds, the question is not only whether we can scream—itself a moral obligation—but whether we can continue to think, to talk of meaning, to practice the discipline of philosophy. This is the central question of *To Mend the World,* the book's driving passion, the stimulus to its philosophical argument, the source of its barely contained fury. Fackenheim poses it this way: "how Jewish (and also Christian and philosophical) thought can both expose itself to the Holocaust and survive." His noble obsession with that central question of our age, these past two decades, has now resulted in a work of unquestioned power and great importance; of painful truth, wrested from "sheer astonishment" at the awful facts.

Fackenheim's method of discussing what cannot be discussed, and of avoiding the danger of saying too little of what must be said, is to proceed via confrontations between pairs of paradigmatic thinkers, both of whom are then exposed to historical realities which call their presuppositions and conclusions into question. The first such confrontation juxtaposes the "extremes of Jewish modernity": secularism, in the person of Spinoza, with "a post-secularist commitment to revelation" represented by the hero of this book, the object of Fackenheim's homage and most brilliant analysis: Franz Rosenzweig. In the second confrontation, Fackenheim widens his focus for a study of the modern philosopher who sought more resolutely than any other to "mediate the clash" between the extremes just described. Hegel had been the subject of Fackenheim's finest work in the past, and is treated in this work with both sure-handedness and sympathy. That his attempt at mediating opposites failed is of less interest to Fackenheim than the method of the attempt and the consequence for Jewry of the failure: a split into religious and secular camps which find themselves forced, inside the renewed Jewish state, into a tense and possibly fruitful coexistence.

Thus far, the reader notes, only glancing contact has been made with the Holocaust. Spinoza's optimism about the limits of tyranny dissipates when confronted with the facts of our time; Hegel's confidence that all could be "overcome" in thought and raised to Spirit's higher synthesis is cruelly mocked by Auschwitz. Direct confrontation with the Holocaust comes after an all-too-brief encounter with the philosopher of our century who most insisted that thought, like life, is situated inescapably in "historicity." How does Heidegger's account of "Being" fare when "related to what Rosenzweig referred to as the history of *Mord und Totschlag*"? We know how Heidegger himself fares. His embrace of the Führer in 1933, and his refusal ever to unequivocally repudiate Nazism, are chronicled by Fackenheim with evident bitterness. But what of his thought of "Being"—of thought itself? It is here that Fackenheim's project reaches its climax: the suggestion that a *tikkun* or mending of the rupture created by the Holocaust *is* possible, and that this *tikkun* arises out of the very horrors which had seemed to render it impossible.

Fackenheim begins with an essay on the "description and definition" of "the spectrum of resistance" during the Holocaust, for if the atrocity itself was a novum, so was its resistance, and resistance provides the possibility and the model for *tikkun:* "thought . . . must take the form of resistance." Can philosophy continue? Yes, because the philosopher Kurt Huber, acting on teachings he derived from Kant and Fichte, led his students in the distribution of anti-Nazi pamphlets in 1943. Can Christianity continue, given the "cowardice, inner falsehood and downright depravity of Christian life and thought then and there?" Yes, because the pastor Bernhard Lichtenberg reacted to *Kristallnacht* by praying publicly on behalf of the Jews until he was arrested for so doing. Finally, are Jewish existence and faith capable of *tikkun?* Yes, because of Jews who prayed in the camps or ghettoes with especial fervor, fully realizing their plight, or who simply knew that Jewish survival had itself become a holy deed, and struggled to live. They prepared the way now widened by the existence of the State of Israel, itself a *tikkun,* fragmentary like the larger *tikkun* it assists but, for Fackenheim, no less a source of both wonder and obligation.

Fackenheim's project, then, is multifaceted and ambitious, combining philosophical analysis, immersion in the facts of the present age, and (particularly in the notes) an abbreviated dialogue with the corpus of modern Jewish thought. His approach to that corpus is highly selective, and his judgments often questionable (that Rosenzweig is the greatest Jewish philosopher since Spinoza, for example, or Buber "the deepest and most representative Jewish thinker to live through the twelve-year Third Reich"). A project so ambitious could not but be uneven in its success, and occasionally peremptory in its judgments. More seriously, the entire work rests on an assumption—the uniqueness of the Holocaust, historical and theological—which is moot. If the "rupture" was not unprecedented, the *tikkun* need not be a novum, and those whose faith was not shattered by the rupture cannot be condemned as "escapist" or self-deceived. If the rupture was as complete as Fackenheim insists, even the courageous figures he describes may not suffice to ensure *tikkun*. The matter rests with each individual soul; no philosophical necessity whatever holds sway.

The issues raised here, clearly, are worthy of our finest argument and deepest passion. Out of a rigorous and principled confrontation with the highest thought and basest horrors of the modern age, Fackenheim has given us both his own greatest achievement to date and a work which ranks with the best of recent Jewish thought. His questions—and responses—will long engage us.

ARNOLD EISEN
Columbia University
Tel Aviv University

E. Feil and I. Toedt (eds.), *Konsequenzen: Dietrich Bonhoeffers Kirchenverstaendnis Heute.* Munich: Chr. Kaiser, 1980. 232 pp.

W. Huber and I. Toedt (eds.), *Ethik im Ernstfall: Dietrich Bonhoeffers Stellung zu den Juden und ihre Aktualitaet.* Munich: Chr. Kaiser, 1982. 264 pp.

Dietrich Bonhoeffer, the great German Protestant theologian who joined the 1944 anti-Hitler plot and died a martyr, continues to occupy Christian theological thought—it is not always clear whether because of the depth and relevance of his theology or because of his personal heroism and eventual martyrdom. No one can question the greatness of his life and death. If a Christian of the stature of Franklin Littell was able to judge that his life was greater than his theology it was, above all, because of a perceived weakness in his theological response to Nazi antisemitism. Indeed, in 1933 Bonhoeffer had not hesitated to invoke the ancient Christian charge of deicide, and when this became widely known in the nineteen sixties in the English-speaking world some Jewish thinkers, the present writer included, pressed Bonhoeffer scholars and followers to investigate whether Bonhoeffer's brave personal struggle against Nazism, in the years after 1933, was matched by a comparable theological struggle against Christian anti-Judaism, his own included.

No one has taken up this challenge with so painstaking an integrity as Bonhoeffer's surviving friend Eberhard Bethge. The author of a voluminous and magisterial Bonhoeffer biography and a septuagenarian, Bethge might well have left the new, disturbing questions to others. Yet the most searching essay in *Konsequenzen* is Bethge's own "Dietrich Bonhoeffer und die Juden." And that it was felt to be so by others is evident from the fact that what was only Bethge's theme in *Konsequenzen* became the overall theme in the next volume in the series.

In his *Konsequenzen* essay Bethge concludes that whereas Bonhoeffer is among those paving the way for a Christian "theology after the Holocaust," he did not himself provide it, not only because he did not and could not know the depth of the catastrophe but also because of crucial "gaps" in his "consciousness," among them his ignorance of Jewish thought past (e.g., the Talmud) and present (e.g., Buber, Rosenzweig, and even his fellow Berliner Leo Baeck). The task of a Christian theology after the Holocaust is incumbent only on the present, and in order to perform it Christian theology must theologize not only *about* Jews but, unlike virtually all its predecessors, also *with* them. ("The non-Jew requires the ceaselessly renewed encounter with Jews and their critical help.") Then how did Bonhoeffer, nevertheless, prepare the way? By progressively abandoning remnants of Christian triumphalism; by bringing his Christ ever closer to the Jewish Bible even as he personally came ever closer to Jews and their suffering; and, perhaps above all, by perceiving the events of his time to be so epoch-making that, had he survived, "he could not have imagined the almost seamless continuation of theology and church, after 1945, where they had left off in 1932."

Beyond deepening our understanding of "Bonhoeffer's attitude toward the Jews," does *Ethik im Ernstfall* contribute toward showing its *Aktualitaet,* i.e., toward a Christian "theology after the Holocaust"? Not, one fears, a great deal. Thus Berthold Klappert asserts that Christian theology must learn to appraise positively the Jewish rejection of Jesus as Christ, but also cites with approval that "Israel must suffer for the nations' salvation"—after Auschwitz an obscenity even in Jewish theology, to say nothing of the Christian. On his part, W. Schrage, to his credit, frankly finds supersessionism over Judaism to be authentic New Testament teaching—but fails to inquire whether, after the Holocaust, the New Testament must not *itself* be subjected to Christian theological criticism. Finally, H. E. Toedt and E. A. Scharffenorth show that within the limits of the Nazi *Zeitgeist* even Bonhoeffer's 1933 utterances express courageous resistance, and this may be fair enough as regards Bonhoeffer the man and even the theologian. But what does it say for Christian *theology* when even in its bravest and deepest representatives it did not or could not recognize the devil's *kairos* or manage to rise to *absolute* resistance?

Perhaps the deepest answer to this question in this volume comes from the title of Bethge's own essay, "Nothing Seems in Order Any Longer." Or else it comes from the concluding words of W. J. Peck's essay, this too inspired by Bethge. Bethge had seen deep significance in the fact that Bonhoeffer's 1940 statement that the expulsion of the Jews from Europe was the expulsion of Jesus Christ coincided with the beginning of the mass deportations, and had not shrunk from asking, what then of the subsequent annihilation, i.e., the Holocaust? Peck cites this and concludes: "here the syllogism breaks off, and we hear Bonhoeffer speak about suffering with God in a world without God, just before he sealed his own testimony with his death."

EMIL L. FACKENHEIM
Hebrew University

Zvi Gitelman, *Becoming Israelis: Political Resocialization of Soviet and American Immigrants.* New York: Praeger, 1982. xvi + 362 pp.

"Man's reach should exceed his grasp, or what's a Heaven for?" These lines come to mind after reading Zvi Gitelman's *Becoming Israelis.* One feels almost palpably the author's frustration at not being able to pin down precisely the institutions and mechanisms which effect the political resocialization of the Soviet and American immigrants to Israel who are the object of his detailed and painstaking study.

Professor Gitelman does, however, succeed in providing reasonably clear answers to the remaining four of the five questions which he poses at the beginning of the book. In addition, he provides his readers with a wealth of information regarding Israel's polity and society; immigration to Israel; the two immigrant groups studied in his research; the background to their moving to Israel; and the experiences which they undergo in the first years of their life in the Promised Land. If the discussion is predominantly centered around the group of immigrants from the USSR, this is natural, since their character and background are more complex and less known to a broad public than are those of the American immigrants.

Looking at the immigrants' experiences from their own perspective as well as from that of Israel's political and cultural systems, Gitelman sought to determine which institutions actually influence such resocialization as takes place, and how they accomplish this. In addition he asks: (1) How does the Israeli political system attempt to integrate the immigrants? (2) Whether, in fact, resocialization takes place? (3) If so, how deeply does the resocialization affect political attitudes, values, and even "primitive beliefs"? (4) Does resocialization result in partial or total change, and if the former, then which aspects of the earlier political culture are maintained, and which altered or abandoned?

Considering that the political resocialization of adults is virtually an unstudied field, this was an ambitious project indeed. Neither was it diminished by being put in the comparative perspective of studying two groups from very different political cultures. A total of 170 immigrants from the USSR and 66 from the United States were interviewed in depth, and a part of the sample was reinterviewed in 1975. The results of these interviews were compared with three other Israeli research projects dealing with the political and social attitudes of immigrants, and bolstered by copious analysis of Israeli press discussions of new immigrants' perceptions of Israel and Israelis' treatment of new immigrants. The last link in the chain was provided by interviews with politicians and administrators from governmental and public bodies actively in contact with the immigrants.

Not surprisingly, Gitelman provides evidence of clear change in the attitudes of both groups of immigrants. For example, there is a convergence of attitudes toward authority, with Americans displaying increased deference to officials and institutions, while former Soviet citizens lose some of their awe of "the powers that be." The longer the immigrant has been in Israel, the more he perceives himself as able to influence politics, but time, it would seem, does nothing to mitigate the distrust which both American and Soviet immigrants feel toward their fellow citizens. Each of the findings is subjected to sophisticated and exhaustive discussion by the author.

In his search for the agencies of resocialization, the author examines the influence of the immigrant associations, the Histadrut labor federation and the political parties. In each case he concludes, largely on the basis of the immigrants' own testimony, that these institutions have little impact on the political attitudes of the immigrants. Later in the discussion, however, as though sensing that he may have missed something, the author draws back from this conclusion, suggesting more than once that perhaps the experience of participation is in itself a socializing factor, that the very rehearsing of Israeli problems in an Israeli framework, and the demonstration of Israeli-style politics within these institutions does, after all, play a part in recasting the immigrants' political perceptions. Such a conclusion would be consonant with most major studies of political participation.

In seeking out the mechanisms and processes of political resocialization Gitelman seems to have ignored some key experiences in Israeli life. Nowhere in the book is there systematic discussion of the socializing influence of colleagues at the place of work, or in army reserve service. Within both of these situations most Israelis are exposed to a broad cross-section of Israeli society and opinion. A great deal of direct information as well as opinion on social and political affairs is exchanged in these frameworks, and it is here that the immigrant first wins peer status as a concrete individual rather than as an abstract category. Questions regarding the immigrants' experience with discussion of politics and society in such informal frameworks might have cast light on the unsolved questions posed by the author. Nevertheless, as he demonstrates convincingly, the immigrants do become Israeli, though this resocialization is a mosaic of shaded changes, with the core of background showing through, and most fundamental beliefs remaining untouched.

Gitelman remarks on the absence of Soviet or American new immigrants in the electoral lists of candidates for the Knesset, and in the leadership of the political parties. It would perhaps be more remarkable were such recent arrivals as his post–1967 group able to make their way into the elite cadres of what is, after all, a fairly rigidly structured and hierarchical party system. In fact there was an abortive movement to set up a separate list of immigrants from the USSR in 1981, and it is perhaps a good measure of the immigrants' integration into Israeli politics that they ignored this communal list and preferred to vote for broader parties with established platforms. On the North American side, this relatively small community of immigrants has been, if anything, overrepresented in the political elite. The late Prime Minister, Golda Meir, and the late Dov Yosef (a Canadian) who was Minister of Rationing and later Minister of Justice among the oldtimers, and the present Defence Minister, Moshe Arens (settled in Israel in 1957), and the recently resigned Deputy Minister of Foreign Affairs, Yehuda Ben-Meir (in Israel since 1962), among the "newcomers," are the most prominent representatives. Another immigrant from the U.S., Tal Brodie, well known as captain of a basketball team, and a national symbol of sportsmanlike conduct, was given a high place on the list of a minor reform party which competed unsuccessfully in the 1981 elections, and another unsuccessful splinter group of the radical right drew both its leadership and its followers almost exclusively from among American immigrants. At political demonstrations of both the secular left and religious right, immigrants from North America are prominently present, and though Soviet immigrants are less prominent, their participation on both sides is noticeable as well.

The new immigrant has become an Israeli not when he begins to hate new immigrants, as the hoary (and cynically tasteless) Israeli aphorism claims, but when, as Gitelman's inquiries show, he ceases trying to emulate some idealized abstract Israeli, decides that he is one himself, and is satisfied to be himself, and to socialize with persons of his own cultural background. Though "many a year passes before the days of his initiation are over" he is finally at home and "his soul is bound up with the soul of the land."

Zvi Gitelman has written a pioneering study which fulfills its promise to "open a window onto a hitherto unexplored, but large, interesting and colorful world—that of the politics of people in transition from one political system and culture to another." His research will undoubtedly remain a foundation stone for further studies of this important facet of modern politics and society.

THEODORE H. FRIEDGUT
Hebrew University

Michael Graetz, *Ha-periferiah haytah la-merkaz. Perakim be-toldot yahadut tzarfat ba-meah ha-XIX: mi-San Simon ad le-yisud Kol Yisrael Haverim.* Jerusalem: Mossad Bialik, 1982.

The focal point of Michael Graetz's book is the foundation of the Alliance Israélite Universelle in 1860. How, he asks, did this organization, dedicated to the defense of Jewish interests throughout the world, emerge from a community emancipated for generations, thoroughly acculturated, French to the core, and wedded to the proposition that Jewish nationhood (at least in the political sense) was a thing of the past? After all, it could not have escaped the attention of its founders that a body which was to be as much political as philanthropic and was to work on behalf of, and draw its membership from, world Jewry was an obvious target for Judeophobic pamphleteers. Why did this fact not deter them? It is not as if they had been driven to desperation by the anti-Jewish trends in France which, although significant in the period 1815–1860, were not perceived as a major threat. And to make all this still more of a puzzle was the fact that the Alliance was founded not by mainstream Jews moved by traditional imperatives but by men closer to the margins of the community.

The basic thesis which Graetz puts forward is that this paradox, however apparent, is not real. There were profound forces at work in the development of French Jewry which, *inter alia,* made the establishment of the Alliance not inevitable, perhaps, but at least natural, and no cause for surprise. If it nonetheless presents the historian with a problem it is because long-standing historiographical traditions had not accustomed him to give due weight to the fact that acculturation (a sociological phenomenon) does not necessarily lead to an ideology of assimilation; that modern Jewish politics preceded the modern Jewish nationalist movement; that emancipationism, while opposed to and by "auto-emancipationism," nonetheless prepared the way for its emergence.

As Graetz describes it, the Alliance was founded as a result of the confluence of two separate processes which can adequately be understood only if traced back over many decades to their respective sources. First, he traces the growth of the established French Jewish leadership and, perhaps still more important, of the myth which attributed real, even vast, power to that leadership. And, second, he describes the emergence of various subgroups within the post-assimilationist intelligentsia which found themselves ensnared in the Jewish question as a result of their attempts to carve out a secure niche for themselves on the French left.

As indicated in the title of the book, the terms which he uses to depict these two factors are, respectively, the "center" and the "periphery." The Alliance was founded, to use this terminology, by important members of the "periphery" who had become convinced that the political power of the "center" was being shamefully underutilized in defense of Jewish interests abroad and that they thus had no choice but to take the initiative themselves.

In describing how a small elite in Paris had attained the leadership of French Jewry by the mid-nineteenth century, Graetz brings an impressive range of themes into play. He shows how French Jewry was shaped by the constant interaction between external, "macrocosmic" and modernizing factors, on the one hand, and by traditional forces immanent within the "microcosm" of Jewish life, on the other.

Thus, at the political level, the extreme centralizing tendencies of the revolutionary and Napoleonic eras left a permanent imprint. What had been a number of totally autonomous communities separated by geography (Alsace, Bordeaux, Avignon) and by history (Ashkenazi and Sephardi) had been forced to act increasingly in union. The consistorial system, retained under the Restoration, was highly centralized, elitist, and like so much else in modern France, directed from Paris.

The influence of the center was further reinforced by rapid demographic changes. If in 1789, the community in Paris represented only 1.25% of French Jewry, by 1861 it had risen to over 25%. (Because of the loss of Alsace-Lorraine to Germany it would reach 67% in 1880.) But still more important in the creation of Parisian hegemony was the emergence of the French capital as a major financial center, second in importance in the world only to London. Graetz describes in fascinating detail how the established "Protestant" banks suffered increasing competition from their new "Jewish" rivals in the early decades of the century; and how, in turn, the more conservative family banks, most notably of course the Rothschilds, were outpaced during the Second Empire by the Péreires with their Crédit Mobilier.

All in all, probably no more than three hundred Jews were engaged in the upper echelons of the financial hierarchy, as bankers, brokers, commodity dealers. But within this small group, a special place was occupied by the few plutocrats: the Rothschilds, Foulds, Goudchaux, d'Eichtals, Koenigswarters and, later, the Péreires. Their influence carried over from the world of high finance and high society into the Jewish community where, at the very least, they would lend their names and prestige to charity balls, banquets, and other such philanthropic endeavors. Thus, to support schooling for Jewish children, particularly when directed to manual and technological skills (productivization) became *de rigueur* even for those millionaires who were otherwise fast shedding their Jewish ties.

There was much more to all this, though, than the busy whirl of fashion. From within this circle were drawn the most prominent leaders of French Jewry, above all the Rothschilds. James de Rothschild, as a non-citizen, could not be a member of the Consistory, but he threw his full support behind such gifted men as Adolphe Crémieux, who was vice-president of the Central Consistory during the 1830s, and he arranged membership for his sons from an early age. It was he who made it possible for Albert Cohn (his children's tutor) to attain his preeminence in the development of Jewish welfare and education, first in France alone, but later in North Africa and the Middle East.

A reputation for power or influence can easily engender real power or influence. Thus, the Paris leadership increasingly found itself subject to appeals for help from Jewish communities abroad in their moments of crisis. The speedy and courageous response to the Damascus affair of 1840 gave a dramatic impetus to this trend. Every few years, the Central Consistory (together with that of the Paris region) found itself called into session to discuss ways of intervening on behalf of the Jews in Russia, the Danubian Provinces, Morocco and the Papal States. In such cases, contacts were established with the Board of Deputies in London; items were released to the press; questions raised in the Chamber of Deputies.

But it is Graetz's contention that all these steps were characterized by great caution, a preference for quiet diplomacy, and an aversion to anything more than a bare minimum of publicity. "The hope throughout was to prevent confrontation with the regime and consign what had happened in 1840 to oblivion." In the long run, a political style of this kind would clearly not be able to meet the rising expectations which had come to concentrate on the "center."

The move toward the institutionalization of political action, with its attendant publicity and publicity-seeking, had thus to be taken in 1860 in direct opposition to the official leadership in Paris, as represented by the Central Consistory. At the same time, it was not surprising that within a few years the establishment would take the new organization under its wing—that the outsiders would become the insiders.

The Alliance was the creation of a group of free-floating intellectuals and professional men: Jules Carvallo, Narcisse and Manuel Leven, Isidor Cahen, Charles Netter, Eugene Manuel. Graetz sees these men as the natural, although not necessarily typical, products of a fast-growing stratum within the intelligentsia: Jewish by origin, but alienated from the Jewish community by their way of life and ideologies; French by inclination and culture, but alienated from the professedly "neutral" milieu in which they moved by its latent contempt for Judaism and the history of the Jewish people.

This double alienation served not infrequently to produce, in turn, an upsurge of respect for the Jewish past, and even a belief in a Jewish future of world-historical, universalist, significance. However, Graetz insists, what was involved here was not a simple retreat to Judaism *per se* (be it Orthodox or Reform) but rather the attempt to appropriate a central place for the Jewish people within their post-metaphysical, positivistic, and "scientific" theories of man and the universe.

To demonstrate this point, Graetz takes the reader on a detailed tour through the writings and discussions of the young Jewish intellectuals who were drawn into the Saint-Simonian movement in the 1820s—Olinde and Eugène Rodrigues, Gustave d'Eichthal, Léon Halévy, and the Péreire brothers (Isaac and Emile). The tendency of Saint-Simon himself and of his leading disciples (Comte, l'Enfantin) to describe their future utopia in terms of a "new Christianity" (albeit anthropocentric and liberated from the Church), was very hard for the Jewish members to accept. This was especially true as the leading Saint-Simonians tended to exalt the universalism of Jesus and Paul by contrasting it with the narrow parochialism and dessicated legalism of ancient Judaism.

The rallying point for the Jews in the Saint-Simonian camp, a *deus ex machina,* proved to be Joseph Salvador who, not a Saint-Simonian himself, was of their generation and, like them, a marginal Jew. (He was a half-Jew by birth.) In 1822, he published the first in a series of books and studies which, coming out over a period of some thirty years, sought to demonstrate that the ancient Jewish "republic" based on Mosaic law represented in microcosm the ideal society. Moses, the great lawgiver of the classical world, had combined in one organic unity the individual and society, faith and law, democracy and order, all inspired by a monotheistic concept of the world and a messianic vision of the future. What had then been attained by one small nation was destined to become the prototype for the reordering of human society as a whole in the era of universal brotherhood and redemption. And the Jewish people, which had upheld its faith so long, would again be able to make its specific contribution (perhaps even restored to its own land and commonwealth).

Drawing on Salvador's research and concepts, d'Eichtal and his comrades undertook to defend the pride of their people. Replacing the established religions, the future world order would subsume within itself both the social ideal of ancient Jewry and the universalism of Christianity. The contribution of Moses would equal that of Jesus.

Salvador's large corpus of works (on Moses, on Jesus, on the Jewish wars against Rome) served a similar function for the next generation of post-assimilationist Jewish intellectuals. The young Jews who moved in the radical circles of Michelet and Renan after the 1848 revolutions likewise found that the positivist science and utopian theories which they there discovered tended to be heavily laden with a contemptuous disdain for Judaism and Jewry remarkably reminiscent of traditional Catholic thought. Once again, the instinctive reaction was to take up the polemical cudgels to prove that the Jews, too, had made an indispensable contribution to human progress and, indeed, still had a specific role to play in creating "the new Jerusalem." (Their favorite text was from Matthew 5:17: "Think not that I am come to destroy the Law or the Prophets. I am come not to destroy but to fulfill.")

From here it was only a relatively short step to active involvement in Jewish life and Jewish politics. But, of course, with such a background, Carvallo and his group would obviously bring with them their own style and vocabulary. Graetz notes, for example, that the name of their new organization seems to have been modeled on that of the Alliance Evangélique Universelle, a fundamentalist Christian organization which advocated the restoration of the Jews to Palestine as a prelude to the Second Coming. Carvallo was in close touch in the 1850s with this organization. Graetz likewise points out that the term "*universelle*" in the title of the Alliance referred not only to the worldwide nature of the organization but also to its universalist aspirations, to the hope that Jewry could serve the redemption of mankind, and be subsumed within it.

Within the compass of a short review it is not possible to do justice to a book remarkable for its depth of perception, breadth of historical perspective, originality of thought, and richness of hitherto unmined detail. It brings home forcefully the need for a new look at the meaning of the Emancipationist era in Jewish history. Unfortunately, the form of the book is much less satisfactory than its content. It is rather as though an architect had left a great building still surrounded by its scaffolding, unpainted, unfinished. Some chapters seem disproportionately long, others relatively too short. There are loose ends. Did the Jewish episode in the lives of the young Saint-Simonians exert any lasting impact on their lives or does Graetz see its importance as purely symptomatic, an early example of a syndrome to be repeated time and again in later generations and in many countries? Why were none of the prominent Saint-Simonians to be found among the founders or leaders of the Alliance? Again, surprisingly, there is in fact rather little space devoted to the group which actually founded the Alliance. And the reader is left wondering at the end whether they were in fact so "peripheral" or so different in experience or views from many members of the "center," most notably Crémieux himself. But when all this is said, the majestic conception and proportions of this book remain imposing. It is a work both of great interest and great importance. It serves to undermine Ahad Ha'am's division of European Jewry in the nineteenth century between those (in the East) who enjoyed "freedom within slavery" and those further West who suffered "slavery within freedom." Profoundly revisionist, it reinforces the view that Jewish life in freedom developed in very complex, contradictory, and dialectical ways.

JONATHAN FRANKEL
Hebrew University

Howard Greenstein, *Turning Point: Zionism and Reform Judaism.* Chico, Calif.: Scholar's Press/Brown University, 1981. 186 pp.

The 1885 Pittsburgh Platform enunciated the well-known anti-Zionist doctrine of late nineteenth century Reform: "We consider ourselves no longer a nation but a religious community, and therefore expect neither a return to Palestine . . . nor the restoration of any of the laws concerning the Jewish state" (p. 19).

Rabbi Isaac Mayer Wise, a central figure in "classical Reform," declared: "Those Zionists came to whip us again into the dark corners of isolation . . ." (p. 10).

The author of the book under review maintains that while the Columbus Platform of 1937 was not a consummation of the "zionization" process in the Reform organizations, it did represent a "turning point." The relevant plank of this platform was based on the 1935 resolution of the Central Conference of American Rabbis (CCAR) in which the Reform rabbinate took a neutral position in the debate over political Zionism. In 1937, going one step further, the rabbis declared it a Jewish obligation to help build a national home in Palestine which would serve as a refuge for the persecuted and a center for Jewish cultural and spiritual life (p. 29). The Columbus Platform, Greenstein relates, was achieved by a "palace coup" carried out by the Zionist minority, who managed to push through their resolution by a majority of one vote (pp. 29–30).

This resolution, of course, did not apply to the Reform movement as a whole, but only to the CCAR. The further development of the trend toward a pro-Zionist position, the radical change in direction that took place between the 1920s and the 1970s, is aptly illustrated by two statements quoted by the author: that of Rabbi David Philipson in 1929 and that of Rabbi Roland Gittelsohn in 1970. Philipson stated that "Palestine represents for us an outgrown phase of Jewish historical experience. . . . To those of us who are Jews in religion and Americans in nationality, political Zionism is anathema." Gittelsohn, president of the CCAR declared, on the other hand, that: "We [Reform Jews] shall use our influence wherever and whenever we can, to persuade this world that its own survival and integrity are irrevocably linked with those of Israel" (p. 6).

Although the book is entitled *Turning Point,* the author in fact deals with a lengthy process of change within the Reform movement. Beginning in the years after the First World War, and particularly after the rise of Nazism in Germany, it became apparent that the path advocated by classical Reform could not answer the pressing needs of European

Jewry. Although Reform, equally with Zionism, sought to win for all Jews a life of freedom and security, the emancipationist solution favored by the early Reform movement failed in the face of twentieth century reality. This led eventually to the collapse of naive notions of utopian universalism incorporated in earlier forms of Reform ideology.

But Greenstein argues that it was not only outside factors but internal change as well that brought about the pro-Zionist tilt among Reform leaders. In particular, he points to the mass immigration of East European Jews to North America which overwhelmed the previous Jewish population. In time, many immigrants or their children entered the Reform organizations and slowly gathered influence. The proponents of Zionism came mainly from this group.

Greenstein's analysis distinguishes between the different processes of ideological change in the three bodies that together comprise the institutional structure of the Reform movement: the CCAR, Hebrew Union College (HUC), and the Union of American Hebrew Congregations (UAHC).

The Columbus Platform was made possible by the transition from one generation to a new one, which included some representatives of the East European immigration. This transition, which took place first at Hebrew Union College—and consequently in the CCAR—was much slower in the UAHC. The UAHC did not adopt an explicitly pro-Zionist position until after the establishment of the State of Israel.

The paralysis in the Reform organizations that followed the first meeting of the American Jewish Conference in August 1943 was produced, Greenstein argues, by the fear that the movement would be permanently split in the event of a walkout of the anti-Zionists. Even Zionists like James Heller and Maurice Eisendrath chose to preserve the unity of the organizations and made concessions to the aggressively anti-Zionist group that formed the American Council for Judaism. Among the rabbis involved in this group were a number of very forceful figures who wielded enormous influence in the movement.

One chapter in the book is devoted to a biography of three figures in the Reform movement: Morris Lazaron, Julian Morgenstern and Maurice Eisendrath. It is not clear why these three were chosen for particular study: only Morgenstern's experience personifies the evolution that took place in the Reform movement. Lazaron was pro-Zionist in the '30s and became a leader of the American Council for Judaism in the '40s. The material on Eisendrath sometimes duplicates the account presented of the Reform position at the American Jewish Conference.

The chapter on the American Jewish Conference itself deals mainly with the affiliation of the UAHC with the Conference in 1943 and the negotiations to prevent its departure from that body—an episode that lasted from the end of 1943 to 1946. Greenstein views the fact that the UAHC did not in fact bolt the Conference as evidence of the growing pro-Zionism of the Reform body. It is unfortunate that he did not, apparently, make full use of the documentation available on the matter. He makes no mention, consequently, of the activities of the Reform leaders during the first meeting of the Conference which are amply attested to in the minutes of the Conference and its committees (preserved in the Zionist Archives in New York).

Nor has he made use of the Robert Goldman papers at the American Jewish Archives in Cincinnati. These files shed light not only on the negotiations between the Reform leaders and Henry Monsky prior to the UAHC affiliation to the American Jewish Conference, but also on the role played by the Reform leaders in persuading the American Jewish Committee to participate in this gathering. During the August-September meetings of the Conference in 1943, Joseph Proskauer of the Committee tried to form a non-Zionist bloc with the Reform representatives to oppose the Zionist demand for a Jewish commonwealth.

Proskauer was prepared to agree with the Reform organizations on the basis of the "declaration of principles" formulated by a subcommittee of the UAHC in the spring of 1943, but despite his efforts, Abba Hillel Silver succeeded in persuading Eisendrath and Goldman to vote in favor of the Zionist demand, and drop the idea of an alternative proposal. Following the first meeting of the Conference, however, pressure was brought to bear on the Reform representatives by their anti-Zionist colleagues, and a large part of them were prepared in the fall of 1943 to dissociate themselves from the commonwealth resolution. The internal battles that took place between the fall of 1943 and early 1944 do not receive detailed attention in Greenstein's study, although the final positions are accurately reported.

The decision was to remain neutral, and this position was maintained throughout the long and fateful period in which the Yishuv was preparing for independence. Though Joseph Proskauer, who had fought against the commonwealth idea during 1942–44, openly supported partition in 1946, the UAHC did not break its neutrality. It is no wonder that Greenstein brings his discussion of the Zionist "revolution" in the Reform movement to a close in 1946, with the UAHC's decision to remain in the American Jewish Conference. This decision, however, had no practical significance: by that time the Conference had ceased to play an important political role.

The Reform neutrality was preserved throughout the deliberations of the Anglo-American Committee—in which the fate of 100,000 DPs hung in the balance—and in November 1947, when the United Nations General Assembly voted in favor of partition. This was the period in which nearly all the non-Zionist Jewish organizations (B'nai B'rith, the American Jewish Committee, the Jewish Labor Committee, even Agudat Israel) decided to support, to some extent at least, the Zionist cause.

Although he cites only one incident in which the Reform movement protested against British policy in Palestine (pp. 120–121), Greenstein nevertheless maintains that "the movement's support for the goals of Jewish nationalism was no longer in serious doubt" (p. 117).

If the movement indeed supported the Zionist venture, it did not express that support in concrete actions. The support to which Greenstein refers did not, by and large, go beyond the discussion of previously staked out positions. Greenstein reports that the CCAR, meeting in June 1948, voiced its approval of the establishment of the State of Israel, and the UAHC followed suit several days later (p. 125). President Truman, of course, had recognized the new Jewish state a few weeks earlier.

A comment by Maurice Eisendrath made in that period is, I think, relevant here:

> It must be pointed out that the Union of American Hebrew Congregations, I believe, is just about the only Jewish organization in America which stood on the sidelines during the recent most critical months, while such organizations composed of mixed constituency, similar to the Union's, as B'nai B'rith, the Council of Jewish Women, American Jewish Committee, etc., did make their voice and influence heard and felt.[1]

Greenstein chose to end his book with a judgment that restores a more objective balance to his work:

> In retrospect, anti-Zionism was not incompatible with Reform Judaism. It was a companion belief . . . , not an essential doctrine. The essential doctrine of Reform Judaism was simply reform—the right to make radical changes in the rituals and forms of Judaism in order to preserve and perpetuate its basic precepts. That principle included the necessity to change the position on Zionism if conditions so required it. Consideration of such conditions was both the basis for the controversy and the process for its eventual resolution. (p. 133)

MENAHEM KAUFMAN
Hebrew University

Note

1. Appendix A, President's Report. Chicago, Ill, June 5, 1948. Reform

Judaism and the Jewish State: *Proceedings of the Union of the American Hebrew Congregations. Annual Report* 1950, p. 109.

Yisrael Gutman, *The Jews of Warsaw 1939–1943*. Bloomington: Indiana University Press, 1982. xi + 487 pp.

At the outbreak of the Second World War, a quarter of a million Jews lived in Warsaw, more Jews than in any city other than New York. These Jews, with their cultural and commercial vitality, constituted the nerve center of what has been called the "Jewish Nation in Poland." Whereas the half-million Jews of Germany had, in effect, nearly seven years between Hitler's coming to power and the outbreak of war to leave Germany (as at least half of them succeeded in doing) the Jews of Poland had no such opportunity. As Professor Gutman writes, in this thoughtful and perceptive study, "the war descended on Polish Jewry like a thunderbolt, leaving no chance to escape."

Warsaw itself was the first city to be bombed in the Second World War. Among some 7,000 civilian victims of the bombing, about 3,000 were Jews. Professor Gutman, who is a cautious historian, does not give these figures. But he does quote from several diarists describing the ferocity of the bombardment. He also comments that it is "impossible to know for certain" whether the bombing of the crowded Jewish section in northern Warsaw on the Day of Atonement was a chance occurrence or "a premeditated act. . . ."

I use the word "cautious" deliberately, and with admiration, to describe Gutman's approach. Not that this book lacks a wealth of detail and precise statistics. It abounds in them: but it is dominated overall by a disciplined professional approach almost universally lacking in previous studies of the Warsaw Ghetto. Some readers may find this historical professionalism all the more surprising given Gutman's own involvement in the events which he described, first as a dweller in the Ghetto, then as an active member in the Jewish Fighting Organization, and subsequently, as an inmate of both Majdanek and Auschwitz.

Professor Gutman is particularly concerned to show the growth of underground activity in the Ghetto and the movement toward armed combat. He also presents new details on the relationship between Poles and Jews, and upon the part played by the Jewish Council and its Chairman, Adam Czerniakow.

Despite the emotive and controversial nature of each of these themes, Gutman's judgment is firmly based upon the bedrock of documentation. His conclusion about Czerniakow speaks of "the fairness and courage of the man who was appointed to represent the largest Jewish community in Europe at a time of terror and supreme trial." Of the Polish response to the destruction of Warsaw Jewry, Gutman, having examined and presented a wealth of old and new evidence, concludes that the Polish National Council in exile in London "sent words of encouragement to the Polish people, but did not ask them to take an active stand and extend aid to the Jewish victims."

Of the reaction of the Poles in Warsaw itself, Gutman writes that the majority "adopted the view that the Jews were an alien body and that their fight neither concerned the Poles nor obliged special action on the part of Poland's political underground or clandestine armed force." As a crucial example of this, Gutman notes that the mass deportation from Warsaw to the Treblinka death camp "was carried out without a word of protest from the Polish public, while the underground did not even bother to adopt a position on the matter."

Having examined the contemporary utterances both of the Polish underground press in Poland and the Polish Government in exile in London, Professor Gutman concludes that if any change could be said to have taken place during the course of the war in the Polish attitude toward the Jews, it was that the Polish "apathy and long standing sense of hostility intensified." This might seem a harsh judgment. But on the basis of the evidence presented in these pages, it does not appear to be an unbalanced one.

In examining the Jewish response to isolation and starvation within the Ghetto, and, from July 1942, to the deportations to Treblinka, Gutman describes both the institutions which were established in the Ghetto and the evolution of resistance circles and plans. He notes at the outset that the escape in September 1939 to Soviet-occupied Poland of the "top echelon of Jewish public and political leaders," among them Menachem Begin, at that time a "rising star" in the Revisionist movement, was a blow to the four hundred thousand Jews who were trapped in the city. Gutman cites the memoirs of one underground activist (memoirs composed while he was in hiding during the war on the "Aryan" side of Warsaw), noting that "the best elements left for distant lands," only second and third rank leaders remaining.

The Ghetto historian Emanuel Ringelblum, on whose published and unpublished diary and documents Gutman draws throughout his work, noted with even greater bitterness at the end of 1941 how the leaders of institutions and enterprises who had left in September 1939 "abandoned everything behind them." Ringelblum added that those who had to rebuild almost from nothing a structure of leadership often debated this aspect of their weakness.

The way of life and sense of community that was constructed by Jews who were isolated, starving, and in many ways leaderless, was a remarkable one, as was the courage of those who strove to create a structure of revolt. Drawing upon a remarkably wide range of documents, including twenty-two Jewish underground newspapers, Gutman analyzes the structure and development of Jewish resistance, and then sets out a perceptive, and at the same time moving, narrative of the revolts of January and April 1943.

Although the great revolt of April 1943 was crushed by overwhelming German military superiority, Gutman concludes that it left its mark on three separate parties to the war. Its effect on the Germans was to make them "more cautious" in their subsequent operations and to take account of the possibility of armed Jewish resistance elsewhere. The ability of the Jews to challenge the Germans in armed combat for so many days had also "seriously undermined" German prestige. The effect of the Ghetto revolt on the Poles, who were impressed by the Jewish struggle, was to stimulate them to develop their own underground activities (which culminated sixteen months later in the Warsaw Uprising). "Perhaps most important of all," in Gutman's view, was the effect of the Ghetto revolt on the Jews themselves throughout German-occupied Poland, in whom it inspired "a sense of self-worth" which generated further initiatives throughout the region in support of Jewish self-defense and rescue.

It is impossible in a short review to do justice to the range of Professor Gutman's research, or to the skill and discipline with which he presents it. This book deserves to become, and will become, a classic textbook of the struggle and destruction of a ghetto in the Second World War. It will also encourage other historians to try to do the same for several of the other large ghettos which still await their historian, and whose tormented stories certainly deserve a historian of Professor Gutman's caliber.

MARTIN GILBERT
Oxford University

H. S. Himmelfarb and S. DellaPergola, *Enrollment in Jewish Schools in the Diaspora. Late 1970s. Research Report Number 1.* 1982.
S. DellaPergola and N. Genuth, *Jewish Education Attained in Diaspora Communities. Data for 1970s. Research Report Number 2.* 1983. Jerusalem: Project for Jewish Education Statistics. Institute of Contemporary Jewry, Hebrew University.

These important research reports provide an indication of the main line of approach and interest in the topic of Jewish education in the Diaspora. The project is a direct response to "concern over rising rates of assimilation and intermarriage."

The aim of a standardized and centralized data bank is worthy and natural, but the problem for such a project is that measurement of any of these indicators is very approximate on the global scale, and fraught with problems of estimation and definition at the national and local level. Happily, the difficulties of trying to cover the great variety of institutional arrangements which exist in the various countries of the Diaspora are appreciated by the authors, as is the problem of comparing the different educational concepts and structures which abound in contemporary world Jewry. Such statistics must also be placed in the context of Jewish and general demographic trends, i.e., the relative numerical decline of Diaspora Jewry.

One only hopes that those who use the tables will bear in mind all the various methodological considerations, qualifications and reservations as they relate to both the reporting systems and the methods of calculation involved for each individual country represented. Nevertheless, the bringing together, within a comparative framework, of Jewish educational data relating to thirty-seven countries is a tribute to the assiduity and ingenuity of the authors.

The first report was largely a contemporary snapshot of enrollment patterns, but the second report attempts to answer the inevitable question of how far exposure to any or certain forms of Jewish education has penetrated the target national Jewish population, and segments of it defined on the basis of age and gender. Such comprehensive national data for the period 1965–76 exist from surveys in the United States, South Africa, Italy, and France. A chapter measuring the Jewish educational attainment for these four very different Jewish populations actually only looks at exposure to two different sets of education: the day school and part-time supplementary classes. Nevertheless, from these and other tables certain features emerge quite strongly, all of which require more in-depth investigation. One is the dropout rate from Jewish educational systems. Another is gender differences, both in access and exposure. The third area is the lack of data on the quality of the education. What are students exposed to in the different settings? Is it worthwhile for the sponsoring bodies to follow up such a project with a general system of tests which would measure pupil attainment? In turn, this opens up the question of input and output relationships and decision makers might go on to look at cost-benefit analysis and even the elements of a common curriculum.

However, before that stage is reached, the need to look at funding, per capita student expenditure, staffing, and numerous other issues must be faced. A start has been made in the current World Census of 3,500 Jewish schools, conducted by the same project. The global nature of the inquiries is itself a massive challenge, but ironically it may be that more reliance on qualitative rather than quantitative techniques might be one answer to the sheer immensity of the task of analysis. One awaits further reports in this series on more controversial and challenging topics—as far as the educational establishment and decision-makers are concerned—with some impatience. Only then can the unstated implications of these reports really be confirmed: that more Jewish education will "stop the rot" and halt the disintegration of the Diaspora.

Barry A. Kosmin
Board of Deputies of
British Jews

Dan Jacobson, *The Story of the Stories: The Chosen People and Its God.* New York: Harper & Row, 1982. 211 pp.

This book is a biblical commentary in the modern style. Dan Jacobson is a novelist, and in the past he has "commented" on the Bible, as Thomas Mann did, by writing a novel *(The Rape of Tamar)* elaborating on one of its stories. Here his enterprise is quite different. *The Story of the Stories* is a philosophical and theological meditation, a sustained engagement with the biblical narrative as a whole, an argument about its deepest meaning. A theological meditation, because Jacobson seeks knowledge of God; but he is a theologian *manqué,* a resolute skeptic, and the God he wants to understand is Israel's own creation. Hence also a philosophical meditation, an account of the human capacity to create and inhabit a meaningful universe.

What is the significance, what are the consequences of conceiving and then living with the God of Israel? Jacobson's response to this question is wide-ranging and richly textured. He knows the "story" intimately, not through a study of the traditional Jewish commentaries, nor of modern biblical scholarship, but through a direct encounter with the words of the text. He finds the Bible to be *one* text, one "story," though told by different authors, marked by "accumulating parallels, echoes, internal allusions, inversions, and almost obsessive reworkings and rewordings of important themes and problems . . ." (p. 4). He reads this text with the skill of a novelist, always alert to its literary form and devices. But his is not a book like Robert Alter's recent *Art of Biblical Narrative,* for Jacobson's first concern is not with the art but with the argument.

The central argument is the God who chooses and the chosen people. Jacobson almost wishes this argument had never been made. Such a God and such a choice have extraordinary consequences for good and evil—but perhaps especially for evil: together they make up "one of the most compelling and also one of the most catastrophic" inventions in human history (p. 3). So *The Story of the Stories* is an argument with the argument of the biblical narrative. I can hardly do justice to that argument here. I shall only recapitulate, crudely, a few of Jacobson's main points, so as to suggest that just as the "story" is worth retelling, so the argument is worth joining.

A God who chooses, Jacobson claims, is also and necessarily a God who rejects. At first, He rejects those He doesn't choose and those He drives out of the land to make room for His chosen people. Though they were its beneficiaries, the biblical writers were deeply uneasy about this original rejection. Their God made them anxious, for it seemed that He could only favor one people by disfavoring another, and His favor was always uncertain. One rejection anticipated the next: "Like the nations that the Lord makes to perish before you, so shall you perish" (Deuteronomy 8:20). The next rejection is of the chosen people themselves, at the time of the destruction of the first Temple and the exile to Babylonia, and this is the focus of Jacobson's book.

Though his argument is ruminative and unsystematic, he seems to discover three consequences of the Deuteronomic and prophetic accounts of the rejection of Israel by Israel's God. The first is self-recrimination and guilt, for was not Israel condemned and conquered because of the sins of the people themselves? The second is a special kind of hope, directed toward a future when punishment is exhausted and the original choice and the original rejection are both renewed. Guilt is aggression introjected, and it gives permanent shape to the religious culture of the Jews. Hope is aggression turned outward, and it gives permanent shape (though Jacobson doesn't quite put things this way) to the political culture of the Jews. It makes for a "triumphalism" that is plainly visible, though often obscured or denied by modern apologists, in prophetic and then in apocalyptic visions of the end of days. Perhaps it makes for parochialism and intolerance too—an intolerance that would one day claim the Jews themselves as its chief victims.

These are the costs of chosenness, for it is never easy, nor is it morally attractive, to live with this guilt or this hope. But that very lack of ease makes for a third consequence: the special morality of the biblical story, a morality that matches the divine "reciprocity" summed up for Jacobson by the prophet Obadiah (1:15): "As you have done, it shall be done to you, your deeds shall return upon your own head." What follows from this is the morality of the golden rule: do as you would be done by. Or, in the earlier language of the Exodus: "You know the heart of the stranger, for you were strangers in the land of Egypt." It is the strength of Jacobson's books to make us see that these different consequences fit together and that we can't pry them apart to suit ourselves. "Being the victim or loser," he writes, "will produce a hunger for justice that is virtually indistinguishable from a dream of revenge and recompense; these, too, are to be found in the Scriptures" (p. 157).

MICHAEL WALZER
Institute for Advanced Study,
Princeton

Jenna Weissman Joselit, *Our Gang: Jewish Crime and the New York Jewish Community, 1900–1940*. Bloomington: Indiana University Press, 1983. 224 pp.

Our Gang, the witty and fitting title of Jenna Weissman Joselit's study of Jewish crime in New York and of the response of the Jewish community, is a valuable contribution to a subject which only recently has aroused the interest of historians. A decade ago a perceptive observer wrote critically of the self-censoring of the American Jewish past that had eliminated any mention of Jewish crime. The strictures were correct only in part. True, fear of antisemitism and the consequent defensive posture of a group eager for acceptance surely influenced those who presented the saga of American Jewry as a story of unrivalled success achieved by dint of hard and honest work. Operative, too, was the unwillingness to abandon the self-image of a people whose spiritual heritage still served as a prophylaxis against the social pathologies of urban life.

Nevertheless, in the early decades of the century when widely publicized disclosures of vice and crime among Jews appeared with increasing regularity and notoriety, New York's organized Jewry did face up to the issue. The established leaders founded institutions for the rehabilitation of delinquents, social workers pored over crime statistics, and the Jewish press analyzed the causes of criminal behavior with remarkable candor. Nor did a later generation sweep its Jewish criminals under the carpet. How could it? New York Jews read about the escapades of their Buchalters, Schultzes, and Lanskys on the front pages of *The Times* as well as the *Morgen Zhurnal,* found them portrayed in the fiction of Michael Gold and Damon Runyon, and followed their rise and fall in popular biographies, and, more recently, on the screen.

The fact that historical scholarship came upon the theme so late should not surprise us. Serious American Jewish historiography is barely a generation old, and the interest in American social history is even younger. Joselit's study is the product of the simultaneous maturation of both fields. Eschewing apologetics on the one hand, and sensationalism on the other, which have flawed earlier studies, *Our Gang* examines two interconnected themes: the acculturation of New York's Jewish underworld over the course of two generations, and, more importantly in the author's eyes, "the changing self-perception and self-image of the New York Jewish community over time" evoked by the presence of Jewish criminality.

In her treatment of crime, Joselit draws upon the insights of sociologists like Daniel Bell whose functional analysis presented crime as an illicit but viable sector of the economy supplying such services to consumers as gambling, sex, drugs and protection. For poor, unbridled youth, this economy of crime promised opportunities for wealth and power otherwise unattainable.

Until 1920, gambling, prostitution, and gangsterism—with their links to politics and to the police—were localized in immigrant neighborhoods. On the Jewish Lower East Side, in addition, the garment industry with its small, highly competitive manufacturing units and other fragmented business enterprises like poultry marketing, proved to be especially vulnerable to an incipient industrial racketeering. Jewish *shtarke* (thugs) provided the "protection" required by Jewish gambling parlors and houses of prostitution, taxed the small merchants and pushcart operators, and extorted money from deliverymen by threatening to poison their horses. Pickpocketing and the stealing and fencing of dry goods and fabrics were endemic to the Jewish quarter. On election day party bosses hired Jewish gangs to intimidate voters, and during the fiercely fought strikes in the garment industry both sides used them. In the pre–World War I era, the Jewish neighborhood, Joselit informs us, defined the structure of Jewish crime. And in fact, being Jewish and operating in their own neighborhood influenced the criminal behavior of the Jewish underworld. Using hitherto untapped court records, Joselit confirms what contemporary observers often commented upon: Jews were far less prone to violent crimes than Italian or native Americans.

With the advent of prohibition the economy of crime underwent drastic changes. There is general agreement that the modern era of "organized crime" begins with the creation of the vast distributive networks required by the multi-million dollar bootleg liquor industry. With the end of prohibition the accumulated knowhow, manpower, and capital moved into other illegal activities like drugs and gambling.

What happened to "our gang"? Two striking changes occurred, according to Joselit. The crime rate among Jews fell as upwardly mobile Jews moved to the new middle-class neighborhoods of Brooklyn and the Bronx, and immigration restriction ended the mass migration of the poor. Furthermore, shocking as the record of the postwar Jewish criminal element was, "there was little intrinsically 'Jewish' about the crimes it committed." In their criminal behavior Jewish hoodlums, too, were acculturating. And yet Joselit's evidence indicates stronger continuities than she herself suggests. The same Lower East Side habitat of the first generation of Jewish gangsters, together with its latter-day Brownsville replica, spawned the second generation of Jewish criminals. Arnold Rothstein and Meyer Lansky did far better than the East Side heroes of their youth. The scope of their criminal activity was national and "trans-ethnic," but their ties to the Jewish community remained real and intimate, and they continued to retain a grip on New York's Jewish economy. The more typical Jewish gangsters of the interwar years still found the garment industry and other business enterprises owned by Jews their surest prey. More murderous than their predecessors, if fewer in number, they moved into the wider world of crime when it paid. However, they felt most at home in the garment district and kosher-poultry market, infiltrating the flour and bakery distributors' trade, and running the numbers and loan-shark rackets in their old neighborhoods. Clearly, by 1940, when Joselit concludes her account, only a dwindling remnant of "our gang" remained, product of a one-time cultural, social, and geographic milieu that had disintegrated.

Nevertheless, crime—which never reached the proportions it did among the population as a whole—obsessed the New York Jewish community in the years prior to the First World War. Then, beginning in the 1920s, it disappeared from the community's agenda, Joselit argues. This change, she believes, mirrored the psychic integration of New York's Jews into American society since the public fixation with crime "served to highlight New York Jewry's understanding of itself even as it shaped the outside world's view of its Jewish neighbors." On a sensitivity-to-crime scale, a high score reflected the insecurity of native and immigrant Jews not yet at home in America, and their distress over the failure of traditional Jewish institutions to provide the social control they once had. This anxiety peaked in the years 1908 to 1914.

What stands out in Joselit's account of the prewar years is the Jewish community's use of typically American methods to demonstrate its civic virtue and to reform its Jewish communal structure. The first all-Jewish reformatory incorporated the most advanced social work theories of the time. Gathering and interpreting statistics to disprove accusations of a high rate of crime reflected the belief in the efficacy of social science analysis. Finally, the establishment of the New York Kehillah by leaders of the Jewish establishment and their downtown counterparts was a singularly ambitious attempt to cope with the social disorganization in Jewish life. No less revealing than the Kehillah's anti-crime activities, which Joselit describes in detail (adding little to this reviewer's earlier account), was the attention it gave to Jewish education. In the former instance, the Kehillah adopted the methods and programs that volunteer anti-crime committees were using at the time—gathering criminal intelligence to force the police to act more aggressively in fighting crime. In the latter instance, the Kehillah raised large sums of money to revamp Jewish religious education in order to stem the moral decline of the young (a form of crime prevention), echoing the views of those social reformers who tied religious instruction to moral uplift. Thus the crime issue became linked with the thrust of acculturation and the yearning for acceptance in American society. At the same time it spurred Jewish communal unity and ethnic self-consciousness.

Seen in this light, Joselit interprets the Jewish public's placid response to Jewish criminality during the interwar years—low on the sensitivity-to-crime scale—as proof that second generation New York Jews were "at home in America." They "in no way felt," Joselit concludes, "that the existence of a Jewish underworld challenged their stake in American society." However, the evidence Joselit assembles suggests a more ambivalent picture than the one she sketches.

Her account of the debate that raged among Jewish leaders over the use of sacramental wine during Prohibition is a case in point. Here indeed was a direct confrontation between Jewish religious law and custom and the law of the land. It exposed the raw nerve of the community's leaders who feared the issue of Jewish exceptionalism and its illegal exploitation. Striking as Joselit's findings are of the absence of that agonizing self-examination which marked the Jewish press's response to crime scandals of an earlier decade, it must be balanced with her brief remarks about the defensive note implied by the annual publication of Jewish crime statistics and the self-praise that generally followed. Furthermore, the community's agencies were in fact monitoring the crime problem albeit in a significantly different way than they had in the 1910s. Joselit points to the Jewish Boards of Guardians' handling of the delinquent and potentially delinquent by professional social workers. One should add the prominence of the Jewish community center which emphasized character building through recreational programs receiving Jewish public support because it claimed to be a haven from the perils of the city street. Thus the community strove to cure or immunize its exposed youth through casework and group work.

Clearly, the making of second generation American Jews was a complex process, and its study requires subtlety and imagination. Using the community's response to its criminal element to illuminate this process is an original but also an eccentric strategy, or, in Daniel Bell's words about crime in American life, a "Coney Island mirror caricaturing the morals and manners of a society." *Our Gang* provides valuable insights into the differences in the mentalities between pre–World War I New York Jewry (Americanized "uptown" Jews coexisting uneasily with the massive "downtown" immigrant population), and the interwar New York Jewry (the coming into their own of the immigrants and their children). But Joselit does not always compensate for the distorting effect of using crime as a mirror of social processes. Finally, although Joselit recognizes the anxieties antisemitism caused within the Jewish community during the interwar years—surely the classic sign of Jewish insecurity—she does not satisfactorily explain the discrepancies between that keenly felt threat and the equanimity that marked the attitude towards crime. If some of Joselit's broad judgments are less than conclusive, her solidly researched study illuminates a number of topics like the Hawthorne school, the structure of Jewish crime, and the sacramental wine issue during Prohibition. Here, her contribution is original and conclusive.

Arthur A. Goren
Hebrew University

Elie Kedourie and Sylvia C. Haim (eds.), *Palestine and Israel in the 19th and 20th Centuries.* London: Frank Cass & Co. Ltd., 1982. $39.50.

Elie Kedourie and Sylvia C. Haim (eds.), *Zionism and Arabism in Palestine and Israel.* London: Frank Cass and Co. Ltd., 1982. $42.50.

Palestine and Israel in the 19th and 20th Centuries is a misleading title. In a collection of twelve essays, the reader might have expected roughly equal attention to each century. Emile Marmorstein's "European Jews in Muslim Palestine" alone centers on the earlier period. It is a chatty review of three books in Hebrew—A. R. Malachi's assessment of the Old Yishuv, Galiyah Yardeni's treatment of the rise of the Hebrew press (1863–1904), and Arthur Ruppin's autobiography and diaries—that skims the surface with erudition but without ever attempting to define the central issues dividing the two cultures. A second piece by Marmorstein, an evaluation of the career and writing of Rashid Husayn, a young Muslim poet in Israel who was translating Bialik into Arabic, lives up to Marmorstein's own standards of originality. Yaacov Ro'i is the only other contributor who deals with Ottomon Palestine. But he focuses on Zionist perceptions of the Arabs in the half-dozen years before the outbreak of World War I.

Of the two articles on Nazi policies toward the Palestine mandate, both drawing heavily and informatively upon official German archives captured by the allies in 1945, the one by David Yisraeli is more analytical and innovative than that by R. Melka. At the time of appearance, Mayir Verete's inquiry into the framing of the Balfour Declaration revised the conventional wisdom of the day, for he rested his study on a penetrating examination of the then recently released evidence in the Public Record Office in London, not available a generation earlier to Leonard Stein. Verete's paper has since been superseded by Isaiah Friedman's definitive book-length treatment of the subject.

Gabriel Ben Dor reviews the role of the educated Druze in Israel in the political and social change of their community; despite the disciplinary jargon, now somewhat dated, the author handles with sophistication a problem neglected by scholars. In a useful but hardly innovative evaluation of the Lohamei Herut Yisrael, Y. S. Brenner leans for supportive testimony on the broadsides and internal brochures of the guerrilla group as well as the memoirs and other books on the subject that started appearing in 1950.

Of the remaining four essays, two deal with the mandate (Ya'acov Firestone on Arab crop-sharing and Fred M. Gottheil on Arab immigration) and two others with Jordanian settlement policies on the West Bank (in which Elisha Efrat points out that the Hashimis did little "to stimulate the economy and develop local resources," helping explain why the rural population grew more rapidly than the urban) and on the political status of Jerusalem (where Naim Sofer found 'Abdallah's policies creative and Husayn's reactive).

The selection as a whole comes from the first thirteen volumes of *Middle Eastern Studies* (1964–76). The editors would have enhanced the value of the book by identifying the authors and, in a speedily changing environment of scholarship on the Middle East, by giving the dates of the first appearance of each entry. Moreover, there is something amateurish and disconcerting about a book that is produced with variable type face, letter size, and margin, and does not even include running heads. These criticisms do not apply to *Zionism and Arabism in Palestine and Israel,* which includes brief notes on the contributors and whose production is uniform throughout. Though submitted and accepted for publication, the ten essays—six by Israeli scholars—were never published in the journal. Instead, the editors point out, since the essays formed a coherent group, they could stand on their own as a book and, it is implied, release space in the quarterly for other articles.

The authors, almost all alumni of postwar regional training programs, have illumined afresh aspects of the Arab-Zionist dispute since the First World War by calling upon the indispensable resources of the declassified official archives (chiefly in London, Jerusalem, and Washington, in that order). Neil Caplan reconsiders Sir Herbert Samuel's term in Jerusalem (1920–25), explains the cooling relations between the high commissioner and the Yishuv, and evaluates his failed efforts at promoting a Zionist-Arab accommodation. The religious crusade of violence against the Yishuv in the second postwar decade, mounted by Syrian-born ash-Shaykh 'Izz al-Din al-Qassam, who won recruits from the underprivileged sector of the Arab community, is explored in detail by Shai Lachman. Militant religious opposition to Zionism is also the subject of an analysis by Thomas Mayer, who investigates the Ikwan al-Muslimun's position on the Palestine dispute in the final three years of the mandate.

Regional and international politics are the themes of three papers. Aaron S. Klieman pursues the mediatory efforts during the Palestine Arab revolt (1936–39) of the heads of the eastern Arab states in the British imperial sphere and their governments. Joseph Heller takes a fresh look at Zionist reactions in 1945–46 to the Anglo-American Commission of Inquiry. Amitzur Ilan follows step by step the Attlee government's formulation of its decision in 1947 to refer the Palestine question to the United Nations while simultaneously announcing its intention to surrender the mandate "without recommendations." Secret testimony given by a Syrian politician to the Anglo-American Commission of Inquiry and contradictory entries in the personal diaries of two of its American members is adduced in Allen H. Podet's "Husni al-Barazi on Arab Nationalism in Palestine"; the slender paper raises more questions than it answers.

Focusing on the early stages of Jewish emigration from the USSR to Israel (1954–67), Yaacov Ro'i assesses its impact on Soviet-Arab relations. In the light of the dramatic improvement in 1983 in Israel's diplomatic standing in Africa, Ibrahim A. Cambari's review of Nigeria's unfolding record from close cooperation with Israel in the 1960s to the abrupt severance of diplomatic relations with it in 1973 is timely. Finally, Yael Yishai probes the experiment of attempting to integrate Arabs into a Zionist political system and society, which Mapam conducted in 1948–54 and had to abandon.

Of the two books, *Zionism and Arabism* is the more original: its articles appear in print for the first time and its authors, by and large, have gone to unpublished archives and occasionally to vernacular publications for much of their supportive evidence.

J. C. HUREWITZ
Columbia University

Ian Kershaw, *Popular Opinion and Political Dissent in the Third Reich: Bavaria, 1933–1945*. Oxford: Clarendon Press, 1983.

Kershaw's study is an excellent reexamination of a view widespread in the literature on the Third Reich, which stresses the success of the Nazi regime in creating a totalitarian society, whether because of the effectiveness of terror or because of the identification of the public at large with Nazi ideology. This book is based on a remarkable account of archival material, consisting of periodic reports on the public mood—known as *Stimmungsberichte* or *Lageberichte*—which were composed by the German security services and the various state, party, and administrative bodies of Nazi Germany. Another source used by Kershaw, which not only supplements the information in the reports but also facilitates their critical evaluation, is the reports published by the German Social Democratic Party in exile (the SOPADE reports). They provide a running account of what transpired in Germany between 1933 and 1940.

In this study, limited to Bavaria only, the author brings together diverse data from these sources, providing a basis for comparison with other areas in Germany, to which his conclusions are, he believes, also relevant.

Because of the extensive scope of this documentary material, Kershaw has broken down the types of information they contain, and has concentrated on the analysis of public political dissent in three aspects: First, he examines the response of different social sectors to Nazi ideology and policy; then he considers the various reactions of the churchgoing public to Church-State relations in the Third Reich; and finally he evaluates the impact of Nazi antisemitism on German society and its reaction to it.

In his conclusions, Kershaw argues that the material conditions operating in Germany, rather than Nazi ideology, were the most influential factors shaping public opinion. He found that there was a considerable amount of discontent and disillusionment in almost all segments of society, but that this was never transformed into active political opposition. Only attacks on the Church aroused significant public hostility toward the government, showing that the religious values and allegiances of the population remained intact, despite Nazi propaganda. But here, too, the negative reactions to the government's Church policy did not endanger the Nazi system.

In his analysis of the reactions to Nazi antisemitism, Kershaw finds that there was a general lack of active interest in the "Jewish Question." According to his reading of the reports, Nazi propaganda succeeded in reinforcing attitudes where it was directed to the already converted (i.e., Nazi activists), although it did not succeed in mobilizing the masses. Nor did antisemitism function as an integrating factor: while the public sympathized with Nazi goals, it refused to accept Nazi methods of implementation.

Without going into the issue of the reliability of the reports—still a matter of scholarly controversy—it seems that on occasion Kershaw's own sources suggest different readings and conclusions. Thus, Kershaw apparently overemphasizes the rejection of Nazism among German workers. Obviously, the analysis of the reactions in this particular social sector requires consideration of the structural differences in various regions and the fluctuations in the level of employment and wages. But, on the whole, it appears that the majority of the working class resigned itself to the regime, welcoming the improved employment situation and the new drive in building and development which produced an economic advance. The SOPADE documents, in particular, indicate that acceptance of the Third Reich overshadowed dissatisfaction. Some reporters are extremely pessimistic, claiming that even under free elections, Hitler would receive a majority of workers' votes.

This contrasts sharply with Kershaw's statement (pp. 75–76) that "worker dissent confirmed the essentially negative attitude towards Nazism which was widespread in the working class." Dissatisfaction and criticism of certain policies, such as compulsory contributions to the party, ought not to be seen as criticism of the regime in principle.

Kershaw's conclusions concerning the attitude toward Nazi antisemitism raise still more complex issues. In the first place, because of the nature of the documents, they convey information on concrete incidents (boycotts, physical attacks on Jews, and the like) while the facts of daily life in a segregated society—humiliations at work, schools, cinemas, restaurants—go unmentioned. Second, the conclusions drawn from the situation in Bavaria, with its relatively small Jewish population, may not explain the situation in other German areas, such as Berlin, where the Jewish community was ten times larger. Moreover, most of the information in the reports deals with attitudes toward Jewish cattle dealers, which cannot be taken to be representative of German reactions in the urban sector (lawyers, doctors), which was affected to a much greater extent but is seldom mentioned.

Leaving all these reservations aside, it appears that there are grounds within the documents themselves for questioning Kershaw's conclusions. His thesis of apathy toward Nazi antisemitic policy is stretched far beyond the empirical data. This sometimes leads to awkward contradictions: "Indifference," he writes at one point, in connection with the Nuremberg Laws, "seems, in fact, to have been the most common response" (p. 239), yet he quotes a source that states that the laws "had been generally welcomed and had met with the approval of the population" (p. 240). Later, Kershaw himself claims that "the Nuremberg Laws had been widely acclaimed" (p. 272). Welcoming, approval, and acclamation hardly add up to indifference.

Despite these lapses of judgment and some factual errors, this is a very important contribution to historical research, and will certainly be welcomed as an indispensable tool for the research of German social history during the Nazi era.

David Bankier
Hebrew University

Marcus Klein, *Foreigners: The Making of American Literature 1900–1940*. Chicago: University of Chicago Press, 1981. xi + 332 pp.

One of the controversies that has continually perplexed literary criticism is the extent to which literature reflects the social world (which often seems to be its explicit subject or at least its explicit background) versus the degree to which it is a part of a tradition which is not only quite separate from the historical field but which is often in an antagonistic relationship to it. In *Foreigners: The Making of American Literature 1900–1940,* Marcus Klein has chosen to approach literature as continuous with, perhaps even coextensive with, social history. "I have wanted to say that American literature of this century," Klein concludes, "has been created by people who have known themselves to be marginal Americans":

> The cultural fact of America has consequently been either rejected or, repeatedly, created—but never merely accepted because in an abruptly urbanized, industrialized, radicalized, and ghettoized society, there has been no American culture available for mere acceptance. Approximately at the moment of the turn of the new century, America vanished, and that fact created a fine opportunity both for some literary people who had lived in the place for generations and for some greater number of literary people who felt themselves to be just arriving. History presented both kinds of Americans with a problem for exploitation: Richard Wright equally with, say, T. S. Eliot, discovered motif and drama in his construction of a home place for himself, or of a tradition, and hence in his assertion of a cultural right and a cultural authority.

Though Klein's major premise here, that early twentieth-century American writers wrote out of a cultural vacuum in which social realities substituted for a literary heritage, must, I think, be carefully examined, the results of his excursions into the ghettos and byroads of modern American writing are an extraordinarily informative and illuminating commentary on over forty years of American cultural productivity. Not only does he survey a field which includes political, social, educational, journalistic, and literary creativity, but he argues, most persuasively, that American modernism represents only one branch of a much more extended family of intellectual thought, the majority of whose members belonged to what we might, in Klein's phrase, call the "Tradition on the Left." Indeed, modernism itself, as Klein describes it, was largely influenced by the existence of this "Tradition on the Left," the "Foreigners" of Klein's title, who represent not only an important immigrant population (with a high density of Jewish brethren), but Blacks, Southerners, Midwesterners, and an assortment of other American relatives who had not yet made it into the mainstream of American life.

But while Klein's study has everything to do with what we might call the "making of American social thought and popular culture, 1900–1940," it does not seem to me to define what he announces is the subject of his book, "the making of American literature." For while Klein skillfully analyzes a surprising number of writers, he deals almost not at all with the writers who, in the 1980s, seem to us to constitute the tradition: Eliot, Pound, Stevens, and Williams (in poetry), and Hemingway, Fitzgerald, and Faulkner (in the novel). Indeed, Klein's study is based on a group of writers (including such figures as Floyd Dell, Max Eastman, Michael Gold, Nathanael West, Richard Wright, James Cain, Dashiell Hammett, Horace McCoy), almost none of whom are poets, and many of whom are essayists or critics rather than creative writers; some of whom constitute (at best) the second or third tier of early twentieth-century writing, many not even that widely known or well regarded.

My disagreement with Klein admittedly has much to do with the definitions of the terms "literature" and "tradition," a subject which any critic who wishes to relate literature to society (as do many critics of ethnic literature) must, I think, contemplate, and which has, of late, occupied one of Klein's famous Buffalo colleagues, Leslie Fiedler, who lectured on this subject in Jerusalem last spring. For anyone who shares my bias that there is a significant difference between great literature and popular literature, and that this difference meaningfully determines our terms of discourse, the problem of Klein's approach becomes immediately obvious, even in the paragraph which I quoted above. Richard Wright is undeniably an important writer. And there is every reason to discuss him seriously in literary criticism. But the moment we have to speak in terms of an equivalency between Wright and Eliot (of "Richard Wright *equally,* with, say T. S. Eliot"), in relation either to their achievement or their social and cultural situation, we are involved in an approach to tradition which is problematical at best and which is fair neither to the special talents of an Eliot nor to the specific cultural identity of a Wright. For whether or not Eliot was affected, as Klein suggests, by the sudden foreignness of America, a tradition quite separate from America's political or ethnic or even cultural identity existed for Eliot which could and did readily absorb him. The consequence is that the "homeplace" or "tradition" which contains Wright and the one which contains Eliot, though they may be related to one another, are not the same, and the assertion of cultural right and cultural authority which issues in each case is also different.

It is not an accident, I think, that the corollary of Klein's flattening of the distance between high culture and low is to submerge ethnic distinction—Jewish, Black, Irish, Polish, immigrant versus native son, city dweller versus country farmer in a similar sea of sameness. For the problem is not only that Wright did not "equally" with Eliot construct a "homeplace" for himself within the tradition, but that Wright, like Eliot, did not come to his role as writer as a total "foreigner." Richard Wright did possess a tradition, as contemporary Black scholarship points out. Similarly American Jewish fiction (as practiced by Meyer Levin or Henry Roth) did not grow out of either a cultural or intellectual vacuum. Narrative models within the Jewish tradition, religious sensibilities, language patterns, and historical experiences contributed not only to the content of the works but to their literary form as well. These special talents and virtues of Jewish writers do not necessarily elevate them to the level of Eliots (indeed, I think they do not), but they do provide a basis for defining American Jewish literature as its own tradition, uniquely qualified for serious investigation and study.

There are, then, many traditions in American literary history which are worthy of scholarly discussion. But to speak of the "making of American literature" is to imply one inclusive tradition, and indeed Klein works hard to synthesize the disparate elements of twentieth-century America into a coherent and meaningful whole. But if there is *one* tradition of American literature, then Klein's "foreigners" do not seem to me its makers precisely because they do not constitute the tradition. It is not that literature must be written out of a tradition (out of what tradition did Hawthorne speak?), but that it must be written into a tradition; it must, in Eliot's terms, become a part of a tradition, which, emphatically changed by the new author's inclusion, makes us retrospectively reevaluate and reinterpret that tradition as a whole. It may well be that one or two of Klein's "foreigners" will in the coming decades become a part of the tradition, not in spite of the rigors of Eliot's conservative definition (Klein makes much of the fact that modernism aligned itself on the right, the other tradition on the left), but because of its open-endedness. The American tradition, which ranges from Poe and Hawthorne to Whitman and Twain to Eliot and Faulkner, is sufficiently eclectic that it can hardly be accused of being "fascistic" or undemocratic. Indeed, it is the sign and strength of its being democratic in this sense that we do not have to democratize our concept of tradition in order to defend the democratic character of the American tradition.

E. Miller Budick
Hebrew University

Jean Lacouture, *Léon Blum*. New York and London: Holmes and Meier, 1982. 571 pp. Cloth, $39.50. Paper, $24.50.

By the 1930s, Léon Blum was, in Jean Lacouture's words, "the most insulted man in France." Permanent foes such as the *Action Française*'s Charles Maurras suggested that he "should be shot, but in the back," and sometimes allies like the Communist Maurice Thorez felt compelled, on the eve of World War II, to characterize Blum as "a repugnant reptile, jackel, lackey of the London bankers. . . ." With the shadows cast by Hitler, Mussolini and Stalin abroad, and the virulence of the anti-democratic, anti-socialist and antisemitic agitation at home, it is difficult to imagine Blum not becoming a symbol; he was a Jewish apostle of democracy and socialism.

Blum served three times as French premier, but it was in his first ministry—which lasted all of a year—that the Popular Front he led fundamentally transformed the face of France, particularly through the Matignon Agreements giving French workers benefits and leverage which they had never had before. For obvious reasons, the Right never forgave him. For entirely different reasons some left-wing historians vent fury at him; during the tumultuous year of 1936–37 he failed to make the revolution. Blum brings to mind a story told by former Austrian Chancellor Bruno Kreisky to France's current socialist president François Mitterrand about a tightrope walker named Karl whose habit was to mount his rope for entire mornings. Challenged by a friend to do so all day, Karl proposed it be on one foot while playing Mozart on the violin. After not a day but a week, he descended and faced his friend, who promptly objected that Karl's playing wasn't up to that of Menuhin.[1]

Jean Lacouture's intelligent and appealing biography of France's first socialist and first Jewish prime minister was published originally in French in 1977 and has now appeared in English translation. In it the author—perhaps France's leading biographer and author of studies of De Gaulle, Ho Chi Minh, Nasser, and Mendès-France among others—successfully gives the reader a balanced, highly sympathetic, yet critical portrait of his subject. *Léon Blum* admirably synthesizes Blum's life story with an exposition of his political thinking and modern French political history.

The son of middle class Alsatian Jews who moved to Paris, Blum's political initiation occurred during the Dreyfus affair, although his political rise took place following World War I. Before the war, he was a literary and theater critic. After earning a law degree, the future premier worked as a magistrate for the important administrative court, the *Conseil d'État,* and then as *chef de cabinet* for the socialist Minister of Public Works Marcel Sembat during the war. His tutors in socialism were the influential Lucien Herr, librarian at the École Normale, and, of course, Jean Jaurès. As Lacouture emphasizes, "From the beginning, the critic, the moralist, the aesthetician, and the political thinker were one" (p. 11).

While his dramatic first term as prime minister was the high point of his political power, it was not the apogee of his career as a whole. In some ways his role as moral emblem, during his trial at Riom by the Vichy regime—in the course of which he sought to make his accusers the defendants—and then as a prisoner at Dachau and Buchenwald, was as dramatic as his periods as head of government. And one can hardly ignore his centrality in French politics in the decade and a half preceding his premiership when he devoted himself to rebuilding a socialist movement traumatized by the morass of World War I and the 1920 split at Tours establishing the French Communist Party.

Blum's vision was ever that of Jaurès—a *French* socialism which saw itself as the historical heir and extension of republicanism, the fulfillment of the promise of the French Revolution. Jaurès argued that "it is socialism which will give the Declaration of the Rights of Man its full meaning and which will finally realize human rights."[2] Blum followed him, as Lacouture notes, in seeking syntheses between materialism and idealism, reformism and revolutionism, patriotism and internationalism. Thus emerged one of Blum's important contributions to socialist tactics. He distinguished the mere *participation in power* by socialists, which he opposed under the conditions of a bourgeois order, from the plausibly desirable and possibly necessary *exercise of power before* the revolution by socialists who could dominate a given situation. Finally he differentiated participation in and exercise of power from its *conquest,* which was the ultimate goal. Blum insisted that, though no "legalist" when it came to "the conquest of power," he was just that when it came to "the exercise of power."

This helps us understand the politics of the Popular Front under Blum. Originally a defensive arrangement of Socialists, Communists, and Radicals faced with the rise of right-wing extremism, the Front won the 1936 elections amid profound domestic and international crisis. Blum's ascension to power was itself a surprise since it had been assumed that the Radical Party would come out ahead of the Socialists.[3] Lacouture is deft in defending Blum against charges of historians like Daniel Guerin who claimed that the premier betrayed a revolutionary moment when, shortly after taking office, the workers seized factories throughout the country, bringing the economy to a halt. No revolutionary situation existed, insists Lacouture, because the strikes were a consequence of Blum's victory and not an effort to go beyond it; the electoral triumph was not a landslide and produced a Popular Front majority, but not a "proletarian majority" (pp. 244–54).

Blum's resignation in June 1937, after the Senate refused him temporary extraordinary powers to deal with France's financial crisis, does indeed seem like a failure of nerve. Lacouture (although not particularly persuasively) attributes the resignation to Blum's foreign policy failures, a domain in which he provides some of his most cogent and vigorous criticisms of the socialist leader. Under pressure, especially from the British Conservative government and his Radical allies, Blum followed an ambiguous "non-intervention" policy—against his own instincts—during the Spanish Civil War.

In a related vein, Lacouture castigates Blum's willingness in the early 1930s to stand unshakably for disarmament despite all that the Germans, Italians, and Japanese were doing—and despite his own clear comprehension of and vigorous opposition to the extreme Right. One shudders to read Blum writing in 1931 that Hitler in power would be no great trauma since "nothing indicates that once installed as Chancellor, the absurd wandering apostle of racism would not feel a heavy mantle of prudence and circumspection fall on his shoulders. . . ." As his biographer perceptively notes, Blum displayed "a surprising incapacity to go beyond the assumptions of his political and strategic thought. From the late twenties on, Blum saw better than anyone the extent of the Nazi phenomenon, its implications, its connections. But until 1935 he was never capable of drawing the simplest and most natural conclusions from this knowledge" (p. 220). The conclusion was, of course, the need to rearm—something that ought to have been obvious to a socialist, let alone a Jewish one.

From their greatest representative—Jean Jaurès—to their least illustrious—Guy Mollet—French socialist leaders in this century have had special ties to the Jews in one way or another. Jaurès cut a heroic figure as a *Dreyfusard,* Blum was a Jew, Mollet was premier during the 1956 Mideast war and helped create the Franco-Israeli alliance, and Mitterrand has a long record of friendship with Jews and Israel. In light of this, Lacouture's treatment of Blum the Jew is nothing less than scandalous, badly marring an otherwise fine book.

The problem goes far beyond several several errors of fact and dates. While Lacouture never hides the antisemitism to which Blum was subjected, one gets the distinct impression that to the extent that we have Blum the Great Frenchman who happened to be a Jew, we have an admiring Lacouture, but insofar as we have a Blum who asserts himself as a Jew, we have a profoundly uncomfortable Lacouture. The biographer is at great pains—virtually in contortions—to downplay Blum's consistent and entirely *un*embarrassed expressions of Jewishness and Zionism. We should draw no "unwarranted" conclusions about Blum's writings on Zionism, he writes. It is evident that the Zionist is something of a bogeyman for Lacouture who asks his reader—he thinks rhetorically—"Can one be a Zionist when one appears on every occasion as a pure product of assimilation which was one of the master strokes of the French Revolution? Can one be a Zionist when, as a deportee, one dreams and hungers only for French soil?" (p. 258).

Blum apparently saw no contradiction between Zionism (indeed, his Jewishness) and his French identity—something Lacouture cannot fathom. But perhaps he should have further explained what a "pure product" of assimilation is. A "pure" Frenchman perhaps? Did the "historical master stroke" to which he refers prevent the cries of "Death to the Jews" at Dreyfus's degradation—a century after "Liberty, Equality, and Fraternity" were proclaimed? Did it prevent the Vichy episode fifty years later?

Charles Maurras is quoted by Lacouture as stating the following in *L'Action Française* in May 1936: "It is as a Jew that we have to see, conceive, understand, fight and cut down the Blum." The implications of this remark were grasped by their author and Blum, but not by Jean Lacouture, even though he writes that Blum was "the man most hated by the French bourgeoisie and by international fascists" (p. 540). The issue is hardly hunger for French soil and Blum was despised not only because he was a socialist and a democrat. Had he been anti-socialist and anti-democratic he would still have been sent to the camps, which can hardly be said for his non-Jewish democratic and socialist comrades. Perhaps Lacouture cares to proffer some warranted conclusions about that fact.

Mitchell Cohen
Baruch College,
City University of New York

Notes

1. François Mitterrand, *The Wheat and the Chaff.* New York: Seaver Books, 1982. pp. 115–116.
2. Jean Jaurès, *Études socialistes.* Paris/Geneva: Ressources, 1979. p. 137.
3. Despite its name, the French Radical Party was, of course, a middle class party composed of anything but radicals.

Lawrence Langer, *Versions of Survival: The Holocaust and the Human Spirit.* Albany: State University of New York Press, 1982.

This is a most important work on the literature of the Holocaust. If it is also a most important work on the Holocaust itself it is because of its most characteristic feature—relentless critique of the tendency, displayed not only by many writers, novelists, and poets but also theologians and even historians, to divert attention to victims, survivors, bystanders, and even "the World" or capitalized "Man" from what is the *conditio sine qua non* of *all* comprehension, the criminals and the crime. Thus Bruno Bettelheim asserts, in a generalization meant to include the Holocaust, that "each environment requires different mechanisms for safeguarding autonomy, those that are germane to success in living, according to one's values in the particular environment." Langer asks: "What 'values' are involved when fellow-inmates of a Jewish woman having given birth to a child must kill the child lest mother and child be both murdered for the 'crime'?" No values at all but only "a necessity, the lesser of two unacceptable evils." On his part, Victor Frankl writes: "If there is a meaning in life at all, then there must be a meaning in suffering. Suffering is an ineradicable part of life, even as fate and death. Without suffering and death human life cannot be complete." Langer translates the last sentence into "without Auschwitz and extermination in the gas chamber, human life cannot be complete," and with this translation he shows that works with opinions such as these are far less responses to the unprecedented "atrocity" of Auschwitz than witting or unwitting evasions of it. And if the evasions are "insensitive" and even "almost sinister," it is because, relying as they do on time-honored but inapplicable clichés such as "autonomy" and "clinging to values," they are compelled to ignore the doom of those too unfortunate to survive, for "to ascribe to the victims an inner weakness or an abandonment of values is to introduce an implicit reproach too infamous to consider."

The Holocaust world, Langer stresses, is a rupture of past values, past beliefs, past concepts of man and God, for Auschwitz was—to the victims though not to the perpetrators, for these had far more space for choices than, subsequently, they were prepared to admit—not a place where to make time-honored choices, but rather "the death of choice." Confronting this grim fact, he proceeds to examine, and increase respect for, those writers who themselves face that fact while yet groping for a post-Holocaust life, among them Tadeusz Borowski and Primo Levi, Elie Wiesel and Nelly Sachs. Through this examination, Langer also redirects the reader's own quest for a post-Holocaust life, if and when such redirection is necessary. Already in 1947 Frankl was no longer "concerned with the great horrors which have already been described often enough." Bettelheim wrote much the same thing as early as 1943. Langer asks both of them and his reader: "Can *any* story of the camps, *any* history of the period, *any* attempt to confront the enigma of the Holocaust evade the horrors and still speak with authority about their implications?"

EMIL L. FACKENHEIM
Hebrew University

Dov Levin, *Bein ha-patish veha-magal. Yehudei ha-arazot ha-baltiot tahat ha-shilton ha-sovieti be-milhemet ha-olam ha-shniyah.* Jerusalem: "Makor," 1983. 508 pp.

Published separately over the past fourteen years, the thirty-six essays collected in this volume—together with Dov Levin's two previous books (*Lohamim ve-omdim al nafsham,* 1974, and *Im ha-gav el ha-kir,* 1978*—represent the fruit of an extended research project on the Jews of the Soviet-annexed territories from 1939 to 1945/46.

Some two millions Jews lived in these areas (from Estonia in the north to Bessarabia in the south) in 1939, and they, along with thousands of Jewish refugees from Nazi-occupied Poland, found themselves at the vortex of historical forces that were poised to sweep them out of existence. For most of them, the period preceding the outbreak of the Soviet-German war in June of 1941 was only a brief respite. For a few, it presented an opportunity to escape further east. For still others, the "east" meant Siberian exile, a punishment for their political past. Finally, life under the Soviets schooled some (particularly younger Jews) in political and military skills and methods of underground activity, while their presence within the USSR fuelled a renaissance of Jewish consciousness and cultural activity that was shortlived but had a long-range impact on the emigrant generation of the 60s and 70s.

These are some of the themes in these closely documented studies, which offer a wealth of fact and interpretation. Levin's work sheds light on crucial aspects of Jewish history in the Holocaust era, on relations between Jews and the Baltic nations, and on the way in which

*See his forthcoming translated work, *Lithuanian Jewry's Armed Resistance to the Nazis* (Holmes and Meier, 1984).

the meandering Soviet policies of those years affected Jewish life (and Jewish lives).

The fact that Levin is one of the few scholars working in this field—due, no doubt, partly to the formidable linguistic skills required—makes the volume all the more important. Anyone interested in any aspect of the topics mentioned will welcome the publication of these studies in this form.

It is therefore disappointing that no general overview is given at the outset (although the first three essays are well placed to introduce the more narrowly focused studies which follow). The lack of an index is also a drawback to an otherwise useful and absorbing collection.

ELI LEDERHENDLER
Jewish Theological Seminary of America
Hebrew University

Ezra Mendelsohn, *The Jews of East Central Europe between the World Wars.* Bloomington, Ind.: Indiana University Press, 1983. 300 pp. $27.50.

This is an excellent volume that will fill an important gap in our knowledge of the history of East Central Europe. The title of the book adequately describes the topic, though not the scope of the endeavor, for Professor Mendelsohn undertakes nothing less than to trace Jewish-gentile relations, the social evolution of both communities, and the political ramifications of this evolution in seven countries (Poland, Hungary, Czechoslovakia, Romania, and the three Baltic republics) chiefly during the two decades of the interwar period. Although, except for the chapter on Poland, the book is based on secondary sources in non-area languages, the author performs his task very well, giving us a judicious and enlightening study of his subject.

A brief survey of the individual chapters may touch only on the most salient points of the narrative, without being able to convey the complexity of historical reality, or the subtlety of the author's analysis. The first substantive chapter is on Poland. In it we are introduced to a Jewish community that is deeply divided not only between traditionalists and secular modernizers, but among several political factions in each of the major cultural groups. Under the impact of Polish nationalism, Zionism was on the rise, though until the end of the interwar period the socialist ideology of the Bund, and to a lesser extent communism, remained important political forces among the Jewish minority. The social structure of Polish Jewry perhaps most closely resembled that of Romania. In that country, too, Jews were divided in a number of ways, between more and less "westernized" segments, as well as between the Jews of the Old Kingdom and those of the new territories acquired after 1918. Suspicion of Jews as "unassimilable aliens" was deeply ingrained, but after 1918, and still more obviously after 1933, the "Jewish question" was made central to Romanian politics by the Christian National Defense and Iron Guard movements. While the old liberal establishment, the monarchy, and the army all fought the right-wing radicals tooth and nail, in the end they all succumbed, or else made concessions to, radical sentiments at the expense of the Jews.

In contrast to Poland and Romania, Hungary was a country that, prior to World War I, had been "good" to its Jewish population, in the sense that its ruling classes, for economic and national reasons, fostered cultural assimilation and integration into the political community. Yet the liberal model was not without ambiguities, and in response to these ambiguities, the younger Jewish intelligentsia of the turn of the century became attracted to the radical Left, mainly because its ideologies seemed to promote political rights disassociated from cultural and ethnic identity. Whether the conspicuous association of the Jewish intelligentsia with the proletarian dictatorship of 1919 was a cause or an effect of a deteriorating relationship is not easy to say, but the revolutions and the subsequent Treaty of Trianon represented significant watersheds in the relationship between Jews and Hungarians. As in Romania, after 1920 a new, antisemitic Right was on the rise, and it eventually overwhelmed the moderates of the old establishment, who tried to mitigate or modify the practical effects of this antisemitism. Thus Hungary, with its "westernized," middle-class Jewish community, and its past record of tolerance, would follow closely the areawide trends of the period. The only country not to do so was Czechoslovakia with its democratic form of government, though here, too, ambivalence lingered, mainly because Jews were perceived to have been more sympathetic to Austro-German and Hungarian than to Czech and Slovak aspirations. Thus, conspicuous assimilationism in the Czech lands coexisted with the rise of Zionism in lesser developed Slovakia and Sub-Carpathia. In all of these provinces, of course, official tolerance came to an end with the dissolution of the Republic in 1938–1939.

For many readers perhaps the most novel and interesting findings in this book will emerge from the chapters on the Baltic republics. In these republics, especially in Lithuania and Latvia, the highly traditional and unacculturated Jewish communities were at first embraced by the new national governments (against Poland and Soviet Russia). But by the mid-twenties, the relationship between gentiles and Jews began to erode, even though the "Jewish question" failed to become subject to the same "obsessive attention" (236) as it did in Poland, Romania, and Hungary. Disappointment fostered Zionism as well as sympathies toward the Soviet state, whose policies in this period are described by the author as favorable to Jews as individuals, even though hostile to Judaism as a form of cultural, religious, and political identity (6). Indeed, as the author recounts, part of the Jewish Left responded favorably to the first Soviet occupation of the republics in 1940, inviting subsequent "disaster for the entire Jewish community" (239).

One of the major conclusions that Professor Mendelsohn draws from these materials is "that what Jews did in interwar East Central Europe had little impact on attitudes and policies toward them" (256). While this conclusion appears to be too sweeping even in the light of some of the author's observations, it is certainly true that the social structure, economic status, or place of a Jewish community on the traditionalist-assimilationist continuum show remarkably little correlation with the manifestations of native antisemitism. Indeed, to understand the latter, we may have to step out of the narrower confines of the area and its national states, and examine the problem of Jewish-gentile relationships within the larger context of the history of modern liberalism and capitalism. If the continent-wide strength of these currents brought forth Jewish emancipation, assimilationism, and entrepreneurship, in the early twentieth century the crisis of these ideas, and growing doubts about the relevance of western economic and political models to the societies of East-Central Europe, were responsible for the gradual drift of Jews from capitalist enterprise into radical politics, and from liberal assimilationism into socialist internationalism. This, in turn, provided lingering antisemitism with a new political idiom, the idiom of conspiracy against the weak national state, which acquired a measure of credibility through the presence of Jews in both capitalist enterprise and socialist parties. Zionism arose and spread as an obvious response to this no-win situation. But whatever its appeals were from country to country, worldwide it was as yet too weak to have a significant impact on historical perceptions and outcomes.

Within this general context, of course, one can easily agree with Professor Mendelsohn that the ultimate fate of the individual Jewish communities had less to do with local tradition, or with a country's level of economic development, than with a political-military situation as it unfolded between 1939–1944. Thus Czech, Polish, and Baltic Jews fell under German military occupation, and their fate was sealed early on. Romanian, Hungarian, and to a lesser extent Slovak Jews, on the other hand, remained under the partial control of national elites, and they became, or remained, pawns in internal political struggles, or in struggles between the governments of these countries and Germany. In Romania, thus, the Jews of the East perished while those of southern Transylvania and Wallachia survived, reflecting Antonescu's calculations of the vagaries of international and internal politics. In Hungary, the Jews of the provinces were deported in May–June 1944, but those of Budapest partly survived, as the deteriorating military situation provided Horthy with some leverage and, still later, made mass deportations impracticable. Much of this, to be sure, will be familiar to the specialist, but the story will come alive again in vivid detail in this volume, which I once again recommend to all who are interested in either East European or Jewish history.

Andrew C. Janos
University of California,
Berkeley

Paul R. Mendes-Flohr (ed.), *A Land of Two Peoples: Martin Buber on Jews and Arabs.* New York: Oxford University Press, 1983. 319 pp. $29.95.

"For Buber," writes Paul R. Mendes-Flohr in his illuminating introduction to this collection of writings, "politics was an essential dimension of the life of dialogue and service to God." Yet Buber's conception of politics, Mendes-Flohr insists, was not (as is sometimes suggested) naively idealistic but rather "a believing realism." In his efforts to promote Arab-Jewish rapprochement, Buber did not preach an unworldly moralism, argues Mendes-Flohr, but rather a "Hebrew humanism" whose foundation principle, as expressed by Buber himself, was: "We cannot refrain from doing wrong altogether, but we are given the grace of not having to do more than absolutely necessary."

This collection draws together sixty-five essays, letters, speeches, and notes, some hitherto unpublished, covering the period from February 1918 to February 1965. Most are by Buber himself but the editor has most usefully included a few writings by correspondents or interlocutors of Buber, where publication of both sides of an exchange will help elucidate Buber's ideas: among these are thought-provoking statements by Hans Kohn and Nathan Rotenstreich.

The development of Buber's thought on the Arab-Jewish conflict in Palestine emerges clearly from this collection. From the outset he rejected talk of a Jewish historical "right" to Palestine. Until 1948, moreover, he remained convinced that (as Mendes-Flohr puts it) "the pursuit of political sovereignty [by the Jews] was a fatuous, unwarranted extravagance." He rejected the "tragic view" of the Arab-Jewish conflict, the notion that the claims of the two peoples were irreconcilable and that an armed struggle was inevitable. At the outset of the British mandatory period he subscribed to the commonly held view that Arab opposition to Zionism was factitiously fomented by the Arab landowning "effendi" class; later he deepened his understanding of the popular roots of Arab anti-Zionism—without, however, losing faith in the possibility of accord.

The pieces collected here chronicle Buber's involvement with the *Brith Shalom* in the 1920s, the League for Arab-Jewish Rapprochement and Cooperation from 1939, the *Ichud* from 1942, and his efforts particularly after 1948 to secure fair treatment for Arabs within Israel. Inevitably the various pieces are of differing weight, ranging from profound expressions of a philosophical position to ephemeral public statements.

The collection certainly bears out the editor's contention that Buber had a far from naive (sometimes uncannily prophetic) grasp of the real political world. And yet it must be said that in the last resort, faced with the collapse of successive cherished notions, Buber fell back on what were perhaps simplistic interpretations of that world. In a lecture in 1947 he speaks of the "possibilities for cooperation, flowing from the two peoples' common origin and shared task . . . were it not for the intervention of the political element." In the 1950s he fell back on the idea that the root of the unsatisfactory Israeli attitude toward the Arabs could be traced back to the Polish and German immigrations of the 1920s and 1930s, whose understanding of the matter (so he suggested) was in general inferior to that of the *halutzim* of the second *aliya*. (*Mutatis mutandis* we may detect here an embryonic version of the idea, common in the 1980s, that the root of the trouble is the *aliya* of Jews from Arab lands).

This book has been edited with exemplary care and is furnished with helpful explanatory notes. Apart from some misprints which should be corrected in any further impression this may stand as the definitive source for an understanding of the views of a much misunderstood Zionist thinker.

BERNARD WASSERSTEIN
Brandeis University

Werner E. Mosse, Arnold Paucker, Reinhard Rürup (eds.), *Revolution and Evolution: 1848 in German-Jewish History* (Schriftenreihe wissenschaftlicher Abhandlungen des Leo Baeck Instituts, Bd. 39). Tübingen: J. C. B. Mohr, 1981. 431 pp.

Walter Grab/Julius H. Schoeps (Hrsg.), *Juden im Vormärz und in der Revolution von 1848*. Stuttgart-Bonn: Burg Verlag, 1983. 400 pp.

Revolution and Evolution: 1848 in German-Jewish History, the fruit of a 1979 Leo Baeck Institute symposium held in Oxford, does not really present us with a snapshot of the 1848 revolutions. It does, however, provide us with something far more valuable: a composite portrait of German Jewry in the first three-quarters of the nineteenth century. We owe this happy circumstance to the conviction, virtually unanimous among the contributors, that the shaping of modern German Jewry had more to do with evolutionary factors than with revolutionary ones. Jewish emancipation, Reinhard Rürup argues in his superb introductory chapter, was part of a wider dynamic process, a concomitant of the gradual, although seldom smooth, consolidation of the liberal-bourgeois order in Western and Central Europe. As a result of this emphasis, long-term processes such as cultural and economic *embourgeoisement,* urbanization, industrialization, and demographic change are given priority here. Scholars have now been provided with indispensable data for all these areas.

If the revolution did not create or determine the overall framework of Jewish emancipation it could nevertheless speed or equally impede and delay its achievement. Rürup's essay represents an attempt to deal with the dialectics and complexities of that process. He argues that as far as legislative emancipation measures were concerned, 1848 produced far more modest gains than might have been expected. Only a few of the minor German states upheld the full equality of the Jews and while the revised Prussian constitution of 1850 confirmed Jewish equality under the law it simultaneously seemed to weaken that principle by proclaiming Christianity as the state religion. This inconclusive state of affairs also applied in most other European countries. The revolutionary legislative program of 1848 was left "at an intermediate stage that was not free of ambiguities." In Germany it was not until the early 1870s, under the imprimatur of a regime hardly liberal in nature, that full legal emancipation was achieved. To the conventional argument that the revolutions nevertheless settled the cause of emancipation in *principle,* Rürup convincingly demonstrates that they also produced popular anti-Jewish outbreaks, rural and urban, which were comparable in scale to some medieval persecutions and the subsequent pogroms of the 1880s. At least 180 localities throughout Europe witnessed some kind of physical action against Jewish persons or property. These reactions were, to be sure, short-lived and, as Rürup points out, largely the response of groups threatened by the perceived economic consequences of "modernization." The evidence, however, remains clear enough. No simplistic uni-directional interpretation of the revolutions is possible.

Even more pertinent is Rürup's contention that 1848 saw the emergence of an entirely new kind of antisemitic ideology, one no longer directed at traditional, unemancipated Jewry but at Jews who had already achieved emancipation. The critique of the very principle of assimilation "cut the ground from under the liberal emancipation theory" and became the staple of all subsequent antisemitic rhetoric. The new stereotype of the modern Jew (moneyed and/or intellectual and/or radical but in all cases subversive of the traditional order and its values) was already present, Rürup argues, in the antisemitic utterances of the revolutionary period. The novelty of modern Jew-hatred is acutely diagnosed here but Rürup underestimates the degree to which the critique of assimilation *preceded* the revolution. The myth of the "cultured" Jew emerged very clearly in the nineteenth century and became part of German popular culture almost simultaneously with the early stages of Jewish acculturation. The revolution served to sharpen that image but it did not create it.

All this does not mean that the 1848 revolutions had no positive significance for German Jewry. Jews emerged for the first time, and in relatively large numbers, as political activists and produced leaders such as Gabriel Riesser, Ludwig Bamberger, Johann Jacoby, and others. This participation, in Rürup's view, was vital for it signalled the moment at which "Jews ceased to be mere passive objects of politics, and . . . took a hand in fashioning their own destiny as well as that of the wider body politic." This represented a major shift in Jewish self-awareness and self-assertiveness. In 1850, twelve years before Moses

Hess wrote his *Rome and Jerusalem*, Ludwig Philippson, editor of the *Allgemeine Zeitung des Judentums*, enunciated a German-Jewish liberal doctrine of auto-emancipation. After the renewed curtailment of Jewish rights in Prussia, Philippson scolded those who supported these measures, declaring that the Jews had long since emerged from the ghetto: "But do you not know that inner emancipation came a long time before your measures? *You* do not emancipate the Jews, *they* emancipated themselves a long time ago. All *you* do is to complete the outward emancipation" (p. 51). Yet inferences from this quotation must be drawn with some caution, as Rürup's comments about the new self-assertiveness do not pertain to collective Jewish matters and communal political life. It was only in the Wilhelminian period that German Jews fitfully came to grips with this persistently problematic dimension.

I have concentrated on Rürup's essay because it is in this sensitive introduction and Werner Mosse's thoughtful conclusion that the overall problem of the 1848 revolutions and its relationship to general German-Jewish history is considered. Despite Rürup's emphasis on the contradictory nature of the revolution he concludes "that if only equality of legal status for the Jews had been irreversibly established by the revolutions of 1848/1849, the ensuing social conflicts would have been mitigated in great measure by the lasting prosperity of the following two-and-a-half decades. . . ." This venture into speculative history is problematic: it ignores the very real internal tensions which, as Rürup himself so clearly shows, were an integral part of the revolution itself. Werner Mosse, in his concluding remarks, paints the overall prospects of German-Jewish emancipation in far deeper colors:

> There is little to suggest that the men of the *Paulskirche* suffered from a greater addiction to pluralism than did the constitution-makers of 1869/1871. . . . Given the realities of German religious, social, political and cultural development, the mode of emancipation might make at best a marginal difference. Emancipation under the Black, Red and Golden banner might differ but little from that under Black, White and Red. No more than the Weimar Republic, again under the colors of Black, Red and Gold, was the *Paulskirche* likely to produce a society in which Jews would enjoy equality and security.

Most of the other essays in this volume analyze (and provide information about) longer-term processes underlying Jewish emancipation and "modernization" in Germany. On the whole they succeed in providing us with a sensible and sorely needed social history of the period. Lawrence Schofer's piece on "Emancipation and Population Change" demonstrates that modern Jewish population movements, prolonged old age, and lower birth rates, began in the 1840s: a full generation before similar developments occurred in the non-Jewish German population. The data is doubtless correct but the problem of historical explanation, of causality, as Peter Pulzer points out in his commentary, is exceedingly complex. Did Jews exhibit these demographic characteristics because, as Schofer maintains, they were a separate ethnic group with distinctive sociocultural traits? Or did they, as Pulzer suggests, display these demographic characteristics simply because they became middle class earlier than most sections of the gentile population (just as one would also expect the North German Protestant middle class to be in advance of society as a whole)? The relation between demographic data and historical explanation remains problematic.

Less speculative is Monika Richarz's article on rural Jews—the silent majority of Jews in most German states until well into the nineteenth century. Richarz succeeds in bringing these usually mute subjects to life. Her analysis of the distinction between urban and rural modes of Christian-Jewish interaction is convincing. In the villages, she writes, "there were two social groups that were totally different in religion, occupation and way of life . . . [precluding] any thought of assimilation in the urban sense." This strict social separation did not prevent "neighborly and even friendly relationships between individual members of the two groups, who knew each other much better than Jews and non-Jews knew each other in the cities." Perhaps the most ubiquitous and "archetypal" rural Jews were the cattle dealers. Their business jargon, a combination of Hebrew, Yiddish, and German, was the only "foreign language" the peasants ever thought worth learning: a measure of the Jewish importance as mediators between the rural and urban economies.

Whatever the centrality of *Dorfjuden* in the first part of the century, the dominant direction after that was toward the towns and cities. Avraham Barkai's stimulating essay on "The German Jews at the Start of Industrialization: Structural Change and Mobility 1835–1860" points out that prior to the 1860s Jews were not yet a metropolitan group but they were already predominantly urban and very mobile. Barkai attempts to account for one of the most outstanding features of German Jewish existence: its consistent upward mobility and economic success. Previous Jewish history, of course, helped the Jews to take advantage of the general trend toward economic modernization. Yet this in itself is not a sufficient explanation for the almost homogeneous middle-class composition of late nineteenth century German Jewry. What contributed to this "levelling" process? At the lowest level of Jewish society, Barkai suggests, some of the *Betteljuden* (vagrants) and other elements were absorbed into the equivalent ranks of gentile society. Even more important is Barkai's insistence on the importance of emigration as "the single most important factor [in] the remarkable decline of the Jewish lower classes."

The other essays in this volume (Julius Carlebach on "Family Structure and the Position of Jewish Women," Ismar Schorsch on "Emancipation and Religious Authority—The Emergence of the Modern Rabbinate," Steven Lowenstein on "The 1840s and the Creation of the German-Jewish Religious Reform Movement," Uriel Tal on "German Jewish Social Thought in the Mid-Nineteenth Century" and Hermann Greive on "Religious Dissent and Tolerance in the 1840s") deal with modernization and *embourgeoisement* in their distinctive Jewish intellectual, religious, and cultural modes. Siegbert Prawer's sparkling essay on "Heine's Portraits of German and French Jews on the Eve of the 1848 Revolution" stands somewhat apart from the more general subject matter of the other contributions. It would have been instructive to have included a piece on the nature of the Eastern Jewish presence as a conditioning factor in the formation of German Jewish attitudes and institutions. Moreover, a systematic consideration of the role of *Bildung,* the enduring cultural sign of German Jewish *embourgeoisement,* would have completed the picture. But these are mere quibbles. This fine volume is definitive and an indispensable tool for all (especially English-speaking) readers interested in the serious study of modern German Jewry.

Juden im Vormärz und in der Revolution von 1848 has a quite different emphasis. This volume, based upon a symposium held in early 1982, does not attempt to present the reader with a history of the period or to delineate the collective development of German Jewry. It is rather a series of discrete studies of various Jewish individuals who, in one way or another, can be regarded as "radicals" or, at least, as politically engaged. The result, however, is uneven for these essays, despite the welter of factual information which they provide, lack a unifying conceptual framework. The jacket, to be sure, tells us that the overall problematic has to do with the nature of Jewish democratic predispositions. Did Jews support democratic principles because these promised the realization of Jewish political and civil rights? Or is there a special affinity between democracy and Jewish religion and tradition? These are reasonable and interesting questions. The problem is that they are nowhere systematically addressed or linked by the various individual contributions. In his article on Ferdinand Lassalle, Shlomo Na'aman makes some interesting general comments on the Jewish revolutionary as a specific type of Jewish intellectual but never develops this. Jewish history need not necessarily be confined to the study of Jewish collectivities or institutions. The study of individual "non-Jewish Jews" can be extremely rewarding—if it is linked to a specific historical problematic. Lacking this dimension such history is prone to succumb to the laundry-list syndrome, or even to an inverted version of Jewish chauvinism.

This does not mean, of course, that all the contributions here are exercises in mere cataloguing. Many—one thinks here especially of Michael Werner on Heine, Jacob Toury on Moritz Saphir and Karl Beck, Walter Grab on Johann Jacoby—make for rewarding reading. Others, such as the attempt by Helmut Hirsch to regard Marx's anti-Jewish invective in his *Judenfrage* and elsewhere as mere exercises of transmuted metaphor, are somewhat more problematic.

Moses Hess, whose early anti-Jewish diatribe and later proto-Jewish nationalism certainly qualify him as a legitimate and important subject, is treated here by Zwi Rosen entirely without reference to the Jewish dimension. This is, of course, in other contexts quite proper and Rosen's study of Hess's influence on Marx's theory of alienation is illuminating. But in a book explicitly dedicated to examining the *Jewish* dimension one is left wondering what, apart from the fact of ethnic origin, the editors and contributors understand it to mean. This particular reader, at any rate, remains in the dark.

STEVEN E. ASCHHEIM
Hebrew University

Paul Panish, *Exit Visa*. New York: Coward, McCann and Geoghegan, 1981. 299 pp.

The reader who can bring to this book anything resembling the open, sensitive mind, the capacity for empathy, and the lively moral involvement with which it is written, will come away richly rewarded indeed. This is not a book which one enjoys. It deals with the anguish, degradation, suffering, frustration, confusion, and alienation which every Soviet Jew endures in greater or lesser measure in the course of ending his Soviet life, descending into the spiritual maelstrom of the transit facilities in Vienna and Rome, and in struggling with his new beginnings in America.

Paul Panish follows the journey of three families as they make this painful pilgrimage. The families, though fictional composites, reflect the true-life experiences of tens of thousands of Jews. If his particular heroes do not reflect every type of immigrant and every variety of experience, it is because the historical reality is too complex to be captured in any single popularization.

The author has, however, delved deeply into the subject, and, even more important, he has understood the depths and subtleties of what his interviewees have shared with him. So sensitive is he to their psychological makeup that he understands the unflattering comparison of the smooth, sterile plastic of America to the living, textured wood which is the Russian's image of Russia. Between the lines of his story, Panish deftly interweaves a great deal of factual information regarding the status of Jews in the USSR, regulations and procedures of emigration and the processing of the emigrants through Europe, in Israel, and in the United States. He also provides a brief account of the historical context in which the Exodus movement grew up, and all this clearly, accurately, and unobtrusively.

The stories of the Gorelskys of Odessa, the Levins of Leningrad, and the Mendelyevitches of the Lubavitcher ḥasidic underground all ring true, as do those of the other characters whom he works into the narrative. We become acquainted with the complex schizophrenic nature of Soviet Jewish life—the intricate strategies of circumspection, the multiple anxieties, the grasping at rumors, the feverish family strategy conferences, and finally the explosive impact of the exodus movement which shocked and shattered the carefully constructed shelter of even the most assimilated Soviet Jew.

Nadia Gershman had been waiting six years for a full-time teaching appointment. ("Listen Nadia, . . . my hands are tied. Your father's name is Avrom, your husband's name is Naum. . . . Now really what can I do?") At long last she is put on the promotion list, but when Tania Petrov (Levin) applies for an exit visa, the cautious director immediately crosses out Nadia's name—lest he be accused of "political blindness" for promoting a potential emigrant.

The overwhelmingly negative cast of the book may seem depressing, but one must remember that the author is not giving his own version of the events, nor is he necessarily drawing a full and balanced picture of reality. He is, however, a faithful camera recording his subjects' perceptions in excruciating detail, and with a delicate mastery of shadings. Each one of the characters is subjected to stress, pressure, and hardship that not infrequently produce both physical and psychological illnesses as well as deviant behavior patterns familiar to anyone who has studied humans in such situations. It is to the credit of both the author and his interviewees that no effort is made to hide the seamy side of the emigrants' behavior or to turn them into unsullied heroes. Their shortcomings are presented as frankly and fully as is their courage. This is not an attempt to demythologize the exodus movement, but perhaps just the opposite, by throwing light on the terrible personal price paid by each of the emigrants for his decision to strike out for a new life. In this book we meet Jews who lie, who cheat the institutions which are assisting them, who fight and betray one another, all in an elemental struggle for survival. "They had already shoved and wept their way through questionnaires, bureaucracies and officials, and would even have broken past the ferryman on the Styx, if he'd dared to block their path to God knows where." Let all those officials who would think to solve the "dropout" problem by bureaucratic regulations ponder this statement, and realize its full truth and implications.

But the Soviet Jew's troubles do not end when he lands on the golden shores of America. Here too the new immigrant finds bureaucratic regulation and a near total communications gap. Over and over the author draws sharp portraits of the immigrants' disoriented values and loss of status. Professors, writers, truck drivers, and butchers all must grope confusedly for a new handle on life, new orientations toward people and institutions. Even the book's ending does not betray this black mood, for though most of the characters do get their feet on the ground, each is steeped in the consciousness of beginning, and of the long path which lies before him. Essentially, Panish shows us a generation of the desert, doomed, however young they may be, to the feeling of being foreigners. Nevertheless these are immigrants coming to be absorbed in a new country, and not emigres who want to cling to the old life in a new setting. The "Odessa by the Sea" of Brighton Beach is a transitory and marginal phenomenon, a brief way-station on the way to becoming a new American. "Irina quickly mastered an unaccented English. On the subway she was almost indistinguishable from any of the young office workers. . . . Nonetheless it seemed to her parents that she was striving for ordinaryness."

Panish writes exclusively of the immigrants who settled in the U.S., touching on Israel only as "one more important influence on the lives and the psyche of the emigres to the West." He makes no attempt to give a balanced or detailed picture of the experiences of Soviet immigrants in Israel. This story, more important in modern Jewish history, and almost surely of a happier nature, still remains to be written. Let us hope that whoever writes the history of Soviet Jews in Israel will be familiar with Paul Panish's work and will draw a carefully comparative picture.

Exit Visa should be compulsory reading for every social worker, community official, and Soviet Jewry activist wherever he may be. A Russian language edition of the book would undoubtedly be avidly read and vociferously debated among new Americans, and would become a *samizdat* "Guide to the Perplexed" among the tens of thousands of Soviet Jews who anxiously await a new turn of the emigration tide. For the lay reader it is a superbly written, informative, and truthful treatment of one of the central events of Jewish life after World War II.

THEODORE H. FRIEDGUT
Hebrew University

Béatrice Philippe, *Être juif dans la société française du Moyen-Age a nos jours.* Paris: Editions Montalba, 1979/1981. 315 pp.

This new history of French Jewry has already seen two editions. The second, in paperback, has been published without the illustrations that graced the first, hardbound edition.

Drawing upon the best of sources, Philippe clearly traces the path traveled by French Jews over the course of fifteen centuries. The history of French Jewry is closely linked with that of France, and the author emphasizes this link as she describes Jewish life and Jews' relations with French society. The first part of the work provides a rapid survey of the history of French Jewry from its origins (from the 4th century) to 1789. The second part analyzes the progressive integration of French Jewry into French society in the twentieth century, up until the eve of World War II. The final part deals with the Holocaust, the reconstruction of the Jewish community in the postwar period, and relations between France and Israel.

Enhanced by a chronology and a bibliography, this volume will serve as a reference work for anyone interested in French Jewry.

DORIS BENSIMON
Université de Caen

Jack Nusan Porter, *The Jew as Outsider: Historical and Comparative Perspectives. Collected Essays, 1974–1980.* Washington, D.C.: University Press of America, 1981. xiv + 219 pp.

Porter belongs to the younger generation of ex-radical Jewish intellectuals; a sociological journalist, he seems widely read, but lacks the imagination and creativity to mold the many books he quotes into new concepts, approaches, or ideas. This collection of his essays, which are based mostly on secondary sources, relates primarily to facets of the contemporary American Jewish scene. It is permeated by the vague idea that Jews are "outsiders." The concept, in Porter's use, relates primarily to Jewish marginality in its various manifestations. Indeed, he claims in the "Prologue" (pp. ix–xii), somewhat grandiloquently, that "These essays represent an entire opus," of which marginality is the leitmotif (p. xii). In fact, most of the essays are a hodgepodge of sociological banalities, occasionally engaging comments on Jewish-American life, and lengthy and sometimes interesting quotations from other people's work.

Porter first presents a variety of what could be called "Jewish cultural types," the Jewish rebel, intellectual, sociologist, comic, and poet (pp. 3–136), all of which are intended to illuminate various aspects of Jewish outsider status; he then discusses what he considers to be various minorities within the Jewish minority—women, young adults, the upper class, and even the Jewish homosexual (pp. 139–207). He winds up with a sweeping epilogue on Jewish "creative paranoia" (pp. 211–218), ranging from Jesus to the contemporary American scene. Several of the essays focus on one particular personality—e.g., the comic Lenny Bruce, the countercultural poet d.a. levy, and the German-Jewish homosexual sexologist Magnus Hirschfeld. Since they deal with minor figures in Jewish history, they are of factual interest, even if they are rarely based on original material.

Porter's pretentious generalizations and analyses, however, can hardly be taken seriously, and sometimes verge on the ludicrous, like the apodictic statement, "The death of Lenny Bruce may have been the beginning of the end for Jewish prominence in American culture" (p. 116). But Porter is a dilettante and there is no point in submitting his sociology to a professional critique. His book should be read as part of the contemporary American Jewish cultural scene rather than a sociological analysis of it.

As a writer, Porter attracts little sympathy. The ponderous notes prefacing his essays (part of which have been previously published in various American Jewish magazines) are occasionally embarrassing. He has little original to say—most of his material comes from other people's books, from which he quotes generously. It is sometimes hard to see the point of an essay. The unattractiveness of the book is compounded by faulty editing. German words in particular are frequently misspelled. Lengthy bibliographies take up much of his book.

Altogether, this is a disappointing book; only a few of the essays, based on the author's personal involvements and experiences, e.g., the ones on the poet d.a. levy and the Jewish upper class (written from data collected while Porter lectured at a private college in Boston) are worth attention.

ERIK COHEN
Hebrew University

W. D. Rubinstein, *The Left, the Right and the Jews*. London: Croom Helm, 1982.

Jewish political behavior has received considerable scholarly attention. Most treatments of this subject, however, have focused on the disproportionate involvement of Jews in socialist or leftist movements, the long-standing tendency of America's Jews to overwhelmingly lend their support to the Democratic party, and the relationship between Jewish political behavior and the Judaic tradition. *The Left, the Right and the Jews* is therefore a welcome study, for its scope is both historical and cross-national while it avoids the common assumption that only a left-liberal political stance is authentically Jewish. Unfortunately, this promising approach meets only partial fulfillment in the substance of this book.

Rubinstein's central concern is the significance of two coincident processes—one chiefly economic, and the other chiefly political—that have played upon Jewish political interests and behavior with increasing force since the Second World War, and which should, as he sees it, dictate their future political allegiances. Economically, Rubinstein finds that, since 1945, the Jews in Western countries have, for the first time in their respective histories, moved virtually *en masse* into the upper middle class. This upward mobility has been so pronounced that the Jews in the West now enjoy overrepresentation among the institutional elites of their societies. The main consequence of this growing affluence and influence among Western Jewry has been to render radical and leftist politics and programs no longer relevant to their socioeconomic interests.

At the same time, this change has been bolstered by a dramatic political development with an almost total realignment in the sources of antisemitism and anti-Zionism. Where once anti-Jewish and anti-Israel sentiment almost exclusively derived from right-wing quarters and the conservative mainstream, from the late 1960s, vociferous anti-Zionist policy and activity has come to constitute the virtual mainstay of the

Socialist and, often, Social Democratic Left's platforms. Conservative parties, on the other hand, have in turn become generally supportive of Israel. Accordingly, these dual processes have served to undercut the historical attachment of Jews to the Left, and caused them in recent years to shift their political allegiances toward the Right of the political spectrum. For Rubinstein, this is not just a shift to be described, but indeed to be encouraged. Jewish security and well-being, including that of Israel, depends on Western Jewry's ability to maintain its privileged position and its access to the elites. Given their otherwise vulnerable status as a minority group, this pursuit of their interests, Rubinstein stresses, is entirely legitimate. The present and foreseeable alignment of forces are such that capitalism and its conservative guardians satisfy Jewish concerns, whereas socialism and left-liberal champions of egalitarianism act only to undermine the very bases of Jewish power. It is hence in the "Jewish interest" to forge a solid and long-term relationship with conservatism.

In presenting his argument, Rubinstein covers considerable ground. His analysis, which depends almost entirely on secondary sources, nevertheless brings together some interesting material gleaned from sub-scholarly journals, newspapers, and "informed" impressions of Jewish communal leaders. The book begins with a useful survey of modern Jewish history from 1815. There are chapters devoted to the nature of power and elites with respect to Western Jewry in the post-war period, the realignment in the political sources of anti-Jewish sentiment, and the developing Jewish political reaction. The book concludes with chapters discussing, from a comparative stance, the Western democracies (especially the United States, Britain, and Australia), the Soviet Union, and Israel.

Still, the summary statement of Rubinstein's position offered above belies what is an uneasy tension in the construction of his thesis. At one level this occurs simply in terms of complicating factors and important exceptions to the general trends and alliances that he wishes to emphasize. Rubinstein is forced to note, for example, that not all those on the Left are hostile to Israel and by no means to the Jews. Here, Mitterrand's France is probably the most striking current example of a socialist government decidedly more friendly to Israel than was its conservative counterpart. Also, the French Jewish community serves to confound the overall pattern of Western Jewry's upward social mobility by maintaining among its ranks a sizable working class. Similarly, the United States provides a paradoxical case where the rise to affluence of its Jews did not diminish their support for the liberal programs of the Democrats, a support offered consistently and overwhelmingly at least since the New Deal.

These exceptional cases, moreover, preempt a whole theoretical dimension relevant to Rubinstein's explanation of Jewish political behavior, but about which, unfortunately, he has nothing to say. His account of Jewish political behavior since World War II depends on the economic "pull" of upper middle class interests working in tandem with, or being reinforced by, a political "push" from hostile leftist quarters. But France and the United States are instructive here precisely because they are examples of places where these forces do not mainly coincide. In the case of France, there is the economic pull of wide-scale upward Jewish social mobility (even allowing for its working class component), but absent is a political push from a hostile (non-Communist) Left.

In the case of the United States, Rubinstein effectively removes "economics" from the entire equation. He does so by arguing, in his account of the seeming anomaly between American Jewry's pronounced rise to affluence and their loyalty to the Democrats, that the Democratic Party hardly constitutes a left-wing party of social and economic reform in the European mold. What remain, therefore, to determine Jewish political behavior in the American context are political forces, and this is exactly how Rubinstein explains the noted and noticeable shift to the Right among American Jews since the sixties. It occurs because of Black antisemitism, the discriminatory aspects of Affirmative Action, and the less than unequivocal statements of support for Israel during the Carter Administration. Thus, in France (where the majority of Jews continue to support the non-Communist Left) and in the United States, it is the political and not the economic factor which appears to be primary in determining Jewish political behavior.

This consideration, then, should invite reexamination of Rubinstein's seemingly straightforward argument that it is the realignment in the sources of anti-Jewish and anti-Israel sentiment *and* Western Jewry's ascendency into the upper middle class which has caused a conservative shift in their political behavior. Rather, may it not be that the realignment in the sources of antisemitism and anti-Zionism was, and continues to be, sufficient in itself to effect a/the conservative Jewish political response? Should this be so, Rubinstein's advocacy of an intimate long-term association with conservatism would be doubly misguided. First, because of the expedient character of the political factors in question: the Left and the Right, after all, have already exchanged positions once vis-à-vis Israel. Second, because conservative economic principles and politics would not be perceived by Western Jews as being crucial to their interests. Rubinstein's failure to treat the implications of his subject leaves his analysis thereby diminished, and his analysis without adequate foundation.

A second source of tension is to be found in Rubinstein's treatment of the nature and extent of Jewish elite status and political power. On the one hand, he speaks of the ascendency of Western Jewry into the upper middle class and elite groups as if this were identical with political muscle: hence, the maintenance of their newly won elite status is imperative if Western Jews are to "guarantee" the survival of Israel and to minimize antisemitism. On the other hand, he frequently notes the severely circumscribed extent of Jewish influence: but for Israel, Jews rarely act in concert on any issue, and even here, we are advised, it is easy to overstate the influence of the Israel lobby and similar bodies in the United States. Rubinstein leaves his readers, as it were, vacillating between impressions of Jewish political potency and relative weakness.

A more subtle discussion of this question would need, at the very least, to emphasize that the mere representation and even overrepresentation among the elite sectors and groups in Western societies should not be confused with actual and real influence within the corridors of power. That a small number of Jews have managed to enter their nation's key economic and political elites does not speak for the vast majority of Jews who must live according to the decision-making (and "non-decision-making") of non-Jews. As for those few Jews who do enjoy privileged positions, it is neither self-evident that they represent "Jewish interests" nor, to the extent that they do, that they have decisive impact on policy-making. And, finally, to take again the now classic example of Jewish influence, it is extremely unlikely that Jewish lobbying on behalf of Israel, either within or outside of AIPAC, could be as effective as it is if it did not also coincide with deep-seated American religious attachments to the land and people of Israel and with American foreign policy interests.

What is best about *The Left, the Right and the Jews* is that it gives serious attention to the gross economic and political forces that have helped shape the contemporary Jewish situation in the West. Its chief fault is to make these twin processes do too much; whether it be accounting for Jewish political behavior, dictating Jewish political preferences, or defining the relationship between Israel and the Diaspora.

Little or no attention is given in this book to why so many Jews *remain* committed to the Left (of various complexions), and there is no attempt to critically appraise what leftist parties may *still* have to offer Western Jewry.

Rubinstein has written a helpful and, at times, insightful book, but the same ground could profitably be covered again with more depth and greater finesse.

GEOFFREY LEVEY
Hebrew University

Ellen Schiff, *From Stereotype to Metaphor: The Jew in Contemporary Drama.* Albany: State University of New York Press, 1982.

Ellen Schiff's book is a vivid portrait of the transformed image of the Jew on the modern stage. It encompasses an impressive range of dramatic literature, but, while this encyclopedic scope furnishes a broad base for the book's conclusions, it does not allow for an adequate critical evaluation of the plays. The result is not a book of literary criticism or interpretation, but rather a socioliterary study that ranges rather indiscriminately over the surveyed works. A large number of the plays mentioned will not be familiar to American or European theatergoers, and in most cases the oblivion that has attached itself to these plays is not entirely undeserved.

It could be argued—although Schiff does not—that the less memorable plays are more representative of certain popular cultural trends than the more serious literature. In any event, the literature surveyed here generally supports the basic thesis of the book which, as suggested in its title, establishes the claim for a transition in the presentation of the stage Jew from stereotype to "metaphor": from a stereotype of the Satanic *other,* the *"sitra aḥra"* of European or American society, to a character who, in his alienation, in his suffering or his antiheroic status, represents Everyman, the self in modern society.

This hypothesis confirms, through the analysis of dozens of plays written since World War II, a projection made by Leslie Fiedler in 1949:

> In all the countries of the West, and pre-eminently in America, we [Jews] have been passing in the last three or four generations from the periphery to the center of culture. . . . Indeed, in this apocalyptic period of atomization and universal alienation, the image of the Jew tends to become the image of everyone; and we are perhaps approaching the day when the Jew will come to seem the central symbol, the essential myth of the whole Western world.

The extent of the shift in the status of the Jew that has occurred in the period following the Second World War can best be measured against the background of what emerges as a continuous literary tradition—and Schiff goes as far back as the twelfth century in her historical survey of the stage Jew. In a condensed but comprehensive manner, she isolates the principal characteristics of the Jew since he first appeared in medieval Christian drama. Every aspect of his character was grounded in Scripture or in Christian legend (Judas Iscariot or Ahasver, the one who betrays or assaults Jesus), or in a particular social role (the Jew as usurer). By the seventeenth century, certain dramatic conventions had crystallized around the figure of the Jew as wanderer, as malefactor, as traitor—and around his beautiful and seductive daughter ("la belle juive"). The Jew was instantly recognizable on the stage by his appearance (flowing cape, red beard, and long, crooked nose) and by his speech (a garble of unintelligible sounds)—external evidence of his accursed state. Throughout this period he was presented as a stock character with no attempts at individuation. As a stereotype, the Jew embodied the darker, demonic, repressed side of the European psyche, the negative counterpart to any Christian notion of good. The dramatization of this mythical figure was a response to deep-seated socio-psychological needs independent of the actual presence of Jews in the immediate social environment.

At the end of the eighteenth and beginning of the nineteenth centuries, non-Jews began to encounter Jews in a greater range of social activity, and here and there in the dramatic literature more positive, if still one-dimensional, portrayals of the Jew appeared. This trend reaches its peak in the modern era when the character who appears on stage is not simply and self-evidently "a Jew," but "a Jew who . . ."; nthe meaning of his appearance before an audience can no longer be taken for granted as it once was, and his role is now defined by his individual qualities. Schiff pinpoints the major change that has taken place in the modern period in the portrait of the Jew who is "no longer routinely characterized by his profession (paid malefactor), his address (elsewhere) or his point of view (the antithesis of whatever is right [at the] time)."

This process was accelerated by such historical events as the Dreyfus Affair in France at the beginning of the present era and the massive westward migration of Jews at the turn of the century—and by the appearance of Jewish writers and playwrights (and their audiences) who acquired cultural citizenship in Western Europe and America during this same period. In America the comics of vaudeville and of radio and their successors in literature and on stage shaped the figure of the Jew who could laugh at himself and, in time, produced new stereotypes such as the "Jewish mother," who is largely the creation of immigrant writers and their sons.

There is also an ironic appropriation of types from the gallery of classical Jewish characters on the part of both Jewish and non-Jewish writers who have invested these characters with more human, personalized features. This humanizing trend can be traced, for example, with reference to Shylock. While Shakespeare had converted him from a demonic to a more human character ("Hath not a Jew eyes? . . .") with defined social status, over the years he persists as the embodiment of the despised characteristics of his people. Late twentieth century playwrights have gone to great lengths in their attempts to rehabilitate him: George Tabori's *Merchant of Venice* is staged against the backdrop of a concentration camp; in Arnold Wesker's play *The Merchant,* the main character is portrayed as a vigorous, multifaceted human being. The more particular Shylock becomes, then, the less conventionally representative he is as a Jew.

The same kind of revisionist process has reshaped other Jewish types, divesting them of the stigma which they had carried over the centuries. In this last stage of his transformation, the Jew has not completely lost his status as "other"; rather, his stance at the borders between cultures has granted him a kind of prominence in an era in which a sense of alienation, of "otherness," is common fare. "Under our very eyes," Diana Trilling wrote in 1950, "we see the Wandering Jew become the wandering man, the alien Jew generalizing into the alienated human being."[1] The Jew who no longer embodies the demonic "other" becomes modern man located at the margins of society; in this moment of flux Hannah Arendt even confers honorary Jewish identity on Charlie Chaplin.[2]

In becoming the bearer of general human traits, the Jew seems, then, to have lost not only his stage mask but all ethnic identity. When Willy Loman appears on stage in Arthur Miller's *Death of a Salesman,* it is not at all clear whether this antihero, this *shlemazel,* is a Jew at all—neither his name nor his attire, neither his language nor his behavior betrays his ethnic origin (he is, for this reason, "disqualified" by Schiff). The alienated, anonymous personae who populate the world of Eugene Ionesco or Samuel Beckett have no identifying marks whatsoever; they appear as "Old Man" and "Old Woman" *(The Chairs),* as M_1 and W_2 *(Play).* The question that naturally arises from these developments is whether there is still room for the Jew *as Jew* on the modern stage.

The answer to this question may be sought in the central role assigned to the Jew in the drama of recent history, which has assured that he would not disappear into the anonymity that he seemed to have won. In exploring the dramatic literature reflecting the Holocaust, Schiff concentrates on those plays in which the question of identity is central. Such a selective principle raises a number of problems. In the first place, plays such as *The Man in the Glass Booth* by Robert Shaw (which focuses on a Jew disguised as a Nazi disguised as a Jew . . .) or *Throne of Straw* by Harold and Edith Lieberman (which revolves around the figure of Chaim Rumkowski, chairman of the *Judenrat* in the Lodz Ghetto) do not provide a serious aesthetic or philosophical response to the issues they raise (and here the absence of vigorous critical evaluation is keenly felt). Second, the mistaken impression is created in this chapter that the subject of the Holocaust is limited in the theater primarily to the representation of the Jew as victimizer or as potential victimizer, or to the survivor's search for identity. In fact, most of the literary and dramatic works concentrate on the suffering of the victims and their struggle for survival.

Nevertheless, Schiff's focus on the ambiguous roles of Jewish characters in plays dealing with the Holocaust serves to highlight a growing preoccupation of American and European dramatists and filmmakers with Nazism as an indwelling, ubiquitous threat, particularly in the past decade or so. I would argue that this should be seen within the larger context of trends in both serious and popular theater, film and literature toward the psychologization of contending forces in history and the domestication or internalization of demonic impulses. What might emerge in an overview of this cultural process is the realization that modern man, who sees himself as Abel, the eternal victim, the eternal alien, the eternal Jew—now also sees himself as Cain, the eternal oppressor, the eternal Nazi. Here, after hundreds of generations, we begin to see the merging of Cain and Abel, of the self and the other, the two sides of the human psyche, beyond any ethnic or group identity.

Schiff's purview does not extend to the Israeli stage, but, despite the changed locus of the "self" and the "other," the same issues can be raised here with even greater urgency. "Jew is only the name we give to that stranger, that agony we cannot feel, that death we look at like a cold abstraction. Each man has his Jew; it is the other. And the Jews have their Jews." So claims Leduc, the Jewish psychiatrist in Arthur Miller's play *Incident at Vichy*. For the Israeli reader of Ellen Schiff's book, the question that persists is, who are the Jews of the Jews? How is the "other" portrayed on the Israeli stage? And finally, can one anticipate, within the foreseeable future, a transformation in the Israeli theater of the figure of the "other" from stereotype to metaphor?

Sidra DeKoven Ezrahi
Hebrew University

Notes

1. Quoted in Edgar Rosenberg, *From Shylock to Svengali: Jewish Stereotypes in English Fiction* (Stanford, 1960), p. 303.
2. Hannah Arendt, "The Jew as Pariah: A Hidden Tradition," in *The Jew as Pariah: Jewish Identity and Politics in the Modern Age,* edited with an introduction by Ron H. Feldman (New York: Grove Press, 1978).

U. O. Schmelz, *World Jewish Population—Regional Estimates and Projections* (*Jewish Population Studies* #13). Institute of Contemporary Jewry. Jerusalem: Hebrew University, 1981. 72 pp.

The number of Jews in the various parts of the Diaspora is in most cases a rough estimate that is not based on actual enumeration or a sample survey. In order to arrive at an assessment of Jewish population size, one must search for and examine a large number of sources, each giving only partial information of limited or even unknown quality. The *American Jewish Year Book* regularly publishes figures on Jewish communities all over the world, and for many years served as the only source of such data. As such, it was quoted extensively, despite the fact that the figures—often no more than guestimates—were compiled with no pretense that thorough scientific methods had been used and, moreover, were frequently based on outdated assumptions. Over the past two decades, the Section of Demography (now directed by Professor Schmelz) in the Institute of Contemporary Jewry has assumed the task of collecting the available fragments of information on the size and composition of each Jewish community in the world. The data have been obtained from a variety of sources: official censuses where a question on religion or ethnicity was included (for example, USSR, Canada); sample surveys of the Jewish population of entire countries (U.S., France, Italy, South Africa) conducted in collaboration with the Institute; local community surveys; and indirectly, e.g., through the examination of the registered vital events of Jewish communities.

After collecting these pieces of information, relating to different years, Schmelz has reconstructed the various parts of a very complicated puzzle into a comprehensive set of estimates for world Jewry, using sophisticated demographic methods and models. The revised Jewish population estimates resulting from this extensive study are given in the publication reviewed here, together with projections of the size of the Jewish communities through the year 2000. These estimates have since also been adopted by the *American Jewish Year Book.*

The investigation arrived at an extensive revision of the previous figures. In general, the new figures are lower than the old ones. For the year 1975, the new estimate of world Jewry is thirteen million (compared with 14.1 million according to the old figures). The Jewish population of the USSR is put at under two million, rather than the 2.7 million previously accepted. For U.S. Jewry, the updated estimate is 5.6 rather than 5.84 million.

The projections until the year 2000 are based on the findings related to low fertility in the main Jewish Diaspora communities, their pronounced aging trend (resulting in relatively high crude mortality rates), and losses due to assimilatory factors. The projections point to a drop in Jewish population of the Diaspora from ten million in 1975 to about eight million in the year 2000. At the same time, the Jewish population in Israel is expected to increase from three million in 1975 to about 4.5 million. Separate projections are given for different parts of the world. A systematic analysis of the realities underlying these demographic trends was given by Professor Schmelz in his article, "Jewish Survival: The Demographic Factors" in the *American Jewish Year Book* of 1981.

This painstaking task of factfinding deserves appreciation, since it fills a gap in our knowledge of world Jewry. The task, however, is not one which can be accomplished with a one-time study. It requires periodic revision and recurrent efforts for the creation of new basic data.

M. SICRON
Hebrew University

U. O. Schmelz, P. Glikson and S. DellaPergola (eds.), *Papers in Jewish Demography, 1981. Jewish Population Studies* #16 (Proceedings of the Demographic Sessions held at the 8th World Congress of Jewish Studies, Jerusalem, August 1981). The Institute of Contemporary Jewry/World Union of Jewish Studies/ Association for Jewish Demography and Statistics. Jerusalem: 1983. 457 pp.

The World Congress of Jewish Studies has met regularly every four years since 1957 (after the first congress met in 1947). Devoting special sessions to the demography of Jews in the Diaspora and Israel has become a tradition. In these sessions, demographers, sociologists, and statisticians from various institutions in various parts of the world meet to present new studies and research, to exchange views, and to discuss problems of common interest. The papers presented to the 1981 Congress which were of wide interest—though of varying quality—are reproduced in the present volume. The editors, who also organized the sessions, are to be thanked for the effort.

Included here are thirty papers presented at the Congress, introduced by three general papers. Prof. R. Bachi, founder of the Demography Section at the Hebrew University's Institute of Contemporary Jewry, reviews the changing trends in research on Jewish demography. Prof. U. O. Schmelz describes the projections of the world Jewish population, and H. Muhsam presents an essay on Zionism and Jewish population.

The next section comprises six papers in historical demography, covering areas and periods ranging from East Galicia in the sixteenth and seventeenth centuries (M. Horn), to France in the eighteenth century (G. Nahon), to Baden at the turn of the twentieth century (A. Goldstein). Also included are papers on migration of Jews to Cincinnati in 1840–1875 (S. G. Mostow); the Jews of Piedmont in the eighteenth and nineteenth centuries (R. Davies); and a general summary of recent trends in historical demographic research on Jewish populations (R. Cohen).

Reports on studies of contemporary Jewish demography appear in the following section. F. Massarik and F. Kobrin present data on U.S. Jewry, the latter comparing U.S. census data on Yiddish as a mother tongue with data from the U.S. National Jewish Population Study. I. I. Millman reports on the Jews in Romania, while Jewish immigration to South Africa from 1928 to 1948 is the subject of a paper by S. Buxbaum.

The analysis of vital events forms the substance of two sections in the volume. Intermarriage in the U.S. population is described by A. I. Goldberg and by A. Grossman-Shechtman. B. A. Kosmin discusses the problems of measuring divorce among Jews in Britain. Six papers are devoted to research on fertility: C. Goldscheider, on contraception; R. Cheskis, on the impact of Jewish identification; M. Verbit, on the correlates of desired fertility among Jewish university students: all three dealing with U.S. Jews; two devoted to fertility in Israel: G. Kenan and E. Sabatello; S. DellaPergola gives an international overview of Jewish fertility.

Another section is devoted to internal migration and urban ecology. Papers describe the redistribution of American Jews (S. Goldstein); the urban ecology of the Jews in the Paris region (D. Bensimon); the ecology of Warsaw Jewry in the interwar period (D. Bloch); and residential ethnic segregation in Israel (A. Kirschenbaum). V. Klaff gives a comparative analysis of the urban ecology of Jewish populations.

A final section that is not strictly demographic includes papers on Jewish education, identity, and community organization. H. Himmelfarb gives a brief account of the international statistics on Jewish education, collected by the Institute of Contemporary Jewry; while S. M. Cohen discusses mobility and Jewish affiliation in the United States; and A. S. York analyzes data on voluntary association membership in the U.S.

The papers on U.S. Jewry dominate the volume, while those on Israel had been prominent in the previous such collection (from the 1977 Congress). Given both the limited number of researchers in the field and the practical limitations of congresses, some inequality in the coverage of subjects and countries is almost unavoidable. When viewed together, however, the volumes that have resulted over the years from these congresses come closer to providing a comprehensive picture of research activity in the world of Jewish demographics.

M. Sicron
Hebrew University

U. O. Schmelz, P. Glikson and S. J. Gould (eds.), *Studies in Jewish Demography: Survey for 1972–1980*. New York: Ktav Publishing/Institute of Contemporary Jewry—Hebrew University/Institute of Jewish Affairs, London, 1983. 303 pp.

For the third time in fifteen years, the Institute of Contemporary Jewry and the Institute of Jewish Affairs have published their *Studies in Jewish Demography*. Earlier volumes covered the years 1961–68 and 1969–71. The present volume brings us up to date till 1980. Up to date is perhaps the key phrase for a series that aims to provide scholars and interested laymen with a survey of the new literature and statistics published during the given period. The present volume consists of three sections; the first contains three scholarly papers, each in its own way contributing to the volume by reporting on a specific area of research. U. O. Schmelz assesses the present size of the Jewish Diaspora population. Readers familiar with Professor Schmelz's work will not be surprised by this paper's message: the number of Jews in the world has been greatly overestimated. The *American Jewish Year Book* estimated the 1975 world Jewish population at more than fourteen million. Schmelz's sober and sobering estimate convincingly shows that this was much too high a figure: by the end of 1980 there were only about thirteen million Jews in the world. Compared with the situation in 1970, the Diaspora has decreased from ten and a quarter million to nine and three quarter million (i.e., by half a million), while the Jewish population in Israel grew by 700,000. A small increase in the world Jewish population is due solely to the growth in Israel. It is hardly surprising that the internal increase of the Diaspora has been inhibited in part by assimilatory factors.

In the second article, S. DellaPergola adopts a similar revisionist attitude. He and Professor Bensimon had already published preliminary results of the French Jewish Population Study, sponsored by the Groupe de Sociologie des Religions of the CNRS in Paris and the Institute of Contemporary Jewry in Jerusalem. This research shows an identifiable Jewish population in Greater Paris of between 253,000 and 279,000 (i.e., 47.3–52.1% of the total estimated French Jewish population in the mid-seventies). As in the first article, these figures are considerably below earlier estimates that ranged as high as 380,000.

In the previous volume of this series (covering 1969–71), I. I. Millman had presented an analysis of the findings of official censuses of different countries with regard to the Jews. In this volume he has updated his material, including new information from South Africa, the United States, Canada, Iran, Australia and a number of European countries. Preliminary data on the USSR Jewish population from the Soviet census of 1979 are particularly useful. Once again, the detailed findings confirm Schmelz's general estimate: between 1959 and 1979, the Jewish population fell by a fifth, while the total population rose by over a quarter. The tenor of all three articles is the same: Jewish Diaspora populations are in a state of quantitative decline.

Conversely, Jewish population studies are on the rise, as the second part of the book shows. For many readers of the *Studies* volumes, this bibliographical survey of the field is the most important section of the book. All the bibliographies in this series were the work of the late Paul Glikson, who died while putting the finishing touches to this one.

As in the previous volumes, the entries are listed by country, and have also been divided into three categories: (a) current publications of official governmental or municipal statistics; (b) all other publications dealing with recent demographic or socioeconomic characteristics of Jewish populations; and finally (c) publications on the historical evolution of Jewish populations. This last category is indicative of the change in Jewish population research. In earlier years Jewish demographic research concerned itself mainly with contemporary aspects. Obviously, this will remain of importance, and Professor Bachi calls in his Foreword for a concentrated effort to expand and update demographic statistics on world Jewry. In recent years, however, Jewish population studies have gained a new dimension through the emphasis on historical demographic research that not only adds to our knowledge of the past, but also deepens our understanding of the present. Paul Glikson's last bibliography provides, therefore, a certain counterbalance to the somber picture in the first part of the volume: it shows the vitality and vigor of Jewish population studies.

The book closes with a number of current research reports relating to studies carried out in the 1970s in various countries.

Robert Cohen
University of Haifa

Dominique Schnapper, *Juifs et israélites.* Paris: Gallimard, 1980. 281 pp.

This sociological study makes a methodological and theoretical contribution to the study of Jewish identity as it has been expressed in France. Dominique Schnapper defines Jews as "those who declare themselves Jews and those whom others perceive as such." The body of the work consists of about one hundred in-depth conversations held in diverse Jewish *milieux,* chosen according to origin and social categories. Basing herself on Max Weber, the author constructs a typology of French Jewry.

The first "type" is made up of practicing Jews: those who transmit Jewish religious tradition. Often, they belong to "popular" *milieux,* but among the younger generations it is often the intellectuals who renew Jewish tradition consciously and out of knowledge.

The second "type" analyzed by Schnapper are the militants: those who have transposed tradition to the political plane. Pro-Israel or anti-Israel, they affirm their solidarity with the Jewish people and dream of a society based on equality and justice.

The first two groups comprise subgroups, which define themselves primarily by their ties to Judaism. A third category, on the other hand, the *Israélites,* define themselves first and foremost by their ties to

France, while continuing to affirm a Jewish identity, however vaguely manifested. Jews in this more assimilated *milieu,* however, have also experienced a degree of "return" to a more conscious Jewish identity, particularly in the period since the Six Day War of 1967. Among the *Israélites,* the author distinguishes two separate subgroups: the new *Israélites,* heirs to the Jewish bourgeoisie of the early part of the century, who are today strongly integrated into the intellectual and moneyed bourgeoisie; and a commercial category, which constitutes a Jewish social environment particularly sensitive to antisemitic manifestations, even though its members are comparatively unattached to specific traditions.

Schnapper places the reaffirmation of Jewish identity which she found among some of the interviewees in the context of a more general religious awakening in France. She interprets this movement as characteristic of a later phase of industrial society in which distinctive cultural groups reject uniformity.

Schnapper's typology, like all typologies, can be contested. The cleavages observed between Jews and *Israélites* are real. But the extrapolation of a "commercial" group is certainly debatable. This socioprofessional category in France today is quite elderly. It is stratified according to country of origin and meaningful social characteristics. The method employed by the author does not allow for measuring the importance of each type analyzed: understandably so, as this was not an objective of her study. Nevertheless, despite these shortcomings, the study provides an interesting approach to the life of French Jewry today.

Doris Bensimon
Université de Caen

Eli Shaltiel (ed.), *Yehudim bi-tnu'ot mahapkhaniot.* Jerusalem: Merkaz Zalman Shazar, 1982.

Just before the end of the First World War, Rosa Luxemburg wrote to a friend that, with all the suffering in the world, "I have no room to spare in my heart for the ghetto, and I feel everywhere at home in the great world wherever there are clouds, birds, and the tears of men." This sensitive woman, a revolutionary to the very marrow of her bones, wholly attuned to the newest developments in Marxist theory, was Jewish by birth, Russian-Polish by education, and found her field of revolutionary activity in Germany.

In the volume of essays under review, I. Getzler compares Rosa Luxemburg to Julius Martov—both "Jewish internationalists" well known for their firm denial of the sources of their identity. This, indeed, is the central problem dealt with in this book: the way in which Jews wrestled with the tragic dilemma they faced when they were drawn to revolutionary activity in movements produced by other nations. This dilemma was—and remains—the choice between universalism and particularism, or, to use a different terminology, between internationalism and nationalism. The question is, is this a "tragic dilemma"?

This is a weighty problem, and one that has affected not only revolutionaries. One might have wished that some definition of the basic concepts involved in the discussion were offered to the reader at the outset. I have in mind such expressions as "revolutionary movement," "radicalism," "intellectual," perhaps even "Jew." There is, to be sure, an attempt to explain the selection of personalities dealt with in the volume, but it did not entirely convince this writer. Other than this discussion of the question of selection, there is no further attempt to establish general conceptual parameters for what follows. There is by now a broad sociological literature on the role of the intellectual in radical movements, and thousands of historical studies of the involvement of Jews (all of them intellectuals?) in the development of ideologies, socialist and Marxist in particular, to which this book is (unjustifiably) limited. None of this seems to be reflected here.

The main point I wish to pose is, however, this: Can one force one hundred years of national and social revolution (from Aaron Liberman, in Jonathan Frankel's excellent essay which opens the volume, to Harold Laski, in Hedva Ben-Israel-Kidron's innovative study), years which saw the rise of so many radical movements, into one mold? Can it really be maintained that the single underlying factor in the mutual attraction between socialism and Jewish intellectuals was the Jewish emergence from the ghetto?

The editor states: "In essence, every one of the branches of radical Jewish thought was marked by a burning messianic faith. . . . It is likely that many Jews who served the socialist cause were drawn toward an extremism that bordered on the pathological." Only Jews? And were there so many?

Have the well-known theories of the late Jacob Talmon been subjected to rigorous concrete study in a variety of historical and geographical contexts? It seems to me that there is a world of difference between such Jews as Luxemburg and Trotsky on the one hand and

Lassalle, Landauer, and Bauer on the other; and the difference does not necessarily lie in their Jewish background. Is it possible, for example, that the process of polarization in the late Tsarist empire led to a "pathological" radicalization among the revolutionary intelligentsia—Jews included—searching for a way out?

I agree with Getzler that socialist internationalism does not of itself lead Jews dedicated to the cause of world revolution to self-hatred. This does not invalidate the statement at the end of S. Naaman's essay on Lassalle: "Not to be a 'good German,' a 'good Jew,' a 'good cosmopolitan'—not, in fact, to be 'good' anything (i.e., acceptable, normal)—this is what it means to be a Jewish radical. It is no wonder that the others hated them even while they admired them."

The editor asks in surprise why such a man as Gustav Landauer, "a born (?) anarchist, and a man of strict moral principle" should become a "revolutionary personality." (I might note that it is a pity that Charles Bloch did not address the issue of Landauer's Jewishness, the influence of Buber on him, etc., which ought to have been a major question in this book. The same is true of the essay on Otto Bauer, and several others.) On the contrary: the intellectual struggles of these people on their road to radicalization attest to their honor and sensitivity. The question of what it means to be a Jew, in relation to the question of what it is to be a human being, is not at all idle "speculation" of those with nothing else on their minds. It is well to point out that the lives of Syrkin and Borokhov (see M. Mintz's fascinating essay) demonstrate how some of those who sought to unite nationalism with socialism were able to arrive at a social radicalism tempered by autoemancipation (in the Jewish-national or Zionist sense).

Aaron Liberman was respected precisely because of his attempts to derive those social-radical elements from Jewish tradition that seemed to fit with populist socialism. Frankel, in his essay, describes how his revolutionary activity ("universalism"), side by side with his loyalty to the oppressed of his own "particular" people, led him to publish a socialist periodical in Hebrew.

As indicated, the topic dealt with in this volume is not a new one. Much has been written on "Jews in the revolution." There are a number of well-known theories that ought to be tested in the light of specific studies. These include the theory of the "Judeophobia" of the founders of socialism (see the work of E. Silberner and, to a degree, that of R. Wistrich); the theory of "self-hatred" as a common characteristic of Jewish intellectuals trying to escape the negative image of the Jew projected by all the anti-capitalist movements; the view of A. Liebman *(The Jews and the Left)* that the Jews were pushed to the political Left by their encounter with capitalism—a Weberian analysis that merges the ethnic factor with the socioeconomic one, and which argues for an inherent Jewish predilection for socialism. I would place in this group, as well, the tendency to treat the problem of Jewish radicals as one of a "tragic choice" between national liberation and socialist liberation—as if the condition of the Jews is not bound up with the nature of the particular regimes under which they live, and as if non-Jewish socialists were not branded as traitors.

As for the idea of the revolutionary as a "non-Jewish Jew" (Deutscher), the connection between the Jewish origin and the radicalism of the individual in question has never been clear to me. Nor has a satisfactory explanation been offered, in the context of the discussion on "revolutionism" (which itself is impossible to measure), of the presence of many outstanding Jews in the moderate socialist camp: the Austro-Marxism of Adler and Bauer, Leon Blum, Jewish "socialist-constructivism" in Israel. Partly, this may be because of the paucity of studies on those individuals who looked for, and sometimes found, a synthesis between universalism and particularism—not in theory, for this does not seem possible, but in history, i.e., in the experience of putting theory into practice.

This dilemma is succinctly captured in the words of one who also struggled with this problem, Y. H. Brenner: "Yes, Karl [Marx] is holy and his torah is holy, but what of Mendele Moykher Sforim?"

AVRAHAM YASSOUR
University of Haifa

Akiva Ernst Simon, *Ha-im'od yehudim anahnu?* Tel Aviv: 1982.

Akiva Ernst Simon—philosopher, scholar, educator—is the representative par excellence of Jewish-religious humanism, as is evident throughout this collection of essays. The work focuses on the problems of Jewish education in the State of Israel. Most of the essays were written following the establishment of the state, and their relevance seems greater today than ever before.

The essay "Goethe and Religious Humanism," which confronts the eminent artist's conception of the world, examines the essence of religious humanism in general. Man is man in that he was created in God's image; his humanity is anchored in the transcendental sphere. Here the author cites the precept in *Yoma:* he who harms his fellow man sins against God. Today, too, man's religious trial lies in the struggle against idolatry which, in our times, takes the form of the deification of relative values such as those embodied in the nation, homeland, state, and so forth. The moral test of humanism lies in our ability to "penetrate the arena with the spirit of ethics to the maximum possible degree," an "almost unbearably difficult" task in view of the need to contest almost constantly superior forces in the short range. This contest is fundamentally the product of a religious decision, "whether to worship God and be a free man, or [to be] free of God and worship man."

Simon defines the principles of Jewish religious humanism: Consistent with the statement in *Sanhedrin,* "Man was created in the image; the value of his life is as the value of an entire world; each man is equal in worth to every other, and all resemble the one and only heavenly authority but differ from one another in their private being. Accordingly every man is responsible for the entire Creation."

The practical implication of these principles is: "Firstly, to recognize the right of every individual to self-determination; secondly, to acknowledge the principle that one must not do harm to an individual's life, honor or freedom (except in cases defined in law, consistent with the moral code, and only then); and thirdly, to treat with utter tolerance . . . views and methods at variance with our own, be they of individuals or groups. . . ."

The significance of Jewish humanism in the reality of the State of Israel is dealt with in the lengthy essay, "Are We Still Jews?" which gives the book its title. The article begins with an analysis of the problematics inherent in the major streams of contemporary Jewry. Traditional Judaism, the Judaism of the Halakhah, in principle encompasses all areas of life and leaves its mark on them. But the secularization process has expropriated various areas of utmost importance—in society, government, and culture—from its jurisdiction. Liberal Judaism takes exception both to the all-embracing claim of the all-embracing religion, and to the "displacement of religion even from the private sphere in the wake of its failure in the public sphere"; but it has not been able to overcome its theological weaknesses. Many saw a solution in Zionism which, from the start, combined religious and secular motives, calling on the individual to fulfill the *mitzvot* of self-realization in his personal life. However, the seed of practical messianism, embedded in Zionism, found expression in two ostensibly contradictory, though in fact complementary, trends; and both are problematic. The "secular" trend ran into the danger of elevating the nation to the place of God, substituting a relative value for an absolute one. The essentially "religious" trend interpreted the principle of sanctifying the people of Israel and the land of Israel not as an ultimate purpose but as an immanent reality, thus blurring the boundaries between the sacred and the secular, between justice and evil.

Simon does not make light of the authentic force of these trends. Like Franz Rosenzweig, he is aware of how profound the schism is, splitting every generation of Jewry in two: those whose belief and longing are so great that, over and over again, they are liable to be misled and disappointed, until the day when their faith will prove to be true; and those whose hope is so great that they are strong enough neither to forestall the future nor see a present devoid of redemption as the dawn of redemption. Fully sympathetic to the motives of the "believers," Simon firmly identifies the place of Jewish humanism with the "hopers." "To drain the concept of the messianic era of its moral content and religious mission, and to identify it exclusively with political achievement, is to court the gravest of dangers which threaten all human enterprise: the stilling of the conscience by imbuing human deeds with an almost divine glory."

In "Az itam," Simon speaks of a "second innocence," a rare level of inner wholeness and harmony, usually reached only after a tortuous journey. He who has achieved this second innocence lives without illusions, and remains strong by force of his hope. He recognizes the "messianic islands in the unredeemed sea of time," but "renounces the security of seclusion and enters the arena of life, including the political arena. . . . [H]e refuses to despair of man as such. . . . he will never exchange his critical messianism and sceptical optimism for a condemnation of the present without a vision of the future, or for a total scepticism devoid of hope." Even in his old age, perhaps then even more than ever, he will adhere to a "policy of love."

Those who have been privileged to know Simon will find in these lines, without, perhaps, the author's intent, a summation of the way of his life.

ARYEH SIMON
Tel-Aviv

Shmuel Stampler (ed.), *Ha-yishuv ba'et ha-hadashah. Ẓiyunei derekh be-terem medinah.* Tel-Aviv: Israel Defense Ministry, 1983. 330 pp.

The publications section of the Ministry of Defense has issued a collection of articles which have appeared, in recent years, in the IDF officers' monthly, *Skirah hodshit.* The book consists of twenty-six articles, written in a popular style, focusing on Jewish settlement in Palestine prior to the establishment of the State of Israel. Eighteen of the articles deal with the history of Palestine before 1918.

Some of the foremost scholars of the history of the modern Jewish *yishuv* in Palestine contributed to the collection. The result is professional and often interesting. There are excellent articles by I. Bartal, E. Shaltiel, S. Laskov, I. Kolatt, A. Shapira, I. Shavit, Y. Bauer, Z. Ganin, and others. Unfortunately, the anthology as such is conceptually limited and superficial, and contributes nothing remarkably new. It would have been preferable for it not to have been published in its present form.

The publication of books on the history of the *yishuv* is currently in vogue—which seems to have prompted those responsible for producing this collection. It joins a long list of other, similarly motivated books. Like them, it is marked by a narrow Palestinocentric approach which ignores the relationship between the history of the Jewish people outside Palestine and the development of the Jewish *yishuv* here, presenting this development as an independent phenomenon which sprouted and grew of itself, as it were. Indeed, three of the articles do attempt to deviate from this conception—those on Herzl (Shaltiel, Eilam) and on the Balfour Declaration (Shapira)—but they are no more than a drop in the bucket in a collection of this size.

Another and perhaps more blatant shortcoming is the notable absence of articles on the internal dissension which plagued the modern *yishuv* from its very inception. One gets the impression that "the state in the making," to use the editor's phrase, developed without any internal dilemmas. Where conflict is described, it involves friction with external forces: the Turks, the British, and (chiefly) the Arabs. The reader is apt to conclude that, internally, from the First Aliyah on, the Jewish *yishuv* in Palestine sailed on calm waters, which was hardly the case. Mention is made of the *Nili* affair (J. Nedava), but what of the struggles between Right and Left in Palestinian society and politics? What of the conflicts *within* the Right and the Left? What of the rift between the secular and the religious sectors on the question of religion and state? Can a history of the "state in the making" contain no articles on the contest for control of the centers of social, economic and military power—all foci of considerable strife?

A more difficult problem pertaining to the collection concerns the attempt to blur the hegemony of the Labour Party during the thirties and forties. The tendency to rewrite the history of the *yishuv* in the light of changes in Israeli politics since 1977 is obvious in the choice of subject matter made by the editors. Can "milestones in pre-statehood" be described without the Histadrut or the predominance of the Labour movement and its leaders? In a volume which purports to present "milestones," we find the stories of Alexander Zeid, Joseph Trumpeldor, Joseph Lishansky, Itzhak Vilkansky, and other more or less marginal figures in the *yishuv*'s history, but none of such figures as Ben-Gurion, Katznelson, and Tabenkin, or Ben-Zvi, Shazar, and Arlozorov. The editor apparently saw no purpose in presenting these "marginal" figures in the *yishuv*'s history to the young officers of the IDF.

The division of the subject matter provides still more insight into the editor's approach. Sixteen articles deal with the period from 1881 to 1971; whereas the following years, the twenties, thirties and forties—apparently less important as "milestones in pre-statehood"—are awarded only six.

The often excellent articles in this volume do not conform to a single historiographic conception, historiosophic discipline, or political line. And yet the lacunae mentioned above, resulting from an idiosyncratic selection, place the book within an all-too-clear political conception, deriving from Israeli politics of the late 1970s and the early 1980s. The result is a collection which does no honor to its editors, and even less to Zionist historiograpy.

Yossi Goldstein
Hebrew University

Michael Sutton, *Nationalism, Positivism and Catholicism: The Politics of Charles Maurras and French Catholics, 1890–1914*. Cambridge: Cambridge University Press, 1982. viii + 334 pp.

This close study of Charles Maurras' intellectual debt to Auguste Comte is not as dauntingly specialized as might first appear. Exploring all the ramifications of Maurras' early Positivism turns out to be quite illuminating, for Maurras' thought was always more *a priori* than occasional, and his basic principles were frozen at an early age.

Auguste Comte might seem an odd *maître à penser* for Maurras. The architect of the "system of positive philosophy" is often thought of as the last of the *philosophes,* with his vision of human progress through three stages—theological, metaphysical, and positive—culminating in a scientifically based good society. Maurras, by contrast, devoted his life to rooting the legacy of 1789 out of French life. Nevertheless, the teenage Maurras, prey to twin crises of sudden deafness and loss of faith, experienced some kind of revelation upon reading Comte. In typically selective and arbitrary fashion, Maurras seized upon one aspect of Comte's system: the "subjective synthesis," the subordination of the individual to Humanity, of reason to community feeling. Then Maurras substituted the Nation for Comte's Humanity. Maurras had been badly frightened by the abyss opened up by the exercise of his own critical intelligence, and he thought he found in Comte a justification for discipline as efficacious for atheists as the Catholic justification was for believers. Settled in Paris as a journalist as the Dreyfus Affair opened, Maurras called upon Catholics to join Positivists in defense against corrosive individualism.

Dr. Sutton shows that Maurras (contrary to a widespread impression) was no traditionalist. His monarchism and Catholicism were instrumental, not matters of conviction. The anarchic effects of unfettered reason were his enemy. From the beginning Maurras traced this enemy to Protestantism and its ancestor, "Hebrew thought and all that it carried of dreams of justice, beatitude, equality, and inner revolt" (as he wrote in 1899). Maurras' antisemitism was closer to Renan's accusation that the Jews were marked by "unbridled feelings of selfhood" and to the secular antisemitism of the nineteenth century French Left than to either the traditional Catholic or modern racial forms; but it was an integral element of his world view from the start.

Catholics were far from homogeneous in their response to Maurras' appeal for an alliance with Positivists. The Jesuit journal *Etudes* found him a useful ally against Republic anticlericalism, though Dr. Sutton belives that Hannah Arendt oversimplified in finding all French Jesuits Maurrasian. In the opposite camp were influential modernists, such as Maurice Blondel and Lucien Laberthonnière, who saw clearly that Maurras' primacy of the community subordinated morality to political expediency. Dr. Sutton's learned exploration of these anti-Maurrasian Catholic intellectuals, the second half of the book, shows that even at the height of the Separation Crisis in 1905 and in the face of official disapproval, the French Church still carried the seeds of its later development toward political pluralism and acceptance of Separation.

Dr. Sutton tells us more about Maurras the intellectual than about *Action française* the movement. Though his attention to contemporary philosophy reminds one of Ernst Nolte, Sutton is unwilling to make easy correlations between *Action française* and fascism. His most important point about the movement is to show that it was Maurras' deliberate courting of Catholic opinion during the Separation Crisis of 1905 that turned *Action française* into a mass organization prepared for street violence. But the mass of new followers did not resemble Maurras. They were not atheist, nor did they share Maurras' thirst for philosophical certainty. They did not care that Maurras had discovered a Comtean alternative for Catholic order. As for Maurras himself, he muted his 1898–99 statements about the "frenzy" of Christ, the evils of monotheism, and the virtue of Catholicism's suppression of Judeo-Christian individualism that had upset Blondel and Laberthonnière. But Dr. Sutton leaves unresolved the "enigma" (p. 238) of whether Maurras ever personally found his way back to the faith of his childhood.

ROBERT O. PAXTON
Columbia University

Yitskhok (Antek) Tsukerman, *Kapitlen fun izovn,* Beit Lohamei hagettaot/Hakibbutz Hameuhad, 1982 (actual date of issue: 1983).

A year after his death on June 17, 1981, the colleagues and comrades of Yitskhok Tsukerman (Hebrew: Yitschak Tsukerman; in English, in the *Encyclopaedia Judaica* for example, Itzhak Cukierman) published a Hebrew translation of memoirs found among his papers. A year after the appearance of *Perakim min haizavon,* which was well received by the Israeli public, its publishers have issued the Yiddish original.

Tsukerman did not prepare his memoirs for publication and they represent in effect seven loosely connected chapters which span a period of three years. Although they did not benefit from final editing by the author, his memoirs nonetheless record their author's voice, thereby lending a measure of unity to the work.

Tsukerman's memoirs move from a frozen January day in 1940 in Lwów to the volcanic spring day of April 19, 1943, when the Warsaw Ghetto revolted. In Lwów in 1940 a tiny group of young Jews, the twenty-five-year-old author among them, warmed themselves with a toast to "that which they were," which was nothing less than the leadership of the chalutz underground in the western Ukraine and western Belorussia, then under Soviet rule. Throughout these memoirs one is awed, as is the author himself, by the extreme youth of those charged by their tragic times to execute dangerous missions, often at the cost of their lives. Tsukerman tersely and unselfconsciously describes several such missions which he himself undertook.

From under the shadow of the Soviet NKVD Antek stole across the border into Nazi-occupied Poland to carry out youth movement work in the Warsaw Ghetto. He is always the exemplary youth movement leader, that special kind of generalist who is ready at all times to assume whatever task is thrust upon him. In Soviet Poland, the Hechalutz aim had been to keep open the lifelines to the Land of Israel and to keep alive the spirit of Zionism in the face of a seductive assimilationism. In the Warsaw Ghetto, energies were mustered to rebuild a shattered movement and give purpose to thousands of dislocated youth.

Under the cover of *Di yidishe sotsyale aleynhilf,* the relief organization sanctioned by the Judenrat in the Warsaw Ghetto, and operating out of its soup kitchen at Dzielne 13, first Hechalutz and later other youth movements organized kibbutz groups and resumed educational work. Dzielne 13 served as a nerve center for all of Nazi-occupied Poland. From its crowded and always busy rooms went forth the emissaries who reorganized youth movement work in the provinces and established farm communes. Under the very noses of the Germans and their Jewish lackeys, the socialist-Zionist youth movements worked at fever pitch. Inevitably, the Jewish social self-help administration clashed with the Judenrat. By 1943 it was crystal clear to the leaders of the Jewish Fighting Organization that internal enemies would have to be destroyed before the German rulers could be confronted.

Tlomcka 5, headquarters of the Jewish Social Self-Help Organization, a beehive of activity, is described in a chapter rich in portraits of communal leaders. While the acutely political author cannot describe anyone without first "placing" him ideologically, he does not draw his portraits with a narrowly partisan eye. Yitskhok Giterman, the director of the Joint Distribution Committee in the Warsaw Ghetto, emerges as a symbol of communal unity against the dangers of rabid partisanship. We are reminded in this book that the Bund maintained its own archives and the Revisionists their own fighting organization in the Warsaw Ghetto. So encrusted were ideological blinders that the Bund took a "principled" stand against the chalutz program of organizing farm communes. These communes proved to be bulwarks against despair for all the chalutz movements. The Bundists argued that by volunteering for farm labor under the German regime, the chalutzim were entering into competition with the Polish peasants, forcing them out of their position and placing them in danger of deportation to Germany.

Tsukerman's memoirs become intensely personal when he first learns of the systematic murders in the Wilno Ghetto. Two non-Jewish friends of the movement traveled to Wilno and returned with news of the methodical destruction of its Jewish population. The author writes: "Thousands of people have already been sent out in an unknown direction. In the Ghetto there are rumors that the Jews are being murdered in Ponar, seven kilometers from Wilno, where the train descends into a tunnel and high on the mountain tall trees rustle. I know the area. I can see it with my eyes closed. I used to spend my summers there, clambering up the mountain, climbing trees, gathering nuts. My Wilno is being murdered there. I can see the city, its streets, its people, familiar faces, friends, my parents, my sister—in the final desolate moments of their agony."

Attempts to convince the head of the Ostrowiec Judenrat of the truth of the genocidal reports from Wilno met with failure. In Ostrowiec, the Nazi death machine had not yet begun to operate and its Jewish functionaries wilfully refused to see the cruel truth before their eyes. Courageous young movement women, some still in their teens, served as couriers between the Warsaw Ghetto and Wilno. The epic of their bravery deserves to be better known. In the Warsaw Ghetto the Wilno news was not dismissed as exaggerated and the chalutz leadership began to prepare for armed struggle. Antek was delegated to enlist aid on the "Aryan" side of the Ghetto wall and his memoirs end with the perfidy of the London-led Polish underground and the hastily prepared revolt. The Warsaw Ghetto struck at the Germans with miserably inadequate arms and fortifications and, Antek notes, with an overly fatalistic spirit which ignored the possibilities of survival.

The story of the Warsaw Ghetto has been told often and has been written about and analyzed from a number of perspectives. Because of his open and unassuming character and the central position which he occupied in the events he describes, Antek's account of the Warsaw Ghetto Uprising and its background carries the force of truth. We do not doubt that the events described happened as described. We are moved not because the writer has organized his materials with great effect, not because of his skill in shaping sentences or choosing words, but because of the powerful documentary impact of the work.

LEONARD PRAGER
University of Haifa

Melvin I. Urofsky, *A Voice That Spoke for Justice: The Life and Times of Stephen S. Wise.* Albany: State University of New York Press, 1982. 439 pp.

In his biography, Urofsky focuses on Wise's part in events and developments relating to American politics, U.S. Jewry, and the Jewish people during the first half of this century. The author portrays Wise as a champion of justice for his people, as well as for other victims of discrimination in the United States: workers, Blacks and other minorities. He was a Zionist from his early youth, but his self-identification as an American did not leave room for contemplating immigration to Palestine. Wise agreed wholeheartedly with Louis Brandeis's view that: "To be good Americans we must be good Jews, to be good Jews we must become Zionists."

This view informed his activities as rabbi, Zionist leader, and public activist in New York and throughout the United States. It is not necessary to accept Urofsky's view of Wise as one of the "giants" of American Jewry to become absorbed by the life story of a man who in his time stirred considerable controversy. The base of his public activity was the Free Synagogue in New York which he founded and where he served as rabbi for decades. Grandson of a Hungarian Orthodox rabbi and son of one of the founders of the Jewish Theological Seminary in New York who was a Conservative rabbi all his life, Wise's religious views diverged considerably from those of his fathers. Urofsky emphasizes that Stephen Wise transformed the rabbi's sermon into the focus of ritual. Himself a brilliant preacher, perhaps the greatest of his time, he drew large crowds, including non-Jews, to each of his sermons.

He founded the Free Synagogue in 1907 following his refusal to serve as rabbi in the prestigious Temple Emanuel. He was unwilling to allow the board of trustees to censor his sermons. At that time, the Temple Emanuel board was chaired by Louis Marshall and the dispute between those two figures was but the first of many to follow in the public life of American Jewry. Wise's insistence on freedom to express his views on any political or social issue remained firm throughout his career. Even in Portland, Oregon, where he served as rabbi of Temple Beth Israel in the years 1900–1906, the community leaders who had not always been pleased with his sermons, surrendered to the young and talented rabbi and allowed him to express controversial opinions from the pulpit.

Social ideals played an important role in Wise's activity in the Free Synagogue. He held Sabbath services for his New York congregation on Friday evenings and Sunday mornings only. He preferred reading from the Prophets rather than from the Torah since the teachings of the Prophets accorded better with his social views. From Urofsky's book we learn that Wise blessed his congregation in Hebrew for the first time in his last sermon, shortly before his death. His open clash with American Jewish Orthodoxy came in 1925, following his sermon on "A Jew's View of Jesus." The Orthodox rabbis condemned this sermon as heretical and demanded Wise's dismissal as head of the United Palestine Appeal. Their demand, however, was rejected by the Appeal's board.

Yet Wise was equally ill at ease in the Reform movement to which he belonged. Already at the beginning of his career, his Reform colleagues aroused his ire for not backing him in his dispute with the board of Temple Emanuel. Another factor contributing to his estrangement from the Reform movement was its opposition to Zionism, which remained in force through the middle 1930s. Wise sought to overcome the anti-Zionist influence, but the undisputed dominance of anti-Zionists over Hebrew Union College in Cincinnati led him to found an independent rabbinical seminary, the Jewish Institute of Religion, in New York in 1920. Urofsky relates the unsuccessful attempts to heal the rift between Cincinnati and the JIR, especially in the years 1923–1929. Only in 1948, during Nelson Glueck's term as president of HUC, was the unification of the two seminaries accomplished.

During the turbulent 1940s, Wise fought against the anti-Zionist American Council for Judaism. This biography gives one the impression that Wise criticized the Reform anti-Zionists from without. Urofsky does not mention the conflict within the Central Conference of American Rabbis in 1942, concerning the resolution in favor of the establishment of a Jewish army (a resolution which led to the formation of the American Council for Judaism); nor does he deal with the conflict within the UAHC stimulated by the extreme anti-Zionist steps undertaken by Temple Beth Israel in Houston, Texas. Similarly, the author fails to deal with Wise's part in the efforts undertaken to prevent the withdrawal of the Reform movement from the American Jewish Conference in 1943.

His activities were not, of course, confined to Jewish struggles. Woodrow Wilson's reform program spurred Wise to dissociate himself from the Republican Party and to lend his support to Wilson's Democrats; he remained loyal to the Democratic Party until his death. In the 1920s he took part in the presidential campaigns, working against Harding and Coolidge and in favor of Al Smith, as well as in Franklin D. Roosevelt's race for the governorship of New York State. Afterwards, he became a staunch supporter of Roosevelt, whom he came to revere as the hero of the New Deal. Here Urofsky portrays Stephen Wise as a deeply committed American who was prepared to fight for his views.

It is doubtful whether his Zionist activity took precedence over his other numerous preoccupations. He was unwilling, for example, to mobilize the Jewish vote or Jewish public opinion to further Zionist goals. Wise was never willing to cause embarrassment of any kind to U.S. presidents, even if such action would benefit Zionist strategies. Thus in 1917 he refrained from exerting pressure on Wilson to support the Zionist program, since the United States was not then in a state of war with Turkey. This approach continued to inform Wise's activity during Roosevelt's term as president. After World War II he vigorously opposed Silver's demands to exert pressure on the Administration to suspend granting loans to Britain (at the time, pursuing an unmistakably anti-Zionist policy).

Urofsky's assertion that during his visit to London in 1936 Wise succeeded in securing a postponement of the publication of the White Paper should be treated with due caution. During his term as president of the ZOA, in 1937–1938, he indeed prevailed upon Roosevelt to appeal to the British Government and to express his "hope" that immigration to Palestine would not be impaired. It seems, however, that Wise did not distinguish between the lip service the American president paid to the Zionist cause and the substance of his Middle East policy.

Urofsky's book also deals with the helplessness of the American Zionist movement following the publication of the White Paper in 1939. Wise's fear of appearing to be disloyal to the United States seems to have been an important factor in his opposition to Jabotinsky's proposal to establish a Jewish volunteer army immediately after the outbreak of the war in 1939. Before Pearl Harbor, his concern was that the establishment of such Jewish units would undermine the neutrality of the United States and create the impression that American Jews constituted an ethnic group with particularistic political interests. He focused his energy on the struggle against the group of Revisionists in the United States led by Peter Bergson (Hillel Kook) on one hand, and against the American Council for Judaism, on the other. He flinched from a head-on confrontation with the Administration. According to Urofsky, Wise also accepted the demand of the president of the American Jewish Committee that the American Jewish Conference to be convened later that year not discuss the subject of Palestine (p. 338). Although Wise was willing to accept this arrangement, neither the Zionist Emergency Committee nor ZOA concurred with his position. Wise, who in 1929 had been considered a maximalist in the Zionist movement, switched to the minimalist camp in 1943. But by then his influence in the Zionist movement was waning.

Like most other accounts dealing with this subject, Urofsky's treatment of developments within American Jewry prior to the Conference in summer 1943, reflects a failure to consult the extensive documentation in the Central Zionist Archives in Jerusalem, as well as other sources. Thus the author erroneously claims that it was only during the Conference that Silver managed, with his impressive speech, to sway the delegates and, consequently, to secure an almost unanimous vote in favor of the proposal to establish a Jewish Commonwealth in Palestine. Similarly, the author's claim that Wise played a central role in stopping the Anglo-American anti-Zionist statement planned for the summer of 1943 is not sufficiently substantiated. Well-documented studies published in the last few years indicate that Wise's role in the affair was not decisive.

Despite his diminished influence, Wise's appearance before the Anglo-American Commission of Inquiry was most impressive. Urofsky provides (p. 351) a gripping account of Wise's testimony, which so eloquently conveyed the anguish of the Jewish people. Wise called upon the deeply impressed Committee members to recommend establishment of Jewish and Arab states in Palestine (a proposal not taken up by the Committee, as it will be recalled).

The controversy surrounding Wise's role in the efforts to rescue Jews during the Holocaust receives thorough discussion here. To put it briefly, his attempts to persuade the Roosevelt Administration to relax immigration restrictions came to naught. Although Breckenridge Long, one of the State Department's most vociferous opponents of Jewish refugee immigration, complained of the "rabbi from New York" stirring up trouble, Wise, in fact, resigned himself to Roosevelt's policy and did not issue a call to the American Jewish community to fight the Administration's immigration policy openly. It was not Wise, but Secretary of the Treasury Henry Morgenthau, Jr., who brought about the establishment of the War Refugee Board in 1944. Urofsky, however, attempts to prove that Wise did all he could under the circumstances.

The fact remains that Wise, acting upon Sumner Wells's request, delayed for a month the publication of information about the implementation of the Nazi "final solution." Urofsky argues that Wise and the American Jews were ultimately powerless to influence Administration policy, which was summed up by the oft-repeated contention that only victory in the war would solve the problem of Jews in Europe. It should be borne in mind, however, that within the Zionist movement in the United States there were people who rejected this approach, notably Haim Greenberg. Wise failed to criticize publicly the "do-nothing" policy of his President, as far as rescue was concerned.

A few mistakes have crept into this book which can be easily corrected in future editions. The Anglo-American Commission of Inquiry did not, as is known, recommend partition of Palestine into two states (p. 351). The account of the American Jewish Conference, as noted above, is incomplete. It implies that Wise and his friends planned the Conference in 1941 and that from 1941 till January 1943—when the Jewish organizations convened in Pittsburgh—no further developments occurred (p. 332). In fact, contacts related to preparing the Conference were first initiated in the fall of 1942, once it had become clear that talks with the American Jewish Committee had yielded no results. Although as early as May 25, 1941, at the conference at the San Regis Hotel in New York (in which Weizmann participated), the subject of collaboration between Zionists and groups like B'nai B'rith had been discussed, the possibility of convening a broader conference was not raised there. There are, as well, quite a few errors in German quotations.

The author ends his book with a statement: "Wise was the last of a generation of titans in American Jewish life." The center of gravity in the life of American Jews had shifted, according to Urofsky, from charismatic leaders toward "the organizational manager." This statement may adequately sum up the situation *today;* it is doubtful whether it could be accurately applied to the situation at the end of the 1940s. Urofsky's list of giants includes Marshall, Brandeis, and Wise. Is it an accident that he has omitted from this list the name of Abba Hillel Silver, leader of American Jewry during the struggle for the establishment of the State of Israel?

MENAHEM KAUFMAN
Hebrew University

Bernard J. Weiss (ed.), *American Education and the European Immigrant: 1840–1940*. Urbana: University of Illinois Press, 1982. 217 pp. + index.

The subject of this collection of essays ably edited by Bernard J. Weiss—American education and the European immigrant—has provoked controversy among historians of education and immigration. Especially in the past decade, scholars have questioned accepted interpretations of the way in which the public schools responded to the task of educating the millions of immigrants who came to the United States in the years after 1840. These revisionist historians have emphasized the repressive character of public schooling, the concern of reformers for social control over working class immigrants and their children, and the centrality of Americanization to the public school curriculum. American educators, they contend, were committed to turning "little savages" into "little citizens" irrespective of the human costs, including the disruption of immigrant family life and the dismantling of immigrant cultures. At the heart of this critique is an attack on the "great school legend" which pictured the schools as vehicles of upward social mobility, offering immigrants and their children a chance to escape poverty and the stigma of foreignness. As Weiss indicates in his excellent introduction, the dispute among historians over the impact of American education on the European immigrants arose in response to the problems the public schools encountered in the 1960s. Provoked by the schools' failure to educate the Hispanic immigrants and Black children, that is, to provide them with a secure ladder of social mobility out of the slums, historians reexamined earlier decades when history appeared to vindicate the claim of the public school to Americanize immigrants and guide them into the comfortable precincts of the white-collar middle class. The best of the essays in this volume address the issues raised by revisionist historians while contributing new knowledge to a field where much primary research remains to be done.

John McClymer's analysis of the Americanization movement and the education of the foreign-born adult, 1914–25, studies the pressures for cultural conformity blossoming in the heated atmosphere of World War I. His insight into the politicization of American culture is sustained by his research into the curricula and textbooks promoted by the government Americanizers. If Americanism, especially the 100-percent variety, implied a total way of life then immigrants would have to learn not merely how to read and speak English to become citizens but how to brush their teeth, clean their fingernails, and air out their bedding. These things were not trivial in an environment that proclaimed cultural diversity a national crisis. McClymer moves deftly from a discussion of the broad meaning of the Americanization movement to a cogent discussion of its strengths and an assessment of its success in reaching immigrant adults. His conclusions, that the movement inadvertently strengthened ethnicity in the United States while redefining political loyalty to include conformity to an American way of life embedded in white, Protestant, middle-class cultural ideals, point to the ironies that revisionist history often uncovers. Similarly, Victor Greene's incisive account of several ethnic confrontations with state universities in the midwest during the nineteenth century reveals the political character of ethnic studies—in this case Scandanavian and Bohemian—and the limits of symbolic success. Greene suggests that the politicization of ethnic culture may have preceded similar trends among American educators, though he, too, sees the irony of immigrant intellectuals rejecting communal schools in favor of American universities as the best means of educating the second generation.

Jewish immigrants, as the one group who appeared to fulfill the promises of the "great school legend," are well represented in the book by two essays. Leonard Dinnerstein's synthetic treatment of the theme of education in the advancement of American Jews restates the conventional interpretation of Jewish social mobility in the United States. Selma Berrol modifies this view by showing through an analysis of school attendance and advancement records that immigrant Jews moved up the economic ladder through skilled trades and petty commerce. The subsequent success of the second generation derived from their use of the schools to enter white collar and professional jobs. Berrol also credits the New York City economy rather than the schools with acculturating immigrants. Nonetheless, she is much less harsh on the reformers than most revisionists.

Berrol's nuanced account points to the possibility of rising above the battle of the revisionists. The encounter of immigrants with American education did not occur only in the classroom as Oscar Handlin points out in the opening essay. By developing sensitivity to the multiple dimensions of education, the historian can avoid the pitfalls of succumbing to the powerful ideological vision of harmony embraced by American educators and recognize the ever-present gap between intention and implementation produced by the context of American society itself. This rewarding anthology might have been appropriately subtitled: "unexpected ironies."

Deborah Dash Moore
Vassar College

Yosef Hayim Yerushalmi, *"Zakhor," Jewish History and Jewish Memory.* Seattle: University of Washington Press, 1982. 192 pp.

This concise volume deals with a question which has perplexed all Jewish historians: the inordinate discrepancy between the historical consciousness essential to the Jewish religion and clearly evident in both the source literature and Jewish ritual, and the almost total absence of Jewish historiographical literature from the time of Josephus until the start of the nineteenth century. For contemporary historians, this problem is primarily one of sources. However, beyond this consideration, it challenges historical thinking: how does one explain the change in attitude of Jewish scholars who came after Ezra and Nehemia to historiographic literature? What is the meaning of this "apathy" toward actual historical events? And how does one reconcile it with the Jewish people's unique sense of history?

The author begins his discussion by suggesting a fruitful distinction which remains the chief message of his book: a people's historical memory which is molded by an attitude of veneration toward ancient origins and by rituals marking specific historical instances, and historiographic literature which documents the chronicles of that people, are two separate matters. A ritualistic historical memory consciously orients one on a given historical course which proceeds from certain founding events and follows various signposts towards some destination; this awareness, however, is not dependent on an explicit record of changing historical events. There is thus no contradiction between a people's sense of history as a purposeful continuum in time, and their lack of concern with historiography. The Jewish people prudently preserved their historical consciousness by means of their rites, even when they totally neglected, or belittled, the historical documentation of their experiences.

Nevertheless, even if the *mitzvah* of "zakhor" (remember) can be practiced without a continuous historiographic record, the question still arises as to the significance of the sharp change between the biblical and later periods. Would it not be reasonable to expect that a people conscious of pursuing a historical course would display a constant interest in the historical events which befall them? The various chapters of the book attempt to provide fresh insights into these questions.

The author assumed that by analyzing the few literary works which can be defined as historiography, even if only partially and in fragmentary fashion, he would find an explanation for the waning of interest in this field. In all truth, it must be said that in the end he merely succeeded in reaffirming the book's initial assertion, that is, the little historiography that was written, including the relatively prolific compositions of the sixteenth century, proves that the Jews were not interested in historiography and attached no importance to it. They felt a need to record only the "chain of tradition" of the Oral Law. All other historical documentation was considered frivolous amusement. Only at the beginning of the nineteenth century was historiography assigned a highly respectable status. At this point, however, the author claims, the Jewish people's sense of history began to fade.

In his introduction, the author explains that he had intended to rewrite and broaden the scope of the book, but had reconsidered and decided to publish the shorter version of lectures as it was. This decision is to be regretted. While there are many advantages to brevity, the present question would have benefited from a comprehensive study. If the problem could have been solved by an analysis of the Jewish historiograpic literature composed between the biblical period and the nineteenth century, brevity would have been appropriate; it is difficult, however, to understand why the author imagined that analyzing such a sparse literary form would yield anything more than a conclusion that it was unimportant. It was thus an error to assume that the question of the absence of historiography could be solved within the framework of an absentee historiography. The question should have been raised within the wider context of the culture studied: how does Jewish literature as a whole relate to ancient history and to current history? Only an enquiry which takes into account the Halakhah and the *aggadah,* the philosophical and ethical works, and the *piyutim,* can provide an explanation. Indeed, the author even sensed this. He hints that the writings of the rabbis, the medieval philosophers, and the kabbalists, in principle relate to the history of the Jewish people. If so, he should have first considered the attitude to history in the philosophical works. Secondly, the Halakhah, *aggadah,* and *piyutim* treated actual historical events in their own fashion, and at times even documented them in their own fashion. There is a wealth of historical, indeed historiographical, material in all forms of Jewish literature, and while it is not presented as historiographical discourse, it nevertheless expresses the views of Jewish scholars on the history of their times. An analysis of the attitude to history in the Halakhah, the philosophical works, and the *piyutim,* would therefore have contributed toward solving the problem at hand, and in the same context, the little historiography which is available may have revealed more than came to light in the analysis of this restricted literary form.

A separate problem is the claim that the development of Jewish historiography in the nineteenth century was concomitant with the fading of the Jewish people's historical memory, and that in the formation of their social and political movements during the modern period, ideology had the upper hand, while historiography in fact exerted little influence.

This claim comprises three correct assertions, and is nevertheless astonishing. It is true that history has been the most flourishing of the Jewish academic disciplines since the start of the nineteenth century. It is also true that the ritualistic historical memory has begun to fade from the consciousness of most Jews, who are no longer observant and are susceptible to processes of assimilation, though it would be a vast exaggeration to claim that the memory of central orienting events of Jewish history has totally disappeared from the consciousness of Jews who continue to see themselves as Jews. And finally, it is true that the life of the Jewish people in the present is molded by various ideological movements, and that ideology is not historiography. What is astonishing is that the author makes no attempt to examine the connection between historical research and the ideologies of the predominant movements among contemporary Jewry. To do so, he would have had to look not only at expressly historiographical works, but also at the extensive literature of modern, philosophical and ideological Jewish thought. This examination would have immediately shown the extent to which it views history as a central field of study, and the extent to which it, in turn, influenced historiographical methodology and the interpretation of the significance of historical events within the historiographical framework. In other words: there is a patent, rich and complex connection between the guiding ideologies of the prominent movements in contemporary Jewry and historical research, and these ideologies have an overwhelming sense of history. It is thus no accident that historical research has achieved such an important status in modern Jewish scholarship, even though historical awareness in modern times is obviously of a totally different nature than in the past, and the cultural mechanism which creates this consciousness among the people is not simply traditional ritual, but also a modern social-educational system.

In conclusion: The book *Zakhor* is interesting and well-written, and offers a refreshing and new analysis of the sparse Jewish historiographical literature composed since the biblical period. Particularly interesting in this respect is the chapter devoted to Jewish historiography in the sixteenth century. However, from the point of view of his overall purpose in writing the book, the author was more successful in reformulating the question than in supplying an answer.

Eliezer Schweid
Hebrew University

Victor Zaslavsky and Robert J. Brym, *Soviet Jewish Emigration and Soviet Nationality Policy*. London: Macmillan, 1983. viii + 185 pp.

Here is a new addition to the wave of recent publications devoted to the history-making emigration of over a quarter of a million Jews from the USSR in the past fifteen years. Broad in conception, and solidly based in its scholarly analysis, Zaslavsky and Brym's work stands up well alongside such recent works as Robert O. Freedman's edited collection *Soviet Jewry in the Decisive Decade* (Duke, 1984), and Zvi Gitelman's ground-breaking *Becoming Israelis* (Praeger, 1982).

The authors draw together a mass of published analyses, memoirs by recent emigrants, Zaslavsky's own experiences in the USSR, and interviews with 155 emigrants in Rome. The authors' unique contribution, however, is the casting of their analysis in the perspective of the development of Soviet society and Soviet nationality policy, utilizing John Armstrong's concept of the Jews as a "mobilized Diaspora." By integrating analysis of the exodus movement into the general political and ideological development of the Soviet system, Zaslavsky and Brym supply a much-needed scholarly corrective to the flood of descriptive literature which isolates the emigration phenomenon from its environment and treats it in emotional, rather than analytical, terms. Altogether, the authors' attempt at a dispassionate and judicious weighing of all the relevant elements is one of the attractive elements of this study, even though such weighing does not, in this reviewer's opinion, always succeed.

The presentation of Soviet interpretations of Marxist nationality theory is concise and clear, though the reader may be startled that following a transition from the Leninist period to Stalin, there is a leap to Brezhnev, as though Nikita Khrushchev had never reversed Stalin's extreme Russification policies, had never encouraged the use of national languages and cultures, and had not experimented in emigration by allowing the repatriation of tens of thousands of Poles (and Polish Jews, who were the first wave of post–World War II Soviet-Jewish emigration), while all the time embodying in his personality the Soviet paradox of an awareness that treatment of the Jews is the litmus test of Soviet social development, mixed with the crudest belief in antisemitic stereotypes.

In examining the elements that motivated and precipitated the exodus movement, the authors undertake a painstaking analysis of the relative force and sequence of numerous extrinsic and intrinsic factors. The outcome of their analysis is a refutation of those who give predominance or exclusivity to external precipitants of emigration, such as American pressure, world public opinion and detente agreements. Instead, they point to the domestic factors of political and social development which fostered the decision to permit Jewish, German, and Armenian emigration. While this analysis is well done and valuable, the authors endanger their whole undertaking by this attempt to rigidly separate what was essentially a complex extended chain of linkages and interdependencies. The Zionist core of the exodus movement, encouraged by such domestic phenomena as de-Stalinization and the emergence of the Soviet Democratic Movement constituted itself as a pressure group, and undertook dramatic actions such as press conferences, petitions, and public demonstrations, thereby gaining the sympathy of external groups which amplified the exodus appeal. Emigration thus became a political issue in the United States and Western Europe, and was entered on the agenda of the detente negotiations which were then beginning. The attention of communities and political figures outside the USSR then acted as feedback, strengthening the morale and activity of the exodus movement. In addition to this complex conjunction of factors, the simultaneous impact of the Six-Day War, the end of the post-Stalin thaw, and the growth of detente all played no small part in determining the growth cycles of the emigration.

Similarly, the scope and emphasis of the discussion of motivations for emigration, which show quite clearly that motivations other than national, religious or cultural were predominant among the emigrants, particularly at the end of the 1970s (though almost all those surveyed were individuals who had opted against going to Israel, and thus almost surely not motivated by Zionism), does not accurately reflect the nature of the exodus movement. From its beginning, through to the present, the movement quite literally owes its existence to a handful of dedicated activists for whom Jewish culture and the Land of Israel are fundamental. This small and changing group (though there are a few who have been refuseniks from the end of the 1960s) are the catalyst without which emigration would long ago have ceased to be an issue. However weakened the exodus movement may be by the emigration of the greater part of those who had a solid grounding in Jewish life, and an organic connection to a living Jewish community, the pressure for emigration continues thanks to a few Zionists who maintain the teaching of Hebrew and explorations of Jewish culture and religion. As a precipitant of the emigration and as examples of civic courage, they and their ideals deserve to be treated as more than a passing initial episode in Jewish emigration.

The concluding chapter of the book offers us two propositions:

(a) Despite biological attrition, assimilation and emigration, the Jews will survive indefinitely in the USSR as a distinctive ethnic group, largely on the basis of negative (i.e., restrictive and antisemitic) pressures.
(b) The emigration movement reveals the possibility of a liberalization, or perhaps even a democratization of the Soviet political system, because of a loosening of control over the population, and the increased stream of living contacts and information between the emigrants and the USSR.

Both propositions are cautiously presented and argued with due attention to the limitations and uncertainties involved. Presented in this manner they are certainly food for thought. Nevertheless the premises on which both ideas are based are so tenuous, and run counter to such basics as the continuing will of the Party bureaucracy to maintain its political monopoly, that they strain our imagination and credulity.

Despite these criticisms, the book remains a challenging and well-conceived piece of research offering a unique insight into the interweaving of social development, ideology and the consequences of state response to multiple contradictory pressures.

THEODORE H. FRIEDGUT
Hebrew University

Partial List of Recently Completed Doctoral Dissertations

John M. Baker University of Connecticut, 1982
"*Bürgerlich* Ethos in the Novels of Karl Gutzkow"

Alan M. Ball University of North Carolina at Chapel Hill, 1982
"The Nepmen: Private Enterprise in the Soviet Union, 1921–1929"

David Bankier Hebrew University of Jerusalem, 1984
"*Ha-hevrah ha-germanit ve-ha-antishemiut ha-natsional sotsialistit, 1933–1938* (German Society and National Socialist Antisemitism, 1933–1938)"

Bruce L. Berg Syracuse University, 1983
"Jewish Identity: Subjective Declarations or Objective Life Styles"

Jay R. Berkovitz Brandeis University, 1983
"French Jewry and the Ideology of *Régénération*"

Etta Z. Bick City University of New York, 1983
"Ethnic Linkage and Foreign Policy: A Study of the Linkage Role of American Jews in Relations Between the United States and Israel, 1956–1968"

Steven M. Borish Stanford University, 1982
"Stones of Galilee: A Study of Culture Change on an Israeli Kibbutz"

David M. Bunis Columbia University, 1981
"The Hebrew and Aramaic Component of Judezmo: A Phonological and Morphological Analysis"

Charles E. Case University of Arizona, 1983
"Changes in Egalitarian Attitudes Toward Racial and Ethnic Minorities From 1956 to 1980: The Interaction of Education and Cultural Environment"

Michael A. De Sosa University of Oregon, 1982
"New Keys to the Nazi Revolution: Factors Facilitating the Nazi Seizure of Power in Germany During 1933–1934"

Sue Zohar Desheh Columbia University Teachers College, 1982
"Some Contexts for Special Education in Jewish Religious Education"

Carol G. Diament Yeshiva University, 1983
"Polemics of Rebirth: David Gordon and Proto-Zionism, 1858–1886"

Paula J. Draper University of Toronto, 1983
"The Accidental Immigrants: Canada and the Interned Refugees"

Maureen K. Fastenau Duke University, 1982
"Maternal Government: The Social Settlement Houses and the Politicization of Women's Sphere"

Linda Y. Fisch Columbia University Teachers College, 1983
"Patterns of Religious and Feminist Socialization Among Jewish College Women"

Steven C. Fraser Rutgers University, 1983
"Sidney Hillman and the Origins of the 'New Unionism' "

Seymour I. Friedman Fordham University, 1983
"The Effect of Jewish Religious Education on the Moral Reasoning and Social Interest of Yeshiva High School Students"

Patricia L. Gerrity University of Pennsylvania, 1983
"By Ourselves: An Ethnographic Study of Self-Care in an Elderly Jewish Population"

Yossi Goldstein Hebrew University of Jerusalem, 1984
"*Ha-tnu'ah ha-tsiyonit be-rusiah, 1897–1904* (The Zionist Movement in Russia, 1897–1904)"

Kim R. Holmes Georgetown University, 1982
"The NSDAP and the Crisis of Agrarian Conservatism in Lower Bavaria: National Socialism and the Peasants' Road to Modernity"

Jack L. Jacobs Columbia University, 1983
"Kautsky on the Jewish Question"

Allen F. Ketcham University of Arizona, 1982
"World War II Events as Represented in Secondary School Textbooks of Former Allied and Axis Nations"

Cole C. Kingseed Ohio School University, 1983
"Eisenhower and Suez: A Reappraisal of Presidential Activism and Crisis Management"

Jerome M. Kutnick Brandeis University, 1983
"Non-Zionist Leadership: Felix M. Warburg, 1929–1937"

Barry R. Leventhal Dallas Theological Seminary, 1982
"Theological Perspectives on the Holocaust"

Dirk H. Lindemann Ball State University, 1983
"Intellectual Roots of Nazism: Interpretations"

Yosef Litvak Hebrew University of Jerusalem, 1984
"*Plitim yehudiim bivrit hamoatsot, 1939–1946* (Polish-Jewish Refugees in the USSR, 1939–1946)"

Sharon R. Lowenstein University of Kansas, 1983
"A New Deal for Refugees: The Promise and Reality of Oswego, 1944–1945"

Edward D. Menarchik George Washington University, 1983
"The Politics of the Israeli Rescue Operation at Entebbe: Crisis Resolution Between State and Terrorist Organizations"

David N. Miller University of California, Santa Cruz, 1982
"Fear of Fiction: Narrative Strategies in the Works of Isaac Bashevis Singer"

Dina D. Miraglia Columbia University, 1983
"An Analysis of Ethnic Identity Among Yemenite Jews in the Greater New York Area"

Stephen J. Morewitz University of Chicago, 1983
"Medicine, Social Control and Social Change: A Case Study of Michael Reese Hospital and the Chicago Jewish Community"

Ronald E. Myers University of Pennsylvania, 1983
"Immigrant Occupational Achievement: A Comparative Case Study of Koreans, Soviet Jews and Vietnamese in the Philadelphia Area"

Sanford B. Parsons New York University, 1983
"The Role of Shraga Feivel Mendlowitz in the Founding and Development of Hebrew Day Schools in the United States"

Leslie S. Perelman University of Wisconsin-Madison, 1983
"Something Old, Something New: The Domestic Side of Moroccan-Israeli Ethnicity"

Gloria W. Pollack Columbia University, 1981
"Eliezer Zvi Hacohen Zweifel: A Case Study in Conflicts and Contrasts"

Terrie G. Raphael Columbia University, 1983
"Rise Before the Hoary Head: Socialization to Old Age in an Israeli Town"

Jerome Rosenthal University of Cincinnati, 1983
"The Public Life of Louis Marshall"

Kathy Rugoff Florida State University, 1983
"The Holocaust in American and British Poetry"

Bernard I. Sandler Bar-Ilan University, 1979
"The Jews of America and the Resettlement of Palestine 1908–1934: Efforts and Achievements"

Rachel C. Schlesinger University of Toronto, 1983
"Jewish Women in Transition: Delayed Entry into the Workforce"

Sanford M. Schwartz The Catholic University of America, 1983
"Organizational and Social Structural Characteristics Influencing

Resource Mobilization: A Case Study of the American Jewish Federation Movement"

Charles Selengut Drew University, 1983
"The Unification Church and Jewish Orthodoxy in America: A Sociological Study of Belief, Life-Style and Reality Maintenance in Cognitive Minority Communities"

Gerald L. Showstack Brandeis University, 1983
"Ethnicity and Business Enterprise: A Study of the Jewish Mutual Insurance Companies of New York"

Jack Sierad University of California, Los Angeles, 1982
"The Enhancement of Ethnic Identity: The Brandeis-Bardin Experiment"

Mark Silber Boston University, 1983
"Ethnicity and Childbirth: The Birthing Process of American Jews"

Rosalind M. R. Silberman Temple University, 1983
"Teacher Expectations of Jewish Afternoon School Principals: Role Responsibilities, Relationships and Decision-Making"

Sarah L. Small University of Missouri-Kansas City, 1983
"Attitudes of Professional and Lay Leaders of Congregations in a Major Metropolitan Jewish Community, Chicago, Toward the Employment of Women as Administrators of Congregational Religious Schools"

David J. Sorkin University of California, Berkeley, 1983
"Ideology and Identity: Political Emancipation and the Emergence of a Jewish Sub-Culture in Germany, 1800–1848"

Orhan Soysal Princeton University, 1983
"An Analysis of the Influence of Turkey's Alignment with the West and of the Arab-Israeli Conflict Upon Turkish-Israeli and Turkish-Arab Relations, 1947–1977"

Paul R. Spickard University of California, Berkeley, 1983
"Mixed Marriage: Two American Minority Groups and the Limits of Ethnic Identity, 1900–1970"

Edward Staski University of Arizona, 1983
"Alcohol Consumption Among Irish-Americans and Jewish-Americans: Contributions from Archaeology"

John D. Sullivan University of Pittsburgh, 1983
"The Perceptual Basis of British Foreign Policy, A Case Study of the Suez Crisis"

Hadassa Z. Sussman Columbia University Teachers College, 1983
"The Relationships Between Ethnic Origin and the Level of Socio-Economic Status and Certain Parental Practices of Oriental and European Parents in Israel"

James W. Warhola Ohio State University, 1983
"Soviet National Relations: Elite Attitudes and Perceptions in the 1970s"

Jacquelin W. Weisheit Johns Hopkins University, 1984
"Julius Bab, German Intellectual and Critic, 1900–1939"

Sheila F. Weiss Johns Hopkins University, 1983
"Race Hygiene and the Rational Management of National Efficiency: Wilhelm Schallmayer and the Origins of German Eugenics, 1890–1920"

Lenore E. Weissler University of Pennsylvania, 1982
"Making Judaism Meaningful: Ambivalence and Tradition in a Havurah Community"

Naomi J. Williams Columbia University, 1981
"Intervention by Syria in the Lebanese Civil War of 1975–1976"

Shlomo Yotvat University of Wisconsin-Madison, 1983
"British and American Attitudes and Disputes Concerning the Palestine Question, 1942–1947"

other essays include

Eliyahu Feldman, on Russian pogroms and British diplomats (documents from the Foreign Office)

Lloyd P. Gartner, on the writing of Jewish social history

Victor Karady, on Hungarian Jews after World War II

Dov Levin, on Lithuanian Jewish refugees in the Soviet Union

Erwin Schmidl, on Jews in the Austro-Hungarian army

Stephen J. Whitfield, on the American Jew as journalist

review essays by

Judy Doneson, on portraits of the Jew in film

Michael Marrus, on America and the Holocaust

Robert Wistrich, on Jews in Vienna

a section on books in review and a list of recent dissertations on Jewish subjects

YAHADUT ZEMANENU

Contemporary Jewry
A Research Annual (in Hebrew)

Volume II (1984)

Editor: Shmuel Almog
Editorial Board: Israel Gutman,
Menahem Kaufman

CONTENTS

ESSAYS

RESEARCH

Antisemitism and the Holocaust

Yair Auron—The Attitudes of Organized Jewish Youth in France to the Holocaust

Zionism and the Yishuv

Yosef Goldstein—The Struggle between Orthodox and Secular Jews over the Character of the Zionist Movement, 1882–1922

Jehuda Reinharz—Chaim Weizmann: The Shaping of a Zionist Leader before World War I

Nakdimon Rogel—Yosef Trumpeldor and the Defense of Metullah in the Winter of 1920

Yitzhak Gil-Har—The Northern Boundary of Palestine

Yosef Heller—Between Messianism and Realpolitik: The Stern Group and the Arab Question, 1947–1948

Demography

U. O. Schmelz and Sergio DellaPergola—Demography and Jewish Education: The Project for Jewish Educational Statistics

Nitza Genuth and Allie Dubb—The Census of Jewish Schools in the Diaspora: Some Methodological Problems and Initial Findings

BOOK REVIEWS